KU-260-288

Pocket
THESAURUS of
ENGLISH WORDS

NEWNES
Pocket
THESAURUS of
ENGLISH WORDS

Edited by
MH Manser

NEWNES BOOKS

NEWNES·BOOKS

First published in 1979 by
The Hamlyn Publishing Group Limited
Published in 1984 by Newnes Books,
Michelin House,
81 Fulham Road,
London SW3 6RB

Reprinted 1992

ISBN 0 600 38779 8

Printed at Thomson Press (India) Ltd.
Faridabad (Haryana)

Introduction

A thesaurus is a book of words arranged according to ideas. You use it when you can think of an idea but cannot find the exact word to express it or when you have a word in mind that isn't close enough to the one you really want. This is where a thesaurus comes in: it gives words in lists according to the ideas they stand for.

This thesaurus covers the central part of the vocabulary of English – the 'core' of the language we all use most of the time – and groups this under 990 categories, each representing a different idea. It does not include highly technical words, but does reflect the fact that the English language used today is becoming more colloquial. By looking up a word in the index and referring to one of the categories in the book you will find a list of words with a similar meaning and you will then be able to choose the one you want.

The first thesaurus was written by Peter Mark Roget (1779–1869), and published in 1852. Its full original title was *The Thesaurus of English Words and Phrases Classified and Arranged so as to Facilitate the Expression of Ideas and Assist in Literary Composition*. It has since been published in many editions and the concept has been taken over and used for other languages. Many changes have been made in writing this thesaurus: categories have been re-ordered, many have been given more intelligible names, and there is a thorough coverage of new words that have entered the language. A large number of older words and phrases have been rejected as no longer used.

This thesaurus is written for those who use language – those who speak and write English and want to use a variety of words, for those who solve crosswords, and for those who just like browsing through its pages to pore over the richness of the language. After all, the word 'thesaurus' itself comes from the Greek word for 'treasure', and we hope that something of the deep resources of the language will be discovered in these pages.

M. H. Manser

How to use this thesaurus

Imagine that you have a word in mind, let us say, 'beautiful'. You have used this word already and don't want to use it again, or you want something more expressive. The first thing to do is to look up this word – 'beautiful' – in the index. The index is arranged in alphabetical order. Every entry in the index consists of a word or words, a part of speech, and a number or numbers. Parts of speech have been abbreviated as follows: *n.* = noun; *adj.* = adjective; *vb.* = verb; *adv.* = adverb; *prep.* = preposition. The numbers refer to categories. The entry for 'beautiful' looks like this:

beautiful adj. 844

If you turn to category **844** in the main part of the book and look under the appropriate part of speech – here *adj.* – you will find a list of alternative words that you can use: beautiful, attractive, good-looking, . . . Some of the entries in the index have numbers printed in a darker, bold type. These show the main references for particular words.

The words listed have slightly different meanings from each other. If you are not familiar with a word it would therefore be advisable to look up the word in a good modern dictionary before using it. Otherwise you may risk using the word in the wrong context. Two further abbreviations are used. Informal or colloquial words are marked as (*inf.*) and slang words (*sl.*). At the end of many entries there are cross-references to other categories (e.g. see also **56, 112**). These can usefully be followed up to find further lists of related words. You should also consult the words given at the other parts of speech in an entry, as some words there may suggest others to you.

If you look at the adjacent categories, too, you will find further help or perhaps the possibility of using a word meaning something opposite, e.g., the categories **534 resolution, 535 perseverance, 536 irresolution.**

A list of the 990 categories is given after the index and you can check that the number of the category you are looking up is the one you want.

Plan of categories

Thesaurus

I Abstract Relations

A Existence

1 existence

n. existence, being, essence, self-existence, reality, actuality, presence; subsistence, givenness, historicity, factuality; actualization, creating, becoming, potentiality, possibility; ontology, existentialism, metaphysics, realism.

fact, truth, *fait accompli*, real thing, entity, vital principle.

adj. existing, being, in being, in existence, afoot, given, uncreated; ontological, metaphysical; extant, living, current, present, standing, surviving; subsisting, subsistent, obtaining, prevailing, prevalent; real, actual, true, authentic, genuine, mere, objective; essential, substantial, substantive, self-existing, self-existent, intrinsic, factual.

vb. be, exist, have being, live, breathe, abide, remain, stay, prevail, be so, be the case; subsist, obtain; consist in, inhere in, reside in; stand, find itself, lie, be situated, be found; occur, take place, happen, continue, go on, endure, last.

adv. actually, really, in fact, in reality.

2 non-existence

n. non-existence, inexistence, non-being, nonentity, nothingness, nullity, nihility, neverness; vacuum, vacuity, emptiness, void, blank; extinction, destruction, abolition, obsolescence.

adj. non-existent, void, vacuous, blank; extinct, dead, obsolete, vanished; unreal, wrong, untrue, false, specious, imaginary, fictitious, hypothetical, groundless, unfounded.

vb. come to nothing, pass away, die, vanish, disappear, dematerialize, evaporate, dissolve; bring to nothing, nullify, destroy, abolish, kill.

3 material existence

n. materiality, substantiality, actuality, essentiality, reality, objectivity, substantivity, corporeity, corporality, concreteness, solidity, tangibility.

substance, thing, body, solid, stuff, matter, entity, flesh and blood (*inf.*).

adj. material, substantial, actual, solid, corporeal, objective, substantive, concrete, physical, real, natural; visible, tangible.

see also 327

4 non-material existence

n. immateriality, insubstantiality, inessentiality, intangibility.

shadow, token, dream, vision, apparition, spirit, illusion, optical illusion, mirage, breath, mist, vapour, wisp.

adj. immaterial, insubstantial, abstract, intangible, imponderable, airy, vaporous, ethereal, spiritual, ghostly, spectral, bodiless, disembodied, visionary, shadowy, vague.

see also 328

5 being according to internal form

n. intrinsicality, inherence, inwardness, internality, essentiality, immanence.

essence, substance, basis, being, soul, fundamental, principle, quality, quintessence, essential, heart, core, character, nature, constitution, structure, make-up, bearing, framework, frame; attribute, element, aspect, quality, feature, manner, temper, temperament, mood, humour, disposition, personality, particularity, idiosyncrasy, endowment, heredity, gene.

adj. intrinsic, essential, inherent, inward, central, fundamental, immanent, implicit, internal, original, integral, innate, distinctive, specific, characteristic, particular, peculiar, unique; native, genetic, hereditary, inborn, congenital, ancestral.

vb. inhere, be intrinsic; internalize.
see also **223, 224**

6 being according to external form

n. extrinsicality, externality, objectivity, outwardness, transcendence, projection, extrapolation; accessory, external.

adj. extrinsic, external, objective, transcendent, exterior, outward, extraneous, foreign, independent, additional, outside.

vb. be extrinsic, transcend, surpass; make extrinsic, objectify, project, extend, extrapolate.

see also **222, 825**

7 absolute state

n. state, standing, condition, station, status, case, position, stand, rank, class, degree, estate, style, fashion, mode, aspect, facet, posture, attitude.

8 circumstance

n. circumstance, circumstances, situation, environment, surroundings, setting, background, backdrop, *milieu,* context, how the land lies, ambience, atmosphere, climate; conditions, factors, details, items, features, particulars, requirements, necessities; cause, reason, motives, grounds.

adj. circumstantial, modal, surrounding, environmental, contextual, incidental, background, contingent; detailed, itemized, particular.

adv. under the circumstances, this being the case, incidentally, under these conditions, in the event of.

B Relation

9 relation

n. relation, relatedness, association, relationship, arrangement; connection, link, dependence, involvement, implication, bearing; relativity, correspondence, analogy, correlation; relevance, suitability, appositeness.

adj. relative, related, connected, involved, arranged, linked, bearing upon, concerning, belonging, appertaining; reciprocal, mutual; analogous, comparable; relevant, suitable, apposite, appropriate, proper, applicable, pertinent.

vb. be related to, concern, refer to, touch upon, bear upon, deal with, treat, have to do with, apply, hold true for, be a factor in; relate, associate, link, refer; correspond to, be analogous to; belong, pertain.

adv., prep. concerning, regarding, as regards, on, about, with reference to, with respect to, on the subject of, in the matter of, à propos, re, in re.

10 absence of relation

n. irrelation, dissociation, unrelatedness, non-involvement, independence, arbitrariness; disproportion, difference, misfit, irreconcilability, irrelevance, unsuitability, inconsequence.

adj. unrelated, independent, unconcerned, uninvolved, unconnected, inappropriate, incongruent; isolated, arbitrary, free, unallied, unilateral; irrelevant, unsuitable, inapplicable, inapposite, inconsequential.

vb. be unrelated to, have no relation with, not concern, have no bearing upon, have nothing to do with, not be one's business.

adv. by the way, incidentally.

11 kindred relations

n. consanguinity, blood relationship, blood, ties of blood, kinship, kindred, relations, relatives, kith and kin; ancestry, parentage, antecedents, forbears, patrimony, heritage, lineage; descent, descendants; affiliation; children, offspring, issue, progeny; sibling, brother, sister, twin, cousin, uncle, aunt, nephew, niece, parent, father, mother; kinsman, clansman, fellow, compatriot; family, matriarch, patriarch, fatherhood, paternity, motherhood, maternity, brotherhood, fraternity, sisterhood, sorority; in laws; household, one's folks (*inf.*), home, family circle; race, stock, generation, strain, breed, line, side, clan, tribe, stirps.

adj. related, akin, kindred, consanguineous; parental, maternal, paternal, brotherly, fraternal, sisterly, sororal, cousinly, avuncular; collateral, allied; ethnic, racial, minority, tribal.

vb. be related to, be akin, generate, adopt, affiliate.

12 correlation

n. correlation, relation, correspondence, mutuality, reciprocity, interchange, interrelation, interdependence, interaction, interplay, exchange, alternation, equivalence.

adj. correlative, reciprocal, reciprocating, mutual, relative, corresponding, equivalent, interchangeable.

vb. correlate, interrelate, interconnect, interplay, interact, reciprocate, correspond, alternate.

adv. correlatively, mutually, reciprocally, alternately.

13 identity

n. identity, identicalness, oneness, sameness, selfsameness, equality, unity, homogeneity, uniformity, invariability, interchangeability.

adj. same, identical, one, very, constant, invariable, unchangeable, unvarying, homogeneous; like, alike, indistinguishable; equivalent, duplicate, equal, twin.

vb. be identical, coincide, coalesce, equate; not distinguish, not know from Adam.

14 absolute difference

n. contrariety, inequality, inequity, contrariness, oppositeness, adverseness; incompatibility, irreconcilability; contradiction, inconsistency, polarity, antithesis.

adj. contrary, different, contrasting, inconsistent, contradictory, mutually exclusive, opposite, reverse, diametrical, adverse, opposing.

vb. be contrary, differ, contrast, contradict, oppose, go against the grain; clash.

adv. on the other hand, on the contrary, contrariwise, conversely, in the opposite way.

15 variance

n. variance, difference, variation, unlikeness, heterogeneity, diversity; disparity, deviation, divergence, deflection, discrepancy, disagreement; differentiation, discrimination.

variant, irregularity, special case.

adj. different, unlike, unidentical, dissimilar, variable, changeable, varying, variant; heterogeneous, diverse, indiscriminate; changed, modified; contrasting, incongruous, contrary, deviating, divergent, disparate, incompatible.

vb. differ, vary, change, modify; diverge, deviate; differentiate, discriminate, distinguish.

16 uniformity

n. uniformity, homogeneity, constancy, sameness, invariability, stability, regularity; symmetry, evenness, unity, congruity; conformity; monotony, routine, ritual, standardization, stereotype.

adj. uniform, homogeneous, same, consistent, invariable, steady, stable, regular, symmetrical, even, unchanging, unvarying; monotonous, routine, standardized, stereotyped.

vb. be uniform, accord, conform; make uniform, characterize, standardize, normalize, level, smooth.

17 non-uniformity

n. non-uniformity, heterogeneity, inconstancy, variability, diversity, instability, irregularity, asymmetry, unevenness, disunity, incongruity.

adj. non-uniform, heterogeneous, inconsistent, variable, diversified, motley, unsteady, irregular, asymmetrical, uneven, changing, varying, incongruous.

18 similarity

n. similarity, likeness, resemblance, affinity, analogy, similitude; disguise, camouflage; correlation, comparison,

equivalent, correspondence; counterpart.

adj. similar, like, alike, resembling, twin, analogous, *à la*, equivalent, typical, representative; lifelike, realistic, faithful, true, exact, simulating, imitative; camouflaged, disguised, mock.

vb. be similar, look like, seem, pass for, take after, approximate; liken, assimilate to, imitate; answer to the description of.

19 dissimilarity

n. dissimilarity, difference, unlikeness, dissimulation, diversity, disparity; variety, variation.

adj. dissimilar, different, unlike, disparate, incongruent; atypical; unrealistic, inexact.

vb. be unlike, differ from, bear no resemblance, have nothing in common with.

20 imitation

n. imitation, imitativeness, copying, representation, portrayal, mimicry, impersonation, caricature, parody; simulation, patterning; likeness, replica, reflection, portrait, echo, copy, reprint, facsimile, counterpart; translation, paraphrase, interpretation; cribbing, plagiarism; counterfeit, forgery, fake, sham.

imitator, simulator, ape, copycat (*inf.*), parrot, conformist, sheep, mimic, impersonator, translator, paraphraser, interpreter; plagiarist; forger, counterfeiter, faker.

adj. imitative, apish, parrot-like, counterfeit, pseudo-, sham, fake, mock, phoney (*sl.*); modelled on, based on.

vb. imitate, emulate, portray, depict, represent, simulate, do likewise, take after, follow suit, take a leaf out of someone's book; parrot, take off (*inf.*), send up (*inf.*), mimic, parody, caricature; repeat, mirror; pretend, disguise; copy, quote, reproduce, paraphrase, translate; crib, plagiarize; counterfeit, fake.

21 non-imitation

n. originality, creation, creativeness, inventiveness, ingenuity, independence, newness, novelty, individuality, authenticity, genuineness; real thing.

adj. unimitative, uncopied, underived, authentic, primary, genuine, creative, inventive, original, independent, first hand, incomparable, unique, rare, exceptional.

22 copy

n. copy, reprint, facsimile, reproduction, transcript, translation, paraphrase, interpretation, crib, forgery; semblance; study, representation, portrait, echo; parody, caricature, travesty; counterpart, duplicate, replica, reflection, likeness, impression, dummy, cast, tracing, model, transfer; analogue, correlate.

23 prototype

n. prototype, archetype, type, primitive form, original; precedent, first occurrence; principle, basis, standard, pattern, frame of reference, criterion; blueprint, design, plan, example, instance, illustration; dummy, mock-up; model, poser, sitter, mannequin, die, stamp, mould, shell, negative, plate, mint.

vb. be an example, set an example; act as a mould; model for, sit, pose; typify, exemplify.

24 agreement

n. agreement, understanding, harmony, unity, integration, uniformity, unanimity, consensus, unison, accord, concord, correspondence, concurrence, consonance; coincidence, congruity; reconciliation, sympathy; treaty, contract.

adj. agreeing, like-minded, unanimous, agreed, corresponding, conforming, concurrent, coinciding, concerted, harmonious, unifying, consonant, concurring, united, collective, undisputed, in step, in concert, of one accord, with one voice, sympathetic, reconcilable, compatible, consistent.

vb. agree, concur, assent, accord, tally, harmonize, match, reconcile, coincide, correspond, fit in with, dovetail, square with, synchronize, adapt, adjust, go hand in hand with, say yes to, see eye to eye, get along with, get on with, click (*inf.*), hit it off (*inf.*); keep in with (*inf.*), keep on the right side of (*inf.*).

see also **643, 699**

25 disagreement

n. disagreement, discord, misunderstanding, division, tension, dissidence, argument, dispute, contention, quarrel, disunion, dissension, strife; discrepancy, dissonance, dissimilarity, disparity, incongruence.

adj. disagreeing, differing, disputing, contradictory, inconsistent, incongruous, out of character, disproportionate, at odds, at variance, at loggerheads, out of step; hostile, inimical, factious, dissenting, non-conformist.

vb. disagree, object, not accept, say no to, speak against, contradict, defy, reject; oppose, fight, quarrel, dispute, come into conflict with, come up against; not conform, be contrary to.

see also **642**

C Quantity

26 quantity

n. quantity, amount, number, sum, extent, scope, expanse, size, dimensions, measure; length, breadth, width, height, depth, volume, capacity, area; mass, bulk, weight; mouthful, handful, spoonful, dose, portion, lot, batch, deal, whole, heaps (*inf.*), masses (*inf.*), load (*inf.*), abundance, profusion, greatness, magnitude, largeness.

adj. quantitative, quantified, measured, some, any.

vb. quantify, measure.

see also 32

27 relative quantity

n. degree, level, grade, point, stage, measure, rate, proportion, ratio, scale, measure, standard, comparison, criterion; extent, scope, range, intensity, frequency, size, speed, shade, nuance, tint; gradation, graduation, calibration, measurement.

adj. graded, graduated, calibrated, measured, scaled, comparative, proportional, relative; gradual, tapering, shading off, fading.

vb. graduate, grade, measure, calibrate; compare, rank, classify; taper off, shade off, fade, narrow, reduce, lessen, thin out.

adv. gradually, in stages, little by little, step by step.

28 equality

n. equality, parity, uniformity, sameness, equivalence, equalization, equation, adjustment, equilibrium, balance, symmetry, steadiness, synonymity, six of one and half a dozen of the other (*inf.*), six and two threes (*inf.*).

equivalent, draw, tie, dead heat, stalemate, no decision; counterpart, opposite number, equal, complement, twin, double, peer; synonym.

adj. equal, equivalent, equilateral, regular, symmetrical, fifty-fifty, on equal terms, even, level, flush, parallel, reciprocal, uniform, comparable, commensurate, proportionate, coextensive, tantamount, synonymous.

vb. be equal, agree with, coincide, suffice, rank with, match, rival, meet, touch, live up to, measure up to, come up to, be the equivalent of. keep pace with, come to the same thing, go halves; tie, draw, balance.

equalize, make equal, adjust, square.

29 inequality

n. inequality, disparity, non-uniformity, unlikeness, disproportion, dissimilarity, deviation, divergence, dissemblance, inferiority, shortcoming, deficiency; unevenness, imbalance, lopsidedness, unsteadiness.

adj. unequal, disparate, non-uniform, uneven, odd, inferior, deficient, insufficient, inadequate; disproportionate, lopsided, top-heavy, crooked, overbalanced.

vb. be unequal, outclass, outstrip, have the advantage, fall short of, not come up to, not hold a candle to (*inf.*).

30 mean

n. average, mean, golden mean, medium, happy medium, median, balance, norm, par, middle term, middle point, midpoint, centre, halfway, middle, compromise.

adj. mean, average, median, middle, grey, intermediate, halfway, lukewarm, middling, fair to middling, medium; typical; mediocre, run of the mill.

vb. average out, take the average, split the difference, strike a balance, go halfway.

31 compensation

n. compensation, weighting, equalization, balance, counterbalance, ballast, allowance, amends, costs, damages, remuneration, reimbursement, indemnification, indemnity, reparation, restitution, recompense, repayment, refund, offset, satisfaction, atonement, requital.

adj. compensatory, indemnificatory, restitutory, balancing.

vb. compensate, make amends, balance, neutralize, equalize, counterbalance, counteract, overcompensate, pay costs, indemnify, remunerate, recompense, reimburse, redeem, refund, recoup, satisfy, make up for, make reparation, allow for, set off, offset, take back.

32 greatness

n. greatness, largeness, bigness, vastness, enormity, immenseness, magnitude, size, bulk; spaciousness; might, mightiness, power, strength, intensity; amplitude, fullness, plenitude.

great quantity, profusion, abundance, masses, lots, quantities, oodles (*inf.*), stacks (*inf.*); excess, redundance, superfluity, superabundance.

adj. big, large, great, considerable, numerous, massive, enormous, vast, colossal, huge, sizeable; tall, lofty, high, towering; strong, mighty, powerful, energetic; ample, plentiful, abundant, profuse, plenteous, copious; noble, sublime, high, stately, exalted; remarkable, notable, unspeakable; extensive, far-reaching, widespread, prevalent, sweeping, universal, worldwide; marvellous, exceptional, surpassing, wonderful, overwhelming, unbelievable, stupendous, astounding.

vb. be great, be big, be large; mount,

soar, tower, exceed, rise above, transcend.

adv. enormously, vastly, highly, on a big scale, in a big way; heavily, strongly, mightily, powerfully, actively; greatly, very, much, in a great measure, extremely, exceedingly, considerably; plenteously, plentifully, abundantly, immeasurably, unspeakably, ineffably, awfully (*inf.*), tremendously; excessively, inordinately, immoderately; unbelievably, exceptionally.

see also 75

33 smallness

n. smallness, littleness, tininess, diminutiveness, minuteness; shortness, slightness, slenderness; meagreness, scantiness, paucity, scarcity, fewness, sparseness, rareness.

small quantity, dash, trace, *soupçon*, shade, morsel, crumb, iota, jot, tittle; point, dot, spot, fleck, speck, grain, atom, particle, modicum, chip, flake, shred, bit, rag, fragment, trifle.

adj. small, little, diminutive, minimal, infinitesimal, imperceptible, tiny, minute, miniature; slim, slender, thin, slight, scanty, meagre, insufficient, few, sparse, rare, inconsiderable, minor, trifling; modest, poor, pitiful.

adv. slightly, little, to a small extent, faintly, on a small scale, in a small way; humbly, modestly; scarcely, hardly, barely, pitifully.

see also 76

34 superiority

n. superiority, supremacy, dominance, transcendence, excellence, perfection, nobility, sublimity, eminence, pre-eminence; advantage, privilege, prerogative, favour, upper hand, head start, start.

superior, better, elder, master, overlord, chief, boss, management, senior, top dog (*inf.*).

adj. superior, eminent, upper, higher, greater, major; better, preferred, surpassing, exceeding; supreme, pre-eminent, greatest; first, chief, principal, main, capital, leading, mainline, cardinal, paramount; best, excellent, superlative, first-class, matchless, unrivalled, unsurpassed, beyond compare.

vb. be superior, rise above, tower, transcend, exceed, excel, surpass, eclipse, top, cap, overshadow, outmatch, get the better of, lord it over; prevail, predominate; have the advantage, have the edge on (*inf.*).

adv. eminently, superlatively, prominently, above all, *par excellence*, principally, especially, particularly.

35 inferiority

n. inferiority, deficiency, imperfection, shortcoming; mediocrity, poorness; lowliness, subordination, subjection, back seat (*inf.*).

inferior, subordinate, servant, slave, junior, auxiliary, accessory, workers, poor relation, underdog (*inf.*).

adj. inferior, low, lower, junior, minor, lesser, subordinate, secondary, accessory, auxiliary, ancillary, unclassified; lowly, humble, menial, subject, obedient; deficient, mediocre, substandard, imperfect, worse, worst, common, below par, not a patch on (*inf.*).

vb. be inferior, fall short of, not come up to, not compare with, not come near, want, lack, not hold a candle to (*inf.*); take a back seat (*inf.*).

see also **571**

36 increase

n. increase, rise, augmentation, growth, progression, development, spread, proliferation, build-up, prolon-

gation, extension, expansion, enlargement, escalation, magnification, heightening, swelling, incorporation, merger, cumulative effect, snowball (*inf.*).

adj. increasing, rising, growing, progressing, developing, proliferating, expanding, escalating, enlarging, intensifying, cumulative, crescent.

vb. increase, grow, rise, gain; thrive, flourish; multiply, enlarge, magnify, amplify, aggrandize; develop, escalate, boost, build, build up, expand, swell, add, compound, upsurge, strengthen, intensify, accumulate, accrue, snowball (*inf.*); prolong, lengthen, broaden, widen, thicken, deepen, heighten; enhance; exacerbate, aggravate.

37 decrease

n. decrease, decline, fall, drop, reduction, wane, restriction, restraint, curtailment, paring, pruning, squeeze; fade-out, regression, depression, depreciation, shortening.

adj. decreasing, falling, declining, reducing, dwindling, fading, on the wane.

vb. decrease, lessen, fall, drop, diminish, moderate, subside, decline, abate, recede, dwindle, wane, shrink, ebb, drain away, tail off; peter out, taper off; deteriorate; reduce, restrain, limit, check, curb, curtail, cut back, economize, consume, use up, shorten, trim, squeeze, compress, erode, dilute, quell.

38 numeration

n. numeration, numbering, enumeration, counting, count, census, figuring, reckoning, calculation, computation; mathematics, arithmetic, algebra, geometry, trigonometry, calculus, analysis; addition, subtraction, multiplication, division; statistics, figures, data, tables, measurements; abacus, ready reckoner, computer, electronic brain, microprocessor, calculator; addend, subtrahend, product, quotient.

adj. numerable, countable, calculable, computable, statistical, numbered, mathematical, arithmetical, algebraical, geometrical, analytical.

vb. number, count, tell, score, tally, cast, enumerate, poll; calculate, add, total, subtract, multiply, divide, compute, figure, work out, reckon, estimate; inventorize, list; classify; measure.

39 number

n. number, numeral, figure, digit, cipher, integer, whole number, prime number, symbol, character, sign, notation; function, variable, expression, formula; fraction, denominator, numerator, decimal, power, root.

adj. numerical, arithmetical, even, odd, prime, whole, positive, negative, rational, irrational, transcendental, exponential, integral, digital, decimal, binary; multiple, reciprocal, fractional.

40 addition

n. addition, summation, total; increase, enlargement, annexation, accession, accretion, accruing, supplement; prefixion, suffixion, affixation.

adj. additional, additive, adopted, extra, new, further, added, fresh, other, extraneous, accessory, auxiliary, supplementary.

vb. add, add up, sum, total; append, annex, attach, tack on, clap on (*inf.*), slap on (*inf.*), join, insert, contribute, supplement, increase, accumulate; accrue; affix, suffix, prefix, infix.

adv. in addition, moreover, furthermore, further, besides, as well, also, additionally, extra, and, too, over and above, in conjunction with.

41 thing added

n. adjunct, addition, attachment, fixture, extension, accretion, accession, accessory, appurtenance, increment, rise, interest, bonus, contribution, supplement; qualification, rider; annexe, wing; *addendum,* appendix, appendage, postscript, note; prefix, suffix, infix.

42 subtraction

n. subtraction, deduction, removal, withdrawal, curtailment, reduction, decrease, cutback, deletion, discount; amputation; abbreviation.

vb. subtract, deduct, take away, detract from, remove, exclude, withdraw, withhold, cut back; unload, unpack; shorten, abbreviate, delete; sever, amputate.

adv., prep. minus, without, with the exception of, bar, excepting, save.

43 thing subtracted

n. deduction, decrement, cut, decrease, reduction, rebate, discount, allowance, credit, depreciation, remission, forfeit, write-off; loss, shortcoming, defect.

44 remainder

n. remainder, rest, remnant, vestige, remains, residue, relic, hangover; result; balance, surplus, excess, margin; left-overs, waste, garbage, rejects, salvage, debris, sediment, dregs, slag, scum, leavings, clippings, crumbs, pairings, trimmings, castoffs.

adj. remaining, left, left over, over, residual, surviving; outstanding, carried over; surplus, unused, spare, to spare, superfluous; outcast.

45 mixture

n. mixture, mingling, combination, fusion, infusion, amalgamation, merger, integration; adulteration, transfusion.

blend, compound, composite, composition, conglomeration, amalgam, alloy, tincture, admixture; medley, miscellany, patchwork, pastiche, jumble, tangle, pot-pourri, *mélange*, mishmash, gallimaufry; hybrid, mongrel.

adj. mixed, composite, fused, merged, combined, united, amalgamated, half-and-half; stirred, blended, heterogeneous, adulterated, hybrid, mongrel; miscellaneous, assorted, motley, varied, jumbled, hotch-potch.

vb. mix, mix up, join, fuse, alloy, merge, combine, unite, amalgamate, conjoin, mingle, intermingle, stir, transfuse, shake, scramble; adulterate, water down; jumble; be mixed, permeate, infect, infiltrate; interbreed, cross with.

46 freedom from mixture

n. simpleness, purity, homogeneity, simplicity, plainness, purification, sifting, elimination.

adj. simple, pure, clean, clear, plain, uniform, absolute, homogeneous, uncomplicated, unadulterated, unqualified; mere, only, sheer.

vb. simplify, purify, unmix, unscramble, disentangle, eliminate, sift, winnow.

47 junction

n. junction, joining, connection, union, reunion, contact, tying, fastening, coupling, merging, fusion, bonding, marriage, concatenation; assemblage, structure, tie-up.

adj. joined, connected, linked, coupled, allied, married, wed, attached, fixed, secure, tied, hooked, stuck, firm, fast, close, rooted; tight, inextricable, inseparable; united, together, whole.

vb. join, attach, fix, stick on, affix, bolt, nail, screw; connect, link, make contact, span, bridge; put together, merge, fuse, combine, marry, juxtapose, cement; secure, tie, hook, couple, fasten, bind, splice, yoke, harness, knit, string, tether, clamp, clinch, twist; assemble, confederate, band together; dovetail, fit, set; unite, become one, meet, converge; unify, associate, ally with.

48 separation

n. separation, disconnection, dissociation, disjoining, detachment, segregation, disunion, disengagement, removal, withdrawal, dislocation, dismemberment, severance, division, cut, parting, divorce; dissolution, disintegration, break-up, dissection, breakdown, analysis; rupture, fracture, cleavage; burst, puncture, blowout.

adj. disjoined, discontinuous, unattached, unconnected; separable, detachable, divisible; apart, distinct, discrete, detached, divorced, isolated, alone, broken, fractured, in pieces, interrupted, torn, rent, cut, split, dismembered.

vb. separate, part, disunite, detach, disengage, break away, set apart, keep apart, disconnect, partition, demarcate, hive off, divide, subdivide, dissociate, divorce, isolate; disintegrate, decompose; fracture, rupture, break, fragment; unravel, disentangle; uncouple, unhitch, dislocate, unbind, loose, free, set free, release; tear, undo, rend; cut, dissect, hew, fell, reap, dice, chop, snip, slit, split, burst, puncture, sever, saw, chip, dissect, behead, carve; distribute, disperse; diverge; decollate.

49 bond

n. bond, link, connection, channel, passage, bridge; line, cable, string, rope, cord, chain, thread, ribbon, band, bandage, ligature, strip, girdle, belt, harness, lace, braid, tie, plait; knot, fastening, zip, hook, hook and eye, nut, bolt, screw, clasp, coupling; joint, junction, nexus, node, weld, seam, splice, swivel, hinge; adhesive, fixative, glue, paste, cement, epoxy, sticky tape.

50 coherence

n. coherence, cohesion, cohesiveness, consistency, adhesiveness; continuity, attachment, solidarity, inseparability, indivisibility.

adj. cohesive, adhesive, sticky, clinging, tenacious; inseparable, indivisible, inextricable, close, compact, solid.

vb. cohere, hold, hold fast, hold together; congregate; fit tight; adhere, stick, cleave, cling, fasten, unite, glue, gum, paste, weld, solder; hug, embrace, grasp, clasp, grip, clinch.

see also 332

51 incoherence

n. incoherence, non-coherence, non-adhesion, separability, divisibility, looseness, laxity.

adj. non-adhesive, slippery, loose, disconnected, lax, runny, inconsistent.

vb. unstick, unglue, detach, disjoin, disunite, peel off; come unstuck, fall apart, shake.

52 combination

n. combination, coalescence, fusion, mixture, synthesis, amalgamation, merger, integration, union, incorporation, embodiment, association, affiliation.

adj. combined, linked, integrated, connected, synchronized, harmonious, unified.

vb. combine, join, link, integrate, fuse, put together, merge, consolidate, unify, compound, group, incorporate, embody, coalesce, amalgamate; mix, blend, absorb; harmonize, synchronize; affiliate, cooperate, work together; kill two birds with one stone; make the best of both worlds, have one's cake and eat it.

see also 639

53 decomposition

n. decomposition, resolution, dissolution, analysis, breakdown, disintegration; decentralization; destruction; decay, putrefaction, corrosion, rottenness, putrescence, mould, rot, blight, mildew.

adj. decomposed, rotten, off, bad, rancid.

vb. decompose, resolve, break down, analyse, reduce, simplify, dissolve, dissect, atomize; decentralize, disband; disintegrate, break up; degenerate, waste away, decay, erode, corrode, rust, rot.

see also 588

54 whole

n. wholeness, completeness, entirety, totality, unity, comprehensivity, inclusiveness, panorama, catch-all; all, everyone, everybody, everything, total, whole, aggregate, sum, ensemble.

adj. whole, all, every, entire, full, complete, single, integral, total, universal, aggregate, gross, outright, inclusive, undivided, indivisible, inseparable, indissoluble; comprehensive, all-inclusive, all-embracing, sweeping, extensive, widespread, far-reaching, omnibus, wholesale, indiscriminate, blanket, catch-all, compendious, encyclopedic; intact, solid, perfect, safe, good, unbroken, undamaged, unblemished, unimpaired, flawless.

adv. wholly, entirely, completely,

altogether, a hundred per cent, all in all.

55 part

n. part, portion, share, cut, division, section, sector, segment, compartment, department, class, group, family, branch; genus, phylum; piece, fragment, bit, scrap; detail; splinter, sliver, chip, chunk, lump, wedge, slice; instalment, part payment, foretaste, downpayment, deposit; excerpt, extract; constituent, component, factor, element, member, ingredient, integral part; aspect, facet, feature.

adj. in parts, fragmentary, broken, in bits and pieces, defective; partial, incomplete, half-finished; constituent, integral, inherent, built-in, inclusive.

vb. part, divide, separate, allot, share.

adv. partly, piecemeal, in part, bit by bit.

see also **73, 717**

56 completeness

n. completeness, wholeness, fullness, plenitude, saturation, one's fill, replenishment, refill; entirety, universality, comprehensivity, nothing lacking, nothing to add, integration; perfection, integrity, soundness; last touch, finish.

adj. complete, full, utter, entire, whole, plenary, all, gross, replete; comprehensive, exhaustive; absolute, extreme, thorough, thoroughgoing, radical, sweeping, wholesale, unqualified, unconditional; integral, perfect; abounding, profuse, brimful, saturated, swamped, drowned, sated, laden.

vb. be complete, come to maturity, culminate; overflow, bulge; make complete, consummate, add, perfect; conclude, fulfil; fill, replenish, top up, soak, overwhelm, saturate, swamp,

drown; cloy, glut, gorge, sate, cram, pack, stuff.

adv. completely, wholly, entirely, fully, utterly, perfectly, altogether, quite, undividedly, exclusively, absolutely, out and out; hook, line, and sinker; with a vengeance, from beginning to end.

see also **659**

57 incompleteness

n. incompleteness, defectiveness, deficiency, shortcoming, deficit, shortage, shortfall, omission, defect, want, need, lack, break, decrease.

adj. incomplete, defective, imperfect, deficient, short, lacking, not enough, sparing, depleted; superficial, unfinished, half-done, under construction, in preparation, in progress; imperfect, sketchy, meagre, skimpy, scrappy, rough.

vb. be incomplete, lack, want.

adv. incompletely, partially, imperfectly, inadequately.

see also **660**

58 composition

n. composition, constitution, organization, make-up; nature, character, condition, quality, personality; design, pattern; compilation.

vb. constitute, compose, form, make up, comprise, consist, comprehend, include, incorporate, belong to, be a component of; arrange, mix, organize, systematize, construct, compile, assemble, devise, design, plan, write.

59 unity

n. unity, oneness, wholeness, homogeneity, unification, integration, uniqueness, singularity, individuality, singleness, isolation, solitude, indivisibility.

unit, item, bit, piece, one, point,

entity, whole, entirety; assembly, system.

adj. one, singular, individual, peculiar, specific, special; sole, single, only, unique, unprecedented, unequalled, *sui generis*, indivisible; lone, alone, lonely, lonesome, homeless, rootless, on one's own, single-handed, unaccompanied.

60 accompaniment

n. accompaniment, togetherness, concomitance, coexistence, society, association, partnership, cooperation, fellowship.

concomitant, accessory, adjunct, attachment, appendage, belongings, appurtenance, attendant, complement; satellite; *sine qua non;* coincidence; consequence.

adj. accompanying, concomitant, coexistent, attendant, accessory, connected, related, associated, belonging, attending, coincidental, incidental, ancillary; contemporary, concurrent, synchronous, simultaneous; symptomatic; united.

vb. accompany, be found with, exist with, happen with, coexist, belong, characterize, coincide, be connected with, go hand in hand, go together, be related, follow.

adv. together, hand in hand, collectively.

61 duality

n. duality, dualism, doubleness, double-sidedness; two, deuce, pair, couple, couplet, twosome, tandem.

adj. dual, duple, dualistic, binary, both, twin, paired, duplex, bilateral, bipartite, bipartisan, bi-.

vb. pair, couple, match, mate, dualize; combine.

62 duplication

n. duplication, doubling, reduplication, repetition, iteration, encore, copy.

adj. double, duplicate, twofold, twin, second.

vb. double, repeat, twin, duplicate, reduplicate, copy.

adv. twice, again, once more.

63 bisection

n. bisection, halving, forking, bifurcation; half, hemisphere, dichotomy; dividing line, equator.

adj. bisected, half, bifurcated, semi-, demi-, hemi-.

vb. bisect, halve, cut in two, divide, split, sunder, bifurcate; go halves; diverge, fork.

64 triality

n. triality, trinity; three, triad, threesome, trio, triplet, trilogy, triangle.

adj. three, tertiary, tripartite, trilateral, triangular, triplex, triform, tri-; triune.

65 triplication

n. triplication, triplicity, hat trick.

adj. treble, threefold, triplicate, third.

vb. treble, triple, triplicate.

66 trisection

n. trisection, tripartition, third, trichotomy.

vb. trisect, cut in three.

67 quaternity

n. quaternity; four, tetrad; square, quadrilateral, quadrangle; quartet, foursome, quadruplet, tetragon.

adj. four, quaternary, quaternal; quadratic, biquadratic, square, quadrilateral, quadri-, tetra-.

68 quadruplication

n. quadruplication, quadruplicity.

adj. fourfold, quadruplicate, fourth, quadruple.

vb. quadruple, quadruplicate.

69 quadrisection

n. quadrisection, quadripartition; fourth, quarter, quart.

vb. quadrisect, quarter, cut in four.

70 five and over

n. five, fiver, pentad, quintuplet, pentagon, quintet, quincunx, Pentateuch; six, half a dozen, hexad, sextuplet, hexagon, sextet; seven, heptad, septuplet, heptagon, septet; eight, octad, octagon, octet, octave; nine, ennead, nonagon, enneagon, nonet; ten, decade, decagon; double figures; eleven, endecagon; twelve, dozen, dodecagon; thirteen, baker's dozen; teens; twenty, score; hundred, century, centenary; three figures, treble figures; gross; thousand, grand, millenium; ten thousand, myriad; million; billion; trillion.

adj. five, quintuple; six, sextuple; seven, septuple; eight, octuple; ten, decimal; twelve, duodecimal; -fold.

71 multisection

n. multisection, quinquesection.

vb. multisect, quinquesect.

72 plurality

n. plurality, plural, number, multiplicity, variety, abundance, some; majority.

adj. plural, pluralistic, pluralistical, multiple, many, some, numerous; more.

73 fraction

n. fraction, fragment, part, section, portion, segment.

adj. fractional, partial, fragmentary, constituent, sectional.

see also 55, 717

74 zero

n. zero, nil, nought; nothingness, nullity, void; nothing, none, no one, nobody; no score, duck, love.

adj. zero, null, not one.

75 multitude

n. multitude, numerosity, multiplicity; great amount, quantity, lot; great number, hundreds, thousands, myriads, millions; crowd, mob, army, throng, flock, legion, host, posse; plenty, a great deal, abundance, profusion, bonanza (*inf.*); majority, main part, mass, bulk, main emphasis, weight.

adj. many, not a few, several, considerable, numerous, manifold, countless, legion; much, sufficient, enough, ample, galore (*inf.*); profuse, abundant, overflowing, prevalent, plentiful; crowded, populous, peopled; dense, teeming with, alive with, thick.

vb. be many, crowd with, throng with, flock, mass, swarm with, teem with, crawl with; overflow with; pack, stuff; outnumber.

76 fewness

n. fewness, paucity, scarcity, sparseness, thinness, rarity; a few, handful, smattering, sprinkling; remnant, minority, insufficiency, absence, lack.

adj. few, not many, sparse, scant, thin, inconsiderable, negligible, infrequent, few and far between.

vb. diminish, reduce, lessen; lack, need.

77 repetition

n. repetition, recurrence, repetitiveness, reappearance; reproduction, copy, duplication; renewal, resumption; reiteration, rehearsal, recapitulation.

repeat, encore, replay; reprint, reissue, rehash.

adj. repeated, reiterated, restated, reworded, retold; reproduced, remade, redone, copied; repetitious, repetitive, boring.

vb. repeat, reiterate, restate, reword, retell, iterate; recite, say after, echo; rehearse, go over, take it from the top (*inf.*); recapitulate; redo, remake, renew, rework, remodel; rehash, revive; reissue, republish, copy; reoccur, reappear.

adv. again, over again, anew; ditto, encore; repeatedly.

78 infinity

n. infinity, endlessness, limitlessness; eternity; infinitude, perpetuity.

adj. infinite, immense, vast, untold, boundless, endless, immeasurable, unexhaustible, interminable; countless, numberless, unnumbered; eternal, perpetual.

vb. go on and on, know no bounds.

adv. infinitely, *ad infinitum*, without end.

D Order

79 order

n. order, organization, arrangement, array, state of order; tidiness, orderliness, neatness; method, pattern, regularity, system; uniformity, routine, habit; discipline.

adj. orderly, organized, methodical, systematic, regular, harmonious; under control, businesslike; neat, tidy, shipshape, well-ordered.

vb. order, organize, harmonize; take shape, fall into place.

adv. in order, all right, all correct, O.K., orderly, systematically, methodically.

80 disorder

n. disorder, disarrangement, muddle, clutter, mess, disarray, disharmony, disorderliness, untidiness; chaos, crisis; confusion, disturbance, shambles, Bedlam, mix-up.

turmoil, tumult, turbulence, agitation, to-do, ferment, storm, upheaval, *mêlée*, *fracas*, uproar, hullabaloo, frenzy, row, riot; anarchy, unruliness.

adj. orderless, out of order, unorganized, disorganized, in disarray, out of order, untidy; unsystematic, unmethodical, irregular, non-uniform; incoherent, muddled, confused, mixed up (*inf.*), disconnected; chaotic; tumultuous, turbulent; anarchical, lawless.

adv. confusedly, anyhow, irregularly, in disorder, higgledy-piggledy, upside down.

81 arrangement

n. arrangement, ordering, reduction to order, composition, preparation, organization, reorganization, regulation, marshalling, disposal, distribution; plan, method, system.

adj. arranged, well-arranged, ordered, organized, well-organized, methodical, regular, systematic, well-regulated, classified, sorted, coordinated, connected, disposed; disciplined; disentangled, unravelled, straightened out.

vb. arrange, plan, prepare, compose, put in order, set in order, reduce to order, array, dispose; assign, set, establish, formulate, coordinate, line up, regulate, marshal, range; organize, systematize, standardize, formalize, coordinate, connect; collocate; classify, pattern; disentangle, unravel, untwist, uncoil, straighten out; put one's own house in order.

82 disarrangement

n. disarrangement, derangement, disorganization, dishevelment, discomposure; irregularity, tangle, entanglement.

adj. disarranged, discomposed, disorganized, disorderly.

vb. disturb, disorganize, disorder, jumble, shuffle, mix up, muddle, derange, upset, unsettle, agitate, disconcert, discompose; ruffle, dishevel; confuse, perturb, confound, trouble; disperse, scatter; destroy, disrupt, dislocate; disband; overturn, overthrow; stir up, put the cat among the pigeons (*inf.*).

83 list

n. list, enumeration, classification, record, register, catalogue, directory, file; statement, schedule, agenda, table; roll, roll-call; roster, rota; enrolment; inventory, stock list, checklist; programme, prospectus, syllabus, synopsis; index, table of contents, bibliography, thesaurus, dictionary, glossary, lexicon.

vb. list, enumerate, catalogue, itemize, classify; enter, register, book, inscribe, record, file, log; enrol, enlist, matriculate; schedule.

84 precedence

n. precedence, antecedence, priority, precedency, previousness; coming before, anteriority; pre-eminence, precedent, preference, superiority.

adj. preceding, precedent, antecedent, anterior; previous, earlier, former, foregoing, prior, aforementioned.

vb. come before, go before, go ahead, precede, have precedence, take pre-

cedence; lead, be in front, head, place before; herald, pioneer, forerun, blaze the trail (*inf.*), clear the way, show the way, set the fashion; preface, introduce, prelude, preamble, usher in.

adv. before, in advance, above.

85 sequence

n. sequence, going after, following, placement, succession; successiveness, consequence; order, series, progression, set, string, row, chain, train, flow, concatenation.

adj. following, succeeding, ensuing, resulting, subsequent, successive, consequent; next, later, posterior; sequential, consecutive, serial; connected.

vb. come after, go after, go behind; ensue, follow, result; place after, append; succeed, come next, supersede, displace, supplant, become heir to.

adv. after, afterwards, behind, subsequently.

86 precursor

n. precursor, predecessor; pioneer, herald, vanguard, scout, pathfinder, forerunner, harbinger; parent, ancestor, forbear.

precedent, antecedent; prelude, preliminary, introduction, prologue, foreword, preface, exordium, prolegomena, preamble; prefix; authoritative example; preparation.

adj. precursory, preliminary, prefatory, introductory; exploratory, preparatory.

87 sequel

n. sequel, consequence, effect, result, end, issue, outcome, upshot, aftermath; after-effect, by-product, spin-off; inference, deduction, conclusion; afterthought, second thoughts; follow-up; continuation, tail, tailpiece, supplement, postscript, epilogue, appendage; suffix.

88 beginning

n. beginning, start, commencement, outset, onset, outbreak; foundation, establishment, origination, invention, birth, origin, genesis, cause, source, root, spring; infancy, primitiveness, youth; starting-point, square one.

inauguration, initiation, début, coming out, unveiling, *première*, opening, inception.

preliminaries, introduction, prelude, foreword, preface; rudiments, first principles, ABC, primer, basics.

adj. beginning, first, starting, initial, maiden; introductory, precursory, opening, inaugural; foundational, elementary, fundamental, basic, rudimentary; original, embryonic, primitive.

vb. begin, start, commence, go ahead, make a beginning, make a start, kick off (*inf.*); come into existence, arise, break out, burst forth, rise, be born, see the light of day; make one's début, come out; undertake, do, set about, tackle, enter upon, set in motion, start up, get under way, start the ball rolling, activate; take the first step, break the ice; begin again, go back to square one (*inf.*).

initiate, conceive, introduce, found, establish, institute, inaugurate, open, originate, invent.

adv. initially, in the first place, first, *ab initio*, at the outset, to begin with, for a kick-off (*inf.*).

see also 605

89 end

n. end, conclusion, close, termination, ending, finish, stop, cessation, completion, closure, adjournment; dissolution; expiration, death, decease, demise; retirement; finale, swan song, last word, death blow, curtains (*inf.*), *finis*, end of the line (*inf.*).

extreme, extremity, terminus, terminal, furthest point, achievement; consummation, perfection, culmination, climax, *dénouement;* goal, limit, point, boundary, top, peak, summit, head, bottom, base, tail; postscript, epilogue, appendage.

adj. ending, final, last, ultimate, terminal, concluding, consummate, ended, settled, concluded; extreme.

vb. end, finish, stop, conclude, terminate, cease, discontinue, desist, refrain, come to an end; expire, breathe one's last, die; run out, run its course, come to a close, draw to a close, break off; settle, determine, bring to an end, put an end to, dispose of, suspend, postpone, cancel, bring to a standstill, arrest, quell; switch off, wind up; end up.

adv. finally, lastly, at last, in conclusion, ultimately.

see also 144

90 middle

n. middle, midpoint, centre, middle distance, equidistance, halfway house; pivot, heart, kernel, core; focus, focal point; average, mean, median; midst, thick of things.

adj. middle, centre, central, mid, equidistant, halfway, medial, intermediate; focal; mean, average; moderate, neutral, compromising.

adv. in the middle, midway, halfway, in between.

91 continuity

n. continuity, continuousness, consecutiveness, progression, continuance, one thing after another, constancy, flow, succession, endlessness, perpetuation, perpetuity; routine, daily round, monotony; sequence, queue, crocodile, procession, march, cortège, column, train, suite, retinue, single file, tail, tailback.

adj. continuous, consecutive, running, serial, successive, progressive, constant, endless, perpetual, sustained, persisting, unbroken, uninterrupted; regular.

vb. continue, carry on, maintain, sustain, remain, succeed, follow in a line; file, march, parade, queue; endure.

adv. continuously, in succession, successively, in file, in train.

92 discontinuity

n. discontinuity, disconnectedness, disjunction; interruption, intervention, break, interval, intermission, pause, breather, rest, stop-over; gap, missing link.

adj. discontinuous, disconnected, unconnected, interrupted, broken; intermittent, irregular, infrequent, few and far between; spasmodic, jerky, uneven, desultory.

vb. discontinue, break, interrupt, pause, stop over; disconnect.

adv. at intervals, irregularly, in fits and starts, discontinuously.

see also 200

93 position in a series

n. term, serial position, order, rank, grade, station, position, situation, status, standing, footing, level, tier, rung, degree.

94 assemblage

n. assemblage, bringing together, juxtaposition, mobilization.

gathering, assembly, association, collection, company, society; circle, clique; meeting, reception, party; council, committee, conference, congress, commission, convention, congregation, convocation, symposium.

group, body, mass, crowd, throng, mob, crush, huddle, band, gang, troop, horde; team, cast, crew, squad; swarm, colony, herd, flock, pack, brood, shoal, school; set, cluster, bunch, lot, batch, bundle.

adj. gathered, assembled, met, convened; crowded, dense, swarming.

vb. gather, assemble, meet, come together, associate, congregate, converge, rendezvous; group, crowd, throng, rally, flock in, pour in; swarm, huddle, bunch; accumulate, pile up, amass; collect, bring together, call up, summon, convene, muster, round up.

95 dispersion

n. dispersion, dispersal, scattering, dissemination, broadcasting, dissipation, diffusion, divergence, decentralization.

adj. dispersed, scattered.

vb. disperse, scatter; disseminate, broadcast, sow, seed; sprinkle, strew, spread, dissipate; separate, divide; shed, distribute, propagate, dispense, dole out, dispel, diffuse, decentralize, disband; evaporate; sprawl, diverge.

96 focus

n. focus, focal point, centre; meeting place, forum, market, club, rendezvous; heart, hub, centre of interest, headquarters, nerve centre; Mecca, promised land.

vb. focus, converge, concentrate, centre, attract, draw attention.

see also 224

97 class

n. class, sort, kind, type, category, section, division, group, grouping, department, branch; mark, brand, make; strain, breed, line, family, genus, species, phylum, caste; hierarchy, rank.

classification, categorization, specification, taxonomy, systematization, list.

adj. classificatory, taxonomic.

vb. class, sort, classify, categorize, hierarchize, rank, grade, group, divide.

98 inclusion

n. inclusion, admission, reception, incorporation, embodiment, composition.

adj. inclusive, comprehensive, all-inclusive, all-embracing, overall, wholesale, sweeping.

vb. include, admit, incorporate, embody, comprehend, comprise, consist of, constitute, contain, involve, take in, entail, embrace, enclose, subsume.

99 exclusion

n. exclusion, exclusiveness; omission, rejection, ejection; prohibition, boycott, embargo, blockade; eviction, dismissal, suspension, expulsion, excommunication, ostracism, segregation, apartheid; bar, ban, closed shop, lock-out.

adj. exclusive, restrictive, segregated, prohibitive.

vb. exclude, omit, leave out, remove, eliminate, except, disregard; disqualify, reject, dismiss, suspend, deport, banish, expel, excommunicate, send to Coventry, ostracize; feel left out, feel out of things; restrict, forbid, prohibit, bar, segregate, ban, black, blacklist, boycott; prevent, preclude, obviate.

prep. except, excluding, apart from, save, bar.

100 extraneousness

n. extraneousness, foreignness; outsider, foreigner, alien, stranger, immigrant, expatriot, migrant, emigrant, refugee; newcomer, guest, visitor; squatter, interloper, invader.

adj. extraneous, extrinsic, external, outward, outside; foreign, alien, strange, immigrant; exotic, imported, borrowed, adopted, introduced, naturalized; alienated, estranged.

101 generality

n. generality, universality; ubiquity; broadness; generalization, abstraction, observation, simplification, overview; average man, man in the street, everybody, every mother's son (*inf.*), all the world and his wife (*inf.*).

adj. general, overall, universal, global, catholic; worldwide, international, cosmopolitan; typical, representative, generic; broad, wide; comprehensive, widespread, ubiquitous, blanket, average.

vb. be general, prevail, predominate; generalize, expand, broaden; conclude, infer.

102 speciality

n. speciality, particularity, originality, individuality, peculiarity, distinctiveness, uniqueness, idiosyncrasy, characteristic.

particulars, specifications, details, minutiae.

adj. special, particular, peculiar, especial, distinct, unique, original, *sui generis*, individual, individualistic, characteristic, idiosyncratic; specific, precise.

vb. specify, define, particularize, itemize, designate, enumerate, go into detail; single out, isolate, put one's finger on (*inf.*).

103 rule

n. rule, regulation, law, direction,

instruction, ordinance, code, order, precept, norm, principle, maxim, proposition, formula, guide, criterion, model, standard, procedure, system, convention.

adj. regulated, normative, prescriptive; legislative; formulaic, conventional.

see also **626, 954**

104 diversity
n. diversity, variation, variousness, heterogeneity, multiformity, variability, difference; medley, mixture, variety, miscellany.

adj. diverse, diversified, various, manifold, heterogeneous, multifarious, motley, irregular; different, disparate, variable, changeable.

see also **45**

105 conformity
n. conformity, correspondence, congruity, consistency, coincidence, compatibility, agreement, affinity, resemblance, similarity, adjustment, acclimatization.

conformist, conventionalist, traditionalist, loyalist, conservative.

adj. conforming, agreeing, harmonious, corresponding, appropriate, applicable, consonant; similar, resembling, well-matched, conformable, adaptable, adjustable, compatible, consistent.

vb. conform, comply, agree, accord; accommodate, adapt, adjust, fit, suit, integrate, bend, square, accustom, acclimatize, harmonize, reconcile; follow, obey, observe, fall into line, toe the line, adhere to.

106 unconformity
n. unconformity, difference, contrast, dissimilarity, disagreement, incon-

sistency, incongruity, incompatibility; nonconformity, unorthodoxy, heresy, schism; eccentricity, peculiarity, unconventionality, abnormality, irregularity.

nonconformist, dissenter, rebel, angry young man, separatist, demonstrator, maverick; eccentric, crank; homosexual, queer (*sl.*), gay (*sl.*), lesbian.

adj. unconformable, different, dissimilar, inconsistent, incongruous, incompatible, inappropriate, inapplicable; nonconformist, unorthodox; heretical, dissident, unconventional, eccentric, peculiar, abnormal, irregular, unusual, unfamiliar.

E Time

107 time
n. time, duration, continuance, extent, life, span, season, date.

adj. temporal; dated.

vb. elapse, pass; continue, last; spend time, employ, fill, occupy oneself, use, what do with oneself, while away, idle, fritter, squander; happen, occur, transpire.

adv., prep. during, when, while, whilst, in the course of, throughout, in the process of; meanwhile, in the meantime, in the interim.

see also **109**

108 absence of time
n. timelessness, neverness, nothingness, eternity.

adv. never, at no time, never again, nevermore.

109 period
n. period, era, epoch, time, season, interval, phase, age, generation; term, span, spell, stint, stretch; cycle; second,

minute, hour, day, week, fortnight, month, year, leap year, decade, decennium, jubilee, centenary, millenium, aeon.

adj. periodic, seasonal, recurring, recurrent, cyclic, regular.

110 course of time

n. course of time, lapse of time.

vb. elapse, pass, lapse; flow, proceed, run, fly.

see also 109

111 contingent duration

adv., prep. as long as, provisionally, for the present, for the time being.

112 long duration

n. lifetime, ages, eternity, month of Sundays (*inf.*), prolongation, permanence; endurance.

adj. long-term, long-standing, long-lasting, abiding, lasting, durable, permanent; enduring, steadfast, unyielding, persistent, surviving.

vb. last, endure, continue, stay, persist, remain, abide, never end, prevail, persevere; survive, outlive, outlast, outstay, live on, linger.

113 short duration

n. transience, ephemerality, evanescence, impermanence; brief period, flash in the pan (*inf.*), nine days' wonder (*inf.*).

adj. transient, transitory, brief, temporary, quick, short, short-term, momentary, short-lived; fading, passing, fleeting, cursory, ephemeral, evanescent, impermanent, perishable, before one can say Jack Robinson (*inf.*).

vb. be transient, pass, pass away, fly, fleet, flit, fade, vanish, disappear.

114 endless duration

n. perpetuity, endlessness, eternity, infinity, everlastingness, timelessness, immortality, constancy, endurance.

adj. perpetual, eternal, endless, interminable, continual, unceasing, incessant, unremitting, infinite everlasting, enduring, around-the-clock, timeless, ageless, immortal, incorruptible, imperishable; perennial.

vb. perpetuate, immortalize, eternalize, preserve, keep alive; never end, go on forever.

adv. always, forever, on and on, perpetually.

115 point of time

n. instantaneousness, suddenness, abruptness; instant, second, moment, flash, jiffy (*inf.*), twinkling, point of time.

adj. instantaneous, immediate, spontaneous, sudden, abrupt, prompt, punctual.

adv. instantaneously, instantly, immediately, at once, directly, forthwith, without delay, promptly, suddenly, abruptly, at the drop of a hat, on the spur of the moment.

116 chronometry

n. chronometry, horology, chronology, timing, timekeeping, dendrochronology; date, day, time; local time, summer time, daylight saving.

timepiece, timekeeper, chronometer, clock, alarm clock, digital clock, watch, wristwatch, digital watch, stopwatch, hour-glass, sun-dial, egg-timer; time-signal, pips, siren, hooter; calendar, schedule, timetable, diary, journal, register, almanac, chronicle, annals, log, memoirs.

adj. chronological, horological, temporal, horometrical, chronometrical.

vb. time, date; put the clocks back, put the clocks forward, set the alarm, wind up, keep time, gain, lose; clock in, clock out.

117 anachronism

n. anachronism, wrong date, misdating, mistiming, parachronism, prochronism.

adj. anachronistic, misdated, undated, early, beforehand; late, overdue.

vb. misdate, antedate, predate, postdate.

118 priority

n. priority, antecedence, anteriority, previousness; pre-existence, preoccurrence; precedent, antecedent, foretaste, preview.

adj. prior, earlier, before, preceding, previous, anterior, past, antecedent, ahead of; pre-existing; one-time, ex-, retired, former; foregoing, abovementioned, above, aforesaid.

vb. go before, come before, precede, forerun, antecede, herald.

see also **84, 124**

119 posteriority

n. posteriority, succession, subsequence; sequel, follower, successor.

adj. following, subsequent, later, after, coming after, next, posterior; designate, elect, to-be; consequential, resulting.

vb. come after, go after, succeed, ensue, follow, result.

see also **85, 123**

120 present time

n. contemporaneity; present time, present moment, present, the time being, this day and age, modern times, today.

adj. present, contemporary, modern, current, present-day, latest, newest, actual, contemporaneous, existent.

adv. now, at present, at the moment, today, nowadays, right now, at this moment in time.

121 different time

n. different time, not now, other time.

adv. not now, yesterday, earlier, tomorrow, later, sometime, sooner or later, at one time or other, at a different time.

122 synchronism

n. synchronism, simultaneousness, coexistence, concurrence, coincidence, contemporaneity; same age; contemporary, own generation, peers, fellows, year, class, set.

adj. synchronous, contemporary, concurrent, coincident, coexistent, simultaneous, contemporaneous; accompanying.

vb. synchronize, coexist, exist together, coincide; accompany.

adv. at the same time, simultaneously, concurrently, in phrase, in step.

123 future

n. futurity, future, tomorrow, time to come; prospect, fate; the shape of things to come; afterlife, world to come, next world, hereafter.

adj. future, later, coming, to come, approaching, unfolding, at hand; prospective, designate; imminent, impending; likely, expected, inevitable.

vb. lie in the future, be near, draw near, approach; impend, threaten.

adv. tomorrow, in the future, in the course of time, hereafter.

124 past

n. past, history, antiquity, prehistory, archaism; retrospection, memory; olden times, yesterday good old days (*inf.*).

adj. past, historical, ancient, prehis

toric, primitive, proto-; gone, bygone, lost, forgotten, no more; former, late, old, once, one-time, ex-, retired, sometime, erstwhile.

vb. be past, have run its course, have had its day (*inf.*), be a thing of the past.

adv. yesterday, formerly, in the past, ago, of old.

125 newness

n. newness, modernity, renovation, modernization, novelty, innovation.

fad, craze, passing fancy, vogue, fashion, the latest thing (*inf.*), all the rage (*inf.*), the last word (*inf.*), the in-thing (*inf.*); innovator, pioneer, leader, futurist, trendsetter, pacesetter, *avant-garde*, upstart, fledgling.

adj. modern, new, novel, current, topical, recent, original; contemporary, present-day, up-to-the-minute, up-to-date, brand-new, just out, hot off the press (*inf.*); newfangled (*inf.*); untraditional, in fashion, in vogue, stylish, chic, smart, modish, trendy (*inf.*), in (*inf.*), *à la mode*, *avant-garde;* advanced, forward-looking, progressive, ultra-modern, streamlined, futuristic, space-age; convenient, automatic, electronic; fresh, virgin, budding, inexperienced.

vb. modernize, bring up to date, adapt, renew, reissue, republish, refurbish, renovate, streamline, update; innovate.

adv. recently, newly, lately, afresh, anew, of late.

126 oldness

n. oldness, antiquity; obsolescence, extinction, decay, deterioration, decline; maturity, ripeness; tradition, footsteps; old age, senility, infirmity.

adj. old, archaic, prehistoric, antique, ancient, primitive, primeval,

aboriginal, extinct; time-worn, time-honoured, venerable, forgotten, antediluvian, distant, former, unrecorded, of earliest time; old-fashioned, antiquated, obsolete, obsolescent, outmoded, discarded, disused, unstylish, *passé*, out of date, old hat (*inf.*), out of fashion, behind the times, anachronistic, dated, outdated; traditional, handed down, established, customary, Victorian; dilapidated, secondhand, used, decrepit, decayed, faded; patched, mended, in holes, rusty, moth-eaten.

see also 30

127 morning; spring; summer

n. morning, morn, a.m., sunrise, dawn, daybreak, break of day, cock-crow, the small hours, forenoon, matin, matins, aurora; noon, midday, meridian; spring, springtime, spring-tide, flowering, budding; summer, summertime, summertide, midsummer, Indian summer, St. Luke's summer, St. Martin's summer.

adj. morning; spring, springlike, vernal; summer, summery, aestival.

128 evening; autumn; winter

n. p.m., afternoon, evening, eventide, eve, evensong, vesper, vespers; sunset, sundown, twilight, dusk, dimness, half-light, gloaming, curfew, night, nightfall, nighttime; midnight, witching time of night, dead of night; autumn, fall, harvest; winter, wintertime, wintertide, midwinter.

adj. afternoon, vespertine, evening; crepuscular; night, nocturnal; autumn, autumnal; wintry, winter, brumous.

129 youth

n. youth, youthfulness, young blood, juniority, juvenility; infancy, tender age, childhood, adolescence, puberty, pubescence, boyhood, girlhood, school-going age, teens, boyishness, girlishness, next generation; freshness, salad days, awkward age, growing pains, younger generation, immaturity, inexperience, callowness, greenness, prime, spring, springtime; minority, wardship, nonage, pupilage.

adj. young, youthful, boyish, girlish, childlike, teenage, adolescent, pubescent, in one's teens; formative, budding, flowering, unwrinkled, ageless, tender, developing; childish, unripe, green, callow, awkward, raw, unfledged, immature, inexperienced, puerile, juvenile; minor, under-age, younger, minor, junior, youngest.

see also 131

130 age

n. age, oldness, old age, senility, second childhood, senescence, seniority, dotage, infirmity; middle age, middle years, older generation; responsibility, experience, wisdom, maturity, caution.

adj. old, aged, elderly, advanced in years, senile, senescent, matured, seasoned, grey, balding, wrinkled, toothless; superannuated; inactive, infirm, debilitated, feeble, enfeebled, doddery, decrepit, moribund, dying, with one foot in the grave; experienced, qualified, expert, respected, venerable; major, senior, older, elder, oldest, eldest, first-born.

vb. age, grow old, decline, progress, advance in years, have seen better days, show one's age; superannuate; mellow, develop, mature.

see also 132

131 infant

n. baby, babe, infant, suckling, mite, toddler, tot, bairn; child, youngster,

kid, brat (*sl.*); young person, juvenile, pupil, schoolchild, minor, teenager, adolescent, student; boy, schoolboy, lad, junior, master; young man, youth, stripling, fellow; girl, schoolgirl, young lady, lass, miss.

adj. baby, newborn, childlike; infantile, babyish, childish, puerile, juvenile; boyish, girlish; adolescent, youthful, teenage, pubescent; immature, naive, innocent, spontaneous.

132 veteran

n. old person, elder, senior, retired person, old age pensioner, senior citizen, dependant; veteran, patriarch, old hand (*inf.*), old timer (*inf.*), grand old man, elder statesman; old woman, matriarch.

133 adulthood

n. adulthood, years of discretion, manhood, womanhood, maturity, age of majority, majority.

adult, grown-up, man, woman.

adj. adult, grown-up, manly, womanly, mature, responsible; marriageable.

vb. come of age, grow up, attain majority; mature.

see also 380, 381

134 earliness

n. earliness, primitiveness, anticipation, presentiment, recency, immediacy, punctuality, promptness, promptitude, prematurity; foresight, hunch; early riser, early bird (*inf.*).

adj. early, prior, previous, recent, primitive; new, fresh, budding; premature, in advance, precocious, preceding, anticipatory, preparatory, advanced, prevenient; immediate, precipitant, speedy; imminent; punctual, prompt, timely, on time, sharp.

vb. be early, anticipate, foresee,

forestall, prepare for; precede, take precedence, get a head start, pre-empt, jump the queue.

135 lateness

n. lateness, belatedness, tardiness, retardation, slowness, dilatoriness, backwardness; late hour, high time, last minute; delay, deferment, postponement, adjournment, discontinuation, suspension, procrastination, cooling-off period, moratorium, respite, days of grace, stay, reprieve, remission, wait and see, filibuster; slow starter, late riser.

adj. late, advanced, tardy, dilatory; too late, overdue, belated, delayed, behind, behindhand; last-minute; unready, unpunctual.

vb. be late, stay up, burn the midnight oil; tarry, be slow, linger, saunter, dawdle, dally, shilly-shally; delay, defer, postpone, procrastinate, retard, stay, adjourn, put off, suspend, withhold, hold back, wait and see, play for time, filibuster; put in cold storage, mothball (*inf.*), put in mothballs (*inf.*), put on ice (*inf.*), shelve.

136 timeliness

n. timeliness, opportuneness, opportunism, expediency, fortuity.

opportunity, chance, occasion, right time; crisis, emergency, turning point, dilemma, eleventh hour, nick of time, moment of truth, hour of decision.

adj. opportune, fortuitous, timely, well-timed, punctual, on time, propitious, auspicious, providential, suitable, expedient, advantageous, convenient; critical, crucial, decisive, momentous, significant, key, urgent.

vb. grasp the opportunity, use to the full, take advantage of, cash in on, exploit, capitalize, make capital out of,

opportunize, play on, profit by; hang in the balance.
see also 577, 915

137 untimeliness

n. untimeliness, inopportuness, inexpediency, mistiming; disturbance, interruption, intrusion.

adj. mistimed, ill-timed, untimely, unpunctual, too early, premature, too late; wrong, ill-chosen, improper, untoward, unseemly, intrusive, interrupting, disturbing, inconvenient, disadvantageous, unsuitable, inappropriate, unseasonable, unfavourable, inopportune, inauspicious.

vb. mistime; interrupt, disturb, intrude, break in on (*inf.*); miss an opportunity, let an opportunity slip, miss the boat, fail to exploit.
see also 578, 916

138 frequency

n. frequency, recurrence, reoccurrence, regularity, constancy, oftenness.

adj. frequent, regular, recurrent, successive, reiterated, rhythmic; common, commonplace, customary, not rare, familiar, habitual, general, expected, usual, periodic; incessant, non-stop, perennial, constant, monotonous, continual, steady.

vb. recur, repeat; go on, continue, occur regularly.

adv. often, frequently, usually, generally, as a rule, commonly, regularly, repeatedly; sometimes, now and again, occasionally, at times, from time to time.
see also 140

139 infrequency

n. infrequency, rarity, uncommonness, scarcity, intermittence, unpredictability, irregularity.

adj. infrequent, occasional, rare, sparse, scarce, few, few and far between, scanty, sporadic, meagre, precious; unique, single, individual; uncommon, unusual, bizarre; intermittent; casual, chance, incidental.

adv. infrequently, scarcely, hardly, hardly ever, occasionally, uncommonly, now and then, rarely, seldom.

see also **141**

140 regularity

n. regularity, recurrence, periodicity, repetition, frequency; stabilization, evenness, steadiness, constancy; timing, phasing, alternation, oscillation; current, wave, rota, cycle, rotation, swing, circuit, pulsation, beat, rhythm, pulse; routine, daily round; anniversary, birthday, commemoration.

adj. periodical, regular, routine, periodic, systematic, methodical, organized, steady, constant, uniform, serial, cyclic, rotational, pulsating, rhythmic, alternating.

vb. recur, repeat, reiterate, come round again, alternate, undulate, regulate, revolve, throb, beat, pulsate, swing.

adv. periodically, systematically, regularly, at regular intervals, like clockwork; hourly, daily, weekly, monthly, annually.

see also **138**

141 irregularity

n. irregularity, fitfulness, jerkiness, unsteadiness, inconstancy, unevenness, variability; jerk, fits and starts, spasm, stop, break, bump.

adj. irregular, sporadic, off and on, fitful, jerky, spasmodic, irregular, uneven; unsteady, shaky; inconstant, random, fluctuating, faltering, waver-

ing, flickering; capricious, changeable, casual.

vb. fluctuate, come and go.

see also **139**

F Change

142 change

n. change, variation, alteration, modification, adjustment, qualification, transformation, refinement, evolution, alternation; fluctuation, wavering, modulation; exchange, transference, substitution, mutation, permutation, conversion; transition, diversion, deviation; renewal, innovation, novelty, reconstruction, improvisation, reformation, revision, rearrangement, reorganization, readjustment, metamorphosis, vicissitude, transmutation; deterioration, withdrawal, removal.

modifier, changer, converter, transformer, catalyst, agitator, leaven, adapter.

adj. variable, varying, changeable, modifiable, qualifiable, alternating, inconstant, mutable, plastic, transformable, movable, mobile.

vb. change, alter, vary, modify, qualify, transform, adapt, adjust, improvise; exchange, transfer, substitute; turn, shift, veer; convert, commute; renew, revise, rearrange, reorganize, reform, translate, reconstruct, renovate; refine, moderate, temper; evolve; alternate, fluctuate, waver, modulate.

143 permanence

n. permanence, constancy, invariability, continuity, steadiness, stability; immobility, solidity, consistency; durability, endurance; conservatism, *status quo*, traditionalist, conservative, reactionary, die-hard, stick-in-the-mud.

adj. permanent, immovable, unchangeable, changeless, certain, fixed, uninterrupted, unchanging, continual, constant, lasting; enduring, unwavering, abiding; stable, unremitting; strong, robust, firm, steady, steadfast; conservative, traditional, unprogressive, reactionary, conventional; obstinate, stubborn.

vb. stay, remain, abide, persist; stabilize, maintain, preserve, uphold, sustain, support.

144 cessation
n. cessation, discontinuation, discontinuance, expiration, termination, conclusion.

stop, halt, standstill, closure, interruption, suspense, lapse; industrial action, stoppage, shut-down, strike, go-slow, work-to-rule, sit-in, walkout, unofficial strike, wildcat strike, general strike, lock-out; deadlock, confrontation; ceasefire, armistice, truce; rest, pause, holiday, vacation, respite, lull, breathing space, remission, recess; intermission, interlude, interval, interim, interregnum.

vb. cease, terminate, stop, discontinue, desist, refrain, finish, knock off (*inf.*), break up, quit, shut down, close down, shut up shop, call it a day (*inf.*); pack it in (*inf.*), knock it off (*sl.*); halt, check, restrain, put a stop to, arrest, stall, interrupt; strike, down tools, come out, go out, walk out, lock out, picket, boycott; pause, break, take five (*inf.*), rest, relax, let up (*inf.*); fizzle out (*inf.*).

see also **89**

145 continuance

n. continuance, continuation, perpetuation, maintenance, persistence, duration, prolongation.

adj. continual, uninterrupted, unbroken, connected, steady, constant, unceasing, incessant, ceaseless, sustained, inexhaustible.

vb. continue, carry on, keep on, go on, maintain, sustain, uphold, keep at it; stay, remain, last, survive, abide; endure, progress, persist, persevere, stay the course.

see also **535**

146 conversion
n. conversion, convertibility, processing, development, change-over, transformation, alteration; regeneration, new birth, rebirth, evangelization; convert, disciple, follower, believer, proselyte, catechumen.

adj. converted, altered, changed, transformed; regenerate, born again.

vb. convert, turn into, alter, transform, transmute; evangelize, proselytize, save, redeem; camouflage, disguise, mask, hide, conceal, obscure; remodel, improve, mend, reconstruct, reshape, reform, mould, metamorphose.

see also **142**

147 reversion
n. reversion, return, regress, regression, reaction, rebound, flashback, boomerang, recoil, backfire, backlash; restoration, restitution, re-establishment, reconditioning, refreshment, rejuvenation, recovery, reopening; atavism, throwback; resurrection, renewal, revival, comeback; reversal, *volte-face*, about-turn, backsliding, apostasy, lapse, relapse.

adj. reverted; atavistic; apostate, degenerate.

vb. revert, go back, return, turn

back, reverse; recur, reappear, restore, restitute, reinstate, replace; recoil, rebound; regress, retrogress, throw back; backslide, fall away, lapse, relapse, degenerate.

148 revolution

n. revolution, disaster, *débâcle*, explosion, eruption; *coup*, shake-up, overthrow, upheaval, revolt, rebellion, insurrection, anarchy, plot, subversion.

radical, revolutionary, extremist, fanatic, demonstrator, agitator, rebel, anarchist, guerrilla, freedom fighter, insurrectionist, traitor.

adj. revolutionary, radical, progressive, extreme, thorough, deep, complete, rabid; earth-shaking, catastrophic, cataclysmic, shattering; militant, rebellious, revolting, anarchistic, insurgent, underground, subversive, seditious.

vb. revolutionize, subvert, overthrow, upset, shake up; rise up, revolt.

149 substitution

n. substitution, exchange, transference, alternation, commutation, shift, shuffle, switch, rearrangement, transposition, vicariousness.

substitute, transfer, alternative, replacement, understudy, proxy, ghostwriter, locum, reserve, stand-in, standby; relief; deputy, agent, delegate; double, dummy, stopgap, makeshift; scapegoat, whipping boy.

adj. substitutional, alternative, vicarious, reserve, provisional, temporary, makeshift; dummy, mock, imitation.

vb. substitute, exchange, transfer, replace, commute, transpose, shuffle, shift, switch, act for, stand in for, cover for, fill in, relieve, fill in for, put in the place of, ghost, double for, serve

in one's stead; take it out on (*inf.*), work off.

adv. instead, in the place of, in lieu.

150 interchange

n. interchange, exchange, transfer, reciprocation, swap, mutuality, interrelation, interchangeability, tit for tat; barter, trade, commerce, correspondence, give and take (*inf.*).

adj. in exchange, mutual, reciprocal, reciprocating, interchangeable, commutable.

vb. interchange, exchange, swap, commute, interact, trade, barter, correspond; give and take (*inf.*).

151 changeableness

n. changeableness, changeability, variability, mutability, irregularity, instability, inconstancy, mobility, fluctuation, vacillation, wavering; fickleness, indecision, unreliability, erraticness, waywardness.

adj. changeable, variable, irregular, inconstant, mobile, vacillating, wavering, fluctuating, volatile, many-sided, versatile, flexible, malleable, adaptable, plastic, unstable, unsteady, protean; fickle, flighty, indecisive, fidgety, capricious, unreliable, erratic, wayward.

vb. vary, range, mutate, chop and change, waver, shift, vacillate, fluctuate, variegate, differ, depart, diverge, dissent.

152 stability

n. stability, immutability, invariability, firmness, permanence, constancy, irreversibility, immobility, immovableness, solidity; regularity; reliability, resoluteness, endurance; stabilization, equilibrium, balance, homeostasis.

fixture, establishment, constant,

invariant; rock, pillar; stabilizer, ballast, counterbalance, counterweight, sandbags.

adj. unchangeable, invariable, changeless, stable, constant, steady, immovable, immobile, stationary; unwavering, inflexible, unadaptable; resolute, reliable, steadfast; stereotyped, uniform; fixed, fast, set, sure, established, entrenched, inveterate.

vb. stabilize, fix, set, steady, secure, sustain, support, fasten; balance; establish, entrench, anchor, transfix.

see also 535

153 present events

n. eventuality, incidence; event, occurrence, incident, episode, happening, situation, circumstance, development, chance, proceeding, transaction, phenomenon, adventure, experience, triumph, celebration; affair, matter, concern; predicament, accident, misadventure, misfortune, mishap, calamity, emergency, catastrophe.

adj. happening, current, present, afloat, in the air, in the wind, about, prevailing.

vb. happen, take place, occur, come about, follow, ensue, arrive, transpire, fall on, befall, arise, come up, turn up, crop up; be realized, come off, turn out, feel, undergo, experience, meet.

154 future events

n. prospect, outlook, forecast, prediction, approach, promise; fate, destiny; imminence, threat, menace.

adj. impending, approaching, coming, near, close, forthcoming, imminent; threatening, brewing, ominous, certain, inevitable, inescapable, unavoidable, fateful, destined, fated; in prospect, in store, to come, in the offing, on the horizon.

vb. impend, approach, draw on,

near, advance, hover, be in store; loom, threaten, hang over, overshadow, menace; forecast, prognosticate; anticipate, expect.

see also **902**

G Causation

155 cause

n. causation, causality, origination, motivation, authorship.

cause, origin, source, root, spring, foundation, seed; beginning, birth, derivation, nativity, genesis; means, basis, grounds, ground, agent, occasion, influence, mainspring, determinant, antecedent; first cause, prime mover, producer, creator, author, originator, inventor, discoverer, founder; motive, inducement, activation; factor, element, rudiment, principle; reason, explanation.

adj. causal, original, determinant; basic, fundamental, primary, radical, initial.

vb. cause, make, create, produce, originate, effect, determine, bring about, provoke, generate, evoke, elicit, induce, call forth, give rise to, arouse, occasion, motivate, suggest, influence, lead to; conduce, contribute to, involve.

156 effect

n. effect, result, consequence, end, outcome, upshot, issue, product; consummation, after-effect, aftermath, repercussion, wake, reaction, backlash, sequel, fruit, harvest, emanation; by-product, spin-off.

adj. caused, consequent, consequential, resultant, resulting, following, ensuing, subsequent, derivative.

vb. result, follow, ensue, spring from,

proceed from, derive from, emanate from, originate in; become of, come of.

157 assignment of cause

n. assignment, attribution, imputation, reference, ascription; association; explanation, theory, hypothesis, rationale.

adj. attributable, assignable, referable, imputable, derivable, culpable; linked, associated; explanatory.

vb. attribute, assign, ascribe, impute, refer, charge, blame, trace, credit with, derive from, lay at; connect, associate, link; explain, account for, solve.

158 chance

n. chance, fortuity, randomness, unpredictability; odds, risk-taking, probability; fate, lot, fortune, luck, good luck, bad luck, pot luck; fluke (*inf.*), gamble.

adj. casual, chance, accidental, coincidental, fortuitous, random, haphazard, unthinking, hit-or-miss, aimless, fluky (*inf.*); unmotivated, inexplicable, unintentional.

vb. chance, fall to one's lot; chance upon, stumble on, venture, happen on, gamble, risk; stand a chance.

adv. by chance, by accident, unexpectedly, unintentionally, fortuitously, randomly, casually, perchance.

see also 553

159 power

n. power, potency, might, strength, energy, vigour, life, liveliness, dynamism; dominance, domination, omnipotence; sway, control, teeth, muscle, influence; ability, capability, skill, potentiality, competence, efficiency, capacity, faculty, efficacy; force, potential, thrust, pressure, horsepower, steam, electricity, juice (*sl.*),

gas, nuclear power, solar energy, hydro-electricity; power station, grid, pylon.

adj. powerful, mighty, energetic, vigorous, strong, lively, dynamic, empowered, forceful, dominant, potent; omnipotent, almighty; able, capable, up to (*inf.*), equal to, potential, competent, efficient, effective.

vb. be able, be up to (*inf.*), be capable of, lie in one's power; be powerful, perform, operate, accomplish; empower, confer, enable, power, charge, invest, arm, strengthen, electrify.

see also 161

160 impotence

n. impotence, lifelessness, powerlessness, ineffectuality, ineffectivity, helplessness; inability, incapability, incompetence; unproductiveness, infertility, barrenness; eunuch, gelding.

adj. powerless, unenergetic, unable, incapable, incompetent, inefficient, ineffective, inadequate, disabled, incapacitated, inept; infirm, helpless, unprotected, defenceless; spineless, nerveless, feeble; impotent, sterilized, sterile, barren, infertile, frigid.

vb. not be able, cannot, not find it in oneself to; disable, impair, exhaust, wear down, run down, incapacitate, disarm, unman, paralyze, put out of action, throw a spanner in the works; disqualify, invalidate; castrate, emasculate, spay, geld.

161 strength

n. strength, might, energy, vigour, force, vitality, toughness, stamina, hardness, brawn, muscle; invincibility.

adj. strong, mighty, powerful, forceful, energetic, firm; unyielding, unresisting, persistent; brawny, muscular, stout, hardy, tough, robust, stalwart, strapping, burly, beefy, big, solid, hefty, virile, athletic; secure, durable.

vb. strengthen, fortify, confirm, reinforce, establish, substantiate, empower, energize, stimulate, build up, brace, refresh, invigorate.

see also 535, 537

162 weakness

n. weakness, feebleness, frailty, faintness, fragility, flimsiness, delicacy, tenderness; infirmity, debility; effeminacy, femininity.

weakling, coward, cry-baby, sissy (*sl.*), pansy (*sl.*).

adj. weak, powerless, helpless, delicate, puny, frail; fragile, flimsy, brittle, insubstantial, makeshift, unsteady; effeminate, womanly; weak-minded, spineless, anaemic (*inf.*), faint-hearted, insipid, diluted, wishy-washy (*inf.*); worn, rotten, decrepit.

vb. faint, sicken, languish, crumble, decline; weaken, exhaust, enfeeble, impoverish, debilitate, enervate, disable, handicap; dilute, water down, blunt, sap; fade, give way, fizzle out (*inf.*).

163 production

n. production, productivity, output, performance, through-put; foundation, manufacture, establishment, construction, fabrication, processing; propagation, generation, procreation, fertility, reproduction, breeding, copulation.

product, creation, work, article, piece, goods, merchandise, handiwork, fruit, harvest, produce, yield, result, opus; edifice, building, structure, erection, invention, concoction, brain-child (*inf.*), baby (*sl.*), thing (*sl.*).

adj. productive, generative, creative, manufacturing; fruitful, rich, prolific, fertile; pregnant, expecting, with child,

with young, in the family way (*inf.*), in the club (*sl.*).

vb. produce, create, make, manufacture, put together, make up, fabricate, construct, build; devise, compose; furnish, effect, perform, return, render, provide; invent, concoct, cook up; carve, chisel; yield, blossom, flower; reproduce, generate, procreate, propagate, multiply, conceive, beget, breed.

164 destruction

n. destruction, annihilation, elimination, liquidation, extirpation, disintegration, demolition, eradication, obliteration, nullification, abolition, dissolution, suppression; slaughter; waste, overthrow, subversion, desolation, havoc, wreckage, sabotage, ruin, ravage, downfall, collapse, ruination.

adj. destructive, hurtful, troublesome, harmful, detrimental, ruinous, deadly, fatal, lethal, poisonous, venomous, toxic, internecine, shattering, annihilative.

vb. destroy, terminate, nullify, abolish, suppress, eradicate, wipe out, blot out, obliterate, wipe off the face of the earth, dissolve; annihilate, eliminate, liquidize, extirpate, exterminate, atomize, pulverize, decimate, decapitate; demolish, break, dismantle, knock down, pull down; crush, overthrow, overturn; blitz, bombard, smash, shatter, mutilate, undo; damage, lay waste, devastate, raze, plunder, ruin, pillage, ravage, despoil, sack.

be destroyed, perish, disintegrate, deteriorate, decay, crumble, go to rack and ruin.

165 reproduction

n. reproduction, reconstruction,

remaking, renovation, reforming; regeneration, resurrection; rediscovery, revival, renaissance; duplication, reduplication, reprinting.

adj. reproductive, regenerative, renascent.

vb. reproduce, reconstruct, rebuild, remake, redo, refashion, remould, reform, renovate, renew, revive, rediscover, regenerate, repeat; propagate, multiply; proliferate, duplicate, reprint, copy.

166 producer

n. producer, creator, maker, instigator, mover, manufacturer, constructor, builder, architect, composer, author, writer, originator, inventor, discoverer.

167 destroyer

n. destroyer, breaker; anarchist, terrorist, desperado, gunman, murderer; disrupter, ravager, vandal, defacer, wrecker, iconoclast, nihilist, abolitionist.

plague, pestilence, moth, locust, erosion, rust, cancer, poison, virus, fungus, mildew, blight; demolition expert, demolisher.

see also 370

168 productiveness

n. productiveness, productivity, generative capacity; prolificness, fruitfulness, fertility, proliferation, fecundity; lushness, luxuriance, exuberance, profusion, richness, abundance, wealth, plenty, horn of plenty, cornucopia, bounty, plethora, hotbed, warren; prosperity, boom.

adj. productive, fruitful, prolific, profuse, fertile, rich, fecund; bounteous, spawning, abundant, plenty, copious, lush, luxurious, fulsome,

exuberant, booming; prosperous, wealthy.

vb. be fruitful, blossom, prosper, thrive, flourish, proliferate, grow, swarm.

see also 163

169 unproductiveness

n. unproductiveness, stagnation, unprofitability, incapacity, barrenness, desolateness, infertility; sterilization, contraception; slump, recession, depression, austerity.

adj. unproductive, unprofitable, fruitless, profitless; desolate, barren, poor, unfruitful; ineffectual, ineffective; infertile, unbearing, sterilized, sterile, impotent, frigid, childless, celibate.

vb. stagnate, vegetate, fail; exhaust; castrate, emasculate, spay, geld.

170 parenthood

n. parenthood, ancestry, origin, genealogy, parentage, line, lineage; fatherhood, paternity; parent, progenitor, procreator, begetter; father, dad, daddy, pop (*sl.*); motherhood, maternity; mother, mum, mummy.

adj. generative, procreative, lifegiving; ancestral, genealogical; family, familial; parental, paternal, fatherly, maternal, motherly.

171 offspring

n. offspring, issue, progeny, posterity; lineage, generation, next generation; adoption; descent, sonship, filiation; family, child, son, daughter; heir, descendant; bastard.

adj. descended, familiar, lineal; filial, daughterly; bastard, illegitimate; adopted.

172 operation

n. operation, agency, action, execution, application, performance, running, management, conduct, function, process, instrumentality, means.

adj. operative, active, functioning, in operation, in action, in force; live, running, working, effective; executive, operational, functional, agential.

vb. operate, function, work, go, move, run; act, behave, perform, handle; produce, bring about.

see also 564, 565

173 vigour

n. vigour, energy, power, dynamism, vehemence, strength, lustiness, élan, dash, verve, vitality, get-up-and-go (*inf.*), go (*inf.*), zest, pep, bounce, zip; drive, push, thrust, enterprise, initiative, aggression.

stimulant, invigorator, activator, incentive, stimulus, fillip, pick-me-up, catalyst, booster, drug, shot.

adj. vigorous, powerful, potent, dynamic, strong, vehement, intense, lively, brisk, energetic; enterprising; aggressive, pushy (*inf.*), self-assertive; stimulating, invigorating, activating.

vb. invigorate, energize, activate, strengthen, fortify, reinforce, stimulate, animate, enliven, vitalize, drive, push, intensify.

see also 159, 161

174 inertness

n. inertness, inertia, inactivity, motionlessness, lifelessness, immobility, dullness, passivity, indolence, idleness, lethargy, listlessness.

adj. inert, lifeless, immobile, motionless, dead, inactive, idle, languid, torpid, lethargic, listless, indolent, passive, slow, still, pacific, dull, sluggish, dormant.

vb. slumber, languish, idle, stagnate, vegetate.

see also 267

175 violence

n. violence, force, boisterousness, turbulence, destructiveness; outburst, outbreak, uproar, explosion, eruption, disruption, clash, clammer, assault, onslaught; disorder, disturbance, turmoil, ferment, fury, frenzy, tumult; storm, blizzard, gale, hurricane, tornado, thunderstorm, hailstorm, cloudburst, tempest.

savage, barbarian, brute, beast, monster, animal, maniac, fiend, terrorist, bully, ruffian.

adj. violent, extreme, severe; vehement, forceful, boisterous, turbulent; rough, raging, wild, stormy, furious, outrageous, rampageous, destructive; aggressive; brutal, brutish, savage, fierce, barbarous.

vb. run wild, rush, mob; erupt, explode, blast, break out; roar, fume, boil, seethe; incite, stir up, whip up, lash; force, coerce; provoke.

176 moderation

n. moderation, assuagement, alleviation, pacification, placating, soothing; reduction; gentleness, calmness, mildness; control.

moderator, balm, consolation, relief, cure, tranquillizer, restraint.

adj. moderate, modest, reasonable; calm, gentle, tranquil; restrained, temperate.

vb. be moderate, be at peace, keep a low profile; keep a happy medium; moderate, restrain, temper, alleviate, reduce, decrease, abate, tone down, cushion, soften the blow, mitigate, mollify, soothe, relieve, console, assuage, pacify, placate, still, quieten; relax, let up.

177 influence

n. influence, weight, dominance,

power, control, force, pressure, sway, authority, pull (*inf.*); significance; prestige, reputation.

adj. influential, weighty, dominant, powerful, forceful, controlling, prevailing, authoritative, impòrtant, significant, momentous; prominent, reputable.

vb. influence, determine, affect, convince, persuade, sway, compel, turn, dominate, govern, control, lobby, bring pressure to bear, put pressure on, carry weight with, pull strings (*inf.*), get in with (*inf.*).

see also **420**

178 tendency

n. tendency, trend, direction, bent, drift, aim; tenor, thrust, spirit; inclination, bias, leaning, propensity, proneness, predisposition, predilection, penchant, fondness, liking, preference, weakness, proclivity.

adj. tending, conducive, predisposed.

vb. tend, lean, incline, drift, predispose, point to, aim, gravitate towards.

179 liability

n. liability, liableness, susceptibility, amenability; subjection, responsibility.

adj. liable, apt, inclined, disposed, prone, likely to, subject to; answerable, responsible, amenable.

vb. be liable, run the risk of, incur, fall on, be subject to, succumb to, fall prey to, expose oneself to, lay oneself open to.

180 concurrence

n. concurrence, collaboration, cooperation, partnership, working together, joint action; union, concert.

adj. concurrent, combined, allied, united, joint, cooperative; mutual.

vb. concur, cooperate, collaborate,

work together, unite, combine; agree, harmonize, accord.

see also **639**

181 counteraction

n. counteraction, opposition, polarity, antagonism, contradiction; retroaction, offsetting, neutralization; friction, resistance, drag, counterweight, cross-current, countermeasure; antidote, cure, medicine, relief, preventive, antibiotic, injection.

adj. counter, counteractive, neutralizing, retarding.

vb. counteract, work against, militate against, run counter to; neutralize, cancel out, invalidate, hinder, prevent, frustrate; interfere, oppose, contradict; drag; counterbalance, countervail.

II Space

A Space in general

182 indefinite space

n. space, expanse, extent, expansion, span, area, surface; range, scope, compass, reach, sweep, stretch, gamut, spread; room, open space, clearance, elbow-room, breathing space, latitude, margin, leeway.

adj. spatial; spacious, ample, extensive, roomy, capacious, vast, expansive, deep, broad, wide, long, far-reaching, widespread.

vb. reach, extend, spread, stretch, sweep, flow, range, encompass, span; open, expand, widen.

183 definite space

n. region, area, district, zone; patch, section, sector, quarter, square.

territory, country, state, kingdom,

realm, principality, duchy, province, county, shire, community, city, capital, centre, borough, town, village, hamlet; constituency, ward; diocese, parish; conurbation, metropolitan county, metropolitan district, metropolis, suburb, suburbia; locality, surroundings, environment, neighbourhood, environs, locale, milieu.

adj. territorial, regional; provincial, local, municipal, urban, suburban, rural; parochial, insular.

184 limited space
n. place, spot, position, point, stand, locus, corner; enclosure, field, compound, pen, close, sty, pound, paddock, plot, zone, square, quadrangle, yard, patio, precinct; niche, groove, socket.

185 situation
n. situation, position, location, station, setting, site, place, scene, scenery; whereabouts, bearings.

adj. situated, located, placed, positioned, sited, set, situate.

vb. be situated, be, be found, lie, be there, stand, sit, be located.

186 location
n. location, position, site, place, seat, station, locus, stand, scene, placing, placement, emplacement; encampment, mooring, lodging.

adj. located, positioned, entrenched, installed, settled, encamped.

vb. locate, position, establish, determine, set, place, unearth, discover, search out, come across, find; park, encamp, set up, install, settle, entrench, camp, moor, lodge.

187 displacement
n. displacement, dislocation, derangement, misplacement, shift, unloading, unpacking; loss, mislaying.

adj. displaced, disturbed; dislocated,

uprooted, homeless, rootless; out of place, uncomfortable.

vb. displace, disarrange, disturb, confuse; dislodge, dislocate, disestablish, unseat, uproot, unsettle, derail; shift, move, remove, replace, transpose, transport; discharge, unload, unpack, extract, withdraw, evacuate, vacate; misplace, lose, mislay; feel out of place.

188 presence
n. presence, attendance, participation; occupancy, residence, inhabitance, habitation; ubiquity, omnipresence.

adj. present, in attendance, attendant, resident; available, at one's disposal, at hand, ready, on call, on tap.

vb. be present, be there, be, be around, kick around (*inf.*); attend, visit; haunt, hang around (*inf.*), frequent; live, inhabit, occupy, reside; appear, make an appearance, turn up, show up (*inf.*), present oneself.

189 absence
n. absence, disappearance, non-appearance; absenteeism, non-attendance, truancy, defection, desertion; non-residence, inexistence; emptiness, vacuity, vacuum, bareness, void, loss, vacancy; lack, need, deficiency.

adj. absent, not here, away, missing, lost, out, not in, elsewhere, not at home, moved, removed, vanished, disappeared; wanting, lacking, minus, unavailable, omitted; empty, vacant, bare, vacuous, unoccupied, uninhabited.

vb. be absent, stay away, be missing, lack, want; absent oneself, take no part in, play truant, play hooky (*sl.*), take French leave.

190 inhabitant

n. inhabitant, native, national; citizen, resident, house-dweller, householder; tenant, lodger, paying guest, incumbent, boarder, occupier, squatter; tax-payer, commuter, voter; city-dweller, townsman, town-dweller, suburbanite; denizen; population, populace.

settler, colonist, pioneer; immigrant, foreigner, guest worker; aborigine, autochthon, primitive, ancient.

adj. native, vernacular, common, popular, national, indigenous, domestic, home, local, domesticated, naturalized, aboriginal.

191 habitation

n. habitation, abode, habitat, accommodation, dwelling, residence, residency, domicile, establishment.

house, address; mansion, country house, hall, lodge, grange, manor, castle, villa, chalet, cottage, bungalow; flat, apartment, suite, maisonette, pad (*sl.*), penthouse, bedsitter, block of flats, tenement, mews, skyscraper, high-rise flats; shelter, hut, shanty; home, fireside, hearth, homestead; lodgings, rooms, quarters, billet, berth, barrack, camp, digs (*inf.*), diggings (*inf.*).

inn, hotel, guest house, boarding house, bed and breakfast, hostel, motel, pension; public house, pub (*inf.*), local (*inf.*), tavern, hostelry, club; bar.

restaurant, café, cafeteria, snack bar, buffet, canteen, refreshment room, tea-room, teashop, coffee-bar, ice-cream parlour, take-away; pull-up.

vb. live, dwell, inhabit, people, populate; settle, colonize; reside, abide, stay, visit, sojourn, stop (*inf.*); settle down, take up residence, put down roots; occupy, rent, lodge, keep, squat.

192 contents

n. contents, items, pieces, ingredients, parts, elements, constituents, components; equipment, material, implements, accessories, articles; load, cargo, freight, stuffing.

vb. load, charge, store, freight, ship, weight, pile, mass, take on, pack.

193 container

n. container, receptacle, holder, cover, envelope; depository, reservoir; packet, package, parcel; bag, sack, purse, wallet, pouch, case, suitcase, trunk, briefcase, grip; box, carton, tin, can, chest, coffer, locker, capsule, canister, crate, bin, hopper, bunker, granary, basket, hamper, pannier; pot, jug, glass, beaker, cup, bucket, pail, bowl, plate, vessel, jar, pitcher, urn, basin, boat, crock, vase; bottle, flask, flagon; cauldron, vat; cistern.

B Dimensions

194 size

n. size, proportions, dimension, measurement, distance, area, extent, mass, weight, volume, capacity; largeness, greatness, hugeness, bigness, enormity, vastness, amplitude, immensity, capaciousness, solidity, bulkiness, corpulence, plumpness, obesity, fleshiness, stoutness.

giant, monster, colossus, leviathan, whale.

adj. big, large, great, huge, enormous, vast, jumbo; fat, obese, stout, plump, podgy, corpulent, fleshy, beefy, pot-bellied; overgrown, larger-than-life; bulky, heavy, solid.

see also 32

195 littleness

n. littleness, shortness, smallness, minuteness, tininess, slightness, scantiness, exiguity, diminutiveness, brevity.

dwarf, pigmy, midge, midget; atom, particle; reduction, miniature.

adj. little, small, tiny, slight, miniature, limited, puny; dwarfed, stunted, squat, dumpy; minute, microscopic, diminutive, atomic, infinitesimal, wee.

see also 33

196 expansion

n. expansion, increase, growth, spread, enlargement, augmentation, extension, supplementation, reinforcement, development, escalation, elaboration, amplification, intensification; dilation; inflation.

adj. expanded, expansive, dilated, stretched, swollen, tumescent.

vb. expand, grow, spread, increase, develop, boost, enlarge, blow up, extend, augment, supplement, reinforce, escalate, elaborate, amplify, intensify, magnify; dilate, distend, let out, gather, swell, bloat, stretch, protract, inflate.

197 contraction

n. contraction, reduction, lessening, decrease, shortening, abridgment, curtailment, compression, confinement, narrowing; shrinkage, constriction, recession, deflation; compressor, roller, constrictor.

adj. contracted, shrunken, shrivelled, astringent, wizened.

vb. contract, weaken, lessen, reduce, decrease, decline, abate, subside, dwindle; curtail, abridge, shorten; shrink, shrivel, wrinkle; constrict, confine, compress, squeeze, pinch, nip.

198 distance

n. distance, length, reach, extent, range, space, way, mileage; horizon, skyline, background; farness, remoteness, back of beyond, world's end, outpost, foreign parts, outskirts, limit; aloofness, reserve.

adj. distant, far, far-away, far-flung, far-off, furthest, farthest, furthermost, long-distance, long-range, out of range, out of sight, ultimate, hindmost; remote, inaccessible, out-of-the-way, God-forsaken; unapproachable, aloof.

vb. distance, outstrip, outpace, outrun, outspeed; keep one's distance, keep out of the way of.

adv. far, away, at a distance, to the ends of the earth, to the back of beyond; out of reach, out of range, out of bounds.

199 nearness

n. closeness, proximity, vicinity; adjacency, juxtaposition, contiguity.

near place, foreground, neighbourhood, locality; close quarters, close range, short step, stone's throw, earshot, spitting distance, hair's breadth.

adj. near, close, nearest, nearby; local, neighbouring; adjacent, adjoining, next; short-distance, short-range; intimate.

vb. be near, approach, approximate; adjoin, abut, connect, border, neighbour; juxtapose.

adv. nearby, in the neighbourhood, locally; at close quarters, at hand, close at hand; within hearing, within range, within earshot.

nearly, almost, approximately, virtually, practically, nigh; tantamount to, to all intents and purposes, substantially, in effect, all but.

200 interval

n. interval, space, separation, clearance, margin, leeway, gap, hole, ditch, cleft, break, crack, chink, rift, fault, passage, pass, gorge, ravine, gulf, chasm, valley, leap, interstice.

vb. space, keep apart, separate, split, intervene, interspace.

201 contact

n. contact, juxtaposition, contiguity, tangency, junction, connection, meeting, touching.

adj. contiguous, in contact, tangential.

vb. contact, touch, meet, brush, graze, kiss; adjoin, abut, border; juxtapose, bring together; unify.

202 length

n. length, space, measure, span, reach, extent; line, mark, stroke, strip, row, file, string, channel; longness, linearity, longimetry, linear measure; lengthening, extension, prolongation, elongation.

adj. long, lengthy, extensive; high, tall, lofty; lengthened, extended, outstretched, elongated, stretching, drawn out, long drawn out, protracted, enlarged; interminable, limitless, boundless, unending.

vb. be long, stretch out; lengthen, extend, stretch, elongate, draw out, prolong, spin out, protract, enlarge, expand.

203 shortness

n. shortness, briefness, brevity, abridgment, curtailment, reduction, shortening.

adj. short, small, low, slight, tiny, little, stunted, dwarf, compact, square, stunted, dumpy, stubby, chunky, thickset; curt, concise, succinct, terse.

vb. shorten, abbreviate, abridge, condense, abstract, summarize, telescope, epitomize, concentrate, boil down; curtail, cut back, truncate, slash; contract, reduce; cut down, shave, prune, shear, trim, strip, clip, nip, pare, whittle, crop, stunt.

204 breadth; thickness

n. breadth, broadness, width, wideness, expanse, latitude, amplitude; bore, calibre, diameter, girth; thickness, plumpness, density, solidity, crassitude; bulk, mess, body.

adj. broad, wide, extended, large, spacious, extensive, roomy, bulky, massive, full, thick, thickset, stout, compact, squat, dumpy, chunky, stubby.

vb. broaden, widen, thicken, fatten.

205 narrowness; thinness

n. narrowness, confinement, restriction, contraction, thinness, slimness, emaciation, leanness, tenuity, shallowness, delicacy; neck, strait, narrows, bottleneck.

adj. narrow, confined, limited, restrained, close; thin, slender, slim, meagre, lanky, lean, threadlike, fine, delicate, skinny, scraggy, weedy, emaciated, bony, spindly, flimsy; wasted, withered, haggard, shrivelled, wizened.

vb. make narrow, taper, confine, straiten; make thin, attenuate, compress; slim, reduce weight, lose weight, take off weight, diet, go on a diet, bant, watch one's weight, starve; shrink, contract.

206 layer

n. layer, stratum, thickness, bed, course, band, substratum, fold, overlap, overlay; row, tier, level, class, zone, storey, floor; coat, coating, ply, seam, laminate, lamina, sheet, slab, foil, panel, slate, plate, scale, flake, squama; lamination, stratification.

adj. layered, laminated, laminate, flaky, scaly, squamous, laminar, lamellar, lamellate, lamelliform, lamellose, laminose.

vb. laminate, layer, overlay, overlap, cover, stratify, scale, flake; veneer.

207 filament

n. filament, wire, thread, cord, strand, string, rope, cable, twine, twist, wisp, lock, shred, hair, whisker, fibre, tendril, eyelash, gossamer; sinew, tendon; strip, tape, band, ribbon, belt, sash, bandage, scarf, strap.

adj. fibrous, threadlike, wiry, stringy, hairy, capillary, sinewy, tendinous.

208 height

n. height, elevation, altitude; loftiness, highness, tallness, stature; uplands, hill, mountain, rise, slope, escarpment, fell, moor; tower, spire, steeple, mast, skyscraper, pillar, column; summit, top.

adj. high, giant, towering, soaring, elevated, sky-high; multi-storey, high-rise; tall, lanky; eminent, distinguished, sublime, exalted, lofty.

vb. tower, soar, extend above, mount, look over, look out on, overlook, command, dominate, overshadow.

adv. high, up, aloft.

209 lowness

n. lowness, depression, netherness, debasement; lowlands, valley, hollow; depths, floor.

adj. low, low-lying, depressed, sunken, nether; squat, crouched; underlying; lesser, inferior.

vb. be low, lie low, crouch, squat, grovel; lower, depress, debase, sink.

adv. under, underneath, beneath, below, down; underfoot, underground.

210 depth

n. depth, lowness, profundity; drop, depression, bottom, abyss, gorge, pit, space, charm, hollow, trench, mine, chamber, ravine; deeps.

adj. deep, low, profound; deep-seated, deep-rooted; bottomless, fathomless; sunken, buried, immersed; submerged, underwater, deep-sea; subterranean, underground; yawning, gaping.

vb. deepen, hollow, dig, excavate, scrape out, sink, plunge.

adv. deeply, out of one's depth.

211 shallowness

n. shallowness, superficiality; shallow, shoal; covering, veneer, gloss, façade, surface.

adj. shallow, superficial, surface, skin-deep; cosmetic; light, inconsiderable, cursory, slight.

vb. skim, brush, touch on, scratch the surface.

212 summit

n. summit, top, peak, apex, zenith, pinnacle, tip, vertex, acme; consummation, maximum, limit, climax; crown, head, crest, brow, cap, spire.

adj. top, topmost, uppermost, highest, maximal, tip-top; apical, acmic, zenithal; head, capital.

vb. crown, top, tip, head, cap; culminate.

213 base

n. base, root, foundation, support, prop, stand, stay, pier, rest, bottom, basement, floor, basin, substratum, bed, channel, ground, understructure, shaft, substratum, groundwork; foot, toe, pedestal.

adj. bottom, undermost, fundamental, basic, underlying.

214 being vertical

n. verticality, uprightness, perpendicularity, erectness, plumbness, straightness, sheerness; steep, cliff, precipice.

adj. vertical, perpendicular, upright, erect, upstanding, plumb, on end, straight up; steep.

vb. be vertical, stick up, rise; make vertical, erect, raise, elevate.

215 being horizontal

n. horizontality, planeness, flatness, evenness; level, plane.

adj. horizontal, plane, level, even, flush; prostrate, prone, supine, recumbent.

vb. be horizontal, lie down, recline, repose; flatten, level, even out, smooth, plane, squash, prostrate, roll out, straighten.

216 hanging

n. pendency, suspension, hanging; pendant, locket, earring; curtain, hangings; pendulum, stalactite.

adj. hanging, suspended, pendent, dangling, drooping, swaying, pendulous, stalactitic, overhanging.

vb. hang, suspend, fall, hover, float, poise, dangle, drape; droop, sag, swing, sway, oscillate, flap.

217 support

n. support, sustenance, maintenance, reinforcement, back-up; supporter, guide, backing, stiffener, strengthener, sustainer; foundation, base, carriage, bearing, undercarriage, underframe, chassis, bogie, truck; stilt, stay, mainstay, buttress, pole, post, prop, stake, boom, column, pillar, corner-stone, pier, pile, timber, brace, beam, rafter, girder, strut, joist; breakwater, pier, wall; splint, crutch, truss; back, rest, headrest, backrest, backbone; wedge, chock; pivot, lever, hinge, axis, fulcrum; stand, board, table, seat, saddle, cushion, pillow; shelf, ledge, rack; backer, provider, patron.

adj. supporting, sustaining.

vb. support, hold up, prop, sustain, maintain, carry, bear, keep up; bolster, shore, brace, stay, truss, underpin, undergird, back, buoy up, shoulder; uphold, establish, promote, advance, further, encourage, confirm, strengthen, corroborate, back up, stand by, stick by (*inf.*), stand up for, stand behind, stick up for (*inf.*).

see also 636

218 parallelism

n. parallelism, equidistance, coextension; likeness, correspondence, similarity, affinity; parallelogram; parallelopiped.

adj. parallel, equidistant, not meeting, not converging, coextensive; corresponding, similar, uniform.

vb. parallel, correspond, be equal; match, equate, compare.

219 being oblique

n. obliqueness, obliquity, skewness, curvature, asymmetry; curve, bend, twist, squint, divergence, diagonal; slope, inclination, slide, acclivity, decline, declivity.

adj. oblique, inclined, leaning, angled, skew, askew, skew-whiff (*inf.*), asymmetrical, awry, crooked, askance; sloping, upward, acclivitous, downward, declivitous, divergent, sideways, slanted, bent, curved, twisted, contorted; cross-wise, diagonal, transverse.

vb. incline, lean, slope, tilt, angle, bend, curve, twist, warp; diverge, deviate, slant.

220 inversion

n. inversion, transposition, reversion, reversal; palindrome, about-turn, *volte-face*; upset, capsizal, somersault.

adj. inverted, inverse, opposite, upside-down, back-to-front, topsy-turvy.

vb. invert, transpose, rearrange, exchange, reverse, revert, put the cart before the horse (*inf.*); turn over, overturn, overthrow, turn upside down, stand on its head, tip, topple, tilt, capsize, keel over, somersault; turn inside out.

221 crossing

n. crossing, junction, intersection, confluence, crossroads, crossover; cross, crux, crucifix, cruciform, swastika; network, system, intercommunication; wickerwork, lattice, grid, grill, web, net, netting, mesh, textile, fabric, weave, loom, plait.

vb. cross, intersect, interlink, cut, pass across, mesh, weave, loom, knit, sew, plait, twist, interlace, spin, twine, intertwine, interlock, tangle, entangle.

222 being exterior

n. exteriority, extraneousness, externality, outwardness; outside, exterior, surface, top, front, face, appearance, façade, covering.

adj. exterior, outside, external, outward, outer, outermost, outlying; extrinsic, foreign.

vb. be outside; externalize, extrapolate, project, objectify, embody.
see also 825

223 being interior

n. interiority, internality, inwardness; inside, interior; substance, contents, heart, centre, soul.

adj. interior, inside, internal, inward,

inner, innermost; intrinsic, inborn, innate; central, integral; inland.

vb. be inside; internalize.
see also 5, 224

224 centrality

n. centrality, centralization; centre, middle, bull's eye; focus, concentration, convergence; nucleus, core, heart, hub, nub, gist, kernel, marrow, pith.

adj. central, centre, middle, inner, focal, pivotal.

vb. centre, centralize, concentrate, focus, converge, draw, attract.
see also 96

225 covering

n. covering, superimposition, cover, lid, flap, box, wrapping; ceiling, roof, shelter, dome, awning, tent, marquee, tarpaulin, canopy, mask, hood, shade, film, blind, umbrella, parasol, sunshade, sheath; sheet, blanket, robe, carpet, rug, mat; coating, varnish, paint, veneer, lacquer, glaze, enamel, wash, polish, stain, distemper, gloss; skin, peel, shell, rind, coat, husk, hull, pod, jacket, integument, tegument.

adj. covered, sheltered, hooded, wrapped, enveloped, veiled, varnished, painted, surfaced.

vb. cover, put on, lay over, protect, shield, shelter, wrap, envelop, enshroud, enclose, veil, superimpose, superpose; roof, carpet, pave, paper; coat, surface, varnish, paint, plate, gloss, glaze, spray, veneer, wax; mask, hide, conceal.

226 lining

n. lining, insulation, interlining; inner surface, inside; filling, stuffing, wadding, padding, quilting, inlay.

vb. line, insulate, interline, inlay,

stuff, wad, pad, fill, quilt, reinforce, overlay, face, encrust.

227 dressing

n. dressing, toilet; dress, clothing, wardrobe, outfit, vesture, garb, gear, guise, raiment, apparel, attire; clothes, garment, vestment, costume, suit, dress; uniform, livery.

adj. dressed, well-dressed, dressed-up, clad.

vb. dress, clothe, turn out, deck out (*inf.*), equip, fit out; wear, have on, be dressed in; put on, get dressed, don, slip on, throw on, assume; dress up, get dressed up, smarten oneself up; change into; wrap up.

228 undressing

n. undressing, divestment; bareness, undress, nakedness, nudism, nudity, naturism, *déshabillé*, stripping, striptease; nude, nudist, naturist; baldness, alopecia, shaving, tonsure.

adj. bare, exposed, unveiled, uncovered, unprotected, revealing, *décolleté*; undressed, naked, nude, stark naked, stripped, in one's birthday suit (*inf.*), in the altogether (*inf.*), starkers (*sl.*); bald, hairless, bald-headed, balding, shaven, tonsured, shining, smooth; threadbare, denuded.

vb. uncover, expose, unveil, reveal, remove, take off, cast off; undress, unclothe, strip, disrobe, divest; pluck, peel, pare, shed, bare, skin, flay, scalp, shell, stone, excoriate, decorticate; denude, ravage.

229 being around

n. environment, ambience, circumstances, surroundings; circumjacence; scene, *milieu*, background, setting, habitat, situation; atmosphere, climate; environs, suburbs, vicinity.

adj. environmental, ambient, surrounding, background, situational.

vb. surround, circle, enclose, close in, envelop, girdle, encompass.

adv., prep. around, about.

see also **8**

230 being between

n. interposition, intermediacy, intercurrence, intervention, interruption, interjection, interpolation; mediation, intercession; partition, wall, watershed, fence, hurdle; insert, inset, wedge.

adj. intermediary, intermediate, intervening.

vb. place between, mediate, interpose; insert, intersperse; interrupt, interject, intervene.

prep. between, among.

see also **653**

231 circumscription

n. circumscription, encircling, circumnavigation; limitation, demarcation, boundary, restriction.

vb. circumscribe, encircle, ring, encompass, surround, circumambulate, circumnavigate, circumvent; surround; limit, restrict, bound, mark off, confine.

232 outline

n. outline, perimeter, periphery, outside, circumference, circuit, border, boundary, contour; sketch, skeleton, silhouette, profile, framework, tracing, delineation.

vb. outline, sketch, trace, delineate.

233 edge

n. edge, extremity, end, limit, verge; border, frontier, boundary; threshold, brink, brim, rim, side, corner, point, tip, margin, skirt; edging, skirting, fringe, hem.

vb. border, verge, edge, skirt; rim, hem, margin, fringe.

234 enclosure

n. enclosure, confinement; envelope, wrapping; area, ground, pitch, arena; plot, court, yard, garden, park; cell, prison, dungeon, den; pen, cage, pound, aviary, coop, warren.

fence, wire, wall, hedge, fencing, paling, rail, railing, balustrade, barrier, ditch, moat, trench, ha-ha.

vb. enclose, envelop, wrap, enfold, confine, contain, blockade, shut in, shut up, lock up, fence, impound, hedge in, hem in; package, parcel; bottle; jail, imprison.

235 limit

n. limit, end, utmost, extremity, destination, terminus, conclusion; limitation, delimitation, restriction, definition, control; hurdle, barrier, frontier, boundary, border, borderline; threshold, upper limit, ceiling; demarcation line, mark, fringe, edge.

adj. limited, set, defined.

vb. limit, set, settle, define, delimit, demarcate, bound, confine, restrict, draw the line at, curb.

236 front

n. front, frontage, exterior, façade, anterior, foreground, face, head, forehead, vanguard, front line; visage, countenance, physiognomy; semblance.

adj. front, forward, fore, foremost, frontal, frontmost, head, obverse, anterior, leading, advance.

vb. face, front, look out on, border; head, lead; meet, confront, encounter, come face to face with.

adv. in advance, ahead; in the foreground.

237 rear

n. rear, back, tail, end, reverse, posterior, backside, bottom, dorsum; wake, rearguard; background, hinterland, backstage.

adj. rear, back, hind, tail, posterior, after, terminal, final, bottom, dorsal, backmost, hindmost, rearmost, background, backstage.

vb. be behind, follow, back on to; bring up the rear.

adv. at the rear, behind, in the background.

238 sidedness

n. sidedness, laterality; juxtaposition, adjacency; side, hand, flank, shoulder.

adj. side, lateral, sidelong, sidewise, sideways, flanking; adjacent.

vb. be side by side, flank, skirt; juxtapose.

adv. laterally, sideways, abreast, alongside, side by side.

239 being opposite

n. opposition, contraposition, polarity; opposite, converse, reverse, contrary, contrast, contradiction, antipode, antipole.

adj. opposite, contrary, opposing, contradictory.

vb. be opposite, oppose, confront, face.

adv., prep. opposite, over against, facing, *vis à vis.*

240 right side

n. right-handedness, dexterity, dextrality; right, right hand; right-hander, dextral; starboard.

adj. right, right-hand, right-handed, off, offside, dextral, dextrorse.

241 left side

n. left-handedness, sinistrality; left, left hand; left-hander, sinistral; port.

adj. left, left-hand, left-handed, near-side, sinistrorse.

C Form

242 form
n. form, shape, style, look, appearance, fashion, design, outline, profile, contour; structure, construction, formation; morphology.

adj. formed, shaped, developed; formative, impressionable, plastic, mouldable.

vb. form, make, create, fashion, pattern, model, mould; cast, stamp, impress, carve, cut; arrange, construct, build, assemble; take shape, develop, express, grow, materialize.

243 absence of form
n. formlessness, shapelessness, amorphism, fuzziness; chaos, liquid; fluid.

adj. formless, shapeless, amorphous; vague, unclear, indistinct, blurred, fuzzy; indeterminate, indefinite; chaotic, misshapen, unshapely, deformed.

244 symmetry
n. symmetry, regularity, conformity, proportion, equality, evenness, balance, harmony, arrangement, order; shapeliness.

adj. symmetrical, balanced, even, proportioned, harmonious, shapely, regular, well-proportioned.

245 asymmetry
n. asymmetry, disproportion, lopsidedness, irregularity, distortion, contortion, twist, deformity, malformation.

adj. asymmetrical, disproportionate, irregular, misproportioned, uneven, unshapely, grotesque, ugly, hideous, distorted, deformed, malformed, dis-figured, crippled, mangled, hunch-backed, crooked, awry, askew.

vb. distort, contort, twist, pervert, deform, misshape, disfigure, buckle, cripple; writhe, scowl, grimace.
see also 845

246 angular form
n. angularity, pointedness, serration; angle, crotch, elbow, fork, corner, point, zigzag; right angle, acute angle, obtuse angle, reflex angle; triangle; quadrilateral, parallelogram, rhomboid, rectangle, oblong, square, diamond, lozenge, rhombus, rhomb, polygon, pentagon, hexagon, heptagon, octagon, nonagon, enneagon, decagon, endecagon, dodecagon; polyhedron, cube, tetrahedron, pyramid, prism, wedge.

adj. angular, pointed, sharp-cornered, scraggy, jagged, serrated, zigzag, wedge-shaped, cuneiform, cuneate; triangular, rectangular, multilateral.

vb. angle, bend, intersect, serrate, zigzag.
see also 259

247 curved form
n. curvature, bending, flexion, flexure, arcuation; curve, bend, sweep, bow, curl, camber, arc, chord, arcade, rainbow, arch, crook, trajectory; catenary, parabola, hyperbola, circle, ellipse, epicycle; crescent, half-moon, lune, lunula, meniscus, lens, lunate.

adj. curved, bent, rounded, arched, vaulted, crescent, lunate.

vb. curve, turn, arch, bow, curl, crook, buckle, twist, warp, flex; waver, meander, swerve, deviate, veer.

248 straight form
n. straightness, rectilinearity; verticality, perpendicularity; horizontality; bee-line.

adj. straight, even, level, direct; upright, vertical, perpendicular, erect; horizontal; unbroken, uninterrupted.

vb. straighten, order, make straight; untwist, unbend, uncoil, disentangle, unravel, uncurl, unfold.

adv. in a straight line, as the crow flies.

249 round form

n. rotundity, roundness; round, globe, sphere, orb, ball, marble, balloon, bubble, drop, droplet, globule; cylinder, barrel, roll, drum.

adj. round, rotund, rounded, spherical, globular, orbicular, globe-shaped, globoid, globose, cylindrical.

vb. round, ball, roll, coil up.

250 simple circularity

n. circularity, roundness; circle, orbit, circuit, ring, loop, halo, crown, corona, aureola, circus, bowl, hoop, quoit, wheel, disc, equator; ellipse, oval, egg; band, belt, wreath, garland; circumference, perimeter, rim, periphery.

adj. round, circular, cyclic, orbicular; oval, elliptical.

vb. encircle, go round; make round.
see also 322

251 complex circularity

n. convolution, intricacy, twisting, sinuosity, torsion; coil, turn, twine, twist, plait, kink, loop, spiral, helix, screw, curl, tendril, scroll.

adj. convoluted, intricate, involved; winding, spiral, coiled, helical, flexuous, sinuous, tortuous; serpentine, snake-like; meandering, undulating, wavy.

vb. turn, wind, curl, loop, twist, twirl, fold, twine, plait, intertwine, entwine, sinuate, wrinkle, contort,

wreathe; crimp, ripple; meander, undulate; wriggle, squirm, wiggle.

252 convexity

n. convexity, protuberance, bulginess, outgrowth.

swelling, growth, bump, hump, lump, ridge, protuberance, rising, bulge; tumour, cancer, corn, boil, inflammation, carbuncle, bunion, wart, pimple, bulb; dome, cupola, vault.

adj. convex, arched, raised, curved, bent; bulbous, swollen, bloated; bulging, swelling, excrescent, tumescent, tumid.

vb. swell, bulge, rise, project, protrude, jut.

253 prominence

n. prominence, salience; projection, protuberance, protrusion, extension, spur, spit, promontory, tongue, headland, relief; leader, figure-head, model, example.

adj. prominent, conspicuous, protuberant, extended, jutting, protruding, projecting, salient, obtrusive.

vb. protrude, extend, jut, project, stand out, stick out.

254 concavity

n. concavity, hollowness; hollow, hole, aperture, opening, depression; pit, abyss, mine, shaft, well, trench; corner, niche, recess, alcove, indentation, pocket; valley, dale, bowl, drop, gulf, basin, glen, ravine, crevasse, fissure, crater, gorge, canyon, gully, chasm; dip, dent, dimple; cave, burrow, cavern, grotto, furrow, covert, warren, pothole; excavation, tunnel, passage, retreat, dug-out, dig (*inf.*).

adj. concave, hollow, depressed, excavated, sunken, carved out, indented.

vb. hollow out, excavate, dig, spade,

gouge, delve, mine, tunnel, bore; indent, depress; cave in, fall in, collapse.

255 sharpness

n. sharpness, acuteness; point, tip, prick, thorn, sting, spike, nail, pin, needle, fork, prong; barb, thorn, bramble, prickle, brier, spine; tooth, edge, scissors, shears, knife.

adj. sharp, acute, pointed, fine, keen, cutting, biting, piercing, incisive, trenchant; spiked, spiky, spiny, prickly, thorny, needle-pointed, barbed; pronged, tapered, tapering, acuminate.

vb. be sharp, prick, sting, taper; sharpen, grind, edge, file, hone, whet, strop; barb, point; puncture.

256 bluntness

n. bluntness, obtuseness, flatness.

adj. blunt, unsharpened, unpointed, dull, unsharp, obtuse; toothless.

vb. blunt, dull, take the edge off, round, turn, obtund; be blunt, not cut.

257 smoothness

n. smoothness, flatness, levelness, regularity; stillness, glossiness, silkiness; glass, ice, marble; gloss, varnish, polish, finish.

adj. smooth, flat, plane, level, even, uniform, steady, stable, continuous; quiet, still, sleek, polished, glossy, glassy, lustrous, silky, soft, slippery, oily.

vb. smooth, even, level, plane, scrape, shave, flatten, iron, sand, file, press; polish, shine, burnish, glaze, gloss, varnish; glide, slide, float, skim, drift, stream.

258 roughness

n. roughness, asperity, unevenness, coarseness, harshness, bumpiness, brokenness, irregularity, jaggedness, corrugation.

adj. rough, uneven, coarse, harsh, bumpy, broken, jagged, rugged, choppy, ruffled; bristly, prickly, hairy, hirsute.

vb. roughen, coarsen, break, notch, serrate, crumple, ruffle.

259 notch

n. notch, indentation, cut, zigzag, cleft, trench, trough, gouge, saw, nick, incision, depression, serration.

adj. notched, jagged, saw-toothed, serrated.

vb. notch, serrate, cut, tooth, cog, indent, nick.

260 fold

n. fold, gather, pleat, lapel, overlap, tuck; crease, crimp, wrinkle, corrugation, turn.

adj. folded, gathered, creased, wrinkled, corrugated, pleated, puckered, overlapping.

vb. fold, double, crease, lap, overlap, plicate, pleat, curl, crimp, wrinkle, ruffle, pucker, gather, corrugate.

261 furrow

n. furrow, groove, slit, slot, trench, rut, gouge, moat, channel, canal, ditch, gutter; corrugation.

adj. furrowed, grooved, ribbed, fluted, corrugated, ridged.

vb. furrow, groove, slot, flute, corrugate, channel, plough.

262 opening

n. opening, aperture, orifice, hole, gap, hollow, slit, perforation, slot, break; mouth, throat, gullet; outlet, vent; window, porthole; door, doorway, gate, exit, entrance, hatch, hatchway, channel, passage.

adj. open, unlocked, unfastened, unsealed; clear, accessible; ajar, gaping, wide, yawning; torn, rent.

vb. open, unlock, unbolt, unbar,

unfasten, undo; clear, admit, free, loosen; expose, reveal, unfold; gape, yawn.

see also 264, 462

263 closure

n. closure, occlusion, stoppage, blockage, obstruction.

adj. closed, unopened, shut, fastened, bolted, blocked, sealed.

vb. close, shut, lock, fasten, bar, bolt.

see also 265

264 perforator

n. perforator, sponge, sieve, strainer, colander; borer, awl, gimlet, drill, lancet, needle, pin, punch; perforation, porosity.

adj. perforated, porous, pervious, permeable, penetrable, spongy, absorbent, holey.

vb. cut, perforate, pierce, prick, slit, puncture, crack, stick, inject, drill, stab, lance, spear, spike, skewer, impale, bore, mine, tunnel; hole, riddle.

265 stopper

n. stopper, plug, cork, bung, tap, valve, stopcock, wedge, rammer, stuffing, filling, stopping.

adj. stopped up, blocked, obstructed, sealed, impenetrable, impervious, watertight.

vb. block, obstruct, blockade, stop, choke, clog, stuff, ram, fill, dam, seal, cork, plug, bung, occlude, obturate.

D Motion

266 motion

n. motion, mobility, movableness, movement, action, activity, unrest, restlessness, move, passage, progress, advance, ascension, descension; velocity, speed.

adj. moving, in motion, transitional, movable, mobile, restless, nomadic.

vb. move, go, run, progress, proceed; push, impel, stir, set in motion, activate, propel.

267 rest

n. rest, immobility, motionlessness, cessation, stillness, standstill, stop; discontinuance, interval, pause; silence, calm; quiet, calmness, peace, tranquillity.

adj. quiet, peaceful, still, quiescent, asleep; immovable, immobile, motionless, unruffled, peaceful, placid, serene.

vb. rest, stand still, pause, halt, stop, cease; not stir, keep quiet; still, soften, quiesce, relax, lull, becalm, hush.

see also 174

268 transference

n. transference, transferal, conveyance, movement, removal, shift, relay, conduct, remittance, dispatch, delivery, hand-over; transport, transportation, transit, carriage, shipment, trans-shipment, haulage, freight, consignment.

adj. transferable, transmittable, transmissible, conveyable, movable, portable.

vb. transfer, move, remove, conduct, carry, take, convey, shift; send, direct, remit, relay, dispatch, forward, deliver, hand over, consign; ship, cart, truck, haul, load, post, mail; convoy, escort; import, export; transmit, communicate; relocate, transplant; ply, shuttle.

see also 714

269 land travel

n. travel, tourism, touring, sightseeing, globe-trotting, roaming; journey, tour, trip, outing, expedition, excursion, day out, picnic; pilgrimage;

venture, adventure; visit, sojourn; exploration, quest, safari.

walk, step, pace, stride, gait, march; stroll, hike, jaunt, saunter, amble, ramble, wayfaring, tramp; promenade, constitutional, perambulation; peregrinations, wanderings.

riding, horse-riding, horsemanship, horse-racing, equestrianism, show-jumping, dressage; cycling, spin, ride; drive; driving, motoring; itinerary, route, course, circuit, direction, map.

adj. journeying, travelling, visiting; peripatetic.

vb. travel, journey, tour, rove, visit, cruise, explore, traverse; walk, step, pace, march, tread, amble, ramble, wander, hike, trek, stroll, ambulate, perambulate, promenade; gad about (*inf.*), gallivant about (*inf.*); ride, cycle, bike (*inf.*); drive, motor.

270 traveller

n. traveller, tourist, sightseer, globe-trotter, holiday-maker, daytripper, visitor, voyager, explorer, adventurer; itinerant, wanderer, roamer, pedlar, vagabond, vagrant, tramp, hobo; migrant, emigrant, immigrant, refugee, gypsy, nomad, bedouin.

pedestrian, walker, foot-passenger, hiker, trekker, rambler, pilgrim, way-farer, runner, athlete; rider, horse-rider, jockey, show-jumper, hitch-hiker; passenger, commuter, season-ticket holder; motorist, driver.

271 water travel

n. navigation, sailing, cruising, circumnavigation; seamanship, seafaring, exploration; voyage, cruise; water sports, aquatics, sailing, yachting, boating, rowing, canoeing, swimming, diving, surfing.

adj. navigational, sailing, nautical, naval, marine, maritime.

vb. sail, cruise, voyage, ply, run, ferry; set sail; launch, cast off; navigate, steer, pilot, make for, head for, set a course; drop anchor, moor; swim, bathe, dive, dip, paddle, wade, surf, water-ski.

272 mariner

n. mariner, sailor, seaman, seafarer, pilot, boatman, marine, crew, captain, boatswain, navigator, helmsman.

273 air travel

n. air travel, aeronautics, aviation, flying, gliding, flight.

pilot, airman, aviator, flier, aeronaut.

adj. flying; aerial, aeronautical, aero-dynamic.

vb. fly, pilot, taxi, take off, climb, rise, soar, zoom; spin, loop, roll; glide, dive, dart, shoot; plunge, plummet, parachute, bail out; touch down, land, come down, crash-land; talk down.

274 space travel

n. space travel, astronautics, cosmonautics; countdown, space flight, space walk; grand tour; re-entry, splashdown.

astronaut, spaceman, cosmonaut, space traveller.

adj. astronautical, cosmonautic, cosmonautical.

vb. take off, orbit, splash down.

275 carrier

n. carrier, bearer, porter, messenger, runner; basket, bag, container; horse, packhorse, llama, beast of burden.

vb. carry, transport, move, convey, transfer, bear.

276 vehicle

n. vehicle, conveyance; cycle, bike bicycle, pushbike (*sl.*), velocipede, tandem, tricycle; moped, scooter, motor scooter, motorcycle, motorbike; car, automobile, motor, saloon, sports car, G. T., coupé, hard-top, convertible, hatchback, estate car, station wagon, shooting-brake, minibus; taxi, taxicab, minicab, cab, hackney carriage, rickshaw; bus, coach, motor bus, tram, trolley-bus; van, lorry, pickup, dump truck; train, underground, rapid transit; engine, locomotive, diesel locomotive, electric locomotive, steam engine.

cart, trolley, pram, barrow, trailer; carriage, wagon, buggy, trap, gig, hansom.

adj. vehicular, locomotive, wheeled.

277 ship

n. ship, boat, vessel, craft; motorboat, steamer, steamboat, steamship, freighter, barge, lighter, packet, ferry, mail-ship, tanker, supertanker, liner; pilot, tug, launch; destroyer, warship, frigate, battleship, aircraft carrier, submarine; sailing ship, clipper, yacht, rowing boat, paddle boat, canoe, kayak, gondola, junk, galleon.

adj. nautical, marine, maritime, naval, seagoing, seaworthy.

278 aircraft

n. aircraft, aeroplane, plane, airliner, jet, jumbo jet, turbo-prop, shuttle, glider, bomber, seaplane; hovercraft, hydrofoil, helicopter; airship, balloon, Zeppelin.

adj. aviational, aeronautical.

279 spaceship

n. spaceship, spacecraft, capsule, module, space shuttle, space probe; space station, satellite, sputnik; flying saucer, UFO; rocket.

280 velocity

n. velocity, speed, quickness, rapidity, hurry, haste, rush, expedition,

celerity; acceleration, hastening, quickening, speeding up, spurt, burst, charge.

adj. quick, fast, speedy, brisk, swift; nimble, agile, deft, spirited; light-footed, prompt, expeditious.

vb. go fast, speed, hurry, hasten, quicken, race, tear, fly, dash, rush, run, sprint, dart, whiz, zip, pelt, bomb, run like mad, go all out, do a ton (*sl.*), go full pelt (*inf.*); accelerate, go faster, speed up, spurt, put on speed, step on it (*inf.*), put one's foot down (*inf.*), get a move on (*inf.*), get one's skates on (*inf.*), make it snappy (*inf.*); overtake, gain on, catch up, reach, pass, overhaul, go after, outstrip, outpace, outdistance, capture, beat; run for dear life.

adv. fast, quickly, speedily, swiftly, at full speed, flat out, at full pelt.

see also **613**

281 slowness

n. slowness, sluggishness, lethargy, apathy, hesitation, reluctance; deceleration, retardation, slackening, delay, go-slow, brake, curb, restraint.

slowcoach, tortoise, snail, dawdler, lingerer, loiterer, loafer, idler.

adj. slow, slow-moving, dawdling, lingering; sluggish, listless, lethargic, apathetic, inactive, leisurely, hesitant, reluctant.

vb. go slowly, idle, stroll, saunter, dawdle, linger, tarry, take one's time, loiter, loaf, crawl, inch, falter, limp, hobble, shuffle, plod; decelerate, slow down, reduce speed, slacken, relax, let up, ease off, delay, retard, brake, put on the brakes; curb.

282 impulse

n. impulse, thrust, impetus, charge, rush, drive, pressure, momentum, impulsion; bump, shove, shock, jolt, impact, brunt, clash, crash, collision, pile-up, smash-up; hit, knock, rap, blow, smack.

vb. impel, push, drive, press, propel, move, set in motion, activate, get going, start; collide, crash, run into, bump into, smash, dash, meet, encounter, touch, impinge, clash, butt, bump, jog, shove, jolt, force, scrape, jar.

hit, strike, beat, smite; tap, rap, jab; slap, thump, clout, smack, pummel, thrash, whip, whack, wallop (*sl.*), sock, clap, box, punch, club, cudgel; hammer, pound, bash, slosh (*sl.*), flail; bang, knock, bruise; kick, knee.

283 recoil

n. recoil, reaction, rebound, spring, bounce, repercussion, echo, reverberation, boomerang, backlash, rebuff, answer, reply.

vb. recoil, react, respond, rebound, bounce, spring, kick back, backfire, echo, reverberate; shrink from, draw back, pull back, wince, flinch.

284 direction

n. direction, bearing, orientation, point of the compass, cardinal point, north, south, east, west; destination, aim, object, intention; tendency, thrust, tenor; outlook, standpoint, point of view.

vb. orientate oneself, take one's bearings, locate; direct, signpost, lead, aim for, go for, head for, make for, point to, steer; tend.

adv. towards, in the direction of, via, heading for, on the way to.

285 deviation

n. deviation, misdirection, disorientation, deflection, divergence, turning, departure, diversion, detour; digression, tangent; irregularity, deterioration.

adj. deviating, aberrant, deviant, divergent, misguided, mistaken, lost; tangential, off-beam.

vb. deviate, deflect, swerve, bend, wander, stray, err, depart from, veer, shift, lose one's bearings, get lost, turn aside; disorientate, misdirect; digress, get sidetracked, go off the point, go off at a tangent.

286 precedence

n. precedence, priority, leading, heading, vanguard.

vb. precede, go before, come first, take precedence, herald, go in advance, lead, lead the way, head, take the lead.

adv. in advance, ahead, before.

see also **84, 118**

287 following

n. following, succession; follower, disciple, hanger-on, attendant, dependant, adherent, supporter, recruit.

vb. follow, go after, come after, ensue, succeed, attend, wait on; shadow, chase, pursue, track, tail (*sl.*), dog; lag behind, trail.

see also **85, 119**

288 progression

n. progression, progress, advance, headway, gain; development, growth, furtherance, advancement, improvement.

adj. forward, progressive, tolerant, broad-minded, forward-looking, enterprising; ongoing.

vb. progress, advance, proceed, move on, forge ahead, press on, strive forward, push ahead, make progress, make headway, gain ground, never look back (*inf.*); further, promote, develop, grow, evolve, become, mature, improve, move with the times.

adv. forward, onward, on, in progress.

289 regression

n. regression, retreat, withdrawal, retirement, return; regress, retrogression, reversal; departure, escape; about-turn, *volte-face*, about-face, U-turn.

adj. backward, backward-looking, reactionary, narrow-minded, reverse, retrograde, retrogressive.

vb. go backwards, regress, recede, retire, back out, withdraw, retreat, draw back, secede, fall back, lose ground; retrogress; go back on one's word, turn around.

290 propulsion

n. propulsion, impulsion, impetus, drive, push, thrust, pressure; missile, projectile, bullet, shell, torpedo, arrow, dart, propellant, shot.

vb. propel, push, move, impel, drive, direct, thrust, press, shove; launch, throw, cast, pitch, toss, chuck (*inf.*); shoot, discharge.

291 pulling

n. pulling, traction, drawing, tow, haul; tug, tractor, traction engine, draught animal; trailer, caravan, train.

vb. pull, draw, haul, drag, heave, tow, tug, take in tow; attract, magnetize; trail.

292 approach

n. approach, advance, arrival, coming; nearness, approximation.

adj. approaching, nearing, forthcoming, coming, looming, drawing near; accessible, get-at-able, approachable, obtainable, available, attainable, convenient, at one's disposal.

vb. approach, draw near, come near, advance, come forward, come into sight, close in on, sidle up to, loom up; approximate, verge on, near.

293 retreat

n. retreat, recession, withdrawal, departure, escape, retirement, removal, evacuation, flight.

vb. retreat, recede, withdraw, back out, depart, run away, fall back, evacuate, escape, retire, remove; fade, die away, sink.

294 attraction

n. attraction, drawing power, gravitation, affinity, pull, draw, influence; magnet, gravity, bait, lure, decoy.

adj. attracting, appealing, magnetic, charismatic.

vb. attract, pull, drag, draw, bring; interest, fascinate.

see also 547

295 repulsion

n. repulsion, rebuff, snub, beating off, dismissal.

adj. repulsive, offensive, repelling.

vb. repel, repulse, drive back, put to flight, beat off, hold off, push back, throw off, turn away, drive away; dismiss, send packing; rebuff, snub; resist.

see also 892

296 convergence

n. convergence, concurrence, confluence, concentration, confrontation, collision course, focalization; union, meeting, encounter.

adj. convergent, concurrent, converging.

vb. converge, come together, focalize, unite, gather, concentrate, meet, tend, narrow the gap, come to a point.

297 divergence

n. divergence, radiation, ramification; fork, bifurcation; fan, spoke, ray.

adj. divergent, deviating, radiating; centrifugal.

vb. diverge, radiate, branch, fork, bifurcate, diffuse, spread, fan out, disperse, scatter, ramify, divaricate.

298 arrival

n. arrival, coming, approach, entrance, entry, appearance, emergence; start, onset; reaching, attainment; return, homecoming; landing, touchdown, disembarkation, alighting, dismounting, docking, mooring.

destination, goal, terminus, journey's end, objective, resting place, harbour, port, dock, berth, landing place, airport.

vb. arrive, come, reach, get to, enter, approach, appear, show up (*inf.*), turn up, return, come home; land, touch down, disembark, alight, dismount, get down, set foot on, dock, moor, drop anchor.

299 departure

n. departure, going, leaving, setting out, exit, withdrawing, abandonment, removal, retreat, flight, take-off, embarkation, sailing; leave-taking, parting, separating, farewell, send-off, dismissal, valediction, parting shot, *congé*; exodus; emigration.

vb. depart, go, leave, move, quit, retire, withdraw, evacuate, go away, take one's leave, make tracks, set out, start out, be off, push off (*inf.*), push along (*inf.*), shove off (*sl.*); rush off, run away, beat it (*sl.*), scram (*sl.*).

300 entrance

n. entrance, entry, ingress, incoming, induction, initiation, immigration; admittance, admission; introduction; influx, intrusion, infiltration, incursion, penetration, invasion, raid.

vb. enter, come in, step in, go in, set foot in, make one's way into, visit, drop in; intrude, invade, trespass, gatecrash; force into, break in; wriggle in, worm in; insert, put in, admit, introduce, implant, penetrate, infiltrate, percolate.

301 emergence

n. emergence, egress, outflow, emanation, issue, discharge, outflow, effluence, flow; escape, gush, spout, welling, oozing, outpour, leakage, seepage, eruption, secretion.

vb. emerge, go out, come out, come out into the open; emit, eject, discharge, expel, flow out, run out, effuse, give out, exhale, send forth, pour out, gush, spurt, shoot, secrete, seep, erupt, squirt; bleed, leak, empty, weep; exude, ooze.

see also **312**

302 reception

n. reception, admission, admittance, acceptance, receptivity; access, welcome, open arms, hospitality, registration, enlistment, enrolment; initiation, baptism, barmitzvah; incorporation, assimilation, absorption, digestion.

adj. admissible, acceptable, receivable; suitable; receptive, sympathetic.

vb. admit, receive, accept, take in; allow in, accommodate, welcome, make welcome; initiate, baptize, introduce, induct, install; assimilate, incorporate, swallow, absorb, digest.

see also **716**

303 ejection

n. ejection, expulsion, eviction, removal, elimination; dismissal, discharge, sack (*inf.*), push (*sl.*), deportation, exile, banishment, extradition;

ejector, bouncer (*sl.*), chucker-out; nausea, sickness, vomiting.

vb. eject, emit, expel, remove, exclude, eliminate, eradicate, wipe out, evict; dismiss, get rid of, dispose of, discharge, sack (*inf.*); depart, exile, banish, extradite, relegate; urinate, excrete; be sick, vomit, bring up (*inf.*), throw up (*inf.*), spew, retch, heave.

304 eating; drinking

n. eating, ingestion, nourishment, feeding, nutrition, consuming, partaking; feasting, devouring, banqueting; digestion, chewing, mastication; drinking, imbibation, potation; gastronomy, epicurism, gourmandise, gluttony.

eater, partaker, consumer, nibbler, chewer, glutton; drinker, sipper, drunkard; connoisseur, gourmet, gourmand, epicure.

vb. eat, consume, feed on, partake; chew, masticate, champ; bite, digest, swallow; gorge, gobble, bolt, put away (*inf.*), eat up, tuck into (*inf.*), polish off (*inf.*), devour, dispose of; breakfast, lunch, sup; eat out, dine out, wine and dine, feast, banquet, gourmandize; stuff, eat one's fill.

nourish, feed, satisfy, provide, maintain, nurture, strengthen, sustain, tend, gratify; suckle, breast-feed, give suck, nurse.

drink, gulp, take in, imbibe, wash down (*inf.*); tipple, guzzle.

305 provisions

n. provisions, food, stores, sustenance, stock, foodstuffs, groceries, subsistence, rations, board; fodder, feed, pasture, pasturage, roughage, provender; portion, helping, share, slice, quota, division, ration; larder, pantry, refrigerator, freezer.

306 food

n. food, meat and drink, foodstuffs, edibles, comestibles, provisions, nutrition, aliment, nutriment, cooking, grub (*sl.*), tuck (*sl.*); victuals, pabulum, viands; delicacy, delicatessen, luxury, delight.

portion, mouthful, piece, bite, morsel, spoonful.

meal, refreshment, fare; repast, refection; breakfast, brunch, elevenses, lunch, luncheon, packed lunch, tea, afternoon tea, high tea, dinner, supper; snack, sandwich, bite, nibble, buffet, tiffin; feast, banquet, orgy, blow-out (*inf.*), beanfeast, beano (*sl.*); picnic, barbecue; menu, bill of fare, table, cover, spread; dish, course, hors-d'oeuvre, appetizer, soup, broth, pottage, aperitif, entrée, main course, sweet, dessert, afters (*inf.*), pudding, savoury.

meat, flesh, game, poultry, fowl; egg; flour, starch; fish, sea-food; milk product, butter, cream, cheese; oil, fat, grease, blubber, margarine, vegetable fat, vegetable oil; bread, staff of life, loaf, roll; pastry, patisserie, biscuit, wafer, cracker, cake; fruit, soft fruit, berry, jam, conserve, spread, extract, jelly, gelatin; vegetable, herb, edible root, greens, tuber, root; cereal, grain; nut, dried fruit, seed, stone, kernel, pip; sweet, confectionery, sweetmeat, confections; cookery, cuisine, catering, domestic science, home economics.

adj. edible, eatable, comestible, digestible, nutritious, delicious, succulent, palatable, appetizing, satisfying, tempting, scrumptious (*inf.*); culinary; prandial, pre-prandial, post-prandial.

vb. cook, prepare, fix, heat up, warm up; simmer, steam, boil, coddle; stew, casserole, braise; bake, roast, spit; grill, barbecue, broil; fry, sauté, sizzle; poach, scramble; toast, crisp, dry; curry, fricassee; dice, mince; lard, baste.

307 condiment

n. condiment, flavouring, seasoning, additive, sauce, relish, herb, plant, pickle, salt, pepper, mustard.

vb. season, flavour, spice, salt, pepper, bring out the flavour.

308 tobacco

n. tobacco, nicotine, snuff, cigarette, cigar, pipe.

vb. smoke, smoke a pipe, inhale, puff, draw, suck; take snuff.

309 drink

n. drink, beverage, potion, liquid, fluid, juice, sap, whey; infusion, decoction; soft drink, water, milk, tea, coffee, thirst-quencher, nightcap; alcoholic drink, beer, wine, champagne, toast, cocktail; sip, gulp, drop; draught, dram.

310 excretion

n. excretion, urination, evacuation, voiding, discharge, secretion, defecation, expulsion, ejection, excrement, exudation; faeces, excreta; waterworks (*sl.*); urine; bowel movement, diarrhoea, dysentry; offal, dung, droppings, manure; ordure, stool; smegma; perspiration, sweat.

adj. excretive, excretory, secretory; faecal.

vb. excrete, expel, defecate, discharge, evacuate, urinate, secrete, pass, spend a penny, go to the lavatory, be excused.

311 insertion

n. insertion, injection, infusion, introduction, insinuation.

vb. insert, put in, inject, infuse,

introduce, interpolate, include, insinuate, pour in, impregnate, stick in, throw in; force in, drag in (*inf.*), embed, install, fix, implant, bury, sink, immerse.

312 extraction

n. extraction, removal, withdrawal, expulsion, discharge, ejection, extrication, pulling; quarrying, mining; scoop, digger, chisel, extractor, gouge, excavator, dredger.

vb. extract, remove, withdraw, pull out, draw out, pluck, wrench, extricate, cut out, extort, dislodge, uproot, displace, lever out; quarry, mine, excavate, dredge, gouge, chisel; get money out of a stone (*inf.*).

313 passage

n. passage, crossing, journey, trek, voyage; way, thoroughfare, traffic, flow; traffic control, traffic regulation, rule of the road, highway code.

vb. pass, cross, traverse, go through, penetrate, emerge, proceed, drive, weave, thread, ford, span.

314 overstepping

n. overstepping, overrunning, infestation, invasion; transcendence; encroachment, violation, transgression.

vb. go beyond, overstep, encroach, go too far, exceed the limit, overrun, overshoot; invade, infest, plague, swarm, ravage; excel, surpass, outdo, transcend, rise above, eclipse; outdistance, outstrip; trespass, violate, infringe, transgress.

315 shortcoming

n. shortcoming, inadequacy, imperfection, falling short; loss, deficit, shortfall, shortage, dearth, default; need, lack, requirement, deficiency, fault, weakness, lapse, weak point; privation, destitution.

adj. short, deficient, missing, lacking, inadequate, not up to scratch; imperfect, incomplete.

vb. fall short, come short, be deficient, fail, need, miss, lack; lag behind, lose ground; collapse, come to nothing.

316 ascent

n. ascent, ascension, climbing, rise, mount, lift, jump, surge, towering, soaring; ladder, step-ladder, steps, stairs, staircase, escalator, moving staircase, travelator, lift, elevator; hill, mountain, acclivity.

adj. ascending, rising, upward.

vb. ascend, go up, rise, tower, soar, rocket, surge, grow, sprout; take off; climb, mount, scale, surmount, progress, top, scale, conquer, scramble, clamber, creep, work one's way up.

317 descent

n. descent, drop, fall, lapse, swoop, sinking, plunge, downfall, tumble; slump, recession, reduction, declination; subsidence, landslide, hole, cave, chasm.

adj. descending, downward.

vb. descend, go down, fall, drop, subside, decline, swoop, plunge, slump, sink, droop, land, come down, touch down; parachute; crash-land; splash down; topple, push over; tumble, overbalance, lose one's balance, stumble, capsize, turn over, tilt, lurch.

318 elevation

n. elevation, lift, raising, erection; exaltation, ennoblement, sublimation.

adj. raised, lifted, elevated, high, aerial, tall, erect, upstanding, upraised; exalted, noble, sublime, lofty.

vb. lift, elevate, raise, pick up, pull up, help up, uplift, hoist, heave, erect;

support, prop; leaven; boost; glorify, heighten, enhance, exalt.

get up, stand up, get to one's feet, arise; jump up, spring to one's feet.

319 depression

n. depression, lowering, dip; hole, cavity; curtsy, bow, genuflexion; debasement.

adj. depressed; smoothed, even; sitting, sedentary, settled, inactive; prostrate.

vb. depress, lower, press, squash; settle, sink, dip, sag, droop, decline; push down, bring low, ground; fell, cut down, chop down, topple, pull down, demolish, raze to the ground.

drop, let fall, shed, loosen, release, let go, spill; fall, drip, dribble, leak, ooze, seep, drain, permeate, percolate, filter.

sit down, be seated, squat, crouch, kneel, genuflect; perch, roost; bend over, stoop, incline, hunch, bow, curtsy.

320 leap

n. leap, jump, dance, spring, vault, bound, hop, rise, pounce, hurdle, leap-frog, saltation.

adj. lively, frisky, saltatory.

vb. leap, jump, spring, vault, dance, hop, bounce, skip, leapfrog, surge, rise.

321 plunge

n. plunge, jump, rush, dive, drop, fall, plummet, leap, pitch, dip, swoop; ducking, immersion, submergence.

vb. plunge, dive, dip, jump, fall, pounce, cast down; duck, submerge, immerse, drown, souse, dunk; go down, sink, go under; splash down; crash-land; go to the bottom.

322 circulation

n. circulation, circumnavigation; spiral; compass, lap, course, circuit, loop, round trip, orbit, ambit, full circle; by-pass, ring road, detour, diversion.

vb. circle, circulate, go around, revolve around, circumnavigate, circumscribe, circumambulate, lap, tour, ring, gird, wind; by-pass.

see also **250**

323 rotation

n. rotation, revolution, turn, circle, spin, cycle, roll, circuit, whirl, twirl, gyration, pirouette; spiral, orbit; whirlpool, eddy, whirlwind, cyclone, tornado, vortex.

adj. rotary, gyratory, rotating, revolving.

vb. rotate, revolve, twist, circle, circulate, spin, cycle, roll, whirl, twirl, loop, swing, spiral; swivel, pivot; swirl, eddy; pirouette.

324 evolution

n. evolution, development, growth, unfolding, unfurling; disentanglement; evolutionism, Darwinism; missing link.

adj. evolving, evolutionary.

vb. evolve, develop, grow, emerge; advance, progress, mature; unfold, open out, unfurl, unroll, unwind, uncurl, uncover, unwrap; unravel, disentangle, free, release, straighten.

325 oscillation

n. oscillation, fluctuation, vacillation, wavering, undulation, quiver, shake, swing, lurch, roll; vibration, tremor, thunder; faltering, hesitancy, uncertainty.

pulse, pulsation, throb, beat, drumming, pound, surge, palpitation, flutter, ripple, wave; earthquake, seismology.

pendulum, oscillator, vibrator, shuttle, see-saw, cradle, rocking-chair, rocking-horse.

adj. oscillating, fluctuating, throbbing, pulsatory; seismic; vacillating, hesitant, undecided, irresolute.

vb. oscillate, alternate, fluctuate, vacillate, vibrate, pulse, throb, beat, pound, surge, flutter, wave, waver, undulate, librate; nod, swing, sway, see-saw, wobble, totter, lurch, roll, rock, quake, quiver, teeter, zigzag; ebb and flow, back and fill; hesitate, falter.

adv. back and forth, to and fro, up and down, from side to side.

326 agitation

n. agitation, disturbance, vibration; jar, jolt, jog, bump, bounce; shudder, quake, tremble, wobble, tremor, jerk; shakes, jitters (*inf.*), shivers, heebie-jeebies (*sl.*), butterflies (*inf.*), apprehension; fit, convulsion, spasm, palsy, seizure, fever, attack, stroke; itch, twitch.

confusion, tumult, turmoil, turbulence; excitement, melodrama, emotion, commotion, fuss, bother, flap (*inf.*), dither (*inf.*), tizzy (*sl.*).

adj. agitated, shaking, unsteady, wavering, shaky, tremulous; jelly-like, itchy, twitching, nervous, apprehensive, jittery (*inf.*).

vb. shake, tremble, vibrate, quiver, quake, shiver, chatter, shudder, palpitate, flap, toss, flutter, totter, wobble, stagger; itch, twitch; twinkle, flicker, glimmer, sparkle.

agitate, sway, rock, swing, beat, disturb, jolt, jar, jerk, bounce; convulse, seize, throw a fit; go out of control.

III Matter

A Matter in general

327 materiality

n. materiality, substantiality, concreteness, corporeality, corporality, tangibility; materialism, Marxism, dialectical materialism.

matter, body, material, stuff, mass, flesh and blood, flesh; thing, object, something, article, commodity, item, being; element, atom, molecule; component, part, ingredient, factor.

adj. material, substantial; corporeal, bodily; physical, concrete, tangible, real, objective, somatic; materialistic, unspiritual, worldly, mundane.

vb. materialize, realize, become real, take form, become flesh, take flesh, objectify, substantialize.

328 immateriality

n. immateriality, insubstantiality, dematerialization, intangibility, disembodiment; spirituality, otherworldliness; shadow, ghost.

adj. immaterial, incorporeal, insubstantial, bodiless, disembodied, intangible, ethereal, shadowy, ghostly, unreal; otherworldly, spiritual.

vb. dematerialize, disintegrate, disembody; spiritualize.

329 universe

n. universe, creation, space, outer space, cosmos, galaxy; world, earth, sphere, globe, orb, nature; heavenly body, celestial body, planet, planetoid, asteroid, moon, satellite, falling star, shooting star, meteor, meteorite, star, sun, constellation, nebula, quasar, pulsar, black hole; heavens, firmament, vault; atmosphere, air, ether, sky, night sky; astronomy, astrophysics, stargazing, observatory, planetarium,

telescope; astrology, horoscope, signs of the Zodiac; cosmology, cosmogony, cosmography, geography; map, atlas.

adj. universal, cosmic, galactic; terrestrial, earthly, worldly, mundane; heavenly, celestial, empyrean; extraterrestrial, planetary, solar, astral, lunar; astronomical; geographical.

330 weight

n. gravity, gravitation, attraction; weight, heaviness, pressure, force, mass, bulk; ballast, load, freight, sinker, counterweight, paperweight, stone, rock, sandbags, anchor, plumb; burden.

balance, scales, weighing machine, weighbridge.

adj. heavy, weighty, ponderous, bulky, cumbersome, top-heavy; burdensome, oppressive, troublesome.

vb. weigh, balance, poise, measure, put on the scales, counterpoise, counterbalance; weigh down, weight, load, overload; burden, overwhelm, saddle.

331 lightness

n. lightness, levity, weightlessness, imponderability; buoy, cork; leaven, lightener, ferment, yeast.

adj. light, insubstantial; underweight; weightless; feathery, dainty, airy, fluffy; gentle, delicate, soft; floatable, buoyant, unsinkable; lightweight, summerweight; small, portable.

vb. be light, float, surface, swim; levitate, defy gravity; lighten, raise, ferment; unburden, take off, remove, unload, disencumber, jettison.

B Inorganic matter

332 density

n. density, solidity, thickness, compactness, concreteness, heaviness, concentration, congestion, substantiality; incompressibility, impenetrability, impermeability; consolidation, crystallization, coagulation, solidification, thickening, stiffening; mass, solid, body, substance, lump, conglomerate.

adj. dense, solid, thick, compact, close, heavy, impenetrable, impermeable, condensed, compressed; clotted, curdled; frozen; indivisible, insoluble.

vb. solidify, thicken, coagulate, freeze, clot, fix, crystallize, harden, stiffen, set, congeal, jell (*inf.*), curdle, petrify, ossify; compress, condense, compact.

see also 50

333 rarity

n. rarity, thinness, fineness; low pressure, vacuum, emptiness; rarefaction, attenuation.

adj. rare, thin, light, rarefied, fine, attenuated, airy, ethereal; weak, tenuous, sparse, shrill, flimsy, fragile, insubstantial, subtle; empty, void.

vb. rarefy, lessen, reduce pressure, purify, refine, thin, attenuate.

334 hardness

n. hardness, stiffness, firmness, toughness, rigidity, solidity, impenetrability, inflexibility; hardening, stiffening.

adj. hard, solid, thick, dense, compact; rigid, firm, stiff, taut, tight; tough, unyielding, unbreakable, impenetrable, unbending, inflexible, inelastic, unmalleable, impermeable.

vb. harden, toughen, strengthen, set, stiffen, temper; concentrate, consolidate, solidify, crystallize, freeze,

coagulate, congeal, fossilize, ossify, petrify, starch.

see also 537

335 softness

n. softness, penetrability, flexibility, plasticity, tractability, suppleness, pliancy, litheness; looseness, laxity.

adj. soft, smooth, fluffy, spongy, mellow; gentle, delicate; flimsy, limp; tender, pliant, flexible, plastic, elastic, supple, pliable, lithe, limber, mouldable.

vb. soften, ease, modify, temper, tenderize; subdue, assuage, mollify, appease; knead, mash; give, yield, relax, relent.

336 elasticity

n. elasticity, flexibility, pliability, springiness, spring, bounce, resilience, buoyancy; stretch, extensibility, tensility.

adj. elastic, flexible, pliant, resilient, buoyant; stretching, extensile, tensile.

vb. stretch; spring, bounce.

337 toughness

n. toughness, durability, strength, tenacity, cohesion; bone, gristle, cartilage.

adj. tough, durable, hard, firm, solid, robust, strong, stiff, enduring, unbreakable, tenacious; impervious, unyielding, resistant; fibrous, gristly, sinewy.

vb. toughen, strengthen, stiffen, harden.

338 brittleness

n. brittleness, frailty, fragility, delicacy.

adj. brittle, delicate, frail; breakable, fragile; crispy, crumbly; flimsy, frangible; shaky, unsteady; friable.

vb. break, break easily, split, snap,

shatter, fragment, burst, fall to pieces, splinter, crumble.

see also 48

339 texture

n. texture, pattern, weave, organization, composition, constitution, make-up, form, structure; feel, sense, taste, shape, mould, fibre, fabric, web, weft, tissue.

adj. structural, organizational, constructional, tectonic; textural, granular.

340 powderiness

n. powderiness, pulverulence; crumbling, pulverization; powder, dust, grain, particle, granule, crumb, flake, pollen.

adj. powdery, fine, granulated, pulverized, pulverulent; dusty; impalpable; crumbling, friable.

vb. grind, crush, pulverize, granulate, pound, beat, grate, scrape, crunch, crumble, atomize.

341 friction

n. friction, rubbing, abrasion, erosion, wearing away, grinding, filing, irritation; massage, polishing; stroke.

adj. frictional, abrasive, rubbing.

vb. rub, abrade, scour, grate, graze, rasp, chafe, grind, file, scrape, scrub; wear away, erode; polish, shine, smooth, massage; burnish; brush, clean, wipe.

342 lubrication

n. lubrication, anointment, unction; lubricant, grease, oil, wax, fat, ointment, cream, lotion, balm, salve, unguent; petrol, juice (*sl.*).

vb. lubricate, grease, oil, cream, daub, smear, coat, rub, anoint.

343 fluidity

n. fluidity, liquidity, wateriness, juiciness, solubility, dilution; fluid, liquid, liquor, vapour, solution, solvent, drink, flow.

adj. fluid, liquid, running, flowing, molten, liquefied, watery, juicy, liquescent.

vb. flow, run, pour, stream, swell; liquefy.

344 gaseity

n. gaseity, gaseousness, vaporousness, aeration; gas, vapour, steam, fume, air, smoke, fluid.

adj. gaseous, vaporous, vapory, gassy, gas-like, steaming, aeriform, airy, light, windy, volatile.

vb. gasify, aerate.

345 liquefaction

n. liquefaction, solubility, dissolution, thawing; solvent, dissolvent.

adj. runny, molten, liquefied, melted, thawed, disintegrated; liquefacient, soluble.

vb. liquefy, dissolve, melt, run, thaw, defrost, fuse, flux, condense, fluidify, fluidize, deliquesce, disintegrate.

346 vaporization

n. vaporization, evaporation, condensation, sublimation, gasification, volatization, distillation; vapour, moisture, exhalation, mist, smoke, sublimate.

adj. vaporous, steaming, steamy, gassy, volatile.

vb. vaporize, evaporate, sublimate, distil, diffuse, dissipate, gasify, exhale, smoke, fume, steam.

347 water

n. water, liquid, rain, wet, dampness; ice, steam, water vapour.

adj. watery, aquatic, aqueous,

hydrated, liquid, fluid, wet, moist, hydrous, aqua-, hydro-.

see also 349

348 air

n. air, oxygen, fresh air; airing, exposure, ventilation, air conditioning, aeration; atmosphere, stratosphere, ozone, ether, sky; pneumatics, aerodynamics.

weather, climate, elements; meteorology, forecasting.

adj. airy, aerial; exposed, ventilated, open, aerated; draughty, breezy, windy; pneumatic, aero-; metereological.

vb. air, aerate, ventilate, open, refresh, freshen, cool, aerify, purify, fan.

see also 359

349 moisture

n. moisture, humidity, dampness, wetness, precipitation; drip, damp, dew, rain, wet; moistening, saturation, wettening, humidification.

adj. moist, damp, wet, humid, muggy, dank, misty; saturated, soaked, sodden, waterlogged, awash, drowned, drenched, wet through, like a drowned rat.

vb. moisten, dampen, wet, humidify; sprinkle, dabble, shower, dip, sponge, splash; saturate, drench, soak, bathe, souse, steep, stream, seep, sog; duck, immerse, submerge, drown; waterlog, flood, swamp, inundate, deluge.

350 dryness

n. dryness, aridity, aridness, parchedness, desiccation, dehydration; thirst, drought.

adj. dry, arid, parched, unmoistened, rainless, sapless, evaporated; barren, desert, dusty, baked, scorched,

bleached; dried, dehydrated, thirsty; waterproof, rainproof, watertight.

vb. dry, dehydrate, freeze-dry, dripdry; desiccate, parch, bake, scorch, torrefy; air, evaporate; shrivel, wither; soak up, absorb.

351 ocean

n. ocean, sea, deep, brine, high seas; oceanography.

adj. oceanic, marine, maritime, pelagic; oceanographical.

352 land

n. land, terrain, *terra firma*, mainland, continent; inland, interior; peninsula, neck, isthmus; ground, soil, earth, gravel, sand, rock, pebble; fields, pasture; shore, beach, seaside, strand, bank, coastline, seaboard.

adj. terrestrial, earthy; inland, interior, landlocked, central; coastal, seaside, littoral, riverside, riparian.

353 gulf

n. gulf, inlet, bay, estuary, bight, mouth, harbour, lagoon, sound, fiord, firth, loch, strait, narrows, arm, kyle; cove, cave.

354 lake

n. lake, tarn, loch, lagoon, pool, pond, creek, mere, inland sea, reservoir, basin; puddle.

355 marsh

n. marsh, fen, swamp, mire, bog, quagmire, quicksand, morass, slough, moor, mud.

adj. marshy, soft, fenny, swampy, boggy, wet, waterlogged, squelchy, slushy, muddy, miry, paludal.

356 plain

n. plain, expanse, open country, flat, lowland, champaign, grassland; meadow, field, grass, pasture; steppe, prairie, savannah, pampa, llano; moor, moorland, common, heath, wold; upland, plateau, tableland, downs; tundra, veld.

357 island

n. island, isle, islet, holm, eyot, ait, archipelago; reef, atoll, ridge, sandbank, cay, key.

358 water in motion

n. river, watercourse, waterway, tributary, branch, fork, effluent; stream, brook, rivulet, beck, runnel, rill, runlet, bourn, creek.

tide, current, flow, course, undercurrent; spring, fountain, spout, gush, rush, jet, outpouring, uprising; whirlpool, eddy, vortex, swirl, maelstrom; wash, backwash.

wave, billow, swell, roller, surge, crest, ripple, undulation, breaker, tidal wave, white-caps, white horses; waterfall, cataract, fall, shoot, cascade, torrent, rapids, weir.

rain, rainfall, precipitation, drizzle, shower, downpour, thunderstorm, cloudburst, flood, deluge, inundation, monsoon; mist.

adj. runny, streaming; rainy, moist, wet, showery, cloudy, thundery, stormy; torrential.

vb. flow, run, stream, sweep, rush; gush, well, spurt, squirt, jet, spout, issue, flood, inundate; wave, undulate, billow, swell, ripple, ebb; swirl, eddy, surge, roll, whirl, tumble; dash, break, splash; drop, drip, seep, leak, trickle, dribble, gurgle; spill, overflow, spew, exude; fall, cascade; drain, empty, clear, tap, expel, deplete, decant, bleed.

rain, pour, patter, spit, drizzle, shower.

359 air in motion

n. wind, draught, current, breeze, whisk, whiff, puff, flutter, waft, zephyr;

gust, blast, flurry, flaw; gale, storm, squall, blizzard, whirlwind, cyclone, typhoon, tornado, hurricane, tempest; trade wind, mistral, föhn.

breathing, respiration, inhalation, expiration, exhalation, afflatus; breath, gasp, sigh, pant, cough, sneeze, wheeze.

adj. windy, open, exposed, fresh, blustery, squally, gusty, stormy, tempestuous; draughty, well-ventilated; wheezy, asthmatic.

vb. blow, breeze, whiff, waft, flutter, flap, buffet, sweep, whisk, fling; blast, rush, roar, howl, wail, stream, whirl; breathe, respire, inhale, exhale, expire, puff, pant, gasp; sigh; cough, sneeze, wheeze; pump, inflate, blow up, swell, fill.

360 water channel

n. conduit, channel, way, passage, bed, ditch, trench, trough, moat; course, canal, aqueduct; tunnel, pipe, pipeline, tube, main, duct, culvert; spout, tap, funnel, siphon; drain, drainpipe, gutter, sewer; flume, gully, cloaca.

361 air-pipe

n. air-pipe, shaft, tube; vent, chimney, flue, ventilator.

362 semiliquidity

n. semiliquidity, viscosity, glutinousness, stickiness, adhesiveness; semiliquid, glue, paste, size, colloid, emulsion, syrup.

adj. semiliquid, semifluid, gelatinous, viscous, viscid, glutinous, coagulated, slimy, syrupy, creamy, sticky, tacky, slushy, gummy, colloid.

363 bubble; cloud

n. bubble, globule, sac, froth, foam, spray, surf, spume; fizz, head; lather, suds; effervescence, fermentation, bubbling.

cloud, haze, haziness, mist, fog, smog, pea-souper (*inf.*), film.

adj. bubbly, foaming, bubbling, soapy, effervescent, sparkling, fizzy, spumous, spumy; cloudy, overcast, dull, grey, unclear, murky, gloomy, dim, misty, hazy, foggy, nebulous.

vb. effervesce, bubble, boil, fizz, foam, ferment.

364 pulpiness

n. pulpiness, sponginess, softness, succulence; pulp, mash, sponge, paste, pap, mulch, mush, jelly, dough, batter, poultice.

adj. pulpy, mushy, doughy, soggy, spongy, pulpous, ripe, fleshy, succulent; thick, smooth.

vb. pulp, mash, crush.

365 unctuousness

n. unctuousness, oiliness, greasiness; oil, fat, grease, blubber; unction, oil, unguent, embrocation, salve, nard, ointment, lubricant, balm, emollient, remedy, cream; resin, gum, pitch, varnish, lacquer, shellac, asphalt, bitumen.

adj. unctuous, oily, greasy, fatty, unguent, creamy.

vb. grease, oil, lubricate; resin, varnish; anoint.

C Organic matter

366 animate matter

n. creation, nature, animals, plants, fauna, flora; creature, organism, cell, protoplasm; biology, natural history, nature study, ecology, genetics, evolution, biochemistry, anatomy, physiology, botany, zoology.

adj. animate, organic, biological.

367 inorganic matter

n. mineral, rock, deposit, ore, metal, coal; geology, mineralogy, metallurgy.

adj. inorganic, inanimate, mineral, metallurgical.

368 life

n. life, existence, being; organism, human, body, creature, man, person, individual, personage, mortal.

soul, spirit, life-blood, breath, heart; élan, verve; vivification, animation, liveliness, vigour, vitality, force, energy.

adj. living, alive, surviving, in the flesh, vital; lively, animated, vigorous, vivacious, forceful, energetic, spirited, alive and kicking, active.

vb. live, exist, be, have life, breathe, respire; move, subsist; be spared, survive.

be born, come to life, come into the world, see the light; bear, beget, conceive, give birth to, bring to life.

vivify, quicken, animate, reanimate, vitalize, enliven, revive, breathe life into.

369 death

n. death, mortality; decease, dying, passing, departure, end, expiration, exit, extinction, parting, separation, release, homecall; loss, bereavement; fatality; demise, dissolution.

last hour, death bed, last breath, swan-song; death list, death toll, casualty list; obituary; the dead, departed, deceased, ancestors, forefathers, those gone before.

adj. mortal, sick, perishing, deathly, moribund, at death's door, on one's last legs; dead, deceased, departed, late, lamented; lifeless, breathless; defunct, extinct, cold, extinguished, terminated, ended, exterminated, lost.

vb. die, depart, go, expire, pass away, give up the ghost, breathe one's last, go the way of all flesh, be taken, kick the bucket (*sl.*); perish, succumb, come to nothing, be no more; be killed, lose one's life; push up daisies (*inf.*).

370 killing

n. killing, slaying, slaughter, destruction, assassination, murder, homicide, manslaughter; bloodshed, carnage, massacre, genocide, butchery, holocaust, liquidation, extermination, annihilation, decimation; shooting, knifing, lynching, poisoning, execution, hanging, strangulation, electrocution, crucifixion, burning, drowning, vivisection; euthanasia, mercy killing; abortion; suicide, self-destruction, hara-kiri, kamikaze.

killer, murderer, assassin, slayer, butcher, cut-throat, poisoner, strangler; gunman, terrorist, gangster, homicidal maniac; hangman, executioner.

adj. killing, lethal, fatal, mortal, deadly, destructive; homicidal, murderous, internecine; suicidal.

vb. kill, murder, slay, destroy, take life, put to death, bump off (*sl.*), knock off (*sl.*), do in (*sl.*), do away with (*inf.*), slaughter, assassinate, massacre, butcher, mow down (*inf.*), gun down (*inf.*), liquidate, annihilate, decimate, exterminate; execute, behead, guillotine, decapitate; shoot, gun, knife, hang, lynch; poison; strangle, suffocate, choke, asphyxiate; put to sleep (*inf.*), put down, put away.

kill oneself, commit suicide, take one's life, do oneself in (*sl.*), blow one's brains out, shoot oneself, cut one's throat.

371 corpse

n. corpse, remains, body, carcass, skeleton, relics, ashes, dust, mummy, cadaver, stiff (*sl.*).

adj. cadaverous, corpse-like, deathlike, deathly, pale.

372 burial

n. burial, funeral, interment, entombment, sepulture; cremation, incineration; embalment, mummification.

burial service, funeral rites, last rites, mourning, obsequies; requiem, elegy, last post, knell, passing bell; epitaph, obituary, in memoriam, RIP; coffin, urn, sarcophagus, pall, mummy case.

mortuary, morgue; undertaker, funeral director; gravestone, headstone, tombstone, monument, memorial; tomb, grave, sepulchre, vault, crypt, mausoleum, barrow; burial ground, graveyard, churchyard, God's acre, cemetery, catacomb, necropolis; pyre, crematorium; war memorial, cenotaph; exhumation, disinterment.

adj. buried, interred; funereal, funeral, mourning, mournful, sad.

vb. bury, inter, inhume, entomb, enshrine, embalm, lay out, lay to rest, sepulture; cremate; exhume, disinter, unearth.

373 animality; animal

n. animality, fauna, zoology; animal, creature, beast, vertebrate, invertebrate; quadruped, biped, man; mammal, marsupial; carnivore, herbivore, omnivore; fish, amphibian, mollusc, crustacean; bird, fowl, bird of prey, waterfowl; insect; reptile; cattle, herd, livestock, poultry, game; pet, domestic animal; rodent, vermin, parasite.

adj. animal, zoological, mammalian; piscine, fishy, amphibian; avian.

374 vegetability; plant

n. vegetability, vegetation, botany;

plant, shrub; plantation, shrubbery, undergrowth, corn, grain, cereal, crop, field; flower, bloom, bud, petal, blossom; flower-bed, garden; foliage; foliation, leafage; grass, pasture, verdure, sod, turf, lawn; herb; weed; tree, sapling, scion; branch, limb, bough, twig, sprig, spray, shoot, stem, stalk, leaf; wood, forest, bush, jungle; copse, spinney, coppice, woodland, thicket, covert, arboretum; forestry, dendrology, conservation; seed, root, bulb.

adj. vegetal, vegetative, botanical, horticultural, floral, verdant, grassy, weedy, arboreal.

375 zoology

n. zoology, life science, anthropology, anatomy, physiology, ichthyology, ornithology, bird-watching, entomology, embryology, taxonomy.

adj. zoological, ornithological.

376 botany

n. botany, plant science, horticulture, ecology, phytology.

adj. botanical, horticultural.

377 management of animals

n. animal husbandry, breeding, stockbreeding, grazing, taming, domestication.

farm, ranch, homestead; fishery, aquarium; zoo, zoological gardens; veterinary science, vet; shepherd, herdsman, herd, cattleherd, cowherd.

vb. keep, husband, breed, rear, raise, herd, drive, ranch, farm, tend, shepherd; feed, fodder, graze, fatten, market; shear, chip, fleece; milk; tame, domesticate, train; groom.

378 agriculture

n. agriculture, farming, cultivation, horticulture, gardening, growing, crop raising, husbandry; strip farming, rotation crops, contour ploughing; landscape gardening.

farm, ranch, homestead, holding, smallholding, grange; kibbutz; farmland, meadow, grassland, farmstead, estate, croft, enclosure, land, field, soil, patch, plot, allotment, plantation; garden, orchard, nursery; greenhouse, vineyard, arboretum.

farmer, husbandman, agriculturalist, cultivator, tiller, planter, grower, rancher, homesteadman, peasant, serf, hiredman, labourer, farmhand; gardener, nurseryman, horticulturalist, landscape gardener.

adj. agrarian, farming, agricultural, rustic, rural, peasant; horticultural, garden.

vb. cultivate, till; fertilize, manure; water, irrigate; dig, plough, harrow; seed, sow, broadcast, disseminate, plant, drill, bed, transplant; weed, hoe; graft; harvest, reap, gather in, glean, winnow, thresh, mow, cut, scythe, bind, stack, pick, pluck.

379 mankind

n. mankind, humanity, human race, human beings, populace, population, the world, flesh; person, man, human being, individual, creature, mortal, body, earthling, *homo sapiens*, Adam, anthropoid; people, public, folk.

society, community, civilization, politics; nation, state, body politic, nationality, statehood; chauvinism, nationalism, imperialism; anthropology, social anthropology, ethnology, sociology.

adj. human, mortal; individual, personal; social, civilized; political, national, state, general, public, civil, federal, social, communal, societal, civic; nationalistic, chauvinist, racialist.

380 male

n. male, man, gentleman, sir; chap, fellow, guy (*sl.*), bloke (*inf.*), boy; virility, masculinity, manliness, manhood.

male animal, cock, drake, gander, dog, tom-cat, hart, stag, stallion, billygoat, ox, bull; gelding.

adj. male, masculine; manly, virile; gentlemanly.

381 female

n. female, woman, lady, girl; madam, miss; fair sex, weaker sex; femininity, womanliness, girlishness, womanhood; feminism, women's lib; effeminacy; womankind.

female animal, hen, duck, goose, bitch, she-dog, filly, ewe, sow, hind, doe, mare, nanny-goat, cow.

adj. female, feminine, girlish, womanly, lady-like; effeminate.

IV Intellect

1 Formation of ideas

A Intellectual operations in general

382 intellect

n. intellect, mind, brain, consciousness, mentality, intelligence, intellectuality, instinct, faculties; perception, conception, capacity, judgment, understanding, reasoning, genius, wisdom; psychology, behaviourism; psychiatry, psychotherapy.

soul, spirit, psyche, heart, individuality, personality, conscience,

self, ego, id, superego, unconscious, subconscious.

adj. mental, intellectual, conceptional, abstract, perceptual, critical, rational, conscious, cognitive, cerebral, intelligent; psychological, psychic, subconscious, subliminal; spiritual.

vb. conceive, cognize, perceive, reason, judge; realize, sense, mark, note.

see also 434

383 absence of intellect

n. unintellectuality, unintelligence, imbecility, stupidity, shallowness, mindlessness, brainlessness.

adj. unintellectual, unintelligent, empty-headed, mindless, brainless.

see also 435

384 thought

n. thought, cogitation, concentration, brain-work; reflection, meditation, rumination, contemplation, thoughtfulness, brooding, pondering, absorption, preoccupation, deliberation; consideration, perception, appreciation, discernment, observation, reasoning, concluding.

adj. thoughtful, pensive, contemplative, reflective, studious; absorbed, engrossed, wrapped up in, dreamy; introspective; discerning, penetrating, intellectual.

vb. think, cogitate, consider, give thought to, concentrate, reflect, meditate, deliberate, ponder, muse, ruminate, contemplate, brood, turn over in one's mind, mull, study, examine, bear in mind, put on one's thinking cap (*inf.*), have on one's mind, take it into one's head (*inf.*); esteem, appraise, weigh up; philosophize, reconsider.

occur to, come to mind, strike, suggest itself, enter one's head.

385 absence of thought

n. thoughtlessness, irrationality, incomprehensibility, folly, senselessness, ignorance, inattention, inconsideration, carelessness, neglect.

adj. thoughtless, irrational, unreasoning, incomprehensible, foolish, blank, vacant, switched off (*inf.*).

vb. not think about, ignore, forget, dismiss, get off one's mind, get out of one's mind, get out of one's head; think no more of, not give another thought to, not give a second thought, not enter one's head.

386 idea

n. idea, notion, concept, conception, thought, mental impression, image, impression; conjecture, fancy, guess, theory, hypothesis, postulate; observation, opinion, assessment, plan.

see also 420

387 topic

n. topic, subject, problem, matter, question; argument, theme, burden, concern, thesis, proposition, thrust, *leitmotif*, issue, point, point in question, moot point.

B Preliminary conditions and operations

388 curiosity

n. curiosity, interest, concern, regard; thirst, quest, desire, eagerness, inclination; inquisitiveness, intrusiveness, nosiness (*sl.*), prying.

questioner, busy-body, snoop, intruder, meddler, Nosy Parker (*sl.*); gossip, backbiter, chatterbox, scandalmonger.

adj. curious, interested, concerned, into (*inf.*), questioning; inquisitive, searching, poking, scrutinizing; intrusive, prying, snooping, meddlesome, nosy (*sl.*).

vb. enquire, question, investigate, seek; show interest, be into (*inf.*), have a thing about (*inf.*); intrude, pry, snoop, meddle, gossip, chatter, backbite.

389 incuriosity

n. incuriosity, apathy, dislike, disinclination.

adj. incurious, unconcerned, inattentive, apathetic, indifferent, uninquisitive, uninterested, bored.

vb. ignore, disregard, be blind to, dismiss, take no interest in, not care less.

390 attention

n. attention, regard, notice, observation, inspection; consideration, study, attentiveness; assiduousness, diligence; mindfulness, heed, heedfulness, vigilance; concentration, preoccupation.

adj. attentive, mindful; heeding, wary, vigilant; considerate, observant; studious, assiduous, diligent.

vb. pay attention, listen, catch, give heed to, observe, notice, take notice, mind, heed, look to, regard, note, take into account; consider, study, inspect, examine, mark, scrutinize, concentrate on; drink in (*inf.*), lap up (*inf.*), hang on someone's every word; lose oneself in; keep one's ear to the ground (*inf.*); attract, draw, pull, focus.

391 inattention

n. inattention, carelessness, inconsideration, unconcern, heedlessness, thoughtlessness; slackness, indolence; neglect, disregard; indifference, coolness, coldness, detachment; absent-mindedness, wandering.

adj. inattentive, careless, inconsiderate, thoughtless, heedless, unobservant; negligent, indifferent, cool, cold, detached; absent-minded, distracted.

vb. be inattentive, dream, daydream, let one's mind wander; not catch, miss, disregard, overlook, neglect; go in one ear and out the other; distract, divert, draw away, turn away, call away, detract, attract from, beguile; upset, disconcert.

392 care

n. care, concern, regard, thought, heed, consideration, solicitude, thoughtfulness, pains; carefulness, scrupulousness, prudence, judiciousness, wisdom; watchfulness, vigilance, alertness; forethought, precaution, caution.

exactness, particularity, thoroughness, meticulousness, neatness, fastidiousness, conscientiousness; economy, conservation, frugality, management, husbandry, stewardship.

oversight, direction, surveillance, supervision, inspection, protection, guarding.

adj. careful, concerned, thoughtful, considerate, courteous, kind, solicitous; prudent, judicious, wise, discreet, unobtrusive, self-possessed, watchful, sober, alert, awake, circumspect, vigilant; diplomatic, politic.

thorough, rigorous, particular, precise, exact, exacting, discriminating, conscientious, meticulous, punctilious, scrupulous; neat, tidy, fussy, finicky; pedantic, fastidious, religious; assiduous, diligent, painstaking, dependable, faithful; economical, sparing, frugal, thrifty, stingy (*inf.*).

vb. be careful, mind, heed, tend, look after, take care of; watch, observe; superintend, supervise, direct, manage, stand over; baby-sit, chaperon; keep vigil; keep tabs on, follow up, protect, support, guard.

393 neglect

n. neglect, carelessness, unconcern, disregard, inconsideration, negligence, neglectfulness, apathy, indifference, omission, dereliction, failure, procrastination; imprudence, rashness, hastiness.

adj. negligent, careless, inconsiderate, unthinking, thoughtless, unmindful, forgetful, oblivious; remiss, lax, inattentive; lackadaisical, imprudent, unguarded, hasty, rash, unwary, reckless, unheeding, injudicious, unwise; apathetic, indifferent, casual, slipshod, lazy; wasteful, extravagant, immoderate.

vb. neglect, omit, miss, forget, dismiss, reject, leave undone, lose sight of, evade, gloss over, skip, skimp; disregard, ignore, overlook, not look at, pass over, make light of, brush aside, laugh off, pooh-pooh, shut one's eyes to, give the go-by, turn a blind eye to.

see also 920

394 enquiry

n. enquiry, inquiry, examination, investigation, study, analysis, search, probe, quest, perusal; checking, scrutiny, review, inspection; question, query, request, invitation, petition, challenge, feeler; experiment, quiz, test, exam, viva, questionnaire; interrogation, interview, dialogue, cross-examination, grilling, catechism.

questioner, examiner, enquirer, interrogator, interviewer, researcher, investigator, canvasser, pollster.

adj. inquiring, inquisitive, curious, nosy (*sl.*); exploratory, fact-finding.

vb. enquire, ask, put a question, pose, put it to; call upon, request, invite, challenge, charge, bid, petition, canvass; question, interrogate, quiz, cross-examine, interview, grill; seek, look for, search, hunt, turn inside out, peruse; sniff out (*inf.*), smell out; investigate, examine, study, inspect, analyse, probe, scrutinize, check, review, monitor; try, hear; pry, snoop, spy.

395 answer

n. answer, reply, response, acknowledgement; comeback, feedback, rebuttal, rejoinder, retort; repartee, backchat, retaliation.

answerer, replier, correspondent, examinee, candidate.

adj. answering, responsive.

vb. answer, reply, respond, come back to, write back, acknowledge, remark, rejoin, retort, answer back, rebut.

396 experiment

n. experiment, test, research; observation, analysis, inspection, operation, diagnosis, exercise; check, verification, proof, sifting; rehearsal, practice run, trial run, test case, pilot, pilot scheme; feeler, probe; speculation, guess, conjecture, trial and error, hit and miss, shot in the dark, hypothesis; sounding board, guinea pig.

researcher, research worker, scientist, boffin (*sl.*), back-room boy, experimenter, experimentalist, speculator.

adj. experimental, hypothetical; tentative, trial, provisional, temporary, probationary, preliminary, preparatory, unproved, speculative, trial, test.

vb. experiment, investigate, study, examine, scrutinize, explore, research,

search, sound out, prove; analyse, diagnose; check, verify, prove; guess, speculate, hypothesize; put out a feeler, see which way the wind is blowing, spy out the land.

397 comparison

n. comparison, juxtaposition; weighing, estimation, measurement; relation, connection, association, balance, match, parallel, parallelism, correspondence, equation; identification, resemblance, similarity, likening, analogy, illustration, example, picture, metaphor, simile, allegory; contrast, opposition.

vb. compare, juxtapose, parallel, draw a parallel between, put side by side; measure, weigh, confront, collate; liken, relate, associate, link, balance, match, equate; contrast, oppose, separate.

398 discrimination

n. discrimination, discernment, acumen, astuteness, keenness, shrewdness, penetration; distinction, nicety, differentiation; diagnosis, appreciation, critique, judgment, sense, sensitivity, tact, feel, refinement, taste, selection, choice.

adj. discriminating, careful, selective, particular, exacting, choosy (*inf.*), judicious, tactful, discerning, perceptive, sensitive, critical, tasteful, refined.

vb. discriminate, differentiate, discern, tell apart, tell from, distinguish; compare and contrast; choose, pick carefully, select, separate, set apart.

399 indiscrimination

n. indiscrimination, uncriticalness, insensitiveness, tastelessness.

adj. indiscriminate, undiscriminating, unselective, uncritical, undiscerning, careless; mixed, blanket, promiscuous; random, haphazard; aimless, chaotic, confused.

vb. not discriminate, draw no distinction, disregard differences, lump together; confuse, confound, mix, muddle, jumble together.

400 measurement

n. measurement, mensuration; quantification; estimation, determination, computation, calculation, assessment, evaluation, reckoning; graduation, calibration; measure, dimension, distance, degree, pitch, time; size, length, depth, height, width, breadth, thickness; area; mass, weight, density, volume, capacity, pressure, intensity, speed, strength, calibre, viscosity; quantity, magnitude, range, extent; amplitude, frequency, ratio, diameter, radius; temperature.

meter, gauge, scale, rule, ruler, tape-measure, slide-rule, calculator, computer; scales, balance, mark, grade, step, point, limit, standard, criterion; weights and measures, imperial system, avoirdupois, apothecary, troy, metric system, SI unit; metrication.

adj. mensural, dimensional; measurable, assessable, calculable, computable.

vb. measure, quantify, estimate, compute, assess, count, reckon, determine, evaluate, appraise, calculate, survey; gauge, calibrate, graduate; take a reading; level, square; survey, map; average; check; go metric, metricate.

C Materials for reasoning

401 evidence

n. evidence, fact, clue, reason, justification, explanation, grounds, data, case; support, foundation, backing; sign, indication, trace; document, documentation, information; testimony, witness, statement, plea, assertion, allegation, attestation, exhibit, reference, affidavit; confirmation, corroboration.

adj. suggestive, indicative, symptomatic, corroborative, supporting.

vb. evidence, show, suggest, indicate, evince, illustrate, demonstrate, document, manifest, imply; confirm, verify, support, substantiate, attest, corroborate; testify, bear witness to, witness, affirm; speak for itself (*inf.*), speak volumes (*inf.*).

see also 413

402 counter-evidence

n. counter-evidence, counterclaim, defence, rebuttal, answer, reply.

adj. rebutting, defending, conflicting; uncorroborative, countervailing; contradictory, contrary, answering, replying.

vb. weigh against, contradict, rebut, refute, squash, deny; be contrary to; cancel out.

see also 414

403 qualification

n. qualification, modification, limitation, restriction; proviso, exception, reservation; allowance.

adj. qualifying, qualificatory, provisional, contingent, conditional, mitigating, extenuating.

vb. qualify, modify, adjust; limit, restrict, restrain, moderate, mitigate, lessen, temper; condition, colour, make exceptions, exempt, allow for, make allowances for.

see also 700

404 possibility

n. possibility, potentiality, practicability, feasibility, plausibility, reasonableness, virtuality.

adj. possible, likely, probable; virtual, potential; able, capable, viable, feasible, plausible, practical, practicable, available, attainable, within reach, obtainable, within the bounds of possibility; conceivable, thinkable, imaginable, credible.

vb. be possible, can, may, might, stand a chance; make possible, enable, admit of.

see also **406**

405 impossibility

n. impossibility, impracticability, unavailability, inaccessibility; unreasonableness, no hope, hopelessness, no chance.

adj. impossible, unbelievable, inconceivable, unimaginable, unthinkable; prohibited; insoluble, difficult; unable, implausible, unpracticable, unavailable, insurmountable, insuperable, inaccessible, unobtainable, out of the question, beyond the bounds of possibility.

vb. be impossible, defy possibilities; not dream of (*inf.*); make impossible, exclude.

adv. no way (*inf.*).

see also **407**

406 probability

n. probability, likelihood, likeliness, expectation; prospect, promise, chance, possibility, good chance, hope, opportunity.

adj. probable, likely, expected; reasonable, presumable, on the cards, supposable; promised, well-founded, seeming; feasible, practicable, workable, plausible, credible.

vb. be probable, may well happen, show signs of; make likely, increase the chances of, hope for.

adv. probably, likely, no doubt, in all probability, quite possibly, most likely, to be expected, to be supposed, as likely as not, everything being equal.

407 improbability

n. improbability, unlikelihood, implausibility, inconceivableness, unreasonableness; rarity, infrequency; bare possibility, million to one chance.

adj. improbable, unlikely, unexpected, unreasonable, impracticable, unworkable, implausible, unbelievable, hardly possible, unheard of, doubtful, dubious, questionable; absurd, extraordinary.

vb. be improbable, probably not happen.

408 certainty

n. certainty, certitude; conviction, assurance; reliance, confidence, trust; truth, accuracy, genuineness; dogmatism; unambiguity, conclusiveness; necessity, inevitability, inexorability.

foregone conclusion, safe bet, sure thing (*inf.*), dead cert (*sl.*).

adj. certain, settled, decided, final, definite; absolute, sure, conclusive, solid, irrefutable, indubitable, indisputable, unquestionable, unmistakable, incontrovertible, unassailable, undisputed; reliable, unfailing, unshakable, inerrant, infallible, sound, authoritative, unerring, trustworthy; unambiguous, unequivocal, incontestable; unconditional; ascertained, certified, verified, attested, confirmed, ratified; self-evident, axiomatic.

vb. make certain, guarantee, authenticate, certify, check, confirm, test, prove, verify, corroborate, ratify; ensure, secure, settle, attest, endorse, clinch; commit, engage, take sides; seal, sign, shake hands.

adv. certainly, without doubt, of

course, definitely, at all events, sure thing (*inf.*); in the bag (*inf.*).

409 uncertainty

n. uncertainty, incertitude; unreliability, questionableness, unpredictability, untrustworthiness, ambiguity, vagueness, obscurity; inconclusiveness, indeterminateness, improbability, unlikelihood.

doubt, disbelief, unbelief, suspicion, misgiving, scepticism, agnosticism, faithlessness, doubtfulness, incredulity; indecision, equivocalness, wavering, hesitancy, suspense; perplexity, bewilderment; puzzle, problem, maze, dilemma, quandary, enigma; fog, haziness; anybody's guess.

adj. uncertain, doubtful, undecided; unsure, inconclusive, ambiguous, vague, unclear, indeterminate, unpredictable, unlikely, possible; risky, chancy, insecure; haphazard, random, casual; questionable, unreliable, fallible, erring; shakable, precarious; puzzling, perplexing.

controversial, open, debatable, contentious, problematical, moot; uncertified, unverified, unattested, unconfirmed, unratified.

doubting, unbelieving, suspicious, sceptical, faithless, distrustful, agnostic.

vb. be uncertain, doubt, flounder, grope, fumble; suspect, smell a rat; not know where one stands, not know which way to turn; sit on the fence, waver; fall between two stools; puzzle, bewilder, perplex.

adv. in the air, in question, open to question.

D Reasoning processes

410 reasoning

n. reasoning, rationalizing; judgment, argumentation; reason, rationality, logic, rationalism; thinking, brainwork, cogitation, knowing, realizing; insight, discernment, acumen, penetration, understanding, comprehension, grasp; reflection, deliberation; concluding.

conclusion, inference, deduction, induction, derivation; syllogism; problem, proposition, premise, postulate, thesis, theorem.

discussion, conversation, exchange, dialogue, interview, disputation, argument, dispute, debate, controversy, symposium; apologetics.

adj. rational, reasoning, logical, sound, rationalistic, reasonable; thoughtful, deliberate, collected; arguing, discursive, controversial, polemical; argumentative.

vb. reason, argue, discuss, converse, dispute, talk about, explain; defend, justify, plead, make out a case, support, contend; philosophize; conclude, put two and two together (*inf.*), deduce, infer, derive, syllogize; be reasonable, add up (*inf.*), make sense, hold water.

411 intuition

n. intuition, instinct, sentiment, feeling, sense; insight, inspiration, extra-sensory perception, ESP, sixth sense; automatic reaction, reflex action, hunch, presentiment, premonition, impression.

adj. intuitive, instinctive; involuntary, reflex, automatic, mechanical, unthinking; spontaneous, inspired, impulsive.

vb. feel, sense, feel in one's bones,

guess, just know, have a funny feeling, have the feeling, follow one's nose.

412 false reasoning

n. sophistry, irrationality, unreasonableness, unsoundness, invalidity; delusion, deceit, deception, erroneousness, speciousness, evasion.

fallacy, sophism, ambiguity, solecism, illogicality, paralogism; inconsistency, *non sequitur*, contradiction; circular argument, vicious circle; misinterpretation; miscalculation; preconception; perversion, prejudice, deviation, aberration.

adj. sophistic, fallacious, illogical, specious, inconsistent, loose, contradictory, ambiguous, solecistic; irrational, unreasonable, unsound, untenable, inconsistent, invalid, deceptive, erroneous, heretical.

vb. reason falsely, evade the issue, beat about the bush, miss the point, beg the question; cavil.

413 demonstration

n. demonstration, proof, verification, justification, establishment, affirmation, validation, corroboration; averment; explanation, elucidation, interpretation, illustration, exhibition, presentation, display.

adj. demonstrative; demonstrated, clear, evident, conclusive, certain, decisive; established, concluded, upheld, valid; demonstrable, verifiable, deducible, inferable.

vb. demonstrate, prove, show, verify, make evident, establish, confirm, substantiate, bear out, affirm, authenticate, attest, validate, test, check; declare, testify, witness, document; have a case; settle, determine; justify; explain, illustrate, describe; manifest, exhibit, display.

414 disproof

n. disproof, confutation, refutation, invalidation, rebuttal, contradiction, denial; upset; exposure; clincher.

adj. disproved, confuted, invalidated; shown up, exposed; contradicted.

vb. disprove, prove false, rebut, invalidate, repudiate, contradict, deny; contend, debate, argue, oppose, dispute; show up (*inf.*), discredit, expose; overthrow, overturn, defeat, finish, confound, overwhelm, crush, floor, silence; knock the bottom out of (*inf.*), cut the ground from under one's feet, get the better of.

E   Results of reasoning

415 judgment

n. judgment, consideration, contemplation, appraisal, examination, review, weighing, sifting, assessment, estimation, appreciation, evaluation, determination; adjudication, arbitration; report, opinion, view, belief, idea, decree, decision, finding, recommendation, pronouncement, verdict, ruling, resolution.

judge, assessor, examiner, valuer, surveyor, adjudicator, arbitrator, referee, umpire.

adj. judicial, judicious; critical; unprejudiced, unbiased.

vb. judge, consider, contemplate, size up (*inf.*), examine, review, appraise, survey, analyse, weigh, sift, assess, evaluate, estimate, appreciate; decide, conclude, find, recommend, pronounce, rule, decree, settle, adjudicate, arbitrate.

416 misjudgment

n. misjudgment, miscalculation, misconception, misunderstanding, misinterpretation, distortion, overestimation, preconception; underestimation; prejudice, bias; narrow-mindedness, pettiness, narrowness, bigotry.

adj. misjudging, wrong; uncritical, unrealistic; injudicious, unwise, ill-judged; partial, unfair, one-sided, biased, prejudiced, intolerant; narrow-minded, petty, mean, narrow, short-sighted, bigoted, insular.

vb. misjudge, miscalculate, misconceive, misconstrue, misapprehend, misunderstand, bark up the wrong tree (*inf.*); undervalue, overvalue, overrate; prejudge, presume, suppose, preconceive, jump to conclusions; prejudice, bias, jaundice, twist, sway, warp, influence.

see also **916**

417 overestimation

n. overestimation, overvaluation, overrating, exaggeration, overstatement; optimism.

adj. overestimated, exaggerated.

vb. overestimate, exaggerate, overvalue, overrate; maximize, emphasize, make a mountain out of a molehill, make too much of, paint in glowing colours.

see also **481**

418 underestimation

n. underestimation, undervaluation, understatement, minimization; pessimism.

adj. underestimated, understated; deprecatory; modest.

vb. underestimate, underplay, play down, underrate, understate, minimize; depreciate, disparage, slight; make light of, not do justice to, think too little of.

419 discovery

n. discovery, finding, disclosure, uncovering; manifestation, revelation; detection, identification, catching; invention; exploration.

adj. on the right track, near, close, warm (*inf.*).

vb. discover, find, hit upon; realize, see, perceive, understand, become aware of, get wise to, get on to, twig (*inf.*); meet, come across, happen upon; expose, disclose, detect, spot, lay bare, reveal, uncover, unearth, bring to light, run to earth (*inf.*), run to ground (*inf.*), track down; catch in the act, catch red-handed.

420 belief

n. belief, credence, trust, acceptance, faith, credit; reliance, dependence, conviction, confidence, persuasion; certainty, surety, assurance, hope; admission, confession, avowal.

creed, doctrine, dogma, credo, revelation; tenet, canon, principle; articles of faith, catechism.

opinion, thought, view, sentiment, idea, notion, conception, impression, assumption; attitude, way of thinking; point of view, position, outlook, angle, stand, stance.

adj. believing, accepting, reliant, dependent, convinced, persuaded, certain, confident; believable, credible, tenable, plausible, trustworthy, reliable, unfailing.

vb. believe, accept, hold, trust, depend, rely, be convicted of, be persuaded of, take at one's word, take on trust, take one's word for; think, consider, regard as, suppose, presume, surmise, fancy, assume, deem, conclude; come round to, change one's views, be converted; have faith in, be a believer, profess, confess.

convince, persuade, bring round, prove, argue, assure, satisfy, make realize, bring home to; teach; captivate, have a way with (*inf.*).

see also 854

421 unbelief

n. unbelief, disbelief, doubt, uncertainty, incredulity, scepticism, misgiving, suspicion, mistrust, distrust, qualm, hesitation, reservation, apprehension, irresolution; faithlessness, rejection; agnosticism, atheism.

adj. unbelieving, disbelieving, doubting, questioning, sceptical, distrusting, incredulous; unbelievable, untenable, unreliable, doubtful, dubious, suspicious, questionable, implausible.

vb. disbelieve, doubt, hesitate, waver, not believe, give no credence to, lack confidence in, set no store by; mistrust, suspect, question, challenge.

422 gullibility

n. gullibility, credulity, simpleness, unsophistication.

adj. gullible, credulous, trusting, unsuspecting, simple, naive, unsophisticated, inexperienced, guileless, simple, green.

vb. be gullible, fall for (*inf.*), be easily persuaded.

423 incredulity

n. incredulity, suspicion, scepticism; sophistication.

adj. incredulous, unbelieving, sceptical, unresponsive, ungullible, sophisticated.

vb. refuse to believe, distrust, doubt; reject, turn a deaf ear to.

see also 421

424 assent

n. assent, affirmative, yes; approval, agreement, acceptance, support, approbation; authorization, permission, consent, empowering, legalization, authority, sanction, guarantee, warrant, authentication, ratification, endorsement, affirmation, go-ahead (*inf.*), green light (*inf.*), nod (*sl.*).

like-mindedness, unanimity, consensus, general agreement; supporter, follower, assenter, signer, subscriber, ratifier, signatory, aye.

adj. assenting, acquiescent; approved, accepted, voted, carried, passed; unanimous, of one mind.

vb. assent, say yes to, agree, concur, affirm, accept, support, subscribe to, approve, vote for, pass, rubber-stamp (*inf.*), put up with (*inf.*), go along with, tolerate, stand for (*inf.*), bear, endure, acquiesce; acknowledge, admit, concede, grant, yield, recognize, defer to.

authorize, grant permission, empower, legalize, ratify, sign, endorse, authenticate, seal.

425 dissent

n. dissent, disapproval, disagreement, dissidence, disapprobation; difference, variance, discord, dissension, protest, controversy, vendetta, animosity, division; non-conformity; non-acceptance, withdrawal, secession; objection, reservation, negative, no.

dissenter, objector, protester, rebel, non-conformist, caviller; interrupter, heckler; separatist; recusant.

adj. dissident, disagreeing, differing; protesting, objecting.

vb. dissent, disagree, disapprove, differ, agree to differ, protest, object, oppose, challenge, heckle, shout down, take exception; reject, refuse, contradict; withdraw, secede.

426 knowledge

n. knowledge, knowing, awareness, consciousness, recognition, realization, understanding, grasp, cognition; intelligence, education, instruction, learning, erudition, scholarship, culture, bookishness; accomplishments, attainments; facts, information, encyclopedia; expertise, know-how, skill, proficiency; wisdom, maturity, experience.

adj. knowing, conscious, mindful, aware, cognizant; discerning, perceptive; acquainted, familiar, well versed in, well grounded in, *au fait;* clever, intelligent, informed, instructed, trained, knowledgeable, educated, well-taught, well-read, learned, erudite, scholarly, cultured, intellectual; mature, wise, experienced.

known, widely known, common, proverbial, commonplace, household name, hackneyed; infamous, notorious.

vb. know, realize, understand, grasp, see, perceive, realize, apprehend, be aware of, discern, appreciate, recognize; experience; be well-informed, be well up on, be into (*inf.*), know backwards, know inside out, know like the back of one's hand.

see also 434, 460

427 ignorance

n. ignorance, unawareness, unconsciousness, unknowingness, nescience; unenlightenment, incomprehension, darkness, fog, haziness, vagueness; inexperience, immaturity, greenness, naivety, simplicity, empty-headedness, stupidity; unlearnedness, unintellectuality, illiteracy; unskilfulness, awkwardness.

smattering, shallowness; unknown, unknown quantity, unexplored ground, virgin territory, mystery, closed book, sealed book.

adj. ignorant, unaware, unknowing; unmindful, unconscious, disregarding; inexperienced, immature, green, inept, simple, stupid, thick, dense; unenlightened, in the dark, unfamiliar with, not conversant, a stranger to, none the wiser; untaught, illiterate, uneducated, untrained, backward, unscholarly, unlearned, uncultivated, unread, uncultured, Philistine, unintellectual; unknown, untold, unseen, mysterious, secret, undiscovered, virgin, uncharted.

vb. not know, be ignorant, be in the dark, not have any idea, not have the foggiest idea (*inf.*); pass (*inf.*).

see also 435

428 student

n. student, scholar, schoolchild, learner, disciple; philosopher, scientist, researcher, expert, man of letters, wise man, savant, sage; professor, don, teacher, doctor; bookworm, intellectual, egghead (*inf.*); genius, brain, know-all, mine of information, walking encyclopedia.

see also 473, 474

429 ignoramus

n. ignoramus, know-nothing, dunce, fool, blockhead; greenhorn, raw recruit, babe, simpleton.

see also 437

430 truth

n. truth, fact, reality, the case, gospel truth, plain truth, real thing, real McCoy (*inf.*).

trueness, verity, correctness, exactitude, accuracy, precision, perfection, rectitude, faithfulness, sincerity, honesty; authenticity, infallibility, genuineness, validity.

adj. true, truthful, veracious, real,

right, factual, correct, objective, actual; historical; genuine, authentic, original, official, veritable; unadulterated, unmixed; attested, valid, guaranteed; undisputed, conclusive, final; accurate, exact, precise, faithful, infallible; sincere, honest, upright.

vb. be true, be the case· ring true; hit the nail on the head (*inf.*); come true, come about, happen, occur.

see also **476**

431 error

n. error, mistake, fault, blunder, failure, fall, flaw, lapse, omission, lie, untruth, wrong, deviation, sin; *faux pas*, slip, slip-up (*inf.*); misjudgment, misunderstanding, misconception, inaccuracy, mismanagement; misprint, literal; bloomer (*sl.*), clanger (*sl.*), howler (*sl.*).

erroneousness, falsity, inaccurateness, inexactness.

adj. wrong, incorrect, unreal, untrue; unauthentic, unoriginal, spurious; inaccurate, inexact, imprecise; erroneous, mistaken, lying, untruthful, in error; unfaithful, disloyal, deceitful, corrupt, unsound; deceptive, fallacious, misleading, pretended, sham, counterfeit, faked, mocked; misunderstood; fallible.

vb. go wrong, make a mistake, err, blunder, slip up (*inf.*), bungle; be wrong, be mistaken; misconceive, misunderstand; not hold water, fall down, fall to the ground; mislead, lead astray, lead up the garden path (*inf.*), pervert, deceive, trick, hoax.

see also **477, 478**

432 maxim

n. maxim, proverb, saying, truth, text, dictum, motto, slogan, watchword, moral, aphorism, adage, axiom; banality, truism, platitude, commonplace, cliché; epigram, witticism.

adj. aphoristic, proverbial, epigrammatic; brief, concise, pithy, terse; trite, commonplace.

433 absurdity

n. absurdity, ridiculousness, ludicrousness, outrageousness, folly, silliness, stupidity, nonsense; spoonerism, malapropism; jest, trick, practical joke, prank, farce, buffoonery, clowning, wildness; extravaganza.

adj. absurd, ridiculous, crazy, farcical, nonsensical, senseless, inane, wild, foolish, silly, stupid, bizarre, extravagant, fantastic.

vb. be absurd, talk nonsense, fool around; play tricks.

see also **451**

434 intelligence; wisdom

n. intelligence, understanding, brightness, cleverness, brilliance; genius, talent, brains, grey matter, intellect, sense, common sense, wit.

wisdom, experience, erudition, sagacity, sapience; shrewdness, discernment, judgment, acumen, insight, perspicacity, sharpness, acuteness, penetration, prudence, foresight.

adj. intelligent, clever, bright, brilliant, able, knowledgeable; wise, sagacious, shrewd, prudent, knowing, contemplative, reasoning, thoughtful, sober, sensible, judicious, circumspect, discreet, considerate, astute, perceptive, perspicacious, far-sighted, discerning, quick, acute, sharp, penetrating, keen, discriminating, having one's wits about one, not born yesterday (*inf.*).

vb. be wise, understand, discern; have one's head screwed on the right way (*inf.*).

see also **426**

435 unintelligence; folly

n. unintelligence, stupidity, dullness, slowness, heaviness; foolishness, folly, weakness, shallowness, silliness, simplicity, childishness, puerility, imbecility; imprudence, short-sightedness, indiscretion.

adj. unintelligent, unthinking, unreasoning; stupid, dull, slow, weak, shallow, superficial, vacant, simple, dumb, thick, dense, empty-headed, slow-witted, feeble-minded, simple-minded, weak-minded, half-witted, blockish, oafish, feather-brained, doltish; foolish, crazy, silly, insane, inane, idiotic, imbecile, puerile, childish; backward, retarded, handicapped, subnormal, deprived; unwise, imprudent, short-sighted, undiscerning.

vb. be foolish, act the fool, fool around, lark about (*inf.*).

see also 427

436. sage

n. sage, wise man, man of learning, savant, pundit, expert, doctor, scholar, master, great thinker, authority, oracle, elder statesman, connoisseur, luminary; wiseacre, know-all, sciolist.

see also 428, 473

437 fool

n. fool, simpleton, dunce, idiot, ignoramus, scatterbrain, half-wit, fathead, thickhead, blockhead, nitwit, nincompoop, moron, cretin, imbecile, numskull, bore, dolt, ass, buffoon, chump (*sl.*), lout, oaf, ninny, jerk (*sl.*), twit (*sl.*).

see also 429, 630

438 sanity

n. sanity, saneness, balance, normality, clearmindedness, lucidity,

wholesomeness, *mens sana*, rationality, reason.

adj. sane, normal, sound-minded, healthy-minded, sound, right-minded, sober, lucid, in one's right mind, self-possessed, all there (*inf.*).

439 insanity

n. insanity, insaneness, madness, lunacy; imbecility, cretinism, idiocy; phobia, mania, craze, passion, obsession, infatuation, fixation, compulsion; mental illness, nervous breakdown, nervous disorder; nervousness, nerves; hysteria, frenzy, fever, attack, fit, rage; peculiarity, eccentricity, abnormality, oddity.

adj. insane, mad, unsound, unbalanced, crazy, deranged, confused, demented, rabid, berserk, out of one's mind, off one's head, off one's rocker (*sl.*); obsessed, infatuated; frenzied, wild, raging, furious; eccentric, odd, cranky, peculiar.

vb. be mad, wander, ramble; go mad, lose one's sanity, take leave of one's senses, go out of one's mind, crack up (*inf.*), go off one's rocker (*sl.*); madden, drive mad, unbalance.

440 madman

n. madman, lunatic, mental case, loony (*sl.*), bedlamite; maniac, psychopath, psychotic, paranoid, hysteric, neurotic, manic-depressive, melancholic, hypochondriac, kleptomaniac; imbecile, idiot, moron, cretin, mongol; fool, crank, nut (*sl.*), eccentric, freak, weirdo (*inf.*), crackpot (*inf.*).

F Extension of thought

441 memory

n. memory, recollection, reminiscence, retrospection, recall, review, flashback, afterthought, hindsight, reconsideration, reflection, thought; retention, good memory, photographic memory, *déjà vu*.

memorandum, memo, reminder, record, note, jotting, scribble, mark; notes, summary, agenda, minutes; mnemonic, aid to memory; souvenir, memento, token, keepsake, relic, trinket; testimonial, memorial, monument, trophy, commemoration; warning, advice, suggestion, hint; prompt, prompter; memoirs, reminiscences, recollections, memories, memorabilia; diary, journal, album, scrapbook, notebook.

adj. remembered, recalled, retained, unforgotten, fresh, vivid; half-remembered, at the back of one's mind; reminiscent, reminding, evocative; memorable, unforgettable, indelibly fixed on one's mind; commemorative, memorial.

vb. remember, recollect, recall, bring to mind, be reminded of, think of, not forget; review, retrace, go back, flash back, look back, turn one's thoughts back, reminisce, call up, revive, rake up the past, drag up (*inf.*), dredge up (*inf.*); recognize, identify, know again, make out.

come to mind, ring a bell, stay in the memory, never be forgotten, haunt, recur, penetrate, stay in one's mind, not leave one's thoughts, not get out of one's mind.

memorize, learn, commit to memory, know by heart, learn by rote, master, impress, retain, fix in the mind; keep always, hold dear, treasure, cherish, commemorate, enshrine in the memory, keep the memory alive.

remind, prompt, suggest, hint, bring back, make one think of, jog one's memory, refresh one's memory; warn, throw the book at (*inf.*).

442 oblivion

n. oblivion, forgetfulness, unmindfulness, absent-mindedness, amnesia, memory like a sieve, loss of memory, blankness, complete blank, mental block; insensibleness, indifference, carelessness.

adj. forgotten, unremembered, lost, out of one's mind, clean forgotten, unrecalled, unretained, in one ear and out the other; out of sight, out of mind; almost remembered, on the tip of one's tongue.

oblivious, forgetful, unmindful, heedless, inattentive, preoccupied, distracted, absent-minded.

vb. forget, fail to remember, have no recollection, put out of one's mind, have a short memory, think no more of, not give another thought, one's memory be a blank, escape one; be forgotten, sink into oblivion, fade from one's memory.

443 expectation

n. expectation, expectancy, looking forward, contemplation, anticipation, prospect, outlook; confidence, trust, hope, high hopes; preparedness; suspense, apprehension, pessimism.

adj. expectant, waiting, in anticipation, looking forward to, in suspense, on tenterhooks, itching, on edge, with bated breath; hoping, hopeful, confident; eager, watchful, vigilant, prepared; apprehensive, pessimistic.

expected, awaited, anticipated, foreseen, predicted, prophesied, longed for, looked for; on the cards, prospective.

vb. expect, look forward to, promise oneself, hope for, anticipate, contemplate, foresee, long for, bargain for (*inf.*), predict, prophesy, forecast, see coming, take for granted; wait for, await, bide one's time, mark time, hold one's breath, be in suspense; rely on, bank on, count on; be expected, lead one to expect, not put it past (*inf.*), be just like one.

444 non-expectation

n. inexpectation, unpreparedness, unexpectedness; surprise, shock, start, jolt, blow, bombshell, bolt from the blue, thunderbolt; turn-up for the book (*sl.*).

adj. unexpected, unforeseen, sudden, surprising, astonishing, staggering; unheralded, unpredicted, uncontemplated; unheard of, not thought of; more than one bargained for, not on the cards, without warning, out of the blue.

surprised, startled, thunderstruck, off one's guard, unready, unprepared, caught napping.

vb. not expect, not bargain for; surprise, take by surprise, catch unawares, catch in the act, catch red-handed, make one jump, startle, astonish, bowl over (*inf.*), knock down with a feather; come unexpectedly, turn up.

445 disappointment

n. disappointment, foiling, bafflement; discouragement, despondency; dissatisfaction, unfulfilment, discontent, frustration, disillusionment, regret, distress, displeasure.

bad news, setback, adversity, defeat, failure, anti-climax, miscarriage, letdown (*inf.*).

adj. disappointed, discouraged, dissatisfied, thwarted, baffled, unsuccessful, defeated, foiled, let-down (*inf.*), disconcerted, depressed, frustrated, disillusioned, full of regrets, despon-

dent; disappointing, unsatisfactory, inadequate, insufficient, not up to expectations.

vb. disappoint, fail, let down (*inf.*), thwart, foil, baffle; come short of, dash one's hopes, not come up to expectations, leave much to be desired; frustrate, disconcert, disillusion, dissatisfy, let the side down (*inf.*).

446 foresight

n. foresight, second sight, foresightedness, anticipation; forethought, premeditation, preconsideration, preconception.

adj. foreseeing, foresighted, looking ahead, anticipatory.

vb. foresee, prophesy, forecast, anticipate; see ahead, look into the future, have a premonition, feel in one's bones.

447 prediction

n. prediction, forecast, foretelling, prophecy, prognostication, prognosis, foresight, forethought, foreknowledge, precognition, prescience, prevision; augury, divination, vaticination, astrology, clairvoyancy, soothsaying, fortune-telling, crystal-gazing, palmistry, casting lots; parapsychology, extrasensory perception; telepathy, telesthesia.

omen, sign, indication, symptom, portent, clue, hint, auspice, writing on the wall; warning, forewarning, foreboding, presentiment; guess, estimate, conjecture, budget; foretoken; presage; horoscope, fortune; herald, harbinger.

oracle, forecaster, prognosticator, prophet, prophetess, seer; fortuneteller, soothsayer, clairvoyant, augur, diviner, palmist, astrologer, crystalgazer, gipsy; witch, wizard, medium; sibyl, haruspex; thought-reader, mind-reader, telepath, parapsychologist; weatherman, meteorologist.

adj. predicting, predictive, prognostic, divinatory, clairvoyant, portentous, significant; auspicious, favourable; ominous, foreboding; psychic, second-sighted; supernatural, paranormal, parapsychological; predictable, foreseen, expected, likely; divinable.

vb. predict, forecast, prognosticate, foresee, foretell, prophesy, vaticinate; forewarn; promise; bode, forebode, betoken, portend, foreshadow, presage; divine, augur, tell the future, tell fortunes, cast lots, read one's hand, read one's palm, read tea leaves.

see also **984**

G Creative thought

448 supposition

n. supposition, guesswork, speculation, theorizing, postulation.

guess, surmise, notion, fancy, conjecture, inkling, hint, intimation, shrewd idea, vague idea, sneaking suspicion, rough guess, wild guess, shot in the dark.

premise, presupposition, postulate, proposition; inference, deduction, conclusion; thesis, hypothesis, working hypothesis, theory.

theorist, scientist, theorizer, academic, thinker, speculator, backroom boy, boffin (*sl.*).

adj. suppositional, unproved, tentative, speculative, conjectural, hypothetical, theoretical; supposed, assumed, presupposed, presumed, reputed, alleged, postulated, putative.

vb. suppose, believe, imagine, think, fancy, deem, guess, venture a guess, conjecture, speculate, estimate, divine, surmise, suspect, gather, assume, presume, presuppose; postulate, posit; infer, imply, deduce, theorize.

449 imagination

n. imagination, inventiveness, creativity, originality, visualization; fantasy, diversion, whimsy, daydreaming, castle-building, pipe-dreaming, wishful thinking, escapism; utopia, paradise, world of fantasy, cloud-cuckoo land, dream world.

idea, figment of the imagination, invention, notion, fancy, whim, caprice, vagary, chimera, will-o'-the-wisp, vision, appearance, day-dream, castles in the air, romance, flight of fancy, dream, nightmare.

visionary, prophet, seer, idealist, escapist, Quixote, dreamer, daydreamer.

adj. imaginative, inventive, creative, resourceful, inspired, visionary, idealistic, with one's head in the clouds, quixotic, impractical, unrealistic; imaginary, fanciful, fantastic, capricious, whimsical, chimerical, dreamlike, ideal, utopian, fictitious, pretended, make-believe, illusory, fabulous.

vb. imagine, picture, conjure up, envisage, conceive, suppose, visualize; invent, create, make up, think of, devise, fabricate, coin, hatch; dream, muse, fancy, fantasize, idealize, romanticize, build castles in the air, daydream, pretend, make believe.

2 Communication of ideas

A Nature of ideas communicated

450 meaning

n. meaning, sense, significance, interpretation, implication, explanation; intent, aim, import, drift, tenor, thrust, purport; substance, essence, content.

meaningfulness, expressiveness; signification, connotation, denotation, reference, referendum, definition; unambiguity, equivalence, synonymity; synonym, related word.

adj. meaningful, significant, indicative, expressive, suggestive, evocative; substantial, pithy, full of meaning, pregnant; unambiguous; literal, verbal, word for word, verbatim, exact, faithful, true; semantic, linguistic.

vb. mean, signify, designate, refer to, drive at (*inf.*), denote, connote, indicate, symbolize, suggest, express, convey, declare, state, assert, spell; intimate, hint, betoken, bode, purport, import; imply, involve, speak of, touch on, point to.

451 meaninglessness

n. meaninglessness, senselessness, inexpressiveness, expressionlessness, nonsensicalness; misinterpretation, illogicality, ambiguity.

nonsense, balderdash, rubbish, twaddle, blather, rot (*sl.*), poppycock (*sl.*), trash, inanity, drivel, bunkum, prattle, baloney (*sl.*), bunk (*sl.*), ballyhoo, piffle (*sl.*); hot air (*sl.*), empty talk, humbug, cliché, truism, platitude.

adj. meaningless, insignificant, unindicative, inexpressive, unevocative; insubstantial, empty, void, vacant, blank; irrelevant, unimportant; senseless, aimless, purposeless; vague, ambiguous, tautological; trite, trivial, absurd, nonsensical, foolish; unintended, misinterpreted.

vb. be meaningless, mean nothing; talk nonsense, babble, prattle, blather, twaddle; talk through one's hat (*sl.*).

452 intelligibility

n. intelligibility, comprehensibility; recognizability, cognizability; lucidity, clarity, transparency; precision, plainness, explicitness, unambiguousness; readability, legibility, decipherability; audibility; plain speech; plain English.

adj. intelligible, comprehensible, understandable; clear, obvious, lucid, precise, plain, explicit, clear-cut, distinct, unambiguous, unequivocal; simple, straightforward, popular, made simple, for the beginner, made easy, without tears, for the million; recognizable, readable, legible, decipherable; audible.

vb. understand, apprehend, comprehend, grasp, follow, take in, figure out (*inf.*), catch on (*inf.*), get the meaning of, get the hang of (*inf.*), twig (*inf.*); fathom, penetrate, get to the bottom of, read between the lines, get the idea, get the gist of; know, have knowledge of, realize, perceive, appreciate; discern, distinguish, make out (*inf.*), work out (*inf.*); conceive, be aware of, recognize, sense, be conscious of.

be intelligible, make sense, be clear, click (*sl.*); make clear, put in plain English, put in words of one syllable.

see also 502

453 unintelligibility

n. unintelligibility, incomprehensibility, meaninglessness, unrecognizability, unsearchableness, impenetrability; unclearness, obscurity, illegibility, ambiguity, indecipherability, unreadability; inaudibility; gibberish, incoherence, double Dutch, Greek; puzzle, mystery, enigma, sealed book, closed book.

adj. unintelligible, incomprehensible, meaningless, beyond one's comprehension; indistinct, vague, indefinite, hazy, inexact, ill-defined, loose, unclear, ambiguous, equivocal; incoherent, mixed up; obscure, puzzling, hard, complicated, intricate, profound, academic, over one's head, abstruse, recondite; concealed, mysterious, hidden, enigmatic, esoteric; illegible, indecipherable, unreadable; inaudible; unrecognizable, impenetrable, unsearchable, inexplicable; inscrutable, unfathomable, unutterable, ineffable.

vb. not understand, not have the first idea, not get the hang of (*inf.*), not make head or tail of, be baffled, be beyond one, get hold of the wrong end of the stick (*inf.*); be unintelligible, talk above someone's head; not make sense, escape one, be all Greek to one.

see also 503

454 ambiguity

n. ambiguity, equivocalness, vagueness, uncertainty; ambivalence, equivocation, incongruity, inconsistency, prevarication; play on words, pun, *double entendre.*

adj. ambiguous, ambivalent, equivocal, uncertain, vague, vacillating, prevaricating; two-edged, backhanded; incongruous.

vb. cut both ways; play on words, pun; quibble, equivocate, prevaricate.

455 figure of speech

n. figure of speech, metaphor, transference, figurativeness; symbolism, imagery; rhetoric; comparison, simile, likeness, allegory, trope, fable, parable, allusion, personification; euphemism, irony, satire; understatement; onomatopoeia.

adj. figurative, metaphorical, extended, transferred, allusive; rhetorical;

symbolic; comparative, allegorical, parabolic; euphemistic, euphuistic, ironical, satirical.

456 interpretation

n. interpretation, explanation, exposition, commentary, elucidation, clarification, illumination, explication; background, reason; analysis, diagnosis, review, criticism, critique, survey, investigation, appraisal, evaluation; significance, importance; annotation, note, comment; example, illustration, instance.

translation, equivalent, dynamic equivalent, paraphrase, rendering, rendition, adaptation, rewording, restatement, gloss, transcription, transliteration, version, reading.

interpreter, commentator, reviewer, critic, analyst, exponent, writer, editor, annotator, expositor, preacher, exegete; translator, linguist, polyglot; hermeneutics, exegetics, homiletics.

adj. interpretive, explanatory, expository, explicatory; analytical, diagnostic, critical, evaluatory; defining, descriptive, illuminating, discursive, exegetical; exemplary, illustrative; editorial, glossarial; literal, faithful, word-for-word; free, rough.

vb. interpret, explain, account for, give reasons for, give reasons why, make sense of; expound, lay bare the meaning, give an account of, state the significance of, read between the lines; make clear, elucidate, make plain, clarify, illuminate, throw light on, cast light on; simplify, expand on, emphasize; demonstrate, illustrate, exemplify, show by example; set forth, reveal, expose, lay bare, unfold, spell out.

translate, render, put in other words, put into, reword, restate, rephrase, paraphrase; transliterate, transcribe; decipher, decode, crack, solve; annotate, comment on, remark on, edit, gloss.

457 misinterpretation

n. misinterpretation, misreckoning, misconception, misunderstanding, misconstruction, falsification, distortion, perversion, delusion, error, mistake; mistranslation.

vb. misinterpret, misunderstand, get hold of the wrong end of the stick (*inf.*), misquote, falsify, distort, pervert, read into, misconstrue, not give a true account of, give a false impression of.

see also 453

B Modes of communication

458 manifestation

n. manifestation, revelation, showing, demonstration, disclosure, expression, presentation, exhibition; publishing, telling, announcement; divulgence, betrayal.

appearance, vision, apparition; exhibit, show, layout, example, specimen, showpiece; parade, procession, pageant; evidence, sign, miracle, theophany.

adj. manifest, apparent, clear, visible, perceptible, observable, obvious, patent, open, evident, self-evident, unmistakable, crystal-clear, staring one in the face, written all over one, express, explicit, conspicuous, noticeable, prominent, bold, striking, pronounced, flagrant, glaring, salient.

vb. manifest, appear, reveal, show, disclose, express; present, produce, publish, tell, announce, proclaim, betray, divulge, demonstrate, exem-

plify, indicate, show signs of, evince; make manifest, make plain, lay bare, expose, show forth; display, exhibit, set out, uncover, unfold, unmask, parade; promote, publicize.

see also 462, 823

459 latency

n. latency, secrecy, subtlety, dormancy; insidiousness; undercurrent, implication, suggestion, hint, allusion, connotation, inference, more than meets the eye, snake in the grass.

adj. latent, hidden, veiled, dormant, quiescent, lurking, subtle, insidious, beneath the surface, between the lines, underlying, undercover; underdeveloped, potential, possible; implied, inherent, inferred, suggested, intimated, hinted, supposed, tacit, understood, unmentioned, unspoken, unexpressed; suggestive, indicative, provocative.

vb. be latent, be beneath the surface, lurk, lie low; imply, indicate, infer, suggest, mean, intimate, hint, insinuate, involve, provoke, entail.

see also 461

460 information

n. information, knowledge, facts, info (*inf.*), gen (*sl.*), low-down (*sl.*); briefing, run-down (*inf.*); proof, evidence, notes, details, results, figures, tables, statistics, data; intelligence; news, message, report, notice, communication, notification, declaration, presentation, proclamation, broadcast, transmission; narration, account, description, story, tale, paper; tidings, discovery, revelation, enlightenment; dispatch, release, hand-out, announcement; telephone call, telex, telegram, cable, wire, teletext.

hint, mention, advice, aside, wink, whisper, word in one's ear, tip-off (*inf.*), warning, intimation, suspicion, glimmer, indication, suggestion.

informant, spokesman, narrator, story-teller, messenger, newsman, reporter, authority, announcer, broadcaster, correspondent, journalist; dispatcher, courier, herald, emissary, envoy, ambassador, carrier; guidebook, manual, chart, itinerary, map, timetable.

informer, spy, secret agent, observer, wire tapper, snoop, grass (*sl.*), squealer (*sl.*); gossip, tell-tale, eavesdropper, newsmonger, tattler, scandalmonger.

adj. informative, instructive, enlightening, educational, enriching, newsy (*inf.*), chatty (*inf.*), communicative.

vb. inform, speak, say, tell, notify, let know, communicate, give the facts, put over, put across, get across, get over, present, give to understand, convey, declare, announce, express, proclaim; relate, narrate, recite, report, describe, set forth, make known, let in on, tip off (*inf.*), have a word in someone's ear; enlighten, put in the picture; broadcast, spread the news, circulate, disseminate, promulgate; telephone, ring, call, telex, cable, wire; report back, debrief (*inf.*).

bring up to date, fill in on (*inf.*); keep up with, keep tabs on (*inf.*), keep track of, keep one's finger on the pulse, keep up to date, keep posted; hint, suggest, get at, insinuate, intimate, advise, warn; tell on, inform on, betray, grass on (*sl.*), squeal (*sl.*).

see also 464, 597

461 concealment

n. concealment, covering, hiding, confinement, burying, secretion; suppression, evasion; seclusion, privacy, isolation, solitude; camouflage, disguise, shroud, veil, curtain, screen, mask, cloak, purdah; cabal.

adj. concealed, hidden, out of sight, behind the scenes, covered, eclipsed, buried, obscured, unseen, unexposed; disguised, camouflaged, incognito; furtive, stealthy, secret, hush-hush, clandestine, underhand, sly.

vb. conceal, hide, cover, bury, suppress, screen, cloak, shroud, veil, curtain, evade, withhold, pull the wool over someone's eyes (*inf.*), keep secret, lie low, keep in the dark, keep under one's hat (*inf.*), sweep under the carpet (*inf.*), secrete; cloud, obscure, envelop, ensconce, camouflage, disguise, dissemble; confine, store, harbour, cache, shelter, stash (*inf.*); close, seal, lock.

sneak, prowl, creep, lurk, steal, slink.

see also 463, 466, 826

462 disclosure

n. disclosure, exposure, opening, uncovering, revelation, apocalypse; show-down; betrayal, manifestation, give-away; acknowledgement, admission.

adj. disclosed, uncovered, exposed, conspicuous, open; indicative, betraying, tell-tale.

vb. disclose, reveal, give away, expose, divulge, lay open, lay bare, make plain, uncover, unfold, unveil, unfurl, unmask, take the wraps off; not contain oneself for, bring into the open; declare, make known, spit it out (*inf.*); put one's cards on the table, nail one's colours to the mast, show one's colours; open up (*inf.*), unburden oneself, unbosom, confide, get out of one's system (*inf.*), get off one's chest (*inf.*); come out of one's shell.

confess, admit, acknowledge, concede, grant, own up (*inf.*), come clean, avow, plead guilty, make a clean breast of; one's sins will find one out.

betray, not keep a secret, blurt out, let on, let out, blabber, leak, let the cat out of the bag (*inf.*), spill the beans, come out with, talk out of turn, give the game away.

see also **458, 460**

463 hiding

n. hiding, deceit, faking, deception; hiding place, hide-out, hidey-hole, refuge, retreat, covert, den, shelter.

disguise, camouflage, mask, blind, masquerade, cloak, cover, veil, guise, façade, envelope, shade, blackout, masking; ambush, snare, trap, pitfall, net, noose.

vb. ambush, trap, ensnare, waylay, lay in wait, set a trap for, decoy.

see also **459, 801**

464 publication

n. publication, announcement, communication, revelation, disclosure, notification, proclamation, declaration, promulgation, broadcasting, dissemination.

broadcast; book, booklet; newspaper, periodical, magazine, journal; publicity, promotion, canvassing, advertisement, poster, sign, bill, placard, notice, broadsheet, leaflet, folder, brochure, pamphlet, circular, hand-out, handbill, flysheet, blurb, plug (*inf.*).

adj. published, in print, available, obtainable, in circulation; current, public.

vb. publish, issue, bring out, put into circulation, print, distribute; reissue, reprint, be published, come out, circulate, get around.

make known, announce, notify, proclaim, declare, pronounce, impart, send forth, communicate, reveal,

disclose, spread, broadcast, diffuse, pass the word round, put about, blazon, promulgate, disseminate; publicize, promote, advertise, canvass, circularize, sell, plug (*inf.*), tell the world.

465 news

n. news, tidings, information, facts, events, current affairs; headlines, front-page news, stop press, newsflash, scoop, sensation; description, account, report, story, bulletin, message, release, communiqué, press release, announcement, hand-out, dispatch.

rumour, gossip, hearsay, scandal, whisper, popular report, fabrication, tale, chit-chat; grapevine, bush telegraph.

vb. report, tell, broadcast, publish, circulate, spread; make news, hit the headlines.

466 secret

n. secret, mystery, puzzle, riddle, brain-teaser, enigma, arcanum; code, cipher, cryptogram, hieroglyph; confidence; skeleton in the cupboard; suppression, blackout, censure.

adj. secret, strange, mysterious, hidden, unknown, puzzling, mystical, cryptic, enigmatic; private, confidential, classified, top secret, hush-hush; secretive, reticent, taciturn; secluded.

vb. keep secret, keep to oneself, not tell, hide, conceal, keep mum (*inf.*), suppress, stifle, sit on (*inf.*), hush up, censor.

adv. in secret, in private, confidentially, under one's breath, between ourselves; between you, me, and the bedpost.

see also **461**

467 messenger

n. messenger, dispatcher, dispatch bearer, carrier, courier, runner, crier, bearer, office-boy, message-boy, errand-boy, page-boy, buttons; spokesman, intermediary, go-between, ambassador, envoy, emissary, internuncio; herald, forerunner, precursor, harbinger, trumpet; minister, angel, prophet.

post, mail, correspondence; post office; telecommunications, telephony, telegraphy; broadcasting, radio, transistor, wireless, television, the box; telephone, phone, receiver; radio set, two-way radio, intercom (*inf.*), pocket radio, walkie-talkie, field radio; telegram, wire, cable, cablegram, telegraph; teleprinter, telex, teletext, semaphore, flag, beacon, smoke-signal.

468 affirmation

n. affirmation, assertion, statement, declaration, proposition, profession, pronouncement, explanation, answer, report, observation, expression, formulation; admission, acknowledgement, attestation, avowal; agreement, ratification, endorsement.

swearing, asseveration; oath, vow, testimony, sworn statement, affidavit, promise, contract, pledge.

adj. affirmative, assertive, affirmatory, declarative; emphatic, strong, forceful, dogmatic, positive, assured, solemn, sworn, on oath.

vb. affirm, assert, state, declare, profess, pronounce, express, explain, maintain, contend, submit, asseverate, aver; confirm, endorse, ratify; admit, acknowledge; emphasize, stress, underline, highlight, impress, urge, reinforce, rub in (*inf.*), make much of, plug; speak out, have one's say, put one's foot down (*inf.*); swear, vow, promise, pledge, testify, attest, assure, guarantee,

vouch; swear in, put on oath, charge, adjure.

see also **514, 698**

469 negation

n. negation, denial, contradiction, repudiation, refusal, renunciation, disclaimer, disavowel; abnegation, recusance.

adj. negative, denying, contrary, contradictory, disavowing, recusant, repugnant.

vb. negate, deny, belie, give the lie to, contradict, contravene, gainsay, renounce, repudiate, disown, disavow, disclaim, abjure, abnegate; refuse, reject; cancel, nullify, invalidate.

see also **694**

470 teaching

n. teaching, education, pedagogy, pedagogics, didactics; instruction, training, study, schooling, direction, guidance, tuition, tutoring, coaching, tutelage; preparation, discipline, cultivation, enlightenment, edification; indoctrination, brainwashing, inculcation, conditioning, propagandism, proselytism; spoon-feeding.

course, curriculum, class, lesson, lecture, talk; catechism; sermon; homework, prep (*inf.*), assignment, exercise, task, work.

adj. educational, informative, instructive, enlightening, edifying; academic, pedagogical, didactic, scholastic.

vb. teach, educate, instruct, impart, inform, acquaint, familiarize, direct, guide, discipline, advise, counsel; convince, explain; prepare, initiate; school, coach, cram, prime, put through the mill (*inf.*); enlighten, edify; cultivate, nurture, train, exercise, practise, groom, drill, ground, bring up, foster, rear, breed, lick into shape (*inf.*); indoctrinate, inculcate, din into, force down someone's throat, ram down someone's throat (*inf.*), instill, imbue, condition; proselytize; catechize; hold classes, lecture, hold forth, expound, preach, sermonize, moralize.

471 misdirection

n. misdirection, misguidance, misinstruction, misteaching, misrepresentation, falsification, perversion, mistake, error, blind leading the blind.

vb. misdirect, misinform, mislead, misrepresent, pervert, distort, deceive.

472 learning

n. learning, knowledge, scholarship, training, erudition, lore; self-improvement, self-education, self-instruction; attainments, study, reading, application, studiousness, industry; lesson, class, course, classwork, homework, prep (*inf.*), assignment; revision, refresher course.

adj. knowledgeable, academic, studious, well-read, learned, industrious, scholarly, erudite; self-taught, self-instructed, self-made.

vb. learn, acquire, pick up, attain; experience, understand, grasp, discover, appreciate; master, become familiar with, get off pat (*inf.*), get the hang of (*inf.*); memorize, learn by heart; study, read, go into, go in for, specialize; absorb, assimilate, digest, drink in, imbibe; read up on, revise, review, refresh oneself, cram, prepare, get up, brush up, improve; pore over, bury oneself in; contemplate; burn the midnight oil; browse, scan, thumb through, flick through (*inf.*), dip into; improve one's mind, teach oneself; study under, sit at the feet of.

see also **426**

473 teacher

n. teacher, educator, advisor, guide, counsellor; school-teacher, headmaster, principal, head; professor, lecturer, don, reader, fellow, doctor, dean; tutor, instructor, pedagogue, coach, trainer, guru, governess.

see also **436**

474 learner

n. learner, pupil, scholar, student, schoolchild; undergraduate, fresher, freshman, graduate, postgraduate; swot, bookworm; follower, disciple, adherent; apprentice, trainee, probationer, novice, beginner, recruit, newcomer, tyro; class, set, form, grade, stream.

see also **428**

475 place of learning

n. school; nursery, kindergarten, crèche; college, polytechnic, university, academy, institute, institution, seminary, varsity (*inf.*), *conservatoire*, *lycée*, *gymnasium*; classroom, schoolroom, study, lecture theatre, auditorium; library, carrel.

476 truthfulness

n. truthfulness, veracity, integrity, frankness, openness, candour, straightforwardness, forthrightness; accuracy, honesty, reliability, sincerity, uprightness, guilelessness, impartiality.

adj. truthful, veracious, sincere, guileless, impartial; frank, open, candid, unreserved, plain, direct, straight, straightforward, forthright, blunt, ingenuous.

vb. be truthful, not lie; speak plainly, tell someone straight, not hesitate, make no bones about, speak one's mind, paint in its true colours, call a spade a spade, tell all; not to put too fine a point on it (*inf.*).

see also 430, 508

477 falsehood

n. falsehood, fraudulence, falsification, fabrication, inaccuracy, deception, dishonesty, lying, mendacity, perjury; misrepresentation, distortion, perversion; double dealing, two-facedness, duplicity, hypocrisy, insincerity, guile; mockery, pretence, make-believe, façade.

adj. false, lying, untruthful, mendacious; fabricated, inaccurate, misrepresented, distorted, put on (*inf.*), make-believe, counterfeit, bogus, pretended, fake, invented, spurious; fraudulent, dishonest, insincere, hypocritical; double-dealing, two-faced; roguish, corrupt, oily, smooth, disingenuous, perfidious.

vb. falsify, lie, fib, exaggerate, understate, tell a white lie, bear false witness, perjure oneself, forswear; prevaricate, equivocate; deceive, mislead, misrepresent, distort, manipulate, doctor, adulterate, make up, invent, concoct, construct, contrive, fabricate, hatch, get up (*inf.*), trump up, spin a yarn; fake, counterfeit, forge; feign, put on (*inf.*), put on a brave face, go through the motions, play, pretend, make believe, sham, simulate, dissemble; laugh off (*inf.*).

see also 431

478 deception

n. deception, misleading, deceit, misrepresentation, cheating, trickery, craftiness, treachery, fraudulence, dishonesty; lying, guile, furtiveness, beguilement, betrayal, treason; hoax, crying wolf, delusion, self-deception, wishful thinking, hallucination, illusion.

trick, dodge, ruse, trap, artifice, stratagem, subterfuge; fraud, swindle, fiddle, rip-off (*sl.*), bamboozle (*inf.*), skulduggery (*inf.*), underhand dealing, sharp practice, sleight of hand, legerdemain.

adj. deceiving, deceptive, illusory, false, sham, fake, fraudulent, dishonest, underhand, behind someone's back, furtive, treacherous, crafty, wily, cunning, shifty.

vb. deceive, mislead, delude, fool, trick, trap, trip up, catch, entrap, ensnare, hoodwink, beguile, dupe, pull the wool over someone's eyes (*inf.*); outwit, outmanoeuvre; go behind someone's back.

cheat, trick, defraud, swindle, fleece, rip off (*sl.*), bamboozle (*inf.*), chisel (*sl.*), cozen; go down (*inf.*), diddle (*sl.*), cross (*sl.*), double-cross, pull a fast one (*sl.*), stack the cards against, put one over on (*inf.*), victimize; take advantage of, get the better of, take for a ride (*inf.*); hoax, cry wolf; play a joke on, kid (*sl.*), pull someone's leg, have on (*inf.*), trifle with, cajole; betray, commit treason.

479 dupe

n. dupe, fool, victim, sucker (*sl.*), sitting duck, simpleton, greenhorn, gull.

480 deceiver

n. deceiver, beguiler, dodger, trickster, swindler, crook, cheat, rogue, impostor, con man (*sl.*), phoney (*sl.*), wolf in sheep's clothing, charlatan, chisel (*sl.*), knave, cozener, sharper; hypocrite, actor, dissembler, Tartuffe; liar, fibber, story-teller; betrayer, traitor, quisling, rat (*sl.*), informer, double-crosser, victimizer; underground, fifth columnist, saboteur, terrorist.

481 exaggeration

n. exaggeration, overstatement, extravagance, hyperbole, misrepresentation, misjudgment, stretching; storm in a teacup, much ado about nothing, stretch of the imagination, fantasy, tall story.

adj. exaggerated, extravagant, preposterous, fabulous, hyperbolic, excessive, superlative, overdone, out of all proportion, coloured, high-falutin, boastful, bombastic.

vb. exaggerate, overstate, overestimate, overplay, hyperbolize, make too much of, overdo, strain, misrepresent; amplify, enlarge, magnify, emphasize, highlight, maximize, heighten, intensify, aggravate; colour, embroider; make a mountain out of a molehill, stretch a point, lay it on thick, pile it on (*inf.*), out-herod Herod.

see also 417

C Means of communicating ideas

482 indication

n. indication, calling, identification, designation, symbolization, signification; sign, badge, emblem, figure, design, symbol, representation, type, token, logo; colophon, flag, banner, pennant, standard, ensign, colours, pendant, bunting, streamer, Union Jack, Stars and Stripes; coat of arms, crest, insignia, medal, regalia.

label, ticket, name, card, notice, bill, stub, counterfoil, docket, form, voucher, counter, chip, tab, tag; indicator, marker, pointer, needle, arrow, index, gauge; stamp, seal, imprint, impression, fingerprint, footprint; signature, autograph, initials, monogram.

signal, gesticulation, gesture; wink, nod, wave, call, shout, whistle, nudge; alarm, siren, hooter, bell; light, beacon.

evidence, hint, suggestion, note, explanation, proof, clue, intimation, symptom, hallmark.

adj. indicative, suggestive, symptomatic, symbolic, typical, representative.

vb. indicate, call, mean, signify; identify, designate, show, name, specify, appoint, assign, symbolize, point to; manifest, express, imply, bear the marks of, evince, intimate, denote, betoken; mark, point, gauge, brand, score, scratch, spot.

label, tag, docket, tab, earmark; stamp, seal, print, punch, impress, emboss, emblazon; sign, initial, autograph; annotate, number, letter, paginate.

gesticulate, gesture, signal, motion, wave, beckon, wink, nod, hoot, ring, shout, whistle, nudge.

483 record

n. record, register, catalogue, account, document, report, statement; brief, memo, memorandum, note; newspaper, bulletin, gazette, almanac; diary, journal, log; certificate, ticket; archives, public records, proceedings, minutes, annals, chronicle, scroll, inscription, manuscript; tape-recording, photograph, film, videotape.

souvenir, memento; relic, mark, trace, remains, evidence; trail, footprint, impression, scent; wash, wake; monument, testimony, witness, memorial, statue, column, cenotaph, remembrance, testimonial, mausoleum, shrine.

adj. recorded, documented, noted, reported.

vb. record, note, mark, report,

account, write down, take down, jot down; register, write in, enter, fill in, insert, inscribe, enrol, matriculate; document, list, catalogue, minute, chronicle; tape, tape-record, photograph, film.

adv. on record, in black and white, in writing, on the books.

484 recorder

n. recorder, registrar, secretary, clerk, accountant; diarist, chronicler, annalist, historian, biographer, journalist, archivist, scribe, amanuensis.

tape-recorder, stereo-recorder, cassette-recorder, video-recorder; record, disc.

485 obliteration

n. obliteration, deletion, erasure, effacement, blotting out, eradication, cancellation, expunction; eraser, rubber, sponge, duster.

vb. obliterate, wipe out, rub off, delete, efface, erase, blot out, black out, strike out, write out, leave no traces, remove, iron out, raze, cancel, expunge.

486 representation

n. representation, description, depiction, illustration, portrayal, exemplification, enactment, personification; reproduction, copy, imitation, image, likeness; picture, sketch, diagram, chart, map, model; art, painting, sculpture; photography, photograph, photo, snapshot, slide, transparency.

adj. representative, characteristic, typical, illustrative.

vb. represent, stand for, stand in the place of, serve as; render, realize, draw, depict, describe, portray, illustrate, picture, reproduce, delineate; reflect, mirror; exemplify, typify, embody, symbolize; designate, express.

487 misrepresentation

n. misrepresentation, distortion, perversion, twisting, falsification, exaggeration, understatement; caricature, parody, travesty, burlesque, counterfeit; misinterpretation.

vb. misrepresent, distort, twist, garble, warp, pervert, falsify, caricature, parody, give the wrong impression; misinterpret, misstate.

488 painting

n. painting, art, graphics, fine art; picture, illustration, mural, depiction, canvas, fresco, wall-painting, collage; work, study, sketch, drawing, outline, silhouette, cartoon, representation, copy, composition, likeness; abstract painting, landscape, portrait, self-portrait, still-life; watercolour, oil painting, miniature, masterpiece, old master.

technique, treatment, design, pattern, atmosphere, tone, shadow, values, perspective.

adj. graphic, visual, pictorial, picturesque, scenic.

vb. paint, portray, depict, compose, illustrate, draw, sketch, design, represent, copy, crayon, pencil, silhouette, ink, shade, tint, limn.

489 sculpture

n. sculpture, carving, stone-carving, cutting, casting, moulding; ceramics, pottery; statue, bust, cast, embossment, relief, marble, plaque, cameo; figure, representation, image.

adj. carved, sculptured, glyptic, glyphic.

vb. sculpture, sculpt, carve, chisel, cut, hew, shape, fashion, model, mould, emboss, cast.

490 engraving

n. engraving, etching, carving, chiselling, incising, printing, photogravure, lithography; inscription, print, lithograph, block, woodcut, linocut, plate.

vb. engrave, etch, inscribe, cut, carve, chisel, incise, chase, print, impress, stamp.

491 artist

n. artist, creator, composer, painter, designer, draughtsman, architect, drawer, sketcher, cartoonist, photographer, cameraman; sculptor, carver, modeller, statuary, lapidary; potter, ceramist; engraver, etcher, lithographer, printer, typographer.

492 language

n. language, communication, speech, tongue, talk, style, diction, parlance; utterance, expression, voice, articulation; idiom, dialect, provincialism, *patois*, jargon, pidgin, *koine*, *lingua franca*; mother tongue, vernacular, common speech, British English, American English, Standard English, Queen's English, Received Pronunciation; artificial language, world language, Esperanto; Babel, confusion of tongues.

linguistics, grammar, syntax, semantics, phonetics, phonology, historical linguistics, comparative linguistics, etymology, philology, dialectology, lexicography; linguist, polyglot, philologist, grammarian, lexicographer.

adj. linguistic, lingual, grammatical, standard, current, vernacular, idiomatic.

see also **514**

493 letter

n. letter, symbol, consonant, vowel; capital, upper case, large letter, majuscule; small letter, lower case, minuscule; rune, cuneiform, hieroglyph; syllable, character, ideogram, pictogram; alphabet, ABC; orthography, spelling, spelling-pronunciation.

adj. literal, alphabetical, orthographic, syllabic.

vb. spell, letter, form letters; syllabify.

494 word

n. word, expression, term, name, designation, vocable, sound, syllable, utterance, phrase, construction, locution; neologism, slang, colloquialism, jargon, provincialism, cliché, vogue word, catch phrase, slogan, archaism; root, derivative, derivation; synonym, antonym, homonym.

vocabulary, lexicon, wordlist, dictionary, glossary, thesaurus, concordance, index; lexicology, lexicography, etymology, terminology.

adj. verbal, literal, lexical, lexicographical.

495 neologism

n. neologism, new word, new usage, coinage, neology; formation, translation, loan-word, borrowing, calque, portmanteau, blend, hybrid; corruption, barbarism, nonce word; cliché, vogue word, slang, vulgarism, argot, cant, colloquialism, informal usage, journalese, Americanism, Anglicism, Briticism.

adj. newly-coined, newfangled, colloquial, informal, slang, foreign, borrowed, translated, nonce, vogue.

496 nomenclature

n. nomenclature, naming, calling, appellation, designation, identification, terminology, classification.

name, title; Christian name, first name, given name, forename; surname, last name, family name, signature; sign, style, label, tag; nomen, denomination; nickname, description, epithet.

adj. nominal, titular; named, known as.

vb. name, call, designate, identify, specify, term, title, dub, label, tag, style; classify, characterize, describe, define, nominate, denominate; christen, baptize; be known as, be called, go by the name of, go under the name of.

497 misnomer

n. misnomer, misnaming, malapropism; nickname, pet name, pen name, pseudonym, fictitious name, assumed name, alias, *nom de plume*, stage name, sobriquet, *nom de guerre*.

anonymity, namelessness; what's-its-name, thinggamy (*inf.*), thingumabob (*inf.*), what-d'you-call-it, so-and-so, A. N. Other, Mr. X.

adj. misnamed, in name only, professed, pretended, pseudo-, quasi-, self-styled, so-called, *soi-disant;* anonymous, unknown, unidentified, nameless, unknown.

vb. misname, nickname, dub, mislabel, mistake.

498 phrase

n. phrase, clause, sentence, group of words; idiom, figure of speech; expression, utterance, locution; slogan, maxim, saying, formula, cliché.

vb. phrase, word, reword, express, state, put into words, formulate, verbalize.

499 grammar

n. grammar, usage, syntax, word order, sentence structure, analysis, parsing; inflection, case-ending, morphology, accidence.

part of speech, noun, substantive, proper noun, collective noun, mass noun, count noun, case, gender, number, declension; pronoun; verb, participle, gerund, copula, infinitive, split infinitive, person, tense, active, passive, conjugation; adjective, qualifier, modifier, comparative, superlative, comparison; adverb, particle; preposition; interjection; conjunction; article, definite article, indefinite article, determiner; subject, predicate; affix, prefix, suffix, infix.

adj. grammatical, syntactic, correct, proper, well-formed, acceptable, appropriate.

vb. parse, analyse, inflect, conjugate, decline.

500 solecism

n. solecism, ungrammaticalness, bad grammar, misusage, mistake, error, barbarism, blunder; mispronunciation, slip of the tongue; malapropism, spoonerism, cacology, catachresis.

adj. ungrammatical, incorrect, solecistic; slovenly, slipshod, loose; inappropriate, unacceptable, badly-formed.

vb. use bad grammar, make a mistake, murder the language.

see also **511**

501 style

n. style, manner, characteristics, presentation; command, fluency, mastery, skill; manner of speaking, diction, phrasing, phraseology, wording, composition, writing; usage, mode of expression, expression, vocabulary, word-power, parlance, choice of words, way of putting it, feeling for words, *sprachgefühl;* mannerism, idiosyncrasy, intonation.

see also **510, 514**

502 lucidity

n. lucidity, clearness, clarity, perspicuity, transparency, unambiguousness, intelligibility, directness, plain speech, simplicity, exactness, precision.

adj. lucid, clear, perspicuous, unambiguous, distinct, obvious, direct, plain, intelligible, explicit, easily understood, limpid, pellucid.

see also **452, 802**

503 obscurity

n. obscurity, imperspicuity, vagueness, opaqueness, ambiguity, imprecision, unintelligibility, complexity, abstruseness.

adj. obscure, cloudy, blurred, fuzzy, vague, unclear, imperspicuous, imprecise, indistinct, ambiguous, unintelligible, incomprehensible, complicated, involved, intricate, abstruse.

see also **453, 803**

504 conciseness

n. conciseness, succinctness, brevity, terseness, curtness, pithiness, laconism; contraction, ellipsis.

adj. concise, brief, succinct, condensed, compressed, shortened, short, precise, pithy, terse, compact, summary, laconic, sententious; elliptic, telegraphic.

vb. be concise, condense, compress, shorten, abridge, abbreviate, summarize, come to the point, put in a nutshell.

adv. in short, in brief, in a nutshell, to the point, to cut a long story short.

505 diffuseness

n. diffuseness, profuseness, abundance; wordiness, verbosity, discursiveness; digression, departure, deviation, excursus; tautology, redundancy, verbiage, repetition, padding, circumlocution, periphrasis, pleonasm.

adj. diffuse, discursive, wordy, lengthy, long-winded, verbose, tedious, rambling, digressive, redundant, repetitious, protracted, prolix, pleonastic, roundabout, periphrastic, circumlocutory.

vb. amplify, enlarge on, develop, expatiate; digress, ramble, wander, deviate, go off at a tangent, go off the subject, get off the point, get sidetracked, beat about the bush (*inf.*); go on and on, talk at length, repeat oneself.

see also **516**

506 vigour

n. vigour, power, strength, intensity, force, effectiveness, forcefulness, urgency, piquancy; sparkle, spirit, punch (*sl.*), fervour, vehemence, verve, animation, vitality, fire, glow, warmth.

adj. vigorous, powerful, strong, forceful, trenchant, incisive, bold, tough, lively, inspired, sparkling, racy, fervent, vehement, insistent, impassioned, fiery, ardent, passionate, persuasive; vivid, graphic; pointed.

see also **173, 755**

507 feebleness

n. feebleness, weakness, faintness, frailty, flaccidity, enfeeblement, pauperism, barrenness, lifelessness.

adj. feeble, weak, faint, frail, thin, poor, limp, lifeless, flaccid, insipid, meagre, scant, slight, shallow, diluted, wishy-washy, uninspired, stale, flat, tame, forced.

see also **162**

508 plainness

n. plainness, simplicity, plain speech, naturalness, straightforwardness, modesty, unpretentiousness, severity.

adj. plain, simple, natural, unaffected, artless, naive, straightforward, modest, ordinary, undramatic, severe, restrained, unadorned, unpretentious, unsophisticated, common, homely, homespun, unimaginative, matter-of-fact; direct, frank, open, blunt.

vb. speak plainly, call a spade a spade, come straight to the point.

see also 476

509 ornament

n. ornamentation, adornment, embellishment, elaboration, enrichment, enhancement, decoration, embroidery, floweriness.

ornament, colour, frills, rhetoric, metaphor, euphemism, verbosity, grandiloquence, bombast, fustian.

adj. ornate, adorned, embellished, grand, rich, lofty, elaborate, lavish, grandiose; vivid, dazzling, scintillating; fancy, extravagant, pretentious, showy, flashy, loud, flaunting, boastful, big, high-falutin, high-flown, big-sounding, magniloquent; rhetorical, voluble, pompous, flowery, euphemistic, euphuistic, grandiloquent.

vb. embellish, adorn, enrich, colour; talk big, lay it on (*inf.*).

see also 846

510 elegance

n. elegance, tastefulness, style, grace, graciousness, dignity, beauty, correctness, refinement, propriety, polish, finish; harmony, balance, proportion, rhythm; artificiality, affectation.

adj. elegant, tasteful, gracious, graceful, dignified, artistic, delicate, refined, pure, stylized, polished; proper, appropriate, happy, well-expressed, right, correct, felicitous, seemly; harmonious, balanced, well-proportioned, well-turned, mellifluous; affected, artificial.

see also 848

511 inelegance

n. inelegance, tastelessness, bad taste, gracelessness, impropriety; barbarism, coarseness, vulgarity; incorrectness, stiltedness, formality, awkwardness, clumsiness.

adj. inelegant, tasteless, graceless, unseemly, improper, incorrect, laboured, stilted, forced, heavy, stiff, formal, ponderous, clumsy, awkward, inappropriate; coarse, crude, vulgar, rude, uncouth.

see also 849

512 voice

n. voice, sound, speech, language, utterance; vocal organs, vocal chords, tongue, lips, larynx, lungs, breath; articulation, pronunciation, vocalization, enunciation, delivery, inflection, intonation, pitch, rhythm, tone, accent, timbre, stress, emphasis; vowel, consonant, phoneme; phonetics.

adj. vocal, expressed, uttered, spoken, oral, lingual, vocalic, phonetic, voiced, sonant, sounded; clear, distinct, articulate.

vb. voice, speak, express, sound, pronounce, utter, articulate, get one's tongue round, vocalize, enunciate; nasalize, palatalize, aspirate; roll, trill, burr; stress, emphasize.

513 muteness

n. muteness, aphonia, voicelessness, inarticulation, dumbness, silence.

adj. mute, voiceless, speechless, tongueless, unsounded, unvoiced, unvocal, surd, inarticulate, tongue-tied, dumb, silent, mum, inaudible.

vb. mute, silence, dumbfound, strike dumb, still, soften, deaden, muffle, suppress, smother.

see also 517, 779

514 speech

n. speech, language, talk, discourse, utterance, articulation, expression, pronunciation, communication; eloquence, fluency, expressiveness, facility, vivacity, style, poise, delivery, rhetoric, vigour, force, gift of the gab (*inf.*).

speaker, talker, conversationalist; public speaker, orator, lecturer, after-dinner speaker, expositor, rhetorician, declaimer, preacher; spokesman, mouthpiece.

adj. speaking, talking, verbal, oral; articulating; eloquent, fluent, voluble, expressive, forceful, meaningful.

vb. speak, say, talk; vocalize, pronounce, voice, enunciate; express, utter, tell, affirm, converse, communicate, chat; repeat, rattle off, trot out (*inf.*).

address, discuss, lecture, teach, instruct, plead, argue, make a speech, give a talk, deliver a lecture, have the floor, hold forth, preach, speechify (*inf.*), rant, spout.

see also **468, 516**

515 imperfect speech

n. imperfect speech, speech defect, aphasia, impediment, stammer, stutter, faltering, hesitation, mispronunciation, lisp, twang, nasalization, drawl.

adj. inarticulate, indistinct, throaty, shaking, stuttering, stammering, hesitant.

vb. stammer, stutter, hesitate, pause, falter, stumble, lisp, drawl, slur, speak through one's nose, mispronounce, mumble, mutter, garble, swallow one's words.

516 talkativeness

n. talkativeness, gift of the gab (*inf.*), loquacity, garrulity, verbosity, long-windedness.

chatter, chat, jabber, babble, prattle, blather, prittle-prattle (*inf.*), chit-chat, idle talk, chinwag (*sl.*), palaver, small talk; nonsense, drive, twaddle, hot air (*sl.*), yap (*inf.*), yackety-yack (*sl.*); gossip, scandal.

chatterbox, prattler, jabberer, tattler, windbag (*inf.*), gasbag (*sl.*); gossip, muckraker (*inf.*).

adj. talkative, chatty, voluble, loquacious, garrulous; chattering, babbling; glib, eloquent, fluent; long-winded, verbose; gossipy.

vb. chat, keep on, go on about (*inf.*), chatter, talk idly, waffle, ramble on; babble, jabber, prattle, gabble, yackety-yack (*sl.*), yack (*sl.*), yap (*inf.*); gossip, tell tales.

see also **505**

517 taciturnity

n. taciturnity, reserve, reticence, silence, uncommunicativeness, no comment, curtness, brusqueness; modesty, hesitance.

adj. taciturn, reserved, reticent, silent, dumb, mute, quiet, uncommunicative, secretive, tight-lipped, close-lipped, mum, restrained, hesitant, modest, retiring; curt, brusque, laconic; aloof, distant.

vb. say nothing, refuse to comment, keep quiet, keep one's mouth shut, hold one's tongue, save one's breath; stand aloof.

see also **779**

518 address

n. address, speech, talk, lecture, oration, discourse, reading, recitation, recital, exhortation, paper, pep talk (*sl.*), spiel (*sl.*), appeal, invocation, homily, sermon, allocution; harangue, tirade, declamation.

inaugural address, opening; greeting, salutation; farewell address, goodbye, valediction.

oratory, rhetoric, speech-making,

public speaking, elocution, preaching, homiletics.

519 conversation

n. conversation, chat, talk, discussion, interview, exchange of views, interchange, expression, repartee, colloquy, interlocution; chatter, chitchat, prattle; *tête-à-tête*, heart-to-heart.

conference, debate, dialogue, consultation, conflab (*inf.*), powwow, summit conference, summit, congress, symposium, convention, seminar, parley, council, audience, hearing.

vb. converse, chat, discuss, hold a conversation, communicate, counsel, confer, exchange views, debate, negotiate, put one's heads together, confabulate.

520 monologue

n. monologue, soliloquy, monody; apostrophe, aside.

vb. soliloquize, talk to oneself.

521 writing

n. writing, script, lettering, calligraphy, stroke, flourish; handwriting, hand, fist, longhand; graphology, chirography; mark, scribble, scrawl; transcription, inscription, printing, copying, shorthand, stenography, typing; correspondence, letter-writing; journalism, reporting.

written matter, copy, work, composition, document, paper, manuscript, transcript, typescript, parchment, scroll.

writer, calligrapher, scribe, copyist, transcriber, secretary, stenographer, typist; author, novelist, journalist.

adj. written, graphic, in writing, handwritten, in black and white, roman, italic.

vb. write, pen, compose, prepare, draft, write out, report, document,

write down, record, put pen to paper; scribble, scrawl; transcribe, inscribe, copy, engrave, print, type.

522 printing

n. printing, typography; composition, typesetting; publishing; print, impression, stamp, page, sheet, copy, printed matter; type, lead, leading, rule, letter, fount, space; galley, proof, slip, bromide.

printer, typographer, typesetter, compositor; proofreader, reader; copy editor.

adj. printed, in print, typographical.

vb. print, impress, imprint, stamp, engrave; compose, set type, set up; run off, go to press, put to bed; publish, issue, bring out.

523 correspondence

n. correspondence, communication, exchange of letters, post, mail; letter, postcard, note, message, report, missive, dispatch, epistle, chit, acknowledgement, reply, answer; business letter, love letter, valentine, fan letter, poison pen letter, chain letter, round robin, circular; address, destination.

correspondent, letter-writer, penfriend, pen-pal (*inf.*), addressee, recipient.

adj. epistolary, postal.

vb. correspond, write to, communicate, exchange letters, drop a line, send, post, mail, dispatch.

524 book

n. book, publication, work, volume, tome, copy, text, manuscript, bestseller, paperback, hardback, booklet, edition, reprint, offprint; study book, course book, textbook, set book, primer, workbook; reader, companion volume, selected readings; complete works, omnibus edition.

magazine, periodical, journal, review, gazette; back number, back issue.

reference book, encyclopedia, cyclopedia, handbook, manual, dictionary, bible, guidebook; index, concordance; bibliography, reading list.

library, collection of books, lending library, public library, mobile library, inter-library loan.

writer, author, novelist, biographer, essayist, reporter, ghost-writer, hack; editor, publisher, reviewer, critic; man of letters, man of learning, bookworm, scholar, book-collector, bibliophile.

525 description

n. description, account, report, statement, record, summary, information, explanation, characterization, specification; portrayal, sketch, portrait, representation, illustration, picture, image, profile; narrative, story, tale, yarn, anecdote, saga, epic; fiction, myth, legend, fairy-tale, fairy story, fantasy, fable, parable, allegory; plot, story-line, subject, argument.

narrator, reciter, story-teller, novelist, raconteur, anecdotist, fabricator.

adj. descriptive, narrative, expressive; graphic, vivid, true-to-life, lifelike, telling, detailed, pictorial; fictional, made-up, legendary, mythical, fabulous, parabolic, allegorical.

vb. describe, portray, sketch, set forth, represent, outline, trace, illustrate, picture, draw, paint, imagine, delineate, characterize, define, specify, mark out, express; account, report, state, record, explain, summarize; narrate, tell, recount, relate, recite, rehearse.

526 dissertation

n. dissertation, essay, paper, composition, commentary, exposition, thesis, treatise, monograph, discourse, disquisition; survey, review, analysis, examination, enquiry, investigation, study, discussion, story, comment, write-up, critique.

essayist, expositor, commentator; critic, reviewer.

vb. discuss, treat, handle, concern, deal with, consider, comment; analyse, survey, examine, explain, interpret; review, criticize, write up.

527 compendium

n. compendium, summary, resumé, precis, abridgment, abstract, summing up, syllabus, survey, outline, synopsis, skeleton, reduction, analysis, conspectus, epitome; core, essence; digest, miscellany, anthology, selections, readings.

adj. compendious, concise, brief, succinct, abbreviated.

vb. summarize, sum up, abstract, abridge, condense, reduce, shorten, digest, outline, survey; boil down to.

528 poetry; prose

n. poetry, song, rhyme, poem, verse, stanza, sonnet, ode, lyric, idyll, epic, ballad, jingle, limerick; chorus, refrain; prosody, versification, scansion, rhythm, metre, stress, beat, foot; prose, writing, literature, composition, story.

poet, writer, composer, versifier, poet laureate, bard, minstrel, troubadour.

adj. poetic, rhythmic, lyrical, idyllic, tuneful.

vb. poetize, sing, versify; rhyme, scan; write, conceive, imagine, compose.

529 drama

n. theatre, the stage; hall, opera

house, cinema, playhouse; play, drama, show, opera, melodrama, tragicomedy, tragedy, comedy, farce, slapstick, pantomime, mime, variety, cabaret, pageant, revue, spectacle, carnival; presentation, appearance, exhibition, production; dramatics, stagecraft, showmanship, acting, performance, histrionics.

actor, actress, performer, player, role, part, character, Thespian, lead, star, understudy, extra; cast, characters, *dramatis personae*.

adj. dramatic, theatrical; impressive, spectacular.

vb. dramatize, direct, produce, present, stage, produce, put on, perform, enact, play.

V Volition

1 Individual volition

A Volition in general

530 will

n. will, volition, intention, resolution, power, mind, conviction, determination, willpower, choice, free will, discretion, conation; desire, wish, inclination.

adj. volitional, willing, minded, voluntary, free, intentional, wilful, deliberate, wished, premeditated, conative.

vb. will, wish, want, desire, incline, choose, resolve, make a decision, decide, make up one's mind, determine, purpose, see fit, take it into one's head to (*inf.*), have one's own way; conclude, come to the conclusion.

adv. at will, at pleasure, as one thinks, of one's own accord.

531 necessity

n. necessity, compulsion, obligation; inevitability, unavoidability, certainty, inexorableness, inescapableness; determinism, predestination, foreordination, fatalism; involuntariness, spontaneity, reflex action, instinct, intuition.

no choice, no alternative, Hobson's choice, six of one and half a dozen of the other; must (*inf.*), essential, prerequisite; fate, the inevitable, whatever will be shall be, *che sara, sara.*

adj. necessary, inevitable, unavoidable, inescapable, inexorable, certain, sure, foreordained, predetermined, destined, predestined, irresistible; essential, indispensable, imperative; compulsory, obligatory; deterministic, fatalistic; involuntary, unintentional, instinctive, unconscious, automatic, reflex, mechanical.

vb. necessitate, compel, oblige, constrain, force, dictate; destine, foreordain; need, require, cry out for.

adv. of necessity, necessarily, inevitably, certainly, willy-nilly.

532 willingness

n. willingness, readiness, disposition, inclination, compliance; eagerness, enthusiasm, zeal, earnestness.

adj. willing, prepared, ready, disposed, inclined, game, desirous, compliant, eager, enthusiastic, zealous; voluntary, uninvited, unasked, unprompted.

vb. be willing, like to, want, desire, choose, feel like, show willing (*inf.*), be inclined towards; volunteer, take on the responsibility, offer oneself; be eager, enthuse, jump at, leap at, lean over backwards (*inf.*), fall over oneself to (*inf.*); gush over, go overboard about (*inf.*), go to town on (*inf.*).

adv. willingly, gladly, eagerly, readily; voluntarily, of one's own accord; off one's own bat.

see also 611

533 unwillingness

n. unwillingness, disinclination, unreadiness, hesitation, reluctance, scruple, qualm, aversion, demur; non-cooperation, protest, abstention.

adj. unwilling, unready, disinclined, reluctant, hesitant, averse, opposed, loath, not in the mood, unenthusiastic, indifferent, half-hearted.

vb. be unwilling, not feel like, not want to, would rather not, refuse, hesitate, hold back, balk at, shirk, demur, fight shy of, shy away, shrink, dodge, evade; force oneself.

adv. unwillingly, without enthusiasm, against one's will, against one's better judgment, under protest, grudgingly.

see also 612

534 resolution

n. resolution, determination, resolve, certainty, persistence, constancy, doggedness, conviction, perseverance, boldness, tenacity, fortitude, steadfastness; firmness, willpower, strength of will, mettle; self-control, self-reliance, self-possession.

adj. resolute, determined, steadfast, firm, steady, strong, certain, serious, strong-willed, iron-willed, inflexible, bold, persistent, tenacious, constant, dogged; single-minded, wholehearted, committed, decided; unyielding, unhesitating, unflinching, unwavering, unswerving, unbending.

vb. be resolute, determine, resolve, decide, be bent on; have one's heart set upon, stand fast, take one's stand,

hold one's ground, not give in, stick to one's guns, stand no nonsense, put one's foot down; take the bull by the horns; commit oneself, dedicate, put one's heart and soul into.

535 perseverance

n. perseverance, tenacity, steadfastness, firmness, persistence, continuance, constancy, endurance, indefatigability, undauntedness, doggedness; stamina, guts (*inf.*), staying power, backbone, stickability (*sl.*), moral fibre, stiff upper lip.

stayer, bulldog.

adj. persevering, persistent, determined, tenacious, steadfast, constant, steady, firm, unmoved, undaunted, indefatigable, untiring, obstinate, enduring, continuing; diligent, industrious, assiduous.

vb. persevere, remain, persist, endure, continue to the end, go on, carry on, have what it takes, keep at it, keep going (*inf.*), stick at it (*inf.*), soldier on, plod (*inf.*), plug away (*inf.*), slog away, see it through (*inf.*), stick it out (*inf.*); stick out for, hold out for; hold a job down (*inf.*).

536 irresolution

n. irresolution, indecision, vacillation, wavering, fluctuation; inconstancy, hesitation, fickleness, instability.

adj. irresolute, indecisive, undecided, fluctuating, wavering, vacillating, fickle, hesitant, in two minds, unstable, infirm, inconstant, changeable.

vb. be irresolute, vacillate, waver, fluctuate, hesitate, falter, shilly-shally.

537 obstinacy

n. obstinacy, stubbornness, inflexibility, rigidity, tenacity, hardness, relentlessness, obduracy, intransigence, intractableness; bigotry, dogmatism, narrow-mindedness, intolerance, fanaticism.

dogmatist, bigot, fanatic, die-hard, mule, intransigent; pedant, stickler.

adj. obstinate, stubborn, inflexible, tenacious, uncompromising, intransigent, unyielding, unrelenting, hardened, hard, intractable, headstrong, self-willed, set in one's ways; stiff-necked, pig-headed, recalcitrant, refractory, obdurate, pertinacious; dogmatic.

vb. be obstinate, not give in, stick to one's guns; resist, oppose, dig one's heels in.

see also 534, 535

538 change of mind

n. change of mind, second thoughts, afterthought, change of heart, *volte-face*, repentance; retraction, withdrawal, backing out, reversal, abandonment, desertion, defection, renunciation, recantation; tergiversation, backsliding, apostasy.

turncoat, time-server, rat, renegade, traitor, deserter, apostate.

adj. fickle, irresolute, unfaithful, inconstant.

vb. change one's mind, have second thoughts, think better of, change one's tune; take back, withdraw, back out, back down, climb down (*inf.*), disown, deny, retract, revoke, recant, disclaim; nullify; trim; apologize, eat humble pie, eat one's words; fall away, apostatize.

539 caprice

n. caprice, whim, fancy, vagary, notion, quirk, prank, crotchet, freak, craze, whimsy, whim-wham, flash; jest,

witticism; capriciousness, whimsicality; fickleness, inconstancy.

adj. capricious, whimsical, fanciful, inconstant, fickle, changeable, flighty, frivolous, freakish, crotchety, unpredictable, erratic, fitful.

540 choice

n. choice, option, decision, determination, selection, adoption; alternative, preference, substitute.

vote, ballot, poll, election, representation, referendum, plebiscite; suffrage, franchise; voter, elector, electorate, constituency, ward.

adj. optional, elective, selective, discretional, discriminating, choosy (*inf.*), fastidious; electoral, voting.

vb. choose, pick, decide on, opt, adopt, sort, prefer, take up, go for, plump for (*inf.*), like, fancy, favour, appoint, co-opt, elect, nominate, commit oneself; separate, select, isolate, segregate, cull, glean, sift, winnow, divide the sheep from the goats, separate the wheat from the chaff; weigh, judge, discriminate, make up one's mind; vote, cast votes, poll, ballot, draw lots, vote in, return.

541 absence of choice

n. no choice, Hobson's choice, first come first served; impartiality, neutrality, no preference, indifference; abstention, don't know.

adj. choiceless, neutral, impartial, disinterested, unbiased, indifferent.

vb. be neutral, abstain, not commit oneself, sit on the fence, not take sides.

542 rejection

n. rejection, dismissal, repudiation, denial, refusal, renunciation, rebuff, disownment, disapproval, exclusion, expulsion.

adj. rejected, repudiated, excluded, renounced, spurned.

vb. reject, not accept, dismiss, exclude, repudiate, renounce, deny, refuse, disapprove, rebuff, spurn, decline, disown, disclaim, despise, turn up one's nose at (*inf.*), expel, jettison, discard, brush aside, have nothing to do with, turn one's back on, laugh in someone's face (*inf.*).

see also **556, 694**

543 predetermination

n. predetermination, predestination, preordination, inevitability, necessity, finality; prediction, forecast; doom, fate; premeditation, predeliberation, foregone conclusion.

adj. predetermined, planned, proposed, designed, fixed, deliberate.

vb. predetermine, foreordain, predestine, appoint, destine, predestinate; predict, forecast, foretell, determine beforehand; premeditate, preconceive.

544 spontaneity

n. spontaneity, spur of the moment; improvisation, extemporization; involuntariness, reflex action; impetuosity, impulsiveness, hastiness, suddenness, rashness; impulse buying.

adj. spontaneous, impulsive, unpremeditated, unthinking, unconsidered; involuntary, automatic, instinctive, reflex; extempore, impromptu, improvised, ad lib (*inf.*); hasty, sudden, rash, precipitate; casual, offhand, throwaway.

vb. act impulsively; blurt out, say the first thing that comes into one's mind; improvise, extemporize, ad lib (*inf.*), play by ear.

adv. on impulse, on the spur of the moment, impulsively, rashly, instinctively, automatically.

see also **613, 859**

545 habit

n. habit, custom, mode, practice, wont, usage, fashion, style, rule, procedure; tendency, propensity, bent, disposition, predisposition, weakness, bias, penchant, second nature, instinct; routine, ritual, rut, groove, treadmill, regularity; convention, precedent, tradition, etiquette, protocol, the done thing; conditioning, accustoming, adaptation, familiarization, training, acclimatization.

addict, habitué, fiend, creature of habit, devotee, client, patron, regular (*inf.*).

adj. usual, customary, normal, common, general, accepted, expected, prevalent, current, conventional, orthodox, established; habitual, frequent, regular, routine, stereotyped; mechanical, seasoned, inveterate; confirmed, ingrained, deep-seated; besetting, clinging, persistent; accustomed, used to, adapted.

vb. accustom, get used to, take to, adapt, adjust, accommodate, condition, train, familiarize, orientate, acclimatize, harden, season, inure, habituate; catch on.

be wont to, be in the habit of, make a practice of.

adv. usually, as is usual, generally.

546 absence of habit

n. disuse, unaccustomedness, desuetude; cessation, relinquishment; decay, neglect, deterioration.

adj. unused, unaccustomed, not used to, not in the habit of; unskilled, inexperienced.

vb. break a habit, abandon, neglect, relinquish, discard, discontinue, rid oneself of, throw off, wean from; not get used to, not take to; not catch on.

see also **607**

547 motive

n. motive, cause, reason, purpose, ground, basis, spring, spur, impetus, urge, prod, goad, carrot, lure, bait; influence, stimulus, incentive, inspiration, prompting, instigation; persuasion, inducement, coaxing, cajolery, wheedling; charm, attraction, glamour; enticement, temptation, bribery.

motivator, instigator, prompter, animator, coaxer, wheedler; pressure group, lobby, lobbyist.

adj. motivating, persuasive, convincing, impelling, forceful; provocative, stimulating, rousing; fascinating, alluring, charming, captivating, enthralling; enticing, tantalizing.

vb. motivate, cause, inspire, stimulate, prompt, instigate, insist, induce, drive, push, egg on, spur, urge, prod, goad; provoke, elicit, call forth, evoke; influence, encourage, support; persuade, sway, prevail on, talk into, win over, wear down resistance, brainwash (*inf.*), twist round one's little finger (*inf.*), pull strings; coax, cajole, wheedle; captivate, fascinate, charm, attract, interest, entice, tempt, tantalize, beguile, enrapture; lobby, put pressure on; bribe, buy, get at (*inf.*), oil, corrupt.

548 dissuasion

n. dissuasion, discouragement, hindrance, deterrent, disincentive, damper, restraint, cold water, wet blanket; spoilsport, killjoy.

adj. dissuasive, discouraging.

vb. dissuade, deter, hinder, prevent, advise against, discourage, talk out of, wean from, dampen, stifle, disparage, pour cold water on.

549 pretext

n. pretext, excuse, plea, apology, justification, pretence, gesture, show, guise, veil, cloak, mask, appearance, alibi.

adj. ostensible, alleged, specious.

vb. allege, pretend, claim, profess, excuse; apologize, make excuses, bluff.

550 good

n. good, benefit, gain, profit, success, advantage, service, boon, windfall, godsend, pennies from heaven, providence, blessing, good turn; well-being, welfare, prosperity, fortune, happiness, weal; improvement, betterment, edification, progress.

adj. good, beneficial, advantageous, helpful, useful, edifying.

see also **899, 935**

551 evil

n. evil, misfortune, ill, harm, ruin, nuisance, disadvantage, bane, accident, tragedy, disaster, catastrophe, calamity, affliction, trial, crying shame, raw deal; foul play, wrong, injury, pain, anguish, hurt; wickedness, corruption.

adj. evil, bad, wicked; unfortunate, ill, tragic, catastrophic, disastrous, painful, distressing, hurtful.

see also **900, 936**

B Prospective volition

552 intention

n. intention, purpose, aim, intent, meaning; goal, object, end, objective, mark, destination, target; plan, design, idea, proposal; dream, desire, aspiration, expectation, ambition.

adj. intended, designed, planned, proposed, deliberate; intending, purposeful, teleological.

vb. intend, aim, go for, attempt, try for, pursue; plan, propose, project, design, purpose, mean; dream, expect, hope, aspire, have designs on (*inf.*); consider, think about, contemplate, study, have in mind, have in view, calculate, work out, decide, determine, resolve.

553 chance

n. chance, randomness, uncertainty, fortuity; fate, fortune, luck, coincidence, fluke, toss-up (*inf.*); speculation, venture, risk, hazard; bet, gamble, wager, stake, flutter, draw, lottery.

speculator, gambler, better, backer, punter; bookmaker, turf accountant, bookie (*inf.*).

adj. chance, lucky, fortuitous, unintentional, haphazard, aimless, random, risky, hazardous, touch-and-go.

vb. chance, risk, venture, hazard, speculate, gamble, bet, wager, back.

see also **158**

554 pursuit

n. pursuit, hunt, chase, race, pursuance, quest, search, tracking; hunter, chaser, pursuer, seeker, quester, follower.

adj. pursuing, following.

vb. pursue, look for, search, follow up, seek, quest, prosecute; hunt, go after, chase, give chase, hound, tail, trail, stalk, shadow, track, sniff out (*inf.*), smell out, dog.

prep. after, in pursuit of, on the track of.

555 avoidance

n. avoidance, evasion, escape, flight, withdrawal, retreat, shunning, abstinence, circumvention; shirker, fugitive, runaway, absconder, eloper, deserter, refugee, truant.

adj. avoiding, evasive, elusive.

vb. avoid, escape, evade, elude, keep away, keep off, boycott; flee, shrink, flinch; get out of, shun, shirk, dodge, flunk, turn away, duck, hedge; steer clear of, keep one's distance, take no part in, leave alone, not get involved in, disregard, give the go-by; abstain, refrain; retreat, withdraw.

556 relinquishment

n. relinquishment, abandonment, giving up, surrender, renunciation, discontinuance, withdrawal, desertion, quitting.

vb. relinquish, abandon, give up, renounce, forgo, abdicate, waive, surrender, throw in the towel; turn over to, turn in; leave, quit, withdraw, back out, go back on, retreat, secede, forsake; discontinue, break with, break off with, drop, let go, throw away, cast off, discard, part with, shed, desert, chuck (*inf.*), ditch, jilt; leave in the lurch, have done with (*inf.*), walk out on (*inf.*).

see also **542, 713**

557 business

n. business, affairs, dealings, trade; job, employment, post, appointment, position, situation, engagement, incumbency; vocation, calling, pursuit, occupation, profession, line of business, speciality, *métier*, craft; career, life-work, life, mission; work, task, undertaking, activity, assignment, affair, concern; function, office, role, capacity, responsibility, duty, charge, commission, terms of reference, scope, area, field, realm, province, portfolio.

adj. businesslike, efficient, professional, official, prompt; busy, tied up with (*inf.*).

vb. employ, occupy, appoint, select, recruit, engage, contract, take on, give a job to, commission, enlist, hire, rope in (*inf.*), take on the payroll; work, undertake, be busy, be occupied with, be engaged on, be about.

558 plan

n. plan, scheme, project, design, programme, proposal, schedule; scope, outline, sketch; method, procedure, guidelines, principles; policy, course of action, strategy; representation, chart; master-plan, long-range plan; blueprint, draft, rough draft, pilot scheme, dummy run; plot, conspiracy, intrigue, cabal, little game (*inf.*).

planner, director, designer, organizer, architect, engineer, administrator; conspirer, plotter, schemer.

adj. planned, projected, prospective, on the drawing board, procedural.

vb. plan, design, work out, draw up, organize, arrange, propose, devise, create, dream up (*inf.*), frame, undertake, proceed, outline, sketch, draft; forecast, project, think ahead, phase; scheme, plot, conspire, concoct, hatch.

559 way

n. way, manner, fashion; method, means, procedure, process; tactics, measures, steps; direction, passage, entrance, access, approach, route, itinerary, course.

path, track, footpath, walk; road, street, avenue, lane, drive, crescent, close, alley, terrace, park, garden, green, hill, grove, boulevard, square, place, court, circus, arcade, piazza, market, mall, embankment; ring-road, by-pass, arterial road, motorway, dual carriageway, clearway, primary route, trunk road, highway.

railway, underground, tube; main line, branch line, feeder.

560 mid-course

n. centre, mean, middle course, middle of the road, half-way house.

adj. middle, central, medial, neutral, middle-of-the-road, unextreme, moderate, intermediate, midway, half-way.

561 circuit

n. circuit, detour, by-pass, roundabout way; digression, deviation.

adj. circuitous, roundabout, indirect, out-of-the-way.

see also **250**

562 requirement

n. requirement, requisite, stipulation, need, want, demand; condition; essential, imperative, necessity, must (*inf.*), desideratum; needfulness, obligation, compulsion, indispensability, emergency, urgency, matter of life and death, essentiality.

adj. necessary, essential, imperative, indispensable, vital, needful, urgent; wanted, in demand.

vb. require, need, want, wish; lack, be in need of, miss; demand, call for, ask, invite, cry out for; necessitate, force, compel.

563 instrumentality

n. instrumentality, mediation, subservience, intervention; help, aid, assistance, agency, medium, vehicle, intermediary, organ.

adj. instrumental, intermediate, conducive, assisting, subsidiary, auxiliary, subservient, contributory, helpful; effective.

vb. be instrumental, help, aid, mediate.

see also **172**

564 means

n. means, wherewithal, resources, ways and means, equipment, supplies, assets, reserves, provisions; power, potential; factor, agent, medium, channel, organization.

vb. find the means, provide, equip, supply.

565 instrument

n. instrument, implement, apparatus, equipment, appliance, gadget, device, invention, contrivance, contraption; machine, mechanism, machinery, engine; tool, utensil; computer, robot, automaton.

adj. instrumental, mechanical, automatic.

566 materials

n. materials, resources, supplies, assets, means, wherewithal, stuff, raw materials.

567 store

n. store, collection, accumulation, heap, pile, stack, load, mass, stock, hoard, bulk, deposit, bundle; crop, harvest; hoard, treasure, reserves, savings, nest-egg; backlog; fountain, well, spring, gold-mine, reservoir; abundance, profusion, fullness.

storage, safekeeping; warehouse, stockroom, storeroom, depot, depository; library, museum, archives.

adj. stored, accumulated, saved, kept.

vb. store, keep, put away, put aside, put by, stow away, stash away (*inf.*); accumulate, pile up, heap, stack, amass, bulk, bundle, stockpile, lay in; collect, save, deposit, invest, hoard, salt away (*inf.*); harvest, gather; put by for a rainy day.

adv. aside, in store, in reserve, in stock.

568 provision

n. provision, equipment, supply, furnishings, fittings, fixtures, reserve, store, facilities, belongings, accessories, accompaniments, outfit, paraphernalia, apparatus, appliance; catering, purveying.

adj. provided, furnished, equipped, well-equipped.

vb. provide, equip, supply, furnish, fit, prepare, rig, dress, assemble, deck; give, afford, lend, invest, endow; maintain, stock, cater; supplement, complement; replenish, fill up.

569 waste

n. waste, ruin, decay, devastation, desolation, dilapidation, deterioration, erosion, wear and tear, loss, exhaustion, depletion, decline; consumption, disuse, misuse, squandering, uselessness, dissipation; extravagance, wastefulness, prodigality; excess.

adj. wasteful, extravagant, prodigal, squandering, spendthrift; wasted, squandered, depleted, worthless.

vb. waste, consume, expend, eat up, eat away, exhaust, reduce, deplete, empty, drain, devour, dissipate; squander, lavish, abuse; destroy, erode, decay, dry up, dwindle, wither, run dry, wear out; be of no avail, come to nothing.

570 sufficiency

n. sufficiency, adequacy, enough to go on with; right amount.

adj. sufficient, adequate, enough, satisfactory, acceptable; plenty, abundant, generous, liberal, full, complete, replete.

vb. be sufficient, suffice, be enough, avail, do, comply with, qualify, fill the bill, come up to, live up to, satisfy requirements, make the grade, prove acceptable; lick into shape (*inf.*).

571 insufficiency

n. insufficiency, inadequacy, deficiency, scarcity, meagreness, scantiness, slightness, poverty, paucity, dearth, lack.

adj. insufficient, inadequate, not enough, unacceptable, meagre, thin, slight, scanty, poor, bankrupt, sparing, unsatisfactory, wanting, lacking, missing, failing, disappointing; miserly, parsimonious.

vb. be insufficient, not come up to, fall short, come short, fail, want, need, lack, require.

prep. without, in want of, short of.

see also 35

572 excess

n. excess, redundance; exorbitance, inordinacy, superfluity, oversufficiency, abundance, plenty, lavishness, plethora, profusion, glut, surfeit, surplus, over-supply, saturation, exuberance, superabundance, inundation, flood, deluge, torrent, avalanche, bounty, bonanza, cornucopia, congestion; enough and to spare, more than enough; luxury, extravagance, too much of a good thing.

adj. excessive, inordinate, exorbitant, extravagant, immoderate, unreasonable, saturated, plentiful, superfluous, overfull, congested, surplus, redundant, to spare, extra; plenty, abundant.

vb. abound, teem, swarm; overdo; saturate, glut, inundate, flood, overwhelm, choke, drench.

573 importance

n. importance, significance, consequence; seriousness, gravity; substance, matter, weight, moment, import; prominence, eminence; be-all and end-all, priority, urgency.

adj. important, significant, momentous, decisive, critical, relevant, consequential, crucial, considerable, valuable; great, extensive; serious, grave, weighty, ponderous, heavy, solemn; famous, well-known, eminent, notable, distinguished, prominent, impressive, imposing, influential, illustrious, extraordinary, outstanding, exceptional, top-notch (*inf.*), heavyweight (*inf.*), mainline (*inf.*); basic, essential, fundamental; chief, main, primary, principal, foremost, leading, paramount, salient.

vb. be important, carry weight, influence, matter, deserve attention; make important, emphasize, underline, stress; value, prize, set great store by, think much of.

574 unimportance

n. unimportance, insignificance, triviality, worthlessness, immateriality, paltriness, irrelevance; red herring, trifle, nothing to speak of, nothing to write home about, nonentity, drop in the ocean.

adj. unimportant, insignificant, immaterial, worthless, inconsequential, irrelevant, trivial, worthless, paltry, petty, trifling, inconsiderable, slight, common, ordinary, superficial.

vb. be unimportant, not matter; play second fiddle, make light of, play down, make nothing of.

575 utility

n. utility, usefulness; utilization, employment, helpfulness, efficacy; suitability, applicability, practicability, serviceableness.

advantage, benefit, profit, worth, value, merit; service, application, convenience.

adj. useful, valuable, beneficial, profitable, advantageous, suitable, practicable, convenient, helpful, handy, available, applicable; utilitarian, functional, sensible, pragmatic.

vb. be useful, help, serve a purpose, perform a function, come in handy; profit, benefit, stand one in good stead, avail.

use, employ, have the use of, exploit, exercise, utilize, take advantage of, turn to, take up, adopt, practise, apply, avail oneself of; handle, operate; spend, consume.

see also **606**

576 inutility

n. inutility, uselessness, worthlessness, fruitlessness, ineffectiveness, unsuitability, impracticability; futility, hopelessness, vanity.

lost labour, waste of time, wild-goose chase; dead wood; waste, refuse, rubbish, waste-product, litter, dregs, dust, muck.

adj. useless, of no use, worthless, purposeless, futile, vain, pointless, empty, ineffective, incompetent, counter-productive; thankless, unrewarding; unusable, unsuitable, impracticable, inconvenient, unhelpful, disadvantageous, unavailable; out of order, broken down, inoperative; unnecessary, uncalled for.

vb. be useless, be of no help, come to nothing; flog a dead horse, labour in vain, have no future, beat the air.

577 expedience

n. expedience, suitability, appropriateness, fitness, rightness, advisability, propriety, desirability, advantageousness, usefulness.

adj. expedient, advantageous, suitable, fitting, appropriate, apposite, desirable, advisable, seemly; practical, useful, convenient; wise, politic.

vb. suit, fit; help, do, benefit.

see also **136, 915**

578 inexpedience

n. inexpedience, unsuitability, inappropriateness, inadvisability, undesirability, unfitness, impropriety, inconvenience, disadvantage, prejudice.

adj. inexpedient, unsuitable, inappropriate, undesirable, inadvisable, unfitting, unseemly, unwise, inopportune, imprudent, unfavourable, detrimental, disadvantageous, inconvenient.

vb. not do, not help; inconvenience, put out, embarrass, bother, trouble, hinder.

see also **137, 916**

579 goodness

n. goodness, excellence, fineness, greatness, magnificence, superiority; quality, value, price, worth, merit.

top people, elite, cream, pick of the bunch, salt of the earth, treasure, gem, one in a million, champion, corker (*sl.*).

adj. good, excellent, fine, great, superb, splendid, magnificent, marvellous, wonderful, attractive, lovely; masterly, skilled, competent; praiseworthy, commendable; admirable, desirable, enticing, surprising, astonishing; super, terrific, out of this world (*inf.*), cool (*sl.*), neat (*sl.*), magic (*sl.*).

best, first-class, first-rate, optimum, premium, prime, highest, supreme, superlative, A-1, top-notch (*inf.*), tops; exceptional, incomparable, surpassing, incredible, unbelievable, excelling, exemplary; choice, select, exquisite, superior, capital (*inf.*); valuable, priceless, inestimable.

fair, pretty good, not bad, all right, O.K., passable, tolerable, adequate, middling, fair to middling.

vb. be good, have value, have quality; do good, benefit, help, edify.

see also 550, 844

580 badness

n. badness, nastiness, wickedness, vileness, foulness; inferiority, unsatisfactoriness, mediocrity; bane, ill wind, woe, spanner in the works, fly in the ointment.

adj. bad, wrong, awful, nasty, terrible, horrid, horrible; inferior, imperfect, defective, worthless, poor, second-rate, below average, deficient, unsatisfactory, mediocre, ordinary, unwholesome, shoddy, trashy, crummy (*sl.*), shabby; lousy (*sl.*), rotten; pitiful, contemptible, paltry.

harmful, damaging, detrimental, hurtful, destructive, fatal, deadly, corrupting, poisonous, corroding, toxic, venomous, subversive.

vb. be bad, have no value; do bad, harm, injure, hurt, wound, ruin, destroy, corrupt, subvert; vex, trouble, wrong.

see also 551

581 perfection

n. perfection, excellence, impeccability, faultlessness, stainlessness; maturity, completion, culmination, consummation.

ideal, standard, model, paragon, summit, ultimate, height, acme; showpiece, masterpiece, *pièce de résistance*.

adj. perfect, faultless, pure, flawless, impeccable, immaculate, untainted, unblemished, untarnished, stainless, spotless, unstained, uncontaminated, unadulterated, irreproachable, beyond compare, brilliant; supreme, ideal.

whole, sound, complete, entire, finished, developed, fulfilled, completed, accomplished, consummate.

vb. perfect, develop, complete, finish, bring to fruition, get down to a fine art, consummate.

582 imperfection

n. imperfection, impurity, defectiveness, inadequacy, immaturity; disfigurement, defacement, deformity, discoloration.

blemish, flaw, stain; fault, mistake, defect, lack, drawback, snag, loophole, weak spot, weak link in the chain.

adj. imperfect, flawed, defective, deficient, malformed, distorted, tainted, adulterated, blemished, damaged, injured, impaired.

incomplete, unfinished, unsound, uneven, unsatisfactory, faulty, inadequate, fallible.

vb. be imperfect, show faults, fall short, not come up to, be found wanting.

see also 847

583 cleanness

n. cleanness, cleanliness, pureness, spotlessness, whiteness; neatness, tidiness, orderliness, trimness; cleaning, washing, scrubbing, scouring, sprinkling; sterilization, disinfection; cleansing, purification, purgation, ablution.

adj. clean, tidy, neat; immaculate, white, spotless, stainless, untarnished, unblemished, unstained, unsullied, unpolluted, unsoiled, dirtless, spick and span, starched, laundered, polished; germ-free.

vb. clean, tidy, clear; wash, lather, shampoo; bathe, scrub, scour, sponge, mop, swab; brush, sweep; freshen, ventilate; disinfect, fumigate; sterilize, pasteurize; launder, starch, iron; cleanse, purify, sprinkle, purge, expurgate.

584 uncleanness

n. uncleanness, impurity, untidiness, disorderliness, muckiness, filthiness, pollution, defilement.

dirt, filth, spot, stain, smear, smudge, blot, muck, grime, grease, slime; squalor.

adj. unclean, dirty, soiled, polluted, tarnished, sullied, spotted, smeared, daubed, smudged, besmirched; filthy, grimy, greasy, muddy, sooty; squalid, foul, mucky; contaminated, decayed, rotten, rancid, putrid; sloppy, untidy, messy, slovenly, dishevelled, bedraggled, unkempt, like something the cat brought in (*inf.*), unwashed; defiled, unrefined, unpurified.

vb. be dirty, rust, decay, rot, collect dust; dirty, soil, sully, tarnish, daub, bedaub, smudge, blot, pollute, foul; mess up, untidy; corrupt, defile, debase, taint, contaminate, infect.

585 health

n. health, wholeness, soundness, healthfulness, healthiness, salubrity, wholesomeness, balance, vitality; sanity; fitness, strength, well-being, good health, rosy cheeks.

hygiene, sanitation, public health, cleanliness.

adj. healthy, well, sound, whole, wholesome, fit, strong, robust, vigorous, energetic, hale, hearty; all right, rosy-cheeked, flourishing, never feeling better, in fine fettle, in good shape, fighting fit.

healthful, invigorating, stimulating, bracing, beneficial, salubrious; nutritious, nourishing, body-building, restorative, therapeutic, corrective; good for one, what the doctor ordered; hygienic, sanitary.

vb. be healthy, flourish, feel fine; be good for.

586 ill health

n. ill health, poor health, bad health, frailty, weakness, infirmity, invalidity, unhealthiness, indisposition.

illness, disease, ailment, malady, sickness, complaint, disability, affliction, condition, disorder, breakdown, collapse, relapse; fever, infection, virus (*inf.*), bug (*sl.*), pain; bout, spell; stroke, fit, attack, seizure, spasm, convulsions.

lack of hygiene, insalubrity, uncleanliness, contagiousness, infectiousness.

adj. ill, unwell, ailing, weak, unhealthy, poorly, frail, infirm, sick; suffering, down with, indisposed, disabled; drooping, languishing, declining, bedridden, laid up, confined; run down, exhausted; under the weather (*inf.*), out of sorts, seedy (*inf.*), groggy (*inf.*).

unhygienic, insanitary, polluted, bad for, insalubrious; infectious, contagious, endemic; poisonous, toxic, deadly.

vb. be ill, be down with, suffer; fall ill, catch, become ill with, contract, go down with, get, be stricken with; show symptoms of, sicken for; waste away, droop, languish; be bad for, disagree with.

587 improvement

n. improvement, betterment, change, advance, development, refinement, progress, reformation, face-lift, amelioration; enrichment, promotion, furtherance, reform, modernization; revision, correction, amendment.

adj. improved, corrected, amended, revised, reformed, touched up; progressive, reformatory.

vb. improve, develop, further, better, reorganize, promote, reform, straighten out, mend, ameliorate; revise, update, upgrade, correct, rectify; polish, refine, enrich; decorate, beautify, touch up, refurbish; progress, make progress, get better, advance, profit; pick up, come on, rally; pull one's socks up (*inf.*); mellow, mature.

see also **288**

588 deterioration

n. deterioration, impairment, degeneration, decay, rotting, decomposition, erosion, rust; dilapidation, ruin, collapse, decadence, disintegration; impoverishment, adulteration, defilement, corruption, spoiling, detriment, pollution; retrogression; damage, injury, wound, lesion, cut, gash, sore, bruise.

adj. deteriorated, impaired, spoiled, decadent, ruined; damaged, harmed, desolate, ravaged, plundered, robbed, marred, mutilated; decayed, decomposed, rotten, putrified, foul, putrid; worn away, wasting away, emaciated, depleted; ramshackle, tumbledown.

vb. deteriorate, worsen, degenerate, decay, decline, slide, fall, slump, sink, go downhill, fall away, depreciate; go bad, rot, wither, crumble, the rot set in (*inf.*); wither, shrivel; spoil; go to pieces, break up, decompose, fade away, waste away, die; collapse, break down, founder, go to wrack and ruin, go to the dogs (*inf.*), go to pot (*inf.*); go off the rails (*inf.*).

impair, pervert, ruin, corrupt, distort; lower, pull down, reduce, degrade, dehumanize, adulterate, defile, deprave, infect, contaminate; eat away, erode, corrode.

harm, damage, injure, wound, savage, cripple, lame; maltreat, misuse; disgrace, dishonour, discredit; exacerbate, aggravate; hold against (*inf.*), count against; confuse, mess up (*inf.*).

589 restoration

n. restoration, healing, cure, recovery, convalescence, recuperation; renovation, repair, reconditioning, refurbishing, reconstruction, remaking; rehabilitation, re-establishment, resumption, reinstatement, return, getting back to normal; reparation, restitution, amends; reclamation, salvage, rescue.

revival, renewal, reawakening, reinvigoration, resuscitation, rebirth, regeneration, resurrection, renaissance, resurgence, rejuvenation; Indian summer, face-lift, new look, comeback.

adj. restored, repaired, re-established, back to normal; restorative, corrective, remedial, recuperative, therapeutic, soothing, curative.

vb. restore, rebuild, reconstruct, remodel, refashion, reorganize, recondition, reform, remake, revamp, renovate, modernize; repair, mend, fix; refurbish, touch up; darn, patch, sew.

put right, correct, rectify, amend, redress; return, recompense, refund, make amends, make restitution, reinstate, put back, reinstall, re-establish, resume, return to normal; reclaim, salvage, rescue, retrieve, redeem.

revive, refresh, renew, recreate, reanimate, regenerate, resurrect, resuscitate, rejuvenate, reawaken, revitalize, rekindle.

cure, heal, treat, minister to, nurse, rehabilitate, put on one's feet again.

be restored, recover, convalesce, recuperate, get well, get better, fall on one's feet (*inf.*), pick up, rally, pull through, gain strength, get back into circulation (*inf.*); come up smiling (*inf.*).

see also **618**

590 relapse

n. relapse, return, reversion, retrogression, regression; deterioration, declension; apostasy.

vb. relapse, regress, retrogress, deteriorate, degenerate, sink back, slip back, revert, suffer, relapse; backslide, fall from grace, apostasize.

see also **289**

591 remedy

n. remedy, cure, relief, assistance, treatment, medication; medicine, medicament, preparation, prescription, pharmaceutical, drug; mixture, dose, potion, linctus; pill, tablet, capsule, lozenge; vaccine, injection, inoculation, jab (*inf.*), shot (*inf.*); lotion, ointment, balm salve; tonic, pick-me-up, stimulant, restorative, refresher, tranquillizer. sedative; panacea, cure-all, elixir; operation, surgery.

adj. remedial, therapeutic, healing, medicinal, corrective, curative, restorative.

vb. remedy, cure, heal, restore; treat, attend, practise; relieve, support, help, mitigate, soothe, palliate; send for the doctor, send to hospital, dial 999, hospitalize, operate; undergo treatment, take pills, take one's medicine.

592 bane

n. bane, curse, plague, evil, scourge, affliction, trial, cross, thorn in the flesh; pain in the neck (*inf.*); weakness, besetting sin; poison, venom, virus; blight, mildew, rust, mould, rot, fungus, gangrene, cancer.

adj. baneful, evil, pestilent; deadly, poisonous, venomous; harmful, destructive.

593 safety

n. safety, security, surety, impregnability, invulnerability, immunity; protection, defence, safekeeping, custody, guardianship, supervision, care; law and order.

protector, guard, defender; custodian, warden, curator, keeper, trustee; life-guard, bodyguard, guardian; patrol, lookout, scout, night watchman, watchdog, vigilante, sentry, policeman.

adj. safe, secure, impregnable, invulnerable, unassailable; protected, guarded, safeguarded, defended, shielded, sheltered; unharmed, unhurt, safe and sound, unscathed; waterproof, bulletproof.

vb. make safe, safeguard, protect, keep, guard, defend, shelter, screen, shield, harbour; supervise, care for, mind, look after, take charge of, keep an eye on, attend to, take under one's wing; keep order, patrol, police, be on the lookout, keep vigil, keep cave (*sl.*); hide, lie low, go to earth.

adv. out of danger, in the clear, out of harm's way, in safe hands, under one's wing, under lock and key.

see also **595**

594 danger

n. danger, peril, risk, hazard, jeopardy; menace, threat; dangerousness, perilousness, riskiness, insecurity, precariousness, vulnerability, exposure, openness, helplessness; weak spot.

adj. dangerous, perilous, hazardous, risky, insecure, precarious, alarming, unsafe, treacherous, slippery, shaky, unstable; unsheltered, unshielded, vulnerable, exposed, open, naked, unfortified; menacing, threatening, ominous; critical, serious, delicate, explosive.

vb. endanger, jeopardize, put in jeopardy, expose, lay open to, risk, run the risk of, render liable to, court disaster, tempt providence.

595 refuge

n. refuge, shelter, sanctuary, asylum, retreat; home, ivory tower, port, harbour, haven; den, lair, nest, covert; castle, fortress, stronghold; safeguard, protection, defence; cover, screen, shade, shield, umbrella, wind-break; escape, way out, recourse, last resort.

see also 593, 646

596 pitfall

n. pitfall, trap, snare, ambush, booby-trap; reef, rock, sandbank, quicksand, undercurrent; danger spot, black spot, trouble spot; trouble-maker, wrecker, snake in the grass.

597 warning

n. warning, caution, lesson, example, advice, counsel, caveat; alert, hint, intimation, admonition, tip-off (*inf.*), early warning, writing on the wall, symptom, sign, omen, augury; foreboding, premonition; notice, indication, notification; call, cry, shout.

adj. warning, cautionary, advisory, instructive.

vb. warn, caution, advise, alert, admonish, counsel, encourage, exhort, hint, prompt, suggest; forewarn, tip off (*inf.*); notify, inform, give notice, apprise.

see also 460

598 indication of danger

n. alarm, alert, bell, alarm bell, fire alarm; siren, horn, fog-horn, klaxon, tocsin; light, red light, warning light; red alert; SOS, distress signal; beacon; war-cry, drum-beat; false alarm, hoax, scare.

vb. give the alarm, raise the alarm, dial 999, alert, put on the alert; cry wolf.

599 preservation

n. preservation, protection, maintenance, saving, keeping, conservation; storage, canning, freezing, refrigeration, dehydration.

adj. preservative, protective; preserved, kept, intact, protected; fresh, well-preserved.

vb. preserve, maintain, keep, protect, look after; conserve, keep fresh, bottle, can, tin, season, cure, salt, dry, smoke, freeze, refrigerate, freeze-dry, dehydrate, pickle, spice, marinade; embalm, mummify.

600 escape

n. escape, flight, departure, getaway; evasion, avoidance, abdication, desertion, disappearance; freedom, release, deliverance, rescue; retreat, withdrawal; narrow escape, close shave, near miss, near thing.

exit, way out, overflow, vent, waste-pipe, exhaust, leak, leakage, life-line, loophole.

escaper, runaway, truant, dodger, fugitive, refugee.

adj. escaped, free, out, at large, at liberty, missing, wanted.

vb. escape, flee, take flight, abscond, leave, depart, break loose, break out, decamp, free, get clear of, get away with, make one's getaway, make oneself scarce, give the slip, slip through one's fingers, elude, avoid, evade, elope, play truant; emerge, issue, burst out.

see also 921

601 deliverance

n. deliverance, saving, rescue, release, freeing, liberation, relief; extrication, unbinding, loosening, disentanglement; ransom, forgiveness, pardon; remission, discharge, acquittal, reprieve, exoneration; emancipation, affranchisement, manumission.

vb. deliver, rescue, release, free, discharge, relieve; remit, acquit, let off (*inf.*), exonerate; extricate, loosen, untie; emancipate, liberate; salvage, retrieve; save, redeem, ransom, pardon, forgive.

see also 680, 911

602 preparation

n. preparation, plan, step, arrange-ment; outline, draft, scheme, foun-dation, groundwork, spadework; rehearsal, practice, training, dummy run; approach, run-up (*inf.*); prepared-ness, readiness, fitness, experience, all systems go (*inf.*); red alert.

adj. preparatory, introductory, ini-tial; prepared, ready, alert, waiting, on call, standing by, all set; experienced, skilled, qualified, versed, seasoned, broken in.

ready-made, prefabricated, ready-mixed, treated; frozen, pre-cooked, processed, dehydrated, ready-to-eat, oven-ready, instant; off-the-peg.

vb. prepare, get ready, arrange, plan, make preparations; settle, decide; adapt, adjust, fit, equip, supply, deck out, fit out, provide; take steps, take measures; practise, rehearse, train, study, hold in readiness; clear the decks, lay the foundations, prepare the ground, pave the way, smooth the way, blaze a trail, do the groundwork, do one's homework, break the ice.

see also 558

603 non-preparation

n. non-preparation, unpreparedness, lack of training, inexperience; immaturity, rawness, naivety.

adj. unprepared, unready, napping, surprised, taken aback, unguarded, off one's guard, with one's pants down (*sl.*); unorganized, makeshift, hasty, rush (*inf.*); thoughtless; inexperienced,

unskilled, uninstructed, untrained, unqualified, unequipped; new, naive, raw, immature; undeveloped, half-baked; backward, developing; fallow, virgin.

vb. be unprepared, be taken unawares, be caught napping; not plan, make no provision for; improvise.

604 attempt

n. attempt, try, effort, trial, experi-ment, endeavour, essay, undertaking, enterprise, venture.

adj. experimental, probationary, tentative, trial.

vb. attempt, try, have a try, make an effort, endeavour, venture, seek, aim for, strive, contend, risk, aspire, contest, have a go, lift a finger, put oneself out, have a crack at (*inf.*), have a shot at (*inf.*), have a stab at (*inf.*).

605 undertaking

n. undertaking, enterprise, project, plan, programme, cause, pursuit, campaign, operation, exercise, venture, exploit, feat; occupation, business, job, task, work, concern, matter in hand, proposition, engagement, commit-ment, obligation.

adj. enterprising, adventurous, ven-turesome, daring, go-ahead, pioneer-ing, progressive, up-and-coming; ambitious, aspiring.

vb. undertake, engage in, go in for, do, take part in, participate in, devote oneself to; manage, engage, promise, contract; take upon oneself, put one's hand to, commit oneself to, take on, assume, shoulder, bear the burden of, tackle, embark on, enter upon, set down to (*inf.*), launch into, plunge into, commence, begin, start, set to, broach, set about; get down to business, get one's teeth into (*inf.*), take the bit between the teeth (*inf.*), get down to brass tacks (*inf.*), get to grips with.

adv. in hand, under control, in order.

see also **88**

606 use

n. use, usage, application, practice, exercise, employment, management, conduct, realization, adoption, conversion, treatment, handling, performance, control; method, technique; utility, usefulness.

adj. used, applied, utilized, adopted, accepted, practised; in use, in service, in force; old, second-hand.

vb. use, employ, apply, utilize, put to use, put into service; realize, adopt, draw on, take advantage of; adapt, convert, relate, bring to bear, resort to, have recourse to, fall back on; manage, conduct, deal with, treat, handle; exploit, use to the full, get the most out of, cash in on (*inf.*), capitalize, get the benefit of.

see also **575**

607 disuse

n. disuse, non-use, discontinuance, suspension, abolition, rejection, relinquishment, abandonment, unemployment, abeyance; obsolescence.

adj. disused, neglected, abandoned, idle, abolished, deserted, derelict; unused, unemployed, unspent; out of order, out of service, inactive; extra, spare.

vb. disuse, suspend, abolish, put aside, have done with, reject, get rid of, throw out, jettison, discard, scrap, throw on the scrap-heap, neglect, abandon, desert, relinquish.

608 misuse

n. misuse, abuse, misapplication, misemployment, mishandling, mismanagement, misappropriation; per-version, debasement, degradation, prostitution, desecration, defilement, profanation, pollution; outrage, violation; error, mistake.

vb. misuse, abuse, mistreat, ill-treat, maltreat, mishandle, misemploy, misappropriate; pervert, prostitute, debase, desecrate, defile, violate, deprave, profane; wrong, insult, injure, hurt, harm, malign; squander, waste.

C Voluntary action

609 action

n. action, doing, execution, commission, operation, management, handling.

act, deed, thing, work, job, activity, feat, exploit; performance, achievement, undertaking, accomplishment; move, step, measure; blow, stroke.

doer, performer, worker, workman; instrument.

adj. doing, in operation, in process, operative.

vb. act, do, conduct, operate, work, function.

achieve, accomplish, complete, fulfil, carry out, bring about, execute, realize, effect, perform, dispose of, commit, transact, put into effect, put into action, put into operation.

take action, take steps, do something about, specialize in, concern oneself with, make it one's business, go in for; persist, persevere, keep going.

see also **611, 615**

610 inaction

n. inaction, rest, waiting, inertia, suspension, abeyance; laissez-faire, dormancy, neglect, stagnation.

adj. inoperative, idle, unemployed; suspended, in abeyance.

vb. not act, wait, pause, hang fire, bide one's time, twiddle one's thumbs, hold your horses (*inf.*); wait and see, do nothing, abstain, refrain; leave alone, have nothing to do with, let sleeping dogs lie.

see also 612

611 activity

n. activity, liveliness, agility, nimbleness, alertness, alacrity, readiness, keenness, eagerness; energy, life, vigour, spirit, verve, zest, dynamism, enthusiasm, get-up-and-go (*inf.*); hurry, bustle, flurry, rush, commotion, rat-race.

industry, diligence, assiduousness, perseverance, resolution, determination, application, concentration; enterprise, initiative; activism, militancy, aggressiveness.

busy person, enthusiast, zealot, activist, fanatic, militant, live wire.

adj. active, lively, energetic, dynamic; busy, hard at it, eventful, bustling, dashing, raring to go; alert, agile, nimble, sharp, spry, wire, alive, restless, fidgety.

enthusiastic, keen, zealous; pushy (*inf.*), ambitious, aggressive, forceful, activist, militant, go-ahead, enterprising; industrious, diligent, hardworking, studious.

vb. be active, be busy, rush around, bustle about, have one's hands full, have a finger in every pie; have many irons in the fire; busy oneself in, stir oneself, rouse onself; persevere, keep going, keep at it; work hard, not have a moment to spare, never stop, overwork, overdo it, have no time to call one's own.

see also 532, 609

612 inactivity

n. inactivity, stillness, inertia; lethargy, slackness, sluggishness, torpor, lifelessness, listlessness; apathy, indifference, carelessness; idleness, laziness, indolence, sloth.

fatigue, tiredness, weariness, sleepiness; sleep, slumber, rest, doze, nod, snooze, shut-eye, catnap, forty winks, siesta, repose, dormancy; breather, pause, holiday, vacation.

lazy person, idler, loafer (*inf.*), good-for-nothing, lazy-bones, bum (*sl.*), tramp, sluggard, wastrel, parasite, sponger.

adj. inactive, still, stable; unemployed, unoccupied, fallow, barren; idle, lazy, slothful, indolent, lethargic, slack, sluggish, listless, torpid, languid; unadventurous, unenterprising, stay-at-home; apathetic, indifferent, uninterested.

tired, weary, drowsy, sleepy, fatigued, somnolent, dormant; exhausted, run down, overworked, worn out, washed out, drooping, faint, weak, stale.

vb. be inactive, rest, relax, pause, bide one's time; drift, vegetate, stagnate.

idle, loaf about (*inf.*), mooch about (*sl.*), loiter about, hang about (*inf.*), bum around (*sl.*); dilly-dally, shilly-shally, languish; kill time, waste time, while away the time.

sleep, slumber, doze, drowse, snooze, take a nap, nod off, have forty winks, yawn, dream; go to bed, turn in, kip down (*sl.*), hit the sack (*sl.*).

see also 533, 617, 841

613 haste

n. haste, rush, hurry, scramble, scurry, flurry, hurly-burly; dash, spirit, spurt, run, burst, sprint, bolt, race;

hurriedness, hastiness, urgency, promptness, precipitation, rashness, impulsiveness, impetuosity.

adj. hasty, quick, fast, swift, speedy, hurried, dashing; impetuous, impulsive, rash, inconsiderate, reckless, foolhardy, precipitate, headlong, impatient.

vb. hasten, quicken, speed up, accelerate, expedite, dispatch, stimulate, fillip, urge, goad, whip, incite, push through, rush through, railroad through (*inf.*).

rush, sprint, spurt, scurry, scuttle, dash, bustle, zoom, tear, bomb (*inf.*), go all out (*inf.*), step on it (*inf.*).

see also **280, 544, 859**

614 leisure

n. leisure, free time, spare time, time off, recreation, relaxation, rest, respite, breather, break, pause, lull, recess; holiday, leave, leave of absence, vacation, sabbatical, furlough, home leave.

adj. leisurely, resting, unoccupied.

vb. have time to spare, be off, take one's ease, relax, rest.

adv. off, off duty, on holiday; at leisure, at one's convenience, at an early opportunity.

see also **281, 840**

615 exertion

n. exertion, effort, panic, trouble, toil, labour, work, travail, strife, strain, tension, elbow grease, drudgery; hard work, handful (*inf.*), uphill task, sweat (*sl.*), drudge.

adj. laborious, arduous, hard, difficult, strenuous, onerous, painstaking, gruelling, punishing, uphill, back-breaking.

vb. exert oneself, try, attempt; take pains, work, labour, fight, toil, contend, struggle, strive, sweat blood; knuckle

down (*inf.*), get down to it (*inf.*), buckle down (*inf.*); drudge, grind, plod (*inf.*), plug away (*inf.*), slog away, sweat one's guts out (*sl.*); make heavy weather of, make a meal of; put oneself out, do one's best, do one's utmost, go to all lengths, go all out, leave no stone unturned, move heaven and earth, pull out all the stops (*inf.*); overdo it, have one's work cut out.

see also **535, 611**

616 repose

n. repose, rest, relaxation, inaction; breather, break, pause, coffee-break, tea-break, lunch-break, lunch-hour, rest period; day of rest, Sabbath, Lord's Day; ease, quiet, quietness, tranquillity.

adj. restful, tranquil, quiet, calm, peaceful; sabbatical.

vb. rest, be quiet, stop, halt; take a rest, take it easy, let up, ease off, slow down, stretch one's legs, have a break; get away from it all (*inf.*).

see also **610, 618**

617 fatigue

n. fatigue, tiredness, weariness, sleepiness, heaviness, drowsiness, doziness, somnolence; faintness, weakness. exhaustion, collapse, staleness, jadedness; lassitude, languor.

adj. tired, weary, exhausted, run down, fagged out (*inf.*), worn out, ready to drop (*inf.*), dog-tired, dead beat, all in, whacked (*inf.*); heavy, dozy (*inf.*), drowsy, sleepy; weak, faint, dropping, haggard; washed out, drained, stale, jaded.

vb. be tired, drop, collapse, flag, jade, peg out (*inf.*), flake out (*sl.*); faint, pass out (*inf.*), lose consciousness; work too hard, overdo it.

weary, tire, fatigue, wear out,

exhaust, take it out of (*inf.*), fag out (*inf.*), strain; bore.

see also **612, 841**

618 refreshment

n. refreshment, enlivenment, invigoration, recovery, restoration, convalescence, recuperation, relief.

adj. refreshing, restoring, invigorating, exhilarating, bracing, stimulating, arousing; refreshed, invigorated, like a new man.

vb. refresh, restore, arouse, revive, enliven, animate, strengthen, stimulate, invigorate, renew, reawaken, bring round, give new life to, energize, improve, relieve, resuscitate, vivify; encourage, cheer.

recover, recuperate, pick up, perk up, recharge one's batteries, get one's breath back.

see also **589, 616**

619 agent

n. agent, doer, actor, performer, participant, instrument, medium, practitioner, executor; worker, workman, operator, mechanic, labourer, operative, craftsman, skilled worker; apprentice; hack, drudge, slave, fag.

workforce, employees, staff, personnel, labour, payroll, manpower, resources.

620 workshop

n. workshop, workplace, establishment, installation, institution, plant, factory, works, foundry, yard; shop, house, office, bureau, branch, station, laboratory; firm, company, concern, industry.

621 conduct

n. conduct, behaviour, manner, deportment, demeanour, air, carriage, bearing, posture, attitude, comportment, mien, delivery, appearance,

guise; guidance, control, oversight, supervision, superintendence, execution, government, management, organization; strategy, tactics, policy, campaign, programme.

adj. behavioural; tactical, strategical.

vb. behave, act, conduct; acquit oneself, bear oneself, comport oneself, pose, appear, seem; behave oneself, mind one's manners, mind one's P's and Q's, be on one's best behaviour; manage, guide, supervise, direct, regulate, administer.

622 management

n. management, conduct, guidance, direction, control, order, charge, power, execution, government, organization, administration, decision making, handling, regulation, legislation, jurisdiction; oversight, supervision, superintendence, surveillance, command, authority, leadership; stewardship, husbandry, housekeeping, economics.

adj. directive, managerial, controlling, supervisory; executive, administrative, governmental, gubernatorial, legislative; official, bureaucratic.

vb. manage, conduct, run, guide, direct, lead, control, regulate, order, govern, command, steer, point the way, decide; handle, execute, administer, organize, legislate; supervise, superintend; steward.

623 director

n. manager, director, controller, leader, executive, governor, politician, minister, legislator, commander; dictator; superintendent, supervisor, inspector, overseer, foreman; steward; administrator, official, bureaucrat, functionary, secretary; guide, organizer.

see also **34, 675**

624 advice

n. advice, suggestion, opinion, view, counsel, guidance, encouragement, information, instruction, recommendation; warning, admonition, criticism, dissuasion, caution, notice; notification.

advisor, counsellor, right-hand man, friend, confidant, teacher, informant, helper, consultant; think-tank.

adj. advisory, consultative.

vb. advise, guide, direct, tell, have a word with, suggest; exhort, urge, prompt, encourage, persuade, recommend, counsel; warn, admonish, dissuade; inform, notify, acquaint.

consult, ask, discuss, talk over, seek the opinion of, seek advice, turn to, confide in.

625 council

n. council, cabinet, committee, government, parliament, board, directorate, board of governors; congress, conference, assembly, convention, synod, convocation, diet; panel, forum, brains trust.

councillor, minister, member of parliament, back-bencher, parliamentarian, statesman, senator, congressman; delegate, representative, officer.

626 precept

n. precept, maxim, command, direction, instruction, prescription, principle, law, statute, commandment, rule; canon, doctrine, law, charge, mandate, injunction, edict; formula, recipe.

see also **103, 954**

627 skill

n. skill, capability, proficiency, competence, skilfulness, expertness, ability, aptitude, talent, gift, genius, endowment, flaw, strong point, forte, what it takes, knack; experience, practice, training, qualifications, expertise, know-how, judgment; adeptness, deftness, adroitness, facility.

adj. skilful, capable, able, proficient, competent, effective, clever; experienced, trained, qualified, fit, suited, cut out for (*inf.*), accomplished, well-versed, expert, veteran; gifted, endowed; handy, adept, deft, adroit, agile, dexterous; all-round, versatile; enterprising, inventive.

vb. be good at, shine at, have what it takes; be expert, know backwards, know the ropes (*inf.*), know the ins and outs (*inf.*).

628 unskilfulness

n. unskilfulness, inability, ineptitude, inexperience, greenness, weak point, incompetence, inefficiency, mismanagement; awkwardness, clumsiness; botch-up, hash, mess, cock-up (*inf.*).

adj. unskilful, inexperienced, uneducated, unqualified, incompetent, amateur, unsuited, unused to, lay, amateurish, unprofessional, do-it-yourself, scratch; butterfingers; awkward, clumsy, heavy-handed, bungling, maladroit; impracticable, home-made, Heath Robinson; unwieldy, cumbersome, bulky.

vb. be no good at (*inf.*), spoil, bungle, ruin, botch, mismanage, mishandle, make a mess of, make a hash of, mess up (*inf.*), louse up (*sl.*), screw up (*sl.*), cock up (*sl.*), put one's foot in it; misfire.

629 expert

n. expert, master, adept, proficient,

handyman, Jack-of-all-trades, man of many parts, man of many talents; professional, authority, specialist, scholar, genius, whizz-kid (*inf.*), veteran, old hand; man of the world.

see also **436**

630 bungler

n. bungler, fumbler, botcher, muddler, dunce, idiot, blockhead, scatterbrain, ignoramus; butterfingers; beginner, novice, greenhorn; amateur, layman; lout, lubber.

see also **437**

631 cunning

n. cunning, craftiness, intrigue, deceit, guile, artfulness, craft, subtlety, slyness, wiliness, cleverness, shrewdness, chicanery, finesse.

stratagem, artifice, trick, deception, plot, scheme, ruse, wile, dodge, trap, little game (*inf.*), con (*sl.*), hoax, fabrication, double-dealing, casuistry.

artful dodger, hypocrite, fraud, cheat, plotter, con-man (*sl.*), trickster, slippery customer (*inf.*), smooth talker (*inf.*).

adj. cunning, shrewd, crafty, artful, sly, wily, deceptive, subtle, dishonest, fraudulent, unscrupulous, underhand, shifty, smart, shady, smooth, slippery, sharp, clever (*inf.*), too clever by half (*inf.*).

vb. be cunning, trick, deceive, fraud, cheat, trap, hoax, con (*sl.*), plot, scheme, contrive, pull a fast one (*sl.*), put one over on (*inf.*), put one across (*inf.*), outwit, get the better of.

632 artlessness

n. artlessness, simplicity, innocence, naivety, simple-mindedness, guilelessness, ingenuousness; child, babe.

adj. artless, innocent, simple, naive,

simple-minded, guileless, unaffected, natural, uncomplicated, straightforward, ingenuous, childlike, unsophisticated, genuine, frank, open, candid, forthright.

vb. be natural, wear one's heart on one's sleeve; speak one's mind, not mince words.

D Antagonism

633 difficulty

n. difficulty, problem, headache, trouble, tall order, handful, heavy going; dilemma, predicament, quandary, strait, plight, embarrassment, fix, pickle (*inf.*), scrape, tight spot (*inf.*), hole (*sl.*); hardship, arduousness, laboriousness, troublesomeness; perplexity.

adj. difficult, hard, tough, laborious, arduous, uphill, strenuous; awkward, burdensome, trying, troublesome, bothersome, wearisome; unclear, obscure, knotty, thorny, baffling, perplexing, complicated, intricate.

vb. be in difficulties, flounder, have a hard time, strike a bad patch, make heavy weather of, make a meal of, not keep one's head above water; get into difficulty, get into hot water; put one's foot in it (*inf.*); beset, trouble, harm, disconcert, discourage, inconvenience, embarrass; baffle, perplex, put on the spot (*inf.*).

adv. in deep water, in difficulty, on the horns of a dilemma, in a quandary, in a spot, in hot water, in trouble.

see also **615, 635**

634 ease

n. ease, facility, straightforwardness; child's play, plain sailing, piece of cake (*inf.*), nothing to it (*inf.*), walk-over (*inf.*), push-over (*inf.*), cinch (*sl.*).

adj. easy, simple, cushy (*inf.*), manageable, facile; obvious, apparent; pleasant, comfortable; clear, uncomplicated; effortless.

vb. be easy, require no effort, present no difficulties, give no trouble, run smoothly, go like clockwork; take in one's stride.

ease, facilitate, smooth the way, free, relieve, rid, get rid of, lighten, release, disentangle; take a weight off someone's mind (*inf.*).

635 hindrance

n. hindrance, impedance, intervention, interruption; restriction, prohibition, restraint, check, blockage; retardation, curb, arrest, drag; inconvenience, hitch, setback, hold-up, bottleneck, catch, snag, spanner in the works (*inf.*), encumbrance, chain, menace.

obstacle, obstruction, barrier, impediment, interference, stumbling-block, barricade, hurdle, bar, impasse, cul de sac.

adj. hindering, restraining, preventive.

vb. hinder, prevent, thwart, frustrate, hamper, trammel; stop, check, restrain, foil, confine, retard, arrest; deter, prohibit, restrict, bar, forbid, encumber, burden, chain, fetter, shackle; interfere, meddle; obstruct, block, impede, barricade; spoil, gum up the works (*sl.*).

see also 633, 665

636 aid

n. aid, help, assistance; helping hand, leg up; encouragement, comfort, relief, succour, alleviation, mitigation; favour, benevolence, service; advice, backing, guidance.

financial aid, giving, support, maintenance, charity; compensation, allowance, grant, subsidy, benefit, stipend, honorarium, expenses; patronage, sponsorship, promotion, advancement.

adj. helpful, beneficial, assisting; auxiliary.

vb. help, aid, assist, cooperate; encourage, stand by, back up, sustain, bolster, relieve, comfort, succour, save, rescue, abet; lend a hand, play one's part; befriend, advise, serve, minister to, take under one's wing.

patronize, finance, support, keep, maintain, promote, subsidize, foster, shoulder, sponsor, sanction.

see also 217, 639

637 opposition

n. opposition, antagonism, confrontation, repugnance, defiance, hostility, abhorrence, aversion, incompatibility, polarity; dislike, dissension, contradiction.

adj. opposing, antagonistic, defiant; hostile.

vb. oppose, counter, conflict with, fly in the face of, run counter to; confront, fight, combat, hinder, obstruct, thwart; object, dispute, contradict; resist, defy, deny, not have any part in, part company with, disapprove, disagree.

see also 648, 883

638 opponent

n. opponent, antagonist, adversary, enemy, foe, the opposition, competitor, challenger, candidate, entrant, rival, contestant.

see also 883

639 cooperation

n. cooperation, collaboration, participation, partnership, fellowship, brotherhood, harmony; give and take, teamwork, solidarity; amalgamation, merger, fusion, affiliation, membership; help, assistance.

adj. cooperative, collaborative, participatory; associated.

vb. cooperate, collaborate, give and take, help each other out, play ball with; contribute, help.

join, combine, unite, merge, club together, affiliate, join forces, pool together, pool resources, stand together, stick together (*inf.*), pull together; share, take part in, participate, throw in one's lot, go along with, team up with, take sides; gang up against (*inf.*); put one's heads together (*inf.*).

see also **180, 709**

640 auxiliary

n. auxiliary, helper, assistant, aid, ancillary, collaborator, helping hand, partner, associate, colleague, fellow-worker, co-worker, team-mate, sidekick (*inf.*); accomplice, confederate; friend, companion, ally, comrade; follower, adherent, disciple; hanger-on; patron, backer, supporter; right-hand man, stalwart, tower of strength.

see also **636**

641 party

n. party, group, movement, organization, society, band, body; council, congress, alliance, association, confederation, federation, league, coalition, union; community, fellowship, brotherhood; company, firm, establishment, concern, cooperative, cartel, syndicate.

faction, sect, denomination, tradition, splinter-group, clique, coterie, inner circle.

adj. federal, allied, confederate,

cooperative; exclusive, cliquish, partisan, sectarian.

vb. join, enrol, become a member of, affiliate, subscribe; associate with, side with.

642 discord

n. discord, dissension, trouble, difference, disagreement, misunderstanding, cross purposes, variance, ill feeling, tension, friction; divisiveness, troublesomeness, quarrelsomeness, rivalry.

dispute, quarrel, row, fight, argument, squabble, bickering, tiff, vendetta, feud; schism, split, rift, parting of the ways.

adj. discordant, disagreeing, divisive; contradictory; quarrelsome, troublesome, violent, factious, pugnacious, harsh, uncooperative, bolshie (*sl.*).

vb. differ, clash, conflict, dissent; fall out with, part company with; break up.

dispute, contend, fight, struggle, strive, come to blows, complain, object, argue, disagree; quarrel, wrangle, squabble, bicker; have a bone to pick with, have words with, take issue with; look for trouble (*inf.*), ask for it (*inf.*), rub up the wrong way (*inf.*), tread on someone's toes.

adv. at loggerheads, at odds, at variance, at sixes and sevens, not on speaking terms.

see also **25, 893**

643 concord

n. concord, agreement, harmony, conformity, understanding, consonance, rapport, goodwill, friendship, amity, concert, accord, consensus, unanimity, unity, *détente*, *rapprochement*, entente, entente cordiale.

adj. agreeing, harmonious, friendly,

peaceful, amicable, reconciled, unanimous, united.

vb. agree, get on with, get along with, hit it off (*inf.*), see eye to eye, be at one with; come to an understanding.

see also **24, 699**

644 defiance

n. defiance, disobedience, rebellion, insubordination, insolence, obstinacy; mutiny, revolt, revolution; challenge, dare.

adj. defiant, bold, daring, proud; unruly, rebellious, disobedient, insubordinate; independent, lawless, anarchistic, militant.

vb. defy, confront, brave, challenge, dare, fling down the gauntlet, call one's bluff; resist, disobey, oppose, disregard, flout, spurn, laugh at, scorn, taunt; rebel, revolt, insult, protest, kick against, kick against the pricks.

see also **648**

645 attack

n. attack, assault, onslaught, aggression, advance, charge, push, thrust, drive, outbreak, outburst, raid, offensive, storm, skirmish, foray, sally, sortie; invasion, intrusion, inroad, incursion, encroachment; siege, barrage, bombardment, blitz; mugging, rape.

attacker, aggressor, assailant, fighter, raider, stormer, invader, enemy, intruder, sniper, ravager; mugger, rapist.

adj. attacking, assaulting, aggressive.

vb. attack, assault, advance, charge, rush, push, thrust, assail, fight; raid, invade, storm, sally, sortie, foray; intrude, encroach; besiege, lay siege to, blockade; ravage, lay waste; fire, shoot, snipe; bomb, bombard; beat up, do over (*sl.*), smash somone's face in (*inf.*), mug, rob, rape.

646 defence

n. defence, protection, guarding, security; fortification, castle, fort, fortress, stronghold, keep, bastion, citadel, garrison; trenches, ditch, moat; embankment, rampart, battlement, earthworks; armour.

defender, guard, watch, sentry; protector, champion.

adj. defended, guarded, safe; defensive, armed, watchful.

vb. defend, protect, guard, keep, keep safe, safeguard, secure, shield, shelter, screen; withstand, beat off, ward off, fend off, drive back, take evasive action; spring to someone's defence; strengthen, reinforce, fortify; arm, cover, camouflage.

see also **593**

647 retaliation

n. retaliation, reprisal, revenge, reaction, backlash, counterattack, counterinsurgence, second-strike capability; measure for measure, an eye for an eye, tit for tat, just deserts; requital, repayment, vengeance, punishment, retribution; recrimination; retort, riposte.

adj. retaliatory, retributive, reciprocal.

vb. retaliate, hit back, strike back, fight back, get back (*inf.*), defend oneself; requite, avenge, revenge, punish, return, repay, vindicate, pay back, settle up, get square, get one's own back, give tit for tat, get even with; reciprocate, return the compliment, give someone a dose of his own medicine; retort, counter, recriminate.

see also **912**

648 resistance

n. resistance, withstanding, defence, stand, check; steadfastness, renitence.

adj. resisting, recalcitrant, hard-hearted.

vb. resist, withstand, not give in, not submit, repel, stand up to, not take lying down, stand fast; stay, defend, hold off, oppose, prevent, thwart, foil, frustrate, obstruct, attack; counteract, neutralize; endure, suffer, tolerate; persevere, hold out, stick it out (*inf.*); maintain, take one's stand, stand one's ground, stick one's heels in (*inf.*), stick to one's guns, hold one's own.

see also 535, 644

649 contest

n. contest, engagement, fight, battle, war, encounter, confrontation, action, skirmish, feud, *mêlée*, set-to, tussle, scrap (*sl.*), brush, affray, altercation; duel, joust, warfare, hostilities; conflict, strife, struggle, bloodshed, onslaught, carnage.

game, match, event, rally, race, challenge; competition, round, tournament; sport, recreation.

adj. contending, contestant; competitive.

vb. contend, fight, oppose, combat, confront, challenge, encounter, engage in battle, campaign, battle, brush with, dispute, strive, struggle, scrap (*sl.*), set to, take on, tussle, joust, assert oneself; compete, contest, race, vie with.

see also 651, 655

650 peace

n. peace, absence of hostilities, armistice, truce, treaty; pacification, conciliation, reconciliation, love, friendship, agreement, harmony, accord; cold war, peaceful coexistence.

adj. peaceful, quiet, tranquil; bloodless, nonaggressive; pacifist; appeasing, conciliatory, peace-making.

see also 24, 652

651 war

n. war, hostilities, combat, fighting, warfare, attack, battle, campaign, operation, mission, action, contention.

aggressiveness, warlikeness, belligerence, militancy, warmongering, pugnacity.

adj. warlike, aggressive, militant, pugnacious, belligerent, martial, threatening, contentious, warmongering, unfriendly, bellicose, up in arms, on the warpath; fighting, warring.

vb. wage war, engage in hostilities, attack, invade, contend, strive; declare war, go to war; mobilize, call up, recruit, enlist, conscript, muster.

see also 645, 649

652 pacification

n. pacification, peace-making, appeasement, conciliation, reconciliation, reparation, satisfaction, assuagement, alleviation, mollification, soothing, calming; propitiation, atonement.

peace-offering, sacrifice, placation, gift; white flag, olive branch.

adj. pacificatory, placatory, propitiatory; irenic.

vb. pacify, conciliate; appease, satisfy, sacrifice, atone, propitiate; quiet, calm, still, moderate, quell; soften, alleviate, assuage, mollify, placate, tranquillize; reconcile, harmonize, bring together, bring to terms, settle one's differences, accommodate; make peace, bury the hatchet; make it up, shake hands.

see also 650

653 mediation

n. mediation, arbitration, interposition, intervention, shuttle diplomacy.

mediator, arbitrator, go-between, intermediary, arbiter, negotiator, peace-maker, trouble-shooter, intercessor, third party; judge, referee, umpire; adjudicator, assessor; neutral, independent.

adj. mediatory, intercessory.

vb. mediate, arbitrate, negotiate, reconcile, hear both sides, intercede, interpose, intervene; judge, umpire, rule; interfere, meddle.

see also 230

654 submission

n. submission, yielding, obedience; acquiescence, resignation, deference; submissiveness, docility, meekness, humility, passivity.

adj. submissive, obedient; compliant, amenable, tractable, mouldable; resigned, subdued; acquiescent, reconciled, patient; docile, humble, lowly, tame.

vb. submit, give in, yield, surrender, capitulate, resign, relinquish, give up, throw in the towel, admit defeat.

obey, defer, bow to, comply, acquiesce; take the line of least resistance.

see also 673, 679

655 combatant

n. combatant, fighter, contender, opponent, serviceman, soldier, conscript, recruit, pressed man; casual, irregular; mercenary, hireling; warrior, veteran.

armed forces, services, troops, forces, military force, army, infantry, cavalry, artillery; navy, air force; unit, group, division, section, squad, troop, patrol, party; task force; formation, column, line, array.

656 non-combatant

n. non-combatant, pacifist, conscientious objector, neutral, dove, flower people, conchie (*sl.*); peace-maker.

657 arms

n. arms, weapons, armament, munitions; armour, mail, panoply; small arms, firearm, gun; revolver, rifle, shotgun, machine gun, automatic; cannon, mortar; bazooka; hand-grenade bomb, explsoive, dynamite, gunpowder; atomic bomb, hydrogen bomb, H-bomb, neutron bomb; armoury, arsenal; ballistics.

658 arena

n. arena, battlefield, battleground, scene of action, field of action, theatre of war, trenches, front; field, ground, centre, scene, sphere, track, court, course; stadium, gymnasium, playground, campus, coliseum, amphitheatre, circus, forum, pit.

E Results of action

659 completion

n. completion, finish, end, conclusion, achievement, performance, accomplishment, fulfilment, perfection, realization, execution.

finishing touch, crown, *coup de grâce;* last straw, limit (*sl.*).

adj. complete, finished, accomplished, fulfilled, perfect, entire, whole; conclusive, final, last.

vb. complete, finish, end, conclude, terminate; achieve, perform, carry out, implement, bring off (*inf.*), pull off (*inf.*), succeed; knock off (*inf.*), polish off (*inf.*), wrap up (*inf.*); get over with (*inf.*), get over and done with (*inf.*); accomplish, work out, hammer out, see through, go through with, realize, effect, fulfil, discharge, settle; be resolved, things work out, perfect, consummate, ripen, mature; culminate, come to a head.

see also 56, 609

660 non-completion

n. non-completion, failure, non-performance, neglect, defeat; fault, blemish, deficiency, defect.

adj. uncompleted, failed, neglected, incomplete, half-done, partial, imperfect, deficient.

vb. not complete, leave undone, neglect, miss, fail, drop out, leave, not stay the course.

see also 57, 582

661 success

n. success, completion, achievement, attainment, accomplishment; successfulness, happy ending, favourable outcome, prosperous issue; triumph, victory, conquest, push-over (*inf.*), walk-over (*inf.*); breakthrough, advance, progress; prosperity, luck, happiness, bed of roses; success story, hit, smash hit (*sl.*).

winner, victor, champion, hero, title-holder, conqueror.

adj. successful, winning, victorious, triumphant, champion, in the lead, unbeaten, invincible; beneficial, advantageous; fruitful, prosperous, fortunate, thriving, flourishing.

vb. succeed, make a success of, achieve, attain, accomplish, reach, complete, fulfil, obtain, get, capture, gain, pull off (*inf.*), bring off (*inf.*); be successful, come off (*inf.*), do the trick (*inf.*); advance, get on, make it (*inf.*), make a go of (*inf.*), make a breakthrough, proceed, progress, benefit, reap, profit, prosper, flourish, thrive, prevail, score a hit, hit the jackpot.

win, beat, conquer, defeat, get the better of, gain the upper hand, clobber (*sl.*), overcome, ride out the storm, crush, overwhelm, win hands down, walk away with (*inf.*), come out on top (*inf.*), come off with flying colours; survive, get by, hang on.

662 failure

n. failure, misadventure, breakdown, collapse, fiasco, disaster, débâcle, disappointment, flop (*inf.*), wash-out (*inf.*); defeat, overthrow, downfall, ruin, landslide; unsuccessfulness, ineffectiveness, defectiveness; neglect, omission, shortcoming; no-go (*inf.*), wild goose chase, utter defeat, clobbering (*sl.*), rout.

loser, underdog, has-been (*inf.*), also-ran (*inf.*), non-starter, dud.

adj. unsuccessful, futile, vain, useless, fruitless, profitless; unfortunate, disastrous; inadequate, ineffective, abortive; overthrown, defeated, fallen, outmatched, thwarted, frustrated, foiled, pipped at the post, outvoted.

vb. fail, go amiss, fall down, let one down; abandon, neglect, miss; thwart, frustrate; fall short, break down, fall through (*inf.*), miscarry, come to nothing, flounder, falter, go on the rocks, flop (*inf.*), fizzle out (*inf.*); lose, be defeated, suffer defeat, go down, go under; bark up the wrong tree (*inf.*), not get to first base (*inf.*); get no change out of (*inf.*).

663 trophy

n. trophy, prize, reward, award, honour, medal, badge, cup, memorial, decoration, ribbon, order, crown, palm, laurel, accolade, mention, citation; consolation prize, booby prize, wooden spoon.

booty, loot, spoil, plunder, premium, capture.

see also 724

664 prosperity

n. prosperity, good fortune, happiness, welfare, well-being, successfulness, luckiness, affluence, wealth, riches, luxury, benefits, blessings; golden age, good old days, heyday, boom, bed of roses, halcyon days, summer.

adj. prosperous, flourishing, thriving, successful, well-to-do, well-off, comfortable, rich, auspicious; up-and-coming, born with a silver spoon in one's mouth; golden, glorious, cloudless, sunny, halcyon.

vb. prosper, thrive, flourish, increase, blossom, be successful, fare well, turn out well; get on in the world, make one's mark, be rich, make a fortune; Fortune smile upon.

see also **661**

665 adversity

n. adversity, misfortune, trouble, hardship, unluckiness, bad luck, hard times, bad patch, ill wind, deep water, difficulty, misadventure, unhappiness; disaster, distress, catastrophe, crisis, calamity, burden, pressure, affliction, blight, curse, plague, scourge.

adj. adverse, unfavourable, hostile, unfriendly, sinister; disastrous, catastrophic; afflicted, troubled, wretched, stricken; unfortunate, unlucky, unhappy, ill-starred, ill-fated, down on one's luck, in a bad way, in the wars.

vb. be in trouble, hit a bad patch, be in for it (*inf.*), have a hard time of it, feel the pinch, fall on hard times, decline, sink, stew in one's own juice, go under, get out of one's depth, fall flat on one's face (*inf.*), fall by the wayside.

see also **633**

666 mediocrity

n. mediocrity, commonness, ordinariness, averageness, passableness, tolerableness.

adj. mediocre, average, ordinary, indifferent, middling, fair, poor, feeble, common, commonplace, dull, monotonous, stale, insipid, wishy-washy, tolerable, fair-to-middling, passable, humdrum, run of the mill, so-so, nothing to write home about, much of a muchness,

vb. make do, just exist, struggle along, muddle through, scrape through, manage somehow, get by, just keep one's head above water, stagnate, vegetate.

2 Intersocial volition

A General

667 authority

n. authority, power, control, right, prerogative, command, rule, sway; dominion, sovereignty, ascendancy, upper hand, supreme authority, last word; influence, prestige, power behind the throne, arm of the law.

government, democracy, *vox populi*, officialdom, bureaucracy, administration, establishment, them, powers that be; open government, devolution.

adj. authoritative, commanding, dominant, lawful, powerful, sovereign; in office, in power; official, executive, administrative, bureaucratic, governmental, democratic, gubernatorial, political.

vb. rule, govern, control, direct, dominate, lord it over, domineer, command, sway, reign; assume control, take over, take the reins, have power, rule the roost, authorize, empower, back, devolve, decentralize.

see also **671**

668 laxity

n. laxity, slackness, looseness, flexibility; anarchy, lawlessness, mob rule, disorder, chaos, turmoil.

adj. lax, slack, loose, remiss, soft, flabby, relaxed, flexible; anarchic, uncontrolled, lawless, chaotic, rebellious.

vb. be lax, tolerate, not enforce, stretch a point; misrule, misgovern; give a free hand to, give free rein to; take the law into one's own hands, do what is right in one's own eyes.

see also 670

669 severity

n. severity, strictness, austerity, firmness, rigidity, inflexibility, rigour; hardness, cruelty; firm hand, strong hand, heavy hand, rod of iron, tight rein, pound of flesh, letter of the law.

tyranny, oppression, despotism, fascism; tyrant, dictator, despot, autocrat, taskmaster, authoritarian, disciplinarian.

adj. severe, stern, strict, harsh, hard, austere, extreme, puritanical; firm, rigid, unbending, inflexible, immovable, unchanging; rigorous, exacting, uncompromising, stringent; grim, cruel, forbidding; unfeeling, hard-hearted; tyrannical, overbearing, domineering, despotic, totalitarian, authoritarian, oppressive, heavy-handed.

vb. be severe, be hard on, discipline, come down on (*inf.*), deal harshly with, insist, crack down on (*inf.*), clamp down on (*inf.*), put one's foot down (*inf.*), keep a tight rein on, rule with an iron hand, domineer, lord it over, dominate, oppress, tyrannize.

see also 963

670 lenience

n. lenience, softness, tolerance, mildness, forbearance; mercy, clemency, forgiveness, pardon; kindness, compassion, favour.

adj. lenient, soft, gentle, mild, kind, compassionate, loving, soft-hearted, tender, sympathetic, easy-going; tolerant, forbearing, long-suffering; merciful, forgiving, clement.

vb. be lenient, go easy on, spare the rod; pass over, forbear, refrain; forgive, pardon; tolerate, bear.

671 command

n. command, direction, rule, charge, ordinance, mandate, directive, dictate, injunction, behest; bidding, call, summons; decree, ruling, law, act, fiat, canon, edict, bull, proclamation; writ, warrant, subpoena; demand, claim, request, requirement; final demand, ultimatum.

adj. commanding, powerful, authoritative.

vb. command, rule, direct, dictate, order, charge, decree, proclaim, ordain; lay down, prescribe; demand, claim, request, ask, require, exact; bid, call, summon, invite, send for.

see also 667, 954

672 disobedience

n. disobedience, violation, disregard, neglect, non-observance, infringement, transgression, sin; misbehaviour, naughtiness; waywardness, stubbornness, insubordination, defiance, intractableness, unruliness; mutiny, revolt, rebellion, revolution, desertion, riot, insurgence.

rebel, revolutionary, radical, anarchist, reactionary, extremist, insurrectionist, insurgent, rioter, terrorist, mutineer, deserter; trouble-maker, brawler.

adj. disobedient, insubordinate; naughty, misbehaving; defiant, refractory, unsubmissive, disloyal, rebellious, intractable, unruly, lawless, uncontrollable, obstreperous; stubborn, wayward, insolent; revolutionary, mutinous, riotous, anarchistic, dissident, factious, insurgent.

vb. disobey, defy, fly in the face of, disregard, neglect, ignore, pay no attention to, not heed, violate, infringe, transgress, sin, break rules; misbehave; revolt, rebel, mutiny.

673 obedience

n. obedience, submission, compliance, loyalty, devotion, faithfulness, fidelity, constancy; meekness, docility.

adj. obedient, submissive, complaisant; law-abiding, well-behaved, good; devoted, loyal, faithful, respectful, dutiful, subservient, docile, acquiescent; round one's little finger (*inf.*), at one's beck and call, on a string, henpecked.

vb. obey, submit, do, keep, observe, follow, pay attention to, bow to, heed, comply, fulfil, agree, behave, do what one is told, do one's duty, do what is expected of one.

see also **654, 679**

674 compulsion

n. compulsion, force, drive, necessity, need, obligation, pressure, constraint, coercion, violence, strong arm, duress; urgency; conscription.

adj. compelling, compulsive, necessary, driving, pressing, coercive, unavoidable, irresistible, compulsory, urgent.

vb. compel, force, drive, coerce, constrain, impel, dictate, necessitate, oblige, require, urge, bring pressure to bear on, inflict.

675 master

n. master, mistress, chief, leader, head, superior, principal, lord; direc-

tor, manager, supervisor, boss, management, overseer, authority, officer, official, mayor, mayoress; governor, governess, ruler, president, executive, sovereign, king, queen, prince, princess, emperor, empress, regent; captain, commander, lieutenant; big Chief (*sl.*), bigwig.

see also **34, 623**

676 servant

n. servant, dependant, assistant, right-hand man, subordinate, employee, worker, staff, personnel; slave, serf, vassal, captive, bondman, fag; orderly, menial; drudge, hack; chauffeur, butler, domestic, housekeeper, maid, nurse; porter, janitor, doorman; steward, stewardess, waiter, waitress, barman, barmaid; charwoman, cleaner.

adj. serving, ministering, attending, helping.

vb. serve, work for, be in the employment of, minister, aid, help, wait upon, care for, look after, nurse, mother; attend, do for (*inf.*).

677 sign of authority

n. badge of office, insignia, symbol, emblem, livery, uniform, regalia, rod, sceptre, mace, crown, staff, wand, rod, sword, stripe, decoration, flag.

678 freedom

n. freedom, liberty, independence, autonomy, democracy, self-determination; freedom of choice, free will; immunity, exemption, privilege, *carte blanche*, blank cheque, unrestraint; range, scope, play, field, room, leeway, latitude, opportunity, full play, free rein, elbow room.

adj. free, released, liberated, freed, at liberty, at large, let out, scot free; clear, extricated, unshackled, unfettered, unattached, unengaged, unconfined, unimpeded, unhindered, unrestrained; independent, autonomous, self-governing, democratic, enfranchised.

vb. free, have a free hand, have the run of; be independent, please onself, do as one wishes, fend for oneself, stand on one's own two feet, go it alone.

see also **680**

679 subjection

n. subjection, subservience, servitude, dependence, subordination, inferiority; allegiance, service; bondage, slavery, serfdom, servility, thrall.

adj. subject, dependent, subordinate, submissive, inferior, junior, accessory, subsidiary, satellite, auxiliary; accountable, answerable, liable, contingent.

vb. subject, enslave, dominate, subordinate, master, rule, hold captive, conquer, tame, subdue, subjugate, hold under one's thumb; repress, suppress, sit on.

be subject to, depend on, lean on; be at the mercy of, serve.

see also 35

680 liberation

n. liberation, release, discharge, deliverance, rescue; extrication, disengagement, unravelling, loosing, unfettering, loosening, untying; emancipation, enfranchisement, manumission.

adj. freed, liberated, released, loose.

vb. liberate, free, release, discharge, deliver, save, rescue, set at liberty, restore, let out; extricate, loose, remove fetters, unfetter, untie, remove, unbind, undo, cut loose, disengage, unravel, let slip; ransom, pardon, dismiss, acquit; emancipate, enfran-

chise; shake off, free oneself of, get rid of, lose.

see also 601, 961

681 restraint

n. restraint, control, constraint, discipline, self-control, self-discipline, self-restraint, reticence, reserve, caution; repression.

restriction, limitation, barrier, check, hindrance, impediment, obstacle, block, bar, curb, blockade, embargo, ban, veto; curfew; closed shop; censorship, news blackout; monopoly, cartel, protectionism.

custody, detention, imprisonment, confinement, impounding; chain, bond, irons, fetter, shackle.

adj. restraining, restrictive, controlling, limiting, strict, narrow, repressive; restrained, under control, in check, controlled, disciplined, reserved, cautious, calm, reticent, withdrawn, repressed, pent-up, bottled-up.

in custody, under arrest, imprisoned, detained, confined, in prison, in detention, behind bars, inside (*sl.*), in jug (*sl.*), in clink (*sl.*).

vb. restrain, control, limit, govern, check, arrest, curb, keep in check, hold back, narrow; discipline, bridle; repress, suppress, keep back, bottle up, muzzle, gag, subdue, quell, quash; hinder, impede, restrict, hamper; control oneself, pull oneself together, take a grip on oneself (*inf.*), sort oneself out (*inf.*), get organized.

take into custody, apprehend, help police with their inquiries, run in, turn in (*inf.*), turn over to, pick up, arrest, convict, take prisoner; imprison, detain, confine, put into prison, put away (*inf.*), shut up, lock up, put behind bars, intern, impound; tie, bind, chain, fetter, manacle.

682 prison

n. prison, gaol, jail, lock-up, nick (*sl.*), clink (*sl.*), jug (*sl.*), maximum-security prison, police station; cell, cage, guardroom; dungeon; detention camp, internment camp, concentration camp; Borstal, detention centre, approved home, remand centre.

683 keeper

n. keeper, custodian, warden, curator, attendant, official, guard; caretaker, porter, janitor, concierge, housekeeper, gatekeeper; watchman, lookout, patrol, scout; baby-sitter, governess, nurse, nanny, guardian; escort, bodyguard; gamekeeper, ranger; jailer, warder, prison governor, screw (*sl.*).
see also 593

684 prisoner

n. prisoner, convict, culprit, con (*sl.*), inmate, star, gaolbird, young offender, captive, prisoner of war, internee; defendant, the accused, detainee; criminal, rogue.
see also 906, 940

685 vicarious authority

n. commission, delegation, deputation, representation, authorization, committal, trusteeship; appointment, nomination, assignment; mission, embassy, envoy, legation, agency; devolution, decentralization; inauguration, installation, investiture, induction, ordination, coronation; accession.

trust, charge, mandate, authority, warrant; task, duty, errand, employment.

adj. commissioned, delegated, vicarious, deputed.

vb. commission, delegate, appoint, empower, grant authority to, authorize, charge, commit, assign, entrust; devolve, decentralize; name, nominate; inaugurate, invest, induct, ordain, install, place, establish; crown, enthrone; employ, engage, hire, contract.

represent, deputize, act on behalf of, stand in for.

686 annulment

n. annulment, cancellation, abrogation, dissolution, revocation, retraction, invalidation, nullification, reversal, repeal, abolition, countermand.

dismissal, removal, displacement, the sack (*inf.*), the boot (*sl.*), the push (*sl.*); retirement, lay-off, redundancy, natural wastage; deposal, dethronement, impeachment.

demotion, downgrading, degradation.

adj. annulled, cancelled, null and void; rained off, abandoned, postponed.

vb. annul, cancel, abolish, repeal, revoke, dissolve, rescind, quash, render void, nullify, invalidate; refute, counteract, reverse, repudiate, countermand.

dismiss, oust, overthrow, unseat, remove from office, discharge, depose, dethrone, displace, suspend, sack, fire, give the push to (*sl.*), give the boot to (*sl.*), give papers to, show the door to, strike off the register, write out, pension off; relieve, replace, recall; impeach, unfrock; demote, degrade, downgrade.

687 resignation

n. resignation, abdication, retirement, relinquishment, renunciation, withdrawal, departure, leaving, surrender, desertion; pension, golden handshake, leaving gift, leaving present, gratuity, superannuation.

adj. resignatory; retired, former,

previous, outgoing, one-time, sometime, emeritus.

vb. resign, quit, leave, depart, vacate office, relinquish, abandon, step down, stand down, stand aside, retire, abdicate, give up office, walk out of, hand in one's notice, tender one's resignation, hand in one's papers.

688 consignee

n. consignee, delegate, representative, substitute, deputy; trustee, executor, nominee, proxy; intermediary, middleman, negotiator, broker; committee, board, panel, group, organization, deputation, cabinet, decision maker.

ambassador, envoy, commissioner, delegation, emissary, diplomat, consul, attaché, plenipotentiary, nuncio; embassy, consulate, mission.

see also 619, 689

689 deputy

n. deputy, assistant, second-in-command, right-hand man; delegate, substitute, representative, proxy, surrogate, stand-in, agent, proxy, vicar; ambassador, commissioner; spokesman, mouthpiece.

adj. deputy, deputizing, vice, pro, acting.

vb. deputize, substitute, represent, stand in for, act on behalf of.

B Special

690 permission

n. permission, liberty, leave, freedom, consent; authorization, legalization, confirmation, endorsement, affirmation, sanction; authority, permit, grant, charter, licence, certificate, concession, allowance; pass, passport, visa, password; letter of commendation; go-ahead, green light (*inf.*), all-clear, clearance, nod; free hand, free rein, *carte blanche*, blank cheque.

adj. permitting, allowing; tolerant, lenient, permissive; permitted, granted, allowed, authorized, approved.

vb. permit, let, allow, grant, give permission; consent, approve, favour, have no objections; authorize, warrant, legalize, sanction, certify, charter, franchise, license; give the go-ahead, give the green light (*inf.*), give clearance, rubber-stamp (*inf.*); tolerate, concede, bear, suffer.

691 prohibition

n. prohibition, forbiddance, obstruction, suppression, repression, refusal, interdiction, injunction, disallowance, countermand, ban, veto, embargo, boycott, taboo.

adj. prohibiting, forbidding; prohibitive, excessive, restrictive; prohibited, forbidden, illegal, illicit, unlawful, taboo, impermissible.

vb. prohibit, forbid, refuse, withhold, deny, disallow, prevent, hinder, hamper, preclude, restrain, interdict; ban, veto, boycott, say no to, debar, exclude, shut out; obstruct, oppose, suppress, repress, restrict, stop, halt.

692 consent

n. consent, acceptance, agreement, allowance, permission, approval, assent, concurrence, acquiescence, compliance.

adj. consenting, agreeable, willing, acquiescent.

vb. consent, accept, allow, agree, approve, assent, say yes to, be in favour of, concur, acquiesce, accede; concede, grant, yield, acknowledge, vouchsafe.

see also 690

693 offer

n. offer, tender, bid, submission; approach, advance, overture; proposal, proposition, presentation, suggestion.

adj. on offer, available, for sale, advertised.

vb. offer, hold out, present, suggest, propose, submit, extend, move, put forward, put forth, tender, bid, approach; make overtures, make advances; lay at one's feet, sacrifice, proffer.

volunteer, offer oneself, come forward, stand for.

694 refusal

n. refusal, rejection, denial, declension; rebuff, snub, slap in the face, insult; veto, ban, exclusion.

adj. refusing, unwilling, uncompliant, resisting, hard-hearted, reluctant.

vb. refuse, reject, not want, decline, resist, ignore, turn down, say no to, not hear of, exclude, disallow, shun, repudiate, repel, spurn, rebuff, scorn, snub, repulse, turn one's back on, turn a deaf ear to, set one's face against, wash one's hands of, harden one's heart against; slam the door in someone's face (*inf.*); withhold, deny, hold back.

see also 469, 542

695 request

n. request, call, petition, invitation, bid, application, demand, appeal, plea, address; inquiry, question; offer, proposal, proposition; prayer, entreaty, intercession, invocation, supplication; importunity, urgency.

adj. requesting, petitioning, supplicatory, imprecatory, invocatory, prayerful, begging, on bended knees; urgent, importunate, persistent, clamorous.

vb. request, call, ask, express a wish, apply for, summon, demand, implore, beseech, beg, appeal, entreat, pray, call on, petition, crave, plead, adjure; inquire, invite.

urge, ply, press, persist, pester, bother, coax, clamour.

canvass, solicit, importune, tout, hawk; appeal for money, pass the hat round (*inf.*), have a whip-round (*inf.*), make a collection.

696 protest

n. protest, deprecation, disapproval, objection, complaint, dissent, expostulation, remonstrance.

demonstration, demo (*inf.*), rally, sit-in, mass meeting, march, protest march, strike, hunger strike.

adj. protesting, deprecatory, expostulatory, remonstrative.

vb. protest, depreciate, speak against, lodge a protest, ask not to, disapprove, object, disagree, oppose, criticize, demur, remonstrate, expostulate; groan, jeer, murmur, heckle, sneer; demonstrate, march, strike, go on strike, picket.

see also 144

697 petitioner

n. petitioner, supplicant, suppliant, applicant, claimant, candidate, bidder; inquirer, advertiser; lobby, lobbyist, pressure group, canvasser, hawker, tout, pedlar, vendor; beggar, scrounger, cadger, sponger, loafer, idler, vagabond, tramp, down-and-out.

C Conditional

698 promise

n. promise, covenant, pledge, contract, pact, undertaking, commitment, consent, word, vow, word of honour; gentleman's agreement.

engagement, betrothal; fiancée, fiancé, intended (*inf.*).

adj. promised, committed, pledged, bound; engaged, betrothed.

vb. promise, agree, undertake, commit, declare, covenant, pledge, contract, consent, vow, swear; warrant, guarantee; bind onself, give one's word, pledge one's honour; become engaged, betrothe.

699 contract

n. contract, agreement, covenant, undertaking, pact, concordat, promise, pledge, understanding, arrangement, settlement, transaction, bargain, deal (*inf.*); negotiation, compromise, give and take; treaty, convention, alliance, league, charter, entente; gentleman's agreement.

adj. contractual, conventional, promissory.

vb. contract, agree, covenant, undertake, pledge, promise, arrange, bargain, deal, negotiate, hammer out, stipulate; sign, sign on the dotted line, agree on terms, settle, come to an agreement, accept an offer, shake on it (*inf.*); ratify, confirm.

see also 24, 643

700 conditions

n. conditions, terms, provisions, specifications, frame of reference, strings, proviso, contingencies, arrangements, limitations, restrictions, reservations, exceptions, escape clause, *sine qua non*.

adj. conditional, provisional, contingent, with strings attached, granted on certain terms, dependent on, subject to.

vb. negotiate, discuss; propose conditions, postulate, stipulate, attach strings, insist on, impose.

see also 403

701 security

n. security, surety, warranty, covenant, bond, promise, pledge, earnest, token, certainty; deposit, caution money, money in advance, forfeit, stake, insurance, bail, pawn, mortgage, collateral; liability, responsibility; hostage, captive, prisoner.

adj. guaranteed, pledged, pawned, on deposit.

vb. give security, guarantee, pledge, sign for, insure, assure, underwrite, mortgage, stake, pawn; give bail, go bail; stand surety, bail out; stand for, back.

702 observance

n. observance, attention, performance, doing, carrying out, keeping, heeding, practice; obedience, compliance, devotion.

adj. observant, practising, professing; diligent, conscientious; exact, scrupulous, pedantic; dependable, responsible; loyal, faithful, devoted, obedient.

vb. observe, heed, keep, do, carry out, follow, adhere to, perform, discharge, practise, adopt, conform to, fulfil, comply; keep on the right side of the law; hold fast, stand by, embrace, profess, give allegiance to, be loyal to.

703 non-observance

n. non-observance, neglect, disregard, omission; breaking, infringement, violation, transgression, trespass, breach, sin; disobedience, disloyalty, infidelity; inattention, carelessness, indifference, irresponsibility.

adj. non-observant, negligent,

careless, indifferent; unfaithful, disobedient.

vb. not observe, not practise, not keep; break, disobey, violate, infringe, transgress, breach, contravene; neglect, disregard, omit; break faith, be faithless.

704 compromise

n. compromise, bargaining, agreement, understanding, settlement; give and take, concessions, mutual concessions; middle course, middle ground, half-way house; composition; *modus vivendi.*

vb. compromise, make concessions, give and take, meet half-way, go fifty-fifty, steer a middle course, split the differences; negotiate, come to an agreement, come to an understanding, reconcile, settle, adjust, agree to differ.

D Possessive relations

705 acquisition

n. acquisition, getting, obtainment, procuration; recovery, retrieval, redemption.

gain, benefit, advantage, reward, income, earnings, wages, salary, grant, profit, receipts, proceeds, emolument; collection, gathering, produce, output, yield, fruit, harvest, crop; addition, accrual, accumulation.

adj. obtainable, available; acquisitive, hoarding, grasping.

profitable, fruitful, productive, advantageous, worthwhile, lucrative, paying its way, remunerative.

vb. acquire, get, obtain, take possession of, make one's own, appropriate, lay hold of, procure; force from, grab, seize, capture, pocket, secure, draw, tap; gain, accept, receive, make,

collect, earn, benefit, win, accumulate; gather, harvest, glean, reap.

get back, recover, retrieve, regain, redeem.

buy, purchase; profit, capitalize on, cash in on (*inf.*); inherit, come into, be left.

see also **716**

706 loss

n. loss, mislaying, misplacement; dispossession, deprivation, forfeiture; want, bereavement; insolvency, bankruptcy.

adj. lost, missing, misplaced, mislaid, nowhere to be found, hidden, obscured, vanished, strayed, gone; lacking, wanting, deprived of, bereft; overdrawn, insolvent, bankrupt; unprofitable, disadvantageous, wasted, irretrievable, desperate, hopeless, futile.

vb. lose, mislay, misplace, not find; let slip, drop, miss, fail, forfeit; deprive, displace; waste, squander; incur losses, go bankrupt.

707 possession

n. possession, ownership, occupancy, residence, tenancy, tenure; possessorship, proprietorship; hold, mastery, grasp, control, custody; purchase.

adj. possessing, having, owning; possessive, exclusive, monopolistic, selfish; possessed, owned, purchased, enjoyed, in possession of.

vb. possess, own, have, hold, keep, retain, grasp, occupy, control, maintain, use, boast of; have title to, have rights to, have claim upon; monopolize, hog (*inf.*), have all to oneself, corner; include, comprise, contain; belong, appertain.

708 non-possession

n. non-possession, loss, deprivation, surrender of rights; lease; no man's land.

adj. not owning, lacking; destitute, poor, impoverished, penniless; unowned, unoccupied, unpossessed, unattached, free, ownerless, virgin, unclaimed, lost, independent, unbound.

see also 706

709 joint possession

n. joint possession, co-ownership, cooperation, participation, partnership, sharing; socialism, communism, public ownership, nationalization, worker participation, profit-sharing; community, cooperative, collective, kibbutz; joint fund, kitty, pool; share, portion.

participator, partner, member, partaker, shareholder, worker-director.

adj. cooperative, joint, participatory, common, communal, profit-sharing; involved, committed, dedicated, connected with.

vb. participate, share, cooperate, join, take part in, partake, go halves.

see also 639

710 possessor

n. possessor, owner, holder, master, partner; buyer, purchaser; occupant, occupier, tenant, resident, lodger, lessee, landlord, landlady, landowner, landholder, proprietor, proprietress; heir, heiress, inheritor.

711 property

n. property, land, assets, resources, means, goods, riches, wealth, valuables, inheritance, capital, investment, equity, land, holding, estate.

belongings, equipment, paraphernalia, things, trappings, fixtures, furni-ture, furnishings, goods and chattels; appurtenances, accoutrements; personal effects, luggage, baggage; burden, encumbrance, impedimenta.

712 retention

n. retention, holding, keeping; hold, grasp, clench, clinch, grip, hug, embrace, clasp; confinement, stranglehold, tight grip, straitjacket.

adj. retentive, holding; retained, held, kept.

vb. retain, hold, keep, keep hold of, grasp, clench, grip, clinch, clasp, clutch, embrace, hug, squeeze, press; cling to, stick to, fasten on, secure, hold fast; contain, restrain, enclose, confine; maintain, preserve; cherish, nurture, harbour; detain, reserve, withhold.

713 non-retention

n. relinquishment, abandonment, renunciation, disposal; exemption, dispensation, release; divorce, dissolution.

adj. abandoned, thrown away, rejected, marooned.

vb. not retain, relinquish, abandon, renounce, let go, part with, dispose of, discard, throw away, jettison, release; waive, lift restrictions, derestrict, exempt.

see also 556, 921

714 transfer

n. transference, conveyancing, assignation; changeover, change of hands; devolution, delegation; exchange, conversion, interchange; sale, lease; bequest, endowment, legacy.

adj. transferable, negotiable, interchangeable, exchangeable; transferred, made over.

vb. convey, transfer, sell, sign,

consign, assign, change over, deliver, make over; entrust, commit; exchange, convert; devolve, delegate, decentralize; bequeath, will, make a will, pass on, hand down.
  see also **268**

715 giving

n. giving, bestowal, conferral, granting, imparting, delivery.

gift, present, donation, grant, award, presentation, prize; allowance, subsidy, aid, assistance; tip, gratuity; bounty, largesse, windfall; leaving present, golden handshake; charity, hand-out, alms; bequest, legacy; blessing, favour, grace, mercy.

sacrifice, offering, worship, dedication, consecration; offering, collection, offertory.

giver, donor, contributor.

adj. giving, charitable, generous, liberal, sacrificial; given, free.

vb. give, donate, grant, award, present, contribute, render, remit, convey, supply, furnish, provide, afford, dispense, hand out, dole out, distribute, administer, deal out, mete out, subsidize, give towards; bestow, confer, endow, invest with, impart, communicate; expend, spend, lavish; offer, sacrifice.

716 receiving

n. receiving, reception, acquisition, acceptance, admission, collection; receipts, proceeds, dues, monies, toll.

recipient, receiver, beneficiary; object, target, victim, guinea pig; customer, client; trustee, payee, addressee, earner; heir, heiress.

adj. receiving, receptive, welcoming, hospitable, sensitive.

vb. receive, accept, admit, be given, get, gain, acquire, collect, obtain, draw, take in, derive, come by, attract, come

in for, be on the receiving end; take up, levy, charge; be received, accrue, come in, fall to one.
  see also **302, 705**

717 apportionment

n. apportionment, allotment, sharing, division, distribution, dealing, rationing.

portion, share, allocation, section, piece, part, fraction, fragment; helping, serving, slice, ration; proportion, quota, allowance; cut (*sl.*), split, parcel, lot.

vb. apportion, allot, distribute, divide, share out, hand out, dole out, dish out (*inf.*), farm out, parcel out, deal, assign, dispose, administer, give away, dispense, ration.
  see also **55**

718 lending

n. lending; loan, advance, mortgage, allowance, credit, investment, credit card, credit account, hire purchase, never-never (*inf.*).

bank, building society, pawnbroker, pop-shop (*sl.*); banker, bank manager, lender, financier, money-lender, creditor; usurer, shark, angel (*sl.*), Shylock.

vb. lend, let out, allow to borrow, trust with, entrust, hire out, let, lease, charter; loan, finance, support, back, advance, grant, lend on security, put out at interest, give credit, risk.

719 borrowing

n. borrowing, rental, hire, loan; assumption; appropriation, adoption, importation; imitation, copy.

vb. borrow, rent, hire, lease, charter; take on tick (*inf.*), raise money, pawn, cadge; touch for (*sl.*); obtain, use, adopt.

720 taking

n. taking, possession, acceptance, appropriation, requisition; seizure, grab, capture; kidnapping, abduction; dispossession, deprivation, extortion, confiscation; recovery, retrieval.

taker, possessor; seizer, grabber, raider; kidnapper, abductor.

adj. taking, grasping, greedy, rapacious, extortionate, ravenous.

vb. take, possess, accept, receive, get, obtain, win, gain; seize, lay hold of, appropriate, take for oneself, acquire, avail oneself of, adopt, assume; grip, clasp; catch, apprehend, grasp; grab, trap, snatch, capture, raid; take away, steal, kidnap, abduct; confiscate, commandeer; recover, retrieve; take from, remove, deprive of, divest of, dispossess, extort, strip, disinherit.

see also **722**

721 restitution

n. restitution, restoration, return, giving back, reinstatement; retrieval, recovery, repossession, repatriation; recompense, repayment, refund, amends, compensation, reimbursement, remuneration, reparation, indemnification, redemption, satisfaction.

adj. restitutive, restoring, compensatory, redemptive.

vb. restore, return, give back, reinstate, reinstall; rehabilitate, repair; recover, get back, retrieve, recoup, regain, retake, reclaim.

make restitution, refund, make amends, reimburse, repay, compensate, indemnify, redeem, ransom.

see also **589**

722 stealing

n. stealing, theft, larceny, robbery, burglary, house-breaking, shop-lifting; vandalism, looting, pilfering, ransacking, pillage, plunder, sacking; hijacking, skyjacking (*inf.*); kidnapping, abduction; hold-up, stick-up (*inf.*), mugging (*inf.*), hit-and-run-raid, smash-and-grab-raid, job (*sl.*); embezzlement, misappropriation, extortion, fraud.

adj. thieving, light-fingered.

vb. steal, take, burgle, thieve, rob, remove, go off with, get away with, make off with, run off with, seize, pilfer, pick-pocket, pinch (*sl.*), nick (*sl.*), filch, fleece, nobble (*sl.*), knock off (*sl.*), rip off (*sl.*), screw (*sl.*), shoplift, purloin; abduct, kidnap, mug (*inf.*), hijack, skyjack; embezzle, misappropriate, defraud, swindle, cheat, fiddle, peculate, smuggle; loot, rifle, sack, raid, ransack, plunder, pillage.

be stolen, fall off the back of a lorry (*inf.*).

723 thief

n. thief, robber, stealer; burglar, house-breaker, shop-lifter, mugger, attacker; pilferer, pick-pocket; hijacker, skyjacker (*inf.*), highwayman, safe-blower, safe-cracker; kidnapper, abductor; plunderer, looter; embezzler, swindler, cheater, fiddler; crook, rogue, thug, smuggler, pirate.

see also **684**

724 booty

n. booty, prize, haul, loot, swag (*sl.*), takings, plunder, spoil, winnings, stolen goods, goods fallen off the back of a lorry (*inf.*), capture, premium, contraband, prey.

725 business

n. business, trade, commerce, business affairs, traffic; negotiations, bargaining, transactions, marketing, buying and selling; barter, exchange, swap (*inf.*).

adj. business, trading, commercial, mercantile.

vb. transact business, trade, traffic, deal in, handle, market, buy and sell; negotiate, bargain; exchange, barter, swap (*inf.*).

726 purchase

n. purchase, buying, obtaining, acquisition; shopping, payment, investment, marketing.

buyer, purchaser, consumer, shopper, customer, patron, client, clientele, custom, market, patronage.

vb. purchase, buy, get, obtain, gain, acquire; go shopping, pay for, invest, exchange, bargain, sign; patronize; go window-shopping, buy back, redeem.

727 sale

n. sale, disposal, selling, marketing, trading; clearance, sell-out; bazaar, jumble sale, rummage sale; auction, public sale; sales talk, salesmanship, high-pressure salesmanship, sales patter, promotion, advertising.

seller, vendor, retailer, shopkeeper, shop assistant, salesman, commercial traveller, sales rep.

adj. saleable, marketable, in demand; available, on the market.

vb. sell, dispose, market, flog (*sl.*), retail, trade, dump, vend; ask, demand; transfer, transact, exchange; peddle, hawk; reduce prices, sell off; auction, come under the hammer.

728 trader

n. trader, dealer, retailer, shopkeeper, tradesman, middleman, wholesaler, exporter, importer, shipper, trafficker, merchant; businessman, industrialist, capitalist, manager, financier, entrepreneur, tycoon, stockbroker, speculator.

pedlar, hawker, tinker, huckster; tout; rag-and-bone man.

729 merchandise

n. merchandise, commodities, stock, wares, articles, goods, property, product, possessions; things, stuff; line, supplies; consumer goods, consumer durables.

730 market

n. market, mart, square, mall, arcade, shopping centre, shopping precinct, exchange, emporium; shop, store, supermarket, department store, multiple, chain store, boutique, hypermarket; kiosk, stand, stall, booth, barrow, bazaar; place of business, premises, concern, establishment.

731 money

n. money, currency, legal tender, cash, bank notes, bread (*sl.*), dough (*sl.*), lolly (*sl.*); change, small change; cheque, credit card, hire purchase; pay, salary, wages, pocket money, pin money; sum, amount, balance; funds, credit, finance, reserves, capital, wealth, wherewithal.

adj. monetary, pecuniary, financial.

vb. mint, coin, issue, monetize, put in circulation; withdraw, remove from circulation, call in, demonetize.

732 treasury

n. treasury, bank, exchequer, repository, coffer, vault, strongroom, depository, safe, cash box; cash register, till; money-box, piggy bank; wallet, purse, bag.

733 treasurer

n. treasurer, receiver, cashier, banker, purser, bursar, paymaster, accountant, teller, steward, trustee.

734 wealth

n. wealth, riches, money, affluence, luxury, opulence, prosperity, fortune, money to burn; profits, assets, means, resources.

rich man, millionaire, moneybags, man of means, capitalist.

adj. rich, wealthy, affluent, prosperous, luxurious, well-off, in the money, well-to-do, well provided for, made of money (*inf.*), rolling in it (*inf.*).

vb. get rich, make a fortune, come into money, line one's pocket; live comfortably, afford, bear the expense of, make both ends meet.

735 poverty

n. poverty, impoverishment, poorness; destitution, scarcity, privation, penury, pennilessness, pauperism, indigence, insolvency; beggary, mendicancy; poor man, pauper, beggar.

adj. poor, needy, destitute, underprivileged, distressed; impecunious, poverty-stricken, penniless, hard up, broke (*inf.*), bankrupt, insolvent; begging, mendicant; starving, hungry, empty-handed, down-and-out.

vb. be poor, find it hard going, live from hand to mouth, starve; impoverish, ruin, eat out of house and home.

736 credit

n. credit, trust, reliability; loan, account, credit account, credit card; creditor, mortgagee.

vb. credit, charge, charge to an account, credit one's account; give credit, defer payment, lend.

737 debt

n. debt, liability, obligation, claim, commitment, indebtedness, due, duty; debts, bills, amount due, amount owing, accounts outstanding, score, deficit, arrears.

debtor, borrower, purchaser, buyer, mortgagor.

adj. indebted, liable, answerable, responsible, committed, under obligation; owing, in debt, overdrawn, in the red; unpaid, due, outstanding, payable, unsettled, in arrears, overdue.

vb. be in debt, owe, be under obligation, overdraw, run up a bill, fall into debt, be in Queer Street (*sl.*).

738 payment

n. payment, remittance; settlement, clearance, reckoning; recompense, restitution, compensation, reimbursement, refund, subsidy; deposit, instalment, down payment, first payment.

pay, wages, salary, earnings, remuneration, emolument; fee, stipend, allowance, expenses, honorarium; pay packet, pay slip; payroll.

adj. paying, remunerative, not owing; paid, discharged, out of debt.

vb. pay, make payment for; repay, reward, remunerate; settle, discharge, defray, meet, bear the cost of, foot the bill; recompense, reimburse, compensate, recoup, refund; subsidize; pay on the nail; contribute, chip in (*inf.*), fork out (*inf.*), cough up (*sl.*); spend, expend; stand, treat.

739 non-payment

n. non-payment, failure to pay, default, bankruptcy, insolvency, liquidation, crash, ruin; overdraft, overdrawn account; debts.

non-payer, defaulter, bankrupt, lame duck; embezzler.

adj. non-paying, defaulting, insolvent, bankrupt, failed, ruined, on the rocks (*inf.*), bust (*inf.*), liquidated.

vb. not pay, default, fall into arrears, go bankrupt, go into liquidation, go to the wall, fold up (*inf.*), fail, be wound up, go bust (*inf.*), crash, go under; write off; bankrupt, ruin, wind up, put in the hands of a receiver, liquidate.

740 expenditure

n. expenditure, outlay, payment, disbursement, spending, costs, expenses, outgoings, investment.

vb. spend, expend, pay, pay out, lay out, invest, foot the bill; exhaust, discharge, consume; squander, waste, lavish.

741 income

n. income, receipts, revenue, returns, earnings, salary, wages, profit, assets, proceeds, dividends, gains, takings, turn-over, box-office receipts, gate-money.

receipt, acknowledgement, slip, voucher, record.

742 accounts

n. accounts, bookkeeping; account, bill, invoice, reckoning, statement, balance sheet; ledger, log, cash-book; budget.

accountant, chartered accountant, auditor, bookkeeper, actuary, cashier.

adj. accounting, budgetary.

vb. account, keep the books, enter, debit, credit, balance; budget, cook the books (*inf.*), falsify, fiddle (*sl.*).

743 price

n. price, cost, expense, amount, charge, toll, fee, fare; rent, rental, hire charge; value, face value, worth; evaluation, valuation, estimate, quotation.

taxation, tax, duty, levy, tariff, inland revenue; excise, custom, impost, tribute, dues; rates, rateable value, assessment.

price control, price freeze, austerity,

squeeze; cost of living, price index; price tag, label, ticket.

adj. priced, marked, charged, valued, worth.

vb. price, value, charge, assess, estimate, put a price on, reckon, rate; demand, ask; reduce, mark down; increase, mark up.

cost, be worth, go for, sell for, fetch, come to, amount to.

tax, exact, levy, put a tax on, raise taxes; pay taxes.

744 discount

n. discount, reduction, rebate, allowance, deduction, cut, subtraction, remission, concession; depreciation; subsidy.

vb. reduce, lower, rebate, deduct, cut, take off, knock off, subtract, allow; depreciate.

745 dearness

n. dearness, expensiveness, expense, costliness; exorbitance, excessiveness, extravagance.

adj. dear, expensive, costly, high-priced, pricey (*inf.*); exorbitant, too high, overpriced, excessive, prohibitive, extortionate, immoderate, unreasonable, extravagant, lavish, steep (*inf.*), stiff (*inf.*).

vb. be dear, cost a lot, cost a pretty penny (*inf.*); go up, increase, revalue; overcharge, exploit, bleed, fleece, extort.

746 cheapness

n. cheapness, inexpensiveness, competitiveness, reasonableness; bargain, good value, good buy.

adj. cheap, inexpensive, low-priced, moderate, reasonable, fair, peanuts (*sl.*).

family-sized, economy-sized, economy, bargain, standard; reduced, cut-price, half-price, marked down, dirt cheap.

free, gratuitous, for nothing, without charge, complimentary, gratis, on the house, for love.

vb. be cheap, get one's money's worth; fall in price, decrease, cheapen, depreciate, mark down, devalue.

747 liberality

n. liberality, generosity, benevolence, bounteousness, bounty, largesse; kindness, giving, charity, hospitality, cordiality.

adj. liberal, generous, big-hearted, open-handed, bountiful, lavish, unsparing, unstinting, munificent; kind, benevolent, unselfish, charitable, beneficent.

vb. be liberal, give generously, lavish, heap upon, spare no expense, go beyond what one can afford.

748 economy

n. economy, thrift, care, prudence, housekeeping, stewardship, management, frugality, husbandry, providence; parsimony, stinginess; saving; retrenchment.

adj. economical, economizing, careful, prudent, good, saving, thrifty, frugal, sparing, stingy, mean; convenient, time-saving, labour-saving.

vb. economize, cut back, keep costs down, cut costs, cut corners, tighten one's belt (*inf.*), make ends meet, live within one's means; manage, steward, husband, save, conserve.

749 extravagance

n. extravagance, wastefulness, squandering, prodigality, lavishness, immoderateness; money to burn, shopping spree, spending spree, no thought of tommorow; prodigal, wastrel, spendthrift, squanderer.

adj. extravagant, wasteful, squandering, prodigal, lavish, over-generous, immoderate, exorbitant, reckless, careless, profligate.

vb. waste, squander, throw away, have money to burn, spend money like water, hang the expense, blow (*sl.*), blue (*sl.*); fritter away, dissipate; go too far, overdo it.

750 parsimony

n. parsimony, parsimoniousness, stinginess, scrimping, niggardliness, penny-pinching, cheese-paring, meanness, miserliness, penuriousness; niggard, miser, screw; greed, avarice, covetousness, avidity, voracity, gluttony.

adj. parsimonious, stingy, niggardly, miserly, mean, tight-fisted, close-fisted, penny-pinching, scrimping; sparing, chary,

greedy, avaricious, voracious, possessive, acquisitive, grasping, grabby (*inf.*), itchy (*inf.*), rapacious, covetous, avid.

vb. be parsimonious, scrimp, stint, skimp; over-economize; be greedy, always want more.

VI Affections

A Affections in general

751 affections

n. affections, qualities, character, nature, make-up; personality, psyche, heart, soul, breast, inner self; temperament, disposition, spirit, temper, mood, state of mind, frame of mind, humour; tendency, inclination, bent, bias.

adj. affected, characterized, formed,

moulded, disposed, inclined, predisposed.

see also 5, 58

752 feeling

n. feeling, emotion, affection, sentiment, passion; experience, sense, impression, consciousness, sensation, perception, sympathy, warmth, tenderness, sensitivity, empathy; fervour, ardour, enthusiasm.

adj. feeling, emotional, sentimental, romantic, passionate, fervent, intense, impassioned, dramatic, burning, earnest, moving, tender; felt, experienced, heart-felt, thrilled, moved, affected, touched.

vb. feel, sense, experience, go through, enjoy, suffer, undergo, bear, endure.

move, affect, touch, stir, impress, excite, influence, quicken, touch one's heart, touch to the quick; appreciate, respond; thrill, tingle.

753 sensitivity

n. sensitivity, sensibility, susceptibility, awareness, consciousness, responsiveness, excitability.

five senses, sight, hearing, smell, taste, touch; sixth sense, intuition, feminine intuition; extra-sensory perception.

adj. sensitive, aware, conscious of, alive to, awake to, susceptible, impressionable, receptive, sensible; sensory, sentient.

raw, tender, bare, sore, bruised, delicate, painful, oversensitive, hypersensitive; exposed, open, vulnerable.

754 insensitivity

n. insensitivity, insensibility, unawareness, unresponsiveness, inexcitability, impassivness; apathy, indifference, lethargy, aloofness, coldness; hypnosis, numbness, paralysis; dream, trance, coma, stupor; hardness of heart, callousness; stoic, ascetic; iceberg.

adj. insensitive, insusceptible, unimpressionable, unresponsive, inexcitable, unmoved, unaffected, unaware, unconscious, dead to, blind to, oblivious to, lost to, insensible; lethargic, dull, unenthusiastic, apathetic, indifferent, cool, aloof; unfeeling, unemotional, passionless, unresponsive, frigid, cold, numb, paralyzed; blank, poker-faced, dead pan, expressionless; thick-skinned, hard-hearted, callous, cold-blooded.

vb. deaden, numb, paralyze, stupefy, stun, harden, sear, blunt, dull, drug; turn off (*inf.*), switch off (*inf*); be unaffected, leave cold.

755 excitation

n. excitation, stimulation, activation, animation, inspiration, quickening; incitement, provocation, agitation, excitement; captivation, fascination, interest.

adj. exciting, stimulating, inspiring, moving, sparkling, exhilarating, thrilling, delightful; captivating, fascinating, interesting, absorbing, gripping, stirring, tantalizing, compelling, impressive, dramatic, sensational.

vb. excite, stimulate, arouse, activate, move, stir, work up, whip up, incite, influence, affect, provoke, awaken, touch, interest, animate, quicken, inspire; inflame, intensify, kindle, fire, light up; electrify, galvanize, energize.

absorb, fascinate, attract attention, impress, intrigue; tantalize, tease, anger, cause a stir; catch one's attention, come home, arrest, compel, engage; make one's mouth water, whet the appetite; knock for six (*inf.*), take one's breath away; delight, thrill, exhilarate, turn on (*inf.*), switch on (*inf.*).

see also **756, 829**

756 excitability

n. excitability, impetuousness, boisterousness, instability, emotionalism, restlessness, agitation, irritability, intolerance.

excitement, exhilaration, thrill, ecstasy, transport; rage, fury, outburst, agony; hysterics, delirium; fuss, big song and dance (*inf.*), hullabaloo, tizzy (*sl.*), tiz-woz (*sl.*), dither (*inf.*), fluster, stew (*inf.*), to-do.

adj. excited, moved, stirred, inspired, thrilled, quickened, enthusiastic, eager, impressed, delighted, pleased, happy, joyful, touched.

excitable, sensitive, highly-strung, nervous, easily excited, emotional; impulsive, quick-tempered, impetuous; moody, temperamental; impatient, irritable, touchy, edgy, jumpy, jittery, restless, fidgety; tense, uptight, all worked up (*inf.*), keyed up, a bundle of nerves (*inf.*); distraught, beside onself; mad, fuming, raging.

vb. be excited, thrill; let oneself go, get carried away, abandon oneself, freak out (*sl.*); tingle, glow, palpitate, pant; tremble, quiver, shake.

get excited, work oneself up; feet, flap (*inf.*), shuffle, fuss; rage, fume, explode, flare up, boil over (*inf.*).

see also **755**

757 inexcitability

n. inexcitability, imperturbability, stability, composure, calmness, coolness, level-headedness, even temper, steadiness; peace of mind, serenity, tranquillity; self-possession, self-control, self-restraint, self-assurance; detachment, aloofness; stoicism.

patience, endurance, forbearance, long-suffering, submission, humility, meekness, resignation.

adj. inexcitable, calm, cool, composed, collected, self-possessed, dispassionate, imperturbable, unflappable (*inf.*), unruffled, immovable, stable, level-headed, even-tempered, easygoing, moderate, sedate, serene, tranquil, placid, inoffensive, mild, phlegmatic; patient, forbearing, uncomplaining, meek, submissive, philosophic, stoical; detached, aloof, disinterested, spiritless, nonchalant, blasé, casual.

vb. keep calm, keep one's temper, keep one's cool (*sl.*), keep one's shirt on (*sl.*), not bat an eyelid; calm down, compose oneself, control oneself, relax, take hold of oneself, pull oneself together, cool it (*sl.*), simmer down (*inf.*), cool off.

bear, tolerate, endure, put up with, stomach (*inf.*), stick it out (*inf.*), swallow, brook, resign oneself to, grin and bear it, submit to, make the best of.

B Sensation

758 touch

n. touch, feeling, contact, tactility; feel, touching, stroking, massage, manipulation; tickle, titillation, itching, scratching, pricking, stinging, shivers.

adj. tactile, tactual, tangible, touchable, palpable.

vb. touch, feel, press, squeeze, stroke, rub, finger, paw, smooth, caress, fondle, massage, manipulate, lick, kiss; tap, pat, hit, strike; explore, feel for, grope, fumble; grasp, grip, grab, grapple, clasp, clutch; tickle, titillate, itch; graze, scratch, prick, sting.

759 heat

n. heat, hotness, warmth, tepidity; temperature, thermometer; thermostat; hot weather, summer, heatwave, scorcher (*inf.*), dog days; fire, blaze, glow, light, sparkle, flicker, conflagration; ardour, fervour, zeal, passion, intensity.

adj. thermal; hot, very warm, torrid, parched; burning, fiery, blazing, ignited, lit, alight, on fire, in flames, glowing, incandescent, smoking; heated, molten; sweltering, baking, scorching, sizzling, scalding, grilling, roasting; tropical, humid, sticky, close, sultry, muggy, stifling, oppressive; warm, tepid, lukewarm; temperate, mild, fair, sunny, summery; bright, clear; intense, fervent, vehement, passionate, ardent, excited.

vb. be hot, burn, flame, burst into flames, catch fire, flare up, flicker, glow; smoke, fume, reek, smoulder, smother, suffocate; cook, boil, scald, seethe, fry, sizzle, roast, parch, scorch, bake, swelter.

760 cold

n. cold, coldness, chilliness, frigidity, frozenness, iciness, frostiness, congelation; chill, nip, shivers, shivering; cold snap, arctic conditions; ice, icicle, glacier, iceberg, black ice; frost, rime, hoar-frost; hail, hailstorm; snow, snowflake, snowdrift, snowstorm, blizzard, avalanche, sleet, slush.

adj. cryoscopic, cold, cool, chilly, fresh, crisp, brisk, nippy, frigid; piercing, biting, cutting, numbing, stinging; raw, sharp, keen; wintry, brumal, bleak, Siberian, arctic, polar; freezing, icy, gelid, frosty, hoary.

vb. be cold, freeze, shiver, shudder, quiver; chatter.

761 heating

n. heating, warming; combustion, burning, incineration, flaming, kindling, ignition, scorching, incandescence.

adj. heating, warming, calefactory; combustible, flammable; glowing, incandescent.

vb. heat, warm, heat up, reheat, put on the fire; ignite, kindle, set fire to, strike a light, put a match to, touch off; burn, scorch, consume, scald, incinerate, reduce to ashes, cremate; fire, smelt; thaw, defrost, de-ice, unfreeze, melt, liquefy; insulate.

762 refrigeration; incombustibility

n. refrigeration, cooling, chilling, freezing, glaciation, glacification.

incombustibility, non-flammability; asbestos, safety curtain.

adj. cooled, chilled; frozen, icy.

incombustible, non-flammable, fireproof.

vb. refrigerate, cool, chill, make cold, freeze, deep-freeze, ice, frost, congeal, glaciate.

extinguish, put out, blow out, quench, stifle, smother, damp, choke, snuff, douse, drown.

763 furnace

n. furnace, boiler, kiln, stove, cooker, oven; incinerator; crematorium; fire, heater, radiator; hearth, fireplace, fireside, grate, hob.

764 refrigerator

n. refrigerator, fridge, freezer, deep-freeze, icebox, icepack, cool-bag, cool-box, cooling apparatus, cold storage; air-conditioner, fan, ventilator.

765 fuel

n. fuel, combustible; coal, coke, charcoal, briquette, wood, log, gas, oil, petrol, electricity, juice (*sl.*), hydro-electricity, nuclear power, solar energy.

match, lighter, firelighter, fuse, touch-paper, vesta, detonator, torch, firebrand, tinder, flint.

adj. combustible, flammable, explosive.

vb. fuel, fire, power; feed, stoke.

766 thermometer

n. thermometer, calorimeter, thermostat, mercury, clinical thermometer, pyrometer, thermocouple, thermopile, thermograph; Fahrenheit, centigrade, Celsius, Réamur, kelvin; degree.

767 taste

n. taste, flavour, relish, savour, smack, sapor; tang, after-taste; tongue, palate, taste buds; gustation.

adj. tasty, palatable, delicious, appetizing, gustatory.

vb. taste, relish, enjoy, eat, smack one's lips; try, sample, sip; taste of, savour of.

768 tastelessness

n. tastelessness, insipidity, flavourlessness, dullness, flatness, staleness.

adj. tasteless, unsavoury, insipid, flavourless, dull, flat, bland, stale, wishy-washy, unseasoned, unspiced, plastic (*inf.*), uninteresting.

see also 507, 843

769 pungency

n. pungency, piquancy, sharpness, keenness, spiciness, tanginess; zest, bite, edge, tang, kick (*inf.*), zing (*sl.*), punch (*sl.*).

adj. pungent, sharp, piquant, penetrating, poignant, strong, tangy,

racy; spiced, curried, hot; tart, sour, bitter.

see also 307

770 savouriness

n. savouriness, palatability, deliciousness, tastiness, richness, lusciousness.

delicacy, luxury, treat, rarity, delight, titbit, dainty, *bonne bouche*, chef's special, dish fit for a king; caviar; ambrosia, nectar.

adj. palatable, delicious, savoury, tasty, nice, dainty, delightful, choice, rich, luscious, delectable, exquisite, heavenly (*inf.*), scrumptious (*inf.*), yummy (*inf.*); fit for a king, fit for the gods; well done, done to a turn.

appetizing, mouth-watering, tempting, inviting, enticing, tantalizing, moreish (*inf.*).

vb. taste good; enjoy, like, relish, savour, appreciate.

771 unsavouriness

n. unsavouriness, unpalatability, unpleasantness, flavourlessness; bread and water, bitter pill, yuk (*sl.*).

adj. tasteless, flavourless, bland, dull, inedible; undrinkable; underdone; gone off; yukky (*sl.*); uninteresting, unappealing, unappetizing, uninviting, disagreeable, horrible, revolting.

vb. nauseate, disgust, turn one's stomach; disagree with, turn off (*inf.*); dislike, loathe.

772 sweetness

n. sweetness, sweetening, sugariness; sweet, sweetener, sugar, honey, molasses, syrup, treacle, saccharin.

adj. sweet, sweetened, sugared; sugary, saccharine, sirupy, rich, luscious, delicious; sticky; bitter-sweet, sweet-and-sour.

vb. sweeten, make sweet, sugar; dulcify.

773 sourness

n. sourness, acidity, bitterness, sharpness; acid, vinegar, gall, wormwood.

adj. sour, acid, tart, bitter, caustic, cutting, pungent, sharp, biting, dry; acidulous, vinegary, acetous; unsweetened, unsugared, unripe.

vb. sour, turn sour, set one's teeth on edge; ferment, curdle, tartarize.

774 odour

n. odour, smell, scent, trace, trail, exhalation, emanation, effluvium; fragrance; stench.

sense of smell, smelling, olfaction, detection.

adj. smelling, scented, odorous; strong, pungent, redolent; olfactory.

vb. smell, smell of, give out, give off, emit, scent, exhale; sniff, whiff, detect, perceive, smell out.

see also 776, 777

775 inodorousness

n. inodorousness, no smell; deodorization, ventilation, fumigation; deodorant, deodorizer; fumigant, fumigator, cleanser.

adj. inodorous, odourless, unscented, scentless.

vb. deodorize, fumigate, aerate, clean, purify.

776 fragrance

n. fragrance, aroma, bouquet, scent, perfume, spice, balm.

adj. fragrant, aromatic, scented, perfumed, spicy, sweet-scented, sweet-smelling, redolent, odoriferous, odorous, ambrosial.

vb. smell, scent, be fragrant; scent, perfume, embalm.

777 stench

n. stench, smell, stink, fetor, reek, fume, mephitis, miasma; foulness, uncleanness, smelliness, mustiness, rancidity; B.O. (inf.), body odour; skunk, polecat; stink-bomb.

adj. smelly, stinking, foul, unclean, fetid, strong-smelling, foul-smelling, nasty, vile, repulsive, offensive, rank, noxious, noisome; stale, musty, rancid, putrid, decaying, high, putrescent.

vb. smell, stink, reek, smell to high heaven (inf.).

778 sound

n. sound, noise, vibration, resonance, report, reverberation, echo, ringing; loudness, softness; note, level, accent, cadence, tenor, intonation, tone, timbre; acoustics, phonetics.

adj. sounding, heard, audible, distinct, within earshot; loud, resonant, sonorous, auditory, acoustic, phonetic.

vb. sound, make a noise, give out, emit, produce; hear, listen.

see also 795

779 silence

n. silence, inaudibility, quietness, stillness, noiselessness; peace, quiet, still, hush; loss of signal, blackout, news blackout, security blackout, censorship.

adj. silent, inaudible, noiseless, hushed, quiet, still, soundless, unuttered, unspoken, unvoiced; soundproof.

vb. silence, hush, quiet, still, calm, muffle, reduce to silence, mute, stifle; subdue, deaden, repress, tone down, put the lid on.

see also 513, 517

780 loudness

n. loudness, noisiness, audibility, rowdiness; noise, racket, roar, boom, blast, swell, din, clamour, tumult, outcry, uproar, hubbub, hullabaloo, pandemonium.

adj. loud, noisy, clamorous, vociferous, loud-mouthed; boisterous, rumbustious, rowdy, obstreperous; thundering, deafening, ringing, booming, ear-splitting, resounding, piercing, blaring, crashing, stentorian, enough to wake the dead.

vb. be loud, boom, roar, thunder, fulminate, resound, bellow, blare, peal, crash, rattle, deafen, be unable to hear oneself think.

781 faintness

n. faintness, softness, inaudibility; whisper, breath, undertone, murmur, mutter, sigh, rustle, ripple, hum.

adj. faint, soft, quiet, hushed, inaudible; indistinct, stifled, muted, muffled, deadened, subdued; feeble, weak, low, distant, muttering.

vb. whisper, speak softly, murmur, mutter, sigh, hum, rustle, purr, creak, squeak.

782 sudden and violent sound

n. bang, blast, shot, report, boom, detonation, eruption, explosion; thud, whack, knock, slap, tap, rap, snap; crash, crackle; shout, cry, yelp.

vb. crash, crack, knock, slap, smack, whack, tap, rap, snap; click; plop, plonk, thud; thunder, boom, detonate, bang, pop, slam, burst, explode, blow up, set off.

783 repeated and prolonged sound

n. roll, clang, clatter; rattle, rustle; chuckle, cackle; whistle, hum, whirr, purr, buzz, strum; throb.

vb. roll, clang, clatter; rattle, rustle; ripple, swish, hum, drone, whirr, purr, buzz, strum, whistle, trill; thump, throb, palpitate, tick, beat, pound,

patter; chime, peal, toll; chuckle, cackle; rumble, grumble, growl.

784 resonance

n. resonance, vibration, tintinnabulation; ringing, clanging, echo, resounding, thunder, boom; chime, bell, gong, jingle, tinkle.

adj. resonant, vibrant, reverberating, loud, echoing, ringing, clanging, chiming, deep-sounding.

vb. resound, reverberate, boom, vibrate, echo, re-echo, ring, gong, chime, tinkle, jingle, clang, whirr, buzz, drone, whine, purr, hum.

785 non-resonance

n. non-resonance, thud, bump, plop, plump, thump, plonk, clonk, clunk.

adj. non-resonant, deadened, muffled, dead, heavy, dull.

vb. thud, bump, plonk, plump, plop, thump, clonk, clunk; muffle, stifle, dull, damp, deaden.

786 hissing sound

n. hiss, hissing, sibilance, buzz, swish, rustle, whirr, whistle, splash, squelch, whoosh, zip.

adj. hissing, sibilant.

vb. buzz, hiss, swish, rustle, whistle, splash, whoosh, zip, fizz, whiz, whirr, squelch, sizzle, sneeze, wheeze, effervesce, sibilate.

787 harsh sound

n. harshness, hoarseness, gruffness, discord, dissonance, cacophony; shrillness, whistle, croak, squawk, squeal, screech, shriek.

adj. strident, shrill, high-pitched, piercing, sharp, penetrating; squealing, creaking, grating, scratchy, tinny, metallic; clanging, clashing, screeching, jarring, discordant, dissonant; hoarse, gruff, harsh, raucous, loud, husky, throaty, guttural, dry.

147

vb. clang, clatter, clunk, crash, bang, clash, jangle; croak, quack, squawk, caw, cluck; saw, grind; shrill, whistle, shriek, screech, scream, squeal, yelp, squeak, creak; grate, rasp, irritate, jar, set one's teeth on edge, get on one's nerves.

788 human sound

n. cry, exclamation, utterance, shout, call, noise, shouting, clamour, outcry; scream, shriek, yell, moan, groan, wail, bellow, howl, whimper.

adj. clamorous, noisy, loud, yelling, vociferous.

vb. cry, exclaim, call, speak, utter, shout, scream, yell, shriek, screech, squeal, squeak, caterwaul, bawl, bellow, hoot, vociferate, whoop, hoop, hollo; groan, moan, complain, howl, wail, whine, whimper, sob.

cheer, chant, clamour, support; shout down, hiss, boo, ridicule, disapprove, censure.

789 animal sound

n. call, cry, ululation, barking.

vb. cry, yelp, yap, squeal, squawk; cackle, cluck, quack; caw, crow; screech, croak, coo, cuckoo; gobble, gaggle; chuckle, chirp, chirrup, cheep; tweet, twitter, whistle, pipe, trill, sing, warble; purr, miaow, mew, caterwaul; hum, drone, buzz; bark, bay, howl, woof, roar, bellow, bell; grunt, snort, snap, growl, snarl, whine, oink; neigh, bray, whinny; bleat, baa; moo, low.

790 melody

n. melody, melodiousness, tunefulness, concord, consonance, euphony, harmony, unison, accord, concert, music, blending.

adj. melodious, musical, euphonic, tuneful, rhythmical, melodic, lyrical, harmonious, in tune, accordant; sweet-sounding, dulcet, soothing, pleasing, mellow, soft, rich; catchy, memorable, singable, popular.

791 discord

n. discord, discordance, unmelodiousness, inharmoniousness, dissonance, atonality; noise, din, racket, cacophony.

adj. discordant, dissonant, atonal, unmelodious, inharmonious, unmusical, untuneful, out of tune, off key, flat, sharp; cacophonous, clashing, jarring, grating.

792 music

n. music, composition, work, opus, piece; arrangement, adaptation, setting, transcription, orchestration, instrumentation; incidental music, background music, accompaniment; record, recording; concert, recital.

classical music, chamber music, light music, country and western, folk music, pop music, electronic music, jazz, blues, reggae, punk, rock, soul, ragtime.

symphony, concerto, suite; overture, prelude; sonata; ballet, dance; opera, operetta; song, air, solo, hymn, strain; tune, chorus, refrain, round; duo, trio, quartet; passage, movement, phrase.

adj. musical, tuneful, pleasing; vocal, choral; scored, arranged, adapted.

vb. compose, write, set to music, arrange, score; perform, render, play, make music, interpret; sing, chant, croon; listen.

793 musician

n. musician, artist, player, performer, virtuoso, soloist, instrumentalist, concert artist; singer, vocalist, chorister, bard, minstrel, artiste, choir, chorus, singing group; orchestra, band, ensemble, symphony orchestra, chamber orchestra; group; dancer, ballerina; composer.

794 musical instrument

n. musical instrument, brass, woodwind, stringed instruments, percussion; record player, gramophone, stereo, hi-fi, music centre, stereogram, juke-box; record, disc, single, LP; tape-recorder, cassette-recorder; recording tape.

795 hearing

n. hearing, sense of hearing; good hearing, an ear for; earshot, range, carrying distance, sound; listening, auscultation; eavesdropping, wire-tapping.

listener, hearer, auditor, witness; eavesdropper, wire-tapper, peeping Tom; audience, auditorium; audition, interview, reception.

adj. auditory, hearing, auricular.

vb. hear, listen to, catch, take in, pick up, lend an ear, be all ears, give a hearing to, hark; attend to, pay attention to; perceive, detect, get wind of; overhear, listen in, eavesdrop, tap, bug.

796 deafness

n. deafness, inaudibility, deaf-and-dumbness, deaf-mutism; lip reading, deaf-and-dumb alphabet, deaf-and-dumb language, dactylology.

adj. deaf, hard of hearing, stone-deaf, deaf-and-dumb, deaf-mute; deafening, stunning, ear-splitting; deaf to, unaware of.

vb. deafen, stun.

797 light

n. light, illumination, lighting, radiance, brilliance, splendour, brightness, clearness, lightness; luminosity, phosphorescence.

beam, ray, gleam, shaft, streak, laser, pencil, stream, glint, chink; flash, streak, blaze, flame, flare, glow, spark, sparkle, twinkle, flicker, glimmer, glitter, dazzle, shimmer; glare, gloss, shine, lustre; polish, reflection; daylight, sunshine; sunrise, daybreak, dawn.

adj. luminous, light, bright, clear, shining, brilliant, beaming, glowing, glittering, sparkling, gleaming, dazzling; shiny, glossy, sheeny; illuminated, lighted, lit; cloudless.

vb. shine, burn, glow, blaze, glitter, glimmer, glisten, gleam, sparkle, dazzle, blind; flash, shimmer, flicker, twinkle, scintillate, blink, flare, beam; dance, play, reflect, glare.

illuminate, switch on, lighten, brighten, enlighten, dawn, shed light on, light up, irradiate; polish, burnish.

798 darkness

n. darkness, dark, night, nightfall, Cimmerian gloom, blackness, blackout, eclipse, shade, shadow, umbra, penumbra, adumbration, obscuration; gloom, sombreness.

adj. dark, unlit, unlighted, unilluminated; black, starless, dull, overcast, cloudy; indistinct, obscure, shady, nebulous, shaded, shadowy; tenebrous, obfuscous; dismal, gloomy, sombre, dreary, bleak, desolate, murky, dim.

vb. darken, blacken, black out, switch off, cover, eclipse, obscure, overshadow, becloud, place in shadow, cast a shadow over, obfuscate, adumbrate.

799 dimness

n. dimness, murkiness, shadiness, obscurity; dusk, twilight, half-light, gloaming, gloom.

adj. dim, dull, faint, vague, indistinct, obscure, blurred, opaque, fading, evanescent; grey, cloudy, foggy, hazy, misty, shadowy, gloomy.

vb. dim, dull, fade out, blur, obscure, shade, becloud, cloud over, dull, vanish, wane, evanesce.

800 source of light

n. light, luminary, sun, moon, planet, star, halo, aurora, corona, nimbus; meteor, shooting star; lightning, flash; fireworks.

lamp, torch, bulb, spotlight, searchlight, flashlight, floodlight, headlamp, side-light, indicator; neon light, fluorescent tube, strobe light, lantern; beacon, lighthouse.

candle, wick, spill, taper, wax; match, flame, flare; coal, ember, brand.

801 shade

n. shade, covering, veil, shield, screen, blind, curtain, shutter, drape; sunglasses, blinkers, goggles; visor, hood; shelter, awning, canopy; umbrella, parasol.

adj. shady; screened.

vb. shade, cover, veil, screen, shield, shelter, protect, curtain, blinker.

see also **463**, **593**

802 transparency

n. transparency, clearness, glassiness, vitreosity, translucence, lucidity.

adj. transparent, translucent, clear, see-through, revealing, unobstructed, glassy, vitreous, crystal, lucid, diaphanous, pellucid, limpid.

vb. be transparent, see through, show, show through.

see also **502**

803 opacity

n. opacity, opaqueness, cloudiness, murkiness, obscurity, darkness; smoke, mist, cloud, film.

adj. opaque, non-transparent, absorbing light, impervious, dark, unclear, smoky, misty, cloudy, muddy, blurred, filmy, dull, murky, dim, darkened, turbid.

vb. make opaque, devitrify, obscure, darken, cloud, smoke, obstruct one's vision.

see also **503**

804 semitransparency

n. semitransparency, translucence, pearliness, milkiness; smoked glass, frosted glass, opal glass; dark glasses, sunglasses.

adj. semitransparent, semitranslucid, semiopaque, frosted, pearly, smoked, milky.

805 colour

n. colour, hue, shade, tinge, tone, dash, touch, tint, tincture, cast; paint, pigment, dye, wash, stain, lake; prism, spectrum; glow, brilliance, warmth, intensity; coloration, colouring, pigmentation, complexion, chromatism.

adj. coloured, chromatic, tinted, tinged, touched, dyed, painted, stained; constant, fast.

colourful, bright, warm, glowing, intense, strong, deep, rich, brilliant; garish, glaring, gaudy, loud, showy, flashy, lurid, harsh, clashing, painful.

soft, pastel, subdued, refined, tender, delicate, matt; faded, dingy, dull, drab, cold, uninviting.

vb. colour, shade, tinge, paint, touch up, stain, wash, coat, put on, lay on; contrast, set off, throw into relief; clash, not go with, conflict, grate.

806 absence of colour

n. colourlessness, achromatism, discoloration, fading, paleness, dullness, dimness, faintness, flatness; anaemia, sallowness, whitening, bleaching.

adj. colourless, hueless, toneless, lacklustre, dull, lifeless, cold, dim, faint, weak; faded, washed out, pale, pallid, sallow, ashen, white, anaemic, pasty; transparent.

vb. fade, lose colour, lose brightness, bleach, blanch, wash out, whiten, drain, turn pale, discolour, grow dim, etiolate.

807 white

n. white, whiteness, whitishness, lightness, fairness, paleness; milkiness, chalkiness, silveriness, snowiness.

adj. white, fair, light, blonde, hoary; snowy, snow-white, frosted, milky, lactescent, chalky, silvery, pearly, ivory, albescent; whitish, cream, off-white; pale, ashen, anaemic, sallow, wan; clean, spotless, pure.

vb. whiten, whitewash, bleach, blanch, snow; clean, purify.

808 black

n. black, blackness, darkness, inkiness, sootiness.

adj. black, blackish; jet-black, pitch-black, coal-black; inky, sooty, stained; dark, murky; sable, swarthy.

vb. blacken, ink, ink in, darken, shade.

809 grey

n. grey, greyness, dinginess, drabness, dusk, shade.

adj. grey, greyish, shaded, dull, drab, dingy, sombre, neutral; dusty, smoky; silver-haired, hoary; speckled, pepper-and-salt.

810 brown

n. brown, tan, beige, mahogany.

adj. brown, brownish, beige, khaki, maroon, auburn, buff, bronze, copper, chocolate, coffee, rust-coloured, reddish-brown, bay, chestnut, russet, sepia, ochre, hazel.

811 red

n. red, redness, blush, glow, colour, cochineal, carmine.

adj. red, reddish, ruddy, scarlet, crimson, vermilion, ruby, cherry-red, blood-red, coral, brick-red, maroon, rust, magenta, russet, auburn, pink, salmon-pink, rosy; glowing, warm; blushing, embarrassed, burning.

vb. redden, blush; glow, flush.

812 green

n. green, verdure; lawn, turf.

adj. green, greenish, grassy, verdant, leafy, lime, emerald, sage, olive, beryl, blue-green, aquamarine, sea-green, pea-green; bilious, sickly, pale; fresh, unripe.

813 yellow

n. yellow, cream, tan, lemon; buttercup, daffodil, crocus, jasmine.

adj. yellow, yellowish, cream, saffron, sand, gold, golden, buff, tan, khaki, light-brown; sallow, bilious, jaundiced.

814 purple

n. purple; violet, pansy, lavender.

adj. purple, purplish, reddish-blue, bluish-red, violet, indigo, mauve, lilac, lavender, plum-coloured.

815 blue

n. blue, sky, azure, indigo.

adj. blue, bluish, turquoise, azure, royal blue, navy blue; sapphire, sky-blue, indigo.

816 orange

n. orange, tangerine, apricot, peach, mandarin, carrot, salmon, coral.

adj. orange, orangey, reddish-yellow, gold, old gold, copper, bronze, brass, ginger.

817 variegation

n. variegation, diversification, diversity, motley, spectrum, rainbow, kaleidoscope; chequerwork, tartan, mosaic, parquetry, marquetry.

adj. variegated, kaleidoscopic, many-coloured, multi-coloured; spotted, mottled, motley, patched, piebald, pied, dappled, speckled, freckled; striped, streaked, checked.

vb. diversify, variegate, chequer, checker; stud, mottle, spatter, dapple, speckle, stipple, streak, strip.

818 vision

n. vision, sight, eyesight, perception, recognition; observation, inspection, scrutiny, investigation, notice, once-over (*inf.*); bird's eye view, survey, panorama, overview.

look, view, regard, glance, glimpse, eye; squint, peep, peek; leer; wink, twinkle.

viewpoint, standpoint, position, outlook, perspective, attitude; lookout, observation point, watch-tower, gallery, grandstand.

adj. visual, ocular, opthalmic, optical; observant; watchful, vigilant.

vb. see, look at, view, watch, look on, observe, perceive, discern, recognize, notice, catch sight of, set eyes on, eye; glance, glimpse, catch a glimpse of, peep, blink, wink, twinkle; gaze, gape, stare, fix one's eyes on; leer, ogle, glare, glower.

scrutinize, investigate, survey, inspect; scan, look through, look over, flick through (*inf.*), thumb through (*inf.*).

819 blindness

n. blindness, sightlessness, colour-blindness, night-blindness, snow-blindness; blind spot, blind side, failing, mote in one's eye.

adj. blind, sightless, unseeing, eyeless, colour-blind; blinded, blind-

fold, blinkered, hoodwinked, in the dark.

vb. be blind, lose one's sight, strike blind, put someone's eyes out; obscure, hide, mask, screen, blindfold, blinker, hoodwink.

820 imperfect vision

n. imperfect vision, partial vision; shortsightedness, myopia; longsightedness, presbyopia; double vision; colour-blindness; squint, strabism, cross-eye, astigmatism, conjunctivitis, cataract.

adj. dim-sighted, purblind, half-blind; shortsighted, myopic; long-sighted, presbyopic; colour-blind, astigmatic, cross-eyed, squinting, strabismic.

vb. see double, squint, screw up one's eyes, see blurred.

821 spectator

n. spectator, viewer, onlooker, observer, watcher, eye-witness, bystander, passer-by, looker-on, beholder; sightseer; peeper, peeping Tom; spy, snoop, meddler.

spectators, crowd, public, supporters, fans, followers, turn-out, audience.

822 optical instrument

n. glasses, spectacles, bifocals, goggles, specs (*inf.*), contact lenses, monocle, eye-glasses, lorgnette, pince-nez; binoculars, opera glasses, field glasses, telescope; microscope, magnifying glass, lens; camera; mirror, looking glass, reflector, glass, speculum.

823 visibility

n. visibility, perceptibility, clarity, distinctness, plainness, prominence, conspicuousness.

adj. visible, apparent, in view, in sight, observable, perceptible, noticeable, before one's very eyes; evident, clear, plain, obvious, patent; prominent, conspicuous, pronounced, standing out; unmistakable, glaring; open, exposed; distinct, well-defined, definite, clear-cut.

vb. show, show through, show itself, manifest itself, be revealed, come into sight, come into view; stand out, stand out a mile (*inf.*), stick out like a sore thumb (*sl.*), hit in the face, leap to the eye.

see also **458, 825**

824 invisibility

n. invisibility, concealment, seclusion, latency, obscurity, indistinctness, imperceptibility, indefiniteness, vagueness, indiscernibility, cloudiness, darkness, haziness, fuzziness.

adj. invisible, imperceptible, indiscernible; hidden, out of sight, concealed, obscure; inconspicuous; indistinct, unclear, ill-defined, vague; intangible, unseen, spiritual; cloudy, nebulous, shadowy, mysterious, hazy, blurred, fuzzy.

see also **461, 826**

825 appearance

n. appearance, look, aspect, feature, shape, form, outline, profile, face; condition, presentation, expression; posture, pose, bearing; mien, countenance, manner, behaviour; externals, appearances, outward show, first impression, face value.

phenomenon, spectacle, display, exhibition, show, demonstration, scene, parade, pageant.

adj. apparent, visible, manifest; seeming, ostensible, supposed, specious, plausible, alleged, outward, superficial, external, to look at (*inf.*).

vb. appear, look, seem, show, take

the form of; emerge, arise, come into view, be revealed, turn up, show up, put in an appearance, crop up (*inf.*), pop up (*inf.*), occur, happen, present itself, express itself, manifest itself, materialize, come to light, come into the picture, come onto the horizon, see the light of day.

adv. apparently, to all appearances, superficially, at first sight, on the face of it, for show, to all intents and purposes.

see also **222, 458, 823**

826 disappearance

n. disappearance, vanishing, fading, fade-out, evanescence, evaporation, dematerialization; departure, retirement, flight, escape, removal, withdrawal, loss.

adj. disappearing, fading, evanescent; disappeared, vanished, missing.

vb. disappear, vanish, fade, evaporate, dematerialize, dissolve; pass out of sight, leave no trace, disappear into thin air, go up in smoke, vanish from sight, be eclipsed, be swallowed up, be lost to view.

go away, depart, remove, withdraw, retire, escape, flee; cease, be no more, die, perish, sink.

see also **824**

C Personal

827 pleasure

n. pleasure, joy, happiness, gladness, delight, enjoyment, satisfaction, fulfilment; serenity.

enchantment, bewitchment, exultation, relish, gusto, zest, glee, cheer, thrill, kick (*inf.*), ecstasy, elation, bliss, rapture, euphoria, transport; luxury, ease, convenience, comfort, paradise, bed of roses, golden age, halcyon days, lap of luxury.

gratification, indulgence, self-indulgence, revelry, hedonism, sensuousness, sensuality, sexuality.

adj. pleasant, satisfying, enjoyable, delightful, exciting, adorable, welcome; comfortable, snug, cosy, homely, comfy (*inf.*), congenial, convenient, palatial, luxurious, gratifying, pleasurable, sensuous, bodily, physical, hedonistic, voluptuous, self-indulgent, carnal.

happy, pleased, joyful, glad, delighted, joyous, satisfied; thrilled, excited, tickled pink (*inf.*), exhilarated, starry-eyed, bubbling over, in the seventh heaven; smiling, laughing, genial, convivial, delirious; merry, in good spirits, cheery, jolly, blithe, gladsome, blissful; overjoyed, ecstatic, in ecstasies, enraptured, in raptures enthusiastic, carried away; peaceful, contented, at peace.

vb. enjoy, like, take delight in, derive pleasure from, rejoice in, love, fancy, be keen on, appreciate, relish, revel in, get a kick out of (*inf.*), rave about (*inf.*), enjoy oneself, have a good time, tread on air.

see also **829, 836, 840**

828 pain

n. pain, hurt, distress, discomfort, affliction, anguish, misery, agony, shock, blow, injury, suffering, unhappiness, sorrow, grief, sadness, regret, melancholy, despair, broken heart, weeping, wretchedness, tribulation, trial, ordeal, torment, torture, martyrdom, crucifixion, hell; bereavement, sense of loss, mourning, grieving; ache, twinge, pang, spasm, stitch, wound, sting, burn, illness, sickness.

worry, anxiety, heartache, vexation, fretting, uneasiness, discontent, disquiet, dissatisfaction; problem, care, burden.

sufferer, victim, prey, scapegoat, wretch, guinea pig.

adj. painful, hurtful, tormenting, excruciating, suffering, writhing, agonizing, harrowing; unpleasant, extreme, sharp, severe, grievous, sore, sensitive.

unfortunate, unhappy, sad, miserable, troubled, afflicted, heavy-laden, burdened, anxious, worried, vexed, uneasy; sorrowful, weeping, mournful, wretched, cut up (*inf.*), heart-broken.

vb. undergo, suffer, go through, bear, endure, put up with (*inf.*), persevere; ache, smart, throb, sting, burn; be tender, be sore, be bruised; regret, despair, mourn, weep.

see also **830**

829 pleasurableness

n. pleasurableness, pleasantness, niceness, enjoyableness, loveliness; charm, fascination, glamour, prestige, attractiveness, winsomeness, allurement.

delight, treat, surprise, amusement, fun, gift, joy, honeymoon, benefit, refreshment, titbit, feast, banquet, manna.

adj. pleasant, nice, enjoyable, agreeable, pleasing, lovely, charming, fascinating, attractive, beautiful, picturesque; glamorous, prestigious, appealing, enchanting, winsome, luring, seductive; delightful, exquisite, delicious, luscious, tasty.

vb. please, satisfy, delight, gladden, rejoice, thrill, gratify; turn on (*inf.*), turn on to (*inf.*), switch on (*inf.*), stimulate, excite; interest; attract, charm, enchant, enthrall, captivate, bewitch, enrapture; amuse, tickle, titillate.

see also **755, 827**

830 painfulness

n. painfulness, hurtfulness, unpleasantness, bitterness, disagreeableness; sorrow, pain, disappointment, irritation, annoyance, nuisance, difficulty, problem, care, burden, trouble, load, cross, concern, nightmare, bitter cup, bitter pill; embarrassment.

adj. unpleasant, disagreeable, bothersome, upsetting, disturbing, troublesome, annoying, irritating, trying, tiresome; distressing, awful, grim, shocking, appalling, tragic, extreme, dreadful.

vb. hurt, grieve, injure, wound, afflict, pain; distress, worry, trouble, outrage, bother, upset, disturb, annoy, irritate, vex, needle; torment, harass, pester, tease, pick on (*inf.*), have it in for (*inf.*); harrow, agonize, excruciate, crucify, martyr, torture, obsess, haunt, plague; lose sleep over (*inf.*); discomfort, put out, inconvenience.

see also **828, 893**

831 content

n. content, contentment, peace, peace of mind, happiness, satisfaction; self-satisfaction, complacency; ease, rest, comfort, serenity, solace.

adj. contented, content, pleased, peaceful, satisfied, happy, carefree, without cares, uncomplaining.

vb. be content, be satisfied, sit pretty, have one's wishes granted, have all that one could wish for, have nothing to worry about, have nothing to complain of, can't complain.

satisfy, gratify, indulge, suffice; go down well, put at ease; appease, reconcile.

832 discontent

n. discontent, dissatisfaction, unhappiness, sadness, depression, resentment, regret, unrest, uneasiness, tension, strain; grudge, chip on one's shoulder.

complainer, grumbler, fault-finder, grouch; reactionary, radical, protester, angry young man.

adj. discontented, unhappy, uneasy, restless, disgruntled, dissatisfied, cheesed off (*sl.*), browned off; grumbling, complaining, critical, hyper-critical, hard to please, never satisfied.

vb. be discontented, grumble, criticize, find fault, go on about, pick holes in (*inf.*), speak out against, moan; dissatisfy, disappoint, disconcert, disgruntle, discourage, dishearten.

833 regret

n. regret, sorrow, misgiving, compunction, scruple, qualm, pang of conscience, apology, repentance, change of heart, contrition, penitence, self-reproach, remorse, soul-searching.

adj. regretful, apologetic, penitent, humble, sorry, remorseful, contrite, repentant, broken, conscience-stricken.

vb. regret, apologize, be sorry for, cry over, repent, humble oneself, admit, own up, grieve, weep over, mourn, bewail, bemoan; rue.

834 relief

n. relief, alleviation, mitigation, assuagement; help, aid, comfort, consolation, relaxation, ease, load off one's mind; remedy, cure.

adj. relieving, easing, comforting, consoling, consolatory, soothing, comfortable, breathing easily.

vb. relieve, alleviate, mitigate, ease, soften, comfort, cushion, assuage, soothe, lighten, ease the strain, console, cheer up.

be relieved, feel better, recover; heave a sigh of relief, breathe again.

see also 176

835 aggravation

n. aggravation, exacerbation, worsening, heightening, intensification, sharpening, deepening, strengthening, inflammation; annoyance, irritation, exasperation.

adj. aggravated, worsened, made worse, not improved.

vb. aggravate, worsen, exacerbate, make things worse, complicate, increase, magnify, multiply, heighten, intensify, deepen, go from bad to worse, get worse and worse; annoy, irritate.

836 cheerfulness

n. cheerfulness, good humour, happiness, gladness, joy; high spirits, vitality, animation, sparkle, liveliness, jollity, merriment, mirth, gaiety, glee; laughter, fun and games; light-heartedness, levity, breeziness; stoicism, stiff upper lip.

adj. cheerful, glad, happy, joyful; genial, animated, lively, in good humour, sparkling, vivacious, exuberant, full of beans (*inf.*), in high spirits, high-spirited, on top of the world, jolly, merry, gay, jovial, jocular, playful, sporty; light-hearted, perky, chirpy, breezy, carefree, debonair.

cheering, heartening, encouraging, inspiring, heartwarming.

vb. cheer, gladden, cheer up, perk up (*inf.*); brighten, encourage, comfort; enliven, animate, inspire; uplift, raise the spirits, warm the heart.

be cheerful, take heart, snap out of it (*inf.*); persevere, keep smiling (*inf.*), grin and bear it, keep one's chin up

(*inf.*), keep a stiff upper lip, keep one's end up (*inf.*).

see also 827, 838

837 dejection; seriousness

n. dejection, despondency, melancholy, sorrow, sadness, grief, depression, despair, gloom, misery, heaviness of spirit, low spirits, blues, dumps, doldrums, mopes, *weltschmerz*.

seriousness, earnestness, solemnity, gravity, sedateness, sobriety, coolness; dead pan (*inf.*), straight face.

adj. dejected, unhappy, despondent, downcast, sad, sorrowful, down-hearted, depressed, low, troubled, desolate, dispirited, broken-hearted, crushed, heart-broken, upset, cut up (*inf.*), discouraged, crestfallen, blue, down, moping, down in the mouth, down in the dumps, in the doldrums (*inf.*), out of sorts; melancholy, world-weary, careworn; gloomy, miserable, dismal, forlorn, doleful, wretched, cheerless, dull; suicidal, despairing.

serious, earnest, grave, sober, solemn; thoughtful, pensive; stern, strict; straight-faced, dead pan (*inf.*), expressionless.

vb. be dejected, lose heart; regret, grieve, mourn, sorrow; fret, brood, mope; languish, droop, wilt, pull a long face, beat one's breast.

sadden, oppress, break a person's heart, cut up (*inf.*), discourage, deject, depress, unnerve, dismay, demoralize, get down (*inf.*); cast down; drive to drink (*inf.*); dampen, pour cold water on.

be serious, keep a straight face, take life seriously, not see the joke.

see also 828, 839

838 rejoicing

n. rejoicing, happiness, celebration, congratulation, jubilation, exultation, revelry, festivity, merrymaking, mirth, thanksgiving; cheers, shouts, hurrahs, applause; laughter, laugh, chuckle, chortle, giggle, snigger, cackle, titter, roar, guffaw; smile, grin, smirk, beam.

adj. rejoicing, jubilant, elated, exultant, rollicking.

vb. rejoice, be happy, sing for joy, leap for joy, dance, exult, celebrate, revel, have a party; clap one's hands, applaud, say thankyou to, congratulate.

laugh, chuckle, chortle, guffaw, giggle, titter, snigger; burst out laughing, roar, fall about laughing, double up with laughter, be convulsed with laughter, split one's sides, roll in the aisles (*inf.*), be in stitches (*inf.*); smile, beam, smirk, grin, twinkle; laugh at, ridicule, poke fun at, deride.

see also **840, 842**

839 lamentation

n. lamentation, mourning, grief, sorrow, weeping, sobbing, tears, waterworks (*sl.*); cry, weep, good cry, sob, bawl, wail, whimper; lament, elegy, requiem, dirge, funeral oration.

adj. lamenting, sad, mournful; weeping, sobbing, in tears, tearful.

vb. lament, grieve, sorrow; cry, weep, burst into tears, break down, dissolve into tears, shed tears, turn on the waterworks (*sl.*), sob, cry one's eyes out (*inf.*), sob one's heart out (*inf.*), blubber, snivel, whimper, whine, howl, bawl, wail.

see also **837**

840 amusement

n. amusement, pleasure, fun, good time; leisure; hobby, pastime, diversion, relaxation, entertainment, recreation, sport, play, game; television, radio, cinema, concert, theatre; meal, picnic, party, barbecue, banquet,

feast; fete, fair, carnival, gala, fiesta, festivity; holiday, excursion, outing, pleasure trip, jaunt.

adj. entertaining, amusing, engaging, diverting, pleasant, witty; amused, entertained.

vb. amuse, entertain, delight, cheer, enliven, brighten up.

amuse oneself, enjoy oneself, relax, play games, go out, have fun, have a good time, let off steam (*inf.*), have a ball (*sl.*), let one's hair down (*inf.*), live it up (*inf.*), whoop it up (*inf.*), paint the town red (*sl.*), carouse, revel.

see also **614, 827, 842**

841 weariness

n. weariness, tiredness, exhaustion, fatigue, lassitude; tedium, boredom, apathy, listlessness, world-weariness, ennui, monotony, sameness, humdrum, the same old thing (*inf.*).

misery, wet blanket, drip; pain in the neck.

adj. wearisome, tiresome; tedious, boring, uninteresting, uninspiring, heavy, monotonous, dreary, flat, stale, repetitious, repetitive, soporific; tired, weary, exhausted, drowsy, jaded, worn out.

vb. weary, fatigue, tire, tire out, send to sleep, bore, exhaust, depress, leave cold; flag, droop.

see also **612, 617, 843**

842 wit

n. wit, wittiness, humour, joking, fun; jocularity, whimsicality, facetiousness, flippancy, drollery.

joke, witticism, repartee, pun, play on words, quip, jest, Spoonerism, *double entendre*, whimsy, sally, wisecrack, gag, funny story, shaggy-dog story, chestnut, aphorism, epigram; satire, sarcasm, irony; banter, burlesque, badinage.

humorist, comedian, joker, wag, life and soul of the party, jester, clown, buffoon, satirist.

adj. witty, humorous, funny, amusing, jocular, quick-witted, whimsical, quick, keen, lively, nimble; waggish; clownish; teasing, bantering.

vb. be witty, crack a joke, joke, jest, pun, bring the house down (*inf.*), sparkle, scintillate; tease, pull a person's leg, banter, rib (*inf.*), rag (*sl.*), make fun of, ridicule, kid (*sl.*).

843 dullness

n. dullness, heaviness, tediousness, mediocrity, insipidity, colourlessness, drabness, dreariness, tameness, flatness, dryness, stuffiness, slowness; familiarity, triteness, banality.

adj. dull, heavy, ponderous, tedious, boring, uninteresting, dry, stuffy, stodgy, sluggish, mediocre, flat, uninspired, lifeless, dead, drab, dreary, gloomy; long-winded, prosaic; conventional, stereotyped, common, commonplace, trite, banal, pointless.

844 beauty

n. beauty, elegance, attractiveness, good looks, loveliness, prettiness, fairness, handsomeness, shapeliness, pulchritude; glamour, grace, charm, appeal; magnificence, gloriousness, splendour, brilliance; beautification, face-lift, hair-dressing, adornment; cosmetics, make-up; plastic surgery.

good looker, smasher (*inf.*), stunner (*inf.*), belle, raving beauty, peach (*sl.*), pin-up (*inf.*), dream, Venus; ornament, masterpiece, showpiece.

adj. beautiful, attractive, good-looking, lovely, pretty, swell (*inf.*), smashing (*inf.*), glamorous, fair, handsome, appealing, pleasing, sightly, graceful, elegant, refined, comely, charming; shapely, well-formed, well-proportioned.

splendid, magnificent, brilliant, wonderful, glorious, marvellous, gorgeous, grand, fine, resplendent, excellent, impressive, exquisite.

vb. beautify, improve the appearance of, pretty up (*inf.*), doll up (*inf.*), tart up (*sl.*), dress up (*inf.*), adorn, decorate, ornament, trim, embellish.

see also **579, 846**

845 ugliness

n. ugliness, hideousness, unloveliness, uncomeliness, inelegance, disfigurement, offensiveness; mutilation, deformity, distortion.

eyesore, defacement, horror, mess, blemish, blot, graffiti, slum.

adj. ugly, hideous, inelegant, unbecoming, unprepossessing; frightful, horrid, shocking, offensive; unlovely, unseemly, uncomely; disfigured, deformed, misshapen, monstrous, grotesque.

vb. make ugly, disfigure, deface, distort, mutilate.

see also **245**

846 ornamentation

n. ornamentation, decoration, adornment, embellishment, enhancement, trimming, frill, foil; embroidery, needlework; illumination, lettering, illustration; jewellery, jewel, gem, stone, precious stone; tinsel, ribbon, lace, gilt, tassel, bunting.

adj. ornamental, decorative, adorning, embellishing, garnishing, cosmetic; florid, dressy, ornate, fancy, gaudy, garish.

vb. decorate, adorn, beautify, enhance, brighten up, embellish, garnish, embroider, deck, bedeck, gild, festoon, array, set off.

see also 509, 844

847 blemish

n. blemish, defect, flaw, stain, smudge, blot, blur, taint, daub, spot, speck, smirch, blotch, tarnish, rust, stigma, dent, impurity, disfigurement, deformity.

adj. blemished, spoilt, disfigured, defective, imperfect.

vb. blemish, stain, smudge, blot, daub, smear, smirch, tarnish, sully, soil, spoil, mar, damage, deface, disfigure.

see also 582, 845

848 good taste

n. good taste, refinement, tastefulness, elegance, grace, polish; discrimination, good judgment, culture, sophistication; decorum, decency, soberness, seemliness, properness, restraint, simplicity, delicacy, daintiness.

good judge, connoisseur, expert, critic, gourmand, *bon vivant.*

adj. tasteful, in good taste, refined, polished, elegant, dignified, graceful, delicate; decent, sober, becoming, seemly, proper, simple, aesthetic; cultured, discriminating, sophisticated, cultivated.

see also 510

849 bad taste

n. bad taste, tastelessness; vulgarity, coarseness, rudeness, barbarism; pretension, artificiality; showiness, gaudiness, ugliness, unloveliness, hideousness; dowdiness, unfashionableness; cad, bounder (*sl.*).

adj. tasteless, in bad taste, unrefined, unpolished; vulgar, coarse, rude, gross, crass, uncouth; pretentious, artificial,

florid, ostentatious, flashy, showy; inelegant, ugly, unsightly, unlovely; dull, tawdry, shoddy, low, common, plebeian.

see also 511

850 fashion

n. fashion, style, mode, trend; new look, latest style, the latest; fad, craze, rage, all the rage, the last word; society, high society, set, right people; upper cut, upper crust.

adj. fashionable, stylish, trendy, latest, in fashion, in vogue, in (*inf.*), all the rage (*inf.*), modern, up-to-the-minute.

vb. catch on (*inf.*), become popular, grow in popularity, find favour; jump on the bandwagon (*inf.*), follow the crowd.

851 ridiculousness

n. ridiculousness, ludicrousness, funniness, outrageousness, absurdity.

adj. ridiculous, funny, comic, droll, amusing, hilarious, farcical, whimsical, side-splitting, too funny for words, rich, priceless (*sl.*), killing (*sl.*), absurd, ludicrous, preposterous, outrageous, fantastic.

vb. be ridiculous; laugh; bring the house down (*inf.*); play the fool, look silly.

see also 853

852 affectation

n. affectation, pretentiousness, pretense; artificiality, unnaturalness; show, sham, foppery, put-on (*sl.*), play-acting, front, façade, act, airs, airs and graces.

pretender, actor; play-actor; charlatan, impostor, humbug, dandy, fop.

adj. affected, pretentious, put-on, tongue in cheek, pretended, assumed, artificial, unnatural, theatrical; showy, for effect; awkward; superficial, shallow, hollow; insincere.

vb. be affected, pretend, assume, put on, feign, simulate, act out the part of, pose, fake, sham, go through the motions of; talk big; put up a front.

853 ridicule

n. ridicule, mockery, contempt, scorn, disdain, derision, sneering, jeering, scoffing; satire, parody, caricature, burlesque; irony, sarcasm.

laughing-stock, target, victim, butt, dupe, fool.

adj. derisory, contemptuous; scoffing; ironical.

vb. ridicule, mock, laugh at, deride, sneer, jeer, scoff, revile, gibe; boo, hiss, hoot; pour scorn on, run down, make fun of, pull a person's leg; banter, taunt; laugh on the other side of one's face (*inf.*); parody, caricature, satirize.

see also **924**

854 hope

n. hope, faith, trust, reliance, confidence, assurance; promise; expectation, anticipation; aspiration, dream, vision, pipe-dream, desire, wish, longing, yearning, ambition; optimism, cheerfulness, high hopes; false optimism, wishful thinking, pious hopes; fool's paradise.

hoper, aspirant, competitor, candidate, optimist, idealist.

adj. hoping, trusting, expecting, hopeful, assured, expectant, optimistic, relying on, confident, sanguine, bold, fearless, ambitious; promising, auspicious, favourable.

vb. hope, trust, believe, have faith in, rely, rest on, depend, lean on, bank on, rest assured, expect, anticipate; aspire, dream, wish, desire, long for, yearn for, contemplate; look on the

bright side, see things through rose-coloured spectacles.

raise one's hopes, inspire, promise, lead one to expect, have the makings of, show signs of promise, bid fair, bode well.

see also **420, 836**

855 hopelessness

n. hopelessness, despair, desperation, despondency; irrevocability, irredeemability; defeatism, pessimism; pessimist, Job's comforter.

adj. hopeless, irrevocable, irredeemable, incurable, irreversible, beyond hope, vain, to no avail, futile; unfortunate, bad, disastrous, impossible, helpless, lost, gone; pessimistic, defeatist.

vb. despair, lose heart, give up hope, abandon all hope, give up; dash one's hopes.

see also **837**

856 fear

n. fear, fright, terror, horror, dread, scare, tremor, panic, despair, alarm, blue funk (*sl.*), consternation, awe, trepidation; timidity, fearfulness, timorousness.

anxiety, hesitation, worry, concern, uneasiness; nervousness, apprehension, cold feet, butterflies (*inf.*), nerves, jitters (*inf.*), willies (*sl.*), heebie jeebies (*sl.*), cold sweat.

adj. afraid, frightened, terrified, dreading, scared, scared stiff, shocked, in awe, trembling, panicking, panic-stricken, startled, petrified, shrinking.

uneasy, worrying, anxious, troubled, bothered, disturbed, hesitant, timid, shy, timorous, cautious; nervous, apprehensive, fidgety, jittery (*inf.*), jumpy, edgy, on edge, tense.

terrible, frightful, awful, dreadful, horrifying, ghastly, atrocious, frightening, terrifying, appalling, harrowing, traumatic, inconceivable; disturbing, disquieting.

vb. fear, be afraid, panic; dread, shake, quiver, quake, cringe, tremble, shudder, one's knees be knocking, be scared out of one's wits, break out in a cold sweat; funk, shrink, flinch; go to pieces, crack up (*inf.*), break down.

frighten, scare, terrify, shock, startle, make one jump; intimidate; give cause for alarm, appal, petrify, frighten out of one's wits, make one's hair stand on end, make one's blood run cold; put the fear of God into (*inf.*); disturb, trouble, bother, concern, dismay, daunt, disquiet, unnerve, worry, torment.

see also **858**

857 courage

n. courage, valour, bravery, fearlessness, boldness, intrepidity, audacity, daring, fortitude; pluck, mettle, heart, backbone, guts (*inf.*), what it takes, stamina, staying power, spunk (*inf.*), grit (*inf.*); Dutch courage; gallantry, chivalry, heroism, prowess, manliness, self-reliance, resolution, determination, firmness, strength; enterprise, initiative.

brave person, hero, heroine, stalwart.

adj. courageous, brave, valiant, bold, confident, fearless, intrepid, audacious, daring, dauntless, undaunted, unflinching; determined, resolute, strong, tough; plucky, heroic, chivalrous, gallant; game; enterprising, adventuresome.

vb. be courageous, have what it takes; keep one's chin up (*inf.*); face, brave, encounter, confront, handle, look in the face, face up to, meet face

to face, take the bull by the horns; have the nerve to; make a stand, risk.

pluck up courage, take heart, summon, muster, nerve oneself.

hearten, encourage, strengthen, fortify, inspire, assure, boost.

see also **534, 535**

858 cowardice

n. cowardice, cowardliness, faint-heartedness, weakness, shrinking, funk, cold feet, weak knees, yellow streak; fear, apprehension; shyness, timidity.

coward, scaredy-cat (*inf.*), cry-baby; deserter, shirker, slacker; poltroon, dastard, sneak.

adj. cowardly, craven, faint-hearted, timid, shy, weak, weak-kneed, scared, lily-livered, yellow (*inf.*), chicken (*sl.*); dastardly, pusillanimous.

vb. lose one's courage, get cold feet, back out, chicken out (*inf.*), funk, shrink, quail, show the white feather.

859 rashness

n. rashness, temerity, imprudence, impulsiveness; hurriedness, overhastiness, carelessness, recklessness, foolhardiness; indiscretion; daring, presumption; flippancy, levity; daredevil, harum-scarum (*inf.*).

adj. rash, impulsive, impetuous, hurried, sudden, precipitous, overhasty, premature, breakneck, headlong, frenzied, furious; reckless, foolhardy, careless, thoughtless, imprudent, inconsiderate; headstrong, unthinking, heedless; wild, brash, ill-considered.

vb. be rash, stick one's neck out (*inf.*), jump to conclusions, rush to conclusions, play with fire, burn one's fingers, court danger, court disaster, ask for trouble (*inf.*), ask for it (*inf.*), fools rush in where angels fear to tread, throw caution to the winds, tempt providence.

see also **544**, **613**

860 caution

n. caution, prudence, cautiousness, care, heed, alertness, vigilance, wariness, suspicion; discretion, circumspection, deliberation, forethought, precaution, presence of mind, foresight.

adj. cautious, watchful, wary, circumspect, careful, prudent, vigilant.

vb. be cautious, play safe, take precautions, take care, look out, provide for, look before one leaps, watch one's step.

861 desire

n. desire, wish, need, want; liking, fondness, fancy, weakness, predilection, inclination, urge, aspiration, ambition; ardour, longing, yearning, pining; nostalgia, homesickness; craze, frenzy, lust, covetousness.

hunger, thirst, ravenousness, craving, voracity, relish, appetite, famine, drought.

adj. desiring, wanting, wishing, liking, desirous, fond, inclined, partial, longing, yearning, pining, itching (*inf.*), dying; eager, keen, crazy, mad, keen, craving; covetous.

hungry, greedy, ravenous, starving, famished, voracious, dry, parched; unsatisfied; peckish (*inf.*).

vb. desire, want, wish, need; like, be fond of, enjoy, choose, fancy, take a fancy to, incline towards, love, take to, be sweet on, have a soft spot for, go for in a big way, set one's heart on (*inf.*), set one's sights on, prize, esteem; aspire, dream; long for, crave, yearn, pine, hanker, make one's mouth water, lust, covet; relish.

be hungry, hunger, starve, famish; be thirsty, be dry, thirst.

see also **889**

862 dislike

n. dislike, distaste, disinclination, dissatisfaction; hate, hatred, loathing, aversion, repugnance.

adj. disliking, disinclined, averse to, loath to, fed up with, allergic, squeamish.

disliked, objectionable, repugnant, loathsome, abhorrent, abominable, disagreeable, unpopular.

vb. dislike, not feel like, not care for, hate, loathe, detest, not take kindly to, have nothing to do with, avoid, turn up one's nose at (*inf.*), not go for, not stomach.

see also **892**

863 indifference

n. indifference, unconcern, apathy, coldness, insensitivity, neutrality; half-heartedness, lukewarmness; unambitiousness.

adj. indifferent, cold, neutral; lukewarm, half-hearted; unconcerned, impassive, dispassionate, unresponsive, unmoved, uninvolved, lackadaisical, listless, inattentive; isolated, uncommunicative.

vb. be indifferent, not mind, not care, not care less, not give a damn (*inf.*), take no interest in, not matter, be all the same to, leave one cold; take it or leave it.

see also **754**

864 fastidiousness

n. fastidiousness, fussiness, meticulousness, scrupulousness, punctiliousness, pedantry, conscientiousness; perfectionism, idealism.

perfectionist, idealist, stickler, purist, pedant; fuss-pot (*inf.*).

adj. fastidious, particular, exact, precise, meticulous, exacting, scrupulous, rigorous, choosy (*inf.*), discriminating, selective, squeamish, finicky, pernickety (*inf.*), overscrupulous, overparticular, overprecise, hypercritical; hard to please; pedantic; delicate, nice.

vb. be fastidious, fuss, be hard to please, split hairs, pick and choose; make a fuss about, make a song and dance about (*inf.*).

865 satiety

n. satiety, repletion, saturation, fill, surfeit, glut, plethora, jadedness, too much of a good thing.

adj. sated, satiated, replete, gorged, glutted, cloyed, overfull, overflowing; full, satisfied.

vb. satiate, fill, surfeit, glut, gorge, stuff, cloy, overfill, overfeed, satisfy, gratify; have one's fill, have enough.

866 wonder

n. wonder, surprise, amazement, awe, astonishment, bewilderment, fascination, stupefaction, incredulity.

sensation, miracle, sign, phenomenon, portent, spectacle, freak, marvel, drama, the unbelievable, prodigy, curiosity, oddity, rarity, something to write home about.

adj. surprising, amazing, astonishing, marvellous, fantastic, unbelievable, incredible, dramatic, remarkable, sensational, phenomenal, miraculous, stupendous, unprecedented, unparalleled, extraordinary, unusual, freakish, unique.

surprised, amazed, astonished, lost in wonder, bewildered, flabbergasted, spellbound, speechless, dumbfounded, thunderstruck, aghast.

vb. wonder, marvel, be surprised, be

amazed, be taken aback, stare, gape, not believe, not get over.

amaze, astonish, surprise, bewilder, stupefy, dumbfound, flabbergast, overwhelm, take one's breath away.

867 absence of wonder

n. non-wonder, blankness; expectation; ordinariness, just as one thought, nothing much to write home about.

adj. unastonishing, expected, common, ordinary, usual; unamazed, unsurprised, unimpressed.

vb. not wonder, not be surprised, not bat an eyelid, not turn a hair; expect, take for granted, presume.

868 repute

n. repute, good standing, reputation, name, good name, renown, character, credit, respectability, reliability, trustworthiness, dependability; respect, favour, prestige, honour, glory, regard, kudos (*inf.*); fame, distinction, eminence, prominence, popularity; greatness, dignity, superiority, exaltation, majesty; rank, position, station, status.

big name, somebody, celebrity, star, dignitary, VIP, bigwig, big shot (*sl.*), grand old man.

adj. reputable, respectable, reliable, trustworthy, dependable, respected, well thought of, esteemed, acclaimed; renowned, of renown, famous, popular, celebrated, notable, leading, wellknown; prestigious, honourable, distinguished, illustrious, eminent, prominent.

dignified, noble, great, grand, superior, high, exalted, elevated, sublime, majestic.

vb. be somebody, have a name, leave one's mark, make a name for oneself, go down in history.

honour, regard, respect, esteem, hold in high regard, admire, revere, praise, worship; exalt, glorify, crown, enthrone, ennoble, knight, immortalize.

869 disrepute

n. disrepute, disfavour, dishonour, ill-repute, bad name, bad character, unreliability, poor reputation; notoriety, infamy; disgrace, disrespect, reproach, shame, humiliation, degradation, abasement, ignominy, contempt.

scandal, gossip, backbiting, slander, calumny, defamation; slur, slight, insult, stain, stigma, brand, blot.

adj. disreputable, dishonourable, discreditable, ignominious; humiliating, lowering, degrading; notorious, infamous; shady, questionable; disgraceful, scandalous, shameful, outrageous, shocking, contemptible, despicable, corrupt, offensive, flagrant, base, mean, low, shabby, shoddy.

disgraced, humiliated, unable to show one's face.

undistinguished, obscure, unknown, unheard of, unrenowned.

vb. disgrace oneself, lose one's reputation, lose face, lapse from grace, fall from grace, fade; condescend, stoop, descend, lower oneself.

put to shame, disgrace, discredit, dishonour, expose, mock, show up; ridicule, embarrass, humiliate, humble; debase, degrade, snub, confound, unfrock; stain, tarnish, smear, sully, blot; take down a peg or two (*inf.*), cut down to size (*inf.*), drag through the mire (*inf.*).

870 nobility

n. nobility, dignity, grandeur, greatness, distinction, eminence; rank,

descent, birth, blood, high birth, blue blood; royalty, majesty, court; aristocracy, gentry, landed gentry, peerage, ruling class, privileged class, elite, gentility; society, high society, upper classes, upper ten thousand, upper crust (*inf.*), higher-ups (*inf.*).

nobleman; peer, peeress; archbishop; duke, duchess; marquis, marchioness; earl; count, countess; viscount, viscountess; bishop; baron, baroness; lord, lady; baronet; knight, dame; life peer; dowager.

adj. noble, dignified, grand, great, magnificent, lofty, imposing, distinguished; royal, majestic, monarchic, regal, reigning, princely; aristocratic, courtly, titled, lordly; highborn, of gentle birth, born in the purple.

871 common people

n. commonalty, common people, commons; people, the masses, general public, rank and file, grass roots; bourgeoisie, middle class; working class, lower class, have-nots, underdogs, proletariat; rabble, crowd, herd, riffraff, *hoi polloi*, ragtag and bobtail, the great unwashed, scum, dregs.

commoner, plebeian, citizen, civilian, man in the street, Mr. Average; countryman, rustic, yokel, country bumpkin, peasant, serf.

adj. common, plebeian, bourgeois, ordinary, average, lowly, humble, of low estate, mean, ignoble; rustic.

872 title

n. title, name, designation; courtesy title, handle (*inf.*), honorific; order, privilege, honour; decoration, ribbon, medal, crest, emblem.

873 pride

n. pride, self-respect, self-regard, self-esteem, dignity, self-love; conceit, vanity, haughtiness, vainglory; self-exaltation, self-glorification; ego-trip; arrogance, insolence.

proud person, bighead (*inf.*), swank (*inf.*), boaster, bragger.

adj. self-respecting, pleased with oneself, self-assured, self-satisfied; dignified, lofty, stately, elevated, high-falutin; egotistic, conceited, bigheaded (*inf.*), patronizing.

vb. be proud, hold one's head high; take pride in, pride oneself on, glory in, boast.

see also 875

874 humility

n. humility, humbleness, self-abasement, self-effacement; submission, obedience, meekness, lowliness, modesty, subservience, subjection; unobtrusiveness.

humiliation; abasement; mortification; come-down (*inf.*), let-down (*inf.*), deflation, crushing, shame.

adj. humble, lowly, meek, submissive, modest, self-effacing, subservient, servile; unassuming, unpretentious; humiliated, humbled, let down (*inf.*), deflated, squashed, crushed, crestfallen, chastened; embarrassed, ashamed.

vb. humble oneself, submit, obey; condescend, stoop, deign; eat humble pie, come down from one's high horse; be humiliated, not dare show one's face, feel small, feel squashed.

humiliate, humble, shame, embarrass, deflate, crush, squash, let down (*inf.*), bring low, put to shame, disconcert, make one feel small, take down a peg or two (*inf.*), teach one his place, reduce to tears.

see also 881

875 vanity

n. vanity, conceit, self-importance, self-glorification, egotism, vainglory,

self-applause, boastfulness; self-worship, narcissism; show, ostentation, exhibitionism; futility, emptiness, uselessness.

egotist, show-off, exhibitionist, know-all, smart aleck (*inf.*), toffee-nose (*sl.*), Narcissus.

adj. vain, conceited, haughty, self-centred, self-important, self-glorifying, self-applauding, full of oneself, boastful, cocky, swollen-headed, stuck up (*inf.*), puffed up, too big for one's boots (*sl.*), swanky (*inf.*), snooty (*inf.*), high and mighty (*inf.*), pompous, arrogant, insolent, supercilious, pretentious, snobbish, toffee-nose (*sl.*), stand-offish; showy, exhibitionist.

vb. be vain, be puffed up, get too big for one's boots (*sl.*), have a high opinion of oneself, think too much of oneself, come the high and mighty with (*inf.*), know it all, boast, show off; turn up one's nose at (*inf.*); go to one's head, puff up.

see also 879

876 modesty; shyness

n. modesty, unassumingness, unpretentiousness, unobtrusiveness, restraint, meekness, retiring nature; chastity, purity, virtue.

shyness, timidity, bashfulness, reserve, reticence, coyness; inhibition, nervousness.

adj. modest, retiring, restrained, meek, unassuming, unobtrusive, diffident, shrinking; restrained, tasteful, undecorated; chaste, pure, innocent.

shy, timid, bashful, quiet, reserved, coy, reticent, reluctant, backward, inhibited, secretive, demure, proper; blushing, embarrassed, red.

vb. hold back, hide one's face, keep in the background, take a back seat, hide one's light under a bushel, retire into one's shell; blush, go red.

877 ostentation

n. ostentation, exhibitionism, showiness, pretension; pomp, pompousness, magnificence, splendour, grandeur, majesty, pageantry; blatancy, flagrancy, flashiness, gaudiness, loudness; flourish, parade, fuss, splurge, showing off; bravado, histrionics, theatricality, sensationalism, effect, showmanship; exhibitionist, show-off, showman.

adj. ostentatious, showing off, proud, pompous, grandiose, extravagant, bombastic, high-flown, fancy, jazzy, showy, garish, gaudy, flashy, flamboyant, flaunting, blatant, flagrant, obtrusive, conspicuous, loud, screaming; spectacular, sensational, theatrical, histrionic, for effect, for show.

vb. show off, flaunt, parade, flourish, splurge, play to the gallery, do for show, make an exhibition of oneself, give oneself airs; sensationalize.

878 celebration

n. celebration, commemoration, honouring, keeping, observance; anniversary, jubilee, birthday, red-letter day, centenary, bicentenary, tercentenary; ceremonial; solemnization; ceremony, function, occasion, festive occasion, do (*inf.*); clapping, applause, praise, acclaim, cheers, hurrahs, cries, ovation, standing ovation, salute.

adj. celebrative, commemorative, anniversary, congratulatory, ceremonial, festive.

vb. celebrate, commemorate, observe, keep, remember, honour, congratulate, crown; throw a party, make merry, kill the fatted calf.

879 boasting

n. boasting, self-glory, self-glorification; boast, brag, empty talk, big talk, hot air, bombast, bluster, braggadocio, gasconade.

boaster, big mouth, swank (*inf.*), gas-bag (*sl.*), arrogance, Gascon.

adj. boastful, bragging, big-mouthed, pretentious, inflated, self-glorifying, vaunting.

vb. boast, vaunt, brag, show off, talk big, bounce, exaggerate; blow one's own trumpet, have a high opinion of oneself, pat oneself on the back, congratulate oneself, flatter oneself.

880 insolence

n. insolence, rudeness, boldness, audacity, effrontery, impudence, impertinence, arrogance, presumption, forwardness, shamelessness, officiousness, sauciness, defiance, lip (*sl.*), cheek, nerve (*inf.*), sauce, brass.

upstart, wise guy (*sl.*), pup.

adj. insolent, impudent, impertinent, arrogant, high-handed, disrespectful, insulting, rude, offensive, officious, outrageous, defiant, cheeky, saucy, uppity (*inf.*); presumptuous, forward.

vb. be insolent, have the cheek, have a nerve (*inf.*), get fresh, come the high and mighty with (*inf.*), get on one's high horse (*inf.*), throw one's weight about (*inf.*); give lip (*sl.*), brazen it out, answer back, presume, take for granted.

881 servility

n. servility, obsequiousness, meniality, sycophancy, toadyism; sycophant, toady, back-scratcher, yes-man, sponger, parasite, hanger-on, boot-licker.

adj. servile, menial, beggarly, slavish, subservient, obsequious, cringing, toadyish, boot-licking, ingratiating, fawning, grovelling, snivelling.

vb. be servile, suck up to (*sl.*), crawl (*inf.*), grovel, go down on one's knees, lick the boots of, ingratiate oneself with, toady, fawn, curry favour; flatter.

D Sympathetic

882 friendship

n. friendship, companionship, amity, comradeship, fraternity, intimacy, familiarity; friendliness, affection, amicability, sociability, good terms, neighbourliness, understanding, compatibility, matiness, warmth, cordiality.

friend, companion, mate, pal, chum, buddy, comrade; boy-friend, girl-friend; acquaintance, neighbour; close friend, best friend, bosom friend, confidant, intimate.

adj. friendly, close, familiar, intimate, inseparable, confiding; faithful, loyal, devoted, true, trusted, staunch, firm; amicable, sympathetic, compatible, sociable, affectionate, warm-hearted, brotherly, matey, pally; kind, benevolent.

vb. be friendly, know, be acquainted with, be on good terms with; befriend, get to know, make friends with, get in with (*inf.*), get pally with, chum up with, break the ice; go out with (*inf.*), go with, knock about with (*inf.*), go around with, keep company with, go together, see (*inf.*), run after (*inf.*), go after (*inf.*), chase, try to get, take out, accompany, court, woo, make advances; be just good friends.

see also **889**

883 enmity

n. enmity, hostility, inimicality; antipathy, unfriendliness; hatred, antagonism, dislike, repugnance, animosity; ill-feeling, hard feelings; separation, estrangement, alienation; bitterness, acrimony, coolness.

enemy, foe, antagonist, opponent, adversary, arch-enemy, invader; public enemy; rival, informer.

adj. inimical, hostile, antagonistic, unfriendly, ill-disposed, opposed; irreconcilable, alienated, estranged; at odds, at daggers drawn, at loggerheads, not on speaking terms, on bad terms; cool, cold, chilly, uncordial; opposite, contrary, conflicting; quarrelsome, unsympathetic, grudging, resentful.

vb. be opposed to, differ, be at odds with, conflict, clash; antagonize, provoke, alienate, estrange.

see also **637, 638**

884 sociability

n. sociability, geniality, friendliness, cordiality, gregariousness, conviviality, affability, hospitality, open house, social intercourse.

party, social, get-together, ball, meeting, reunion, rendezvous, reception, at home, soirée; visit, call, appointment, engagement, date, interview, stay; arrangement.

visitor, dropper-in, guest, caller; mixer, good mixer, life and soul of the party; gate-crasher, uninvited guest.

adj. sociable, friendly, genial, cordial, affable, gregarious, neighbourly, hospitable.

vb. be sociable, invite, welcome, receive, entertain, throw a party; keep open house; visit, drop in on, look in, call by.

885 unsociability

n. unsociability, unfriendliness, uncommunicativeness, shyness; distance, unapproachability, aloofness; seclusion, privacy, separateness, isolation, retirement, withdrawal, solitariness, loneliness; backwater, back of beyond, backwoods, refuge, retreat, cloister, ivory tower, shell, desert island.

recluse, hermit, monk, anchorite, backwoodsman; loner, stay-at-home; outcast, castaway; refugee, evacuee; outlaw, bandit; orphan, leper.

adj. unsociable, unfriendly, distant, shy, uncommunicative, unapproachable, aloof, stand-offish, antisocial, inhospitable; lonesome, solitary, lonely, friendless, desolate, retiring, withdrawn; secluded, forsaken, isolated, rustic, out-of-the-way, remote, God-forsaken, unexplored, uninhabited, deserted.

vb. be unsociable, stand aloof, keep oneself to oneself, keep one's distance, go into seclusion, shut oneself up, retire into one's shell; seclude, exclude, expel, excommunicate, repel, cold-shoulder, keep at arm's length, keep at bay, beat off.

886 courtesy

n. courtesy, thoughtfulness, consideration, politeness, manners, good manners, civility, culture, refinement, breeding, gentility, respect, kindness, friendliness, generosity, gallantry, chivalry; condescension, flattery, oiliness.

good turn, favour, compliment; greeting, handshake, smile, embrace, hug, kiss.

adj. courteous, polite, well-mannered, civil, amiable, affable, thoughtful, considerate, kind, friendly, generous, obliging; cultivated, cultured, refined, polished, well-bred; politic, diplomatic; gentlemanly, lady-like; gallant, chivalrous; condescending, obsequious, ingratiating, patronizing.

vb. be courteous, behave oneself, mind one's P's and Q's, be on one's best behaviour; give one's regards, give one's compliments, send best wishes, pay one's respects, compliment; greet, welcome, hail, exchange greetings, hold out one's hand, shake hands, smile, wave, hug, embrace, kiss.

887 discourtesy

n. discourtesy, impoliteness, bad manners, misbehaviour, incivility, ill breeding; disrespect, impudence, unfriendliness, brusqueness; meanness, nastiness, unpleasantness, rudeness, vulgarity, boorishness, coarseness, grossness, shamelessness.

adj. discourteous, impolite, bad-mannered, uncivil, uncultured, unrefined, unbecoming, misbehaved, ungentlemanly, rude, unfriendly, unkind, ungracious, unpleasant, nasty, obstreperous, disrespectful, offensive, crude, coarse, vulgar, shameless; loutish, rowdy, disorderly, boorish; thoughtless, careless, inconsiderate, tactless, gauche, outspoken; brusque, abrupt, curt, offhand, rough, gruff, surly, difficult; audacious, brash; cheeky, high-handed.

vb. be rude, insult, affront, outrage; give the cold shoulder; irritate, annoy, shout down, interrupt; snub, disregard, ignore.

888 congratulation

n. congratulation, felicitation, best wishes, compliments, happy returns; applause, appreciation, bouquet, praise, acknowledgement, toast.

adj. congratulatory, complimentary.

vb. congratulate, compliment, felicitate, pay one's respects, offer one's congratulations, salute, praise, honour, acclaim, sound the praises of, appreciate, admire, adulate; toast, celebrate; mob.

889 love

n. love, fondness, affection, attachment, devotion, adoration; passion, Eros, ardour, amorousness, lust, infatuation, crush (*sl.*), pash (*sl.*); first love, calf-love, puppy love; emotion, sentiment; attractiveness, charm, winsomeness, appeal, sex-appeal, fascination; love affair, affair, romance, liaison, relationship, flirtation, amour, eternal triangle.

lover, admirer, suitor, wooer, boy-friend, girl-friend, date (*inf.*), steady (*inf.*), blind date; Romeo, Juliet, fiancé, fiancée; mistress; cohabitant.

adj. loving, fond, affectionate, devoted, adoring, attached; emotional, sentimental, tender, soft; yearning, longing, passionate, ardent, amorous, glowing.

enamoured, attracted, enchanted, fascinated, caught, charmed, captivated, enraptured, taken with, sweet on, keen on, infatuated, gone on, crazy, wild, mad, smitten, in love, head over heels in love.

lovable, winsome, attractive, charming, appealing, captivating, irresistible, dear; loved, beloved, cherished.

vb. love, like, be fond of, care for, delight in, adore, fancy; treasure, hold dear, take to one's heart (*inf.*), admire, regard, cherish, appreciate, esteem, value, prize; be in love, dote on, be enraptured by; fall in love, fall for, be crazy about, have it bad (*inf.*); lose one's heart to, have a crush on, be swept off one's feet (*inf.*), be infatuated with; long, yearn; copulate, have intercourse, make love to, have sex with (*inf.*), sleep with (*inf.*), sleep together (*inf.*), go to bed with, have it off with (*sl.*); live with, live together, cohabit, live in sin (*inf.*).

attract, appeal, fascinate, captivate, charm, enchant, allure, draw, rouse, enrapture, infatuate, sweep off one's feet (*inf.*).

see also **861, 882**

890 endearment

n. endearment, affection, attachment, fondness, love, soft nothings, embrace, kiss, cuddle, stroke, fondling, petting, necking (*sl.*); courtship, courting, wooing, pass, advance, dating, flirtation, amorous intentions; love-letter, Valentine; proposal, offer of marriage, engagement.

vb. woo, court, go out with (*inf.*), run after (*inf.*), pursue, chase, date, pay attentions to, make overtures, make advances, make passes, make eyes at (*inf*), ogle, flirt; propose, pop the question (*inf.*).

be fond of, cherish; embrace, hug, clasp, draw close, snuggle, kiss, cuddle; stroke, fondle, caress, pat, pet, neck, smooch (*inf.*).

see also **882**

891 darling; favourite

n. darling, dear, love, beloved, dearest, sweetheart, angel, pet, sweet, sweetie (*inf.*), sweetie-pie (*inf.*), sugar (*inf.*), honey (*inf.*), precious (*inf.*), treasure (*inf.*), jewel (*inf.*); favourite, mother's darling, teacher's pet, blue-eyed boy, apple of one's eye.

892 hate

n. hate, hatred, dislike, antipathy, aversion, loathing, abhorrence, repugnance, repulsion, disgust, scorn, detestation, nasty look.

anathema, abomination, menace, pest, *bête noire*, bitter pill.

adj. detestable, hateful, odious, abominable, abhorrent, loathsome, accursed, offensive, repugnant, disgusting, revolting, repulsive, vile; averse to, hostile, antagonistic.

vb. hate, dislike, loathe, abhor, detest, abominate, denounce, condemn, object to, spurn, spit upon, curse, reject, have it in for (*inf.*).

offend, rub up the wrong way, repel, disgust, shock, alienate, estrange, antagonize, make one's blood run cold.

see also 295, 862

893 resentment; anger

n. resentment, bitterness, hurt, soreness, malice, grudge, bone to pick; sore point.

anger, indignation, displeasure, antagonism; rage, fury, wrath, vehemence, passion, vexation, exasperation, annoyance, impatience, ire; bad temper, outburst, fit, tantrum, huff, tiff, quarrel, argument, fight.

adj. resentful, indignant, sore, hurt, grudging, bitter, embittered, with a chip on one's shoulder, acrimonious.

angry, cross, irate, furious, raging, fiery, mad (*inf.*), hopping mad (*inf.*), fuming, displeased; antagonized, enraged, exasperated, infuriated, annoyed, irritated, peeved (*sl.*), impatient, irritable, ratty (*sl.*), shirty (*sl.*), provoked, affronted, riled, vexed, worked up, het up (*inf.*), up in arms, in a huff, hot under the collar, foaming at the mouth (*inf.*).

vb. resent, feel bitter towards, take umbrage, take exception, be insulted, bear a grudge, bear malice, have a bone to pick.

get angry, get cross, lose one's temper, blow one's top (*inf.*), hit the roof (*inf.*), fly off the handle (*inf.*), blow up (*inf.*), explode; get worked up, get het up (*inf.*), get hot under the collar, go up the wall (*inf.*), go off the deep end (*inf.*).

be angry, burn, roar, rage, rant and rave, fume, storm, boil, seethe, foam at the mouth (*inf.*); snap, bite someone's head off (*inf.*), jump down someone's throat (*inf.*); criticize, nag, get at.

anger, enrage, incense, infuriate, madden, antagonize, exasperate, provoke, bother, harass, vex, annoy, incite, irritate, needle, nettle, rankle, rile, stir, get someone's back up (*inf.*), get someone's blood up, make one's blood boil, send up the wall (*inf.*), rub up the wrong way (*inf.*), tread on someone's toes (*inf.*), get on someone's nerves, get under someone's skin, get someone's goat (*sl.*), upset, ruffle, discompose, put out.

see also 642

894 irritability

n. irritability, sensitivity, nervousness, uneasiness, exasperation, impatience, touchiness, bad temper.

adj. irritable, sensitive, susceptible, touchy, oversensitive, prickly, edgy, short-tempered, ratty (*sl.*), shirty (*sl.*), uptight, gruff, grumpy; nervous, anxious, jumpy, jittery (*inf.*); temperamental, moody; irritated, annoyed, needled, riled, rankled, nettled, rubbed up the wrong way, with a chip on one's shoulder; irascible, choleric, querulous, cantankerous.

895 sullenness

n. sullenness, moroseness, glumness, moodiness, unsociability, sourness, bad temper, gruffness, spleen; frown, scowl, grimace, sneer, dirty look (*inf.*), wry face.

adj. sullen, morose, glum, silent,

unsociable; moody, surly, grouchy, churlish, sulky, cross, mopish, ill-humoured, ill-natured, disagreeable, sour, mournful, saturnine; scowling, frowning; gloomy, dismal, sad, dim, dark, cheerless, sombre.

vb. scowl, frown, grimace, make a face, pull a face, glower, growl, sulk, grouch, mope, sneer.

896 marriage

n. marriage, matrimony, wedlock, conjugality, union, match, alliance, marriage tie, marriage bed; wedding, pledging, ceremony, nuptials, espousals; church wedding, civil marriage, registry-office wedding; elopement, abduction; shotgun wedding; reception, wedding breakfast, party, dance; honeymoon, consummation.

man and wife, bride and groom, bridal pair, newlyweds, honeymooners; partner, spouse, mate; husband, man; wife, helpmeet, better half (*inf.*), the missus (*sl.*).

adj. matrimonial, marital, nuptial, conjugal, married, wed, united, matched; newly-wed; honeymooning, going-away, marriageable, eligible, suitable, of marriageable age.

vb. marry, get married, wed, espouse, take to oneself, lead to the altar, plight one's troth, become one, get hitched (*sl.*), get spliced (*sl.*), make an honest woman of (*inf.*); honeymoon, go away, consummate; run away, leave home, elope; join, unite, pronounce man and wife, marry, give in marriage, give away; marry into, marry out of; marry off, match, match-make, find a match for, find a mate for; catch, find, hook (*sl.*).

see also **889**

897 celibacy

n. celibacy, singleness, bachelorhood, virginity, spinsterhood; celibate, bachelor, confirmed bachelor; spinster, bachelor girl, old maid, virgin.

adj. celibate, single, unmarried, unwed, not the marrying kind; eligible, unattached, free; virgin.

898 divorce; widowhood

n. divorce, separation, annulment, dissolution, decree nisi, desertion; breakdown of marriage.

widowhood; survivor, widow, dowager, relict; widower; grass widow, golf widow.

adj. divorced, parted, separated, living apart.

vb. divorce, get a divorce, annul, cancel, put asunder, sue for a divorce, desert, split up (*inf.*), separate, live apart; widow, bereave; leave, survive.

899 benevolence

n. benevolence, kindness, helpfulness, thoughtfulness, kindheartedness, graciousness, courtesy, charity, altruism, philanthropy, fellow-feeling, the golden rule; service, good deed, good turn, aid, relief, favour, benefit, alms.

kind person, good Samaritan, good neighbour, altruist, humanitarian, do-gooder, philanthropist, heart of gold.

adj. kind, benevolent, charitable, helpful, careful, thoughtful, well-meaning, well-intentioned, well-meant, gracious, good, pleasant, generous, obliging, neighbourly, kindhearted, warm-hearted, compassionate, sympathetic, unselfish, altruistic, humanitarian, philanthropic; merciful, pitying.

vb. be kind, help, do a good turn, do a favour, benefit, support, encourage, comfort, relieve, bless, mean well, wish well, do as one would be done by, bend over backwards to help.

see also 550, 905, 935

900 malevolence

n. malevolence, unkindness, hate, animosity, malice, malignity, spite, bitterness, acrimony; cruelty, inhumanity, wickedness, ruthlessness, relentlessness, harshness, severity, callousness; tyranny, oppression, despotism, intolerance; brutality, beastliness, savagery, barbarousness, brutishness, monstrousness.

ill, harm, misfortune, mischief, blow, outrage, foul play, catastrophe, disaster, atrocity, torture.

adj. unkind, unfriendly, unloving, uncharitable, stepmotherly, inconsiderate, thoughtless; spiteful, malicious, catty, hateful, resentful, bitter, acrimonious, caustic.

cruel, malevolent, malicious, inhuman, wicked, harsh, severe, relentless, fierce, savage, barbarous, brutal, beastly; pitiless, unmerciful, intolerant, ruthless, cold, callous, hardhearted, oppressive, despotic, devilish, diabolical.

vb. be malevolent, hurt, harm, abuse, maltreat, damage, injure, oppress, tyrannize, not tolerate, persecute, torture, torment, victimize, have it in for (*inf.*), take it out on (*inf.*).

see also 551, 906, 936

901 curse

n. curse, malediction, denunciation, execration, abuse, vilification, vituperation, scurrility; profanity, swearing, oath, imprecation, expletive, swearword, naughty word, bad language, blasphemy, sacrilege, profanation.

adj. maledictory, imprecatory, damnatory; abusive, scurrilous, profane,

sacrilegious, blasphemous, blue, naughty, indecent, obscene.

vb. curse, wish on (*inf.*), invoke, summon, call down on; abuse, defame, denounce, pour abuse, call names, revile, vituperate, vilify, damn; swear, swear like a trooper, blaspheme.

902 threat

n. threat, menace, warning, intimidation, blackmail; writing on the wall, danger signal, distress signal; threatening, commination.

adj. threatening, menacing, intimidating, frightening; ominous, imminent.

vb. threaten, menace, intimidate, blackmail, frighten, scare, torment, bully, push around (*inf.*), order about (*inf.*); be brewing, loom, be imminent.

see also 154

903 philanthropy

n. philanthropy, humanitarianism, utilitarianism, altruism, social conscience; welfare state, social services; patriotism, love of one's country, loyalty, public spirit; nationalism, chauvinism; internationalism.

philanthropist, humanitarian, dogooder; idealist, altruist, visionary, man with a vision, missionary; patriot, lover of one's country, loyalist, nationalist, chauvinist; internationalist, citizen of the world, cosmopolitan.

adj. philanthropic, humanitarian, humane, kind, altruistic, patriotic; chauvinistic; public-spirited, reforming.

vb. have a social conscience, be public-spirited, show public spirit; love one's country.

904 misanthropy

n. misanthropy, selfishness, egotism, cynicism, unsociability, incivism;

misanthrope, man-hater, misogynist, woman-hater, cynic, egoist.

adj. misanthropic, antisocial, unsocial, unsociable, inhuman, cynical; unpatriotic.

see also **885**

905 benefactor

n. benefactor, benefactress, helper, good neighbour, do-gooder, giver, donor, contributor; protector, guard, watch, champion, guardian; patron, supporter, backer; rescuer, deliverer, liberator, redeemer; angel, guardian angel.

see also **640**

906 evildoer

n. evildoer, wrongdoer, troublemaker, mischief-maker; criminal, lawbreaker, offender, transgressor, sinner, public enemy; crook, villain, rogue; thief, gangster, con man (*inf.*); murderer, assassin; ruffian, thug, hooligan, layabout (*inf.*), nasty piece of work (*inf.*); beast, brute, monster, vampire, viper.

see also **684, 723, 940**

907 pity

n. pity, compassion, goodness, kindliness, benevolence, understanding, charity; tenderness, soft-heartedness, warm-heartedness; condolence, sympathy, commiseration, fellow feeling, comfort, solace, consolation; mercy, favour, grace, clemency, forbearance, forgiveness, second chance.

adj. pitying, compassionate, kind, tender, gentle, lenient; merciful, gracious, clement, forbearing, forgiving, generous; sympathetic, consoling, commiserating, comforting, sorry; pitiful, pitiable.

vb. pity, show mercy, take pity on, pardon, spare, forgive, reprieve, give a second chance; relent, relax, repent; put out of one's misery.

sympathize, feel for, feel with, put oneself in someone's shoes, be understanding, express sympathy, commiserate, share another's sorrow, grieve with, weep for, love, console, comfort, support, uphold, encourage, sit by, put one's arm round.

908 pitilessness

n. pitilessness, ruthlessness, mercilessness, relentlessness, cruelty, heartlessness, callousness, hardness of heart; letter of the law, pound of flesh.

adj. pitiless, unpitying, unmerciful, merciless, relentless, unrelenting, unforgiving, barbarous, tyrannical, vindictive, revengeful; rough, harsh, severe; cruel, brutal, savage; cold, unsympathetic, unfeeling, unmoved, inflexible; hard-hearted, stony-hearted, cold-blooded.

vb. show no pity, stop at nothing (*inf.*), harden one's heart, turn a deaf ear to, give no quarter, exact one's pound of flesh; one's heart bleed for (*inf.*).

909 gratitude

n. gratitude, thankfulness, appreciation, gratefulness, sense of obligation; thanks, thank-you, acknowledgement, response, recognition, praise, tribute, vote of thanks, honour, credit; blessing, grace, prayer, benediction; bread-and-butter letter; reward, trip; leaving-present.

adj. grateful, thankful, appreciative, responsive; indebted, obliged, much obliged; pleased, gratified, overwhelmed.

vb. thank, say thank you, show one's gratitude, respond, appreciate, show one's appreciation, acknowledge, recognize, praise, pay a tribute to, never forget, applaud; reward, tip; give thanks, say grace, return thanks.

910 ingratitude

n. ingratitude, ungratefulness, lack of appreciation, thanklessness, no sense of obligation; thoughtlessness, rudeness.

adj. ungrateful, unappreciative, unmindful, forgetful, rude; thankless, unrewarding, unprofitable, worthless; unthanked, unacknowledged, unrewarded.

vb. be ungrateful, not thank, take for granted, presume upon.

911 forgiveness

n. forgiveness, pardon, free pardon, absolution, remission, acquittal, release, discharge; exoneration, exculpation; justification, reconciliation, redemption, atonement; reprieve, amnesty, indemnity; grace, mercy, patience, forbearance.

adj. forgiven, pardoned, excused, absolved, let off, acquitted, free, not guilty, released, reinstated, reconciled, restored, taken back, welcomed home; redeemed, justified, adopted.

vb. forgive, pardon, excuse, remit, reprieve, clear, absolve, discharge, acquit, free, declare not guilty, let off (*inf.*), let go; let pass, disregard, ignore, shut one's eyes to, grant amnesty to; show mercy, tolerate, forbear; redeem, reconcile, justify; purge, blot one's sins out, wipe the slate clean; bury the hatchet, make it up, kiss and make up; forgive and forget, let bygones be bygones.

see also **921, 961**

912 revenge

n. revenge, vengeance, requital, reprisal, retaliation; vindictiveness, spitefulness, rancour; avenger, vindicator.

adj. revengeful, vengeant, spiteful, retaliatory, unrelenting, rancorous, unappeasable, implacable.

vb. avenge, take revenge, take vengeance, requite, vindicate, retaliate, get even with, get one's own back.

see also **647**

913 jealousy

n. jealousy, resentment, intolerance, distrust, suspicion, green eye, green-eyed monster; rivalry, unfaithfulness, hostility; vigilance, watchfulness, possessiveness.

adj. jealous, green-eyed, resentful, distrustful, suspicious, vigilant, watchful, possessive.

914 envy

n. envy, covetousness, resentment.

adj. envious, covetous, jealous.

vb. envy, covet, lust after, desire, crave, hanker; grudge, begrudge.

E Moral

915 right

n. right, justice, rightfulness, lawfulness, legality, legitimacy, fairness, equity, impartiality, poetic justice; suitability, reasonableness, fittingness; the right thing, what is right, the proper thing, square deal, fair play.

adj. right, correct, precise, true, valid, accurate; appropriate, proper, suitable, apt, fit, on the right track; fair, honest, upright, righteous, just, rightful, lawful, legitimate, equitable, impartial, objective, unprejudiced, unbiased, disinterested, dispassionate, straightforward, plain; fair and square, straight, fair-minded, sporting.

vb. be just, play the game, try to be

fair, do justice to, do the right thing, give the Devil his due.

see also 577

916 wrong

n. wrong, wrongness, injustice, wrongfulness, inequity, unfairness, partiality, partisanship, prejudice, bias, favouritism; foul play, raw deal, irregularity; grievance, injury; preferential treatment, discrimination, reverse discrimination, nepotism.

adj. wrong, unjust, wrongful, unreasonable, unfair, inequitable, partial, biased, prejudiced, partisan, uneven, unbalanced; below the belt, not cricket (*inf.*), unsportsmanlike; erroneous, imprecise, inaccurate, on the wrong track, at fault; injurious, harmful; wicked, sinful; unsuitable, unfitting, inappropriate, improper; unjustifiable, inexcusable, unforgivable; inadmissible, illegal, illicit, illegitimate.

vb. do wrong, break the law, wrong, hurt, injure, harm, treat unfairly, maltreat, cheat; discriminate, favour, prefer, show preference, be biased, show partiality; not play the game properly, not play fair, hit below the belt.

see also 416, 578

917 dueness

n. dueness, due; deserts, comeuppance, just deserts, merits; right, human rights, rights of man, women's rights; dues, fees, levy, contribution; reward, compensation; punishment; privilege, responsibility, prerogative.

adj. due, owing, payable, overdue, outstanding, unpaid, unsettled, in arrears, chargeable; deserved, well-deserved, merited, worthy, just, warranted, entitled, deserving, worthy, needy, rightful, meritorious.

vb. be due, become due, mature, deserve, merit, have the right to, be entitled to; be worthy of, warrant, expect, earn, claim, lay claim to; demand one's rights; have it coming to one (*inf.*), have only oneself to thank, serve someone right.

918 undueness

n. undueness, unfittingness; presumption, assumption, overstepping, arrogation, violation, encroachment; dispossession, disentitlement, forfeiture, disfranchisement.

adj. undue, undeserved, unmerited, unwarranted, uncalled for, improper, unnecessary, immoderate; unworthy, unjust, unfair, undeserving; unentitled, unprivileged.

vb. have no right to, presume, venture, overstep, assume, usurp, violate, not be entitled to, take liberties; not expect; disqualify; invalidate, disentitle, disfranchise.

919 duty

n. duty, obligation, liability, responsibility, burden, onus; accountability; engagement, commitment, pledge, contract, debt; call of duty, sense of duty, moral obligation, conscience, still small voice; loyalty, faithfulness, allegiance.

adj. incumbent, up to one, behoving; obliged, duty-bound, under obligation; liable, responsible, answerable, subject to, accountable; obligatory, binding, compulsory, necessary; dutiful, obedient, submissive, tractable, compliant.

vb. be one's duty, be the duty of, should, ought, had better, behove; be responsible for, rest with, devolve on, rest on the shoulders of, fall to, fall to one's lot; accept responsiblity, commit oneself; do one's duty, do what is expected of one, perform, fulfil, acquit oneself well, meet one's obligations; impose a duty, call upon, enjoin, look to; oblige, bind, saddle with, put under obligation.

920 neglect of duty

n. neglect, disregard, omission, evasion, non-observance, dereliction, negligence; carelessness, slackness, remissness, slovenliness; absence, absenteeism, truancy; defection, desertion, mutiny; disloyalty, unfaithfulness.

adj. negligent, inattentive, careless, slack, undutiful; disloyal, unfaithful; rebellious, mutinous.

vb. neglect, fail, break, violate; pass over, let slip, let go, omit, ignore, evade, shirk; defer, postpone, procrastinate; suspend, discard, dismiss; rebel, mutiny; absent oneself, play truant; let someone down, not trouble oneself.

see also **393**

921 exemption

n. exemption, immunity, privilege; freedom, liberation, release, dispensation, exception, absolution; permission, leave; lifting of restrictions; escape-clause.

adj. exempt, free, clear, non-liable, not subject to, not chargeable; immune, privileged; unaffected, unrestrained, uncontrolled, unbound, unrestricted; outside.

vb. exempt, free, clear, release, acquit, discharge; lift restrictions; shrug off, pass the buck (*inf.*); be exempt, be free, enjoy immunity, get away with murder (*inf.*).

see also **680, 961**

922 respect

n. respect, regard, honour, esteem, appreciation, favour, admiration, recognition, high opinion, high regard, deference, liking, love; praise, reverence, veneration, awe, worship; respects, bow, curtsy, salute, greeting, salutation.

adj. respectful, deferential, courteous, polite, admiring, showing respect for; attentive, reverential; on one's knees, prostrate.

respected, highly regarded, valued, appreciated, esteemed, honoured, time-honoured, important, well thought of.

vb. respect, regard highly, think well of, think a great deal of, have a high opinion of, admire, take off one's hat to (*inf.*), value, appreciate, honour, hold dear; praise, extol, revere, worship; pay one's respects, bow, kneel, curtsy, welcome, greet; scrape, grovel; keep in with (*inf.*), keep on the right side of; stand in awe of.

command respect, impress, overawe, awe, stun, overwhelm, humble.

923 disrespect

n. disrespect, discourtesy, impoliteness, irreverence, dishonour, low opinion, low regard; insult, affront, offence, humiliation, slight, snub, rebuff, slap in the face, backhanded compliment.

adj. disrespectful, discourteous, impolite, irreverent, dishonourable, insulting, offensive, slighting, cutting, humiliating, rude, scornful, impertinent, depreciating, pejorative.

vb. have no respect for, show disrespect for, have a low opinion of, have no time for, underrate, dishonour, offend, insult, affront, slight, snub, rebuff, scorn, despise, look down on (*inf.*), humiliate, interrupt.

924 contempt

n. contempt, scorn, disdain, ridicule, mocking, derision, disrespect, disdainfulness, contemptuousness, scornfulness, snobbishness, haughtiness; sneer, slight, scoff, cold shoulder.

adj. contemptuous, disdainful, scornful, disrespectful, haughty, supercilious, insolent, snooty, snobbish; contemptible, mean, poor, base, worthless, shameful, despicable, beneath contempt.

vb. despise, disdain, spurn, scorn, pour scorn on, turn one's nose up at (*inf.*), sneer at, mock, laugh at, ridicule, deride; pity, look down on (*inf.*), look down one's nose at (*inf.*); disregard, cut dead; avoid, shun, steer clear of; cheapen, belittle, pooh-pooh, not care a fig for.

see also 853

925 approval

n. approval, recognition, acknowledgement; satisfaction; agreement, permission, sanction, adoption, acceptance; admiration, esteem, credit, honour; compliment, bouquet, commendation, citation, write-up; praise, glorification; applause, clapping, ovation, acclaim.

adj. approving, favourable, complimentary, commendatory, laudatory; approvable, commendable, laudable, praiseworthy, creditable, acceptable; approved, popular, praised, uncensored.

vb. approve, recognize, acknowledge; agree, give permission, allow, sanction; accept, adopt, favour; not reject, not sniff at; praise, admire, esteem, compliment, commend, speak well of, write up, crack up (*inf.*), take off one's hat to (*inf.*), give full marks to, must hand it to (*inf.*); find no fault with, have nothing but praises for; sing the praises of, rave about (*inf.*); clap, applaud, cheer, acclaim, hail, give a big hand to.

926 disapproval

n. disapproval, disagreement, non-acceptance, objection, criticism, complaint, opposition, rejection, contradiction, denunciation, censure, fault-finding, reprehension, judgment, blame, reproach, sneer, taunt.

rebuke, reprimand, reproof, admonition, talking to, telling off, lecture, piece of one's mind; brickbat; dissatisfaction, discontent, displeasure.

adj. disapproving, critical, hostile, reproachful, sneering, taunting, reproving, chiding, censorious, condemnatory, defamatory; niggling, fault-finding; unfavourable, uncomplimentary, disparaging; shocked, not amused.

objectionable, blameworthy, reprehensible, not good enough, in person's bad books, not all it is cracked up to be (*inf.*).

vb. disapprove, disagree, not accept, not think much of, not hold with, hold no brief for, frown on; run down, disparage, belittle; object to, oppose, contradict; boo, hiss; blame, reproach, incriminate; snub, taunt, sneer.

criticize, complain, denounce, find fault with, pick holes in; reprehend, reprove, rebuke, reprimand, admonish, upbraid, judge, knock (*sl.*), slam (*sl.*), condemn, censure, punish, put someone in his place; tell off, talk to, tick off (*inf.*), speak to, lecture, have words with (*inf.*), dress down (*inf.*), dust down (*inf.*), tear off a strip (*sl.*), chide, scold, take to task, rap over the knuckles (*inf.*), haul over the coals (*inf.*); give a piece of one's mind to, give a person what for (*sl.*).

927 flattery

n. flattery, adulation, compliment,

soft soap (*inf.*), eyewash (*sl.*), false praise, insincerity, obsequiousness, fawning, cajolery, wheedling.

flatterer, cajoler, wheedler, hypocrite, toady.

adj. flattering, adulatory, blandishing, complimentary, over-complimentary, unctuous, ingratiating, insincere, smooth, smarmy (*inf.*).

vb. flatter, butter up (*inf.*), suck up to (*sl.*), soft-soap (*inf.*), cajole, wheedle, inveigle; lay it on thick (*inf.*), lay it on with a trowel (*inf.*).

see also **881**

928 disparagement

n. disparagement, depreciation, detraction, degradation, debasement, vilification, discrediting, belittling; defilement, denigration, smear campaign, whispering campaign, muck-raking, mud-slinging, backbiting; slander, libel, calumny, defamation; aspersion, slur, smear, insinuation, innuendo, scandal, gossip.

disparager, critic, slanderer, libeller, backbiter, scandal-monger, muck-raker, mud-slinger; mocker, scoffer, cynic, satirist.

adj. disparaging, deprecatory, derogatory, pejorative, denigratory, slanderous, libellous, defamatory, slighting; cynical.

vb. disparage, depreciate, belittle, play down, run down (*inf.*), decry, discredit, cut down to size (*inf.*); denounce, denigrate, blacken; attack, cast aspersions on; criticize, revile, defame, vilify, malign, slight, slur, tarnish, defile, sully, knock (*sl.*); smear; slander, libel; hound; deride, scoff, mock, ridicule.

929 vindication

n. vindication, justification, establishment, support, plea, defence, excuse, extenuation; ground, right, basis; exoneration, exculpation.

adj. vindicating, justifying, excusing; extenuating; justifiable, arguable, defensible, plausible.

vb. vindicate, justify, establish, support, bear out, uphold, confirm, show, prove, demonstrate, maintain, defend, give grounds for; absolve, acquit, clear, exonerate, excuse, make excuses for, make allowances for.

930 accusation

n. accusation, indictment, prosecution, arraignment, impeachment, charge, censure, incrimination, insinuation, slur, exposé, complaint, denunciation, smear, blame, allegation, action, case; frame-up (*inf.*), put-up job.

accuser, plaintiff, prosecutor.

adj. accusing, denunciatory, incriminating, defamatory.

vb. accuse, censure, charge, bring charges, prefer charges, arrest, arraign, impeach, indict, impute, complain, bring a complaint, find fault with, blame, pin blame on, denounce, incriminate, implicate, involve, reprove, slur, attack, recriminate, slander, libel; point the finger at; frame (*sl.*), trump up, concoct, invent, fabricate, construct, bear false witness.

931 probity

n. probity, uprightness, rectitude, honesty, integrity, fidelity, faithfulness, loyalty, morality, goodness, virtue, reliability, conscientiousness, truthfulness, character, principles, high principles.

adj. honourable, upright, moral, right, fair, good, straight, square, virtuous, honest, law-abiding, reputable, reliable, trustworthy, dependable, conscientious, faithful, loyal, straightforward, sincere, frank, candid, principled, scrupulous.

see also **935, 951**

932 improbity

n. improbity, dishonesty, immorality, badness, evil, wickedness, criminality, corruption; cunning, guile; disloyalty, faithlessness, double-dealing, double-crossing, sell-out, duplicity, betrayal, defection, treason, treachery, perfidy, foul play, trick, prank.

adj. dishonest, immoral, bad, wicked, corrupt, evil, criminal, fraudulent; unscrupulous, unprincipled, disreputable; unreliable, undependable, faithless; betraying, treacherous, perfidious, insidious, two-faced, insincere, deceitful, double-dealing; underhand, sly, crafty, devious, shady, dubious, suspicious, questionable, fishy (*sl.*).

vb. be dishonest, lie, cheat, swindle, deceive, betray, double-cross, sell out (*inf.*), two-time (*sl.*).

see also **936, 952**

933 disinterestedness

n. disinterestedness, impartiality, indifference, non-involvement, unconcern, detachment, objectivity, neutrality; selflessness, self-sacrifice, self-denial.

adj. disinterested, impartial, indifferent, unconcerned, unbiased, unprejudiced, dispassionate, objective, fair, unselfish, selfless, self-denying, self-sacrificing, self-effacing, self-forgetful; generous, liberal, magnanimous.

934 selfishness

n. selfishness, self-indulgence, greed, meanness, narrowness; self-worship, narcissism, egoism, vanity, self-interest, self-seeking.

self-seeker, egoist, individualist, time-server, narcissist, number one.

adj. selfish, self-centred, self-indulgent, greedy, miserly, mean, narrow; wrapped up in oneself, self-absorbed, self-seeking, egoistic.

vb. be selfish, look after number one.

935 virtue

n. virtue, morality, goodness, uprightness, righteousness, narrow way, sanctity, rectitude; honesty, temperance, kindness, excellence; quality, character, integrity; purity, chastity, innocence; ethics, morals.

adj. virtuous, moral, good, upright, righteous, holy, saintly, angelic; honest, kind, excellent, worthy, proper; perfect, irreproachable, unblemished, immaculate, impeccable; chaste, pure, innocent.

vb. be good, behave oneself, acquit oneself well, keep to the straight and narrow; set a good example.

see also **931, 951**

936 vice

n. vice, wickedness, corruption, iniquity, evil, immorality, perversity, baseness, meanness, malignity, malevolence, grossness, wantonness; degeneration, deterioration; unrighteousness, transgression, ungodliness; bad habit, besetting sin, failing, weakness, fault.

adj. wicked, evil, bad, corrupt, immoral, wayward, dissolute, perverse, gross, wanton, base, mean, malevolent, perverted, depraved, degenerate, irreligious, sinful, unrighteous, ungodly, unregenerate.

offensive, shocking, outrageous, scandalous, atrocious, abominable, heinous, repugnant, monstrous, unforgivable.

vb. err, stray, fall, lapse, degenerate, transgress, go off the rails (*inf.*); make wicked, corrupt, demoralize, defile, lead astray.

see also 932, 952

937 innocence

n. innocence, guiltlessness, blamelessness, inculpability, irreproachability, faultlessness, integrity, probity, uprightness, perfection, purity, impeccability; clear conscience, clean hands, clean slate.

adj. innocent, not guilty, above suspicion, in the clear, pure, clean, spotless, unsoiled, untainted, undefiled, blameless, irreproachable, faultless, upright, perfect, impeccable; unoffending, simple, unsophisticated, inexperienced, guileless.

vb. be innocent, have a clear conscience, have nothing to confess.

938 guilt

n. guilt, blame, culpability; responsibility, liability, answerability; criminality, sinfulness; bad conscience, guilty conscience.

crime, offence, transgression, trespass, misdeed, sin, misdemeanour, misconduct, misbehaviour, error, fault, lapse, slip.

adj. guilty, wrong, at fault, offending, to blame, culpable, reproachable; blamed, condemned, judged, incriminated; red-handed, caught in the act.

939 good person

n. good person, good example, model, standard, pattern, ideal, paragon; one in a million, salt of the

earth, last word, ultimate; saint, angel, hero, pillar; perfect gentleman; good fellow, good sort, good egg, sport (*sl.*).

see also 905

940 bad person

n. bad person, wrongdoer, evildoer, sinner, transgressor; reprobate; scoundrel, wretch, villain, miscreant, rogue, rascal, blackguard, knave; bully, scallywag, scamp, scapegrace; wastrel, bum (*sl.*), idler, loafer, prodigal, beggar, tramp; ugly customer, nasty piece of work (*inf.*), bad lot, bad egg; good-for-nothing, ne'er-do-well, black sheep; criminal, crook, liar, cheat, traitor, impostor; rat, louse (*sl.*), worm.

941 penitence

n. penitence, repentance, change of heart, confession, contrition; sorrow, regret, remorse; sackcloth and ashes, hair shirt; penitent, convert, prodigal son.

adj. penitent, repentant, confessing, humble, contrite, conscience-stricken, convicted; regretful, sorry, compunctious, apologetic, full of regrets.

vb. repent, confess, acknowledge, plead guilty, humble oneself, own up, admit; feel shame, deplore; be penitent, be sorry, regret, apologize; turn from sin, see the light, be converted.

942 impenitence

n. impenitence, hardness of heart, heart of stone, seared conscience, obduracy; no regrets; hardened sinner.

adj. impenitent, unrepentant, uncontrite; hard, insensitive, callous, stubborn, obdurate, unashamed; incorrigible, irredeemable; dead, lost.

vb. be impenitent, have no regrets, show no remorse; harden one's heart.

943 atonement

n. atonement, satisfaction, amends.

apology, redress, compensation, indemnity, retribution, requital, repayment, restitution, reparation.

propitiation, reconciliation, sacrifice, offering; substitute, representative; scapegoat; expiation; penance; purgatory.

adj. atoning, satisfying, indemnificatory, compensatory; propitiatory, reconciliatory, sacrificial, redemptive; substitutionary, representative, vicarious.

vb. atone, make amends, redress, compensate, indemnify, requite, repay; apologize; propitiate, reconcile, appease, satisfy, redeem.

944 temperance

n. temperance, moderation, abstemiousness, restraint, self-restraint, self-control, self-discipline; self-denial, abstinence, teetotalism; abstainer, total abstainer, teetotaller.

adj. temperate, moderate, restrained, disciplined, careful; self-denying, self-controlled, abstinent; continent; sparing, frugal, plain; abstemious, sober.

vb. be temperate, exercise self-control, control oneself, deny oneself, abstain, refrain; know when to stop, know when one has had enough.

945 intemperance

n. intemperance, excess, extravagance, inordinateness, self-indulgence; sensuality, voluptuousness, carnality, flesh; luxury, high living; dissipation, debauchery; hedonism, epicureanism.

adj. intemperate, immoderate, unrestrained, inordinate, excessive, self-indulgent; sensual, sensuous, voluptuous, carnal, bodily, fleshly,

gluttonous, debauched; high-living, pleasure-loving, epicurean, hedonistic.

vb. be intemperate, indulge oneself, have one's fling, sow one's wild oats, paint the town red (*sl.*), not know when to stop, overeat, drink too much.

946 ascetism

n. ascetism, austerity, abstinence, abstemiousness, mortification, plain living.

ascetic, self-denier, recluse, hermit, anchorite, stylite; fakir, dervish, flagellant.

adj. ascetic, austere, plain, severe, rigid, stern, abstemious, puritanical, rigorous.

947 fasting

n. fasting, abstinence, hunger, starvation; fast, bread and water, short commons, diet, slimming; fast-day, Lent, Ramadan.

adj. fasting, abstinent, abstaining, starving, hungry, unfed, famished, Lenten.

vb. fast, eat nothing, go hungry, starve, famish; go on hunger strike; diet, reduce weight, slim, take off weight.

948 gluttony

n. gluttony, greed, voracity, rapacity, unsatiability, intemperance, excess, indulgence.

glutton, pig (*inf.*), guzzler, hog, greedy-guts (*sl.*); gourmand, epicure.

adj. greedy, gluttonous, ravenous, devouring, guzzling.

vb. overeat, stuff oneself, make a pig of oneself (*inf.*), eat like a horse, devour, guzzle, gobble, gulp down, bolt down; eat out of house and home.

949 soberness

n. soberness, sobriety, temperance, abstinence, teetotalism, prohibition.

sober person, abstainer, teetotaller, total abstainer, prohibitionist, Band of Hope, Temperance League.

adj. sober, temperate, abstinent, teetotal, on the wagon (*sl.*), off drink, clear-headed, in one's right mind, in possession of one's senses, unintoxicated, stone-cold sober, dry.

vb. be sober, not drink, sign the pledge; hold one's drink, have a good head for drink; sober up, sleep it off (*inf.*).

950 drunkenness

n. drunkenness, intoxication, inebriety, insobriety, intemperance; alcoholism, dipsomania; a drop too much, tipsiness, drinking-bout, pub-crawl, party, celebration, orgy; pink elephants; hangover, head, headache.

drunkard, drinker, heavy drinker, hard drinker, tippler, boozer, alcoholic, drunk (*sl.*).

adj. drunk, intoxicated, inebriated, under the influence, tipsy, befuddled; on the bottle; happy, high, lit up (*inf.*); seeing double, glassy-eyed; groggy; the worse for drink, sloshed (*sl.*), tight (*inf.*), stoned (*sl.*), blotto (*sl.*), canned (*sl.*), sozzled (*sl.*), plastered (*sl.*), under the table.

vb. drink, booze, guzzle, tipple, wet one's whistle (*inf.*), hit the bottle, drink like a fish, drown one's sorrows; be merry, be tipsy, have a drop too much, have one over the eight; be drunk, have more than one can hold, see double, get stoned out of one's mind (*sl.*); intoxicate, inebriate, go to one's head.

951 purity

n. purity, cleanness, cleanliness, whiteness; sinlessness, perfection; untaintedness, unsulliedness, spotlessness, immaculateness.

morality, chastity, virtue, decency, abstemiousness, virginity; prudery, primness, prudishness, overmodesty, false modesty, squeamishness; prude, prig, old maid.

adj. pure, clean, perfect, sinless; unsullied, untainted, spotless, undefiled, unadulterated, unc.taminated; decent, demure, abstemious; edifying; chaste, virtuous; continent, celibate, virgin, platonic; prudish, prim, squeamish, shockable, narrow, strict, Victorian, puritanical, strait-laced, old-maidish; simple, innocent, guileless, artless; inexperienced.

see also 931, 935

952 impurity

n. impurity, uncleanness, sinfulness, imperfection, taintedness, sulliedness, contamination, pollution, adulteration.

immorality, unchastity, indecency, looseness of morals, permissive society; lewdness, prurience, profligacy, incontinence, lechery, wantonness, licentiousness, dissoluteness, salaciousness, lasciviousness; lust, sensuality, eroticism; obscenity, filth, dirt, smut, pornography; free love, promiscuity, adultery, wife-swapping (*inf.*), sleeping around (*inf.*), fornication, unfaithfulness, infidelity, affair, relationship, liaison, eternal triangle; seduction, rape, assault, violation, defilement; prostitution, street-walking, harlotry, whoredom; homosexuality, lesbianism, sodomy, incest.

adj. impure, unclean, imperfect, tainted, sullied, contaminated, polluted, adulterated; immoral, unchaste, indecent, loose, slack, of loose morals, easy, fast, wild, promiscuous, of easy virtue, permissive; lewd, profligate, lecherous, licentious, lascivious, wanton, dissolute, salacious, debauched; sensual, erotic; vulgar, coarse, risqué, spicy; obscene, filthy, dirty, smutty, lurid, sexy, pornographic, blue, unprintable, unexpurgated; homosexual, gay (*sl.*), queer (*sl.*), lesbian; extramarital, unlawful, illicit, adulterous, incestuous.

vb. be impure, commit adultery, fornicate, sleep around (*inf.*); seduce, take advantage of (*inf.*), rape, assault, violate; go on the streets, walk the streets, prostitute, adulterate, contaminate; sully, taint, pollute.

see also 932, 936

953 libertine

n. libertine, profligate, Don Juan, rake, womanizer, lecher, adulterer, seducer, rapist, fornicator; homosexual, homo (*inf.*), queer (*sl.*), gay (*sl.*), fairy (*sl.*), pansy (*inf.*), nancy (*sl.*), butch (*sl.*), transvestite, pervert; lesbian.

adultress, woman of easy virtue, loose woman, flirt, tart (*sl.*), slut, pick-up (*inf.*); mistress; prostitute, pro, call-girl, fallen woman, whore, harlot, street-walker, hustler (*sl.*).

954 legality

n. legality, legitimacy, lawfulness, permissibility, validity, constitutionality; legislation, law-giving, law-making, authorization, codification, sanction, enactment; right, authority, justice; jurisprudence.

law, statute, decree, ordinance, act, edict, order, code, regulation, rule, by-law, constitution.

adj. legal, legitimate, lawful, right, just; constitutional; permissible, permitted, valid, sanctioned, codified, authorized, prescribed, within the law, statutory; jurisprudential, nomothetic.

vb. legalize, permit, authorize,

sanction, approve, validate, establish, enforce, pass, license, charter, empower; legislate.

see also 103, 626

955 illegality

n. illegality, unlawfulness, unconstitutionality, miscarriage of justice, injustice; law-breaking, violation, transgression, trespass, contravention, encroachment, infringement, offence, wrong, crime.

lawlessness, antinomianism, irresponsibility, terrorism, anarchism, mob rule, chaos, disorder, breakdown of law and order.

illegitimacy, bastardy; bastard, illegitimate child, natural child, love child.

adj. illegal, unlawful, illicit, forbidden, prohibited, banned, unauthorized, wrong, against the law, outside the law; stolen, black-market, smuggled, contraband; lawless, wild, chaotic, anarchic, irresponsible; illegitimate, bastard, natural, born out of wedlock, born on the wrong side of the blanket, born without benefit of clergy (*inf.*).

vb. break the law, disobey, commit, violate, transgress, contravene, infringe; take the law into one's own hands, be a law unto oneself; nullify, abrogate, void, annul, cancel.

956 jurisdiction

n. jurisdiction, authority, control, direction, supervision; right, power, responsibility, capacity, competence; executive, corporation, administration; domain, extent, scope, range, territory.

police, police force, constabulary; police officer, policeman, constable, officer, copper (*sl.*), cop (*sl.*), rozzer (*sl.*), fuzz (*sl.*); traffic warden, meter maid.

adj. jurisdictional, judiciary, competent, responsible, judicial, executive.

vb. administer, preside, direct, supervise; judge; police, keep order, control.

957 tribunal

n. tribunal, court, assizes, session, bench, bar; judgment seat, mercy seat, throne; dock, witness-box; courthouse.

958 judge

n. judge, justice, J.P., recorder, magistrate, stipendiary, beak (*sl.*); judiciary; marshal; jury, panel, tribunal; juror, juryman, jurywoman, foreman.

see also **653, 960**

959 lawyer

n. lawyer, legal practitioner; the bar, legal profession; defender, counsel, barrister, advocate, bencher; legal adviser, attorney, procurator, solicitor; prosecution; notary, commissioner for oaths; legist, jurist, jurisconsult; pettifogger.

vb. practise law, plead; be called to the bar, take silk; argue, defend, advocate; allege, prosecute.

960 lawsuit

n. lawsuit, case, suit, action, legal proceedings, hearing, indictment; litigation, judicature; summons, writ, subpoena; affidavit, bill; pleadings, argument, prosecution, cross-examination, defence, plea, summing-up; verdict, finding, decision, ruling, pronouncement, sentence, decree, award, precedent; appeal; litigant, party, suitor, plaintiff, defendant.

vb. go to law, prosecute, sue, litigate, bring an action against, bring to trial, file a claim; try, hear, give a hearing to, judge, arbitrate, adjudicate; rest one's case; sum up; rule, find, pron-

ounce, declare, return a verdict, bring in a verdict, pass sentence, sentence, convict, acquit.

961 acquittal

n. acquittal, discharge, reprieve, release, remission, pardon, clearance, dismissal, exoneration, exculpation; innocence; suspended sentence.

adj. acquitted, not guilty, clear, discharged, released, set free, liberated, justified; forgiven.

vb. acquit, declare not guilty, discharge, pardon, absolve, forgive, clear, dismiss, grant remission, reprieve, release, set free, let off (*inf.*), exempt; exonerate, exculpate; justify, vindicate; save, rescue, redeem.

see also **601, 921**

962 condemnation

n. condemnation, denunciation, conviction.

adj. condemnatory, damnatory.

vb. condemn, find guilty, sentence, pass sentence on, judge, convict, punish, doom, damn, curse; proscribe, denounce, criticize, find fault with, blame, rebuke.

963 punishment

n. punishment, reproof, discipline, chastisement, correction, reprimand, retribution; penalty, imposition, fine, damages, costs, compensation; exile, banishment; hard labour; bread and water.

corporal punishment, slap, rap, cuff, blow, clout; capital punishment, death sentence, execution, decapitation, beheading, hanging, electrocution, strangling, strangulation, poisoning, crucifixion, impalement, drowning; torture; slaughter; genocide, mass murder, massacre, annihilation.

punisher; executioner, hangman, firing squad; inquisition.

adj. punitive, penal, castigatory, disciplinary, corrective.

vb. punish, reprove, discipline, chastise, correct, sentence, take to task, admonish, rebuke, reprimand, dress down (*inf.*), come down on like a ton of bricks (*inf.*), crack down on (*inf.*); make an example of; retaliate, get one's revenge, get even with.

expel, exile, banish, deport, transport, outlaw, isolate, send to Coventry; imprison, jail; penalize, fine, endorse one's licence.

strike, hit, slap, rap over the knuckles, box on the ears; flog, whip, beat, thrash, scourge, flay; spank, give a good hiding (*inf.*), thrash the living daylights out of (*sl.*), lick (*sl.*), tan (*sl.*), belt, strap, clout, wallop (*sl.*), cane, whack (*inf.*).

kill, put to death, shoot, execute, behead, guillotine, decapitate; hang, lynch; hang, draw, and quarter; crucify, impale; electrocute, gas; strangle; burn at the stake; drown; poison; slaughter, annihilate, massacre; torture, martyr, put on the rack, break on the wheel, tar and feather.

be punished, suffer, pay the penalty, get one's just deserts, have it coming, deserve; face the music, take the rap.

see also 926

964 means of punishment

n. scourge, birch, whip, lash, belt, cane, rod, stick, switch, cat-o'-nine-tails; pillory, stocks, ducking stool, whipping post; torture chamber, rack, wheel, screw, water torture; axe, guillotine; block, scaffold; cross, stake; gallows, gibbet, noose, rope; electric chair, gas chamber, death chamber; condemned cell.

965 reward

n. reward, pay, payment, compensation, recompense, remuneration, reimbursement, reparation, redress; allowance, expenses, honorarium; tip, gratuity; prize, award, trophy, bonus, premium, bounty, accolade, guerdon.

adj. rewarding, remunerative, compensatory; profitable, advantageous, worthwhile; charitable, liberal, generous, open-handed, unsparing.

vb. reward, pay, recompense, reimburse, redress, compensate; award, recognize, pay tribute, present, give, bestow, confer, grant, thank.

see also 663, 715

F Religious

966 divinity

n. divinity, divineness, deity, godhead; God, Spirit, Supreme Being, Creator, prime mover, Providence.

adj. divine, spiritual; godlike, godly; heavenly, celestial, sublime; transcendent, immanent, self-existent; eternal, everlasting, immortal; almighty, omnipotent, all-powerful, infinite, supreme; omniscient, all-knowing; just, merciful, gracious, loving, personal.

967 God

n. God; Trinity; Father, Lord, Yahweh, Jehovah, Almighty, King of Kings; Son of God, Jesus Christ, Son of Man, Immanuel, Word, Messiah, Saviour, Redeemer; Holy Spirit, Holy Ghost, Comforter, Paraclete.

god, goddess, object of worship; idol, false god; golden calf; pantheon; numen; totem, fetish; mumbo-jumbo.

supreme deity, Zeus, Jupiter; goddess of women and marriage, Hera, Juno; goddess of crops, Demeter,

Ceres; god of the sun, Phoebus, god of music, medicine, and poetry, Apollo; god of war, Ares, Mars; god of commerce, eloquence, and cunning, Hermes, Mercury; god of the sea, Poseidon, Neptune; god of metalworking, Hephaestus, Vulcan; god of wine and revelry, Dionysus, Bacchus; god of the underworld, Hades, Pluto, Dis; god of agriculture, Kronos, Saturn; god of love, Eros, Cupid; goddess of love and beauty, Aphrodite, Venus; goddess of the moon and hunting, Artemis, Diana; goddess of wisdom, Athena, Minerva; god of the countryside, Pan, Faunus.

Allah; Brahma, Atman, Vishnu, Shiva; Buddha.

968 good spirit
n. good spirit, angel, ministering spirit, seraph, cherub, host, principalities, authorities, powers, thrones, dominions; archangel.

adj. angelic, ministering, heavenly, celestial.

969 evil spirit
n. devil, Satan, fallen angel, father of lies, Beelzebub, prince of this world, prince of darkness; demon, evil spirit, unclean spirit, powers of darkness; imp, fiend, vampire; adversary.

adj. satanic, devilish, diabolic, diabolical, wicked.

see also **984**

970 mythical being
n. fairy, spirit, elf, brownie, goblin, hob, bogle, body, kobold, hobgoblin, dryad, pixie, gnome, peri; sprite, genie, jinnee; nymph; wood-nymph, hamadryad; mountain-nymph, oread; water-nymph, naiad; sea-nymph, nereid; siren, mermaid, water-spirit, water-elf, nix, nixie, kelpie; imp, puck,

leprechaun, gremlin, urchin; changeling; sylph; dwarf, troll.

adj. fairy, mythical, imaginary, fabulous; elfin, elfish, impish.

971 ghost
n. ghost, spectre, spook (*inf.*), apparition, vision, phantom, phantasm, appearance, shade, presence, poltergeist, wraith, *doppelgänger*, double, fetch, visitant, spirit, departed spirit, zombie.

adj. ghostly, spooky (*inf.*), supernatural, evil, haunted, eerie, weird, uncanny, phantom.

vb. haunt, visit, walk, return from the dead.

972 heaven
n. heaven, paradise, bliss, glory, kingdom of heaven, Abraham's bosom, heavenly city, next world, world to come, eternal rest, kingdom-come (*sl.*), happy hunting ground, Elysium; rapture, resurrection, translation, ascension, glorification.

adj. heavenly, celestial, blessed, glorious, glorified, empyrean.

973 hell
n. hell, perdition, underworld, lower world, nether regions, bottomless pit, abyss, inferno, everlasting fire, lake of fire and brimstone, place of the lost, place of torment, pandemonium, Sheol, Gehenna.

adj. hellish, infernal.

974 religion
n. religion, belief, faith, dogma, teaching, doctrine, creed, tenet, revelation, articles of faith, confession, theology.

deism, theism, monotheism, polytheism, pantheism; animism; gnosticism.

Christianity, Judaism; Islam

Buddhism, Hinduism, Brahmanism, Taoism, Confucianism.

teacher; prophet, apostle; preacher, lay-preacher, exponent, interpreter, commentator, evangelist, missionary.

adj. religious, spiritual, divine, holy, sacred; theological, doctrinal; devout, godly, believing, practising, faithful, regenerate, converted.

see also **980**

975 irreligion

n. irreligion, ungodliness, godlessness, unholiness, unspirituality, wickedness, sinfulness, idolatry, heathenism, paganism; atheism, unbelief; disbelief, scepticism, doubt, agnosticism; heresy, antichristianity; rationalism, free thinking, materialism.

unbeliever, atheist; agnostic, doubter, sceptic, doubting Thomas; idolater; heathen, pagan; infidel, heretic, dissenter.

adj. irreligious, ungodly, godless, wicked, sinful, idolatrous, heathen, pagan; unbelieving, atheistic; heretical, unorthodox; disbelieving, sceptical, agnostic; materialistic, secular, worldly, profane; unregenerate, unconverted, lost, damned.

see also **981**

976 revelation

n. revelation, disclosure; inspiration, afflatus, prophecy, vision; signs, foreshadowing; Scripture, Bible, Word of God, canon; Talmud, Torah, Ten Commandments; Law, Gospel.

Koran, Vedas.

adj. revelational, inspirational, inspired, revealed, prophetic, biblical, scriptural, canonical; evangelical; authoritative.

977 orthodoxy

n. orthodoxy, soundness, faithfulness, strictness, truth, adherence, observance.

the Church, body of Christ, Church invisible, Church militant, Church triumphant, Christendom; believer, true believer, Christian, practising Christian, church member, the saints, the faithful.

adj. orthodox, sound, correct, right, pure, true, faithful; evangelical, conservative, strict, literal, fundamentalist; practising, believing.

978 heresy

n. heresy, heterodoxy; divergence, aberration, distortion, perversion, unorthodoxy, unauthenticity, apostasy, infidelity.

adj. heretical, heterodox, divergent, different, unorthodox, unsound, unscriptural, unbiblical.

979 sectarianism

n. sectarianism, partisanship, schismatism, separatism; denominationalism; party-spirit.

sect, schism, split, section, faction, division, branch; denomination, communion, tradition; off-shoot, secession; sectarian, party-man, seceder, dissident, non-conformist, rebel.

adj. sectarian, partisan, schismatic, party-minded; denominational; dissident, non-conformist; separatist, secessionist, break-away; exclusive.

980 piety

n. piety, devoutness; devotion, single-mindedness; trust, faith; loyalty, submission, dedication, commitment, faithfulness, adherence, perseverance, allegiance, zeal, ardour, earnestness; adoration, worship, reverence, fear, awe, prayerfulness; holiness, sanctity, consecration, godliness, saintliness, humility, spirituality.

saint, believer, convert, man of prayer, man of God; follower, disciple, pilgrim; pietist.

adj. pious, devout, devoted, faithful, loyal, dedicated, committed, single-minded, zealous, earnest; believing, practising, holy, godly, saintly, spiritual, sanctified, consecrated, other-worldly, humble, meek.

vb. be pious, repent and believe, have faith, trust, fear God; keep the faith, persevere; worship, pray; sanctify, consecrate, make holy, dedicate, hallow.

981 impiety

n. impiety, godlessness, irreverence, unrighteousness, unholiness, sinfulness, disobedience; worldliness; blasphemy, sacrilege, desecration, defilement, violation.

hypocrisy, sanctimoniousness, false piety, self-righteousness, religiosity, formalism, hallowness, churchianity (*inf.*), religious show, façade, lip service, cant.

sinner, blasphemer; scoffer, mocker; materialist, worldling; hypocrite, Pharisee, scribe.

adj. impious, irreligious, ungodly, godless, irreverent, unholy, unrighteous, sinful, wicked, disobedient; unbelieving, atheistic, agnostic, non-practising; unhallowed, unsanctified, unregenerate, hardened; blasphemous, sacrilegious, profane; sanctimonious, hypocritical, pharasaical, false, deceitful, insincere, dishonest.

vb. be impious, sin, blaspheme; desecrate, profane, pay lip service.

982 worship

n. worship, honour, reverence, praise, adoration, exaltation, homage, veneration; service, devotions; prayer, private devotion, quiet time, meditation; confession; thanksgiving, grace; supplication, request, entreaty, appeal, petition, intercession, rogation; hymn, song, psalm, chant, anthem, canticle, chorus.

worshipper, church-goer, Christian, communicant; supplicant, petitioner, intercessor, man of prayer; congregation, church, flock, assembly.

adj. worshipping, devoted, reverent, religious, devout, prayerful, on one's knees, supplicant; worshipful, reverential, solemn, holy, serious, dignified, sublime, majestic, glorious.

vb. worship, adore, praise, glorify, bless, exalt, honour, magnify, revere, venerate, pay homage to, laud, bow down, humble oneself; idolize; pray to, seek; confess; thank, give thanks, ask, invoke, entreat, petition, implore, intercede, say one's prayers, beseech; sing; meditate, contemplate, consider, reflect.

see also 977

983 idolatry

n. idolatry, idolism, idol worship, irreligion, heathenism, paganism, fetishism, demonism, devil-worship, hero-worship, iconolatry, image-worship, mumbo-jumbo; idolization, deification, apotheosis.

idol, false god, image, graven image, icon, statue, golden calf, totem, fetish.

idolater, idolizer, pagan, heathen, image-maker.

adj. idolatrous, heathen, pagan, idol-worshipping.

vb. idolatrize, idolize, worship, enshrine, deify; sing the praises of, pu on a pedestal, admire, dote on, treasure.

984 sorcery

n. sorcery, magic, superstition, witchcraft, diabolism, black magic, occultism, cabbala, exorcism, divination; miracle-working, thaumaturgy; spell, incantation, bewitchment, enchantment, influence, possession, trance, hocus-pocus, mumbo-jumbo, open sesame, abracadabra; charm, amulet, talisman, mascot, fetish, good-luck charm.

spiritism, spiritualism, spirit communication; séance, sitting; ouija board, planchette, automatic writing; levitation.

sorcerer, wizard, witch, enchanter, spell-binder, magician, conjurer; soothsayer, clairvoyant; astrologer; shaman, witch-doctor, medicine-man; voodoo; thaumaturgist, miracle-worker; diviner; exorcist; occultist; necromancer, spiritualist.

adj. sorcerous, devilish, diabolical, occult, necromantic; spell-binding; magical, supernatural, weird, uncanny, eerie; charmed, bewitched, enchanted; mystic, esoteric, transcendental.

vb. divine, conjure; wave a wand; exorcise, lay ghosts; call up spirits; bewitch, enchant, charm, fascinate, mesmerize, obsess, possess, put under curse; hold a séance; go into a trance; materialize, dematerialize.

see also 447

985 churchdom

n. churchdom, Christendom, the church, ministry; call, vocation; office, holy orders; pastorship, pastorate, priesthood, clerical order; cure of souls, spiritual guidance, pastoral case; service, preaching, administration of the sacraments, prayer; fellowship communion.

adj. ecclesiastical, ministerial, pastoral, cleric, priestly, sacerdotal.

vb. call, ordain, consecrate, present, nominate; take holy orders.

986 clergyman

n. clergyman, servant of God, shepherd; pastor, preacher, minister, incumbent, priest, vicar, parson, rector; curate, chaplain, cleric, padre, father, reverend; abbot, prelate, bishop, archbishop, prior, dean, archdeacon, canon, primate, Pope; metropolitan, patriarch, cardinal; monk, friar; nun, sister; rabbi, teacher.

adj. clerical, ordained.

vb. be ordained, enter the ministry.

987 laity

n. laity, layman, lay people, parish, congregation, church, fold, flock, assembly, church member, parishioner, brethren; elder, deacon; lay-preacher, lay-reader.

adj. lay, unordained, non-clerical, secular, temporal, of the world, civil, profane, unholy, unconsecrated, unsacred.

vb. laicize, secularize, deconsecrate.

988 religious service

n. ceremony, ordinance, rite, ritual, custom, institution, observance; order, form, litany; administration, celebration, officiation.

service, divine worship, service of worship, morning service, matins, evening service, evensong, vespers, compline, fellowship, prayer meeting, Bible Study, Sunday School; Holy Communion, Lord's Supper, mass, Eucharist; baptism.

adj. ritual, ceremonial, customary, formal, liturgical.

vb. observe, keep, celebrate, minister, administer, officate, perform, dedicate, bless, pray, baptize, worship; encourage, share, fellowship.

989 vestment
n. vestment, cloth, clerical dress, canonicals, robes, surplice, gown, mantle, cassock, rochet, chasuble, cape, hood; mitre, staff, crook, crosier.

990 church building
n. church, chapel, sanctuary, house of prayer, house of God, Lord's house, bethel, kirk, tabernacle; mission, house-church, meeting-house; cathedral, minster, abbey; monastery, priory, friary, convent, nunnery; synagogue; mosque, shrine, temple.

Index

The index does not list every word or phrase in the main part of the book. In particular, many words derived from other related words, e.g. adverbs ending in -ly derived from adjectives, have been excluded. If you want to look up a word that is not in the index, you should therefore look up the word closest to it, and refer to the categories in the main part of the book, looking at the part of speech of the word you originally wanted. Further, a reference to a particular entry does not necessarily mean that the word looked up will appear at that entry – but since you are interested in other words related to this one, the fact that it does not occur at the entry is of no consequence.

Numbers printed in darker, bold type show the main categories for the particular words. The titles of the categories are also printed in the bolder typeface. For further help on finding the word you want, see the section 'How to use this thesaurus' at the front of the book.

Index

accolade n. 663, 965

accommodate vb. 105, 302, 545, 652

accommodation n. 191

accompaniment n. **60**, 792

accompany vb. 60, 122, 882

accomplice n. 640

accomplish vb. 159, 609, 659, 661

accomplished adj. 581, 627, 659

accomplishment n. 609, 659, 661

accord n. 24, 643; vb. 16, 24, 105, 180

account n. (description) 460, 465, 483, 525; (money) 736, 742; vb. (describe) 157, 456, 483, 525; (pay) 742

accountable adj. 679, 919

accountant n. 733, 742

accounts n. **742**

accretion n. 40, 41

accrue vb. 36, 40, 705, 716

accumulate vb. 36, 40, 94, 567, 705

accurate adj. 430, 476, 915

accursed adj. 892

accusation n. **930**

accuse vb. 930

accustom vb. 105, 545

ache n. 828; vb. 828

achieve vb. 609, 659, 661

achievement n. 89, 609, 659, 661

achromatism n. 806

acid n. 773; adj. 773

acknowledge vb. 395, 424, 468, 692, 909, 925, 941

acme n. 212, 581

acoustics n. 778

acquaintance n. 882

acquiesce vb. 424, 654, 673, 692

acquire vb. 472, 705, 716, 720, 726

acquisition n. 705, 716, 726

acquisitive adj. 705, 750

acquit vb. 601, 680, 911, 921, 961

acquit oneself well vb. 919, 935

acquittal n. 601, 911, **961**

acrimonious adj. 893, 900

act n. 609, 852, 954; vb. 172, 529, **609**, 621

acting n. 529; adj. 689

action n. 172, 266, **609**, 651, 960

activate vb. 88, 266, 282

active adj. 172, 368, 611

activism n. 611

activist n. 611; adj. 611

activity n. 266, 557, 609, **611**

actor n. 529, 619

actress n. 529

actual adj. 1, 3, 120, 430

actuary n. 742

acumen n. 434

acute adj. 255, 434

acute angle n. 246

adage n. 432

Adam n. 379

adapt vb. 24, 105, 125, 142, 602, 606

adaptable adj. 105, 151

adaptation n. 456, 545, 792

add vb. 36, **40**

addendum n. 41

addict n. 545

addition n. 38, **40**, 41, 705

additional adj. 6, 40

additive n. 307

address n. 191, **518**, 523, 695; vb. 514

addressee n. 523, 716

adept n. 629; adj. 627

adequate adj. **570**, 579

adhere vb. 50

adherent n. 474, 640

adhesive n. 49; adj. 50

ad infinitum adv. 78

adjacent adj. 199, 238

adjective n. 499

adjoin vb. 199, 201

adjournment n. 89, 135

adjudicate vb. 415, 960

adjudicator n. 415, 653

adjunct n. 41, 60

adjure vb. 468, 695

adjust vb. 24, 105, 142, 403, 704

ad lib adj. 544; vb. 544

administer vb. 621, **622**, 956, 988

administration n. 622, 667, 956

administrator n. 558, 623

admirable adj. 579

admire vb. 868, 888, **922**, 925

admissible adj. 302

admission n. 98, 300, 302, 420, 462, 468, 716

admit vb. 98, 262, 300, 302, 424, 462, 468, 716, 833

admit defeat vb. 654

admonish vb. 597, 624, 926, 963

adolescent n. 131; adj. 129, 131

adopt vb. 540, 575, 606, 702, 720

adopted adj. 40, 100, 171, 606

adoption *n.* 171, 540, 606

adorable *adj.* 827

adore *vb.* 889, 982

adorn *vb.* 509, 844, 846

adroit *adj.* 627

adulation *n.* 927

adult *n.* 133; *adj.* 133

adulterate *vb.* 45, 477, 582, 952

adulterer *n.* 953

adultery *n.* 952

adulthood *n.* 133

adumbrate *vb.* 798

advance *n.* **288**, 292, 587, 645, 693, 718, 890; *adj.* 236; *vb.* **288**, 292, 587, 645, 661, 718

advanced *adj.* 125

advantage *n.* 34, 550, 575

advantageous *adj.* 550, 575, 577, 661, 965

adventure *n.* 153, 269

adventurer *n.* 270

adventurous *adj.* 605

adverb *n.* 499

adversary *n.* 638, 883, 969

adverse *adj.* 14, 665

adversity *n.* 445, **665**

advertisement *n.* 464

advertising *n.* 727

advice *n.* 460, 597, **624**, 636

advisable *adj.* 577

advise *vb.* 460, 597, **624**, 636

advisor *n.* 473, 624

advisory *adj.* 597, 624

advocate *n.* 959; *vb.* 959

aerate *vb.* 344, 348, 775

aerial *adj.* 273, 318, 348

aerodynamics *n.* 348

aeronautical *adj.* 273, 278

aeronautics *n.* 273

aeroplane *n.* 278

aesthetic *adj.* 848

affable *adj.* 884

affair *n.* 153, 557, 889, 952

affect *vb.* 177, 752, 755

affectation *n.* 510, **852**

affected *adj.* 510, 751, 752, 852

affection *n.* 752, 882, 889, 890

affections *n.* **751**

affidavit *n.* 401, 468, 960

affiliate *vb.* 11, 52, 639, 641

affinity *n.* 18, 105, 218, 294

affirm *vb.* 401, 413, 424, 468, 514

affirmation *n.* 413, 424, **468**, 690

affirmative *n.* 424; *adj.* 468

affix *n.* 499; *vb.* 40, 47

afflict *vb.* 830

affliction *n.* 551, 586, 592, **665**, 828

affluence *n.* 664, 734

afford *vb.* 568, 715, 734

affront *n.* 923; *vb.* 887, 923

affronted *adj.* 893

afloat *adj.* 153

aforementioned *adj.* 84

afraid *adj.* 856

after *adj.* 119; *adv.* 85

after-effect *n.* 87, 156

afterlife *n.* 123

aftermath *n.* 87, 156

afternoon *n.* 128

afterthought *n.* 87, 441, 538

afterwards *adv.* 85

again *adv.* 62, 77

age *n.* 109, 130; *vb.* 130

aged *adj.* 130

ageless *adj.* 114, 129

agency *n.* 172, 563, 685

agenda *n.* 83, 441

agent *n.* 149, 155, 564, **619**, 689

aggravation *n.* 835

aggregate *n.* 54; *adj.* 54

aggressive *adj.* 173, 175, 645, 651

aggressor *n.* 645

aghast *vb.* 866

agile *adj.* 280, 611, 627

agitation *n.* 80, **326**, 755, 756

agitator *n.* 142, 148

agnostic *n.* 975; *adj.* 409, 975, 981

agnosticism *n.* 409, 421, 975

ago *adv.* 124

agonize *vb.* 830

agonizing *adj.* 828

agony *n.* 756, 828

agrarian *adj.* 378

agree *vb.* 24, 105, 180, 424, 692, 925

agreeable *adj.* 692, 829

agreed *adj.* 24

agreement *n.* 24, 105, 424, 643, 650, 692, 699, 704, 925

agriculture *n.* 378

ahead *adv.* 236, 286

ahead of *adj.* 118

aid *n.* 563, **636**, 640, 834, 899; *vb.* 563, **636**

ailment *n.* 586

aim *n.* 178, 284, 450, 552; *vb.* 178, 284, 552

aimless *adj.* 158, 399, 451, 553

air *n.* 329, 344, **348**, 621, 792; *vb.* 348, 350

air conditioning *n.* 348

aircraft *n.* **278**

airing *n.* 348

air in motion *n.* 359

airman *n.* 273

air-pipe *n.* **361**

airport *n.* 298

airs *n.* 852

air travel *n.* 273

airy *adj.* 4, 331, 333, 344, 348

ajar *adj.* 262

akin *adj.* 11

alacrity *n.* 611

alarm *n.* 482, 598, 856

alarming *adj.* 594

album *n.* 441

alcoholism *n.* 950

alcove *n.* 254

alert *n.* 597, 598; *adj.* 392, 602, 611; *vb.* 597, 598

algebra *n.* 38

alias *n.* 497

alibi *n.* 549

alien *n.* 100; *adj.* 100

alienate *vb.* 883, 892

alight *adj.* 759; *vb.* 298

alike *adj.* 13, 18

alive *adj.* 368, 611, 753

all *n.* 54; *adj.* 54, 56

Allah *n.* 967

allegation *n.* 401, 930

allege *vb.* 549, 959

alleged *adj.* 448, 549, 825

allegiance *n.* 679, 919, 980

allegory *n.* 397, 455, 525

all-embracing *adj.* 54, 98

allergic *adj.* 862

alleviate *vb.* 176, 652, 834

alley *n.* 559

alliance *n.* 641, 699, 896

allied *adj.* 11, 47, 180, 641

all-inclusive *adj.* 54, 98

allocation *n.* 717

allot *vb.* 55, 717

allotment *n.* 378, 717

allow *vb.* **690**, 692, 744, 925

allowance *n.* 31, 690, 715, 717, 718, 738, 744, 965

allow for *vb.* 31, 403

alloy *n.* 45; *vb.* 45

all right *adj.* 579, 585; *adv.* 79

all-round *adj.* 627

allure *vb.* 547, 829, 889

allusion *n.* 455, 459

ally *n.* 640

ally with *vb.* 47

almanac *n.* 116, 483

Almighty *n.* 967

almighty *adj.* 159, 966

almost *adv.* 199

alms *n.* 715, 899

aloft *adv.* 208

alone *adj.* 48, 59

alongside *adv.* 238

aloof *adj.* 198, 517, 754, 757, 885

alphabet *n.* 493

also *adv.* 40

alter *vb.* 142, 146

alternate *vb.* 12, 140, 142, 325

alternative *n.* 149, 540; *adj.* 149

altitude *n.* 208

altogether *adv.* 54, 56

altruistic *adj.* 899, 903

always *adv.* 114

amalgamate *vb.* 45, 52

amass *vb.* 94, 567

amateur *n.* 630; *adj.* 628

amaze *vb.* 866

ambassador *n.* 460, 467, 688, 689

ambience *n.* 8, 229

ambiguity *n.* 409, 412, 451, 453, **454**, 503

ambition *n.* 552, 854, 861

ambitious *adj.* 605, 611, 854

ambivalent *adj.* 454

amble *n.* 269; *vb.* 269

ambrosia *n.* 770

ambulate *vb.* 269

ambush *n.* 463, 596; *vb.* 463

amelioration *n.* 587

amenable *adj.* 179, 654

amend *vb.* 589

amendment *n.* 587

amends *n.* 31, 589, 721, 943

amiable *adj.* 886

amicable *adj.* 643, 882

amity *n.* 643, 882

amnesia *n.* 442

amnesty *n.* 911

among *prep.* 230

amorous *adj.* 889

amorphous *adj.* 243

amount *n.* 26, 731, 743; *vb.* 743

amphibian *n.* 373; *adj.* 373

amphitheatre *n.* 658

ample *adj.* 32, 75, 182

amplify *vb.* 36, **196**, 481, 505

amplitude *n.* 32, 194, 204, 400

amputate *vb.* 42

amulet *n.* 984

amuse *vb.* 829, 840

amusement *n.* 829, **840**

amusing *adj.* 840, 842, 851

anachronism *n.* **117**

anachronistic *adj.* 117, 126

anaemic *adj.* 162, 806, 807

analogy *n.* 9, 18, 397

analysis *n.* 38, 48, 53, 394, 396

analyst *n.* 456

analytical *adj.* 38, 456

anarchist n. 148, 167, 672

anarchistic adj. 148, 644, 672

anarchy n. 80, 148, 668

anathema n. 892

anatomy n. 366, 375

ancestor n. 11, 86

anchor n. 330; vb. 152

ancient adj. 124, 126

ancillary n. 640; adj. 35, 60

and adv. 40

anecdote n. 525

anew adv. 77, 125

angel n. 467, 891, 905, 939, **968**

angelic adj. 935, 968

anger n. 893; vb. 755, 893

angle n. 246, 420; vb. 219, 246

angry adj. 893

anguish n. 551, 828

angular form n. **246**

animal n. 175, 373, adj. 373

animality n. 373

animal sound n. **789**

animate adj. 366; vb. 173, 368, 618, 755, 836

animate matter n. **366**

animism n. 974

animosity n. 425, 883, 900

annals n. 116, 483

annex vb. 40

annexe n. 41

annihilate vb. 164, 370, 963

anniversary n. 140, 878; adj. 878

annotate vb. 456, 482

announce vb. 458, 460, 464

announcement n. 458, 460, 464, 465

announcer n. 460

annoy vb. 830, 835, 887, 893

annoyed adj. 893, 894

annually adv. 140

annulment n. **686**, 898

anoint vb. 342, 365

anonymous adj. 497

answer n. 283, 395, 402, 468, 523; vb. 395

answerable adj. 179, 679, 737, 919

answer back vb. 395, 880

antagonism n. 181, 637, 883, **892**, 893

antagonist n. 638, 883

antagonistic adj. 637, 883, 892

antecede vb. 118

antecedent n. 86, 118, 155; adj. 84, 118

antedate vb. 117

antediluvian adj. 126

anterior n. 236; adj. 84, 118, 236

anthem n. 982

anthology n. 527

anthropoid n. 379

anthropology n. 375, 379

anticipate vb. 134, 154, 443, 446, 854

anti-climax n. 445

antidote n. 181

antinomianism n. 955

antiquated adj. 126

antique adj. 126

antiquity n. 124, 126

antisocial adj. 885, 904

anxious adj. 828, 856, 894

any adj. 26

anyhow adv. 80

apart adj. 48

apartheid n. 99

apartment n. 191

apathy n. 281, 389, 393, 612, 754, 841, 863

ape n. 20

aperitif n. 306

aperture n. 254, 262

aphasia n. 515

apocalypse n. 462

apologetics n. 410

apologetic adj. 833, 941

apologize vb. 538, 549, 833, 941, 943

apology n. 549, 833, 943

apostasy n. 147, 538, 590, 978

apostle n. 974

appal vb. 856

appalling adj. 830, 856

apparatus n. 565, 568

apparent adj. 458, 634, 823, 825

apparently adv. 825

apparition n. 4, 458, 971

appeal n. 518, 695, 960; vb. 695, 829

appear vb. 188, 298, 458, 621, **825**

appearance n. 222, 242, 298, 458, 621, **825**

appease vb. 335, 652, 831, 943

append vb. 40, 85

appendage n. 41, 60, 87, 89

appendix n. 41

appertain vb. 707

appertaining adj. 9

appetite n. 861

appetizer n. 306

appetizing adj. 306, 767, 770

applause n. 838, 878, 888, 909, 925

appliance n. 565, 568

applicable adj. 9, 105, 575

applicant n. 697

application n. 172, 472, 575, 606, 611, 695

apply *vb.* 9. 575, 606. 695

appoint *vb.* 540, 557. 685

appointment *n.* 557. 685, 884

apportionment *n.* **717**

apposite *adj.* 9, 577

appraise *vb.* 384, 400. 415

appreciate *vb.* 415, 770, 827, 888, 889, **909, 922**

appreciative *adj.* 909

apprehend *vb.* 426, 452, 681, 720

apprehensive *adj.* 326, 443, 856

apprentice *n.* 474, 619

apprise *vb.* 597

approach *n.* 154, **292.** 298, 559, 602, 693; *vb.* 123, 154, 199, 292, 298, 693

approachable *adj.* 292

appropriate *adj.* 105, 499, 510, 577, 915; *vb.* 705, 720

approval *n.* 424, 690, 692, **925,** 954

approximate *vb.* 18, 199, 292

approximately *adv.* 199

apricot *n.* 816

apt *adj.* 179, 915

aptitude *n.* 627

aquarium *n.* 377

aquatic *adj.* 347

aquatics *n.* 271

aqueduct *n.* 360

arbiter *n.* 653

arbitrary *adj.* 10

arbitrate *vb.* 415, 653. 960

arc *n.* 247

arcade *n.* 247, 559, 730

arch *n.* 247; *vb.* 247. 252

archaic *adj.* 126

archaism *n.* 124, 494

archbishop *n.* 870, 986

archetype *n.* 23

architect *n.* 166, 491. 558

archives *n.* 483, 567

archivist *n.* 484

arctic *adj.* 760

ardent *adj.* 506, 759. 889

ardour *n.* 752, 759, 861, 889, 980

arduous *adj.* 615, 633

area *n.* 26, 182, 183, 194, 234, 400, 557

arena *n.* 234, **658**

arguable *adj.* 929

argue *vb.* 410, 414, 420. 514, 642, 959

argument *n.* 25, 387, 410, 525, 642, 893, 960

argumentative *adj.* 410

arid *adj.* 350

arise *vb.* 88, 153, 318, 825

aristocracy *n.* 870

arithmetic *n.* 38

arm *n.* 353; *vb.* 159, 646

armistice *n.* 144, 650

armour *n.* 646, 657

arms *n.* **657**

army *n.* 75, 655

aroma *n.* 776

around *adv., prep.* 229

arouse *vb.* 155, 618, 755

arraign *vb.* 930

arrange *vb.* 58, 81, 242. 558, 602, 699, 792

arrangement *n.* 9, 79, **81,** 244, 602, 699, 792. 884

array *n.* 79, 655; *vb.* 81, 846

arrears *n.* 737

arrest *n.* 635; *vb.* 89, 144, 635, 681, 681, 755. 930

arrival *n.* 292, **298**

arrive *vb.* 153, 298

arrogant *adj.* 875, 880

arrow *n.* 290, 482

arsenal *n.* 657

art *n.* 486, 488

artful *adj.* 631

article *n.* 163, 327, 499

articles *n.* 192, 729

articulate *adj.* 512; *vb.* 512

artifice *n.* 478, 631

artificial *adj.* 510, 849. 852

artillery *n.* 655

artist *n.* **491,** 793

artistic *adj.* 510

artlessness *n.* 508, **632.** 951

asbestos *n.* 762

ascend *vb.* 316

ascent *n.* **316**

ascertained *adj.* 408

ascetism *n.* **946**

ascribe *vb.* 157

ashamed *adj.* 874

ashen *adj.* 806, 807

aside *n.* 460, 520; *adv.* 567

ask *vb.* 394, 695

askance *adj.* 219

askew *adj.* 219, 245

asleep *adj.* 267

as long as *adv., prep.* 111

aspect *n.* 5, 7, 55, 825

aspersion *n.* 928

asphalt *n.* 365

asphyxiate *vb.* 370

aspirate *vb.* 512

aspire *vb.* 552, 604, 854, 861

aspiring *adj.* 605

ass *n.* 437

assail *vb.* 645

assassin *n.* 370, 906

assassinate *vb.* 370

assault *n.* 175, 645, 952; *vb.* 645, 952

assemblage   n. 47, **94**

assemble   vb. 47, 58, 94, 242, 568

assembly   n. 59, 94, 625, 982, 987

assent   n. **424**, 692; vb. 24, 424, 692

assert   vb. 450, 468

assert oneself   vb. 649

assess   vb. 400, 415, 743

assessor   n. 415, 653

assets   n. 564, 566, 711, 734, 741

asseverate   vb. 468

assiduous   adj. 390, 392, 535

assign   vb. 685, 714, 717

assignable   adj. 157

assignment   n. 470, 557

assignment of cause   n. **157**

assimilate   vb. 302, 472

assist   vb. 636

assistance   n. 563, 636, 639

assistant   n. 640, 676, 689

assizes   n. 957

associate   n. 640; vb. 9, 47, 94, 157, 397

associated   adj. 60, 157, 639

association   n. 52, 60, 397, 641

assorted   adj. 45

assuage   vb. 176, 652, 834

assume   vb. 448, 720, 852

assumption   n. 420, 918

assurance   n. 408, 420, 854

assure   vb. 420, 468, 701, 857

asthmatic   adj. 359

astigmatism   n. 820

astonish   vb. 444, 866

astonishing   adj. 444, 579, 866

astrologer   n. 447, 984

astrology   n. 329, 447

astronaut   n. 274

astronomy   n. 329

astute   adj. 434

asylum   n. 595

asymmetry   n. 17, 219, **245**

atavism   n. 147

at hand   adj. 123, 188; adv. 199

atheism   n. 421, 975

atheist   n. 975

athlete   n. 270

athletic   adj. 161

at home   n. 884

atlas   n. 329

at last   adv. 89

atmosphere   n. 8, 229, 329, 348, 488

atoll   n. 357

atom   n. 33, 195, 327

atomic   adj. 195

atomic bomb   n. 657

atomize   vb. 53, 164, 340

atonal   adj. 791

at once   adv. 115

atonement   n. 31, 652, 911, **943**

atrocious   adj. 856, 936

atrocity   n. 900

attach   vb. 40, 47

attaché   n. 688

attached   adj. 47, 889

attachment   n. 41, 50, 60, 889, 890

attack   n. 326, 439, 586, **645**, 651; vb. 645, 648, 651, 928, 930

attacker   n. 645, 723

attain   vb. 472, 661

attainable   adj. 292, 404

attainments   n. 426, 472

attempt   n. **604**; vb. 552, 604, 615

attend   vb. 188, 287, 591, 676

attendant   n. 60, 287, 683; adj. 60, 188

attending   adj. 60, 676

attend to   vb. 593, 795

attention   n. **390**, 702

attentive   adj. 390, 922

attenuate   vb. 205, 333

attest   vb. 401, 408, 413, 468

attested   adj. 408, 430

at the same time   adv. 122

attire   n. 227

attitude   n. 7, 420, 621, 818

attorney   n. 959

attract   vb. 224, 291, 294, 390, 547, 889

attract attention   vb. 755

attraction   n. **294**, 330, 547

attractive   adj. 579, 829, 844, 889

attributable   adj. 157

attribute   n. 5; vb. 157

atypical   adj. 19

auburn   adj. 810, 811

auction   n. 727; vb. 727

audacious   adj. 857, 887

audacity   n. 857, 880

audible   adj. 452, 778

audience   n. 519, 795, 821

audition   n. 795

auditorium   n. 475, 795

augment   vb. 36, 196

augur   n. 447; vb. 447

augury   n. 447, 597

aunt   n. 11

aurora   n. 127, 800

auspicious   adj. 136, 447, 664, 854

austere   adj. 669, 946

austerity   n. 169, 669, 743, 946

authentic *adj.* 21, 430

authenticate *vb.* 408, 413, 424

author *n.* 155, 166, 521, 524

authoritarian *n.* 669; *adj.* 669

authoritative *adj.* 177, 408, 667, 671, 976

authority *n.* 177, 436, 629, **667**, 675, 685, 690, 956

authorize *vb.* 424, 667, 685, 690, 954

autocrat *n.* 669

autograph *n.* 482; *vb.* 482

automatic *adj.* 125, 411, 531, 544, 565

automaton *n.* 565

automobile *n.* 276

autonomous *adj.* 678

autumn *n.* **128**; *adj.* 128

auxiliary *n.* 35, **640**; *adj.* 35, 40, 563, 636, 679

avail *vb.* 570, 575, 720

available *adj.* 188, 404, 464, 575, 705, 727

avalanche *n.* 572, 760

avant-garde n. 125; *adj.* 125

avarice *n.* 750

avenge *vb.* 647, 912

avenger *n.* 912

avenue *n.* 559

aver *vb.* 468

average *n.* 30, 90, 871; *adj.* 30, 90, 101, 666, 871; *vb.* 30, 400

averse *adj.* 533, 637, 862, 892

aviary *n.* 234

aviation *n.* 273

avid *adj.* 750

avoid *vb.* 555, 600, 862, 924

avoidance *n.* 555, 600

avow *vb.* 462

avowal *n.* 420, 468

avuncular *adj.* 11

await *vb.* 443

awake *adj.* 392, 753

award *n.* 663, 715, 960, 965; *vb.* 715, 965

aware *adj.* 426, 753

awash *adj.* 349

away *adj.* 189; *adv.* 198

awe *n.* 856, 866, 922, 980

awful *adj.* 580, 830, 856

awfully *adv.* 32

awkward *adj.* 129, 511, 628, 633, 852

awl *n.* 264

awning *n.* 225, 801

awry *adj.* 219, 245

axe *n.* 964

axiom *n.* 432

axiomatic *adj.* 408

axis *n.* 217

azure *n.* 815; *adj.* 815

B

baa *vb.* 789

babble *vb.* 451, 516

babe *n.* 131, 429, 632

Babel *n.* 492

baby *n.* 131, 163; *adj.* 131

babyish *adj.* 131

baby-sit *vb.* 392

baby-sitter *n.* 683

bachelor *n.* 897

back *n.* 217, 237; *adj.* 237; *vb.* 217, 553, 667, 701, 718

back and forth *adv.* 325

back-bencher *n.* 625

backbiting *n.* 869, 928

backbone *n.* 217, 535, 857

back-breaking *adj.* 615

back down *vb.* 538

backer *n.* 217, 553, 640, 905

backfire *n.* 147; *vb.* 283

background *n.* 8, 198, 229, 237, 456

backhanded *adj.* 454

back-handed compliment *n.* 923

backing *n.* 217, 401, 636

backlash *n.* 147, 156, 283, 647

backlog *n.* 567

back of beyond *n.* 198, 885

back on to *vb.* 237

back out *vb.* 289, 293, 538, 556, 858

backrest *n.* 217

backside *n.* 237

backslide *vb.* 147, 590

backsliding *n.* 147, 538

backstage *n.* 237

back-to-front *adj.* 220

back up *vb.* 217, 636

backward *adj.* 289, 427, 435, 603, 876

backwardness *n.* 135

backwash *n.* 358

backwoods *n.* 885

bad *adj.* 53, 551, 580, 855, 932, 936

badge *n.* 482, 663

badge of office *n.* 677

bad luck *n.* 158, 665

bad-mannered *adj.* 887

badness *n.* **580**, 932

bad news *n.* 445

bad person *n.* **940**

bad taste *n.* 511, **849**

bad temper *n.* 893, 894, 895

baffle *vb.* 445, 633

bag *n.* 193, 275, 732

baggage *n.* 711

bail out *vb.* 273, 701

bait *n.* 294, 547

bake *vb.* 306, 350, 759

balance n. 28, 31, 44, 152, 244, 330, 400, 731; vb. 28, 31, 152, 330, 397, 742
balance sheet n. 742
bald adj. 228
balderdash n. 451
balk at vb. 533
ball n. 249, 884
ballad n. 528
ballast n. 31, 152, 330
ballerina n. 793
ballet n. 792
ballistics n. 657
balloon n. 249, 278
ballot n. 540
ballyhoo n. 451
balm n. 176, 342, 365, 591, 776
balustrade n. 234
bamboozle vb. 478
ban n. 99, 681, 691, 694; vb. 99, 691
banality n. 432, 843
band n. 49, 94, 207, 250, 641, 793; vb. 47
bandage n. 49, 207
bandit n. 885
bane n. 551, 580, **592**
bang n. 782; vb. 282, 782, 787
banish vb. 99, 303, 963
bank n. 352, 718, 732
banker n. 718, 733
bank on vb. 443, 854
bankrupt adj. 571, 706, 735, 739; vb. 739
banner n. 482
banquet n. 306, 829, 840; vb. 304
banter vb. 842, 853
baptism n. 302, 988
baptize vb. 302, 496, 988
bar n. (inn) 191; (restraint) 681; (tribunal) 957; vb. 99, 263, 635; prep. 42, 99

barb n. 255; vb. 255
barbarian n. 175
barbarism n. 495, 500, 511, 849
barbarous adj. 175, 900, 908
barbecue n. 306, 840
bard n. 528, 793
bare adj. 189, 228, 753; vb. 228
barely adv. 33
bargain n. 699, 746; vb. 699, 725, 726
bargain for vb. 443
bargaining n. 704, 725
barge n. 277
bark vb. 789
barman n. 676
baron n. 870
barrack n. 191
barrage n. 645
barrel n. 249
barren adj. 160, 169, 350, 612
barricade n. 635; vb. 635
barrier n. 234, 235, 635, 681
barrister n. 959
barrow n. 276, 372, 730
barter n. 150, 725; vb. 150, 725
base n. 89, **213**, 217; adj. 869, 924, 936
basement n. 213
bash vb. 282
bashful adj. 876
basic adj. 88, 155, 213, 573
basin n. 193, 213, 254, 354
basis n. 23, 155, 547
basket n. 193, 275
bastard n. 171, 955
baste vb. 306
bastion n. 646
batch n. 26, 94
bathe vb. 271, 349, 583

battle n. 649, 651
battleground n. 658
battlement n. 646
battleship n. 277
bawl vb. 788, 839
bay n. 353; adj. 810; vb. 789
bazaar n. 727, 730
be vb. 1, 185, 188, 368
beach n. 352
beacon n. 467, 482, 598, 800
beaker n. 193
be-all and end-all n. 573
beam n. 217, 797, 838; vb. 797, 838
beanfeast n. 306
bear vb. 217, 275, 368, 828
bearer n. 275, 467
bearing n. 9, 217, 284, 621, 825
bearings n. 185
bear in mind vb. 384
bear malice vb. 893
bear out vb. 413, 929
bear upon vb. 9
bear witness to vb. 401
beast n. 175, 373, 906
beastly adj. 900
beast of burden n. 275
beat n. 140, 325, 528; vb. 140, 282, 325, 340, 661, 783, 963
beat about the bush vb. 412, 505
beat off vb. 295, 646, 885
beat one's breast vb. 837
beat up vb. 645
beautiful adj. 844
beautify vb. 587, 844, 846
beauty n. 510, **844**
becalm vb. 267
beck n. 358

beckon *vb.* 482
becloud *vb.* 798, 799
become *vb.* 1, 142, 288
become of *vb.* 156
becoming *n.* 1; *adj.* 848
bed *n.* 206, 213, 360; *vb.* 378
bed and breakfast *n.* 191
bedaub *vb.* 584
bedeck *vb.* 846
Bedlam *n.* 80
bedlamite *n.* 440
bed of roses *n.* 661, 664, 827
bedouin *n.* 270
bedraggled *adj.* 584
bed-ridden *adj.* 586
be drunk *vb.* 950
be dry *vb.* 861
bedsitter *n.* 191
beefy *adj.* 161, 194
bee-line *n.* 248
Beelzebub *n.* 969
beer *n.* 309
be excited *vb.* 756
be excused *vb.* 310
befall *vb.* 153
before *adj.* 118; *adv.* 84, 286
beforehand *adj.* 117
be found *vb.* 1, 185
befriend *vb.* 636, 882
befuddled *adj.* 950
beg *vb.* 695
beget *vb.* 163, 368
begetter *n.* 170
beggar *n.* 697, 735, 940
beggarly *adj.* 881
begin *vb.* 88, 605
begin again *vb.* 88
beginner *n.* 474, 630
beginning *n.* 88, 155
begrudge *vb.* 914
beg the question *vb.* 412
beguile *vb.* 391, 478, 547

beguiler *n.* 480
behave oneself *vb.* 621, 886, 935
behead *vb.* 48, 370, 963
behest *n.* 671
behind *adj.* 135; *adv.* 85, 237
behind bars *adj.* 681
behindhand *adj.* 135
behind someone's back *adj.* 478
behind the scenes *adj.* 461
behind the times *adj.* 126
beholder *n.* 821
behove *vb.* 919
beige *n.* 810; *adj.* 810
being *n.* 1, 5, 327, 368; *adj.* 1
being according to external form *n.* 6
being according to internal form *n.* 5
being around *n.* 229
being between *n.* 230
being exterior *n.* 222
being horizontal *n.* 215
being interior *n.* 223
being oblique *n.* 219
being opposite *n.* 239
being vertical *n.* 214
belated *adj.* 135
belie *vb.* 469
belief *n.* 415, **420**, 974
believable *adj.* 420
believe *vb.* **420**, 448, 854
believer *n.* 146, 977, 980
believing *adj.* 420, 974, 977, 980
belittle *vb.* 924, 926, 928
bell *n.* 482, 598, 784; *vb.* 789
belle *n.* 844
belligerent *adj.* 651

bellow *vb.* 780, 788, 789
belong *vb.* 9, 58, 60, 202, 707
belonging *adj.* 9, 60
belongings *n.* 60, 568, 711
beloved *n.* 891; *adj.* 889
below *adv.* 209
below average *adj.* 580
below par *adj.* 35
below the belt *adj.* 916
belt *n.* 49, 207, 250, 964; *vb.* 963
bemoan *vb.* 833
bench *n.* 957
bencher *n.* 959
bend *n.* 219, 247; *vb.* 105, 219, 246, 285
bend over *vb.* 319
bend over backwards to help *vb.* 899
beneath *adv.* 209
beneath contempt *adj.* 924
beneath the surface *adj.* 459
benediction *n.* 909
benefactor *n.* **905**
beneficial *adj.* 550, 575, 585, 636, 661
beneficiary *n.* 716
beneficent *adj.* 747
benefit *n.* 550, 575, 636, 705, 829, 899; *vb.* 575, 577, 579, 661, 705, 899
benevolence *n.* 636, 747, **899**, 907
benevolent *adj.* 219, 247, 252
bequeath *vb.* 714
bequest *n.* 714, 715
bereave *vb.* 898
bereavement *n.* 369, 706, 828
bereft *adj.* 706
berry *n.* 306
berserk *adj.* 439
berth *n.* 191, 298

beryl *adj.* 812
beseech *vb.* 695, 982
beset *vb.* 633
besetting *adj.* 545
besetting sin *n.* 592, 936
beside onself *adj.* 756
besides *adv.* 40
besiege *vb.* 645
be situated *vb.* 1, 185
besmirched *adj.* 584
best *adj.* 34, 579
best friend *n.* 882
bestow *vb.* 715, 965
bestseller *n.* 524
best wishes *n.* 888
be subject to *vb.* 179, 679
bet *n.* 553; *vb.* 553
bête noire *n.* 892
be the duty of *vb.* 919
bethel *n.* 990
betoken *vb.* 447, 450, 482
betray *vb.* 458, 462, 478, 932
betrayer *n.* 480
betrothal *n.* 698
betrothed *adj.* 698
better *n.* 34, 553; *adj.* 34; *vb.* 587
better half *n.* 896
betterment *n.* 550, 587
between *prep.* 230
between ourselves *adv.* 466
between the lines *adj.* 459
be up to *vb.* 159
beverage *n.* 309
bewail *vb.* 833
bewilder *vb.* 409, 866
bewitch *vb.* 829, 984
bewitched *adj.* 984
be worth *vb.* 743
beyond compare *adj.* 34, 581
beyond hope *adj.* 855
bi- *adj.* 61

bias *n.* 178, 416, 545, 751, 916; *vb.* 416
biased *adj.* 416, 916
Bible *n.* 524, 976
biblical *adj.* 976
bibliography *n.* 83, 524
bicker *vb.* 642
bicycle *n.* 276
bid *n.* 693, 695; *vb.* 394, 671, 693
bidder *n.* 697
bide one's time *vb.* 443, 610, 612
bifurcate *vb.* 63, 297
big *adj.* 32, 161, 194, 509
bigheaded *adj.* 873
big-hearted *adj.* 747
big-mouthed *adj.* 879
big name *n.* 868
bigot *n.* 537
bigoted *adj.* 416
big-sounding *adj.* 509
big talk *n.* 879
bigwig *n.* 675, 868
bike *n.* 276; *vb.* 269
bilateral *adj.* 61
bilious *adj.* 812, 813
bill *n.* 464, 482, 742, 960
billet *n.* 191
billion *n.* 70
bill of fare *n.* 306
billow *vb.* 358
billy-goat *n.* 380
bin *n.* 193
binary *adj.* 39, 61
bind *vb.* 47, 378, 681, 698, 919
binding *adj.* 919
binoculars *n.* 822
biographer *n.* 484, 524
biology *n.* 366
bipartite *adj.* 61
birch *n.* 964
bird *n.* 373
bird's eye view *n.* 818
bird-watching *n.* 375
birth *n.* 88, 155, 870

birthday *n.* 140, 878
biscuit *n.* 306
bisection *n.* 63
bishop *n.* 870, 986
bit *n.* 33, 55, 59
bit by bit *adv.* 55
bitch *n.* 381
bite *n.* 306, 306, 769; *vb.* 304
bite someone's head off *vb.* 893
biting *adj.* 255, 760, 773
bitter *adj.* 769, 773, 893, 900
bitter-sweet *adj.* 772
bitumen *n.* 365
bizarre *adj.* 139, 433
blabber *vb.* 462
black *n.* 808; *adj.* 798, 808; *vb.* 99
blacken *vb.* 798, 808, 928
blackguard *n.* 940
black hole *n.* 329
blackish *adj.* 808
blacklist *vb.* 99
black magic *n.* 984
blackmail *n.* 902; *vb.* 902
black-market *adj.* 955
black out *vb.* 485, 798
blackout *n.* 463, 466, 779, 798
black sheep *n.* 940
black spot *n.* 596
blame *n.* 926, 930, 938; *vb.* 157, 926, 930, 962
blameless *adj.* 937
blameworthy *adj.* 926
blanch *vb.* 806, 807
bland *adj.* 768, 771
blank *n.* 2; *adj.* 2, 385, 451, 754
blank cheque *n.* 678, 690
blanket *n.* 225; *adj.* 54, 101, 399
blankness *n.* 442, 867

blare *vb.* 780
blasé *adj.* 757
blaspheme *vb.* 901, 981
blast *n.* 359, 780, 782; *vb.* 175, 359
blatant *adj.* 877
blather *n.* 451, 516; *vb.* 451
blaze *n.* 759, 797; *vb.* 797
blazon *vb.* 464
bleach *vb.* 806, 807
bleached *adj.* 350
bleak *adj.* 760, 798
bleat *vb.* 789
bleed *vb.* 301, 358, 745
blemish *n.* 582, 660, 845, **847**; *vb.* 847
blend *n.* 45, 495; *vb.* 52
bless *vb.* 899, 982, 988
blessed *adj.* 972
blessing *n.* 550, 715, 909
blessings *n.* 664
blight *n.* 53, 167, 592, 665
blind *n.* 225, 463, 801; *adj.* 754, 819; *vb.* 797
blinded *adj.* 819
blindfold *adj.* 819; *vb.* 819
blindness *n.* **819**
blind spot *n.* 819
blink *vb.* 797, 818
blinker *vb.* 801, 819
blinkers *n.* 801
bliss *n.* 827, 972
blithe *adj.* 827
blitz *n.* 645; *vb.* 164
blizzard *n.* 175, 359, 760
bloat *vb.* 196
bloated *adj.* 252
block *n.* 490, 681, 964; *vb.* 263, 265, 635
blockade *n.* 99, 681; *vb.* 234, 265, 645
blockage *n.* 263, 635

blockhead *n.* 429, 437, 630
blonde *adj.* 807
blood *n.* 11, 870
blood relationship *n.* 11
bloodshed *n.* 370, 649
bloom *n.* 374
bloomer *n.* 431
blossom *n.* 374; *vb.* 163, 168, 664
blot *n.* 584, 845, 847, 869; *vb.* 584, 847, 869
blotch *n.* 847
blot out *vb.* 164, 485, 911
blow *n.* 282, 444, 609, 828, 900, 963; *vb.* 359, 749
blowout *n.* 48, 306
blow up *vb.* 196, 359, 782, 893
blubber *n.* 306, 365; *vb.* 839
blue *n.* **815**; *adj.* 815, 837, 901, 952
blue blood *n.* 870
blue-eyed boy *n.* 891
blueprint *n.* 23, 558
blues *n.* 792, 837
bluff *vb.* 549
blunder *n.* 431, 500; *vb.* 431
blunt *adj.* 256, 476, 508; *vb.* 162, 256, 754
bluntness *n.* 256
blur *n.* 847; *vb.* 799
blurb *n.* 464
blurred *adj.* 243, 503, 799, 803, 824
blurt out *vb.* 462, 544
blush *n.* 811; *vb.* 811, 876
bluster *n.* 879
blustery *adj.* 359
board *n.* 217, 305, 625, 688
boarder *n.* 190

boast *n.* 879; *vb.* 873, 875, 879
boaster *n.* 873, 879
boastful *adj.* 481, 509, 875, 879
boasting *n.* **879**
boat *n.* 193, 277
bode *vb.* 447, 450
bode well *vb.* 854
bodiless *adj.* 4, 328
bodily *adj.* 327, 827, 945
body *n.* 3, 327, 368, 371
body-building *adj.* 585
bodyguard *n.* 593, 683
body odour *n.* 777
boffin *n.* 396, 448
bog *n.* 355
bogie *n.* 217
bogus *adj.* 477
boil *n.* 252; *vb.* 175, 306, 363, 759, 893
boil down *vb.* 203, 527
boiler *n.* 763
boil over *vb.* 756
boisterous *adj.* 175, 756, 780
bold *adj.* 458, 506, 534, 644, 854, 857
boldness *n.* 534, 857, 880
bolshie *adj.* 642
bolster *vb.* 217, 636
bolt *n.* 49, 613; *vb.* 47, 263, 304
bolt down *vb.* 948
bomb *n.* 657; *vb.* 280, 613, 645
bombard *vb.* 164, 645
bombast *n.* 509, 879
bombastic *adj.* 481, 877
bomber *n.* 278
bombshell *n.* 444
bonanza *n.* 75, 572
bond *n.* **49**, 681, 701
bondage *n.* 679
bone *n.* 337
bone to pick *n.* 893

bonus n. 41, 965
boo vb. 788, 853, 926
booby prize n. 663
booby-trap n. 596
book n. 464, **524**; vb. 83
bookishness n. 426
bookkeeping n. 742
booklet n. 464, 524
bookmaker n. 553
bookworm n. 428, 474, 524
boom n. 168, 217, 664, 780, 782, 784; vb. 780, 782, 784
boomerang n. 147, 283
boon n. 550
boorish adj. 887
boost vb. 36, 196, 318, 857
booster n. 173
booth n. 730
booty n. 663, **724**
booze vb. 950
boozer n. 950
border n. 232, 233, 235; vb. 199, 201, 233, 236
bore n. 204, 437; vb. 254, 264, 617, 841
boredom n. 841
borer n. 264
boring adj. 77, 841, 843
borough n. 183
borrow vb. 719
borrowed adj. 100, 495
borrower n. 737
borrowing n. 495, **719**
boss n. 34, 675
botany n. 366, 374, 376
botch vb. 628
both adj. 61
bother n. 326; vb. 578, 695, 830, 856, 893
bothered adj. 856
bothersome adj. 633, 830
bottle n. 193; vb. 234, 599

bottleneck n. 205, 635
bottle up vb. 681
bottom n. 89, 210, 213, 237; adj. 213, 237
bottomless adj. 210
bough n. 374
bounce n. 173, 283, 326, 336; vb. 283, 320, 326, 336, 879
bouncer n. 303
bound n. 320; vb. 231, 235
boundary n. 89, 231, 232, 233, 235
boundless adj. 78, 202
bounteous adj. 168, 747
bounty n. 168, 572, 715, 747, 965
bouquet n. 776, 888, 925
bourgeois adj. 871
bout n. 586
boutique n. 730
bow n. 247, 319, 922; vb. 247, 319, 654, 673, 922
bow down vb. 982
bowl n. 193, 250, 254
bowl over vb. 444
box n. 193, 225; vb. 282, 963
boy n. 131, 380
boycott n. 99, 691; vb. 99, 144, 555, 691
boy-friend n. 882, 889
brace n. 217; vb. 161, 217
bracing adj. 585, 618
brag vb. 879
braid n. 49
brain n. 382, 428
brain-child n. 163
brainwash vb. 470, 547
braise vb. 306
brake n. 281; vb. 281
bramble n. 255
branch n. 55, 97, 358, 374, 620, 979; vb. 297

brand n. 97, 800, 869; vb. 482
brand-new adj. 125
brash adj. 859, 887
brass n. 794, 880; adj. 816
brat n. 131
brave adj. 857; vb. 644, 857
brawler n. 672
brawn n. 161
brawny adj. 161
bray vb. 789
brazen it out vb. 880
breach n. 703; vb. 703
bread n. 306
breadth n. 26, **204**, 400
break n. 92, 200, 262, 614, 616; vb. 48, 92, 144, 164, 338, 703, 920
breakable adj. 338
break-away adj. 979
break down vb. 53, 588, 662, 839, 856
breakdown n. 48, 53, 586, 662
breaker n. 167, 358
breakfast n. 306
break in vb. 300
break in on vb. 137
breakneck adj. 859
break off vb. 89
break out vb. 88, 175, 600
break the law vb. 916, 955
breakthrough n. 661
break up vb. 53, 144, 588, 642
breakwater n. 217
break with vb. 556
breath n. 4, 359, 368, 512, 781
breathe vb. 359, 368
breather n. 92, 612, 614, 616
breathing space n. 144, 182

burdensome *adj.* 330, 633

bureau *n.* 620

bureaucracy *n.* 667

bureaucrat *n.* 623

bureaucratic *adj.* 622, 667

burglar *n.* 723

burglary *n.* 722

burial *n.* 372

buried *adj.* 210, 372, 461

burlesque *n.* 487, 842, 853

burly *adj.* 161

burn *n.* 828; *vb.* 759, 761, 797, 828, 893

burning *n.* 370, 761; *adj.* 752, 759, 811

burnish *vb.* 257, 341, 797

burr *vb.* 512

burrow *n.* 254

bursar *n.* 733

burst *n.* 48, 280, 613; *vb.* 48, 338, 782

burst forth *vb.* 88

burst into flames *vb.* 759

burst into tears *vb.* 839

burst out *vb.* 600

bury *vb.* 311, 372, 461, 472

bus *n.* 276

bush *n.* 374

business *p.* 557, 605, 725

businesslike *adj.* 79, 557

businessman *n.* 728

bust *n.* 489; *adj.* 739

bustle *n.* 611; *vb.* 611, 613

busy *adj.* 557, 611

busy-body *n.* 388

butcher *n.* 370; *vb.* 370

butler *n.* 676

butt *n.* 853; *vb.* 282

butter *n.* 306

buttercup *n.* 813

butterfingers *n.* 630; *adj.* 628

butterflies *n.* 326, 856

butter up *vb.* 927

buttress *n.* 217

buy *vb.* 547, 705, 726

buyer *n.* 710, 726, 737

buzz *n.* 783, 786; *vb.* 783, 784, 786, 789

by accident *adv.* 158

by chance *adv.* 158

bygone *adj.* 124

by-law *n.* 954

by-pass *n.* 322, 559, 561; *vb.* 322

by-product *n.* 87, 156

bystander *n.* 821

by the way *adv.* 10

C

cab *n.* 276

cabal *n.* 461, 558

cabaret *n.* 529

cabinet *n.* 625, 688

cable *n.* 49, 207, 460, 467; *vb.* 460

cackle *n.* 783, 838; *vb.* 783, 789

cacophony *n.* 787, 791

cad *n.* 849

cadge *vb.* 719

cadger *n.* 697

café *n.* 191

cage *n.* 234, 682

cajole *vb.* 478, 547, 927

cajoler *n.* 927

cake *n.* 306

calamity *n.* 153, 551, 665

calculate *vb.* 38, 400, 552

calculation *n.* 38, 400

calculator *n.* 38, 400

calculus *n.* 38

calendar *n.* 116

calibrate *vb.* 27, 400

calibre *n.* 204, 400

call *n.* 788, 789, 884; *vb.* 482, 496, 788

call away *vb.* 391

call by *vb.* 884

caller *n.* 884

call for *vb.* 562

call forth *vb.* 155, 547

call-girl *n.* 953

calligraphy *n.* 521

call in *vb.* 731

calling *n.* 557

call of duty *n.* 919

call on *vb.* 695

callous *adj.* 754, 900, 942

callow *adj.* 129

call up *vb.* 94, 441, 651

call upon *vb.* 394, 919

calm *n.* 267; *adj.* 176, 616, 681, 757; *vb.* 652, 779

calm down *vb.* 757

calque *n.* 495

calumny *n.* 869, 928

camber *n.* 247

cameo *n.* 489

camera *n.* 822

cameraman *n.* 491

camouflage *n.* 18, 461, 463; *vb.* 146, 461, 646

camp *n.* 191; *vb.* 186

campaign *n.* 605, 621, 651; *vb.* 649

campus *n.* 658

can *n.* 193; *vb.* 404, 599

canal *n.* 261, 360

cancel *vb.* 485, 686, 955

cancel out *vb.* 181, 402

cancer *n.* 167, 252, 592

candid *adj.* 476, 632, 931

candidate *n.* 395, 638, 697, 854

candle *n.* 800

catechism n. 420, 470
categorize vb. 97
category n. 97
catenary n. 247
cater vb. 568
catering n. 306, 568
cathedral n. 990
catholic adj. 101
cattle n. 373
cattleherd n. 377
catty adj. 900
cauldron n. 193
causal adj. 155
causation n. 155
cause n. 155, 547, 605;
   vb. 155, 547
caustic adj. 773, 900
caution n. 392, 597,
   624, 860; vb. 597
cautionary adj. 597
cautious adj. 681, 856,
   860
cavalry n. 655
cave n. 254, 317, 353
caveat n. 597
cave in vb. 254
cavity n. 319
caw vb. 787, 789
cease vb. 89, 144, 267,
   826
ceasefire n. 144
ceaseless adj. 145
ceiling n. 225, 235
celebrate vb. 838, 878,
   888, 988
celebrated adj. 868
celebration n. 838, 878
celebrity n. 868
celestial adj. 329, 966,
   968, 972
celestial body n. 329
celibacy n. 897
celibate n. 897; adj.
   169, 897, 951
cell n. 234, 366, 682
cement n. 49; vb. 47
cemetery n. 372
cenotaph n. 372, 483

censor vb. 466
censorious adj. 926
censorship n. 681, 779
censure n. 466, 926,
   930; vb. 926, 930
census n. 38
centenary n. 70, 109,
   878
central adj. 5, 90, 223,
   224
centrality n. 224
centralize vb. 224
centre n. 90, 96, 183,
   560; adj. 90, 224; vb.
   96, 224
centrifugal adj. 297
century n. 70
ceramics n. 489
ceramist n. 491
cereal n. 306, 374
ceremonial adj. 878,
   988
ceremony n. 878, 896,
   988
certain adj. 408, 413,
   420, 531, 534
certainly adv. 408, 531
certainty n. 408, 420,
   531, 534
certificate n. 483, 690
certified adj. 408
certify vb. 408, 690
cessation n. 89, 144,
   267
chafe vb. 341
chain n. 49, 85, 635,
   681; vb. 635, 681
chalet n. 191
chalky adj. 807
challenge n. 394, 644,
   649; vb. 394, 425, 644,
   649
challenger n. 638
chamber n. 210
champ vb. 304
champagne n. 309
champion n. 579, 646,
   661, 905; adj. 661

chance n. 158, 406, 553;
   adj. 139, 553; vb. 158,
   553
chance upon vb. 158
chancy adj. 409
change n. 142, 731; vb.
   15, 142
changeable adj. 15, 142,
   151, 536, 539
changeableness n. 151
change of mind n. 538
change over vb. 714
channel n. 261, 262,
   360, 564; vb. 261
chant n. 982; vb. 788,
   792
chaos n. 80, 243, 668,
   955
chap n. 380
chapel n. 990
chaperon vb. 392
chaplain n. 986
character n. 5, 58, 493,
   529, 751, 868, 931
characteristic n. 102;
   adj. 5, 102, 486
characterize vb. 525
charcoal n. 765
charge n. 557, 622, 626,
   645, 671, 685, 743, 930;
   vb. 159, 645, 671, 685,
   736, 743, 930
charismatic adj. 294
charitable adj. 715, 747,
   899, 965
charity n. 636, 715, 747,
   899, 907
charlatan n. 480, 852
charm n. 547, 829, 844,
   889, 984; vb. 547, 829,
   889, 984
charming adj. 547, 829,
   844, 889
chart n. 460, 486, 558
charter n. 690, 699; vb.
   690, 718, 719, 954
charwoman n. 676
chary adj. 750

chase *n.* 554; *vb.* 287,
490, 554, 882, 890
chaser *n.* 554
chasm *n.* 200, 254, 317
chassis *n.* 217
chaste *adj.* 876, 935,
951
chastened *adj.* 874
chastise *vb.* 963
chat *n.* 516, 519; *vb.*
514, 516, 519
chatter *n.* 516, 519; *vb.*
326, 388, 516, 760
chatterbox *n.* 388, 516
chatty *adj.* 460, 516
chauffeur *n.* 676
chauvinist *n.* 903; *adj.*
379
cheap *adj.* 746
cheapen *vb.* 746, 924
cheapness *n.* 746
cheat *n.* 480, 631, 940;
vb. 478, 631, 722, 916,
932
cheater *n.* 723
check *n.* 396, 635, 648,
681; *vb.* 37, 144, 394,
396, **408**, 413, 635, 681
checker *vb.* 817
checklist *n.* 83
cheeky *adj.* 880, 887
cheer *n.* 827; *vb.* 618,
788, 834, 836, 840, 925
cheerfulness *n.* 836, 854
cheerless *adj.* 837, 895
cheers *n.* 838, 878
cheese *n.* 306
cheesed off *adj.* 832
cheese-paring *n.* 750
cheque *n.* 731
chequer *vb.* 817
cherish *vb.* 441, 712,
889, 890
cherub *n.* 968
chest *n.* 193
chestnut *n.* 842; *adj.*
810
chew *vb.* 304

chicanery *n.* 631
chicken *adj.* 858
chicken out *vb.* 858
chide *vb.* 926
chief *n.* 34, 675; *adj.* 34,
573
child *n.* 11, 131, 171
childhood *n.* 129
childish *adj.* 129, 131,
435
childless *adj.* 169
childlike *adj.* 129, 131,
632
chill *n.* 760; *vb.* 762
chilly *adj.* 760, 883
chime *n.* 784; *vb.* 783,
784
chimney *n.* 361
chink *n.* 200, 797
chip *n.* 33, 55, 482; *vb.*
48, 377
chip in *vb.* 738
chip on one's shoulder
n. 832
chirp *vb.* 789
chirpy *adj.* 836
chirrup *vb.* 789
chisel *n.* 312, 480; *vb.*
163, 312, 478, 489, 490
chit *n.* 523
chit-chat *n.* 465, 516,
519
chivalry *n.* 857, 886
chocolate *adj.* 810
choice *n.* 398, 530, **540**;
adj. 579, 770
choiceless *adj.* 541
choir *n.* 793
choke *vb.* 265, 370, 572,
762
choleric *adj.* 894
choose *vb.* 398, 530,
532, **540**, 861
choosy *adj.* 398, 540,
864
chop *vb.* 48, 319
chop and change *vb.*
151

choppy *adj.* 258
choral *adj.* 792
chord *n.* 247
chorister *n.* 793
chortle *vb.* 838
chorus *n.* 528, 792, 793,
982
christen *vb.* 496
Christendom *n.* 977,
985
Christian *n.* 977, 982
Christianity *n.* 974
chromatic *adj.* 805
chronicle *n.* 116, 483;
vb. 483
chronicler *n.* 484
chronological *adj.* 116
chronometer *n.* 116
chronometry *n.* 116
chuck *vb.* 290, 556
chuckle *n.* 783, 838; *vb.*
783, 789, 838
chum *n.* 882
chunky *adj.* 203, 204
church *n.* 977, 982, 985,
987, 990
church building *n.* **990**
churchdom *n.* 985
church-goer *n.* 982
church member *n.* 977,
987
churchyard *n.* 372
churlish *adj.* 895
cigar *n.* 308
cigarette *n.* 308
cinema *n.* 529, 840
cipher *n.* 39, 466
circle *n.* 94, 247, 250,
323; *vb.* 229, 322, 323
circuit *n.* 140, 232, 250,
269, 322, 323, **561**
circular *n.* 464, 523;
adj. 250
circulate *vb.* 322, 323,
460
circulation *n.* 322
circumambulate *vb.*
231, 322

circumference *n.* 232, 250

circumlocution *n.* 505

circumscription *n.* **231**

circumspect *adj.* 392, 434, 860

circumstance *n.* **8**, 153

circumstances *n.* 8, 229

circumstantial *adj.* 8

circumvent *vb.* 231, 555

circus *n.* 250, 559, 658

cistern *n.* 193

citadel *n.* 646

citation *n.* 663, 925

citizen *n.* 190, 871

city *n.* 183

city-dweller *n.* 190

civic *adj.* 379

civil *adj.* 379, 886, 987

civilian *n.* 871

civility *n.* 886

civilization *n.* 379

civilized *adj.* 379

clad *adj.* 227

claim *n.* 671, 737; *vb.* 549, 671, 917

claimant *n.* 697

clairvoyant *n.* 447, 984

clamber *vb.* 316

clammer *n.* 175

clamorous *adj.* 695, 780, 788

clamour *n.* 780, 788; *vb.* 695, 788

clamp *vb.* 47

clamp down on *vb.* 669

clan *n.* 11

clandestine *adj.* 461

clang *n.* 783; *vb.* 783, 784, 787

clanger *n.* 431

clanging *n.* 784; *adj.* 784, 787

clap *vb.* 282, 838, 878, 925

clarify *vb.* 456

clarity *n.* 452, 502, 823

clash *n.* 175, 282; *vb.*

14, 282, 642, 787, 791, 805, 883

clasp *n.* 49, 712; *vb.* 50, 712, 720, 758, 890

class *n.* 7, 55, **97**, 122, 206, 470, 472, 474; *vb.* 97

classified *adj.* 81, 466

classify *vb.* 81, 83, 97, 496

classroom *n.* 475

clatter *vb.* 783, 787

clause *n.* 498

clean *adj.* 46, **583**, 937, 951; *vb.* 341, **583**, 775, 807

cleaner *n.* 676

cleanliness *n.* 583, 585, 951

cleanness *n.* 583, 951

cleanse *vb.* 583

cleanser *n.* 775

clear *adj.* 46, 413, 452, 458, 502, 512, 678, 797, 802, 823, 921; *vb.* 320, 583, 921, 961

clearance *n.* 182, 200, 690, 727

clear-cut *adj.* 452, 823

clear-headed *adj.* 949

clearmindedness *n.* 438

cleavage *n.* 48

cleave *vb.* 48, 50

cleft *n.* 200, 259

clemency *n.* 670, 907

clergyman *n.* **986**

cleric *n.* 986; *adj.* 985

clerical *adj.* 986

clerical dress *n.* 989

clerk *n.* 484

clever *adj.* 426, **434**, 627, 631

cliché *n.* 495, 498

click *vb.* 24, 452, 782

client *n.* 545, 716, 726

cliff *n.* 214

climate *n.* 8, 229, 348

climax *n.* 89, 212

climb *vb.* 273, 316

climb down *vb.* 538

clinch *n.* 712; *vb.* 47, 50, 408, 712

clincher *n.* 414

cling *vb.* 50, 712

clip *vb.* 203

clipper *n.* 277

clippings *n.* 44

clique *n.* 94, 641

cloak *n.* 461, 463, 549; *vb.* 461

clock *n.* 116

clog *vb.* 265

cloister *n.* 885

clonk *n.* 785; *vb.* 785

close *n.* 89, 184, 559; *adj.* 47, 50, 154, 199, 419, 759, 882; *vb.* 144, 263, 461

closed book *n.* 427, 453

closed shop *n.* 99, 681

close-fisted *adj.* 750

close friend *n.* 882

close in on *vb.* 292

close-lipped *adj.* 517

close shave *n.* 600

closure *n.* 89, 144, 263

clot *vb.* 332

cloth *n.* 989

clothe *vb.* 227

clothes *n.* 227

cloud *n.* 363, 803; *vb.* 461, 799, 803

cloudburst *n.* 175, 358

cloudless *adj.* 664, 797

cloudy *adj.* 358, 363, 503, 799, 803, 824

clout *n.* 963; *vb.* 282, 963

clown *n.* 842

clowning *n.* 433

cloy *vb.* 56, 865

club *n.* 96, 191; *vb.* 282, 639

cluck *vb.* 787, 789

clue *n.* 401, 447, 482

clumsy *adj.* 511, 628

cluster *n.* 94
clutch *vb.* 712, 758
clutter *n.* 80
coach *n.* 276, 473; *vb.* 470
coagulate *vb.* 332, 334
coagulated *adj.* 362
coal *n.* 367, 765, 800
coalesce *vb.* 13, 52
coalition *n.* 641
coarse *adj.* 258, 511, 849, 887, 952
coastline *n.* 352
coat *n.* 206, 225; *vb.* 225, 342, 805
coating *n.* 206, 225
coat of arms *n.* 482
coax *vb.* 547, 695
cock *n.* 380
cocktail *n.* 309
cock-up *n.* 628
cocky *adj.* 875
coddle *vb.* 306
code *n.* 103, 466, 954
codification *n.* 954
coerce *vb.* 175, 674
coexist *vb.* 60, 122
coextensive *adj.* 28, 218
coffee *n.* 309; *adj.* 810
coffee-bar *n.* 191
coffee-break *n.* 616
coffer *n.* 193, 732
coffin *n.* 372
cog *vb.* 259
cogitation *n.* 384, 410
cognition *n.* 426
cognitive *adj.* 382
cognizability *n.* 452
cognizant *adj.* 426
cohabit *vb.* 889
cohabitant *n.* 889
cohere *vb.* 50
coherence *n.* 50, 337
cohesive *adj.* 50
coil *n.* 251; *vb.* 249
coin *vb.* 449, 731
coinage *n.* 495

coincide *vb.* 13, 24, 28, 60, 122
coincidence *n.* 24, 60, 105, 122, 553
coincidental *adj.* 60, 158
coke *n.* 765
cold *n.* 760; *adj.* 754, 760, 806, 863
cold-blooded *adj.* 754, 908
cold feet *n.* 856, 858
cold shoulder *n.* 924; *vb.* 885
cold war *n.* 650
coliseum *n.* 658
collaborate *vb.* 180, 639
collaborator *n.* 640
collage *n.* 488
collapse *n.* 164, 588, 617, 662; *vb.* 254, 588, 617
collate *vb.* 397
collateral *n.* 701; *adj.* 11
colleague *n.* 640
collect *vb.* 94, 567, 705, 716
collective *n.* 709; *adj.* 24
collectively *adv.* 60
college *n.* 475
collide *vb.* 282
collision course *n.* 296
colloid *n.* 362; *adj.* 362
colloquial *adj.* 495
colloquialism *n.* 494, 495
colonist *n.* 190
colonize *vb.* 191
colony *n.* 94
coloration *n.* 805
colossal *adj.* 32
colour *n.* 509, 805, 811; *vb.* 403, 509, 805
colour-blind *adj.* 819, 820
colourful *adj.* 805

colourlessness *n.* 806, 843
colours *n.* 482
column *n.* 91, 208, 217
coma *n.* 754
combat *n.* 651; *vb.* 637, 649
combatant *n.* **655**
combination *n.* 45, **52**
combine *vb.* 45, 47, **52**, 639
combustible *n.* 765; *adj.* 761, 765
combustion *n.* 761
come *vb.* 298
come about *vb.* 153, 430
come across *vb.* 186, 419
come after *vb.* 85, 119, 287
comeback *n.* 147, 395, 589
come back to *vb.* 395
come before *vb.* 84, 118
come by *vb.* 716
come clean *vb.* 462
comedian *n.* 842
come down *vb.* 273, 317
come-down *n.* 874
come down on *vb.* 669, 963
comedy *n.* 529
come first *vb.* 286
come forward *vb.* 292, 693
come home *vb.* 298, 755
come in *vb.* 300, 716
come into *vb.* 705
come into conflict with *vb.* 25
come into sight *vb.* 292, 823
come into view *vb.* 823, 825
comely *adj.* 844

come near vb. 292
come next vb. 85
come of vb. 156
come of age vb. 133
come off vb. 153, 661
come on vb. 587
come out vb. 88, 144,
  301, 464
come out with vb. 462
come round again vb.
  140
come round to vb. 420
come short vb. 315,
  445, 571
comestible adj. 306
comet n. 329
come to vb. 743
come to a head vb. 659
come to an agreement
  vb. 699, 704
come to an end vb. 89
come to blows vb. 642
come together vb. 94,
  296
come to life vb. 368
come to light vb. 825
come to mind vb. 384,
  441
come to nothing vb. 2,
  315, 369, 576, 662
come to the point vb.
  504
come up vb. 153
come up against vb. 25
come up to vb. 28, 570
comfort n. 636, 834; vb.
  636, 834, 836, 899, 907
comfortable adj. 634,
  664, 827, 834
comforting adj. 834,
  907
comic adj. 851
coming n. 292, 298; adj.
  123, 154
coming out n. 88
command n. 501, 622,
  626, 667, 671; vb. 208,
  622, 667, 671

commandeer vb. 720
commander n. 623, 675
commanding adj. 667,
  671
commandment n. 626
commemorate vb. 441,
  878
commemorative adj.
  441, 878
commence vb. 88, 605
commend vb. 925
commendable adj. 579,
  925
commensurate adj. 28
comment n. 456, 526;
  vb. 456, 526
commentary n. 456,
  526
commentator n. 456,
  526, 974
commerce n. 150, 725
commercial adj. 725
commercial traveller n.
  727
commiserate vb. 907
commission n. 94, 557,
  609, 685; vb. 557, 685
commissioner n. 688,
  689
commissioner for oaths
  n. 959
commit vb. 609, 685,
  698, 714
commit adultery vb.
  952
commitment n. 605,
  698, 737, 919, 980
commit oneself vb. 534,
  540, 605, 919
commit suicide vb. 370
committed adj. 534,
  698, 737, 980
committee n. 94, 625,
  688
commodities n. 729
commodity n. 327
common n. 356; adj.

35, 138, 508, 666, 709,
  843, 867
commoner n. 871
commonly adv. 138
common people n. 871
commonplace n. 432;
  adj. 138, 666, 843
common sense n. 434
commotion n. 326, 611
communal adj. 379, 709
communicant n. 982
communicate vb. 460,
  464, 514, 519, 523
communication n. 460,
  464, 492, 514, 523
communicative adj.
  460
communion n. 979
communiqué n. 465
communism n. 709
community n. 183, 379,
  641, 709
commutable adj. 150
commutation n. 149
commute vb. 142, 149,
  150
commuter n. 190, 270
compact adj. 50, 203,
  204, 332, 334, 504; vb.
  332
companion n. 640, 882
company n. 94, 620,
  641
comparable adj. 28
comparative adj. 27,
  455
compare vb. 27, 218,
  397
comparison n. 18, 27,
  397, 455, 499
compartment n. 55
compass n. 182, 322
compassion n. 670, 907
compassionate adj.
  670, 899, 907
compatible adj. 24, 105,
  882
compatriot n. 11

compel *vb.* 177, 531, 562, 674, 755

compelling *adj.* 674, 755

compendious *adj.* 54, 527

compendium *n.* 527

compensation *n.* 31, 721, 738, 917, 965

compensatory *adj.* 31, 721, 943, 965

compete *vb.* 649

competence *n.* 159, 627, 956

competent *adj.* 159, 579, 627, 956

competition *n.* 649

competitive *adj.* 649

competitor *n.* 638, 854

compile *vb.* 58

complacency *n.* 831

complain *vb.* 642, 788, 832, **926**, 930

complainer *n.* 832

complaint *n.* 586, 696, 926, 930

complement *n.* 28, 60

complete *adj.* 54, **56**, 581, 659; *vb.* 581, 609, **659**, 661

completely *adv.* 54, 56

completeness *n.* 54, **56**

completion *n.* 89, 581, **659**, 661

complex circularity *n.* 251

complexion *n.* 805

complexity *n.* 503

compliance *n.* 532, 673, 692, 702

compliant *adj.* 532, 654, 919

complicate *vb.* 835

complicated *adj.* 453, 503, 633

compliment *n.* 886, 888, 925, 927; *vb.* 886, 888, 925

comply *vb.* 105, 570, 654, 673, 70ᴢ

component *n.* 55, 192, 327

compose *vb.* 58, 81, 163, 521, 528, 792

composed *adj.* 757

composer *n.* 166, 491, 528, 793

composite *adj.* 45

composition *n.* 45, **58**, 81, 339, 488, 521, 522, 526, 528, 792

compositor *n.* 522

composure *n.* 757

compound *n.* 45, 184; *vb.* 36, 52

comprehend *vb.* 58, 98, 452

comprehensible *adj.* 452

comprehension *n.* 410, 452

comprehensive *adj.* 54, 56, 98, 101

compress *vb.* 37, **197**, 205, 332, 504

compressed *adj.* 332, 504

compressor *n.* 197

comprise *vb.* 58, 98

compromise *n.* 30, 699, **704**; *vb.* 704

compulsion *n.* 439, 531, 562, 674

compulsive *adj.* 674

compulsory *adj.* 531, 674, 919

compunction *n.* 833

compunctious *adj.* 941

compute *vb.* 38, 400

computer *n.* 38, 400, 565

comrade *n.* 640, 882

con *n.* 631, 684; *vb.* 631

concatenation *n.* 47, 85

concavity *n.* 254

conceal *vb.* 225, **461**, 466

concealment *n.* **461**, 824

concede *vb.* 424, 462, 690, 692

conceited *adj.* 873, 875

conceivable *adj.* 404

conceive *vb.* 88, 163, 368, 382, 449

concentrate *vb.* 96, 296, 334, **384**, **390**

concentration *n.* 296, 332, **384**, **390**, 611

concept *n.* 386

conception *n.* 382, 386, 420

concern *n.* 387, 392, 557, 605, 620; *vb.* 9, 526, 609, 856

concerned *adj.* 388, 392

concerning *adv., prep.* 9

concert *n.* 180, 643, 790, 792, 840

concerto *n.* 792

concession *n.* 690, 704, 744

conciliation *n.* 650, 652

concise *adj.* 203, 432, **504**, 527

conciseness *n.* 504

conclude *vb.* 56, 89, 410, 530

conclusion *n.* 89, 144, 235, 410, 659

conclusive *adj.* 408, 413, 430, 659

concoct *vb.* 163, 477, 558, 930

concomitant *n.* 60; *adj.* 60

concord *n.* 24, **643**, 790

concordance *n.* 494, 524

concordat *n.* 699

concrete *adj.* 3, 327, 332

concur *vb.* 24, **180**, 424, 692

concurrence *n.* 24, **180**, 296, 692

concurrent *adj.* 24, 60, 122, 180, 296

condemn *vb.* 892, 926, **962**

condemnation *n.* 962

condemned *adj.* 938

condemned cell *n.* 964

condensation *n.* 346

condense *vb.* 203, 332, 345, 504, 527

condescend *vb.* 869, 874, 886

condiment *n.* 307

condition *n.* 7, 562, 825; *vb.* 470, 545

conditional *adj.* 403, 700

conditioning *n.* 470, 545

conditions *n.* 8, **700**

condolence *n.* 907

conduce *vb.* 155

conducive *adj.* 178, 563

conduct *n.* 172, 606, **621**, 622; *vb.* 268, 606, 609, **621**, 622

conduit *n.* 360

confectionery *n.* 306

confederate *n.* 640; *adj.* 641; *vb.* 47

confederation *n.* 641

confer *vb.* 159, 519, 715, 965

conference *n.* 94, 519, 625

confess *vb.* 420, 462, 941, 982

confession *n.* 420, 941, 974, 982

confidant *n.* 624, 882

confide *vb.* 462, 624

confidence *n.* 408, 420, 443, 466, 854

confident *adj.* 420, 443, 854, 857

confidential *adj.* 466

confine *vb.* 205, 234, 681, 712

confirm *vb.* 401, 408, 413, **468**, 699, 929

confiscate *vb.* 720

conflict *n.* 649; *vb.* 637, 642, 805, 883

confluence *n.* 221, 296

conform *vb.* 16, 24, **105**, 702

conformist *n.* 20, 105

conformity *n.* 16, **105**, 244, 643

confound *vb.* 82, 399, 414, 869

confront *vb.* 239, 637, 644, 649

confrontation *n.* 637, 649

confuse *vb.* 82, 187, 399

confused *adj.* 80, 399, 439

confusedly *adv.* 80

confusion *n.* 80, 326

confuted *adj.* 414

congeal *vb.* 332, 334, 762

congelation *n.* 760

congenial *adj.* 827

congenital *adj.* 5

congestion *n.* 332, 572

conglomerate *n.* 332

conglomeration *n.* 45

congratulate *vb.* 838, 878, **888**

congratulate oneself *vb.* 879

congratulation *n.* 838, **888**

congregate *vb.* 50, 94

congregation *n.* 94, 982, 987

congress *n.* 94, 519, 625, 641

congressman *n.* 625

congruity *n.* 16, 24, 105

conjecture *n.* 386, 396, 447, **448**; *vb.* 448

conjugal *adj.* 896

conjugate *vb.* 499

conjunction *n.* 499

conjunctivitis *n.* 820

conjure *vb.* 449, 984

conjurer *n.* 984

con man *n.* 480, 631, 906

connect *vb.* 47, 81

connected *adj.* 9, 47, 52, 60, 81

connection *n.* 9, 47, 49, 201

connoisseur *n.* 304, 436, 848

connotation *n.* 450, 459

conquer *vb.* 316, 661, 679

conqueror *n.* 661

conscience *n.* 382, 919

conscience-stricken *adj.* 833, 941

conscientiousness *n.* 392, 864, 931

conscious *adj.* 382, 426, 753

conscript *n.* 655; *vb.* 651

conscription *n.* 674

consecrate *vb.* 980, 985

consecration *n.* 715, 980

consecutive *adj.* 85, 91

consensus *n.* 24, 424, 643

consent *n.* 424, 690, **692**, 698; *vb.* 690, 692, 698

consequence *n.* 60, 85, 87, 156, 573

consequent *adj.* 85, 156

consequential *adj.* 119, 156, 573

conservation *n.* 374, 392, 599

conservatism *n.* 143

conservative *n.* 105, 143; *adj.* 143, 977

conserve *n.* 306; *vb.* 599, 748

consider *vb.* 384, 390, 415, 420, 526, 982

considerable *adj.* 32, 75, 573

considerate *adj.* 390, 392, 434, 886

consideration *n.* 384, 390, 392, 415, 886

consign *vb.* 268, 714

consignee *n.* **688**

consignment *n.* 268

consist *vb.* 1, 58, 98

consistency *n.* 50, 105, 143

consistent *adj.* 16, 24, 105

consolation *n.* 176, 834, 907

consolation prize *n.* 663

console *vb.* 176, 834, 907

consolidate *vb.* 52, 334

consolidation *n.* 332

consonance *n.* 24, 643, 790

consonant *n.* 493, 512; *adj.* 24, 105

conspicuous *adj.* 253, 458, 462, **823**, 877

conspiracy *n.* 558

conspire *vb.* 558

conspirer *n.* 558

constable *n.* 956

constancy *n.* 16, 91, 114, 140, 143, 152, 535

constant *n.* 152; *adj.* 91, 140, 143, 145, 152, 535

constellation *n.* 329

consternation *n.* 856

constituency *n.* 183, 540

constituent *n.* 55, 192; *adj.* 55, 73

constitute *vb.* 58, 98

constitution *n.* 5, 58, 339, 954

constitutional *n.* 269; *adj.* 954

constrain *vb.* 531, 674

constraint *n.* 674, 681

constrict *vb.* 197

construct *vb.* 58, 163, 242, 477, 930

construction *n.* 163, 242, 494

constructor *n.* 166

consul *n.* 688

consult *vb.* 624

consultant *n.* 624

consultation *n.* 519

consultative *adj.* 624

consume *vb.* 304, 569, 575, 740, 761

consumer *n.* 304, 726

consummate *adj.* 89, 581; *vb.* 56, 581, 659, 896

consummation *n.* 89, 156, 212, 581, 896

consumption *n.* 569

contact *n.* 47, **201**, 758; *vb.* 201

contagious *adj.* 586

contain *vb.* 98, 234, 707, 712

container *n.* **193**, 275

contaminate *vb.* 584, 588, 952

contemplate *vb.* 384, 415, 552

contemplative *adj.* 384, 434

contemporaneous *adj.* 120, 122

contemporary *n.* 122; *adj.* 60, 120, 122, 125

contempt *n.* 853, 869, **924**

contemptible *adj.* 580, 869, 924

contemptuous *adj.* 853, 924

contend *vb.* 414, 615, **649**, 651

contender *n.* 655

content *n.* 450, **831**; *adj.* 831

contented *adj.* 827, 831

contentious *adj.* 409, 651

contents *n.* **192**, 223

contest *n.* **649**; *vb.* 604, 649

contestant *n.* 638; *adj.* 649

context *n.* 8

contiguity *n.* 199, 201

continent *n.* 352; *adj.* 944, 951

contingencies *n.* 700

contingent *adj.* 8, 403, 679, 700

contingent duration *n.* **111**

continual *adj.* 114, 138, 143, **145**

continuance *n.* 91, 107, **145**, 535

continue *vb.* 91, 107, 112, 138, 145, 535

continuity *n.* 50, **91**, 143

continuous *adj.* 91, 257

contort *vb.* 245, 251

contour *n.* 232, 242

contraband *n.* 724; *adj.* 955

contraception *n.* 169

contract *n.* 24, 468, 698, **699**, 919; *vb.* 197, 203, 205 557, 698, 699

contraction *n.* 197, 205, 504

contractual *adj.* 699

contradict *vb.* 14, 25,

12, 18, 24, 105, 397, 521, 523
correspondent *n.* 395, 460, 523
corroborate *vb.* 217, 401, 408
corroborative *adj.* 401
corrode *vb.* 588
corrosion *n.* 53
corrugate *vb.* 260, 261
corrupt *adj.* 431, 477, 869, 932, 936; *vb.* 547, 580, 584, 588, 936
corruption *n.* 495, 551, 588, 932, 936
cosmetic *adj.* 211, 846
cosmetics *n.* 844
cosmic *adj.* 329
cosmology *n.* 329
cosmonaut *n.* 274
cosmopolitan *n.* 903; *adj.* 101
cosmos *n.* 329
cost *n.* 743; *vb.* 743
costly *adj.* 745
costs *n.* 31, 740, 963
costume *n.* 227
cosy *adj.* 827
cottage *n.* 191
cough *n.* 359; *vb.* 359
cough up *vb.* 738
council *n.* 94, 519, 625, 641
councillor *n.* 625
counsel *n.* 597, 624, 959; *vb.* 470, 519, 597, 624
counsellor *n.* 473, 624
count *n.* 38, 870; *vb.* 38, 400
countable *adj.* 38
count against *vb.* 588
countdown *n.* 274
countenance *n.* 236, 825
counter *n.* 482; *adj.* 181; *vb.* 637, 647

counteract *vb.* 31, 181, 648, 686
counteraction *n.* **181**
counterattack *n.* 647
counterbalance *n.* 31, 152; *vb.* 31, 181, 330
counter-evidence *n.* **402**
counterfeit *n.* 20, 487; *adj.* 20, 431, 477; *vb.* 20, 477
counterfoil *n.* 482
countermand *n.* 686, 691; *vb.* 686
countermeasure *n.* 181
counterpart *n.* 18, 20, 22, 28
counterpoise *vb.* 330
counter-productive *adj.* 576
counterweight *n.* 152, 181, 330
countless *adj.* 75, 78
count on *vb.* 443
country *n.* 183
countryman *n.* 871
county *n.* 183
coup *n.* 148
coup de grâce n. 659
coupé *n.* 276
couple *n.* 61; *vb.* 47, 61
couplet *n.* 61
coupling *n.* 47, 49
courage *n.* **857**
courier *n.* 460, 467
course *n.* 269, 306, 358, 360, 470, 559
course of action *n.* 558
course of time *n.* **110**
court *n.* 234, 559, 658, 870, 957; *vb.* 882, 890
court danger *vb.* 859
courteous *adj.* 392, 886, 922
courtesy *n.* **886**, 899
courtship *n.* **890**
cousin *n.* 11
cove *n.* 353

covenant *n.* 698, 699, 701; *vb.* 698, 699
cover *n.* 193, 225, 306, 463, 595; *vb.* 206, 225, 461, 646, 798, 801
cover for *vb.* 149
covering *n.* 211, 222, 225, 461, 801
covert *n.* 254, 374, 463, 595
covet *vb.* 861, 914
covetous *adj.* 750, 861, 914
covetousness *n.* 750, 861, 914
cow *n.* 381
coward *n.* 162, 858
cowardice *n.* **858**
cowardly *adj.* 858
co-worker *n.* 640
coy *adj.* 876
crack *n.* 200; *vb.* 264, 456, 782
crack down on *vb.* 669, 963
cracker *n.* 306
crackle *n.* 782
crack up *vb.* 439, 856, 925
cradle *n.* 325
craft *n.* 277, 557, 631
craftsman *n.* 619
crafty *adj.* 478, 631, 932
cram *vb.* 56, 470, 472
crank *n.* 106, 440
cranky *adj.* 439
crash *n.* 282, 739, 782; *vb.* 282, 739, 780, 782, 787
crash-land *vb.* 273, 317, 321
crass *adj.* 849
crate *n.* 193
crater *n.* 254
crave *vb.* 695, 861, 914
craven *adj.* 858
craving *n.* 861
crawl *vb.* 281, 881

crawl with   vb. 75

crayon   vb. 488

craze   n. 125, 439, 539, 850, 861

crazy   adj. 433, 435, 439, 861, 889

creak   vb. 781, 787

cream   n. 306, 342, 365, 579, 813; adj. 807, 813; vb. 342

creamy   adj. 362, 365

crease   n. 260; vb. 260

create   vb. 155, 163, 242, 449, 558

creation   n. 21, 163, 329, 366

creative   adj. 21, 163, 449

creator   n. 155, 166, 491, 966

creature   n. 366, 368, 373, 379

crèche   n. 475

credence   n. 420

credible   adj. 404, 406, 420

credit   n. 420, 718, 731, 736, 868, 909, 925; vb. 736, 742

creditable   adj. 925

credit card   n. 718, 731, 736

creditor   n. 718, 736

credulous   adj. 422

creed   n. 420, 974

creek   n. 354, 358

creep   vb. 316, 461

cremate   vb. 372, 761

cremation   n. 372

crematorium   n. 372, 763

crescent   n. 247, 559; adj. 36, 247

crest   n. 212, 358, 482, 872

crestfallen   adj. 837, 874

cretin   n. 437, 440

crevasse   n. 254

crew   n. 94, 272

crib   n. 22; vb. 20

crier   n. 467

crime   n. 938, 955

criminal   n. 684, 906, 940; adj. 932

criminality   n. 932, 938

crimp   n. 260; vb. 251, 260

crimson   adj. 811

cringe   vb. 856

cringing   adj. 881

cripple   vb. 245, 588

crisis   n. 80, 136, 665

crisp   adj. 760; vb. 306

crispy   adj. 338

criterion   n. 23, 27, 103, 400

critic   n. 456, 524, 526, 848, 928

critical   adj. 136, 382, 398, 415, 573, 594, 926

criticism   n. 456, 624, 926

criticize   vb. 696, 832, 893, 926, 962

critique   n. 398, 456, 526

croak   vb. 787, 789

crocodile   n. 91

crocus   n. 813

croft   n. 378

crook   n. 247, 480, 723, 906, 940, 989; vb. 247

crooked   adj. 29, 219, 245

crop   n. 374, 567, 705; vb. 203

crop up   vb. 153, 825

cross   n. 221, 592, 830, 964; adj. 893, 895; vb. 45, 221, 313, 478

cross-examination   n. 394, 960

cross-eyed   adj. 820

crossing   n. 221, 313

cross purposes   n. 642

crotchety   adj. 539

crouch   vb. 209, 319

crow   vb. 789

crowd   n. 75, 94, 821, 871; vb. 75, 94

crown   n. 212, 250, 659, 663, 677; vb. 212, 685, 868, 878

crucial   adj. 136, 573

crucifix   n. 221

crucifixion   n. 370, 828, 963

crucify   vb. 830, 963

crude   adj. 511, 887

cruel   adj. 669, 900, 908

cruise   n. 271; vb. 269, 271

crumb   n. 33, 340

crumble   vb. 162, 164, 338, 340, 588

crumple   vb. 258

crunch   vb. 340

crush   n. 94, 889; vb. 164, 340, 364, 414, 661, 874

crushed   adj. 837, 874

crushing   n. 874

crustacean   n. 373

crutch   n. 217

crux   n. 221

cry   n. 597, 782, 788, 789, 839; vb. 788, 789, 833, 839

cry-baby   n. 162, 858

cry out for   vb. 531, 562

cry over   vb. 833

cryptic   adj. 466

crystal   adj. 802

crystal-clear   adj. 458

crystallize   vb. 332, 334

cry wolf   vb. 478, 598

cube   n. 246

cuckoo   vb. 789

cuddle   vb. 890

cudgel   vb. 282

cuff   n. 963

cuisine   n. 306

cul de sac   n. 635

culinary   adj. 306

cull   vb. 540

culminate *vb.* 56, 212, 659

culmination *n.* 89, 581

culpable *adj.* 157, 938

culprit *n.* 684

cultivate *vb.* 378, 470

cultivated *adj.* 848, 886

cultivator *n.* 378

culture *n.* 426, 848, 886

cultured *adj.* 426, 848, 886

culvert *n.* 360

cumbersome *adj.* 330, 628

cumulative *adj.* 36

cuneiform *n.* 493; *adj.* 246

cunning *n.* 631, 932; *adj.* 478, 631

cup *n.* 193, 663

curate *n.* 986

curative *adj.* 589, 591

curator *n.* 593, 683

curb *n.* 281, 635, 681; *vb.* 37, 235, 281, 681

curdle *vb.* 332, 773

cure *n.* 176, 181, 589, 591, 834; *vb.* 589, 591, 599

curfew *n.* 128, 681

curiosity *n.* 388, 866

curious *adj.* 388, 394

curl *n.* 247, 251; *vb.* 247, 251, 260

currency *n.* 731

current *n.* 140, 358, 359; *adj.* 120, 125, 153, 464, 492, 545

current affairs *n.* 465

curriculum *n.* 470

curried *adj.* 769

curry *vb.* 306

curry favour *vb.* 881

curse *n.* 592, 665, 901; *vb.* 892, 901, 962

cursory *adj.* 113, 211

curt *adj.* 203, 504, 517, 887

curtail *vb.* 37, 197, 203

curtain *n.* 216, 461, 801

curtsy *n.* 319, 922; *vb.* 319, 922

curve *n.* 219, 247; *vb.* 219, 247

curved form *n.* 247

cushion *n.* 217; *vb.* 176, 834

custodian *n.* 593, 683

custody *n.* 593, 681, 707

custom *n.* 545, 726, 743, 988

customary *adj.* 126, 138, 545, 988

customer *n.* 716, 726

cut *n.* 43, 55, 259, 717, 744; *vb.* 48, 259, 264, 490, 744

cut back *vb.* 37, 42, 203, 748

cut down *vb.* 203, 319

cut out *vb.* 312

cut out for *adj.* 627

cut-price *adj.* 746

cut-throat *n.* 370

cutting *adj.* 255, 760, 773, 923

cut up *adj.* 828, 837; *vb.* 837

cycle *n.* 109, 140, 276, 323; *vb.* 269, 323

cyclic *adj.* 109, 140, 250

cycling *n.* 269

cyclone *n.* 323, 359

cyclopedia *n.* 524

cylinder *n.* 249

cylindrical *adj.* 249

cynic *n.* 904, 928

cynical *adj.* 904, 928

cynicism *n.* 904

D

dabble *vb.* 349

dad *n.* 170

daffodil *n.* 813

daily *adv.* 140

dainty *n.* 770, 848; *adj.* 331, 770

dally *vb.* 135

dam *vb.* 265

damage *n.* 588; *vb.* 164, 582, 588, 847

damages *n.* 31, 963

damaging *adj.* 580

damn *vb.* 901, 962

damned *adj.* 975

damp *n.* 349; *adj.* 349; *vb.* 762

dampen *vb.* 349, 548, 837

dampness *n.* 347, 349

dance *n.* 792, *vb.* 320, 838

dancer *n.* 793

dandy *n.* 852

danger *n.* 594

dangerous *adj.* 594

dangle *vb.* 216

dank *adj.* 349

dapple *vb.* 817

dare *n.* 644; *vb.* 644

daredevil *n.* 859

daring *n.* 857, 859; *adj.* 644, 857

dark *n.* 798; *adj.* 798, 803, 808

darken *vb.* 798, 803, 808

darkness *n.* 427, 798, 803, 808

darling *n.* 891

darn *vb.* 589

dart *n.* 290; *vb.* 273, 280

dash *n.* 33, 173, 613; *vb.* 280, 282, 613

dashing *adj.* 611, 613

dastardly *adj.* 858

data *n.* 38, 401, 460

date *n.* 107, 116, 884; *vb.* 116

dated *adj.* 107, 126

deep *n.* 351; *adj.* 148, 182, 210, 805

deepen *vb.* 36, 210, 835

deep-freeze *n.* 764; *vb.* 762

deep-seated *adj.* 210, 545

deface *vb.* 845, 847

defamation *n.* 869, 928

defamatory *adj.* 926, 928, 930

default *n.* 315, 739; *vb.* 739

defeat *n.* 445, 660, 662; *vb.* 414, 661

defeatist *adj.* 855

defecate *vb.* 310

defect *n.* 43, 57, 582, 660, 662, 847

defection *n.* 189, 538, 920, 932

defective *adj.* 55, 57, 580, 582, 847

defence *n.* 402, 593, 595, 646, 648, 929, 960

defenceless *adj.* 160

defend *vb.* 410, 593, 646, 647, 648, 929, 959

defendant *n.* 684, 960

defer *vb.* 135, 424, 654, 920

deference *n.* 654, 922

defiance *n.* 637, 644, 672, 880

deficiency *n.* 29, 35, 57, 189, 315, 571, 660

deficient *adj.* 29, 35, 57, 315, 582, 660

deficit *n.* 57, 315, 737

defile *vb.* 584, 588, 608, 928, 936

defilement *n.* 584, 588, 608, 928

define *vb.* 102, 235, 496, 525

defining *adj.* 456

definite *adj.* 408, 823

definite article *n.* 499

definite space *n.* 183

definition *n.* 235, 450

deflate *vb.* 874

deflated *adj.* 874

deflation *n.* 197, 874

deflect *vb.* 285

deformed *adj.* 243, 245, 845

deformity *n.* 245, 582, 845, 847

defraud *vb.* 478, 722

defrost *vb.* 345, 761

deft *adj.* 280, 627

defunct *adj.* 369

defy *vb.* 25, 331, 637, 644, 672

degenerate *n.* 940; *adj.* 147, 936; *vb.* 53, 147, 588, 590, 936

degradation *n.* 608, 686, 869, 928

degrade *vb.* 588, 686, 869

degree *n.* 7, 27, 93, 400, 766

dehydrate *vb.* 350, 599

de-ice *vb.* 761

deification *n.* 983

deign *vb.* 874

deism *n.* 974

deity *n.* 966

déjà vu n. 441

dejection *n.* 837

delay *n.* 135, 281; *vb.* 135, 281

delegate *n.* 149, 625, 688, 689; *vb.* 685, 714

delete *vb.* 42, 485

deliberate *adj.* 410, 530, 543, 552; *vb.* 384

deliberation *n.* 384, 410, 860

delicacy *n.* 162, 205, 306, 338, 770, 848

delicate *n.* 753; *adj.* 162, 205, 331, 338, 510, 594, 735, 848, 864

delicatessen *n.* 306

delicious *adj.* 306, 767, 770, 772, 829

delight *n.* 306, 770, 827, 829; *vb.* 755, 829, 840, 889

delighted *adj.* 756, 827

delightful *adj.* 755, 770, 827, 829

delineate *vb.* 232, 486, 525

delirious *adj.* 827

delirium *n.* 756

deliver *vb.* 268, 601, 680, 714

deliverance *n.* 600, 601, 680

delivery *n.* 268, 512, 514, 621, 715

delude *vb.* 478

deluge *n.* 358, 572; *vb.* 349

delusion *n.* 412, 457, 478

demand *n.* 562, 671, 695; *vb.* 562, 671, 695, 727, 743

demarcation *n.* 48, 231, 235

dematerialize *vb.* 2, 328, 826, 984

demeanour *n.* 621

demented *adj.* 439

demise *n.* 89, 369

democracy *n.* 667, 678

demolish *vb.* 164, 319

demolition *n.* 164

demon *n.* 969

demonism *n.* 983

demonstrate *vb.* 401, 413, 456, 458, 696

demonstration *n.* 413, 458, 696, 825

demonstrator *n.* 106, 148

demoralize *vb.* 837, 936

demote *vb.* 686

demur *n.* 533; *vb.* 533, 696

demure *adj.* 876, 951

den *n.* 234, 463, 595

dendrochronology *n.* 116

denial *n.* 414, 469, 542, 694

denigrate *vb.* 928

denomination *n.* 496, 641, 979

denominational *adj.* 979

denominator *n.* 39

denote *vb.* 450, 482

dénouement *n.* 89

denounce *vb.* 892, 928, 930, 962

dense *adj.* 75, 332, 334, 435

density *n.* 204, 332, 400

dent *n.* 254, 847

denude *vb.* 228

denunciation *n.* 901, 926, 930, 962

deny *vb.* 402, 414, 469, 542, 637, 691, 694, 944

deodorant *n.* 775

depart *vb.* 151, 285, 293, 299, 600, 687, 826

department *n.* 55, 97

departure *n.* 285, 293, 299, 369, 600, 687, 826

depend *vb.* 420, 679, 854

dependable *adj.* 392, 702, 868, 931

dependant *n.* 132, 287, 676

dependence *n.* 9, 420, 679

dependent *adj.* 420, 679, 700

depict *vb.* 20, 486, 488

deplete *vb.* 358, 569

depleted *adj.* 57, 569, 588

deplore *vb.* 941

deport *vb.* 99, 963

deposit *n.* 55, 367, 567, 701, 738; *vb.* 567

depository *n.* 193, 567, 732

depot *n.* 567

deprave *vb.* 588, 608

depreciate *vb.* 696, 744, 746, 928

depreciation *n.* 37, 43, 744, 928

depress *vb.* 209, 254, 319, 837, 841

depression *n.* 37, 169, 209, 210, 254, 259, 319, 837

deprive *vb.* 706, 720

deprived *adj.* 435, 706

depth *n.* 26, 209, 210, 400

deputation *n.* 685, 688

deputize *vb.* 685, 689

deputy *n.* 149, 688, 689; *adj.* 689

derail *vb.* 187

deranged *adj.* 439

derelict *adj.* 607

dereliction *n.* 393, 920

deride *vb.* 838, 853, 924, 928

derivation *n.* 155, 410, 494

derivative *n.* 494; *adj.* 156

derive *vb.* 156, 157, 410, 716

derogatory *adj.* 928

descend *vb.* 317, 869

descendant *n.* 11, 171

descent *n.* 11, 171, 317, 870

describe *vb.* 413, 460, 496, 525

description *n.* 460, 465, 486, 496, 525

descriptive *adj.* 456, 525

desecrate *vb.* 608, 981

desert *adj.* 350; *vb.* 556, 607, 898

deserter *n.* 538, 555, 672, 858

desertion *n.* 189, 556, 600, 672, 898, 920

deserts *n.* 917

deserve *vb.* 573, 917, 963

desiccate *vb.* 350

design *n.* 23, 58, 242, 482, 488, 552, 558; *vb.* 58, 488, 543, 552, 558

designate *adj.* 119, 123; *vb.* 102, 450, 482, 486, 496

designer *n.* 491, 558

desirable *adj.* 577, 579

desire *n.* 388, 530, 552, 854, 861; *vb.* 530, 532, 854, 861, 914

desist *vb.* 89, 144

desolate *adj.* 169, 588, 837

desolation *n.* 164, 569

despair *n.* 828, 837, 855, 856; *vb.* 828, 855

desperate *adj.* 706

desperation *n.* 855

despise *vb.* 542, 923, 924

despondency *n.* 445, 837, 855

despotism *n.* 669, 900

dessert *n.* 306

destination *n.* 235, 284, 298, 552

destined *adj.* 154, 531, 543

destiny *n.* 154

destitute *adj.* 708, 735

destroy *vb.* 82, 164, 370, 569

destroyer *n.* 167, 277

destruction *n.* 2, 53, 164, 370

destructive *adj.* 164, 175, 370, 580

dissemble vb. 461, 477

disseminate vb. 95, 378, 460, 464

dissension n. 25, 425, 637, 642

dissent n. 425, 696; vb. 151, 425, 642

dissenter n. 106, 425, 975

dissertation n. 526

dissident n. 979; adj. 106, 425, 672, 979

dissimilarity n. 19, 25, 29, 106

dissimulation n. 19

dissipate vb. 95, 346, 569, 749

dissipation n. 95, 569, 945

dissociation n. 10, 48

dissolute adj. 936, 952

dissolution n. 48, 53, 164, 345, 369, 686, 898

dissolve vb. 2, 53, 164, 345, 686, 826

dissonance n. 25, 787, 791

dissuade vb. 548, 624

dissuasion n. 548, 624

distance n. 194, 198, 400, 885; vb. 198

distant adj. 198, 517, 781, 885

distaste n. 862

distemper n. 225

distend vb. 196

distil vb. 346

distinct adj. 48, 102, 452, 512, 778, 823

distinction n. 398, 868, 870

distinctive adj. 5

distinguish vb. 15, 398, 452

distinguished adj. 208, 573, 868, 870

distort vb. 245, 457, 471, 477, 487, 588, 845

distorted adj. 245, 477, 582

distortion n. 245, 416, 457, 477, 487, 845

distracted adj. 391, 442

distraught adj. 756

distress n. 445, 665, 828; vb. 830

distressed adj. 735

distressing adj. 551, 830

distress signal n. 598, 902

distribute vb. 95, 464, 715, 717

distribution n. 81, 717

district n. 183

distrust n. 421, 913; vb. 423

disturb vb. 82, 137, 187, 326, 856

disturbance n. 80, 137, 175, 326

disunite vb. 48, 51

disunity n. 17

disuse n. 546, 569, 607; vb. 607

ditch n. 261, 360, 646; vb. 556

dither n. 326, 756

ditto adv. 77

dive n. 321; vb. 271, 273, 321

diverge vb. 15, 48, 95, 151, 219, 297

divergence n. 285, 297

divergent adj. 15, 219, 285, 297, 978

diverse adj. 15, 104

diversified adj. 17, 104

diversify vb. 817

diversion n. 142, 285, 449, 840

diversity n. 15, 17, 19, 104, 817

divert vb. 391

diverting adj. 840

divest vb. 228, 720

divide vb. 38, 48, 55, 63, 95, 97, 717

dividends n. 741

divination n. 447, 984

divine adj. 966, 974; vb. 447, 448, 984

divinity n. 966

divisibility n. 51

division n. 25, 38, 48, 55, 97, 425, 655, 717

divisive adj. 642

divorce n. 48, 713, 898; vb. 48, 898

divulge vb. 458, 462

do n. 878; vb. 570, 577, 605, 609, 673, 702

do away with vb. 370

docile adj. 654, 673

dock n. 298, 957; vb. 298

docket n. 482; vb. 482

doctor n. 428, 436, 473; vb. 477

doctrine n. 420, 626, 974

document n. 401, 483, 521; vb. 401, 483, 521

dodge vb. 478, 631; vb. 533, 555

dodger n. 480, 600

doe n. 381

doer n. 609, 619

dog n. 380; vb. 287, 554

doggedness n. 534, 535

dogma n. 420, 974

dogmatic adj. 468, 537

do-gooder n. 899, 903, 905

do in vb. 370

doing n. 609, 702; adj. 609

do-it-yourself adj. 628

doldrums n. 837

doleful adj. 837

dole out vb. 95, 715, 717

doll up vb. 844

doltish adj. 435

domain n. 956

dome n. 225, 252

domestic n. 676; adj. 190

domestic animal n. 373

domesticate vb. 377 ·

domesticated adj. 190

domestic science n. 306

domicile n. 191

dominance n. 34, 159, 177

dominant adj. 159, 177, 667

dominate vb. 177, 208, 667, 669, 679

domineer vb. 667, 669

dominion n. 667

don n. 428, 473; vb. 227

donate vb. 715

donor n. 715, 905

doom n. 543; vb. 962

door n. 262

doorman n. 676

do over vb. 645

dormancy n. 459, 610, 612

dorsal adj. 237

dose n. 26, 591

dot n. 33

dotage n. 130

dote on vb. 889, 983

double n. 28, 149, 971; adj. 62; vb. 62, 149, 260

double-cross vb. 478, 932

double dealing n. 477, 631, 932; adj. 477, 932

double entendre n. 454, 842

double-sidedness n. 61

doubt n. 409, 421, 975; vb. 409, 421, 423

doubtful adj. 407, 409, 421

dough n. 364, 731

douse vb. 762

dove n. 656

dovetail vb. 24, 47

dowager n. 870, 898

dowdiness n. 849

down adj. 837; adv. 209

down-and-out n. 697; adj. 735

downcast adj. 837

downfall n. 164, 317, 662

downgrade vb. 686

down-hearted adj. 837

down-payment n. 55, 738

downpour n. 358

downward adj. 219, 317

doze n. 612, 617; vb. 612

dozen n. 70

drab adj. 805, 809, 843

draft n. 558, 602; vb. 521, 558

drag n. 181, 635; vb. 181, 291, 294

drag up vb. 441

drain n. 360; vb. 319, 358, 569, 806

drained adj. 617

drake n. 380

dram n. 309

drama n. 529, 866

dramatic adj. 529, 752, 755, 866

dramatis personae n. 529

drape n. 801; vb. 216

draught n. 309, 359

draught animal n. 291

draughtsman n. 491

draughty adj. 348, 359

draw n. 28, 294, 553; vb. 28, 291, 294, 308, 312, 390, 486, 488, 525, 705, 889

drawback n. 582

drawer n. 491

drawing n. 291, 488

drawl n. 515; vb. 515

draw up vb. 558

dread n. 856; vb. 856

dreadful adj. 830, 856

dream n. 4, 449, 552, 854; vb. 391, 449, 552, 612, 854, 861

dream up vb. 558

dreamy adj. 384

dreary adj. 798, 841, 843

dredge vb. 312

dredge up vb. 441

dregs n. 44, 576, 871

drench vb. 349, 572

dress n. 227; vb. 227, 568, 844

dressage n. 269

dress down vb. 926, 963

dressing n. 227

dribble vb. 319, 358

dried adj. 350

drift n. 178, 450; vb. 178, 257, 612

drill n. 264; vb. 264, 378, 470

drink n. 309, 343; vb. 304, 950

drinker n. 304, 950

drink in vb. 390, 472

drinking n. 304

drip n. 349, 841; vb. 319, 358

drip-dry vb. 350

drive n. 173, 269, 282, 290, 559, 645, 674; vb. 173, 269, 282, 290, 295, 377, 547, 674

drive at vb. 450

drivel n. 451

driver n. 270

driving n. 269; adj. 674

drizzle n. 358; vb. 358

droll adj. 851

drone vb. 783, 784, 789

droop vb. 216, 317, 319, 837, 841

drop n. 37, 210, 249, 254, 309, 317, 321; vb.

economize *vb.* 37, 748

economy *n.* 392, 748; *adj.* 746

ecstasy *n.* 756, 827

eddy *n.* 323, 358; *vb.* 323, 358

edge *n.* 233, 235, 255, 769; *vb.* 233, 255

edgy *adj.* 756, 856, 894

edible *adj.* 306

edict *n.* 626, 671, 954

edifice *n.* 163

edify *vb.* 470, 550, 579

edit *vb.* 456

edition *n.* 524

editor *n.* 456, 524

educate *vb.* 470

educated *adj.* 426

education *n.* 426, 470

educational *adj.* 460, 470

eerie *adj.* 971, 984

efface *vb.* 485

effect *n.* 87, 156, 877; *vb.* 155, 163, 609, 659

effective *adj.* 159, 172, 563, 627

effeminate *adj.* 162, 381

effervesce *vb.* 363, 786

efficacy *n.* 159, 575

efficient *adj.* 159, 557

effluent *n.* 301, 358

effort *n.* 604, 615

effortless *adj.* 634

effrontery *n.* 880

egg *n.* 250, 306

egg-timer *n.* 116

ego *n.* 382

egoist *n.* 904, 934

egotism *n.* 875, 904

ego-trip *n.* 873

eight *n.* 70; *adj.* 70

eject *vb.* 301, 303

ejection *n.* 99, 303, 310, 312

elaborate *adj.* 509; *vb.* 196

elapse *vb.* 107, 110

elasticity *n.* 336

elated *adj.* 756, 827, 838

elbow *n.* 246

elder *n.* 34, 132, 987; *adj.* 130

eldest *adj.* 130

elect *adj.* 119; *vb.* 540

election *n.* 540

electorate *n.* 540

electric chair *n.* 964

electricity *n.* 159, 765

electrify *vb.* 159, 755

electrocute *vb.* 370, 963

electronic *adj.* 125

elegance *n.* 510, 844, 848

elegy *n.* 372, 839

element *n.* 5, 55, 155, 327

elementary *adj.* 88

elements *n.* 192, 348

elevated *adj.* 208, 318, 868, 873

elevation *n.* 208, 318

elevator *n.* 316

eleven *n.* 70

elevenses *n.* 306

eleventh hour *n.* 136

elf *n.* 970

elicit *vb.* 155, 547

eligible *adj.* 896, 897

eliminate *vb.* 46, 99, 164, 303

elite *n.* 579, 870

elixir *n.* 591

ellipse *n.* 247, 250

ellipsis *n.* 504

elliptic *adj.* 504

elocution *n.* 518

elongated *adj.* 202

elope *vb.* 600, 896

eloquent *adj.* 514, 516

elsewhere *adj.* 189

elucidate *vb.* 413, 456

elude *vb.* 555, 600

emaciated *adj.* 205, 588

emanation *n.* 156, 301, 774

emancipation *n.* 601, 680

emasculate *vb.* 160, 169

embalm *vb.* 372, 599, 776

embankment *n.* 559, 646

embargo *n.* 99, 681, 691

embarkation *n.* 299

embark on *vb.* 605

embarrass *vb.* 578, 633, 869, 874

embarrassed *adj.* 811, 830, 874, 876

embassy *n.* 685, 688

embed *vb.* 311

embellish *vb.* 509, 844, 846

ember *n.* 800

embezzle *vb.* 722

embezzler *n.* 723, 739

embittered *adj.* 893

emblazon *vb.* 482

emblem *n.* 482, 677, 872

embody *vb.* 52, 98, 222, 486

emboss *vb.* 482, 489

embrace *n.* 886, 890; *vb.* 50, 98, 702, 886, 890

embrocation *n.* 365

embroider *vb.* 481, 509, 846

embryology *n.* 375, 376

embryonic *adj.* 88

emerald *adj.* 812

emerge *vb.* 301, 313, 324, 600, 825

emergence *n.* 298, 301

emergency *n.* 136, 153, 562

emigrant *n.* 100, 270

emigration *n.* 299

eminent *adj.* 34, 208, 573, 868, 870

emissary *n.* 460, 467, 688

emit *vb.* 301, 303, 774, 778

emollient *n.* 365

emolument *n.* 705, 738

emotion *n.* 326, 752, 756, 889

empathy *n.* 752

emperor *n.* 675

emphasize *vb.* 417, 456, 468, 481, 512, 573

employ *vb.* 107, 557, 575, 606, 685

employee *n.* 619, 676

emporium *n.* 730

empower *vb.* 159, 161, **667, 685**, 954

emptiness *n.* 2, 189, 333, 875

empty *adj.* 189, 333, 451; *vb.* 301, 358, 569

empty-handed *adj.* 735

empty-headed *adj.* 383, 427, 435

emulate *vb.* 20

emulsion *n.* 362

enable *vb.* 159, 404

enact *vb.* 529

enactment *n.* 486, 954

enamel *n.* 225

enamoured *adj.* 889

encampment *n.* 186

enchant *vb.* 827, 829, 889, 984

encircle *vb.* 231, 250

enclose *vb.* 98, 225, 229, **234**

enclosure *n.* 184, 234, 378

encompass *vb.* 182, 229, 231

encore *n.* 62, 77; *adv.* 77

encounter *n.* 296, 649; *vb.* 649, 857

encourage *vb.* 217, 547, 618, 624, 636, **836**, 857, 907

encroachment *n.* 314, 645, 918, 955

encrust *vb.* 226

encumbrance *n.* 635, 711

encyclopedia *n.* 426, 524

end *n.* **89**, 156, 235, 237, 369, 552, 659; *vb.* 89, 659

endanger *vb.* 594

endearment *n.* **890**

endeavour *n.* 604; *vb.* 604

endemic *adj.* 586

endless *adj.* 78, 91, 114

endless duration *n.* **114**

endorsement *n.* 408, 424, 468, 690, 963

endow *vb.* 568, 715

endowment *n.* 5, 627, 714

endurance *n.* 112, 114, 143, 152, 337, 535, 757

endure *vb.* 91, 112, 145, 535, 648, 752, 757, 828

enemy *n.* 638, 645, **883**

energetic *adj.* 32, 159, 161, 173, 368, 585, 611

energize *vb.* 161, 173, 618, 755

energy *n.* 159, 161, 173, 368, 611

enfeeble *vb.* 130, 162, 507

enforce *vb.* 954

enfranchise *vb.* 678, 680

engage *vb.* 557, 605

engaged *adj.* 698

engage in battle *vb.* 649, 651

engagement *n.* 557, 605, 649, 698, 890

engine *n.* 276, 565

engineer *n.* 558

engrave *vb.* 490, 521, 522

engraver *n.* 491

engraving *n.* **490**

engrossed *adj.* 384

enhance *vb.* 36, 318, 509, 846

enigma *n.* 409, 453, 466

enjoy *vb.* 752, 770, **827**, 861

enjoyable *adj.* 827, 829

enjoy immunity *vb.* 921

enjoy oneself *vb.* 827, 840

enlarge *vb.* 36, 40, 196, 202, 505

enlighten *vb.* 460, 470, 797

enlist *vb.* 83, 302, 557, 651

enliven *vb.* 173, 368, 618, 836, 840

enmity *n.* **883**

ennoble *vb.* 318, 868, 870

ennui *n.* 841

enormous *adj.* 32, 194

enough *adj.* 75, 570

enquire *vb.* 388, 394

enquiry *n.* 394, 526

enrage *vb.* 893

enrapture *vb.* 547, 827, 829, 889

enrich *vb.* 509, 587

enrol *vb.* 83, 483, 641

ensconce *vb.* 461

ensemble *n.* 54, 793

enshrine *vb.* 372, 983

enshroud *vb.* 225

ensign *n.* 482

enslave *vb.* 679

ensnare *vb.* 463, 478

ensue *vb.* 85, 119, 153, 156, 287

ensure *vb.* 408

entail *vb.* 98, 459

entangle *vb.* 82, 221

entente *n.* 643, 699

enter *vb.* 298, **300**, 483, 742

enterprise *n.* 173, 288, 604, **605**, 611, 627, 857

entertain *vb.* 840, 884

enter upon *vb.* 88, 605

enthralling *adj.* 547, 829, 866

enthrone *vb.* 685, 868

enthusiasm *n.* 532, 611, 752

enthusiastic *adj.* 532, 611, 756, 827

entice *vb.* **547**, 770

entire *adj.* 54, 56, 581, 659

entirety *n.* 54, 56, 59

entitled *adj.* 917

entity *n.* 1, 3, 59

entomb *vb.* 372

entomology *n.* 375

entrance *n.* 262, 298, **300**, 559

entrant *n.* 638

entrap *vb.* 478

entreat *vb.* 695, 982

entrée *n.* 306

entrench *vb.* 152, 186

entrepreneur *n.* 728

entrust *vb.* 685, 714, 718

entry *n.* 298, 300

entwine *vb.* 251

enumerate *vb.* 38, 83, 102

enunciate *vb.* 512, 514

envelop *vb.* 225, 229, 234, 461

envelope *n.* 193, 234

envious *adj.* 914

environment *n.* 8, 183, 229

envisage *vb.* 449

envoy *n.* 460, **467**, 685, 688

envy *n.* **914**; *vb.* 914

ephemeral *adj.* 113

epic *n.* 525, 528

epicure *n.* 304, 945, 948

epigram *n.* 432, 842

epilogue *n.* 87, 89

episode *n.* 153

epistle *n.* 523

epitaph *n.* 372

epithet *n.* 496

epitome *n.* 527

epitomize *vb.* 203

epoch *n.* 109

equal *n.* 28; *adj.* 13, **28**, 159

equality *n.* 13, **28**, 244

equalize *vb.* 28, 31

equate *vb.* 13, 218, 397

equation *n.* 28, 397

equator *n.* 63, 250

equestrianism *n.* 269

equidistant *adj.* 90, 218

equilibrium *n.* 28, 152

equip *vb.* 227, 564, 568, **602**

equipment *n.* 568, 711

equity *n.* 711, 915

equivalence *n.* 12, 28, 450

equivalent *n.* 18, 28, 456; *adj.* 12, 13, 18, 28

equivocal *adj.* 409, 453, 454

equivocate *vb.* 454, 477

era *n.* 109

eradicate *vb.* 164, 303, 485

erase *vb.* 485

erect *adj.* 214, 248, 318; *vb.* 214, 318

erection *n.* 163, 318

erode *vb.* 37, 53, 164, 341, 569, **588**

Eros *n.* 889, 967

erotic *adj.* 952

err *vb.* 285, 431, 936

errand *n.* 685

errand-boy *n.* 467

erratic *adj.* 151, 539

erring *adj.* 409

erroneous *adj.* 412, 431, 916

error *n.* **431**, 457, 471

erudite *adj.* 426, 472

eruption *n.* 148, 175, 301, 782

escalate *vb.* 36, 196

escalator *n.* 316

escape *n.* 293, 301, 555, 595, **600**, 826; *vb.* 293, 555, **600**, 826

escapism *n.* 449

escarpment *n.* 208

escort *n.* 683; *vb.* 268

esoteric *adj.* 453, 984

especial *adj.* 34, 102

Esperanto *n.* 492

espouse *vb.* 896

essay *n.* 526, 604

essence *n.* 1, 5, 450

essential *n.* 5, 531, 562; *adj.* 1, 5, 531, 562, 573

establish *vb.* 81, 88, 152, 161, 413, 685, 929, 954

established *adj.* 126, 152, 413, 545

establishment *n.* 88, 152, 191, 413, 620, 641, 667, 730

estate *n.* 7, 378, 711

esteem *n.* 922, 925; *vb.* 384, 861, 868, 889, 925

estimate *n.* 447, 743; *vb.* 38, 400, 415, 448, 743

estrange *vb.* 883, 892

estuary *n.* 353

etcher *n.* 491

etching *n.* 490

eternal *adj.* 78, 114, 966

eternity *n.* 78, 108, 112, **114**

ethereal *adj.* 4, 328, 333

ethics *n.* 935

ethnic *adj.* 11, 379

etiquette *n.* 545

etymology *n.* 492, 494

Eucharist *n.* 988

eunuch *n.* 160

euphemism *n.* 455, 509

exhibitionist *n.* 875, 877; *adj.* 875

exhilarate *vb.* 618, 755, 827

exhilaration *n.* 756

exhort *vb.* 518, 597, 624

exhume *vb.* 372

exile *n.* 303, 963; *vb.* 303, 963

existence *n.* 1, 368

existent *adj.* 120

existentialism *n.* 1

exit *n.* 262, 299, 369, 600

exodus *n.* 299

exonerate *vb.* 601, 911, 929, 961

exorbitant *adj.* 572, 745, 749

exorcise *vb.* 984

exotic *adj.* 100

expand *vb.* 36, **196**

expand on *vb.* 456

expanse *n.* 26, 182, 204, 356

expansion *n.* 36, 182, **196**

expatriot *n.* 100

expect *vb.* 154, 443, 552, 854

expectation *n.* 406, 443, 552, 854, 867

expected *adj.* 123, 138, 406, 443, 447, 545, 867

expecting *adj.* 163, 854

expedience *n.* 136, 577

expedite *vb.* 613

expedition *n.* 269, 280

expel *vb.* 99, 301, 303, 310, 542, 885, 963

expend *vb.* 569, 715, 738, 740

expenditure *n.* **740**

expense *n.* 743, 745

expenses *n.* 636, 738, 740, 965

experience *n.* 130, 153,

426, 434, 602, 627, 752; *vb.* 153, 426, 472, 752

experiment *n.* 394, **396**, 604; *vb.* 396

expert *n.* 428, 436, **629**, 848; *adj.* 130, 627

expertise *n.* 426, 627

expiation *n.* 943

expiration *n.* 89, 144, 359, 369

explain *vb.* 157, 410, 413, 456, 470, 525, 526

explanation *n.* 155, 157, 413, 450, 456, 525

expletive *n.* 901

explicit *adj.* 452, 458, 502

explode *vb.* 175, 756, 782, 893

exploit *n.* 605, 609; *vb.* 136, 575, 606, 745

exploration *n.* 269, 271, 419

exploratory *adj.* 86, 394

explore *vb.* 269, 396, 758

explorer *n.* 270

explosive *n.* 657; *adj.* 594, 765

exponent *n.* 456, 974

exponential *adj.* 39

export *vb.* 268

exporter *n.* 728

expose *vb.* 228, 262, 414, 419, 458, **462**

exposed *adj.* 228, 348, 414, 462, 753, 823

expose oneself to *vb.* 179

expositor *n.* 456, 514, 526

expostulate *vb.* 696

expound *vb.* 456, 470

express *adj.* 458; *vb.* 242, 450, 458, 460, 514, 525

expression *n.* 242, 458, 468, 492, 494, 498, 825

expressionless *adj.* 451, 754, 843

expulsion *n.* 99, 303, 310, 312, 542

expunge *vb.* 485

expurgate *vb.* 583

exquisite *adj.* 579, 770, 829, 844

extant *adj.* 1

extemporize *vb.* 544

extend *vb.* 6, 182, 196, 202, 208, 253, 693

extended *adj.* 202, 204, 253, 455

extension *n.* 36, 41, 196, 202, 253

extensive *adj.* 32, 54, **182**, 202

extent *n.* 26, 27, 107, 182, 194, 198, 202, 400, 956

extenuating *adj.* 403, 929

exterior *n.* 222, 236; *adj.* 6, 222

exterminate *vb.* 164, 369, 370

external *n.* 6; *adj.* 6, 100, 222, 825

extinct *adj.* 2, 126, 369

extinguish *vb.* 164, 369, 762

extol *vb.* 922

extort *vb.* 312, 720, 722, 745

extra *n.* 529; *adj.* 40, 572, 607; *adv.* 40

extract *n.* 55, 306; *vb.* 187, 312

extraction *n.* **312**

extradite *vb.* 303

extramarital *adj.* 952

extraneousness *n.* 6, 40, **100**, 222

extraordinary *adj.* 407, 573, 866

extrapolate *vb.* 6, 222

extra-sensory perception
n. 411, 447, 753
extraterrestrial adj. 329
extravagance n. 481,
569, 572, 745, 749, 945
extravagant adj. 481,
509, 569, 572, 745, 749,
877
extreme n. 89; adj. 89,
148, 175, 669, 828, 830
extremely adv. 32
extremist n. 148, 672
extremity n. 89, 233,
235
extricate vb. 312, 601,
678, 680
extrinsic adj. 6, 100,
222
exuberant adj. 168, 572,
836
exudation n. 310
exude vb. 301, 358
exultation n. 827, 838
eye n. 818; vb. 818
eye for an eye n. 647
eyelash n. 207
eyesight n. 818
eyesore n. 845
eye-witness n. 821

F

fable n. 455, 525
fabric n. 221, 339
fabrication n. 163, 465,
477, 631
fabulous adj. 449, 481,
525, 970 .
façade n. 211, 222, 236,
477, 852
face n. 222, 236, 825;
vb. 226, 239, 857
face-lift n. 587, 589, 844
facet n. 7, 55
facetiousness n. 842
face value n. 743, 825

facility n. 514, 568, 627,
634
facsimile n. 20, 22
fact n. 1, 401, 426, 430,
460
fact-finding adj. 394
faction n. 641, 979
factious adj. 25, 642,
672
factor n. 8, 55, 155, 327
factory n. 620
factual adj. 1, 430
faculties n. 382
faculty n. 159
fad n. 125, 850
fade vb. 162, 588, 806,
826
fade out vb. 799
faeces n. 310
failing n. 819, 936
failure n. 315, 393, 431,
445, 571, 660, **662**
faint vb. 162, 617
faint-hearted adj. 162,
858
faintness n. 162, 507,
617, 781, 799, 806
fair n. 840; adj.
(average) 30, 666; (of
weather) 759;
(whitish) 807; (good-
looking) 844; (just)
915, 931, 933
fairy n. 953, 970
fairy story n. 525
faith n. 420, 854, 974,
980
faithful adj. 430, 456,
673, 702, 882, 977
faithless adj. 409, 421
fake n. 20; adj. 20, 477,
478; vb. 20, 477, 852
fall n. 37, 317, 321, 358;
vb. 37, 317, 321, 588,
936
fallacy n. 412, 431
fall apart vb. 51
fall away vb. 538, 588

fall back vb. 289, 293
fall back on vb. 606
fall down vb. 431, 662
fallen adj. 662
fallen angel n. 969
fallen woman n. 953
fall for vb. 422, 889
fallible adj. 431, 582
fall ill vb. 586
fall in vb. 254
falling star n. 329
fall in love vb. 889
fall on vb. 153, 179
fallow adj. 603, 612
fall short vb. 29, 35,
315, 571, 582, 662
fall through vb. 662
fall to vb. 716, 919
false adj. 2, 477, 478
falsehood n. 431, 477
false reasoning n. 412
falsification n. 457, 471,
477, **487**
falter vb. 325, 515, 536,
662
fame n. 868
familiar adj. 138, 426,
545, 882
familiarize vb. 470, 545
family n. 11, 55, 97, 171
famished adj. 861, 947
famous adj. 573, 868
fan n. 764; vb. 348
fanatic n. 148, 537, 611
fanciful adj. 449, 539
fancy n. 448, 449, 539,
861; adj. 509, 846; vb.
448, 449, 540, 861, 889
fan out vb. 297
fantastic adj. 433, 449,
851, 866
fantasy n. 449, 481
far adj. 198
farce n. 433, 529, 851
fare n. 306, 743
farewell n. 299
far-flung adj. 198

farm *n.* 377, 378; *vb.* 377

farm out *vb.* 717

far-reaching *adj.* 32, 182

far-sighted *adj.* 434

farthest *adj.* 198

fascinate *vb.* 294, 547, 755, 889

fascinating *adj.* 547, 755, 829

fascism *n.* 669

fashion *n.* 125, 242, 545, 559, **850**

fast *n.* 947; *adj.* 280, 613, 805; *vb.* 947; *adv.* 280

fasten *vb.* 47, 50, 152, 263

fastidiousness *n.* 392, 540, **864**

fasting *n.* **947**; *adj.* 947

fat *n.* 306; *adj.* 194

fatal *adj.* 164, 369, 370

fatalism *n.* 531

fate *n.* 123, 154, **158**, 531, 543, **553**

fat-head *n.* 437

father *n.* 11, 170

fathom *vb.* 452

fathomless *adj.* 210

fatigue *n.* **617**, 841

fatten *vb.* 204, 377

fatty *adj.* 365

fault *n.* 200, 315, 431, 582

faultless *adj.* 581, 937

faulty *adj.* 582

fauna *n.* 366, 373

faux pas *n.* 431

favour *n.* 636, 670, 715, 886, 899, 907, 922; *vb.* 540, 925

favourable *adj.* 854, 925

favourite *n.* **891**

favouritism *n.* 916

fawning *n.* 927; *adj.* 881

fear *n.* **856**, 858, 980; *vb.* 856

fearless *adj.* 857

feasible *adj.* 404, 406

feast *n.* 306; *vb.* 304

feat *n.* 605, 609

feathery *adj.* 331

feature *n.* 5, 8, 55, 825

fecundity *n.* 168

federal *adj.* 379, 641

federation *n.* 641

fed up with *adj.* 862

fee *n.* 738, 743, 917

feeble-minded *adj.* 435

feebleness *n.* 160, 162, 507, 666, 781

feed *vb.* 304, 377

feedback *n.* 395

feeder *n.* 559

feel *n.* 339, 398, 758; *vb.* 411, 752, 758

feel better *vb.* 834

feeler *n.* 394, 396

feel for *vb.* 758, 907

feeling *n.* 411, 752, 758; *adj.* 752

feel like *vb.* 532

feel small *vb.* 874

fees *n.* 917

feign *vb.* 477, 852

felicitate *vb.* 888

felicitous *adj.* 510

fell *n.* 208; *vb.* 48

fellow *n.* 11, 122, 131, 380, 473

fellow-feeling *n.* 899, 907

fellowship *n.* 60, 639, 641, 988; *vb.* 988

fellow-worker *n.* 640

female *n.* **381**; *adj.* 381

femininity *n.* 162, 381

feminism *n.* 381

fen *n.* 355

fence *n.* 230, 234

fend for oneself *vb.* 678

fend off *vb.* 646

ferment *n.* 80, 175; *vb.* 331, 363, 773

ferry *n.* 277; *vb.* 271

fertile *adj.* 163, 168

fertilize *vb.* 378

fervour *n.* 506, 752, 759

festive *adj.* 878

festivity *n.* 838, 840

festoon *vb.* 846

fetch *vb.* 705, 718, 743

fete *n.* 840

fetid *adj.* 777

fetish *n.* 967, 983, 984

fetter *n.* 681; *vb.* 635, 681

feud *n.* 642, 649

fever *n.* 326, 439, 586

few *adj.* 33, 76, 139

fewness *n.* 33, **76**

fiancée *n.* 698, 889

fiasco *n.* 662

fib *vb.* 477

fibber *n.* 480

fibre *n.* 207, 339

fibrous *adj.* 337

fickle *adj.* 151, 536, 538, 539

fiction *n.* 525

fictitious *adj.* 2, 449

fiddle *n.* 478; *vb.* 722, 742

fidelity *n.* 673, 931

fidgety *adj.* 151, 611, 756, 856

field *n.* 184, 352, 356, 378, 557, 658

fiend *n.* 175, 969

fierce *adj.* 175, 900

fiery *adj.* 506, 759, 893

fiesta *n.* 840

fifth columnist *n.* 480

fight *n.* 642, 649, 651; *vb.* 25, 615, **637**, 642, 645, 649

fight back *vb.* 647

fighter *n.* 645, 655

figurative *adj.* 455

figure *n.* 39, 489; *vb.* 38

figure-head *n.* 253

figure of speech *n.* **455**, 498

figure out *vb.* 452

filament *n.* **207**

filch *vb.* 722

file *n.* 83, 202; *vb.* 83, 91, 255, 257, 341

filial *adj.* 171

filibuster *n.* 135; *vb.* 135

fill *n.* 865; *vb.* 56, 107, 265, 865

fill in *vb.* 149, 460, 483

fillip *n.* 173; *vb.* 613

fill up *vb.* 568

filly *n.* 381

film *n.* 225, 363, 483, 803; *vb.* 483

filter *vb.* 319

filth *n.* 584, 952

final *adj.* 89, 237, 408, 659

finality *n.* 543

finance *n.* 731; *vb.* 636, 718

financier *n.* 718, 728

find *vb.* 415, 419, 960

find fault with *vb.* 832, 926, 930, 962

fine *n.* 963; *adj.* 205, 255, 333, 340, 579, 844; *vb.* 963

finesse *n.* 631

finger *n.* 758

fingerprint *n.* 482

finicky *adj.* 392, 864

finish *n.* 56, 89, 257, 510, 659; *vb.* 89, 144, 414, 581, 659

fiord *n.* 353

fire *n.* 506, 759, 763; *vb.* 645, 686, 755, 761, 765

firearm *n.* 657

fireproof *adj.* 762

fireside *n.* 191, 763

fireworks *n.* 800

firing squad *n.* 963

firm *n.* 620, 641; *adj.* 143, 152, 161, 334, 337, 534, 535, 669

first *adj.* 34, 88

first-class *adj.* 34, 579

first hand *adj.* 21

firth *n.* 353

fish *n.* 306, 373

fishy *adj.* 373, 932

fissure *n.* 254

fit *n.* 326, 439, 586, 893; *adj.* 585, 915; *vb.* 47, 105, 568, 602

fitful *adj.* 141, 539

fit in with *vb.* 24

fit out *vb.* 227, 602

fitting *adj.* 577, 915

fittings *n.* 568

five and over *n.* 70

fix *n.* 633; *vb.* 47, 152, 311, 589

fixation *n.* 439

fixative *n.* 49

fixed *adj.* 47, 143, 152, 543

fixtures *n.* 152, 568, 711

fizz *n.* 363; *vb.* 363, 786

fizzle out *vb.* 144, 162, 662

flabbergasted *adj.* 866

flabby *adj.* 668

flaccid *adj.* 507

flag *n.* 467, 482, 677; *vb.* 617, 841

flagellant *n.* 946

flagon *n.* 193

flagrant *adj.* 458, 877

flail *vb.* 282

flake *n.* 33, 206, 340; *vb.* 206

flake out *vb.* 617

flamboyant *adj.* 877

flame *n.* 797, 800; *vb.* 759

flammable *adj.* 761, 765

flank *n.* 238; *vb.* 238

flap *n.* 225, 326; *vb.* 216, 326, 359, 756

flare *n.* 797, 800; *vb.* 756, 797

flash *n.* 115, 539, 797, 800; *vb.* 797

flashback *n.* 147, 441

flashlight *n.* 800

flashy *adj.* 509, 805, 849, 877

flask *n.* 193

flat *n.* 191, 356; *adj.* 215, 257, 768, 791, 843

flat out *adv.* 280

flattery *n.* 881, 886, **927**

flaunt *vb.* 877

flavour *n.* 767; *vb.* 307

flavourless *adj.* 768, 771

flaw *n.* 431, 582, 847

flawless *adj.* 54, 581

flay *vb.* 228, 963

fleck *n.* 33

fledgling *n.* 125

flee *vb.* 555, 600, 826

fleece *n.* 377, 478, 722

fleeting *adj.* 113

flesh *n.* 306, 327, 379

flesh and blood *n.* 3, 327

fleshly *adj.* 945

fleshy *adj.* 194, 364

flex *vb.* 247

flexible *adj.* 151, 335, 336, 668

flexuous *adj.* 251

flicker *vb.* 326, 759, 797

flickering *adj.* 141

flick through *vb.* 472, 818

flight *n.* 273, 293, 299, 555, 600, 826

flighty *adj.* 151, 539

flimsy *adj.* 162, 205, 335, 338

flinch *vb.* 283, 555, 856

fling *vb.* 359

flint *n.* 765

flippancy *n.* 842

flirt *n.* 953; *vb.* 890

fuel   n. 765; vb. 765
fugitive   n. 555, 600
fulcrum   n. 217
fulfil   vb. 56, 659, 661, 673, 702
fulfilment   n. 659, 827
full   adj. 54, 56, 204, 570, 865
fullness   n. 32, 56, 567
fulminate   vb. 780
fulsome   adj. 168
fumble   vb. 409, 758
fumbler   n. 630
fume   n. 344, 777; vb. 175, 346, 756, 759, 893
fumigate   vb. 583, 775
fun   n. 829, 836, 840, 842
function   n. 39, 172, 557, 878; vb. 172, 609
functional   adj. 172, 575
functionary   n. 623
fundamental   adj. 5, 88, 155, 213, 573
fundamentalist   adj. 977
funds   n. 731
funeral   n. 372
fungus   n. 167, 592
funk   n. 858; vb. 856, 858
funny   adj. 842, 851
furious   adj. 175, 893
furlough   n. 614
furnace   n. 763
furnish   vb. 163, 568, 715
furniture   n. 711
furrow   n. 254, 261
further   adj. 40; vb. 217, 288, 587; adv. 40
furthest   adj. 89, 198
furtive   adj. 461, 478
fury   n. 175, 756, 893
fuse   n. 765; vb. 45, 47, 52, 345
fusion   n. 45, 47, 52, 639
fuss   n. 326, 756, 877; vb. 756, 864
fussy   adj. 392, 864

futile   adj. 576, 662, 855
future   n. 123; adj. 123
future events   n. 154
futuristic   adj. 125
fuzzy   adj. 243, 503, 824

G

gabble   vb. 516
gad about   vb. 269
gadget   n. 565
gag   n. 842; vb. 681
gaiety   n. 836
gain   n. 288, 550, 705; vb. 36, 116, 705, 720
gala   n. 840
galaxy   n. 329
gale   n. 175, 359
gallant   adj. 857, 886
gallery   n. 818
galley   n. 522
gallivant about   vb. 269
gallows   n. 964
galore   adj. 75
galvanize   vb. 755
gamble   n. 158, 553; vb. 158, 553
gambler   n. 553
game   n. 306, 373, 649, 840; adj. 532, 857
gamekeeper   n. 683
gamut   n. 182
gang   n. 94
gangster   n. 370, 906
gang up against   vb. 639
gaol   n. 682
gap   n. 92, 200, 262
gape   vb. 262, 818, 866
garb   n. 227
garbage   n. 44
garble   vb. 487, 515
garden   n. 234, 374, 378
gardener   n. 378
garish   adj. 805, 846, 877
garment   n. 227
garnish   vb. 846

garrison   n. 646
garrulous   adj. 516
gas   n. 159, 344, 765; vb. 963
gaseity   n. 344
gash   n. 588
gasify   vb. 344, 346
gasp   n. 359; vb. 359
gastronomy   n. 304
gate   n. 262
gatecrash   vb. 300
gate-crasher   n. 884
gather   n. 260; vb. 94, 196, 260, 296, 448, 567
gaudy   adj. 805, 846, 877
gauge   n. 400, 482; vb. 400, 482
gay   n. 106, 953; adj. 836, 952
gaze   vb. 818
gazette   n. 483, 524
gear   n. 227
geld   vb. 160, 169
gem   n. 579, 846
gene   n. 5
genealogy   n. 170
general   adj. 101
generality   n. 101
generalize   vb. 101
generally   adv. 138, 545
generate   vb. 11, 155, 163
generation   n. 11, 109, 163, 171
generative   adj. 163, 170
generic   adj. 101
generosity   n. 747, 886
generous   adj. 715, 747, 899, 965
genetics   n. 366
genial   adj. 827, 836, 884
genius   n. 382, 428, 434, 627, 629
genocide   n. 370, 963
gentle   adj. 176, 670, 907
gentleman   n. 380
gentlemanly   adj. 380, 886

gentleman's agreement
n. 698, 699

gentry n. 870

genuine adj. 1, 21, 430,
632

geography n. 329

geology n. 367

geometry n. 38

gesticulate vb. 482

gesture n. 482, 549; vb.
482

get vb. 705, 716, 720,
726

get across vb. 460

get along with vb. 24,
643

get around vb. 464

get at vb. 460, 547, 893

get-at-able adj. 292

getaway n. 600

get away with vb. 600,
722, 921

get back vb. 647, 705,
721

get by vb. 661, 666

get down vb. 298, 837

get down to vb. 605

get dressed vb. 227

get even with vb. 647,
912, 963

get in with vb. 177, 882

get on vb. 661, 664

get one's own back vb.
647, 912

get on one's nerves vb.
787, 893

get on with vb. 24, 643

get over vb. 460, 659

get ready vb. 602

get rid of vb. 303, 607,
634, 680

get the hang of vb. 452,
472

get to vb. 298

get-together n. 884

get up vb. 318, 472, 477

get-up-and-go n. 173,
611

get used to vb. 545

get well vb. 589

ghastly adj. 856

ghost n. 328, **971**

ghostly adj. 4, 328, 971

ghost-writer n. 149, 524

giant n. 194; adj. 208

gibberish n. 453

gibe vb. 853

gift n. 627, 652, 715, 829

gifted adj. 627

gift of the gab n. 514,
516

giggle vb. 838

gild vb. 846

ginger adj. 816

gipsy n. 447

gird vb. 322

girder n. 217

girdle n. 49; vb. 229

girl n. 131, 381

girl-friend n. 882, 889

girth n. 204

gist n. 224

give vb. 335, 568, **715**,
965

give and take n. 150,
639, **704**

give away vb. 462, 717,
896

give in vb. 654

given adj. 1, 715

give off vb. 301, 774

give out vb. 301, 774,
778

giver n. 715, 905

give up vb. 556, 654,
855

give up office vb. 687

give way vb. 162

giving n. 636, 715, 747

glaciate vb. 762

glacier n. 760

glad adj. 827, 836

gladden vb. 829, 836

gladly adv. 532

glamorous adj. 829, 844

glamour n. 547, 829,
844

glance n. 818; vb. 818

glare n. 797; vb. 797,
818

glaring adj. 458, 805,
823

glass n. 193, 257, 822

glasses n. 822

glassy adj. 257, 802

glaze n. 225; vb. 225,
369, 257

gleam n. 797; vb. 797

glean vb. 378, 540, 705

glee n. 827, 836

glib adj. 516

glide vb. 257, 273

glider n. 278

glimmer n. 460, 797;
vb. 326, 797

glimpse n. 818; vb. 818

glint n. 797

glisten vb. 797

glitter n. 797; vb. 797

global adj. 101

globe n. 249, 329

globe-trotter n. 270

globule n. 249, 363

gloom n. 798, 799, 837

gloomy adj. 798, 799,
837, 843, 895

glorification n. 925, 972

glorify vb. 318, 868, 982

glorious adj. 664, 972,
982

glory n. 868, 972; vb.
873

gloss n. 211, 225, 257,
456, 797; vb. 225, 257,
456

glossary n. 83, 494

gloss over vb. 393

glossy adj. 257, 797

glow n. 759, 797, 805;
vb. 759, 797, 811

glue n. 49, 362; vb. 50

glum adj. 895

glut n. 572, 865

241

grace n. 844, 848, 907, 911

graceful adj. 510, 844, 848

gracious adj. 510, 899, 907, 966

gradation n. 27

grade n. 27, 93, 400, 474; vb. 27, 97

gradual adj. 27

graduate n. 474; vb. 27, 400

graft vb. 378

grain n. 33, 306, 340, 374

grammar n. 492, 499

grammarian n. 492

grammatical adj. 492, 499

granary n. 193

grand adj. 509, 844, 868, 870

grandeur n. 870, 877

grandiloquent adj. 509

grandiose adj. 509, 877

grandstand n. 818

grange n. 191, 378

grant n. 636, 715; vb. 424, 690, 692, 715

grant permission vb. 424

granular adj. 339

granulate vb. 340

granule n. 340

grapevine n. 465

graphic adj. 488, 506, 521, 525

graphics n. 488

grapple vb. 758

grasp n. 410, 707, 712; vb. 50, 426, 452, 472, 707, 712, 720, 758

grasping adj. 705, 720, 750

grass n. 356, 374, 460

grassland n. 356, 378

grassy adj. 374, 812

grate n. 763; vb. 341, 787, 805

grateful adj. 909

gratify vb. 829, 831, 865

grating adj. 787, 791

gratitude n. **909**

gratuity n. 715, 965

grave n. 372; adj. 573, 837

graven image n. 983

gravestone n. 372

gravitate towards vb. 178

gravity n. 294, 330, 573, 837

graze vb. 201, 341, 377, 758

grease n. 306, 342, 365, 584; vb. 342, 365

greasy adj. 365, 584

great adj. 32, 573, 579, 868, 870

greater adj. 34

greatness n. 26, 32, 194, 579, 868, 870

greedy adj. 720, 750, 861, 934, **948**

greedy-guts n. 948

green n. 559, **812**; adj. 129, 422, 427, 812, 913

greenhorn n. 429, 479, 630

greenhouse n. 378

greet vb. 886, 922

greeting n. 518, 886, 922

gregarious adj. 884

gremlin n. 970

grey n. **809**; adj. 30, 130, 363, 799, 809

grey matter n. 434

grid n. 159, 221

grief n. 828, 837, 839

grievance n. 916

grieve vb. 830, 833, 837, 839

grill n. 221; vb. 306, 394, 759

grim adj. 669, 830

grimace n. 895; vb. 245, 895

grimy adj. 584

grin n. 838; vb. 838

grin and bear it vb. 757, 836

grind vb. 341, 615, 787

grip n. 193, 712; vb. 50, 712, 720, 758

gripping adj. 755

gristle n. 337

groan n. 788; vb. 696, 788

groceries n. 305

groggy adj. 586, 950

groom vb. 377, 470

groove n. 184, 261, 545; vb. 261

grope vb. 409, 758

gross n. 70; adj. 54, 56, 849, 936

grotesque adj. 245, 845

grotto n. 254

grouch n. 832; vb. 895

ground n. (reason) 155, 401, 547, 929; (land) 213, 352, 658; vb. 319, 470

groundwork n. 213, 602

group n. 55, 94, 97, 641, 793; vb. 52, 94, 97

grovel vb. 209, 881, 922

grow vb. 36, 168, 196, 242, 288, 316, 324

growl vb. 783, 789, 895

grown-up n. 133; adj. 133

growth n. 36, 196, 252, 288, 324

grow up vb. 133

grudge n. 832, 893; vb. 914

grudgingly adv. 533

gruelling adj. 615

gruff adj. 787, 887, 894

grumble vb. 783, 832

grumbler n. 832

grumpy *adj.* 894

grunt *vb.* 789

guarantee *n.* 424; *vb.*
408, 468, 698, 701

guard *n.* 593, 646, 683;
vb. 392, 593, 646

guardian *n.* 593, 683,
905

guardroom *n.* 682

guerdon *n.* 965

guerrilla *n.* 148

guess *n.* 386, 396, 447,
448; *vb.* 396, 411, **448**

guest *n.* 100, 884

guffaw *vb.* 838

guidance *n.* 470, 624

guide *n.* 103, 217, 473,
623; *vb.* 470, 621, 622,
624

guidebook *n.* 460, 524

guile *n.* 477, 478, 631,
932

guileless *adj.* 422, 476,
632, 937, 951

guillotine *n.* 964; *vb.*
370, 963

guilt *n.* **938**

guilty *adj.* 938

guinea pig *n.* 396, 716,
828

guise *n.* 227, 463, 549

gulf *n.* 200, 254, 353

gullibility *n.* **422**

gully *n.* 254, 360

gulp *n.* 309; *vb.* 304,
948

gum *n.* 365; *vb.* 50

gun *n.* 657; *vb.* 370

gunman *n.* 167, 370

gunpowder *n.* 657

gurgle *n.* 358

guru *n.* 473

gush *vb.* 301, 358, 532

gust *n.* 359

gusto *n.* 827

gusty *adj.* 359

guts *n.* 535, 857

gutter *n.* 261, 360

guzzle *vb.* 304, 948, 950

gypsy *n.* 270

gyration *n.* 323

H

habit *n.* 79, 138, **545**

habitat *n.* **191**, 229

habitation *n.* 188, **191**

hack *n.* 524, 619, 676

hackneyed *adj.* 426

haggard *adj.* 205, 617

hail *n.* 760; *vb.* 886, 925

hair *n.* 207

hair-dressing *n.* 844

hairless *adj.* 228

hairy *adj.* 207, 258

halcyon days *n.* 664,
827

hale *adj.* 585

half n,63; *adj.* 63

half a dozen *n.* 70

half-and-half *adj.* 45

half-done *adj.* 55, 57,
660

half-hearted *adj.* 533,
863

half-price *adj.* 746

half-remembered *adj.*
441

halfway *n.* 30, 704; *adj.*
30, 90, 560; *adv.* 90

half-wit *n.* 437

half-witted *adj.* 435

hall *n.* 191, 529

hallmark *n.* 482

hallow *vb.* 980

hallucination *n.* 478

halo *n.* 250, 800

halt *n.* 144; *vb.* 144,
267, 691

halve *vb.* 63

hamlet *n.* 183

hammer *vb.* 282

hammer out *vb.* 659,
699

hamper *n.* 193; *vb.* 635,
681, 691

hand *n.* 238, 521

handbook *n.* 524

hand down *vb.* 714

handful *n.* 26, 76, 633

handicap *vb.* 162

hand in one's notice
vb. 687

handiwork *n.* 163

handle *n.* 872; *vb.* 172,
606, 609, 622, 725

hand out *vb.* 715, 717

hand-out *n.* 464, 465,
715

hand over *vb.* 268

handshake *n.* 886

handsome *adj.* 844

handwriting *n.* 521

handy *adj.* 575, 627

handyman *n.* 629

hang *vb.* **216**, 370, 963

hang around *vb.* 188,
612

hanger-on *n.* 287, 640,
881

hanging *n.* **216**, 370,
963

hangman *n.* 370, 963

hangover *n.* 44, 950

hanker *vb.* 861, 914

haphazard *adj.* 158,
399, 409, 553

happen *vb.* 1, 107, 153,
825

happening *n.* 153

happiness *n.* 550, 661,
664, 831, **836**

happy *adj.* 827, 831,
836, 950

happy medium *n.* 30

happy returns *n.* 888

harangue *n.* 518

harass *vb.* 830, 893

harbour *n.* 298, 353,
595; *vb.* 461, 593, 712

hard *adj.* 334, 337, 537,
633, 669, 942

harden *vb.* 332, 334, 337, 754

hardened *adj.* 537, 942

hard-hearted *adj.* 648, 754, 908

hard labour *n.* 963

hardly *adv.* 33, 139

hardness *n.* 334, 537, 633, 669, 754

hardship *n.* 633, 665, 735

hard-working *adj.* 611, 615

hardy *adj.* 161

harlot *n.* 953

harm *n.* 551, 900; *vb.* 580, 608, 900, 916

harmful *adj.* 164, 580, 592, 916

harmonious *adj.* 24, 79, 105, 244, 643, 790

harmony *n.* 24, 244, 510, 643, 650, 790

harness *n.* 49; *vb.* 47

harrow *vb.* 378, 830

harrowing *adj.* 828, 856

harsh *adj.* 258, 642, 669, 787, 900, 908

harsh sound *n.* 787

harvest *n.* 128, 163, 567; *vb.* 378, 567

haste *n.* 280, 613

hasty *adj.* 393, 544, 603, 613

hatch *n.* 262; *vb.* 449, 477, 558

hatchway *n.* 262

hate *n.* 862, 892, 900; *vb.* 862, 892

hatred *n.* 862, 883, 892

haughty *adj.* 873, 875, 924

haul *n.* 291, 724; *vb.* 268, 291

haunt *vb.* 188, 441, 830, 971

have *vb.* 707

have a go *vb.* 604

have fun *vb.* 840

have in mind *vb.* 552

have it in for *vb.* 892, 900

haven *n.* 595

have nothing to do with *vb.* 10, 542, 862

have no time for *vb.* 923

have-nots *n.* 871

have on *vb.* 227, 478

have one's own way *vb.* 530

have one's say *vb.* 468

have on one's mind *vb.* 384

havoc *n.* 164

hawk *vb.* 695, 727

hawker *n.* 697, 728

hazard *n.* 553, 594; *vb.* 553

hazel *adj.* 810

hazy *adj.* 363, 799, 824

H-bomb *n.* 657

head *n.* 89, 236, 675; *vb.* 212, 236, 284, 286

headache *n.* 633, 950

headlines *n.* 465

headlong *adj.* 613, 859

headmaster *n.* 473

headquarters *n.* 96

head start *n.* 34

headstone *n.* 372

headstrong *adj.* 537, 859

headway *n.* 288

heal *vb.* 589, 591

health *n.* 585

heap *n.* 567; *vb.* 567, 747

hear *vb.* 778, 795, 960

hearing *n.* 795, 960

hearsay *n.* 465

heart *n.* 223, 224, 368, 751, 857

heart-broken *adj.* 828, 837

heartening *adj.* 836, 857

hearth *n.* 191, 763

heartlessness *n.* 908

heart-to-heart *n.* 519

heartwarming *adj.* 836

hearty *adj.* 585

heat *n.* 759, 763; *vb.* 306, 761

heath *n.* 356

heathen *n.* 975, 983

heating *n.* 761

heatwave *n.* 759

heave *vb.* 291, 303, 318, 834

heaven *n.* 329, 972

heavenly *adj.* 770, 966, 972

heavy *adj.* 330, 332, 511, 573, 617, 841

heavy drinker *n.* 950

heavy-handed *adj.* 628, 669

heavy-laden *adj.* 828

heavyweight *adj.* 573

heckle *vb.* 425, 696

hedge *n.* 234; *vb.* 555

hedonistic *adj.* 827, 945

heed *n.* 390, 392, 860; *vb.* 390, 392, 673, 702

heedless *adj.* 391, 442, 859

hefty *adj.* 161

height *n.* 26, 208, 400, 581

heighten *vb.* 36, 318, 481, 835

heinous *adj.* 936

heir *n.* 171, 710, 716

helicopter *n.* 278

helix *n.* 251

hell *n.* 828, 973

helmsman *n.* 272

help *n.* 563, 636, 639, 834; *vb.* 563, 575, 577, 636, 639, 676

helper *n.* 624, 640, 905

helpful *adj.* 550, 575, 636

helping *n.* 305, 717

helpless *adj.* 160, 162, 855

hem *n.* 233; *vb.* 233

hem in *vb.* 234

hemisphere *n.* 63

hen *n.* 381

henpecked *adj.* 673

herald *n.* 86, 467; *vb.* 118, 286

herb *n.* 306, 307, 374

herbivore *n.* 373

herd *n.* 94, 373, 377, 871; *vb.* 377

hereafter *n.* 123; *adv.* 123

hereditary *adj.* 5

heresy *n.* 106, 975, **978**

heretical *adj.* 106, 412, 975, **978**

heritage *n.* 11

hermit *n.* 885, 946

hero *n.* 661, 857, 939

heroic *adj.* 857

hesitant *adj.* 515, 533, **536**, 856

hesitate *vb.* 325, 409, 421, 515, 533, 536

heterodox *adj.* 978

heterogeneous *adj.* 15, 17, 45, 104

hew *vb.* 48, 489

hexagon *n.* 70, 246

heyday *n.* 664

hidden *adj.* 453, 459, **461**, 466, 824

hide *vb.* 225, **461**, 466, 593

hideous *adj.* 245, 845

hide-out *n.* 463

hiding *n.* 461, **463**

hierarchy *n.* 97

hi-fi *n.* 794

high *adj.* 32, **208**, 318, 777, 868

high birth *n.* 870

highest *adj.* 212, 579

high-flown *adj.* 509, 877

high-handed *adj.* 880, 887

high hopes *n.* 443, 854

highlight *vb.* 468, 481

high living *n.* 945

highly-strung *adj.* 756

high opinion *n.* 922

high-pitched *adj.* 787

high principles *n.* 931

high-rise *adj.* 208

high spirits *n.* 836

high tea *n.* 306

high time *n.* 135

highway *n.* 559

highway code *n.* 313

highwayman *n.* 723

hijack *vb.* 722

hijacker *n.* 723

hike *n.* 269; *vb.* 269

hiker *n.* 270

hilarious *adj.* 851

hill *n.* 208, 316, 559

hind *n.* 381; *adj.* 237

hinder *vb.* 181, 548, 635, 637, 681

hindmost *adj.* 198, 237

hindrance *n.* 548, **635**, 681

hindsight *n.* 441

hinge *n.* 49, 217

hint *n.* 459, **460**, 482; *vb.* 459, 460

hire *vb.* 557, 685, 719

hire out *vb.* 718

hire purchase *n.* 718, 731

hiss *vb.* **786**, 788, 853, 926

hissing sound *n.* 786

historian *n.* 484

historical *adj.* 124, 430

history *n.* 124

histrionics *n.* 529, 877

hit *n.* 282, 661; *vb.* 282, 758, 963

hit and miss *n.* 396

hit back *vb.* 647

hitch *n.* 635

hitch-hiker *n.* 270

hit it off *vb.* 24, 643

hit-or-miss *adj.* 158

hit upon *vb.* 419

hive off *vb.* 48

hoard *n.* 567; *vb.* 567

hoarse *adj.* 787

hoary *adj.* 126, 807, 809

hoax *n.* 478, 598, 631; *vb.* 478, 631

hob *n.* 763, 970

hobble *vb.* 281

hobby *n.* 840

hoe *vb.* 378

hog *n.* 948; *vb.* 707

hoist *vb.* 318

hold *n.* 707, 712; *vb.* 50, 420, 707, **712**

hold against *vb.* 588

hold back *vb.* 533, 681, 694, 876

hold dear *vb.* 441, 889, 922

holder *n.* 193, 710

hold forth *vb.* 470, 514

holding *n.* 378, 711, 712

hold off *vb.* 295, 648

hold one's breath *vb.* 443

hold out *vb.* 648, 693

hold out for *vb.* 535

hold up *vb.* 135, 217, 635

hold-up *n.* 635, 722

hold water *vb.* 410

hole *n.* 254, 262, 319; *vb.* 264

holiday *n.* 144, 612, 614, 840

holiday-maker *n.* 270

hollow *n.* 210, 254, 262; *adj.* 254, 852; *vb.* 210, 254

holocaust *n.* 370

holy *adj.* 935, 974, 980, 982

Holy Communion *n.* 988

holy orders *n.* 985
Holy Spirit *n.* 967
homage *n.* 982
home *n.* 11, 191, 595;
    adj. 190
homecoming *n.* 298
homeless *adj.* 59, 187
homely *adj.* 508, 827
home-made *adj.* 628
homesickness *n.* 861
homestead *n.* 191, 377,
    378
homework *n.* 470, 472
homicide *n.* 370
homogeneity *n.* 13, 16,
    46, 59
homo sapiens n. 379
homosexual *n.* 106,
    953; *adj.* 952
honest *adj.* 430, 476,
    915, 931
honey *n.* 772, 891
honeymoon *n.* 829,
    896; *vb.* 896
honour *n.* 663, 868,
    872, 909, **922**, 982; *vb.*
    868, 878, 922, 982
honourable *adj.* 868,
    931
hood *n.* 225, 801, 989
hooded *adj.* 225
hoodwink *vb.* 478, 819
hook *n.* 49; *vb.* 47, 896
hooligan *n.* 906
hoop *n.* 250; *vb.* 788
hoot *vb.* 482, 788, 853
hooter *n.* 116, 482
hop *n.* 320; *vb.* 320
hope *n.* 406, 420, 443,
    854; *vb.* 406, 443, 552,
    854
hopeful *adj.* 443, 854
hopelessness *n.* 405,
    576, **855**
horizon *n.* 198
horizontal *adj.* 215, 248
horn *n.* 598
horn of plenty *n.* 168

horology *n.* 116
horoscope *n.* 329, 447
horrible *adj.* 580, 771
horrid *adj.* 580, 845
horrifying *adj.* 856
horror *n.* 845, 856
horse *n.* 275
horsemanship *n.* 269
horse-power *n.* 159
horse-racing *n.* 269
horse-rider *n.* 270
horticultural *adj.* 374,
    376, 378
hospitable *adj.* 716, 884
hospitality *n.* 302, 747,
    884
host *n.* 75, 968
hostage *n.* 701
hostel *n.* 191
hostile *adj.* 637, 665,
    883, 892
hostilities *n.* 649, 651
hot *adj.* 759, 769
hotel *n.* 191
hour *n.* 109
hour-glass *n.* 116
hourly *adv.* 140
house *n.* 191, 620
household *n.* 11; *adj.*
    426
householder *n.* 190
housekeeper *n.* 676,
    683
housekeeping *n.* 622,
    748
hover *vb.* 154, 216
hovercraft *n.* 278
howl *vb.* 359, 788, 789,
    839
hub *n.* 96, 224
huddle *n.* 94; *vb.* 94
hue *n.* 805
hug *n.* 712, 886; *vb.* 50,
    712, 886, 890
huge *adj.* 32, 194
hull *n.* 225
hum *n. vb.* 781, 783,
    784, 789

human *n.* 368; *adj.* 379
human being *n.* 379
humane *adj.* 903
humanitarian *adj.* 899,
    903
humanity *n.* 379
human rights *n.* 917
human sound *n.* **788**
humble *adj.* 35, 654,
    833, 871, **874**, 941, 980;
    vb. 869, 874, 922
humble oneself *vb.* 833,
    874, 941, 982
humid *adj.* 349, 759
humiliate *vb.* 869, **874**,
    923
humility *n.* 654, **874**,
    980
humorous *adj.* 842
humour *n.* 5, 751, 842
hump *n.* 252
hunch *n.* 134, 411; *vb.*
    319
hunchbacked *adj.* 245
hundred *n.* 70
hunger *n.* 861, 947; *vb.*
    861
hunger strike *n.* 696
hungry *adj.* 735, 861,
    947
hunt *n.* 554; *vb.* 394,
    554
hurdle *n.* 230, 235, 320,
    635
hurricane *n.* 175, 359
hurried *adj.* 613, 859
hurry *n.* 280, 611, 613;
    vb. 280, 613
hurt *n.* 828; *adj.* 893;
    vb. 580, 608, 830, 900,
    916
hurtful *adj.* 164, 551,
    580, 828, 830
husband *n.* 896; *vb.*
    377, 748
husbandry *n.* 378, 622,
    748

hush *n.* 779, 781; *vb.*
267, 779
hush-hush *adj.* 461, 466
hush up *vb.* 466
husk *n.* 225
husky *adj.* 787
hut *n.* 191
hybrid *n.* 45, 495
hydrated *adj.* 347
hydro- *adj.* 347
hydro-electricity *n.*
159, 765
hydrogen bomb *n.* 657
hygienic *adj.* 585
hymn *n.* 792, 982
hyperbole *n.* 481
hyper-critical *adj.* 832,
864
hyper-sensitive *adj.* 753
hypnosis *n.* 754
hypochondriac *n.* 440
hypocrisy *n.* 477, 981
hypocrite *n.* 480, 631
hypothesis *n.* 157, 386,
396, 448
hypothetical *adj.* 2,
396, 448
hysteria *n.* 439, 756
hysteric *n.* 440

I

ice *n.* 347, 760; *vb.* 762
iceberg *n.* 754, 760
icon *n.* 983
icy *adj.* 760, 762
idea *n.* 386, 415, 420,
449, 552
ideal *n.* 581, 939; *adj.*
449, 581
idealist *n.* 449, 864, 903
identical *adj.* 13
identification *n.* 397,
419, 482, 496
identify *vb.* 482, 496
identity *n.* 13

idiom *n.* 492, 498
idiosyncractic *adj.* 102
idiosyncrasy *n.* 5, 102,
501
idiot *n.* 437, **440**, 630
idiotic *adj.* 435
idle *adj.* 174, 610, **612**;
vb. 107, 174, 281, 612
idler *n.* 281, 612, 940
idol *n.* 967, **983**
idolatry *n.* 975, **983**
idolize *vb.* 982, 983
idyllic *adj.* 528
ignite *vb.* 761
ignited *adj.* 759
ignoble *adj.* 871
ignominious *adj.* 869
ignoramus *n.* **429**, 437,
630
ignorance *n.* 385, **427**
ignorant *adj.* 427
ignore *vb.* 385, 389,
393, 672, 694, 887, 911
ill *n.* 551, 900; *adj.* 586
illegal *adj.* 691, 916, **955**
illegality *n.* 955
illegible *adj.* 453
illegitimate *adj.* 171,
916, **955**
ill feeling *n.* 642, 883
ill health *n.* **586**
ill-humoured *adj.* 895
illicit *adj.* 691, 916, 952,
955
illiterate *adj.* 427
illness *n.* 586, 828
illogical *adj.* 412, 451
illuminate *vb.* 456, 797
illusion *n.* 4, 449, 478
illustrate *vb.* 413, 456,
486, **488**, 525
illustration *n.* 23, 397,
413, 456, 486, **488**, 525
illustrative *adj.* 456,
486
illustrious *adj.* 573, 868
image *n.* 386, 486, 489,
525, 983

imagery *n.* 455
imaginable *adj.* 404
imaginary *adj.* 2, 449,
970
imagination *n.* **449**
imagine *vb.* 448, **449**
imbecile *n.* 437, 440;
adj. 435
imbecility *n.* 383, 435,
439
imitate *vb.* 18, 20
imitation *n.* **20**, 486,
719; *adj.* 149
immaculate *adj.* 581,
583, 935
immanent *adj.* 5, 966
immateriality *n.* 4, **328**,
574
immaturity *n.* 129, 427,
582, 603
immeasurable *adj.* 78
immediate *adj.* 115, 134
immensity *n.* 194
immerse *vb.* 311, **321**,
349
immersed *adj.* 210
immigrant *n.* 100, 190,
270; *adj.* 100
immigration *n.* 300
imminent *adj.* 123, 134,
154, 902
immobile *adj.* 152, 174,
267
immoderate *adj.* 32,
393, 572, 749, 918, 945
immoral *adj.* 932, 936,
952
immortal *adj.* 114, 966
immortalize *vb.* 114,
868
immovable *adj.* 143,
152, 267, 669, 757
immunity *n.* 593, 678,
921
immutability *n.* 152
imp *n.* 969, 970
impact *n.* 282
impair *vb.* 160, 588

impale *vb.* 264, 963

impart *vb.* 464, 470, 715

impartial *adj.* 476, 541, 915, 933

impassioned *adj.* 506, 752

impassive *adj.* 863

impatient *adj.* 613, 756, 893

impeach *vb.* 686, 930

impeccable *adj.* 581, 935, 937

impede *vb.* 635, 681

impediment *n.* 515, 635, 681

impel *vb.* 266, 282, 290, 674

impend *vb.* 123, 154

impenetrable *adj.* 265, 332, 334, 453

impenitence *n.* 942

imperative *n.* 562; *adj.* 531, 562

imperceptible *adj.* 33, 824

imperfect *adj.* 35, 57, 315, 582, 847, 952

imperfection *n.* 35, 315, 582, 952

imperfect speech *n.* 515

imperfect vision *n.* 820

imperialism *n.* 379

imperishable *adj.* 114

impermeable *adj.* 332, 334

impersonation *n.* 20

impertinent *adj.* 880, 923

imperturbable *adj.* 757

impervious *adj.* 265, 337, 803

impetuous *adj.* 613, 756, 859

impetus *n.* 282, 290, 547

impiety *n.* **981**

impinge *vb.* 282

implacable *adj.* 912

implant *vb.* 300, 311

implausible *adj.* 405, 407, 421

implement *n.* 192, 565; *vb.* 659

implicate *vb.* 930

implication *n.* 450, 459

implicit *adj.* 5

implore *vb.* 695, 982

imply *vb.* 401, 448, 450, 459, 482

impolite *adj.* 887, 923

imponderability *n.* 4, 331

import *n.* 450, 573; *vb.* 268, 450

importance *n.* 456, **573**

important *adj.* 177, **573**, 922

importer *n.* 728

importunity *n.* 695

impose *vb.* 700, 919

imposing *adj.* 573, 870

imposition *n.* 963

impossibility *n.* **405**

impostor *n.* 480, 852, 940

impotence *n.* **160**, 169

impoverish *vb.* 162, 735

impracticable *adj.* 407, 576, 628

impractical *adj.* 449

imprecatory *adj.* 695, 901

imprecise *adj.* 431, 503, 916

impregnable *adj.* 593

impregnate *vb.* 311

impress *vb.* 242, 441, **468**, 482, 490, 522, 752, 755, 922

impression *n.* 22, 386, 411, 420, 482, 483, 522, 752

impressionable *adj.* 242, 753

impressive *adj.* 529, 573, 755, 844

imprint *n.* 482; *vb.* 522

imprison *vb.* 234, 681, 963

improbability *n.* **407**, 409

improbity *n.* **932**

improper *adj.* 137, 511, 916, 918

improve *vb.* 288, 472, 587, 618

improvement *n.* 288, 550, **587**

improvise *vb.* 142, 544, 603

imprudent *adj.* 393, 435, 859

impudent *adj.* 880, 887

impulse *n.* **282**

impulsive *adj.* 411, 544, 613, 756, 859

impurity *n.* 582, 584, 847, **952**

impute *vb.* 157, 930

inability *n.* 160, 628

inaccessible *adj.* 198, 405

inaccurate *adj.* 431, 477, 916

inaction *n.* **610**, 616

inactive *adj.* 174, 281, 607, **612**

inactivity *n.* 174, **612**

inadequate *adj.* 315, 571, 582, 662

in advance *adj.* 134; *adv.* 84, 236, 286

inadvisable *adj.* 578

inane *adj.* 433, 435

inanimate *adj.* 367

inanity *n.* 451

inapplicable *adj.* 10, 106

inappropriate *adj.* 10, 106, 137, 500, 511, 578

in arrears *adj.* 737, 917

inarticulate *adj.* 513, 515

indiscretion n. 435. 859

indiscriminate adj. 15, 54, 399

indiscrimination n. 399

indispensable adj. 531, 562

indisputable adj. 408

indissoluble adj. 54

indistinct adj. 243, 503, 515, 781, 799, 824

indistinguishable adj. 13

individual n. 368, 379; adj. 59, 102, 139, 379

individualist n. 934

indivisibility n. 50, 59

indivisible adj. 50, 54, 59. 332

indoctrinate vb. 470

indolent adj. 174, 612

indubitable adj. 408

induction n. 300, 410, 685

indulge vb. 831, 945

indulgence n. 827, 948

industrialist n. 728

industrious adj. 472, 535. 611

industry n. 472, 611, 620

inebriated adj. 950

inedible adj. 771

ineffable adj. 453

ineffably adv. 32

ineffective adj. 160, 169, 576, 662

inefficient adj. 160, 628

inelegance n. 511, 845, 849

inept adj. 160, 427, 628

inequality n. 14, 29

inequity n. 14, 916

inerrant adj. 408

inertia n. 174, 610, 612

inertness n. 174

inescapable adj. 154, 531

inevitable adj. 123, 154, 408, 531, 543

inexact adj. 19, 431, 453

inexcitability n. 754, 757

inexcusable adj. 916

inexhaustible adj. 145

inexpedience n. 137, 578

inexpensive adj. 746

inexperience n. 129, 427, 603, 628

inexperienced adj. 125, 129, 422, 546, 628, 937

inexplicable adj. 158, 453

infallible adj. 408, 430

infamous adj. 426, 869

infancy n. 88, 129

infant n. 131; adj. 129

infantry n. 655

infatuated adj. 439, 889

infatuation n. 439, 889

infect vb. 45, 584, 588

infection n. 586

infectious adj. 586

infer vb. 101, 410, 448, 459

inferable adj. 413

inference n. 410, 448, 459

inferiority n. 29, 35, 580, 679

infernal adj. 973

inferno n. 973

infertile adj. 160, 169

infest vb. 314

infidel n. 975

infidelity n. 703, 952, 978

infiltrate vb. 45, 300

infinite adj. 78, 114

infinitely adv. 78

infinitesimal adj. 33, 195

infinity n. 78, 114

infirm adj. 130, 160, 586

infirmity n. 126, 130, 162, 586

inflammation n. 252, 835

inflate vb. 196, 359

inflated adj. 879

inflation n. 196

inflect vb. 499

inflection n. 499, 512

inflexible adj. 152, 334, 537, 908

inflict vb. 674

influence n. 155, 159, 177, 294, 547; vb. 155, 177, 547, 573, 755

influential adj. 177, 573

influx n. 300

in force adj. 172, 606

inform vb. 460, 470, 597, 624

informal adj. 495

informant n. 460, 624

information n. 401, 426, 460, 465, 525, 624

informative adj. 460, 470

informed adj. 426

informer n. 460, 480, 883

infrequency n. 139, 407

infringement n. 672, 703, 955

infuriate vb. 893

infusion n. 309, 311

ingenuity n. 21

ingenuous adj. 476, 632

ingratiating adj. 881, 886, 927

ingratitude n. 910

ingredient n. 55, 192, 327

inhabit vb. 188, 191

inhabitant n. 190

inhale vb. 308, 359

inharmonious adj. 791

inhere vb. 5

inherent adj. 5, 55, 459

inherit vb. 705

inheritance *n.* 711
inheritor *n.* 710
inhibition *n.* 876
inhuman *adj.* 900, 904
inimical *adj.* 25, 883
iniquity *n.* 936
initial *adj.* 88, 155, 602;
vb. 482
initiation *n.* 88, 300,
302, 470
initiative *n.* 173, 611,
857
inject *vb.* 264, 311
injection *n.* 181, 311,
591
injudicious *adj.* 393,
416
injunction *n.* 626, 671,
691
injure *vb.* 580, 588, 608,
830, 900, 916
injured *adj.* 582
injury *n.* 551, 588, 828,
916
injustice *n.* 916, 955
ink *vb.* 488, 808
inkling *n.* 448
inland *n.* 352; *adj.* 223,
352
inland revenue *n.* 743
inlay *n.* 226; *vb.* 226
inlet *n.* 353
in lieu *adv.* 149
in love *adj.* 889
inmate *n.* 684
in memoriam *n.* 372
inn *n.* 191
innate *adj.* 5, 223
inner *adj.* 223, 224
innermost *adj.* 223
inner self *n.* 751
innocence *n.* 632, 935,
937, 961
innocent *adj.* 632, 935,
937, 951
innovation *n.* 125, 142
innuendo *n.* 928
inoculation *n.* 591

inodorousness *n.* 775
inoffensive *adj.* 757
in operation *adj.* 172,
609
inoperative *adj.* 576,
610
inopportune *adj.* 137,
578
in order *adv.* 79, 605
inordinate *adj.* 572, 945
inordinately *adv.* 32
inorganic matter *n.* 367
in part *adv.* 55
in progress *adj.* 57; *adv.*
288
inquire *vb.* 695
inquirer *n.* 697
inquiry *n.* 394, 695
inquisition *n.* 963
inquisitive *adj.* 388, 394
inroad *n.* 645
insalubrious *adj.* 586
insane *adj.* 435, 439
insanitary *adj.* 586
insanity *n.* 439
inscription *n.* 483, 490,
521
inscrutable *adj.* 453
insect *n.* 373
insecure *adj.* 409, 594
insensible *adj.* 754
insensitive *adj.* 754, 942
insensitivity *n.* 754, 863
inseparable *adj.* 47, 50,
54, 882
insert *n.* 230; *vb.* 40,
230, 311, 483
insertion *n.* 311
inside *n.* 223, 226; *adj.*
223, 681
insidious *adj.* 459, 932
insight *n.* 410, 411, 434
insignia *n.* 482, 677
insignificant *adj.* 451,
574
insincere *adj.* 477, 852,
927, 932, 981

insinuate *vb.* 311, 459,
460
insinuation *n.* 311, 928,
930
insipid *adj.* 162, 507,
666, 768, 843
insist *vb.* 547, 669, 700
insistent *adj.* 506
insobriety *n.* 950
insolence *n.* 644, 672,
873, **880**, 924
insoluble *adj.* 332, 405
insolvent *adj.* 706, 735,
739
inspect *vb.* 390, 394,
818
inspection *n.* 390, 392,
394, 396, 818
inspector *n.* 623
inspiration *n.* 411, 755,
976
inspire *vb.* 547, 755,
836, 854, 857
inspired *adj.* 411, 449,
506, 756, 976
instability *n.* 17, 151,
536, 756
install *vb.* 186, 302, 311,
685
installation *n.* 620, 685
instalment *n.* 55, 738
instance *n.* 23, 456
instant *n.* 115; *adj.* 602
instantaneous *adj.* 115
instantly *adv.* 115
instead *adv.* 149
instigate *vb.* 547
instigator *n.* 166, 547
instill ' *vb.* 470
instinct *n.* 382, 411,
531, 545
instinctive *adj.* 411,
531, 544
institute *n.* 475; *vb.* 88
institution *n.* 475, 620,
988
in store *adj.* 154; *adv.*
567

instruct *vb.* 470, 514

instructed *adj.* 426

instruction *n.* 103, 426, **470**, 624, 626

instructive *adj.* 460, 470, 597

instructor *n.* 473

instrument *n.* **565**, 609, 619

instrumental *adj.* 563, 565

instrumentalist *n.* 793

instrumentality *n.* 172, **563**

insubordinate *adj.* 644, 672

insubstantial *adj.* 4, 328, 331, 333, 451

insufficiency *n.* 315, **571**

insular *adj.* 183, 416

insulate *vb.* 226, 761

insult *n.* 869, 923; *vb.* 644, 887, 923

insulting *adj.* 880, 923

insuperable *adj.* 405

insurance *n.* 701

insurgence *n.* 672

insurgent *n.* 672; *adj.* 148, 672

insurmountable *adj.* 405

insurrection *n.* 148

insurrectionist *n.* 148, 672

insusceptible *adj.* 754

intact *adj.* 54, 599

intangible *adj.* 4, 328, 824

integer *n.* 39

integral *adj.* 5, 39, 54, 55, 56, 223

integrate *vb.* 52, 105

integration *n.* 24, 45, 52, 56, 59

integrity *n.* 56, 476, 931, 935, 937

intellect *n.* **382**, 434

intellectual *n.* 428; *adj.* 382, 384, 426

intelligence *n.* 382, 426, **434**, 460

intelligent *adj.* 382, 426, **434**

intelligibility *n.* **452**, 502

intemperance *n.* **945**, 948, 950

intend *vb.* 552

intended *n.* 698; *adj.* 552

intense *adj.* 173, 752, 759, 805

intensification *n.* 196, 835

intensify *vb.* 36, 173, 196, 481, 835

intensity *n.* 27, 32, 506, 759, 805

intention *n.* 284, 530, 552

intentional *adj.* 530

interact *vb.* 12, 150

intercession *n.* 230, 653, 695, 982

intercessor *n.* 653, 982

interchange *n.* 12, **150**, 519, 714; *vb.* 150

interdiction *n.* 691

interest *n.* 41, 388, 755; *vb.* 294, 547, 755, 829

interested *adj.* 388

interesting *adj.* 755

interfere *vb.* 181, 635, 653

interior *n.* 223, 352; *adj.* 223, 352

interjection *n.* 230, 499

interlude *n.* 144

intermediary *n.* 653; *adj.* 230

intermediate *adj.* 30, 90, 230, 560, 563

interminable *adj.* 78, 114, 202

intermingle *vb.* 45

intermission *n.* 92, 144

intermittent *adj.* 92, 139

internal *adj.* 5, 223

international *adj.* 101

internationalism *n.* 903

internecine *adj.* 164, 370

internee *n.* 684

internment camp *n.* 682

interplay *n.* 12; *vb.* 12

interpose *vb.* 230, 653

interpret *vb.* 456

interpretation *n.* 450, **456**

interpreter *n.* 456, 974

interrogate *vb.* 394

interrupt *vb.* 92, 137, 144, 230, 887, 923

interruption *n.* 92, 230

intersect *vb.* 221, 246

intersperse *vb.* 230

interval *n.* 92, 109, 144, **200**, 267

intervention *n.* 92, 230, 563, 635, 653

interview *n.* 394, 410, 519, 884; *vb.* 394

interviewer *n.* 394

intimacy *n.* 882

intimate *n.* 882; *adj.* 199, 882; *vb.* 450, 459, 460, 482

intimation *n.* 448, 460, 482, 597

intimidate *vb.* 856, 902

intolerance *n.* 537, 900

intonation *n.* 501, 512, 778

intoxicate *vb.* 950

intractable *adj.* 537, 672

intransigent *adj.* 537

intrepid *adj.* 857

intricate *adj.* 251, 453, 503, 633

intrigue *n.* 558, 631; *vb.* 755

intrinsic   *adj.* 1, 5, 223

introduce   *vb.* 84, 88, 300, 302, 311

introductory   *adj.* 86, 88, 602

introspective   *adj.* 384

intrude   *vb.* 137, 300, 388, 645

intruder   *n.* 388, 645

intrusive   *adj.* 137, 388

intuition   *n.* **411**, 531, 753

inundate   *vb.* 349, 358, 572

in use   *adj.* 606

inutility   *n.* **576**

invade   *vb.* 314, 645, 651

invader   *n.* 100, 645, 883

invalid   *adj.* 412, 586

invalidate   *vb.* 414, 469, **686**

invariability   *n.* 13, 16, 143, 152

invasion   *n.* 300, 314, 645

inveigle   *vb.* 927

invent   *vb.* 163, **449**, 477, 930

invention   *n.* 88, 163, 419, 449

inventive   *adj.* 21, 449, 627

inventor   *n.* 155, 166

inventory   *n.* 83

inversion   *n.* **220**

invertebrate   *n.* 373

invest   *vb.* 159, 568, 715, 726, 740

investigate   *vb.* 388, 394, 396, 818

investigation   *n.* 394, 526, 818

investigator   *n.* 394

investiture   *n.* 685

investment   *n.* 718, 726, 740

inveterate   *adj.* 152, 545

in view   *adj.* 823

invigorate   *vb.* 161, 173, 618

invigorating   *adj.* 173, 585, 618

invincible   *adj.* 161, 661

invisibility   *n.* **824**

invitation   *n.* 394, 695

invite   *vb.* 562, 695, 884

invocation   *n.* 518, 695

invoice   *n.* 742

invoke   *vb.* 901, 982

involuntary   *adj.* 411, 531, 544

involve   *vb.* 9, 98, 155, 450

involved   *adj.* 9, 251, 503, 709

inward   *adj.* 5, 223

iota   *n.* 33

irate   *adj.* 893

iron   *vb.* 257, 583

ironical   *adj.* 455, 853

iron out   *vb.* 485

irony   *n.* 455, 842, 853

irrational   *adj.* 39, 385, 412

irreconcilability   *n.* 10, 14

irreconcilable   *adj.* 883

irredeemable   *adj.* 855, 942

irrefutable   *adj.* 408

irregular   *adj.* 17, 80, 92, 104, 106, 141, 151, 245

irregularity   *n.* 17, 106, **141**, 151, 245, 258, 285, 916

irrelevant   *adj.* 10, 451, 574

irreligion   *n.* **975**, 983

irreligious   *adj.* 936, 975, 981

irreproachable   *adj.* 581, 935, 937

irresistible   *adj.* 531, 674, 889

irresolution   *n.* 421, **536**, 538

irresponsible   *adj.* 955

irretrievable   *adj.* 706

irreverent   *adj.* 923, 981

irreversibility   *n.* 152, 855

irrevocable   *adj.* 855

irrigate   *vb.* 378

irritability   *n.* 756, 893, **894**

irritate   *vb.* 830, 835, 893

irritation   *n.* 341, 830, 835

Islam   *n.* 974

island   *n.* 357

isolate   *vb.* 48, 102

isolated   *adj.* 885

isolation   *n.* 59, 461, 885

issue   *n.* 11, 87, 156, 171, 301, 387; *vb.* 358, 464, 522, 600, 731

italic   *adj.* 521

itch   *vb.* 326, 758

itching   *adj.* 443, 861

item   *n.* 59, 192, 327

itinerant   *n.* 270

itinerary   *n.* 269, 460, 559

ivory   *adj.* 807

ivory tower   *n.* 595, 885

J

jab   *n.* 591; *vb.* 282

jacket   *n.* 225

jaded   *adj.* 617, 841, 865

jagged   *adj.* 246, 258, 259

jail   *n.* 682; *vb.* 234, 963

jailer   *n.* 683

jam   *n.* 306

jangle   *vb.* 787

janitor   *n.* 676, 683

jar   *n.* 193, 326; *vb.* 282, 326, 787, 791

jargon   *n.* 492, 494

jaundice *vb.* 416, 813

jaunt *n.* 269, 840

jazz *n.* 792

jealousy *n.* 913, 914

jeer *vb.* 696, 853

jell *vb.* 332

jelly *n.* 306, 364

jeopardize *vb.* 594

jerk *n.* 92, 141, 326, 437; *vb.* 326

jest *n.* 433, 539, 842; *vb.* 842

jet *n.* 278, 358; *vb.* 358

jettison *vb.* 331, 542, 607, 713

jewel *n.* 846, 891

jilt *vb.* 556

jittery *adj.* 326, 756, 856, 894

job *n.* 557, 605, 609, 722

jockey *n.* 270

jocular *adj.* 836, 842

jog *n.* 326; *vb.* 282, 441

join *vb.* 40, 45, 47, 52, 639, 709

joint *n.* 49; *adj.* 180, 709

joint possession *n.* 709

joke *n.* 842; *vb.* 842

jolly *adj.* 827, 836

jolt *n.* 282, 326, 444; *vb.* 282, 326

jot *n.* 33

jot down *vb.* 441, 483

journal *n.* 116, 441, 464, 483, 524

journalist *n.* 460, 484, 521

journey *n.* 269, 313; *vb.* 269

jovial *adj.* 836

joy *n.* 827, 829, 836

J.P. *n.* 958

jubilant *adj.* 838

jubilee *n.* 109, 878

Judaism *n.* 974

judge *n.* 415, 653, **958**; *vb.* 382, **415**, 540, 653, 956, 960

judgment *n.* 382, 398, 410, **415**, 434, 627, 926

judicious *adj.* 392, 398, 415, 434

jug *n.* 193, 682

juice *n.* 309, 343

jumble *n.* 45; *vb.* 45, 82, 399

jump *n.* 316, 320, 321; *vb.* 320, 321

jump at *vb.* 532

jump the queue *vb.* 134

jumpy *adj.* 756, 856, 894

junction *n.* 47, 49, 201, 221

jungle *n.* 374

junior *n.* 35, 131; *adj.* 35, 129, 679

junk *n.* 277

jurisdiction *n.* 622, **956**

jurisprudence *n.* 954

jurist *n.* 959

juror *n.* 958

jury *n.* 958

just *adj.* 915, 917, 954, 966

just deserts *n.* 647, 917

justice *n.* 915, 954, 958

justification *n.* 401, 413, 549, 911, 929

justify *vb.* 410, 413, 911, 929, 961

jut *vb.* 252, 253

juvenile *n.* 131; *adj.* 129, 131

juxtaposition *n.* 94, 199, 201, 238, 397

K

kaleidoscope *n.* 817

keel over *vb.* 220

keen *adj.* 255, 434, 611, 760, 842, 861

keenness *n.* 611

keen on *adj.* 889

keep *n.* 646; *vb.* 377, 567, 593, 599, 673, 702, 707, 712

keep apart *vb.* 48, 200

keep away *vb.* 198, 555, 885

keep back *vb.* 681

keeper *n.* 593, **683**

keep in with *vb.* 24, 922

keep off *vb.* 555

keep on *vb.* 145, 516

keep one's temper *vb.* 757

keep order *vb.* 593, 956

keepsake *n.* 441

keep up *vb.* 217, 460

kernel *n.* 90, 224, 306

key *n.* 357; *adj.* 136

keyed up *vb.* 756

kick *n.* 769, 827; *vb.* 282

kick against *vb.* 644

kid *n.* 131; *vb.* 478, 842

kidnap *vb.* 720, 722

kidnapper *n.* 720, 723

kill *vb.* 370, 963

killing *n.* 370; *adj.* 370, 851

killjoy *n.* 548

kill time *vb.* 612

kiln *n.* 763

kind *n.* 97; *adj.* 882, 886, 899, 903, 935

kindergarten *n.* 475

kindhearted *adj.* 899

kindle *vb.* 755, 761

kindness *n.* 670, 747, 886, 899, 935

kindred relations *n.* 11

king *n.* 675

kingdom *n.* 183

kingdom of heaven *n.* 972

kink *n.* 251

kinship *n.* 11

kiosk *n.* 730

kip down *vb.* 612

kiss n. 886, 890; vb. 758, 886, 890

kitty n. 709

kleptomaniac n. 440

knack n. 627

knead vb. 335

kneel vb. 319, 922

knell n. 372

knife n. 255; vb. 370

knight n. 870; vb. 868

knit vb. 47, 221

knock n. 282, 782; vb. 282, 782, 926, 928

knock down vb. 164

knock off vb. 144, 370, 659, 722, 744

knot n. 49

know vb. 426, 452, 882

know-all n. 428, 436, 875

know-how n. 426, 627

knowing n. 410, 426; adj. 426, 434

knowledge n. 426, 460, 472

knowledgeable adj. 426, 434, 472

knuckle down vb. 615

Koran n. 976

L

label n. 482, 496, 743; vb. 482, 496

laboratory n. 620

laborious adj. 615, 633

labour n. 615, 619; vb. 615

laboured adj. 511

labourer n. 378, 619

lace n. 49, 846

lack n. 57, 76, 189, 315, 571, 582, 706, 708; vb. 35, 57, 76, 189, 562, 571

lacklustre adj. 806

laconic adj. 504, 517

lacquer n. 225, 365

lactescent adj. 807

lad n. 131

ladder n. 316

laden adj. 56

lady n. 381, 870

lady-like adj. 381, 886

lag behind vb. 287, 315

lagoon n. 353, 354

laid up adj. 586

lair n. 595

laissez-faire n. 610

laity n. 987

lake n. 354, 805

lame vb. 588

lamellar adj. 206

lament n. 839; vb. 839

lamentation n. 839

lamina n. 206

laminate n. 206; adj. 206; vb. 206

lamp n. 800

lance vb. 800

lancet n. 264

land n. 352, 378, 711, 711; vb. 273, 298, 317

landed gentry n. 870

landlady n. 710

landlord n. 710

landscape n. 488

landscape gardener n. 378

landslide n. 317, 662

land travel n. 269

lane n. 559

language n. 492, 512, 514

languish vb. 162, 174, 586, 612, 617, 837

lanky adj. 205, 208

lantern n. 800

lap n. 322; vb. 260, 322

lapel n. 260

lapidary n. 491

lapse n. 110, 144, 147, 315, 431, 938; vb. 110, 147, 869, 936

lap up vb. 390

larceny n. 722

lard vb. 306

larder n. 305

large adj. 26, 32, 194, 204

largesse n. 715, 747

lark about vb. 435

larynx n. 512

lascivious adj. 952

laser n. 797

lash n. 964; vb. 175

lass n. 131

lassitude n. 617, 841

last adj. 89, 659; vb. 107, 112, 143, 145

last-minute adj. 135

last resort n. 595

last rites n. 372

last straw n. 659

last word n. 89, 667, 939

late adj. 117, 124, 135, 369

lately adv. 125

latency n. 459, 824

lateness n. 135

later adj. 85, 119, 123; adv. 121

lateral adj. 238

latest adj. 120, 850

lather n. 363; vb. 583

latitude n. 182, 204, 678

lattice n. 221

laud vb. 982

laudable adj. 925

laugh n. 838; vb. 644, 827, 838, 851, 853, 924

laugh off vb. 393, 477

launch n. 277; vb. 271, 290

launch into vb. 605

launder vb. 583

laurel n. 663

lavender n. 814; adj. 814

lavish adj. 509, 745,

747, 749; *vb.* 569, 740, 747

law *n.* 103, 626, 671, 954, 976

lawful *adj.* 667, 915, 954

lawless *adj.* 80, 644, 668, 672, 955

lawn *n.* 374, 812

lawsuit *n.* 960

lawyer *n.* 959

laxity *n.* 51, 335, 393, 668

lay *adj.* 628, 987

layabout *n.* 906

lay at *vb.* 157, 693

lay bare *vb.* 419, 456, 458, 462

lay claim to *vb.* 917

lay down *vb.* 671

layer *n.* 206; *vb.* 206

lay hold of *vb.* 705, 720

lay in wait *vb.* 463

lay it on *vb.* 481, 509, 927

layman *n.* 630, 987

lay-off *n.* 686

lay on *vb.* 805

lay out *vb.* 372, 740

lay-preacher *n.* 974, 987

lay siege to *vb.* 645

lay waste *vb.* 164, 645

lazy *adj.* 393, 612

lead *n.* 286, 529; *vb.* 34, 84, 236, 284, 286, 573, 622

lead astray *vb.* 431, 936

leader *n.* 125, 253, 623, 675

leading *n.* (printing) 522

lead to *vb.* 155

leaf *n.* 374, 812

leaflet *n.* 464

league *n.* 641, 699

leak *n.* 600; *vb.* (es-

cape) 301, 358; (dis-closure) 462

lean *adj.* 205; *vb.* (tend) 178; (incline) 219

lean on *vb.* 679, 854

leap *n.* 200, 320, 321; *vb.* 320

leapfrog *n.* 320; *vb.* 320

leap year *n.* 109

learn *vb.* 441, 472

learner *n.* 428, 474

learning *n.* 426, 472

lease *n.* 708, 714; *vb.* 718, 719

leave *n.* 614, 690, 921; *vb.* 299, 556, 600, 660, 687

leave alone *vb.* 555, 610

leaven *n.* 142, 331; *vb.* 318

leave of absence *n.* 614

leave out *vb.* 99

leave-taking *n.* 299

leave undone *vb.* 393, 660

leavings *n.* 44

lechery *n.* 952, 953

lecture *n.* 470, 518, 926; *vb.* 470, 514, 926

lecturer *n.* 473, 514

lecture theatre *n.* 475

ledge *n.* 217

ledger *n.* 742

leer *n.* 818; *vb.* 818

leeway *n.* 182, 200, 678

left *n.* 241; *adj.* 44, 241

legacy *n.* 714, 715

legal adviser *n.* 959

legality *n.* 915, 954

legalize *vb.* 424, 690, 954

legal proceedings *n.* 960

legal tender *n.* 731

legation *n.* 685

legend *n.* 525

legerdemain *n.* 478

legible *adj.* 452

legion *n.* 75; *adj.* 75

legislation *n.* 622, 954

legislative *adj.* 103, 622

legislator *n.* 623

legist *n.* 959

legitimacy *n.* 915, 954

leisure *n.* 614, 840

leisurely *adj.* 281, 614

leitmotif *n.* 387

lemon *n.* 813

lend *vb.* 568, 718, 736

lending *n.* 718

length *n.* 26, 198, 202, 400

lengthen *vb.* 36, 202

lengthy *adj.* 202, 505

lenience *n.* 670

lenient *adj.* 670, 690, 907

lens *n.* 247, 822

Lent *n.* 947

leper *n.* 885

leprechaun *n.* 970

lesbian *n.* 106, 953; *adj.* 952

lesion *n.* 588

lessee *n.* 710

lessen *vb.* 37, 76, 197, 333, 403

lesser *adj.* 35, 209

lesson *n.* 470, 472, 597

let *vb.* 690, 718

let down *vb.* 445, 874

let fall *vb.* 319

let go *vb.* 556, 713

lethal *adj.* 164, 370

lethargy *n.* 174, 281, 612, 754

let off *vb.* 601, 911, 961

let on *vb.* 462

let out *vb.* 196, 462, 680, 718

let pass *vb.* 911

let slip *vb.* 680, 706, 920

letter *n.* 493, 522, 523; *vb.* 482, 493

lettering *n.* 521, 846

letter of the law n. 669, 908

let up vb. 144, 176, 281, 616

level n. 27, 93, 206, 215; adj. 28, **215**, 248, 257; vb. 16, 257, 400

level-headed adj. 757

lever n. 217

leviathan n. 194

levitation n. 331, 984

levity n. 331, 836, 859

levy n. 743, 917; vb. 716, 743

lewdness n. 952

lexical adj. 494

lexicography n. 492, 494

lexicology n. 494

lexicon n. 83, 494

liability n. **179**, 701, 737, 919, 938

liaison n. 889, 952

liar n. 480, 940

libel n. 928; vb. 928, 930

liberal adj. 570, 715, 747, 965

liberated adj. 678, 680, 961

liberation n. 601, **680**, 921

liberator n. 905

libertine n. **953**

liberty n. 678, 690

library n. 475, 524, 567

librate vb. 325

licence n. 690

license vb. 690, 954

licentiousness n. 952

lick vb. 758, 963

lick into shape vb. 470, 570

lid n. 225

lie n. 431; vb. 185, 477, 932

lie down vb. 215

lie low vb. 209, 459, 461, 593

lieutenant n. 675

life n. 107, 159, **368**, 557, 611

life-blood n. 368

life-giving adj. 170

life-guard n. 593

lifeless adj. 174, **369**, 507, 612, 843

lifelike adj. 18, 525

life-line n. 600

life peer n. 870

life science n. 375

lifetime n. 112

life-work n. 557

lift n. 316, 318; vb. 318

lift restrictions vb. 713, 921

ligature n. 49

light n. 797, 800; adj. (not heavy) 331, 333, 344; (of colour) 797, 807

lighted adj. 797

lighten vb. 634, 797, 834

lighter n. 277, 765

light-hearted adj. 836

lighthouse n. 800

lighting n. 797

light music n. 792

lightness n. 331, 797, 807

lightning n. 800

light up vb. 755, 797

like adj. 13, 18; vb. 540, 770, 827, 861, **889**

like clockwork adv. 140

likely adj. 123, 404, **406**, 447; adv. 406

likely to adj. 179

like-minded adj. 24, 424

liken vb. 18, 397

likeness n. **18**, 20, 22, 486, 488

like to vb. 532

liking n. 178, 861, 922

lilac adj. 814

lily-livered adj. 858

limb n. 374

limber adj. 335

lime adj. 812

limerick n. 528

limit n. 89, 233, **235**, 400, 659; vb. 231, **235**, 403, 681

limitation n. 231, 235, 403, 681

limitations n. 700

limited adj. 195, 205, 235

limited space n. **184**

limitless adj. 78, 202

limp adj. 335, 507; vb. 281

limpid adj. 502, 802

line n. 11, 170, 202, 655, 729; vb. 81, 226

lineage n. 11, 170, 171

lineal adj. 171

linearity n. 202

liner n. 277

linger vb. 112, 135, 281

lingua franca n. 492

linguist n. 456, 492

linguistic adj. 450, 492

lining n. **226**

link n. 9, 49; vb. 9, 47, 52, 157, 397

lip reading n. 796

lip service n. 981

liquefaction n. 345

liquefied adj. 343, 345

liquefy vb. 343, 345, 761

liquescent adj. 343

liquid n. 309, **343**, 347; adj. 343, 347

liquidate vb. 164, 370, 739

liquidize vb. 164

liquor n. 343

lisp n. 515; vb. 515

list n. **83**, 97; vb. 38, 83, 483

listen vb. 390, 778, 792, 795

listless adj. 174, 281, **612**, 863

lit adj. 759, 797

litany n. 988

literal n. 431; adj. 456, 493, 494, 977

literature n. 528

lithe adj. 335

lithographer n. 491

lithography n. 490

litigation n. 960

litter n. 576

little adj. 33, 195, 203; adv. 33

little by little adv. 27

liturgical adj. 988

live adj. 172; vb. 1, 188, 191, 368

live apart vb. 898

live comfortably vb. 734

lively adj. 173, 368, **506**, 611, 836

livery n. 227, 677

livestock n. 373

live together vb. 889

live up to vb. 28, 570

live wire n. 611

live with vb. 889

llama n. 275

llano n. 356

load n. 26, 192, 330, 830; vb. 192, 268, 330

loaf about vb. 612

loafer n. 281, 612, 697, 940

loan n. 718, 719, 736; vb. 718

loan-word n. 495

loath adj. 533

loathe vb. 771, 862, 892

loathsome adj. 862, 892

lobby n. 547, 697; vb. 177, 547

local n. 191; adj. 183, 190, 199

locality n. 183, 199

locate vb. 186, 284

location n. 185, **186**

loch n. 353, 354

lock n. 207; vb. 263, 461

locker n. 193

locket n. 216

lock out vb. 144

lock-out n. 99, 144

lock up vb. 234, 681

lock-up n. 682

locomotive n. 276; adj. 276

locust n. 167

lodge n. 191; vb. 186, 191

lodger n. 190, 710

lodging n. 186

lodgings n. 191

loftiness n. 208

lofty adj. 208, 318, 870

log n. 116, 483, 742, 765; vb. 83

logic n. 410

logo n. 482

loiter vb. 281, 612

lone adj. 59

loneliness n. 59, 885

long adj. 182, 202; vb. 443, 854, 861, 889

long-distance adj. 198

long duration n. 112

longhand n. 521

longing n. 854, 861; adj. 861, 889

long-lasting adj. 112

longness n. 202

long-range adj. 198

longsighted adj. 820

long-standing adj. 112

long-suffering n. 757; adj. 670

long-term adj. 112

long-winded adj. 505, 516, 843

look n. 242, 818, 825; vb. 818, 825

look after vb. 392, 593, 599, 676

look back vb. 441

look down on vb. 923, 924

looker-on n. 821

look for vb. 394, 554

look forward to vb. 443

look in vb. 884

looking glass n. 822

look like vb. 18

look out vb. 860

lookout n. 593, 683, 818

look out on vb. 208, 236

look over vb. 208, 818

look through vb. 818

look to vb. 390, 919

loom n. 221; vb. 154, 221, 292, 902

loop n. 250, 251, 322; vb. 251, 273, 323

loophole n. 582, 600

loose adj. 335, 453, 500, 668, 680, 952; vb. 48, 680

loosen vb. 262, 319, 601

loot n. 663, 724; vb. 722

lopsidedness n. 29, 245

loquacious adj. 516

lord n. 675, 870, 967

lord it over vb. 34, 667, 669

Lord's Day n. 616

Lord's Supper n. 988

lore n. 472

lorgnette n. 822

lorry n. 276

lose vb. 116, 187, 662, **706**

lose consciousness vb. 617

lose face vb. 869

lose ground vb. 289, 315

lose heart vb. 837, 855

loser   n. 662
lose weight   vb. 205
loss   n. 43, 189, 369, 569,
   706
lot   n. (many) 26, 32,
   75, 94; (fate) 158; (apportionment) 717
lotion   n. 342, 591
lottery   n. 553
loud   adj. 778, **780**, 787,
   788, 805, 877
loudness   n. 778, **780**,
   877
louse   n. 940
louse up   vb. 628
lousy   adj. 580
lout   n. 437, 630
love   n. 650, **889**, 890,
   891, 922; vb. 827, 861,
   889
love affair   n. 889
love child   n. 955
love letter   n. 523, 890
lovely   adj. 579, 829, 844
lover   n. 889
loving   adj. 670, **889**,
   966
low   adj. 35, **209**, 210,
   781, 837, 849, 869; vb.
   789
lower   adj. 35; vb. 209,
   319, 588, 744
lower class   n. 871
lowland   n. 356
lowlands   n. 209
lowly   adj. 35, 654, 871,
   874
low-lying   adj. 209
lowness   n. **209**, 210
low opinion   n. 923
low-priced   adj. 746
low regard   n. 923
low spirits   n. 837
loyalist   n. 105, 903
loyalty   n. 673, 702, 919,
   931
lozenge   n. 246, 591
LP   n. 794

lubber   n. 630
lubricate   vb. 342, 365
lubrication   n. **342**
lucidity   n. 438, 452,
   502, 802
luck   n. 158, 553, 661,
   664
lucrative   adj. 705
ludicrous   adj. 433, 851
luggage   n. 711
lukewarm   adj. 30, 759,
   863
lull   n. 144, 614; vb. 267
luminary   n. 436, 800
luminous   adj. 797
lump   n. 55, 252, 332
lump together   vb. 399
lunacy   n. 439
lunar   adj. 329
lunate   n. 247; adj. 247
lunatic   n. 440
lunch   n. 306; vb. 304
lunch-break   n. 616
lunch-hour   n. 616
lune   n. 247
lungs   n. 512
lurch   n. 325; vb. 317,
   325
lure   n. 294, 547
lurid   adj. 805, 952
luring   adj. 829
lurk   vb. 459, 461
luscious   adj. 770, 772,
   829
lushness   n. 168
lust   n. 861, 889, 952;
   vb. 861, 914
lustiness   n. 173
lustre   n. 257, 797
luxurious   adj. 168, 734,
   827
luxury   n. 572, 664, 734,
   747, 827, 945
lynch   vb. 370, 963
lyric   n. 528
lyrical   adj. 528, 790

M

mace   n. 677
machinery   n. 565
mad   adj. **439**, 756, 861,
   889, 893
madam   n. 381
madden   vb. 439, 893
made-up   adj. 525
madman   n. **440**
madness   n. 439
magazine   n. 464, 524
magic   n. 984; adj. 579
magistrate   n. 958
magnanimous   adj. 933
magnetic   adj. 294
magnetize   vb. 291
magnification   n. 36
magnificent   adj. 579,
   844, 870
magnify   vb. 36, 196,
   481, 835, 982
magnifying glass   n. 822
magnitude   n. 26, 32,
   400
maid   n. 676
maiden   n. 897; adj. 88
mail   n. 467, 523, 657;
   vb. 268, 523
main   n. 360; adj. 34,
   573
mainland   n. 352
maintain   vb. 91, 143,
   145, 217, 304, 468, 568,
   599, 636, 712, 929
majesty   n. 868, 870, 877
major   adj. 34, 130
majority   n. 72, 75, 133
make   n. 97; vb. 155,
   163, 242, 705
make advances   vb. 882,
   890
make a face   vb. 895
make a fortune   vb. 664,
   734
make a go of   vb. 661

make amends *vb.* 31,
589, 721, 943
make a mess of *vb.* 628
make a mistake *vb.* 431,
500
make an example of *vb.*
963
make a noise *vb.* 778
make a speech *vb.* 514
make-believe *n.* 477;
adj. 449, 477
make certain *vb.* 408
make clear *vb.* 452, 456
make do *vb.* 149, 606,
666
make exceptions *vb.*
403
make excuses *vb.* 549
make eyes at *vb.* 890
make for *vb.* 271, 284
make friends with *vb.*
882
make fun of *vb.* 842,
853
make headway *vb.* 288
make it *vb.* 661
make it up *vb.* 652, 911
make known *vb.* 460,
462, 464
make light of *vb.* 393,
418, 574
make love to *vb.* 889
make nothing of *vb.*
574
make off with *vb.* 722
make one jump *vb.* 444,
856
make one think of *vb.*
441
make out *vb.* 288, 441,
452
make over *vb.* 714
make passes *vb.* 890
make peace *vb.* 652
make plain *vb.* 456,
458, 462
make possible *vb.* 404

make preparations *vb.*
602
make progress *vb.* 288,
587
maker *n.* 166, 967
make sense *vb.* 410,
452, 456
makeshift *adj.* 149, 162,
603
make the best of *vb.*
757
make too much of *vb.*
417, 481
make up *vb.* 58, 163,
449, 477
make-up *n.* 5, 58, 339,
751, 844
make up for *vb.* 31
make up one's mind
vb. 530, 540
malady *n.* 586
malapropism *n.* 433,
497, 500
male *n.* **380**; *adj.* 380
malevolence *n.* **900**,
936
malformed *adj.* 245,
582
malice *n.* 893, 900
malign *vb.* 608, 900,
928, 936
malleable *adj.* 151
maltreat *vb.* 588, 608,
900, 916
mammal *n.* 373
man *n.* 133, 368, 373,
379, 380
manage *vb.* 392, 605,
606, 621, 622, 661, 666,
748
manageable *adj.* 634
management *n.* 392,
606, 609, 621, **622**, 675
management of animals
n. 377
manager *n.* 623, 675,
728
manage to *vb.* 661

mandate *n.* 626, 671,
685
mangled *adj.* 245
manhood *n.* 133, 380
mania *n.* 439
maniac *n.* 175, 440
manifest *adj.* 458, 825;
vb. 401, 413, 458, 482,
823, 825
manifestation *n.* 419,
458, 462
manipulate *vb.* 477, 758
mankind *n.* 379
manliness *n.* 380, 857
manner *n.* 501, 559,
621, 825
mannerism *n.* 501
manners *n.* 886
man of learning *n.* 428,
436, 524
man of many talents *n.*
629
man of means *n.* 734
man of the world *n.* 629
manor *n.* 191
manpower *n.* 619
mansion *n.* 191
manslaughter *n.* 370
manual *n.* 460, 524
manufacture *n.* 163; *vb.*
163
manufacturer *n.* 166
manure *n.* 310; *vb.* 378
manuscript *n.* 483, 521,
524
many *adj.* 72, 75
many-coloured *adj.* 817
many-sided *adj.* 151
map *n.* 269, 460, 486;
vb. 400
mar *vb.* 847
march *vb.* 91, 269, 696
mare *n.* 381
margarine *n.* 306
margin *n.* 44, 182, 200,
233; *vb.* 233
marine *n.* 272; *adj.* 271,
277, 351

mariner

mariner *n.* 272
marital *adj.* 896
maritime *adj.* 271, 277, 351
mark *n.* 97, 202, 235, 400, 441, **483**, 521, 522; *vb.* 382, 390, 482, 483
mark down *vb.* 743, 746
marker *n.* 482
market *n.* 96, 559, 726, 730; *vb.* 377, 725, 727
mark up *vb.* 743
maroon *adj.* 810, 811
marooned *adj.* 713
marquee *n.* 225
marquis *n.* 870
marred *adj.* 588
marriage *n.* 47, **896**
marrow *n.* 224
marry *vb.* 47, 896
marsh *n.* 355
marshal *n.* 958; *vb.* 81
marsupial *n.* 373
martial *adj.* 651
martyr *n.* 980; *vb.* 830, 963
martyrdom *n.* 828
marvel *n.* 866; *vb.* 866
marvellous *adj.* 32, 579, 844, 866
Marxism *n.* 327
mascot *n.* 984
masculine *adj.* 380
mash *vb.* 335, 364
mask *n.* 225, 461, 463, 549; *vb.* 146, 225, 819
mass *n.* 26, 75, 94, 194, 327, 330, 332, 567, 988; *vb.* 75, 192
massacre *n.* 370, 963
massage *vb.* 341, 758
masses *n.* 26, 32, 871
massive *adj.* 32, 204
mast *n.* 208
master *n.* 34, 131, 436, 629, 675; *vb.* 441, 472, 679
masterly *adj.* 579

masterpiece *n.* 488, 581, 844
master-plan *n.* 558
mastery *n.* 501, 707
masticate *vb.* 304
mat *n.* 225
match *n.* 397, 649, 765, 800, 896; *vb.* 24, 28, 61, 218, 397, 896
matchless *adj.* 34
mate *n.* 882, 896; *vb.* 61, 889
material *n.* 192, 327; *adj.* 3, 327
material existence *n.* 3
materialist *n.* 981
materialistic *adj.* 327, 975
materiality *n.* 3, **327**
materialize *vb.* 242, 327, 825, 984
materials *n.* **566**
maternal *adj.* 11, 170
mathematics *n.* 38
matriculate *vb.* 83, 483
matt *adj.* 805
matter *n.* 3, 153, 327, 387, 573; *vb.* 573
matter in hand *n.* 605
matter-of-fact *adj.* 508
matter of life and death *n.* 562
mature *adj.* 133, 426; *vb.* 130, 133, 288, 324, 587, 659
maturity *n.* 126, 130, 133, 581
mauve *adj.* 814
maxim *n.* 103, **432**, 498, 626
maximize *vb.* 417, 481
maximum *n.* 212
mayor *n.* 675
maze *n.* 409
meadow *n.* 356, 378
meagre *adj.* 33, 57, 205, 507, 571
meal *n.* 306, 840

mean *n.* **30**, 90, 560; *adj.* (average) 30, 90; (stingy) 748, 750; (disreputable) 869, 871, 924, 936; (selfish) 934; *vb.* **450**, 459, 482, 552
meander *vb.* 247, 251
meaning *n.* **450**, 552
meaningful *adj.* 450, 514
meaninglessness *n.* **451**, 453
meanness *n.* 750, 887, 934, 936
means *n.* 155, 172, 559, **564**, 566, 711, 734
means of punishment *n.* **964**
meanwhile *adv., prep.* 107
measure *n.* 26, 27, 400, 559, 609; *vb.* 26, 27, 330, 397, 400
measure for measure *n.* 647
measurement *n.* 27, 194, 397, **400**
meat *n.* 306
Mecca *n.* 96
mechanic *n.* 619
mechanical *adj.* 411, 531, 545, 565
mechanism *n.* 565
medal *n.* 482, 663, 872
meddle *vb.* 388, 635, 653
meddler *n.* 388, 821
medial *adj.* 90, 560
median *n.* 30, 90
mediation *n.* 230, 563, **653**
mediator *n.* 653
medicine *n.* 181, 591
mediocre *adj.* 30, 35, 580, **666**, 843
mediocrity *n.* 35, 580, **666**, 843
meditate *vb.* 384, 982

medium *n.* 30, 447, 563, 564, 619; *adj.* 30
medley *n.* 45, 104
meekness *n.* 654, 673, 757, 874, 876
meet *vb.* 94, 153, 201, 296, 419
meet half-way *vb.* 704
meeting *n.* 94, 201, 296, 884
meeting place *n.* 96
melancholy *n.* 828, 837; *adj.* 837
mellow *adj.* 335, 790; *vb.* 130, 587
melodious *adj.* 790
melodrama *n.* 326, 529
melody *n.* **790**
melt *vb.* 345, 761
member *n.* 55, 709
member of parliament *n.* 625
membership *n.* 639
memo *n.* 441, 483
memoirs *n.* 116, 441
memorable *adj.* 441, 790
memorial *n.* 372, 441, 483, 663; *adj.* 441
memorize *vb.* 441, 472
memory *n.* 124, 441
menace *n.* 154, 594, 892, 902; *vb.* 154, 902
mend *vb.* 146, 587, 589
menial *n.* 676; *adj.* 35, 881
meniscus *n.* 247
mensuration *n.* 400
mental *adj.* 382
mental block *n.* 442
mental illness *n.* 439
mention *n.* 460, 663; *vb.* 460, 514
menu *n.* 306
mercantile *adj.* 725
mercenary *n.* 655
merchandise *n.* 163, **729**

merchant *n.* 728
merciful *adj.* 670, 899, 907, 966
merciless *adj.* 908
mercury *n.* 766, 967
mercy *n.* 670, 715, 907, 911
mere *n.* 354; *adj.* 1, 46
merge *vb.* 45, 47, 52, 639
merger *n.* 36, 45, 52, 639
meridian *n.* 127
merit *n.* 575, 579, 917; *vb.* 917
mermaid *n.* 970
merry *adj.* 827, 836
merrymaking *n.* 838
mesh *n.* 221; *vb.* 221
mesmerize *vb.* 984
mess *n.* 80, 204, 628, 845
message *n.* 460, 465, 523
messenger *n.* 275, 460, 467
Messiah *n.* 967
mess up *vb.* 584, 588, 628
messy *adj.* 584
metal *n.* 367
metallic *adj.* 787
metallurgy *n.* 367
metamorphosis *n.* 142
metaphor *n.* 397, 455, 509
metaphysics *n.* 1
meteor *n.* 329, 800
meteorologist *n.* 447
meteorology *n.* 348
mete out *vb.* 715
meter *n.* 400
method *n.* 79, 81, 558, 559, 606
methodical *adj.* 79, 81, 140
meticulous *adj.* 392, 864

metre *n.* 528
metric system *n.* 400
metropolis *n.* 183
metropolitan *n.* 986
mettle *n.* 534, 857
mew *vb.* 789
miaow *vb.* 789
microscope *n.* 822
microscopic *adj.* 195
mid *adj.* 90
mid-course *n.* **560**
midday *n.* 127
middle *n.* 30, **90**, 224; *adj.* 30, 90, 224, 560
middle age *n.* 130
middle class *n.* 871
middleman *n.* 688, 728
middle of the road *adj.* 560
middling *adj.* 30, 579, 666
midget *n.* 195
midnight *n.* 128
midpoint *n.* 30, 90
midsummer *n.* 127
midway *adj.* 560; *adv.* 90
midwinter *n.* 128
mien *n.* 621, 825
might *n.* 32, 159, 161
mighty *adj.* 32, 159, 161
migrant *n.* 100, 270
mild *adj.* 176, 670, 757, 759
mildew *n.* 53, 167, 592
mileage *n.* 198
milieu *n.* 8, 183, 229
militant *n.* 611; *adj.* 148, 611, 644, 651
militate against *vb.* 181
milk *n.* 309; *vb.* 377
milk product *n.* 306
milky *adj.* 804, 807
millenium *n.* 70, 109
million *n.* 70
millionaire *n.* 734
mime *n.* 529
mimic *n.* 20; *vb.* 20

mince *vb.* 306

mind *n.* 382, 530; *vb.* 390, 392, 593

mindful *adj.* 390, 426

mindless *adj.* 383

mind-reader *n.* 447

mine *n.* 210, 254; *vb.* 254, 264, 312

mineral *n.* 367

mingle *vb.* 45

miniature *n.* 195, 488; *adj.* 33, 195

minibus *n.* 276

minimal *adj.* 33

minimize *vb.* 418

mining *n.* 312

minister *n.* 467, 623, 625, 986; *vb.* 589, 636, 676, 988

ministerial *adj.* 985

ministry *n.* 985

minor *n.* 131; *adj.* 33, 35, 129

minority *n.* 76, 129; *adj.* 11

minstrel *n.* 528, 793

mint *n.* 23; *vb.* 731

minus *adj.* 189; *adv.*, *prep.* 42

minute *n.* 109; *adj.* 33, 195; *vb.* 483

minutes *n.* 441, 483

minutiae *n.* 102

miracle *n.* 458, 866

miracle-working *n.* 984

miraculous *adj.* 866

mirage *n.* 4

mire *n.* 355

mirror *n.* 822; *vb.* 20, 486

mirth *n.* 836, 838

misadventure *n.* 153, 662, 665

misanthropy *n.* 904

misapprehend *vb.* 416

misappropriation *n.* 608, 722

misbehaviour *n.* 672, 887, 938

miscalculation *n.* 412, 416

miscarriage *n.* 445

miscarriage of justice *n.* 955

miscarry *vb.* 662

miscellany *n.* 45, 104, 527

mischief *n.* 900

mischief-maker *n.* 906

misconception *n.* 416, 431, 457

misconduct *n.* 938

misconstrue *vb.* 416, 457

misdate *vb.* 117

misdemeanour *n.* 938

misdirection *n.* 285, 471

misemployment *n.* 608

miser *n.* 750

miserable *adj.* 828, 837

miserly *adj.* 571, 750, 934

misery *n.* 828, 837, 841

misfire *n.* 628

misfit *n.* 10

misfortune *n.* 153, 551, 665, 900

misgiving *n.* 409, 421, 833

misgovern *vb.* 668

misguidance *n.* 471

misguided *adj.* 285

mishandle *vb.* 608, 628

mishap *n.* 153

mishmash *n.* 45

misinform *vb.* 471

misinstruction *n.* 471

misinterpretation *n.* 412, 416, 451, 457, 487

misjudgment *n.* 416, 431, 481

mislay *vb.* 187, 706

mislead *vb.* 431, 471, 477, 478

mismanagement *n.* 431, 608, 628

misnomer *n.* 497

misogynist *n.* 904

misplace *vb.* 187, 706

misprint *n.* 431

mispronunciation *n.* 500, 515

misquote *vb.* 457

misrepresentation *n.* 471, 477, 478, 481, 487

miss *n.* 131, 381; *vb.* 137, 315, 391, 393, 660, 662, 706

misshapen *adj.* 243, 245, 845

missile *n.* 290

missing *adj.* 189, 315, 571, 600, 706, 826

missing link *n.* 92, 324

mission *n.* 557, 651, 685, 688, 990

missionary *n.* 903, 974

mist *n.* 4, 346, 358, 363, 803

mistake *n.* 431, 457, 471, 500, 582, 608; *vb.* 497

mistaken *adj.* 285, 431

mistiming *n.* 117, 137

mistranslation *n.* 457

mistreat *vb.* 608

mistress *n.* 675, 889, 953

mistrust *n.* 421; *vb.* 421

misty *adj.* 349, 363, 799, 803

misunderstanding *n.* 25, 416, 431, 457, 642

misusage *n.* 500

misuse *n.* 569, 608; *vb.* 588, 608

mite *n.* 131

mitigate *vb.* 176, 403, 591, 834

mitigation *n.* 636, 834

mitre *n.* 989

mix *vb.* **45**, 52, 58, 82, 399

mixed up *adj.* 80, 453

mixer *n.* 884

mixture *n.* 45, 52, 104, 591

mix-up *n.* 80

mnemonic *n.* 441

moan *vb.* 788, 832

moat *n.* 234, 261, 360, 646

mob *n.* 75, 94; *vb.* 175, 888

mobile *adj.* 142, 151, 266

mobilization *n.* 94, 651

mob rule *n.* 668, 955

mock *adj.* 18, 20, 149; *vb.* 853, 869, 924, 928

mocker *n.* 928, 981

mockery *n.* 477, 853

mock-up *n.* 23

modal *adj.* 8

mode *n.* 7, 545, 850

model *n.* 22, 486, 581, 939; *vb.* 23, 242, 489

modeller *n.* 491

moderate *adj.* 176, 560, 746, 757, 944; *vb.* 142, **176**, 403, 652

moderation *n.* 176, 944

modern *adj.* 120, 125, 850

modernization *n.* 125, 587, 589

modest *adj.* 33, 176, 418, 508, 517, 874, **876**

modesty *n.* 508, 517, 874, **876**

modify *vb.* 15, 142, 335, 403

modulation *n.* 142

module *n.* 279

moist *adj.* 347, 349, 358

moisten *vb.* 349

moisture *n.* 346, 349

molecule *n.* 327

mollify *vb.* 176, 335, 652

molten *adj.* 343, 345, 759

moment *n.* 115, 573

momentary *adj.* 113

momentous *adj.* 136, 177, 573

momentum *n.* 282

monarchic *adj.* 870

monastery *n.* 990

money *n.* 731, 734

money-lender *n.* 718

mongol *n.* 440

mongrel *n.* 45; *adj.* 45

monitor *vb.* 394

monk *n.* 885, 986

monocle *n.* 822

monograph *n.* 526

monologue *n.* **520**

monopolize *vb.* 707

monopoly *n.* 681

monotony *n.* 16, 91, 841

monsoon *n.* 358

monster *n.* 175, 194, 906

monstrous *adj.* 845, 936

month *n.* 109

monthly *adv.* 140

monument *n.* 372, 441, 483

moo *vb.* 789

mooch about *vb.* 612

mood *n.* 5, 751

moody *adj.* 756, 894, 895

moon *n.* 329, 800

moor *n.* 208, 355, 356; *vb.* 186, 271, 298

moot *adj.* 409

moot point *n.* 387

mop *vb.* 583

mope *vb.* 837, 895

moral *n.* 432; *adj.* 931, 935

moralize *vb.* 470

moral obligation *n.* 919

moratorium *n.* 135

more *adj.* 72

moreish *adj.* 770

moreover *adv.* 40

more than enough *n.* 572

morgue *n.* 372

moribund *adj.* 130, 369

morning *n.* **127**; *adj.* 127

moron *n.* 437, 440

moroseness *n.* 895

morphology *n.* 242, 499

morsel *n.* 33, 306

mortal *n.* 368, 379; *adj.* 369, 370, 379

mortgage *n.* 701, 718

mortgagee *n.* 736

mortgagor *n.* 737

mortification *n.* 874, 946

mortuary *n.* 372

mosaic *n.* 817

mosque *n.* 990

motel *n.* 191

moth *n.* 167

mothball *vb.* 135

moth-eaten *adj.* 126

mother *n.* 11, 170; *vb.* 676

motion *n.* **266**; *vb.* 482

motionless *adj.* 174, 267

motivate *vb.* 155, 547

motivator *n.* 547

motive *n.* 8, 155, **547**

motley *adj.* 17, 45, 104, 817

motor *n.* 276; *vb.* 269

motorcycle *n.* 276

motoring *n.* 269

motorist *n.* 270

motorway *n.* 559

mottled *adj.* 817

motto *n.* 432

mould *n.* 23, 53, 339, 592; *vb.* 146, 242, 489

mouldable *adj.* 242, 335, 654

mount *n.* 316; *vb.* 32, 208, 316

mountain *n.* 208, 316

mourn *vb.* 828, 833, 837

mournful *adj.* 372, 828, 839, 895

mouth *n.* 262, 353

mouthful *n.* 26, 306

mouthpiece *n.* 514, 689

mouth-watering *adj.* 770

movable *adj.* 142, 266, 268

move *n.* 266, 609; *vb.* 172, 187, 266, 268, 282, 290, 299, 693, 752, 755

moved *adj.* 189, 752, 756

movement *n.* 266, 268, 641, 792

move on *vb.* 288

mover *n.* 166

moving *adj.* 752, 755

mow *vb.* 378

mow down *vb.* 370

Mr. X *n.* 497

much *adj.* 75; *adv.* 32

muck *n.* 576, 584

muckraker *n.* 516, 928

mucky *adj.* 584

mud *n.* 355

muddle *n.* 80; *vb.* 82, 399

muddler *n.* 630

muddle through *vb.* 666

muddy *adj.* 355, 584, 803

mud-slinging *n.* 928

muffle *vb.* 513, 779, 785

muffled *adj.* 781, 785

mugging *n.* 645, 722

muggy *adj.* 349, 759

mulch *n.* 364

mule *n.* 537

mull *vb.* 384

multi-coloured *adj.* 817

multifarious *adj.* 104

multilateral *adj.* 246

multiple *n.* 730; *adj.* 39, 72

multiplication *n.* 38

multiplicity *n.* 72, 75

multiply *vb.* 36, 38, 163, 165, 835

multisection *n.* 71

multi-storey *adj.* 208

multitude *n.* 75

mum *n.* 170; *adj.* 513, 517

mumble *vb.* 515

mumbo-jumbo *n.* 967, 983, 984

mummify *vb.* 372, 599

mundane *adj.* 327, 329

municipal *adj.* 183

munificent *adj.* 747

munitions *n.* 657

mural *n.* 488

murder *n.* 370; *vb.* 370

murderer *n.* 167, 370, 906

murky *adj.* 363, 798, 803, 808

murmur *n.* 781; *vb.* 696, 781

muscle *n.* 159, 161

muse *vb.* 384, 449

museum *n.* 567

mush *n.* 364

music *n.* 790, **792**

musical instrument *n.* **794**

musician *n.* 793

must *n.* 531, 562

mustard *n.* 307

muster *vb.* 94, 651, 857

musty *adj.* 777

mutability *n.* 151

mutation *n.* 142

mute *adj.* 513, 517, 781; *vb.* 513, 779

muteness *n.* 513

mutilate *vb.* 164, 845

mutineer *n.* 672

mutiny *n.* 644, 672, 920; *vb.* 672, 920

mutter *n.* 781; *vb.* 515, 781

mutual *adj.* 9, 12, 150, 180

muzzle *vb.* 681

myriads *n.* 75

mystery *n.* 427, 453, 466

mystic *adj.* 984

myth *n.* 525

mythical being *n.* **970**

N

nag *vb.* 893

nail *n.* 255; *vb.* 47

naive *adj.* 131, 422, 632

naked *adj.* 228, 594

name *n.* 482, 494, 496, 868, 872; *vb.* 482, 496

nanny *n.* 683

nanny-goat *n.* 381

nap *n.* 612

narcissism *n.* 875, 934

narrate *vb.* 460, 525

narrative *n.* 525; *adj.* 525

narrow *adj.* 205, 416, 681, 934; *vb.* 27, 681

narrow-mindedness *n.* 416, 537

narrowness *n.* 205, 416, 934

narrows *n.* 205, 353

nasalization *n.* 515

nasty *adj.* 580, 777, 887

nation *n.* 379

national *n.* 190; *adj.* 190, 379

nationality *n.* 379

nationalization *n.* 709

native *n.* 190; *adj.* 5, 190

nativity n. 155
natural adj. 3, 508, 632, 955
natural history n. 366
naturalized adj. 100, 190
nature n. 5, 58, 329, 366, 751
naturism n. 228
naughty adj. 672, 901
nausea n. 303
nautical adj. 271, 277
naval adj. 271, 277
navigate vb. 271
navy n. 655
near adj. 154, 199, 419; vb. 154, 292
nearby adj. 199; adv. 199
nearly adv. 199
nearness n. 199, 292
nearside adj. 241
neat adj. 79, 392, 579, 583
nebula n. 329
nebulous adj. 363, 798, 824
necessary adj. 531, 562, 674, 919
necessities n. 8
necessity n. 408, 531, 543, 562, 674
neck n. 205, 352; vb. 890
nectar n. 770
need n. 57, 189, 315, 562, 674, 861; vb. 76, 315, 531, 562, 571, 861
needle n. 255, 264, 482; vb. 830, 893
needlework n. 846
needy adj. 735, 917
negation n. 469
negative n. 23, 425; adj. 39, 469
neglect n. 385, 391, 393, 546, 610, 660, 662, 672, 703, 920; vb. 391, 393,

546, 607, 660, 662, 672, 703, 920
negligent adj. 391, 393, 703, 920
negligible adj. 76
negotiable adj. 714
negotiate vb. 519, 653, 700, 704, 725
neigh vb. 789
neighbour n. 882
neighbourhood n. 183, 199
neighbouring adj. 199
neighbourly adj. 884, 899
neologism n. 494, **495**
nephew n. 11
nerve n. 880
nerveless adj. 160
nerves n. 439, 856
nervous adj. 326, 756, 856, 894
nervousness n. 439, 856, 876, 894
nest n. 595
net n. 221, 463
nether adj. 209
netting n. 221
network n. 221
neurotic n. 440
neutral n. 653, 656; adj. 90, 541, 560, 863
neutrality n. 541, 863, 933
neutralize vb. 31, 181, 648
never adv. 108
new adj. 40, 125, 134, 603
newborn adj. 131
newcomer n. 100, 474
newest adj. 120
newly adv. 125
newly-wed adj. 896
newness n. 21, **125**
news n. 460, 465
newspaper n. 464, 483
next adj. 85, 119, 199

nibble n. 304, 306
nice adj. 770, 829, 864
niche n. 184, 254
nick n. 259, 682; vb. 259, 722
nickname n. 496, 497; vb. 497
nicotine n. 308
niece n. 11
niggardly adj. 750
nigh adv. 199
night n. 128, 798; adj. 128
nightfall n. 128, 798
nightmare n. 449, 830
nihilist n. 167
nil n. 74
nimble adj. 280, 611, 842
nimbus n. 800
nine n. 70
nip n. 760; vb. 197, 203
no n. 425
nobility n. 34, **870**
noble adj. 32, 318, 868, 870
nobody n. 74
nocturnal adj. 128
nod n. 424, 482, 612, 690; vb. 325, 482
node n. 49
nod off vb. 612
noise n. 778, 780, 788, 791
noiseless adj. 779
noisome adj. 777
nomad n. 270
nomadic adj. 266
nom de plume n. 497
nomenclature n. 496
nominal adj. 496
nominate vb. 496, 540, 685, 985
nominee n. 688
non-acceptance n. 425, 926
non-adhesive adj. 51
non aggressive adj. 650

nonce adj. 495
nonchalant adj. 757
non-combatant n. **656**
non-completion n. **660**
nonconformist n. 106,
425, 979; adj. 25, 106,
979
none n. 74
nonentity n. 2, 574
non-existence n. 2
non-expectation n. 444
non-flammable adj. 762
non-imitation n. 21
non-material existence
n. 4
non-observance n. 672,
703, 920
non-payment n. **739**
non-possession n. **708**
non-preparation n. 603
non-resonance n. 785
non-retention n. 713
nonsense n. 433, 451,
516
non sequitur n. 412
non-starter n. 662
non-stop adj. 138
non-uniformity n.   17,
29
noon n. 127
no one n. 74
noose n. 463, 964
norm n. 30, 103
normal adj. 438, 545
normalize vb. 16
normative adj. 103
north n. 284
nostalgia n. 861
nosy adj. 388, 394
notable adj. 32,   573,
868
notary n. 959
notation n. 39
notch n. **259**; vb. 258,
259
note n. 41, 441, 456,
460, 482, 483, 523, 778;
vb. 382, 390, **483**

nothing n. 74
notice n. 390, 460, 464,
482, 597, 624, 818; vb.
390, 818
noticeable adj. 458, 823
notify vb. 460, 464, 597,
624
notion n. 386, 420, 448,
449
notorious adj. 426, 869
nought n. 74
noun n. 499
nourish vb. 304
nourishing adj. 585
novel n. 525; adj. 125
novelist n. 521, 524, 525
novelty n. 21, 125, 142
novice n. 474, 630
now adv. 120
nowadays adv. 120
no way adv. 405
noxious adj. 777
nuance n. 27
nucleus n. 224
nude n. 228; adj. 228
nudge n. 482; vb. 482
nuisance n. 551, 830
null adj. 74
nullify vb. 2, 164, 469,
686
numb adj. 754; vb. 754
number n. 26, 39, 72,
499; vb. 38, 482
numbering n. 38
numbing adj. 760
numeral n. 39
numeration n. 38
numerous adj. 32, 72,
75
nun n. 986
nunnery n. 990
nuptial adj. 896
nurse n. 676, 683; vb.
304, 589, 676
nursery n. 378, 475
nurture vb. 304, 470,
712
nut n. 49, 306, 440

nutrition n. 304, 306
nutritious adj. 306, 585
nymph n. 970

O

oaf n. 437
oafish adj. 435
oath n. 468, 901
obdurate adj. 537, 942
obedience n. 654, 673,
702, 874
obedient adj. 654, 673,
702, 919
obesity n. 194
obey vb. 105, 654, 673,
874
obituary n. 369, 372
object n. 327, 552, 716;
vb. 25, 425, 637, 642,
696, 892, 926
objection n. 425, 696,
926
objectionable adj. 862,
926
objective n. 298, 552;
adj. 3, 6, 327, 430, 933
obligation n. 531, 562,
605, 674, 737, 919
oblige vb. 674, 919
obliged adj. 909, 919
obliging adj. 886, 899
oblique adj. 219; vb.
531
obliteration n. 164, 485
oblivion n. 442
oblivious adj. 393, 442,
754
oblong n. 246
obscene adj. 901, 952
obscure adj. 453, 503,
798, 799, 824; vb. 461,
798, 799
obscurity n. 453, 503,
799, 803, 824

obsequious *adj.* 881, 886

observable *adj.* 458, 823

observance *n.* 702, 878, 977, 988

observant *adj.* 390, 702, 818

observation *n.* 101, 384, 386, 390, 396, 818

observatory *n.* 329

observe *vb.* 105, 390, 392, 673, 702, 818, 878, 988

observer *n.* 460, 821

obsess *vb.* 830, 984

obsessed *adj.* 439

obsolete *adj.* 2, 126

obstacle *n.* 635, 681

obstinacy *n.* 537, 644

obstinate *adj.* 143, 535, 537

obstruct *vb.* 265, 635, 637, 648, 691

obtain *vb.* 1, 661, 705, 716, 720, 726

obtainable *adj.* 292, 404, 464, 705

obtrusive *adj.* 253, 877

obtuse *adj.* 256

obtuse angle *n.* 246

obvious *adj.* 452, 458, 502, 634, 823

occasion *n.* 136, 155, 878; *vb.* 155

occasionally *adv.* 138, 139

occult *adj.* 984

occupancy *n.* 188, 707

occupation *n.* 557, 605

occupier *n.* 190, 710

occupy *vb.* 107, 188, 191, 557, 707

occur *vb.* 1, 107, 153, 384, 430, 825

ocean *n.* 351

octagon *n.* 70, 246

octave *n.* 70

octet *n.* 70

odd *adj.* 29, 39, 439

oddity *n.* 439, 866

odds *n.* 158

ode *n.* 528

odious *adj.* 892

odorous *adj.* 774, 776

odour *n.* 774

of course *adv.* 408

off *adj.* 53, 240; *adv.* 614

offal *n.* 310

offence *n.* 923, 938, 955

offend *vb.* 892, 923

offender *n.* 906

offensive *n.* 645; *adj.* 295, 777, 845, 869, 880, 887, 892, 923, 936

offer *n.* 693, 695; *vb.* 532, 693, 715

offering *n.* 715, 943

offertory *n.* 715

offhand *adj.* 544, 887

office *n.* 557, 620, 985

office-boy *n.* 467

officer *n.* 625, 675, 956

official *n.* 623, 675, 683; *adj.* 430, 557, 622, 667

officious *adj.* 880

offset *n.* 31; *vb.* 31

off-shoot *n.* 979

offside *adj.* 240

offspring *n.* 11, 171

often *adv.* 138

ogle *vb.* 818, 890

oil *n.* 306, 342, 365, 765; *vb.* 342, 365, 547

oiliness *n.* 365, 886

oily *adj.* 257, 365, 477

ointment *n.* 342, 365, 591

O.K. *adj.* 579; *adv.* 79

old *adj.* 124, 126, 130, 606

old-fashioned *adj.* 126

old maid *n.* 897, 951

old master *n.* 488

oldness *n.* 126, 130

olive *adj.* 812

olive branch *n.* 652

omen *n.* 447, 597

ominous *adj.* 154, 447, 594, 902

omission *n.* 57, 99, 393, 431, 662, 703, 920

omitted *adj.* 189

omnibus *n.* 524; *adj.* 54

omnipotent *adj.* 159, 966

on *adv.* 288; *adv.*, *prep.* 9

on and on *adv.* 114

once *adj.* 124

one *n.* 59; *adj.* 13, 59

on edge *adj.* 443, 856

on end *adj.* 214

oneness *n.* 13, 59

onerous *adj.* 615

one-sided *adj.* 416

one-time *adj.* 118, 124, 687

ongoing *adj.* 288

onlooker *n.* 821

only *adj.* 46, 59

onomatopoeia *n.* 455

onset *n.* 88, 298

onslaught *n.* 175, 645, 649

on time *adj.* 134, 136

ontological *adj.* 1

onus *n.* 919

onward *adv.* 288

ooze *vb.* 301, 319

opacity *n.* 803

opal glass *n.* 804

opaque *adj.* 799, 803

open *adj.* 262, 348, 409, 458, 462, 476, 508, 632, 753, 823; *vb.* 88, 182, 262, 348

open-handed *adj.* 747, 965

opening *n.* 88, 254, 262, 462, 518; *adj.* 88

openness *n.* 476, 594

open up *vb.* 462

P

palaver *n.* 516

pale *adj.* 371, 806, 807, 812

palindrome *n.* 220

paling *n.* 234

pall *n.* 372

palliate *vb.* 591

pallid *adj.* 806

pally *adj.* 882

palm *n.* 663

palmist *n.* 447

palpable *adj.* 758

palpitate *vb.* 326, 756, 783

palpitation *n.* 325

palsy *n.* 326

paltry *adj.* 574, 580

pampa *n.* 356

pamphlet *n.* 464

panacea *n.* 591

pandemonium *n.* 780, 973

panel *n.* 206, 625, 688, 958

pang *n.* 828, 833

panic *n.* 615, 856; *vb.* 856

pannier *n.* 193

panoply *n.* 657

panorama *n.* 54, 818

pansy *n.* 162, 814, 953

pant *n.* 359; *vb.* 359, 756

pantheism *n.* 974

pantheon *n.* 967

pantomime *n.* 529

pantry *n.* 305

pap *n.* 364

paper *n.* 460, 518, 521, 526; *vb.* 225

paperback *n.* 524

par *n.* 30

parable *n.* 455, 525

parabola *n.* 247

parabolic *adj.* 455, 525

parachute *n.* 273, 317

parade *n.* 458, 825, 877; *vb.* 91, 458, 877

paradise *n.* 449, 827, 972

paragon *n.* 581, 939

parallel *n.* 397; *adj.* 28, 218; *vb.* 218, 397

parallelism *n.* 218, 397

parallelogram *n.* 218, 246

paralysis *n.* 754

paralyze *vb.* 160, 754

paramount *adj.* 34, 573

paranoid *n.* 440

paranormal *adj.* 447

paraphernalia *n.* 568, 711

paraphrase *vb.* 20, 456

parapsychology *n.* 447

parasite *n.* 373, 612, 881

parasol *n.* 225, 801

parcel *n.* 193, 717; *vb.* 234, 717

parch *vb.* 350, 759

parchment *n.* 521

pardon *vb.* 601, 670, 680, 907, 911, 961

pare *vb.* 203, 228

parent *n.* 11, 86, 170

parenthood *n.* 170

parish *n.* 183, 987

parishioner *n.* 987

parity *n.* 28

park *n.* 234, 559; *vb.* 186

parliament *n.* 625

parochial *adj.* 183

parody *n.* 20, 487, 853

parrot *n.* 20; *vb.* 20

parse *vb.* 499

parsimony *n.* 748, 750

parson *n.* 986

part *n.* 55, 73, 327, 529, 717; *vb.* 48, 55, 637, 642, 898

partake *vb.* 304, 709

partial *adj.* 55, 73, 660, 861, 916

participant *n.* 619, 709

participate *vb.* 605, 639, 709

participation *n.* 188, 639, 709

participle *n.* 499

particle *n.* 33, 195, 340, 499

particular *adj.* 5, 8, 102, 392, 398, 864

particularize *vb.* 102

particularly *adv.* 34

parting *n.* 48, 299, 369, 642

partisan *adj.* 641, 916, 979

partition *n.* 230; *vb.* 48

partly *adv.* 55

partner *n.* 640, 709, 710, 896

partnership *n.* 60, 180, 639, 709

part of speech *n.* 499

part with *vb.* 556, 713

party *n.* 94, 641, 655, 840, 884, 896, 950, 960

party-minded *adj.* 979

pass *n.* 200, 690, 890; *vb.* 107, 110, 310, 313, 424, 427, 954

passable *adj.* 579, 666

passage *n.* 200, 262, 266, 313, 360, 559, 792

pass away *vb.* 369

passé adj. 126

passenger *n.* 270

passer-by *n.* 821

pass for *vb.* 18

passing *n.* 369

passion *n.* 752, 889, 893

passionate *adj.* 506, 752, 759, 889

passive *n.* 499; *adj.* 174

pass on *vb.* 714

pass out *vb.* 617

pass over *vb.* 393, 670, 920

passport *n.* 690

pass sentence *vb.* 960

password *n.* 690
past *n.* 124: *adj.* 118, 124
paste *n.* 49, 362, 364; *vb.* 50
pastel *adj.* 805
pasteurize *vb.* 583
pastime *n.* 840
pastor *n.* 986
pastry *n.* 306
pasturage *n.* 305
pasture *n.* 305, 352, 356, 374
pasty *adj.* 806
pat *vb.* 758, 890
patch *n.* 183, 378; *vb.* 589
patched *adj.* 126, 817
patent *adj.* 458, 823
paternal *adj.* 11, 170
path *n.* 559
patience *n.* 757, 911
patient *adj.* 654, 757
patio *n.* 184
patisserie *n.* 306
patriarch *n.* 11, 132, 986
patrimony *n.* 11
patriotic *adj.* 903
patrol *n.* 593, 655, 683; *vb.* 593
patron *n.* 217, 545, 640, 726, 905
patronage *n.* 636, 726
patronize *vb.* 636, 726
patronizing *adj.* 873, 886
patter *vb.* 358, 783
pattern *n.* 23, 58, 79, 339, 488; *vb.* 81
pauper *n.* 735
pause *n.* 92, 144, 267, 612, 614, 616; *vb.* 92, 144, 267, 610, 612
pave *vb.* 225
paw *vb.* 758
pawn *n.* 701; *vb.* 701, 719

pawnbroker *n.* 718
pay *n.* 731, 738, 965; *vb.* 726, 738, 740, 965
payable *adj.* 737, 917
pay attention *vb.* 390
pay back *vb.* 647
payee *n.* 716
paymaster *n.* 733
payment *n.* 726, 738, 740, 965
payroll *n.* 619, 738
peace *n.* 267, 650, 779, 831
peaceful *adj.* 267, 616, 643, 650, 831
peace-maker *n.* 653, 656
peace-offering *n.* 652
peace of mind *n.* 757, 831
peach *n.* 816, 844
peak *n.* 89, 212
peal *vb.* 780, 783
pearly *adj.* 804, 807
peasant *n.* 378, 871; *adj.* 378
pebble *n.* 352
peculiar *adj.* 102, 106, 439
pedagogics *n.* 470
pedagogy *n.* 470
pedant *n.* 537, 864
pedantic *adj.* 392, 702, 864
peddle *vb.* 727
pedestal *n.* 213
pedestrian *n.* 270
pedlar *n.* 270, 697, 728
peek *n.* 818
peel *n.* 225; *vb.* 228
peel off *vb.* 51
peep *n.* 818; *vb.* 818
Peeping Tom *n.* 795, 821
peer *n.* 28, 122, 870
peg out *vb.* 617
pejorative *adj.* 923, 928
pellucid *adj.* 502, 802

pelt *vb.* 280
pen *n.* 184, 234; *vb.* 521
penalty *n.* 963
penance *n.* 943
penchant *n.* 178, 545
pencil *n.* 797; *vb.* 488
penda..t *n.* 216, 482
pendulum *n.* 216, 325
penetrability *n.* 335
penetrate *vb.* 300, 313, 441, 452
penetrating *adj.* 384, 434, 769, 787
penetration *n.* 300, 434
pen-friend *n.* 523
peninsula *n.* 352
penitence *n.* 833, 941
pennant *n.* 482
penniless *adj.* 708, 735
penny-pinching *n.* 750; *adj.* 750
pen-pal *n.* 523
pension *n.* 191, 687
pension off *vb.* 686
pensive *adj.* 384, 837
pentagon *n.* 70, 246
pent-up *adj.* 681
penumbra *n.* 798
people *n.* 379, 871; *vb.* 191
pep *n.* 173
pepper *n.* 307; *vb.* 307
perceive *vb.* 382, 419, 426, 452, 795, 818
perceptible *adj.* 458, 823
perception *n.* 382, 384, 752, 818
perceptive *adj.* 398, 426, 434
perch *vb.* 319
percolate *vb.* 300, 319
percussion *n.* 794
perennial *adj.* 114, 138
perfect *adj.* 581, 659, 937, 951; *vb.* 56, 581, 659

perfection n. **581**, 659, 937, 951

perfectionist n. 864

perforation n. 262, 264

perforator n. **264**

perform vb. 163, 172, 529, 609, 659, 702, 792, 919, 988

performance n. 163, 172, 529, 609, 659, 702

performer n. 529, 609, 619, 793

perfume n. 776; vb. 776

peril n. 594

perimeter n. 232, 250

period n. **109**

periodic adj. 109, 138, 140

periodical n. 464, 524; adj. 140

peripatetic adj. 269

periphery n. 232, 250

periphrastic adj. 505

perish vb. 164, 369, 826

perishable adj. 113

perjury n. 477

perk up vb. 618, 836

permanence n. 112, **143**, 152

permeable adj. 264

permeate vb. 45, 319

permissible adj. 954

permission n. 424, **690**, 692, 921, 925

permissive society n. 952

permit n. 690; vb. 690, 954

permutation n. 142

pernickety adj. 864

perpendicular adj. 214, 248

perpetual adj. 78, 91, 114

perpetuate vb. 114

perpetuation n. 91, 145

perpetuity n. 78, 91, 114

perplex vb. 409, 633

perplexing adj. 409, 633

persecute vb. 900

perseverance n. 534, 535, 611, 980

persevere vb. 145, 535, 611, 648, 980

persist vb. 112, 143, 145, 535, 695

persistence n. 145, 534, 535

person n. 368, 379, 499

personal adj. 379, 966

personal effects n. 711

personality n. 5, 58, 382, 751

personification n. 455, 486

personnel n. 619, 676

perspective n. 488, 818

perspicacity n. 434

perspicuity n. 502

perspiration n. 310

persuade vb. 177, 420, 547, 624

persuasion n. 420, 547

perturb vb. 82

peruse vb. 394

perverse adj. 936

perversion n. 412, 457, 471, 477, 487, 608, 978

perversity n. 936

pervert n. 953; vb. 431, 457, 487, 588, 608

perverted adj. 936

pessimism n. 418, 443, 855

pest n. 892

pester vb. 695, 830

pestilence n. 167

pestilent adj. 592

pet n. 373, 891; vb. 890

petal n. 374

peter out vb. 37

petition n. 394, 695, 982; vb. 394, 695, 982

petitioner n. **697**, 982

petrify vb. 332, 334, 856

petrol n. 342, 765

petty adj. 416, 574

phantom n. 971; adj. 971

Pharisee n. 981

pharmaceutical n. 591

phase n. 109; vb. 558

phasing n. 140

phenomenal adj. 866

phenomenon n. 153, 825, 866

philanthropy n. 899, **903**

philosopher n. 428

philosophic adj. 757

philosophize vb. 384, 410

phlegmatic adj. 757

phobia n. 439

phoneme n. 512

phonetics n. 492, 512, 778

phoney n. 480; adj. 20

phosphorescence n. 797

photograph n. 483, 486; vb. 483

photographer n. 491

photography n. 486

phrase n. 494, **498**, 792; vb. 498

phraseology n. 501

physical adj. 3, 327, 827

physiognomy n. 236

physiology n. 366, 375

piazza n. 559

pick vb. 378, 398, 540

picket vb. 144, 696

pickle n. 307, 633; vb. 599

pick-me-up n. 173, 591

pick on vb. 830

pick-pocket n. 723; vb. 722

pick up vb. 318, 472, 587, 589, 618

picnic n. 269, 306, 840

pictogram n. 493

pictorial *adj.* 488, 525

picture *n.* 397, 486, 488, 525; *vb.* 449, 486, 525

picturesque *adj.* 488, 829

piece *n.* 55, 59, 306, 717, 792

pièce de résistance n. 581

piecemeal *adv.* 55

pier *n.* 213, 217

pierce *vb.* 264

piercing *adj.* 255, 760, 780, 787

piety *n.* **980**

pig *n.* 948

pigment *n.* 805

pigmy *n.* 195

pile *n.* 217, 567; *vb.* 192

pile-up *n.* 282

pile up *vb.* 94, 567

pilfer *vb.* 722

pilferer *n.* 723

pilgrim *n.* 270, 980

pilgrimage *n.* 269

pill *n.* 591

pillage *n.* 722; *vb.* 164, 722

pillar *n.* 152, 208, 217, 939

pillow *n.* 217

pilot *n.* 272, 273, 277, 396; *vb.* 271, 273

pilot scheme *n.* 396, 558

pimple *n.* 252

pin *n.* 255, 264

pinch *vb.* 197, 722

pine *vb.* 861

pink *adj.* 811

pinnacle *n.* 212

pin-up *n.* 844

pioneer *n.* 86, 125, 190; *vb.* 84

pious *adj.* 980

pip *n.* 306

pipe *n.* 308, 360; *vb.* 789

pipe-dreaming *n.* 449, 854

pipeline *n.* 360

piquancy *n.* 506, 769

pirate *n.* 723

pirouette *n.* 323; *vb.* 323

pit *n.* 210, 254, 658

pitch *n.* 234, 321, 365, 400, 512; *vb.* 290

pitfall *n.* 463, **596**

pith *n.* 224

pithy *adj.* 432, 450, 504

pitiable *adj.* 907

pitiful *adj.* 33, 580, 907

pitilessness *n.* **908**

pity *n.* **907**; *vb.* 907, 924

pivot *n.* 90, 217; *vb.* 323

pivotal *adj.* 224

pixie *n.* 970

placard *n.* 464

placate *vb.* 176, 652

place *n.* 184, 185, 186, 559; *vb.* 186

placement *n.* 85, 186

place of business *n.* 730

place of learning *n.* 475

placid *adj.* 267, 757

plagiarize *vb.* 20

plague *n.* 167, 592, 665; *vb.* 314, 830

plain *n.* 356; *adj.* 46, 452, 476, 502, **508**, 823

plain living *n.* 946

plainness *n.* 46, 452, **508**, 823

plain speech *n.* 452, 502, 508

plaintiff *n.* 930, 960

plait *n.* 49, 221, 251; *vb.* 221, 251

plan *n.* 23, 81, 386, 552, **558**, 602, 605; *vb.* 58, 81, 552, **558**, 602

plane *n.* 215, 278; *vb.* 215, 257

planet *n.* 329, 800

planetarium *n.* 329

planned *adj.* 543, 552, 558

plant *n.* 307, 374, 620; *vb.* 378

plantation *n.* 374, 378

planter *n.* 378

plants *n.* 366

plaque *n.* 489

plastic *adj.* 142, 151, 242, 335, 768

plastic surgery *n.* 844

plate *n.* 23, 193, 206, 490; *vb.* 225

plateau *n.* 356

platitude *n.* 432, 451

platonic *adj.* 951

plausible *adj.* **404**, 406, 420, 825, 929

play *n.* 529, 678, 840; *vb.* 477, 529, 792, 797

play-acting *n.* 852

play down *vb.* 418, 574, 928

player *n.* 529, 793

playful *adj.* 836

play games *vb.* 840

playground *n.* 658

playhouse *n.* 529

play on words *n.* 454, 842

plea *n.* 401, 549, 695, 929, 960

plead *vb.* 410, 514, 695, 959

plead guilty *vb.* 462, 941

pleadings *n.* 960

pleasant *adj.* 827, 829, 840

please *vb.* 829

pleased *adj.* 756, 827, 831, 909

pleased with oneself *adj.* 873

please onself *vb.* 678

pleasing *adj.* 790, 792, 829, 844

pleasurableness *n.* **829**

pleasure   n. 827, 840

pleasure trip   n. 840

pleat   n. 260; vb. 260

plebeian   n. 871; adj. 849, 871

plebiscite   n. 540

pledge   n. 468, **698, 699,** 701, 919; vb. 468, **698, 699,** 701

plenary   adj. 56

plenipotentiary   n. 688

plenitude   n. 32, 56

plentiful   adj. 32, 75, 572

plenty   n. 75, 168, 572; adj. 168, 570, 572

plethora   n. 168, 572, 865

pliable   adj. 335

pliant   adj. 335, 336

plight   n. 633

plight one's troth   vb. 896

plod   vb. 281, 535, 615

plonk   vb. 782, 785

plop   n. 785; vb. 782, 785

plot   n. 148, 184, 234, 378, 525, 558, 631; vb. 558, 631

plough   vb. 261, 378

pluck   n. 857; vb. 228, 312, 378

pluck up courage   vb. 857

plucky   adj. 857

plug   n. 265, 464; vb. 265, 464, 468

plug away   vb. 535, 615

plumb   n. 330; adj. 214

plummet   n. 321; vb. 273

plump   n. 785; adj. 194, 204; vb. 540, 785

plunder   n. 663, 722, 724; vb. 164, 722

plunderer   n. 723

plunge   n. 317, **321**; vb. 210, 273, 317, **321**, 605

plural   n. 72; adj. 72

plurality   n. 72

ply   n. 206; vb. 268, 271, 695

pneumatic   adj. 348

poach   vb. 306

pocket   n. 254; vb. 705

pocket money   n. 731

pod   n. 225

podgy   adj. 194

poem   n. 528

poet   n. 528

poetic justice   n. 915

poet laureate   n. 528

poetry   n. **528**

poignant   adj. 769

point   n. 184, 233, 246, 255, 387, 400; vb. 178, 255, 284, 482

pointer   n. 482

pointless   adj. 576, 843

point of time   n. 115

point of view   n. 284, 420

poise   n. 514; vb. 216, 330

poison   n. 167, 592; vb. 370, 963

poisoner   n. 370

poisonous   adj. 164, 580, 586, 592

poke fun at   vb. 838

poker-faced   adj. 754

polar   adj. 760

polarity   n. 14, 181, 239, 637

pole   n. 217

polemical   adj. 410

police   n. 956; vb. 593, 956

policeman   n. 593, 956

police station   n. 682

policy   n. 558, 621

polish   n. 225, 257, 510, 797, 848; vb. 257, 341, 587, 797

polished   adj. 257, 510, 583, 848, 886

polish off   vb. 304, 659

polite   adj. 886, 922

politic   adj. 392, 577, 886

political   adj. 379, 667

politician   n. 623

politics   n. 379

poll   n. 540; vb. 38, 540

pollen   n. 340

pollster   n. 394

pollution   n. 584, 588, 608, 952

poltergeist   n. 971

polygon   n. 246

polytechnic   n. 475

pomp   n. 877

pompous   adj. 509, 875, 877

pond   n. 354

ponder   vb. 384

ponderous   adj. 330, 511, 573, 843

pooh-pooh   vb. 393, 924

pool   n. 354, 709; vb. 639

poor   adj. 169, 507, 571, 666, 735

poorly   adj. 586

pop   n. 170; vb. 782

Pope   n. 986

pop music   n. 792

popular   adj. 190, 868, 925

populate   vb. 191

population   n. 190, 379

pop up   vb. 825

pore over   vb. 472

pornography   n. 952

porous   adj. 264

port   n. 241, 298, 595

portable   adj. 268, 331

portentous   adj. 447

porter   n. 275, 676, 683

portfolio   n. 557

porthole   n. 262

portion   n. 55, 73, 305, 306, **717**

portrait n. 20, 22, 488, 525

portray vb. 20, 486, 488, 525

portrayal n. 20, 486, 525

pose n. 825; vb. 23, 394, 621, 852

position n. 7, 93, 184, 185, 186, 420, 557; vb. 186

position in a series n. 93

positive adj. 39, 468

possess vb. 707, 720, 984

possession n. 707, 720, 729, 984

possessive adj. 707, 750, 913

possessor n. 710, 720

possibility n. 404, 406

possible adj. 404, 409, 459

post n. 217, 467, 523, 557; vb. 268, 523

postdate vb. 117

poster n. 464

posterior n. 237; adj. 85, 119, 237

posteriority n. 119

posterity n. 171

postgraduate n. 474

post office n. 467

postpone vb. 89, 135, 920

postscript n. 41, 87, 89

postulate n. 386, 410, 448; vb. 448, 700

posture n. 7, 621, 825

pot n. 193

pot-bellied adj. 194

potent adj. 159, 173

potential n. 159, 564; adj. 159, 404, 459

pothole n. 254

potion n. 309, 591

pot luck n. 158

potter n. 491

pottery n. 489

pouch n. 193

poultry n. 306, 373

pounce n. 320; vb. 321

pound n. 184, 234, 325; vb. 282, 325, 340, 783

pound of flesh n. 669, 908

pour vb. 343, 358

pour out vb. 301

poverty n. 571, 735

powder n. 340

powderiness n. 340

power n. 159, 173, 177, 506, 530, 564, 622, 667; vb. 159, 765

powerful adj. 159, 161, 173, 177, 506, 667, 671

powerless adj. 160, 162

power station n. 159

practicable adj. 404, 406, 575

practical adj. 404, 577

practical joke n. 433

practically adv. 199

practice n. 396, 545, 602, 627, 702

practise vb. 470, 591, 602, 702

practised adj. 606

practising adj. 702, 974, 977, 980

practitioner n. 619

pragmatic adj. 575

prairie n. 356

praise n. 909, 922, 925, 982; vb. 868, 909, 922, 925, 982

praiseworthy adj. 579, 925

pram n. 276

prank n. 433, 539, 932

prattle vb. 451, 516

pray vb. 695, 980, 982, 988

prayer n. 695, 909, 982, 985, 988

prayerful adj. 695, 980, 982

preach vb. 470, 514

preacher n. 456, 514, 974, 986

preaching n. 518, 985

preamble n. 86; vb. 84

precarious adj. 409, 594

precaution n. 392, 860

precede vb. 84, 118, 134, 286

precedence n. 84, 286

precedent n. 23, 84, 86, 118, 545, 960; adj. 84

preceding adj. 84, 118, 134

precept n. 103, 626

precinct n. 184

precious adj. 139

precious stone n. 846

precipice n. 214

precipitate adj. 544, 613

precipitation n. 349, 358, 613

precipitous adj. 859

precis n. 527

precise adj. 392, 504, 864

preclude vb. 99, 691

precocious adj. 134

preconception n. 412, 416, 446

precursor n. 86, 467

predate vb. 117

predecessor n. 86

predestination n. 531, 543

predetermination n. 543

predicament n. 153, 633

predict vb. 443, 447, 543

predictable adj. 447

prediction n. 154, 447, 543

predilection n. 178, 861

280, 557; *vb.* 441, 547,
597, 624
prompter *n.* 441, 547
promptly *adv.* 115
promulgate *vb.* 460,
464
prone *adj.* 178, 179, 215
prong *n.* 255
pronoun *n.* 499
pronounce *vb.* 415,
464, 468, 512, 514, 960
pronounced *adj.* 458,
823
pronouncement *n.* 415,
468, 960
pronunciation *n.* 512,
514
proof *n.* 396, 413, 460,
482, 522
proofreader *n.* 522
prop *n.* 213, 217; *vb.*
217, 318
propagandism *n.* 470
propagate *vb.* 95, 163,
165
propel *vb.* 266, 282, 290
propellant *n.* 290
propensity *n.* 178, 545
proper *adj.* 499, 510,
848, 876, 915, 935
proper noun *n.* 499
property *n.* 711, 729
prophecy *n.* 447, 976
prophesy *vb.* 443, 446,
447
prophet *n.* 447, 449,
467, 974
prophetic *adj.* 976
propitiation *n.* 652, 943
propitious *adj.* 136
proportion *n.* 27, 244,
510, 717
proportions *n.* 194
proposal *n.* 552, 558,
693, 695, 890
proposition *n.* 103, 410,
448, 468, 605, 693, 695
proprietor *n.* 710

propriety *n.* 510, 577
propulsion *n.* **290**
prosaic *adj.* 843
proscribe *vb.* 962
prose *n.* **528**
prosecution *n.* 930, 959,
960
prosecutor *n.* 930
proselytize *vb.* 146, 470
prosody *n.* 528
prospect *n.* 123, 154,
406, 443
prospective *adj.* 123,
443, 558
prospectus *n.* 83
prosperity *n.* 168, 550,
661, **664**, 734
prostitute *n.* 953; *vb.*
608, 952
prostrate *adj.* 215, 319,
922; *vb.* 215
protect *vb.* 225, 392,
593, 599, 646, 801
protection *n.* 392, 593,
595, 599, 646
protectionism *n.* 681
protector *n.* 593, 646,
905
protest *n.* 425, 533, **696**;
vb. 425, 644, 696
protester *n.* 425, 832
protocol *n.* 545
prototype *n.* **23**
protract *vb.* 196, 202
protrude *vb.* 252, 253
protuberance *n.* 252,
253
proud *adj.* 644, 877
prove *vb.* 396, 396, 408,
413, 420, 929
proverb *n.* 432
proverbial *adj.* 426, 432
provide *vb.* 163, 304,
564, **568**, 602, 715
providence *n.* 550, 748,
966
providential *adj.* 136
province *n.* 183, 557

provincial *adj.* 183
provincialism *n.* 492,
494
provision *n.* **568**
provisional *adj.* 149,
396, 403, 700
provisionally *adv.,*
prep. 111
provisions *n.* 305, 306,
564, 700
proviso *n.* 403, 700
provocation *n.* 755
provocative *adj.* 459,
547
provoke *vb.* 155, 459,
547, 755, 883, 893
prowess *n.* 857
prowl *vb.* 461
proximity *n.* 199
proxy *n.* 149, 688, 689,
689
prudent *adj.* 392, 434,
748, 860
prudish *adj.* 951
prune *vb.* 203
pry *vb.* 388, 394
psalm *n.* 982
pseudo- *adj.* 20, 497
pseudonym *n.* 497
psyche *n.* 382, 751
psychiatry *n.* 382
psychic *adj.* 328, 382,
447
psychology *n.* 382
psychopath *n.* 440
psychotherapy *n.* 382
psychotic *n.* 440
pub *n.* 191
puberty *n.* 129
public *n.* 379, 821; *adj.*
379, 464
publication *n.* 464, 524
public house *n.* 191
publicity *n.* 464
publicize *vb.* 458, 464
public records *n.* 483
public-spirited *adj.* 903

publish *vb.* 458, 464, 465, 522
publisher *n.* 524
publishing *n.* 458, 522
puck *n.* 970
pucker *vb.* 260
pudding *n.* 306
puddle *n.* 354
puerile *adj.* 129, 131, 435
puff *n.* 359; *vb.* 308, 359
puff up *vb.* 875
pugnacious *adj.* 642, 651
pull *n.* 177, 294; *vb.* 291, 294, 390
pull a person's leg *vb.* 478, 842, 853
pull down *vb.* 164, 319, 588
pulling *n.* 291, 312
pull off *vb.* 659, 661
pull oneself together *vb.* 681, 757
pull one's socks up *vb.* 587
pull out *vb.* 312
pull through *vb.* 589
pull together *vb.* 639
pull up *vb.* 318
pull-up *n.* 191
pulp *n.* 364; *vb.* 364
pulpiness *n.* 364
pulsar *n.* 329
pulsate *vb.* 140
pulsation *n.* 140, 325
pulse *n.* 140, 325; *vb.* 325
pulverize *vb.* 164, 340
pummel *vb.* 282
pump *vb.* 359
pun *n.* 454, 842
punch *n.* 264, 506, 769; *vb.* 282, 482
punctiliousness *n.* 392, 864
punctual *adj.* 115, 134, 136

puncture *n.* 48; *vb.* 48, 255, 264
pungency *n.* 769
pungent *adj.* 769, 773, 774
punish *vb.* 647, 926, 962, 963
punishment *n.* 647, 917, 963
punk *n.* 792
puny *adj.* 162, 195
pup *n.* 880
pupil *n.* 131, 474
purchase *n.* 707, 726; *vb.* 705, 726
purchaser *n.* 710, 726, 737
purdah *n.* 461
pure *adj.* 46, 581, 583, 935, 937, 951, 977
purgatory *n.* 943
purge *vb.* 583, 911
purify *vb.* 46, 333, 348, 583, 775, 807
purist *n.* 864
puritanical *adj.* 669, 946, 951
purity *n.* 46, 876, 935, 937, 951
purloin *vb.* 722
purple *n.* 814; *adj.* 814
purport *n.* 450; *vb.* 450
purpose *n.* 547, 552; *vb.* 530, 552
purposeful *adj.* 552
purposeless *adj.* 451, 576
purr *vb.* 781, 783, 784, 789
purse *n.* 193, 732
purser *n.* 733
pursue *vb.* 287, 552, 554, 890
pursuer *n.* 554
pursuit *n.* 554, 557, 605
push *n.* 303, 645; *vb.* 282, 290, 547, 645
push ahead *vb.* 288

push along *vb.* 299
push around *vb.* 902
push back *vb.* 295
push down *vb.* 319
push off *vb.* 299
push-over *n.* 634, 661
pushy *adj.* 173, 611
put *vb.* 186
put about *vb.* 464
put across *vb.* 460
put aside *vb.* 567, 607
put a stop to *vb.* 144
put asunder *vb.* 898
putative *adj.* 448
put away *vb.* 304, 370, 567, 681
put back *vb.* 589
put by *vb.* 567
put down *vb.* 370
put forward *vb.* 693
put in *vb.* 300, 311
put into *vb.* 456
put into action *vb.* 609
put it to *vb.* 394
put off *vb.* 135
put on *vb.* 225, 227, 477, 529 805, 852
put-on *n.* 852; *adj.* 477, 852
put on a brave face *vb.* 477
put oneself out *vb.* 604, 615
put out *vb.* 578, 762, 830, 893
put over *vb.* 460
putrefaction *n.* 53, 777
putrid *adj.* 584, 588, 777
put right *vb.* 589
put together *vb.* 47, 52, 163
put up *vb.* 191
put-up job *n.* 930
put up with *vb.* 424, 757, 828
puzzle *n.* 409, 453, 466; *vb.* 409

pylon *n.* 159
pyramid *n.* 246
pyre *n.* 372

Q

quack *vb.* 787, 789
quadrangle *n.* 67, 184
quadratic *adj.* 67
quadrilateral *n.* 67, 246
quadrisection *n.* **69**
quadruped *n.* 373
quadruple *adj.* 68; *vb.*
  68
quadruplet *n.* 67
quadruplication *n.* **68**
quagmire *n.* 355
quail *vb.* 858
quake *n.* 326; *vb.* 325,
  326, 856
qualification *n.* 41, 142,
  403
qualifications *n.* 627
qualified *adj.* 130, 602,
  627
qualify *vb.* 142, 403,
  570
quality *n.* 5, 58, 579,
  935
qualm *n.* 421, 533, 833
quandary *n.* 409, 633
quantify *vb.* 26, 400
quantitative *adj.* 26
quantity *n.* **26**, 32, 75,
  400
quarrel *n.* 25, 642, 893;
  vb. 25, 642
quarrelsome *adj.* 642,
  883
quarry *vb.* 312
quart *n.* 69
quarter *n.* 69, 183; *vb.*
  69
quartet *n.* 67, 792
quasar *n.* 329
quash *vb.* 681, 686

quasi- *adj.* 497
quaternity *n.* **67**
queen *n.* 675
Queen's English *n.* 492
queer *n.* 106, 953; *adj.*
  952
quell *vb.* 37, 89, 652,
  681
quench *vb.* 762
query *n.* 394
quest *n.* 269, 388, 394,
  554; *vb.* 554
question *n.* 387, **394**,
  695; *vb.* 388, **394**, 421
questionable *adj.* 407,
  409, 421, 869, 932
questioner *n.* 388, 394
questionnaire *n.* 394
queue *n.* 91; *vb.* 91
quibble *vb.* 454
quick *adj.* **280**, 434,
  613, 842
quicken *vb.* **280**, 368,
  613, 752, 755
quicksand *n.* 355, 596
quick-tempered *adj.*
  756
quick-witted *adj.* 842
quiescent *adj.* 267, 459
quiet *n.* 267, 616, 779;
  adj. 517, 616, 650, 779,
  781, 876; *vb.* 652, 779
quieten *vb.* 176
quiet time *n.* 982
quilt *vb.* 226
quintessence *n.* 5
quintet *n.* 70
quintuple *adj.* 70
quintuplet *n.* 70
quip *n.* 842
quirk *n.* 539
quisling *n.* 480
quit *vb.* 299, **556**, 687
quite *adv.* 56
quiver *n.* 325; *vb.* 325,
  326, 756, 760, 856
Quixote *n.* 449
quiz *n.* 394; *vb.* 394

quoit *n.* 250
quota *n.* 305, 717
quotation *n.* 743
quote *vb.* 20
quotient *n.* 38

R

rabbi *n.* 986
rabble *n.* 871
rabid *adj.* 148, 439
race *n.* 11, 554, 613,
  649; *vb.* 280, 649
racialist *adj.* 379
rack *n.* 217, 964
racket *n.* 780, 791
raconteur *n.* 525
racy *adj.* 506, 769
radiate *vb.* 297
radiation *n.* 297
radiator *n.* 763
radical *n.* 148, 672, 832;
  adj. 56, 148, 155
radio *n.* 467, 840
radius *n.* 400
rafter *n.* 217
rag *n.* 33; *vb.* 842
rage *n.* 439, 756, 850,
  893; *vb.* 756, 893
ragtime *n.* 792
raid *n.* 300, 645; *vb.*
  645, 720, 722
rail *n.* 234
railing *n.* 234
railway *n.* 559
rain *n.* 347, 349, 358;
  vb. 358
rainbow *n.* 247, 817
rainfall *n.* 358
rainproof *adj.* 350
raise *vb.* 214, 318, 331,
  377
rake *n.* 953
rally *n.* 649, 696; *vb.*
  94, 587, 589
ram *vb.* 265

recent *adj.* 125, 134

receptacle *n.* 193

reception *n.* 94, 98, **302**, 716, 795, 884, 896

receptive *adj.* 302, 716, 753

recess *n.* 144, 254, 614

recession *n.* 169, 197, 293, 317

recipe *n.* 626

recipient *n.* 523, 716

reciprocal *adj.* 9, 12, 28, 39, 150, 647

recital *n.* 518, 792

recite *vb.* 77, 460, 525

reckless *adj.* 393, 613, 749, 859

reckon *vb.* 38, 400, 743

reckoning *n.* 38, 400, 738, 742

reclaim *vb.* 589, 721

recline *vb.* 215

recluse *n.* 885, 946

recognition *n.* 426, 818, 909, 925

recognize *vb.* 426, 441, 452, 818, 909, 925

recoil *n.* 147, **283**; *vb.* 147, 283

recollect *vb.* 441

recommend *vb.* 415, 624

recompense *n.* 31, 721, 738, 965; *vb.* 31, 589, 738, 965

reconcile *vb.* 24, 105, 652, 653, 704, 831, 911, 943

reconciled *adj.* 643, 654, 911

reconciliation *n.* 24, 650, 652, 911, 943

recondite *adj.* 453

reconditioning *n.* 147, 589

reconsider *vb.* 384

reconsideration *n.* 441

reconstruct *vb.* 142, 146, 165, 589

record *n.* 83, 441, **483**, 484, 525, 792, 794; *vb.* 83, 483, 525

recorder *n.* **484**, 958

recount *vb.* 525

recoup *vb.* 31, 721, 738

recourse *n.* 595

recover *vb.* 589, 618, 720, 721, 834

recovery *n.* 147, 589, 618, 705, 720, 721

recreation *n.* 614, 649, 840

recriminate *vb.* 647, 930

recruit *n.* 287, 474, 655; *vb.* 557, 651

rectangle *n.* 246

rectify *vb.* 587, 589

rector *n.* 986

recuperate *vb.* 589, 618

recur *vb.* 77, 138, 140, 441

recurrent *adj.* 109, 138

red *n.* **811**; *adj.* 811, 876

redeem *vb.* 31, 146, 601, 721, 726, 911, 943

redeemer *n.* 905, 967

rediscover *vb.* 165

red-letter day *n.* 878

redress *n.* 943, 965; *vb.* 589, 943, 965

reduce *vb.* 37, 76, 197, 203, 588, 743, 744

reduction *n.* 37, 42, 195, 197, 527, 744

redundancy *n.* 505, 686

redundant *adj.* 505, 572

reduplication *n.* 62, 165

re-echo *vb.* 784

reef *n.* 357, 596

reek *n.* 777; *vb.* 759, 777

re-entry *n.* 274

re-establish *vb.* 589

refer *vb.* 9, 157, 450

referee *n.* 415, 653

reference *n.* 157, 401, 450

reference book *n.* 524

referendum *n.* 450, 540

refill *n.* 56

refine *vb.* 142, 333, 587

refined *adj.* 398, 510, 805, 844, 848, 886

reflect *vb.* 384, 486, 797, 982

reflection *n.* 22, 384, 441, 797

reflector *n.* 822

reflex *adj.* 411, 531, 544

reform *n.* 587; *vb.* 142, 146, 587, 589

reforming *n.* 165; *adj.* 903

refractory *adj.* 537, 672

refrain *n.* 528, 792; *vb.* 89, 144, 555, 610, 944

refresh *vb.* 161, 348, 472, 589, 618

refresher *n.* 591

refreshment *n.* 147, 306, **618**, 829

refresh one's memory *vb.* 441

refrigeration *n.* 599, **762**

refrigerator *n.* 305, **764**

refuge *n.* 463, 595, 885

refugee *n.* 270, 600, 885

refund *n.* 31, 721, 738; *vb.* 31, 589, 721, 738

refurbish *vb.* 125, 587, 589

refusal *n.* 469, 542, 691, **694**

refuse *n.* 576; *vb.* 425, 469, 533, 542, 691, **694**

refutation *n.* 414

refute *vb.* 402, 686

regain *vb.* 705, 721

regal *adj.* 870

regalia *n.* 482, 677

regard *n.* 388, 390, 392,

868, 922; *vb.* 390, 420, 868, 889

regarding *adv., prep.* 9

regenerate *adj.* 146, 974; *vb.* 165, 589

regent *n.* 675

reggae *n.* 792

region *n.* 183

register *n.* 83, 116, 302, 483; *vb.* 83, 483

registrar *n.* 484

regress *n.* 147, 289; *vb.* 147, 289, 590

regression *n.* 37, 147, **289**, 590

regret *n.* 445, 828, 832, **833**; *vb.* 828, 833, 837, 941

regular *n.* 545; *adj.* 16, 79, 81, 91, 138, **140**, 244, 545

regularity *n.* 16, 79, 138, **140**, 244, 257, 545

regulate *vb.* 81, 140, 621, 622

regulation *n.* 81, 103, 622, 954

rehabilitate *vb.* 589, 721

rehearse *vb.* 77, 525, 602

reign *vb.* 667

reigning *adj.* 870

reimburse *vb.* 31, 721, 738, 965

reinforce *vb.* 161, 173, 226, 468, 646

reinforcement *n.* 196, 217

reinstate *vb.* 147, 589, 721

reissue *n.* 77; *vb.* 77, 125, 464

reiterate *vb.* 77, 140

reject *vb.* 25, 99, 393, 425, 469, **542**, 694

rejection *n.* 99, 421, **542**, 694, 926

rejects *n.* 44

rejoice *vb.* 829, 838

rejoicing *n.* **838**

rejoin *vb.* 395

rejuvenation *n.* 147, 589

rekindle *vb.* 589

relapse *n.* 147, 586, **590**; *vb.* 147, 590

relate *vb.* 9, 397, 460, 525

related *adj.* 9, 11, 60

relation *n.* 9, 11, 12, 397

relationship *n.* 9, 889, 952

relative *n.* 11; *adj.* 9, 12, 27

relative quantity *n.* **27**

relax *vb.* 144, 176, 267, 335, 612, 614, 840, 907

relaxation *n.* 614, 616, 834, 840

relay *n.* 268; *vb.* 268

release *n.* 460, 465, 600, 601, 680, 713, 911, 921, 961; *vb.* 601, 634, 680, 713, 921, 961

relegate *vb.* 303

relent *vb.* 335, 907

relentless *adj.* 900, 908

relevant *adj.* 9, 573

reliable *adj.* 152, 408, 868, 931

reliance *n.* 408, 420, 854

relic *n.* 44, 371, 441, 483

relief *n.* 149, 176, 181, 253, 489, 591, 601, 618, 636, **834**, 899

relieve *vb.* 149, 176, 591, 601, 618, 634, 636, 686, **834**, 899

religion *n.* 974

religious *adj.* 392, 974, 982

religious service *n.* **988**

relinquishment *n.* 546, **556**, 607, 687, 713

relish *n.* 307, 767, 827, 861; *vb.* 767, 770, 827, 861

relocate *vb.* 268

reluctant *adj.* 281, 533, 694, 876

rely *vb.* 420, 443, 854

remain *vb.* 91, 112, 143, 145, 535

remainder *n.* 44

remains *n.* 44, 371, 483

remake *vb.* 77, 165, 589

remark *vb.* 395, 456

remarkable *adj.* 32, 866

remedy *n.* 365, **591**, 834; *vb.* 591

remember *vb.* 441, 878

remembrance *n.* 483

remind *vb.* 441

reminiscences *n.* 441

reminiscent *adj.* 441

remiss *adj.* 393, 668

remission *n.* 43, 144, 601, 744, 911, 961

remit *vb.* 268, 601, 715, 911

remittance *n.* 268, 738

remnant *n.* 44, 76

remodel *vb.* 77, 146, 589

remonstrate *vb.* 696

remorse *n.* 833, 941

remote *adj.* 198, 885

remould *vb.* 165

removal *n.* 42, 48, 142, 268, 293, 299, 303, 312

remove *vb.* 42, 99, 187, 228, 268, 293, 300, 312, 485, 680, 720, 722, 826

remuneration *n.* 31, 721, 738, 965

remunerative *adj.* 705, 738, 965

renaissance *n.* 165, 589

rend *vb.* 48

render *vb.* 456, 486, 715, 792

rendezvous *n.* 96, 884; *vb.* 94

renegade *n.* 538

renew *vb.* 77, 125, 142, 165, 589

renounce *vb.* 469, 542, 556, 713

renovate *vb.* 125, 142, 165, 589

renown *n.* 868

rent *n.* 743; *adj.* 48, 262; *vb.* 191, 719

renunciation *n.* 469, 538, 542, 556, 713

reoccurrence *n.* 77, 138

reorganization *n.* 81, 142

reorganize *vb.* 142, 587, 589

repair *n.* 589; *vb.* 589, 721

reparation *n.* 31, 589, 721, 943, 965

repartee *n.* 395, 519, 842

repatriation *n.* 721

repay *vb.* 647, 721, 738, 943

repeal *n.* 686; *vb.* 686

repeat *n.* 77; *vb.* 20, 62, 77, 138, 140, 165

repeated and prolonged sound *n.* 783

repel *vb.* 295, 648, 885, 892

repent *vb.* 833, 907, 941

repercussion *n.* 156, 283

repetition *n.* 62, 77, 140, 505

repetitive *adj.* 77, 841

replace *vb.* 147, 149, 187, 686

replay *n.* 77

replenish *vb.* 56, 568

replete *adj.* 56, 570, 865

replica *n.* 20, 22

reply *n.* 283, 395, 402, 523; *vb.* 395

report *n.* 415, 460, 465, 468, 483, 523, 525, 778, 782; *vb.* 460, 465, 483, 521, 525

reporter *n.* 460, 524

repose *n.* 612, **616**; *vb.* 215

repository *n.* 732

reprehensible *adj.* 926

represent *vb.* 20, **486**, 488, 525, 685, 689

representation *n.* 20, 22, **486**, 488, 489, 525, 558, 685

representative *n.* 625, 688, 689; *adj.* 18, 101, 482, 486

repress *vb.* 679, 681, 691, 779

reprieve *n.* 135, 601, 911, 961; *vb.* 907, 911, 961

reprimand *n.* 926, 963; *vb.* 926, 963

reprint *n.* 20, 22, 77, 524; *vb.* 165, 464

reprisal *n.* 647, 912

reproach *n.* 869, 926; *vb.* 926

reproduce *vb.* 20, 163, 165, 486

reproduction *n.* 22, 77, 163, **165**, 486

reprove *vb.* 926, 930, 963

reptile *n.* 373

repudiate *vb.* 414, 469, 542, 686, 694

repugnance *n.* 637, 862, 883, 892

repugnant *adj.* 862, 892, 936

repulse *vb.* 295, 694

repulsion *n.* 295, 892

repulsive *adj.* 295, 777, 892

reputable *adj.* 177, 868, 931

reputation *n.* 177, 868

repute *n.* **868**

request *n.* 394, 671, **695**, 982; *vb.* 394, 671, 695

requiem *n.* 372, 839

require *vb.* 531, 562, 571, 671, 674

requirement *n.* 8, 315, **562**, 671

requital *n.* 31, 647, 912, 943

rescue *n.* 589, 600, 601, 680; *vb.* 589, 601, 636, 680

research *n.* 396; *vb.* 396

researcher *n.* 394, 396, 428

resemblance *n.* 18, 105, 397

resentful *adj.* 883, 893, 900, 913

resentment *n.* 832, **893**, 913, 914

reservation *n.* 403, 421, 425, 700

reserve *n.* 149, 198, 517, 568, 681, 876; *adj.* 149; *vb.* 712

reserves *n.* 564, 567, 731

reservoir *n.* 193, 354, 567

reside *vb.* 188, 191

residence *n.* 188, 191, 707

resident *n.* 190, 710; *adj.* 188

residual *adj.* 44

residue *n.* 44

resign *vb.* 654, 687

resignation *n.* 654, **687**, 757

resilience *n.* 336

resin *n.* 365; *vb.* 365

resist *vb.* 295, 537, 637, 644, **648**, 694

140, 545; *adj.* 16, 140, 545

rove *vb.* 269

row *n.* 85, 202, 206, 642

rowdy *adj.* 780, 887

rowing *n.* 271

royal *adj.* 870

rub *vb.* 341, 342, 758

rubber *n.* 485

rubbish *n.* 451, 576

rub in *vb.* 468

ruby *adj.* 811

rude *adj.* 511, 849, 880, 887, 910, 923

rudiment *n.* 155

rudimentary *adj.* 88

rue *vb.* 833

ruffian *n.* 175, 906

ruffle *vb.* 82, 258, 260, 893

rug *n.* 225

rugged *adj.* 258

ruin *n.* 164, 551, 569, 588, 662, 739; *vb.* 164, 588, 628, 735

rule *n.* 103, 400, 522, 626, 667, 671, 954; *vb.* 415, 653, 667, 671

ruler *n.* 400, 675

rumble *vb.* 783

ruminate *vb.* 384

rumour *n.* 465

run *n.* 613; *vb.* 110, 172, 266, 280, 343, 345, 358, 622

run away *vb.* 293, 299, 896

runaway *n.* 555, 600

run down *vb.* 160, 853, 926, 928

run-down *n.* 460; *adj.* 586, 612, 617

rung *n.* 93

run in *vb.* 681

run into *vb.* 282

runner *n.* 270, 275, 467

running *n.* 172; *adj.* 91, 172, 343

runny *adj.* 51, 345, 358

run off with *vb.* 722, 896

run out *vb.* 89, 301

rupture *n.* 48; *vb.* 48

rural *adj.* 183, 378

ruse *n.* 478, 631

rush *n.* 280, 282, 358, 611, 613; *adj.* 603; *vb.* 280, 358, 359, 613, 645

russet *adj.* 810, 811

rust *n.* 167, 588, 592, 847; *adj.* 810, 811; *vb.* 53, 584

rustic *n.* 871; *adj.* 378, 871, 885

rustle *vb.* 781, 783, 786; *vb.* 781, 783, 786

rusty *adj.* 126, 810, 811

rut *n.* 261, 545

ruthless *adj.* 900

S

Sabbath *n.* 616

sabbatical *n.* 614; *adj.* 616

sable *adj.* 808

sabotage *n.* 164

saboteur *n.* 480

saccharin *n.* 772

sack *n.* 193, 303, 686; *vb.* 164, 303, 686, 722

sackcloth and ashes *n.* 941

sacred *adj.* 974

sacrifice *n.* 652, 715, 943; *vb.* 652, 693, 715

sacrilege *n.* 901, 981

sad *adj.* 828, 837, 839, 895

sadden *vb.* 837

saddle *n.* 217; *vb.* 330, 919

safari *n.* 269

safe *n.* 732; *adj.* 54, 593, 646

safe-blower *n.* 723

safeguard *n.* 595; *vb.* 593, 646

safekeeping *n.* 567, 593

safety *n.* 593

safety curtain *n.* 762

sag *vb.* 216, 319

saga *n.* 525

sage *n.* 428, 436

sail *vb.* 271

sailing *n.* 271, 299

sailing ship *n.* 277

sailor *n.* 272

saint *n.* 939, 977, 980

saintly *adj.* 935, 980

salacious *adj.* 952

salad days *n.* 129

salary *n.* 705, 731, 738, 741

sale *n.* 714, 727

salesman *n.* 727

sales talk *n.* 727

salient *adj.* 253, 458, 573

sallow *adj.* 806, 807, 813

sally *n.* 645, 842; *vb.* 645

salmon *n.* 811, 816

saloon *n.* 276

salt *n.* 307; *vb.* 307, 599

salt away *vb.* 567

salt of the earth *n.* 579, 939

salubrious *adj.* 585

salutation *n.* 518, 922

salute *n.* 878, 922; *vb.* 888

salvage *n.* 44, 589; *vb.* 589, 601

salve *n.* 342, 365, 591

same *adj.* 13, 16, 28

sample *vb.* 767

sanctify *vb.* 980

sanctimonious *adj.* 981

scrape *n.* 633; *vb.* 257, 341

scrape out *vb.* 210

scrape through *vb.* 666

scrappy *adj.* 57

scratch *adj.* 628; *vb.* 482, 758

scratch the surface *vb.* 211

scratchy *adj.* 787

scrawl *n.* 521; *vb.* 521

scream *n.* 788; *vb.* 787, 788

screech *vb.* 787, 788, 789

screen *n.* 461, 595, 801; *vb.* 461, 593, 646, 801

screw *n.* 49, 251

scribble *n.* 441, 521; *vb.* 521

scribe *n.* 484, 521, 981

script *n.* 521

Scripture *n.* 976

scroll *n.* 251, 483, 521

scrounger *n.* 697

scrub *vb.* 341, 583

scrumptious *adj.* 306, 770

scruple *n.* 533, 833

scrupulous *adj.* 392, 702, 864, 931

scrutinize *vb.* 390, 394, 396, 818

scrutiny *n.* 394, 818

sculptor *n.* 491

sculpture *n.* 486, 489; *vb.* 489

scum *n.* 44, 871

scurrilous *adj.* 901

scurry *n.* 613; *vb.* 613

scythe *vb.* 378

sea *n.* 351

seaboard *n.* 352

seafaring *n.* 271

sea-food *n.* 306

seagoing *adj.* 277

seal *n.* 482; *vb.* 265, 408, 424, 461, 482

sealed book *n.* 427, 453

seam *n.* 49, 206

seaman *n.* 272

séance *n.* 984

sear *vb.* 754

search *vb.* 394, 396, 554

searching *adj.* 388

searchlight *n.* 800

seared conscience *n.* 942

seaside *n.* 352; *adj.* 352

season *n.* 107, 109; *vb.* 307, 545, 599

seasoned *adj.* 130, 545, 602

seat *n.* 186, 217

secede *vb.* 289, 425, 556

secession *n.* 425, 979

secluded *adj.* 466, 885

seclusion *n.* 461, 824, 885

second *n.* 109, 115; *adj.* 62

secondary *adj.* 35

secondhand *adj.* 126, 606

second nature *n.* 545

second-rate *adj.* 580

second thoughts *n.* 87, 538

secrecy *n.* 459

secret *n.* 466; *adj.* 427, 461, 466

secret agent *n.* 460

secretary *n.* 484, 521, 623

secrete *vb.* 301, 310, 461

secretive *adj.* 466, 517, 876

sect *n.* 641, 979

sectarian *n.* 979; *adj.* 641, 979

sectarianism *n.* 979

section *n.* 55, 73, 97, 183, 717

sectional *adj.* 73

sector *n.* 55, 183

secular *adj.* 975, 987

secure *adj.* 47, 161, 593; *vb.* 47, 152, 408, 646, 705, 712

security *n.* 593, 646, **701**

sedateness *n.* 757, 837

sedative *n.* 591

sedentary *adj.* 319

sediment *n.* 44

seditious *adj.* 148

seducer *n.* 953

seduction *n.* 952

seductive *adj.* 829

see *vb.* 419, 426, 818, 882

see ahead *vb.* 446

seed *n.* 155, 306, 374; *vb.* 95, 378

see double *vb.* 820, 950

seedy *adj.* 586

see fit *vb.* 530

see it through *vb.* 535

seek *vb.* 388, 394, 554, 604, 982

seem *vb.* 18, 621, 825

seeming *adj.* 406, 825

seemly *adj.* 510, 577, 848

seep *vb.* 301, 319, 349, 358

seer *n.* 447, 449

see-saw *n.* 325; *vb.* 325

seethe *vb.* 175, 759, 893

see through *vb.* 659, 802

segment *n.* 55, 73

segregate *vb.* 99, 540

segregation *n.* 48, 99

seismic *adj.* 325

seize *vb.* 326, 705, 720, 722

seizure *n.* 326, 586, 720

seldom *adv.* 139

select *adj.* 579; *vb.* 398, 540, 557

selection *n.* 398, 527, 540

selective *adj.* 398, 540, 864

self *n.* 382

self-abasement *n.* 874

self-assurance *n.* 757, 873

self-centred *adj.* 875, 934

self-control *n.* 534, 681, 757, 944

self-deception *n.* 478

self-denial *n.* 933, 944

self-destruction *n.* 370

self-determination *n.* 678

self-discipline *n.* 681, 944

self-effacing *adj.* 874, 933

self-esteem *n.* 873

self-evident *adj.* 408, 458

self-forgetful *adj.* 933

self-glory *n.* 879

self-important *adj.* 875

self-improvement *n.* 472

self-indulgent *adj.* 827, 934, 945

self-instruction *n.* 472

self-interest *n.* 934

selfishness *n.* 904, 934

selfless *adj.* 933

self-love *n.* 873

self-made *adj.* 472

self-portrait *n.* 488

self-possessed *adj.* 392, 438, 757

self-regard *n.* 873

self-reliance *n.* 534, 857

self-respect *n.* 873

self-sacrifice *n.* 933

selfsameness *n.* 13

self-satisfied *adj.* 831, 873

self-seeking *n.* 934; *adj.* 934

self-styled *adj.* 497

self-taught *adj.* 472

sell *vb.* 464, 714, 727

sell-out *n.* 727, 932

semantic *adj.* 450

semantics *n.* 492

semaphore *n.* 467

semblance *n.* 22, 236

semi- *adj.* 63

semiliquidity *n.* **362**

seminar *n.* 519

seminary *n.* 475

semitransparency *n.* **804**

senator *n.* 625

send *vb.* 268, 523

send for *vb.* 671

send forth *vb.* 301, 464

send-off *n.* 299

send up *vb.* 20

senility *n.* 126, 130

senior *n.* 34, 132; *adj.* 130

sensation *n.* 465, 752, 866

sensational *adj.* 755, 866, 877

sense *n.* 398, 411, 434, **450**, 752; *vb.* 382, 411, 452, 752

senseless *adj.* 433, 451

sense of duty *n.* 919

sense of hearing *n.* 795

sense of smell *n.* 774

sensibility *n.* 753

sensible *adj.* 434, 575, 753

sensitive *adj.* 398, 716, 753, 756, 828, 894

sensitivity *n.* 398, 752, 753, 894

sensory *adj.* 753

sensual *adj.* 945, 952

sensuality *n.* 827, 945, 952

sentence *n.* 498, 960; *vb.* 960, 962, 963

sententious *adj.* 504

sentient *adj.* 753

sentiment *n.* 411, 420, 752, 889

sentimental *adj.* 752, 889

sentry *n.* 593, 646

separability *n.* 48, 51

separate *vb.* 48, 55, 95, 398, 540, 898

separation *n.* 48, 898

separatism *n.* 979

separatist *n.* 106, 425; *adj.* 979

sepia *adj.* 810

septet *n.* 70

sepulchre *n.* 372

sequel *n.* 87, 119, 156

sequence *n.* 85, 91

seraph *n.* 968

serenity *n.* 267, 757, 827, 831

serf *n.* 378, 676, 871

serfdom *n.* 679

serial *adj.* 85, 91, 140

serial position *n.* 93

series *n.* 85

serious *adj.* 534, 573, 594, **837**, 982

seriousness *n.* 573, **837**

sermon *n.* 470, 518

serrate *vb.* 246, 258, 259

servant *n.* 35, **676**

serve *vb.* 636, 676, 679

serve as *vb.* 486

service *n.* 550, 575, 679, 982, 988

service of worship *n.* 988

services *n.* 655

servility *n.* 679, **881**

serving *n.* 717

session *n.* 957

set *n.* 94, 474, 850; *adj.* 152, 185, 235; *vb.* 47, 81, 152, 186, 235, 332, 334

set about *vb.* 88, 605

set apart *vb.* 48, 398

setback n. 445, 635

set fire to vb. 761

set forth vb. 456, 460, 525

set free adj. 961; vb. 48, 961

set great store by vb. 573

set in motion vb. 88, 266, 282

set in order vb. 81

set no store by vb. 421

set off vb. 782, 805, 846

set one's heart on vb. 861

set one's teeth on edge vb. 773, 787

set out vb. 299, 458

set sail vb. 271

setting n. 8, 185, 229, 792

settle vb. 186, 191, 319, 408, 413, 652, 659, 699, 738

settle down vb. 191

settlement n. 699, 704, 738

settler n. 190

settle up vb. 647

set to vb. 605, 649

set up vb. 186, 522

seven n. 70; adj. 70

sever vb. 42, 48

several adj. 75

severe adj. 175, 508, 669, 828, 908, 946

severity n. 508, 669, 900

sew vb. 221, 589

sewer n. 360

sex-appeal n. 889

sextet n. 70

sexuality n. 827

sexy adj. 952

shabby adj. 580, 869

shackle n. 681; vb. 635

shade n. 225, 463, 595, 798, 801; vb. 799, 801

shadow n. 4, 328, 798; vb. 287, 554

shadowy adj. 4, 328, 798, 799, 824

shady adj. 631, 798, 801, 869, 932

shaft n. 213, 254, 361, 797

shake vb. 45, 51, 326, 756, 856

shake hands vb. 408, 652, 699, 886

shake off vb. 680

shake-up n. 148

shaky adj. 141, 326, 338, 594

shallow adj. 211, 435, 507, 852

shallowness n. 211, 383, 427, 435

sham n. 20, 852; adj. 20, 431, 478; vb. 477, 852

shambles n. 80

shame n. 869, 874; vb. 874

shameful adj. 869, 924

shameless adj. 887

shampoo vb. 583

shanty n. 191

shape n. 242, 339, 825; vb. 489

shapeless adj. 243

shapely adj. 244, 844

share n. 55, 305, 709, 717; vb. 55, 639, 709, 988

shareholder n. 709

share out vb. 717

sharing n. 709, 717

shark n. 718

sharp adj. 255, 434, 769, 773, 787, 791, 828

sharpen vb. 255

sharpness n. 255, 434, 769, 773

sharp practice n. 478

shatter vb. 164, 338

shattering adj. 148, 164

shave vb. 203, 257

shaving n. 228

shear vb. 203, 377

shears n. 255

sheath n. 225

shed vb. 95, 228, 319, 556

shed light on vb. 797

sheep n. 20

sheer adj. 46, 214

sheet n. 206, 225, 522

shelf n. 217

shell n. 23, 225, 290, 885; vb. 228

shellac n. 365

shelter n. 191, 225, 463, 595, 801; vb. 225, 461, 593, 646, 801

shelve vb. 135

Sheol n. 973

shepherd n. 377, 986

shield n. 595, 801; vb. 225, 593, 646, 801

shift n. 149, 187, 268; vb. 142, 149, 151, 187, 268, 285

shifty adj. 478, 631

shilly-shally vb. 135, 536, 612

shimmer n. 797; vb. 797

shine n. 797; vb. 257, 341, 797

shine at vb. 627

ship n. 277; vb. 192, 268

shipment n. 268

shipper n. 728

shirk vb. 533, 555, 920

shirker n. 555, 858

shirty adj. 893, 894

shiver vb. 326, 760

shoal n. 94, 211

shock n. 282, 444, 828; vb. 856, 892

shockable adj. 951

shocked adj. 856, 926

shocking *adj.* 830, 845, 869, 936

shoddy *adj.* 580, 849, 869

shoot *n.* 374; *vb.* 290, 370, 645, 963

shooting star *n.* 329, 800

shop *n.* 620, 730

shop assistant *n.* 727

shop-lifter *n.* 723

shop-lifting *n.* 722

shopper *n.* 726

shopping *n.* 726

shopping centre *n.* 730

shopping spree *n.* 749

shore *n.* 352; *vb.* 217

short *adj.* 57, 113, 203, 315, 504

shortage *n.* 57, 315

shortcoming *n.* 29, 35, 43, 57, 315, 662

short duration *n.* 113

shorten *vb.* 37, 42, 197, 203, 504, 527

shortfall *n.* 57, 315

shorthand *n.* 521

short-lived *adj.* 113

shortness *n.* 33, 195, 203

short-sighted *adj.* 416, 435, 820

short-sightedness *n.* 435, 820

short-tempered *adj.* 894

short-term *adj.* 113

shot *n.* 173, 290, 782

shoulder *n.* 238; *vb.* 217, 605, 636

shout *n.* 482, 597, 782, 788; *vb.* 482, 788

shout down *vb.* 425, 788, 887

shove *n.* 282; *vb.* 282, 290

show *n.* (manifestation) 458; (drama) 529; (vanity) 852, 875; *vb.* (be visible) 458, 802, 823, 825; (demonstrate) 413; (indicate) 482

show-down *n.* 462

shower *n.* 358; *vb.* 349, 358

show-jumper *n.* 270

show-jumping *n.* 269

showman *n.* 877

showmanship *n.* 529, 877

show off *vb.* 419, 875, 877, 879

show-off *n.* 875, 877

show one's colours *vb.* 462

showpiece *n.* 458, 581, 844

show through *vb.* 802, 823

show up *vb.* 188, 298, 414, 825, 869

show willing *vb.* 532

showy *adj.* 509, 852, 875, 877

shred *n.* 33, 207

shrewd *adj.* 434, 631

shrewd idea *n.* 448

shrewdness *n.* 398, 434, 631

shriek *n.* 787, 788

shrill *adj.* 333, 787; *vb.* 787

shrine *n.* 483, 990

shrink *vb.* 37, 197, 205, 283, 533, 555, 856, 858

shrivel *vb.* 197, 350, 588

shroud *vb.* 461

shrub *n.* 374

shrug off *vb.* 921

shudder *vb.* 326, 760, 856

shuffle *vb.* 82, 149, 281, 756

shun *vb.* 555, 694, 924

shut *vb.* 263

shut down *vb.* 144

shut-eye *n.* 612

shut in *vb.* 234

shut oneself up *vb.* 885

shut out *vb.* 691

shutter *n.* 801

shuttle *n.* 278, 325; *vb.* 268

shut up *vb.* 144, 234, 681

shy *adj.* 856, 858, 876, 885

shy away *vb.* 533

shyness *n.* 858, 876, 885

sibilant *adj.* 786

sick *adj.* 369, 586

sicken *vb.* 162, 586

sickly *adj.* 812

sickness *n.* 303, 586, 828

side. *n.* 11, 233, 238

side by side *adv.* 238

sidedness *n.* 238

side-splitting *adj.* 851

sideways *adj.* 219, 238; *adv.* 238

side with *vb.* 641

sidle up to *vb.* 292

siege *n.* 645

siesta *n.* 612

sieve *n.* 264

sift *vb.* 46, 415, 540

sigh *vb.* 359, 781

sight *n.* 753, 818

sightly *adj.* 844

sightseeing *n.* 269

sightseer *n.* 270, 821

sign *n.* 401, 447, 458, 482, 597; *vb.* 424, 482, 699, 701, 714, 726

signal *n.* 482; *vb.* 482

signatory *n.* 424

signature *n.* 482, 496

significance *n.* 450, 456, 573

significant *adj.* 136, 450, 573

signify *vb.* 450, 482

sign of authority *n.* 677

signpost *vb.* 284
silence *n.* 267, 513, 517, 779; *vb.* 414, 513, 779
silent *adj.* 513, 517, 779, 895
silhouette *n.* 232, 488; *vb.* 488
silky *adj.* 257
silly *adj.* 433, 435
silver-haired *adj.* 809
silvery *adj.* 807
similarity *n.* 18, 105, 218, 397
simile *n.* 397, 455
simmer *vb.* 306
simmer down *vb.* 757
simple *adj.* (not mixed) 46; (gullible) 422, 632, 937, 951; (foolish) 427, 435; (easy to understand) 452, 502, 508; (easy) 634
simple circularity *n.* 250
simple-minded *adj.* 435, 632
simpleton *n.* 429, 437, 479
simplify *vb.* 46, 53, 456
simulate *vb.* 20, 477, 852
simultaneous *adj.* 60, 122
sin *n.* 431, 672, 703, 938; *vb.* 672, 981
sincere *adj.* 430, 476, 931
sine qua non *n.* 60, 700
sinew *n.* 207
sinful *adj.* 916, 936, 938, 952, 975, 981
sing *vb.* 528, 789, 792, 982
singer *n.* 793
single *adj.* 54, 59, 139, 897
single-minded *adj.* 534, 980

single out *vb.* 102
singular *adj.* 59
sinister *adj.* 665
sinistral *n.* 241
sink *vb.* 209, 210, 317, 319, 321, 588
sink back *vb.* 590
sinker *n.* 330
sinless *adj.* 951
sinner *n.* 906, 940, 981
sinuate *vb.* 251
sip *n.* 309; *vb.* 767
siphon *n.* 360
sir *n.* 380
siren *n.* 116, 482, 598, 970
sirupy *adj.* 772
sister *n.* 11, 986
sit *vb.* 23, 185
sit down *vb.* 319
site *n.* 185, 186
sit-in *n.* 144, 696
sit on *vb.* 466, 679
sit on the fence *vb.* 409, 541
sit pretty *vb.* 831
sitting *n.* 984
sitting duck *n.* 479
situation *n.* 8, 93, 153, 185, 229, 557
six *n.* 70; *adj.* 70
sixth sense *n.* 411, 753
size *n.* 26, 27, 32, 194, 362, 400
size up *vb.* 415
sizzle *vb.* 306, 759, 786
skeleton *n.* 232, 371, 527
sketch *n.* 232, 486, 488, 525, 558; *vb.* 232, 488, 525, 558
sketchy *adj.* 57
skew *adj.* 219
skewer *vb.* 264
skilful *adj.* 627
skill *n.* 159, 426, 501, 627
skilled *adj.* 579, 602

skilled worker *n.* 619, 629
skim *vb.* 211, 257
skimp *vb.* 393, 750
skimpy *adj.* 57
skin *n.* 225; *vb.* 228
skinny *adj.* 205
skip *vb.* 320, 393
skirmish *n.* 645, 649
skirt *n.* 233; *vb.* 233, 238
skunk *n.* 777
sky *n.* 329, 348, 815
skyjacking *n.* 722
skyline *n.* 198
skyscraper *n.* 191, 208
slab *n.* 206
slack *adj.* 391, 612, 668, 920, 952
slacken *vb.* 281
slacker *n.* 858
slag *n.* 44
slam *vb.* 782, 926
slander *n.* 869, 928; *vb.* 928, 930
slanderer *n.* 928
slang *n.* 494, 495; *adj.* 495
slant *vb.* 219
slap *n.* 782, 963; *vb.* 282, 782, 963
slap in the face *n.* 694, 923
slapstick *n.* 529
slash *vb.* 203
slate *n.* 206
slaughter *n.* 164, 370, 963; *vb.* 370, 963
slave *n.* 35, 619, 676
slavery *n.* 679
slavish *adj.* 881
slay *vb.* 370
sleek *adj.* 257
sleep *n.* 612; *vb.* 612
sleep around *vb.* 952
sleep together *vb.* 889
sleep with *vb.* 889
sleepy *adj.* 612, 617

sleet n. 760

sleight of hand n. 478

slender adj. 33, 205

slice n. 55, 305, 717

slide n. 219, 486; vb. 257, 588

slide-rule n. 400

slight n. 869, 923, 924; adj. 33, 195, 203, 571; vb. 418, 923, 928

slim adj. 33, 205; vb. 205, 947

slime n. 584

slimy adj. 362

slink vb. 461

slip n. 431, 500, 522, 741, 938

slip back vb. 590

slippery adj. 51, 257, 594, 631

slipshod adj. 393, 500

slip-up n. 431

slit n. 261, 262; vb. 48, 264

sliver n. 55

slogan n. 432, 494, 498

slog away vb. 535, 615

slope n. 208, 219; vb. 219

sloppy adj. 584

slot n. 261, 262; vb. 261

slothful adj. 612

slough n. 355

slovenly adj. 500, 584, 920

slow adj. 174, 281, 435; vb. 281, 616

slowcoach n. 281

slowness n. 135, 281, 435, 843

sluggard n. 612

sluggish adj. 174, 281, 612, 843

slum n. 845

slumber vb. 174, 612

slump n. 169, 317; vb. 317, 588

slur n. 869, 928, 930; vb. 515, 928, 930

slush n. 760

slushy adj. 355, 362

slut n. 953

sly adj. 461, 631, 932

smack vb. 282, 782

smack one's lips vb. 767

small adj. 33, 195, 203, 331

small arms n. 657

small change n. 731

smallholding n. 378

smallness n. 33, 195

small talk n. 516

smarmy adj. 927

smart adj. 125, 631; vb. 828

smart aleck n. 875

smash vb. 164, 282, 645

smash-and-grab-raid n. 722

smash hit n. 661

smash-up n. 282

smattering n. 76, 427

smear n. 584, 928, 930; vb. 342, 847, 869, 928

smell n. 753, 774, 777; vb. 774, 776, 777

smell out vb. 394, 554, 774

smelly adj. 777

smelt vb. 761

smile n. 838, 886; vb. 838, 886

smirch n. 847; vb. 847

smirk n. 838; vb. 838

smite vb. 282

smitten adj. 889

smog n. 363

smoke n. 344, 346, 803; vb. 308, 346, 599, 759, 803

smoke-signal n. 467

smoking adj. 759

smoky adj. 803, 809

smooth adj. 228, 257, 335, 364, 477, 631, 927; vb. 16, 215, 257, 341, 758

smoothness n. 257

smother vb. 513, 759, 762

smoulder vb. 759

smudge vb. 584, 847

smuggle vb. 722

smuggled adj. 955

smuggler n. 723

smut n. 952

snack n. 306

snack bar n. 191

snag n. 582, 635

snail n. 281

snake in the grass n. 459, 596

snake-like adj. 251

snap vb. 338, 782, 789, 893

snap out of it vb. 836

snapshot n. 486

snare n. 463, 596

snarl vb. 789

snatch vb. 720

sneak n. 858; vb. 461

sneer n. 895, 924, 926; vb. 696, 853, 895, 924, 926

sneeze vb. 359, 786

sniff vb. 774

sniff out vb. 394, 554

snigger n. 838; vb. 838

snip vb. 48

sniper n. 645

snivel vb. 839

snobbish adj. 875, 924

snoop n. 388, 460, 821; vb. 388, 394

snooty adj. 875, 924

snooze n. 612; vb. 612

snort vb. 789

snow n. 760; vb. 807

snowball n. 36; vb. 36

snowdrift n. 760

snowflake n. 760

snowstorm n. 760

snub n. 295, 694, 923;
   vb. 887, 923, 926
snuff n. 308; vb. 762
snug adj. 827
snuggle vb. 890
soak vb. 56, 349
soak up vb. 350
so-and-so n. 497
soapy adj. 363
soar vb. 32, 208, 273,
   316
sob n. 839; vb. 788, 839
sober adj. 837, 848, 944,
   949
soberness n. 848, **949**
so-called adj. 497
sociability n. 882, **884**
social n. 884; adj. 379
social conscience n.
   903
socialism n. 709
social services n. 903
society n. 379, 641, 850,
   870
sociology n. 379
socket n. 184
sod n. 374
sodden adj. 349
sodomy n. 952
soft adj. 257, 331, 335,
   670, 781, 805, 889
soft drink n. 309
soften vb. 267, 335, 513,
   652, 834
soft-hearted adj. 670,
   907
softness n. 335, 364,
   670, 778, 781
soft nothings n. 890
soft soap n. 927
sog vb. 349
soggy adj. 364
soi-disant adj. 497
soil n. 352, 378; vb. 584,
   847
soirée n. 884
sojourn n. 269; vb. 191
solace n. 831, 907

solar adj. 329
solar energy n. 159, 765
solder vb. 50
soldier n. 655
soldier on vb. 535
sole adj. 59
solecism n. 412, **500**
solemn adj. 468, 573,
   837, 982
solicit vb. 695
solicitor n. 959
solicitous adj. 392
solid n. 3, 332; adj. 3,
   50, 161, 332, 334, 337
solidarity n. 50, 639
solidify vb. 332, 334
solidity n. 3, 152, 204,
   332, 334
soliloquize vb. 520
soliloquy n. 520
solitary adj. 885
solitude n. 59, 461
solo n. 792
soloist n. 793
soluble adj. 345
solution n. 343
solve vb. 157, 456
solvent n. 343, 345
sombre adj. 798, 809,
   895
some adj. 26, 72
somebody n. 868
somersault n. 220; vb.
   220
something n. 327
sometime adj. 124, 687;
   adv. 121
sometimes adv. 138
somnolence n. 612, 617
son n. 171
sonata n. 792
song n. 528, 792, 982
sonnet n. 528
sonorous adj. 778
soothe vb. 176, 591, 834
soothing adj. 589, 790,
   834
soothsayer n. 447, 984

sooty adj. 584, 808
sophism n. 412
sophisticated n.   848;
   adj. 423, 848
sophistry n. 412
soporific adj. 841
sorcery n. **984**
sore n. 588; adj. 753,
   828, 893
sore point n. 893
sorrow n. 828, 830, 833,
   837, 839, 941; vb. 837,
   839
sorry adj. 833, 907, 941
sort n. 97; vb. 97, 540
sortie n. 645; vb. 645
SOS n. 598
soul n. 223, 368, 382,
   751
sound n. 353, 512, 778,
   795; adj. 410, 438, 581,
   585, 977; vb. 512, 778
sounding board n. 396
sound out vb. 396
soundproof adj. 779
soup n. 306
soupçon n. 33
sour adj. 769, 773, 895
source n. 88, 155
source of light n. **800**
sourness n. 773, 895
souvenir n. 441, 483
sovereign n. 675; adj.
   667
sow n. 381; vb. 95, 378
space n. **182**, 198, 200,
   202, **329**
space-age adj. 125
spaceman n. 274
spaceship n. 279
space travel n. 274
space traveller n. 274
spacious adj. 32, 182,
   204
spade vb. 254
spadework n. 602
span n. 109, 182, 202;
   vb. 47, 182, 313

spank *vb.* 963

spanner in the works *n.* 580, 635

spare *adj.* 44, 607; *vb.* 670, 907

spare time *n.* 614

sparing *adj.* 748, 750, 944

spark *n.* 797

sparkle *n.* 506, 759, 797, 836; *vb.* 326, 797, 842

sparse *adj.* 33, 76, 139, 333

spasm *n.* 141, 326, 586, 828

spasmodic *adj.* 92, 141

spatial *adj.* 182

spatter *vb.* 817

spay *vb.* 160, 169

speak *vb.* 460, 512, 514, 788

speak against *vb.* 25, 696

speaker *n.* 514

speak for itself *vb.* 401

speak one's mind *vb.* 476, 632

speak out *vb.* 468

speak out against *vb.* 832

speak volumes *vb.* 401

spear *vb.* 264

special *adj.* 59, 102

specialist *n.* 629

speciality *n.* 102, 557

specialize *vb.* 472, 609

species *n.* 97

specific *adj.* 5, 59, 102

specification *n.* 97, 525

specifications *n.* 102, 700

specify *vb.* 102, 482, 496, 525

specimen *n.* 458

specious *adj.* 412, 549, 825

speck *n.* 33, 847

speckle *vb.* 817

spectacle *n.* 529, 825, 866

spectacles *n.* 822

spectacular *adj.* 529, 877

spectator *n.* **821**

spectre *n.* 971

spectrum *n.* 805, 817

speculation *n.* 396, 448, 553

speculator *n.* 396, 448, 553, 728

speech *n.* 492, 512, **514**, 518

speech defect *n.* 515

speechless *adj.* 513, 866

speech-making *n.* 518

speed *n.* 27, 266, **280**, 400; *vb.* 280

speed up *vb.* 280, 613

speedy *adj.* 134, 280, 613

spell *n.* 109, 586, 984; *vb.* 450, 493

spell-binder *n.* 984

spellbound *adj.* 866

spelling *n.* 493

spell out *vb.* 456

spend *vb.* 575, 715, 738, 740

spendthrift *n.* 749; *adj.* 569

spend time *vb.* 107

spew *vb.* 303, 358

sphere *n.* 249, 329, 658

spice *n.* 776; *vb.* 307, 599

spick and span *adj.* 583

spicy *adj.* 769, 776, 952

spike *n.* 255; *vb.* 264

spill *n.* 800; *vb.* 319, 358

spin *n.* 269, 323; *vb.* 221, 273, 323

spine *n.* 255

spineless *adj.* 160, 162

spinney *n.* 374

spin-off *n.* 87, 156

spin out *vb.* 202

spinster *n.* 897

spiral *n.* 251, 322, 323; *adj.* 251; *vb.* 323

spire *n.* 208, 212

spirit *n.* 4, 368, 382, 506, 611, 751, 966, 968, 969

spirited *adj.* 280, 368

spiritism *n.* 984

spiritless *adj.* 757

spiritual *adj.* 4, 328, 382, 966, 974, 980

spiritualist *n.* 984

spirituality *n.* 328, 980

spit *n.* 253; *vb.* 306, 358

spiteful *adj.* 900, 912

splash *n.* 786; *vb.* 349, 358, 786

splash down *vb.* 274, 317, 321

spleen *n.* 895

splendid *adj.* 579, 844

splendour *n.* 797, 844, 877

splice *n.* 49; *vb.* 47, 896

splint *n.* 217

splinter *n.* 55; *vb.* 338

splinter-group *n.* 641

split *n.* 642, 717, 979; *adj.* 48; *vb.* 48, 63, 200, 338

split hairs *vb.* 864

spoil *n.* 663, 724; *vb.* 588, 628, 635, 847

spoilsport *n.* 548

spoke *n.* 297

spokesman *n.* 460, 467, 514, 689

sponge *n.* 264, 364, 485; *vb.* 349, 583

sponger *n.* 612, 697, 881

spongy *adj.* 264, 335, 364

sponsor *vb.* 636

spontaneity *n.* 531, **544**

spontaneous *adj.* 115, 131, 411, **544**

spooky *adj.* 971

spoonerism *n.* 433, 500, 842

spoon-feeding *n.* 470

spoonful *n.* 26, 306

sporadic *adj.* 139, 141

sport *n.* 649, 840, 939

sporting *adj.* 915

spot *n.* 33, 184, 584, 847; *vb.* 419, 482

spotless *adj.* 581, 583, 807, 937, 951

spotlight *n.* 800

spotted *adj.* 584, 817

spouse *n.* 896

spout *n.* 301, 358, 360; *vb.* 358, 514

sprachgefühl *n.* 501

sprawl *vb.* 95

spray *n.* 363, 374; *vb.* 225

spread *n.* 36, 182, 196, 306; *vb.* 95, 182, 196, 297, 460

sprig *n.* 374

spring *n.* (season) 127; (cause) 155, 547; (recoil) 283, 336; (leap) 320; (water) 358; *adj.* 127; *vb.* 156, 283, 320, 336

sprinkle *vb.* 95, 349, 583

sprinkling *n.* 76, 583

sprint *n.* 613; *vb.* 280, 613

sprout *vb.* 316

spry *adj.* 611

spur *n.* 253, 547; *vb.* 547

spurious *adj.* 431, 477

spurn *vb.* 542, 644, 694, 892, 924

spur of the moment *n.* 544

spurt *vb.* 280, 301, 358, 613

sputnik *n.* 279

spy *n.* 460, 821; *vb.* 394, 396

squabble *n.* 642; *vb.* 642

squad *n.* 94, 655

squalid *adj.* 584

squall *n.* 359

squander *vb.* 107, 569, 608, 706, 740, 749

squanderer *n.* 749

square *n.* 67, 183, 184, 246, 730; *adj.* 67, 931; *vb.* 24, 28, 105, 400

square deal *n.* 915

square one *n.* 88

squash *vb.* 215, 319, 402, 874

squat *adj.* 195, 204, 209; *vb.* 191, 209, 319

squatter *n.* 100, 190

squawk *n.* 787; *vb.* 787, 789

squeak *vb.* 781, 787, 788

squeal *vb.* 460, 787, 788, 789

squealer *n.* 460

squeamish *adj.* 862, 864, 951

squeeze *n.* 37, 743; *vb.* 37, 197, 712, 758

squelch *vb.* 786

squelchy *adj.* 355

squint *n.* 219, 818, 820; *vb.* 820

squirm *vb.* 251

squirt *vb.* 301, 358

stab *vb.* 264

stability *n.* 16, 143, 152, 757

stabilizer *n.* 152

stable *adj.* 16, 143, 152, 257, 612, 757

stack *n.* 567; *vb.* 378, 567

stadium *n.* 658

staff *n.* 619, 676, 677, 989

stag *n.* 380

stage *n.* 27, 527; *vb.* 529

stagger *vb.* 326

staggering *adj.* 444

stagnate *vb.* 169, 174, 610, 666

stain *n.* 225, 582, 584, 805, 847, 869; *vb.* 805, 847, 869

stainless *adj.* 581, 583

staircase *n.* 316

stake *n.* 217, 553, 701, 964; *vb.* 701

stalactite *n.* 216

stale *adj.* 612, 617, 666, 768, 841

stalemate *n.* 28

stalk *n.* 374; *vb.* 554

stall *n.* 730; *vb.* 144

stallion *n.* 380

stalwart *n.* 640, 857; *adj.* 161

stamina *n.* 161, 535, 857

stammer *n.* 515; *vb.* 515

stamp *n.* 23, 482, 522; *vb.* 242, 482, 490, 522

stance *n.* 420

stand *n.* 7, 184, 186, 213, 217, 420, 648, 730; *vb.* 1, 185, 318, 738

standard *n.* 23, 27, 103, 400, 482, 531, 939; *adj.* 492, 746

standardize *vb.* 16, 81

stand by *vb.* 217, 636, 702

stand-by *n.* 149

stand down *vb.* 687

stand fast *vb.* 534, 648

stand for *vb.* 424, 486, 693, 701

stand-in *n.* 149, 689

stand in for *vb.* 149, 685, 689

standing *n.* 7, 93

stand-offish *adj.* 875, 885

stand out *vb.* 253, 823

standpoint   n. 284, 818

standstill   n. 144, 267

stand together   vb. 639

stand up   vb. 318

stand up for   vb. 217

stand up to   vb. 648

stanza   n. 528

star   n. 329, 529, 684, 800, 868

starboard   n. 240

starch   n. 306; vb. 334, 583

stare   vb. 818, 866

starless   adj. 798

start   n. 34, **88**, 298, 444; vb. **88**, 282, 605

startle   vb. 444, 856

start out   vb. 299

starve   vb. 205, 735, 861, 947

stash away   vb. 567

state   n. 7, 183, 379; adj. 379; vb. **468**, 498, 525

statehood   n. 379

stately   adj. 32, 873

statement   n. 83, 401 **468**, 483, 525, 742

statesman   n. 625

station   n. 7, 93, 185, 186, 620, 868

stationary   adj. 152

statistics   n. 38, 460

statue   n. 483, 489, 983

stature   n. 208

status   n. 7, 93, 868

status quo   n. 143

statute   n. 626, 954

statutory   adj. 954

staunch   adj. 882

stay   n. 135, 213, 217, 884; vb. (of time) 112, 135, 143, 145; (dwell) 191; (support) 217; (resist) 648

stay-at-home   n. 885; adj. 612

stay away   vb. 189

staying power   n. 535, 857

stay up   vb. 135

steadfast   adj. 112, 143, 152, 534, 535

steady   n. 889; adj. 16, 140, 143, 145, 152, 534, 535; vb. 152

steal   vb. 461, 720, 722

stealing   n. **722**

stealthy   adj. 461

steam   n. 159, 344, 347; vb. 306, 346

steam engine   n. 276

steamer   n. 277

steep   adj. 214, 745; vb. 349

steeple   n. 208

steer   vb. 271, 284, 622

steer clear of   vb. 555, 924

stem   n 374

stench   n. 774, **777**

stenography   n. 521

step   n. 269, 400, 602, 609; vb. 269

step by step   adv. 27

step down   vb. 687

step in   vb. 300

stepmotherly   adj. 900

step on it   vb. 280, 613

steppe   n. 356

steps   n. 316, 559

stereogram   n. 794

stereo-recorder   n. 484

stereotyped   adj. 16, 152, 545, 843

sterile   adj. 160, 169

sterilization   n. 169, 583

stern   adj. 669, 837, 946

stew   n. 756; vb. 306

steward   n. 623, 676, 733; vb. 622, 748

stewardship   n. 392, 622, 748

stick   n. 964; vb. 47, 50, 264

stick by   vb. 217

stick-in-the-mud   n. 143

stick it out   vb. 535, 648, 757

stickler   n. 537, 864

stick one's heels in   vb. 648

stick one's neck out   vb. 859

stick out   vb. 253, 823

stick out for   vb. 535

stick to   vb. 712

stick together   vb. 639

stick to one's guns   vb. 534, 537, 648

stick-up   n. 722

stick up for   vb. 217

sticky   adj. 50, 362, 759, 772

stiff   n. 371; adj. 334, 337, 511, 745

stiffen   vb. 332, 334, 337

stiff-necked   adj. 537

stiff upper lip   n. 535, 836

stifle   vb. 466, 548, 762, 779, 785

stifled   adj. 781

stifling   adj. 759

stigma   n. 847, 869

still   adj. 174, 257, 267, 612, 779; vb. 176, 267, 513, 652, 779

still-life   n. 488

stilt   n. 217

stilted   adj. 511

stimulant   n. 173, 591

stimulate   vb. 173, 547, 618, 755, 829

stimulus   n. 173, 547

sting   n. 255, 828; vb. 255, 758, 828

stinginess   n. 748, 750

stink   n. 777; vb. 777

stint   n. 109; vb. 750

stipend   n. 636, 738

stipendiary   n. 958

stipple   vb. 817

stipulate   vb. 699, 700

suffer *vb.* 586, 590, 648, 752, **828**, 963
suffer defeat *vb.* 662
sufferer *n.* 828
suffice *vb.* 28, 570, 831
sufficiency *n.* **570**
sufficient *adj.* 75, 570
suffix *n.* 41, 87, 499; *vb.* 40
suffocate *vb.* 370, 759
suffrage *n.* 540
sugar *n.* 772, 891; *vb.* 772
sugary *adj.* 772
suggest *vb.* 155, 401, 441, 450, 459, 460, 597, 624, 693
suggestion *n.* 441, 459, 460, 482, 624, 693
suggestive *adj.* 401, 450, 459, 482
suicide *n.* 370
sui generis *adj.* 59, 102
suit *n.* 227, 960; *vb.* 105, 577
suitable *adj.* 136, 302, 575, 577, 896, 915
suitcase *n.* 193
suite *n.* 91, 191, 792
suitor *n.* 889, 960
sulk *vb.* 895
sullenness *n.* **895**
sullied *adj.* 584, 952
sully *vb.* 584, 847, 869, 928, 952
sultry *adj.* 759
sum *n.* 26, 54, 731; *vb.* 40
summarize *vb.* 203, 504, 525, 527
summary *n.* 441, 525, 527; *adj.* 504
summer *n.* **127**, 664, 759; *adj.* 127
summer time *n.* 116, 127
summery *adj.* 127, 759
summing up *n.* 527, 960

summit *n.* 89, 208, **212**, 519, 581
summon *vb.* 94, 671, 695, 857, 901
summons *n.* 671, 960
sum up *vb.* 527, 960
sun *n.* 329, 800
Sunday School *n.* 988
sunder *vb.* 63
sundown *n.* 128
sunglasses *n.* 801, 804
sunken *adj.* 209, 210, 254
sunny *adj.* 664, 759
sunrise *n.* 127, 797
sunset *n.* 128
sunshine *n.* 797
sup *vb.* 304
super *adj.* 579
superabundance *n.* 32, 572
superannuated *adj.* 130
superannuation *n.* 687
superb *adj.* 579
supercilious *adj.* 875, 924
superficial *adj.* **211**, 435, 574, 825, 852
superfluity *n.* 32, 572
superimpose *vb.* 225
superintend *vb.* 392, 622
superintendent *n.* 623
superior *n.* 34, 675; *adj.* 34, 579, 868
superiority *n.* 34, 84, 579, 868
superlative *n.* 499; *adj.* 34, 481, 579
supermarket *n.* 730
supernatural *adj.* 447, 971, 984
superpose *vb.* 225
supersede *vb.* 85
superstition *n.* 984
supervision *n.* 392, 593, 621, 622, 956
supervisor *n.* 623, 675

supper *n.* 306
supplant *vb.* 85
supple *adj.* 335
supplement *n.* 40, 41, 87; *vb.* 40, 196, 568
supplementary *adj.* 40
supplicant *n.* 697, 982; *adj.* 982
supplication *n.* 695, 982
supplies *n.* 564, 566, 729
supply *n.* 568; *vb.* 564, 568, 602, 715
support *n.* 213, **217**, 401, 424, 636, 929; *vb.* 152, **217**, 392, 401, 410, 424, **636**, 907
supporter *n.* 217, 287, 424, 640, 821, 905
suppose *vb.* 416, 420, **448**, 449
supposed *adj.* 448, 459, 825
supposition *n.* **448**
suppress *vb.* 164, 461, 466, 513, 679, 681, 691
supreme *adj.* 34, 579, 581, 667, 966
sure *adj.* 152, 408, 531
surety *n.* 420, 593, 701
surf *n.* 363; *vb.* 271
surface *n.* 182, 211, 222; *adj.* 211; *vb.* 225, 331
surfeit *n.* 572, 865; *vb.* 865
surge *vb.* 316, 320, 325, 358
surgery *n.* 591
surly *adj.* 887, 895
surmise *n.* 448; *vb.* 420, 448
surmount *vb.* 316
surname *n.* 496
surpass *vb.* 6, 34, 314
surpassing *adj.* 32, 34, 579
surplice *n.* 989
surplus *n.* 44, 572

303

T

tab *n.* 482; *vb.* 482
table *n.* 83, 217, 306
tablet *n.* 591
taboo *n.* 691; *adj.* 691
tacit *adj.* 459
taciturnity *n.* 517
tackle *vb.* 88, 605
tack on *vb.* 40
tacky *adj.* 362
tactful *adj.* 398
tactical *adj.* 621
tactics *n.* 559, 621
tactless *adj.* 887
tag *n.* 482, 496; *vb.* 482, 496
tail *n.* 87, 89, 91, 237; *adj.* 237; *vb.* 37, 287, 554
taint *n.* 847; *vb.* 584, 952
take *vb.* 268, 720, 722
take action *vb.* 609
take advantage of *vb.* 136, 478, 575, 606, 952
take after *vb.* 18, 20
take away *vb.* 42, 720
take back *vb.* 31, 538
take care *vb.* 860
take care of *vb.* 392
take charge of *vb.* 593
take exception *vb.* 425, 893
take for granted *vb.* 443, 867, 880, 910
take from *vb.* 720
take heart *vb.* 836, 857
take in *vb.* 98, 302, 304, 452, 716, 795
take it out of *vb.* 617
take it out on *vb.* 149, 900
take liberties *vb.* 918
take life *vb.* 370

take measures *vb.* 602
take notice *vb.* 390
take off *vb.* 20, 228, 273, 744
take on *vb.* 557, 605, 649
take out *vb.* 882
take over *vb.* 667
take pains *vb.* 615
take part in *vb.* 605, 639, 709
take place *vb.* 1, 153
take precautions *vb.* 860
take sides *vb.* 408, 639
take steps *vb.* 602, 609
take to *vb.* 545, 861
take umbrage *vb.* 893
take up *vb.* 540, 575, 716
take upon oneself *vb.* 605
taking *n.* 720
takings *n.* 724, 741
tale *n.* 460, 465, 525
talent *n.* 434, 627
talisman *n.* 984
talk *n.* 470, 492, 514, 518, 519; *vb.* 514
talkativeness *n.* 516
talk down *vb.* 273
talker *n.* 514
talk into *vb.* 547
talk out of *vb.* 548
talk over *vb.* 624
tall *adj.* 32, 202, **208**, 318
tally *vb.* 24, 38
tame *adj.* 507, 654; *vb.* 377, 679
tan *n.* 810, 813; *adj.* 813; *vb.* 963
tandem *n.* 61, 276
tang *n.* 767, 769
tangency *n.* 201
tangent *n.* 285
tangerine *n.* 816
tangible *adj.* 3, 327, 758

tangle *n.* 45, 82; *vb.* 221
tangy *adj.* 769
tanker *n.* 277
tantalize *vb.* 547, 755
tantamount *adj.* 28; *adv.* 199
tantrum *n.* 893
tap *n.* 265, 360, 782; *vb.* 282, 358, 758, 782
tape *n.* 207; *vb.* 483
tape-measure *vb.* 400
taper *vb.* 37, 205, 255
tape-recorder *n.* 484, 794
tape-recording *n.* 483
tardy *adj.* 135
target *n.* 552, 716, 853
tariff *n.* 743
tarnish *n.* 847; *vb.* 584, 847, 869, 928
tarpaulin *n.* 225
tarry *vb.* 135, 281
tart *adj.* 769, 773
tartan *n.* 817
tart up *vb.* 844
task *n.* 557, 605
tassel *n.* 846
taste *n.* 339, 398, 753, 767; *vb.* 767
tasteful *adj.* 398, 510, 848, 876
taste good *vb.* 770
tasteless *adj.* 511, 768, 771, 849
tastelessness *n.* 399, 511, **768**, 771, 849
tasty *adj.* 767, 770, 829
taunt *n.* 926; *vb.* 644, 853, 926
taut *adj.* 334
tautological *adj.* 451
tautology *n.* 505
tavern *n.* 191
tawdry *adj.* 849
tax *n.* 743
taxi *n.* 276; *vb.* 273
taxonomy *n.* 97, 375

tea *n.* 306, 309
tea-break *n.* 616
teach *vb.* 420, 470
teacher *n.* 428, 473, 624, 974, 986
teaching *n.* **470**
team *n.* 94
team-mate *n.* 640
team up with *vb.* 639
teamwork *n.* 639
tear *vb.* 48, 280, 613
tea-room *n.* 191
tears *n.* 839
tease *vb.* 755, 830, 842
technique *n.* 488, 606
tedious *adj.* 841, 843
teem *vb.* 75, 572
teenager *n.* 131
teens *n.* 70, 129
teeter *vb.* 325
teeth *n.* 159
teetotalism *n.* 944, 949
telecommunications *n.* 467
telegram *n.* 460, 467
telegraphic *adj.* 504
telepathy *n.* 447
telephone *n.* 467; *vb.* 460
telescope *n.* 329, 822; *vb.* 203
television *n.* 467, 840
tell *vb.* 38, 460, 465, 514, 525, 624
tell apart *vb.* 398
teller *n.* 733
tell fortunes *vb.* 447
telling *adj.* 525
tell off *vb.* 926
tell on *vb.* 460
tell-tale *n.* 460; *adj.* 462
tell tales *vb.* 516
tell the future *vb.* 447
temerity *n.* 859
temper *n.* 5, 751; *vb.* 142, 176, 334, 335, 403
temperament *n.* 5, 751

temperamental *adj.* 756, 894
temperance *n.* 935, **944**, 949
temperate *adj.* 176, 759, 944, 949
temperature *n.* 400, 759
tempest *n.* 175, 359
tempestuous *adj.* 359
temple *n.* 990
temporal *adj.* 107, 116, 987
temporary *adj.* 113, 149, 396
tempt *vb.* 547
temptation *n.* 547
tempting *adj.* 306, 770
tempt providence *vb.* 594, 859
ten *n.* 70; *adj.* 70
tenable *adj.* 420
tenacious *adj.* 50, 337, 534, 535, 537
tenancy *n.* 707
tenant *n.* 190, 710
tend *vb.* **178**, 284, 377, 392
tendency *n.* **178**, 284, 545, 751
tender *n.* 693; *adj.* 129, 335, 670, 752, 753, 889; *vb.* 693
tenderize *vb.* 335
tendril *n.* 207, 251
tenement *n.* 191
tenet *n.* 420, 974
tenor *n.* 178, 284, 450, 778
tense *n.* 499; *adj.* 756, 856
tension *n.* 25, 615, 642, 832
tent *n.* 225
tentative *adj.* 396, 448, 604
tenuous *adj.* 333
tenure *n.* 707
tepid *adj.* 759

tergiversation *n.* 538
term *n.* 93, 109, 494; *vb.* 496
terminal *n.* 89; *adj.* 89, 237
terminate *vb.* 89, 144, 164, 659
terminology *n.* 494, 496
terminus *n.* 89, 235, 298
terms *n.* 700
terms of reference *n.* 557
terrace *n.* 559
terra firma n. 352
terrain *n.* 352
terrestrial *adj.* 329, 352
terrible *adj.* 580, 856
terrific *adj.* 579
terrify *vb.* 856
territory *n.* 183, 956
terror *n.* 856
terrorism *n.* 955
terrorist *n.* 167, 175, 370
terse *adj.* 203, 432, 504
test *n.* 394, 396; *vb.* 408, 413
testify *vb.* 401, 413, 468
testimonial *n.* 441, 483
testimony *n.* 401, 468, 483
tether *vb.* 47
text *n.* 432, 524
textbook *n.* 524
textile *n.* 221
textural *adj.* 339
texture *n.* 339
thank *vb.* 909, 965
thankful *adj.* 909
thankless *adj.* 576, 910
thanks *n.* 909
thanksgiving *n.* 838, 982
thaw *vb.* 345, 761
theatre *n.* 529, 840
theatrical *adj.* 529, 852, 877
theft *n.* 722

theism n. 974

theme n. 387

theology n. 974

theorem n. 410

theoretical adj. 448

theorist n. 448

theorize vb. 448

theory n. 157, 386, 448

therapeutic adj. 585, 589, 591

thermal adj. 759

thermometer n. 759, 766

thermostat n. 766

thesaurus n. 83, 494

thesis n. 387, 410, 448, 526

thick adj. 204, 332, 364, 435

thicken vb. 204, 332

thicket n. 374

thickness n. 204, 206, 332

thickset adj. 203, 204

thick-skinned adj. 754

thief n. 723, 906

thin adj. 33, 76, 205, 333, 507, 571; vb. 27, 333

thing n. 3, 163, 327, 609

thing added n. 41

thing subtracted n. 43

think vb. 384, 420, 448

thinkable adj. 404

think about vb. 552

think ahead vb. 558

thinker n. 448

think-tank n. 624

thinness n. 76, 205, 333

third n. 66; adj. 65

third party n. 653

thirst n. 350, 388, 861; vb. 861

thirst-quencher n. 309

thirsty adj. 350

thorn n. 255, 255

thorn in the flesh n. 592

thorny adj. 255, 633

thorough adj. 56, 148, 392

thoroughfare n. 313

thought n. 384, 386, 392, 420, 441

thoughtful adj. 384, 392, 410, 434, 837, 886

thoughtless adj. 385, 391, 393, 603, 859, 887, 900, 910

thousand n. 70

thrall n. 679

thrash vb. 282, 963

thread n. 49, 207; vb. 313

threadbare adj. 228

threadlike adj. 205, 207

threat n. 154, 594, 902

threatening adj. 154, 594, 651, 902

three n. 64; adj. 64

thresh vb. 378

threshold n. 233, 235

thrifty adj. 392, 748

thrill n. 756, 827; vb. 752, 755, 756, 829

thrive vb. 36, 168, 661, 664

throat n. 262

throaty adj. 515, 787

throb n. 325, 783; vb. 140, 325, 783, 828

throne n. 957

throng n. 75, 94; vb. 75, 94

throughout adv., prep. 107

throw vb. 290

throw away vb. 556, 713, 749

throwaway adj. 544

throw in vb. 311

throw in the towel vb. 556, 654

throw light on vb. 456

throw off vb. 295, 546

throw out vb. 607

throw up vb. 303

thrust n. 173, 178, 282, 290, 645; vb. 290, 645

thud vb. 782, 785

thug n. 723, 906

thumb through vb. 472, 818

thump vb. 282, 783, 785

thunder n. 325, 784; vb. 780, 782

thunderbolt n. 444

thunderstorm n. 175, 358

thunderstruck adj. 444, 866

thundery adj. 358

thwart vb. 445, 635, 637, 648, 662

tick vb. 783

ticket n. 482, 483, 743

tickle vb. 758, 829

tick off vb. 926

tide n. 358

tidy adj. 79, 392, 583; vb. 583

tie n. 28, 49; vb. 28, 47, 681

tier n. 93, 206

tie-up n. 47

tight adj. 47, 334, 950

tight-fisted adj. 750

tight-lipped adj. 517

till n. 732; vb. 378

tilt vb. 219, 220, 317

timber n. 217

timbre n. 512, 778

time n. 107, 109, 116, 400; vb. 116

time-honoured adj. 126, 922

timekeeping n. 116

timelessness n. 108, 114

timeliness n. 136

timepiece n. 116

time-saving adj. 748

time-server n. 538, 934

timetable n. 116, 460

timid adj. 856, 858, 876

timing n. 116, 140

timorous adj. 856

tin n. 193; vb. 599

tincture n. 45, 805

tinder n. 765

tinge n. 805; vb. 805

tingle vb. 752, 756

tininess n. 33, 195

tinker n. 728

tinkle n. 784

tinny adj. 787

tinsel n. 846

tint n. 27, 805; vb. 488

tinted adj. 805

tiny adj. 33, 195, 203

tip n. 212, 233, 255, 715, 965; vb. 212, 220, 909

tip-off n. 460, 597

tipple vb. 304, 950

tipsy adj. 950

tirade n. 518

tire vb. 617, 841

tired adj. 612, 617, 841

tiresome adj. 830, 841

tissue n. 339

titbit n. 770, 829

tit for tat n. 150, 647

titillate vb. 758, 829

title n. 496, 872

titled adj. 870

title-holder n. 661

titter n. 838

titular adj. 496

tizzy n. 326, 756

toady n. 881, 927; vb. 881

to and fro adv. 325

toast n. 309, 888; vb. 306, 888

tobacco n. 308

today n. 120

toddler n. 131

to-do n. 80, 756

toe n. 213

together adj. 47; adv. 60

togetherness n. 60

toil n. 615; vb. 615

toilet n. 227

token n. 4, 441, 482, 701

tolerable adj. 579, 666

tolerant adj. 288, 670, 690

tolerate vb. 670, 690, 911

toll n. 716, 743; vb. 783

tomb n. 372

tomorrow n. 123; adv. 121, 123

tone n. 488, 512, 778, 805

tone down vb. 176, 779

toneless adj. 806

tongue n. 253, 492, 512, 767

tongue in cheek adj. 852

tongue-tied adj. 513

tonic n. 591

tonsure n. 228

too adv. 40

tool n. 565

tooth n. 255; vb. 259

toothless adj. 130, 256

top n. 89, 208, 212, 222; adj. 212; vb. 34, 212, 316

top-heavy adj. 29, 330

topic n. 387

topical adj. 125

top-notch adj. 573, 579

topple vb. 220, 317, 319

topsy-turvy adj. 220

top up vb. 56

Torah n. 976

torch n. 765, 800

torment n. 828; vb. 830, 856, 900, 902

torn adj. 48, 262

tornado n. 175, 323, 359

torpedo n. 290

torpid adj. 174, 612

torrent n. 358, 572

torrential adj. 358

tortoise n. 281

tortuous adj. 251

torture n. 828, 900, 963; vb. 830, 900, 963

toss vb. 290, 326

toss-up n. 553

tot n. 131

total n. 40, 54; adj. 54; vb. 38, 40

totalitarian adj. 669

totality n. 54

totem n. 967, 983

totter vb. 325, 326

touch n. 753, 758, 805; vb. 201, 752, 755, 758

touch-and-go adj. 553

touch down vb. 273, 298, 317

touched adj. 752, 756

touch on vb. 211, 450

touch up vb. 587, 589, 805

touchy adj. 756, 894

tough adj. 161, 334, 337, 506, 633, 857

toughen vb. 334, 337

toughness n. 161, 334, 337

tour vb. 269, 322

tourism n. 269

tourist n. 270

tournament n. 649

tout n. 697, 728; vb. 695

tow vb. 291

towards adv. 284

tower n. 208; vb. 32, 34, 208, 316

towering adj. 32, 208

tower of strength n. 640

town n. 183

townsman n. 190

toxic adj. 164, 580, 586

trace n. 33, 401, 483, 774; vb. 157, 232, 525

tracing n. 22, 232

track n. 559, 658; vb. 287, 554

track down vb. 419

tractable adj. 654, 919

tractor n. 291

trade n. 150, 557, 725;
vb. 150, 725, 727
trader n. 728
tradition n. 126, 545,
641, 979
traditional adj. 126, 143
traditionalist n. 105,
143
traffic n. 313, 725; vb.
725
trafficker n. 728
traffic warden n. 956
tragedy n. 529, 551
tragic adj. 551, 830
trail n. 483, 774; vb.
287, 291, 554
trailer n 276, 291
train n. 85, 91, 276, 291;
vb. 377, 470, 545, 602
trained adj. 426, 627
trainee n. 474
trainer n. 473
training n. 470, 472,
545, 602, 627
traitor n. 148, 480, 538,
940
tramp n. 269, 270, 612,
697, 940
trance n. 754, 984
tranquil adj. 616, 757
tranquillize vb. 652
tranquillizer n. 176, 591
transact vb. 609, 727
transaction n. 153, 699,
725
transcend vb. 6, 32, 34,
314
transcribe vb. 456, 521
transcriber n. 521
transcript n. 22, 521
transcription n. 456,
521, 792
transfer n. 22, 149, 150,
714; vb. 142, 149, 268,
275, 714
transferable adj. 268,
714
transferal n. 268

transference n. 142,
149, 268, 455, 714
transfix vb. 152
transform vb. 142, 146
transformer n. 142
transfusion n. 45
transgression n. 672,
936, 955
transgressor n. 906, 940
transient adj. 113
transit n. 268
transition n. 142
transitional adj. 266
transitory adj. 113
translate vb. 20, 142,
456
translation n. 456, 495,
972
translator n. 456
transliterate vb. 456
translucent adj. 802,
804
transmission n. 460
transmit vb. 268
transmutation n. 142
transmute vb. 146
transparency n. 452,
486, 502, 802
transparent adj. 802,
806
transpire vb. 107, 153
transplant vb. 268, 378
transport n. 268, 756,
827; vb. 187, 275, 963
transpose vb. 149, 187,
220
transverse adj. 219
transvestite n. 953
trap n. 276, 463, 478,
596, 631; vb. 463, 478,
631, 720
trappings n. 711
trash n. 451
trashy adj. 580
traumatic adj. 856
travail n. 615
travel vb. 269
traveller n. 270

traverse vb. 269, 313
travesty n. 22, 487
treacherous adj. 478,
594, 932
treachery n. 478, 932
treacle n. 772
tread vb. 269
treason n. 478, 932
treasure n. 567, 579,
891; vb. 441, 889, 983
treasurer n. 733
treasury n. 732
treat n. 770, 829; vb.
526, 589, 591, 606, 738
treated adj. 602
treatise n. 526
treatment n. 488, 591,
606
treaty n. 24, 650, 699
treble adj. 65; vb. 65
tree n. 374
trek n. 313; vb. 269
tremble vb. 326, 756,
856
tremendously adv. 32
tremor n. 325, 326, 856
tremulous adj. 326
trench n. 210, 234, 254,
259, 261, 360
trenchant adj. 255, 506
trenches n. 646, 658
trend n. 178, 850
trepidation n. 856
trespass n. 703, 938,
955; vb. 300, 314
trial n. 551, 592, 604,
828; adj. 396, 396, 604
triality n. 64
triangle n. 64, 246
tribe n. 11
tribulation n. 828
tribunal n. 957, 958
tributary n. 358
tribute n. 743, 909
trick n. 433, 478, 631,
932; vb. 431, 478, 478,
631
trickery n. 478

trickle *vb.* 358
trickster *n.* 480, 631
trifle *n.* 33, 574; *vb.* 478
trigonometry *n.* 38
trill *vb.* 512, 783, 789
trim *vb.* 37, 203, 538, 844
trimming *n.* 846
trimmings *n.* 44
trimness *n.* 583
trinity *n.* 64, 967
trio *n.* 64, 792
trip *n.* 269, 909; *vb.* 478
triplication *n.* 65
trisection *n.* 66
trite *adj.* 432, 451, 843
triumph *n.* 153, 661
trivial *adj.* 451, 574
troll *n.* 970
trolley *n.* 276
troop *n.* 94, 655
trophy *n.* 441, 663, 965
tropical *adj.* 759
trot out *vb.* 514
troubadour *n.* 528
trouble *n.* 615, 633, 642, 665, 830; *vb.* 82, 578, 580, 633, 830, 856
troubled *adj.* 665, 828, 837, 856
trouble-maker *n.* 596, 672, 906
trouble-shooter *n.* 653
troublesome *adj.* 164, 330, 633, 642, 830
trouble spot *n.* 596
trough *n.* 259, 360
truancy *n.* 189, 920
truant *n.* 555, 600
truce *n.* 144, 650
truck *n.* 217; *vb.* 268
true *adj.* 1, 430, 450, 882, 915
true-to-life *adj.* 525
truism *n.* 432, 451
trump up *vb.* 477, 930
truncate *vb.* 203
trunk *n.* 193

truss *n.* 217
trust *n.* 408, **420**, 443, 685, 736, 854; *vb.* **420**, 854, 980
trustee *n.* 688, 733
trusteeship *n.* 685
trustworthy *adj.* 408, 420, 868, 931
truth *n.* 1, 408, **430**, 432, 977
truthful *adj.* 430, 476
truthfulness *n.* 476, 931
try *n.* 604; *vb.* **604**, 615, 767, 960
trying *adj.* 633, 830
tube *n.* 360, 361, 559
tuck *n.* 260, 306; *vb.* 304
tug *n.* 277, 291; *vb.* 291
tuition *n.* 470
tumble *vb.* 317, 358
tumid *adj.* 252
tumour *n.* 252
tumult *n.* 80, 175, 326, 780
tumultuous *adj.* 80
tundra *n.* 356
tune *n.* 792
tuneful *adj.* 528, 790, 792
tunnel *n.* 254, 360; *vb.* 254, 264
turbulence *n.* 80, 175, 326
turf *n.* 374, 812
turmoil *n.* 80, 175, 326, 668
turn *n.* 251, 260, 323; *vb.* 142, 177, 247, 251, 256
turn around *vb.* 289
turn aside *vb.* 285
turn away *vb.* 295, 391, 555
turn back *vb.* 147
turn down *vb.* 694
turn in *vb.* 556, 612, 681
turning *n.* 285

turning point *n.* 136
turn inside out *vb.* 220, 394
turn into *vb.* 146
turn off *vb.* 754, 771
turn on *vb.* 755, 829
turn out *vb.* 153, 227
turn-out *n.* 821
turn over *vb.* 220, 317
turn-over *n.* 741
turn to *vb.* 575, 624
turn up *vb.* 153, 188, 298, 444, 825
turn upside down *vb.* 220
turquoise *adj.* 815
tussle *n.* 649
tutor *n.* 473
twaddle *n.* 451, 516
twang *n.* 515
tweet *vb.* 789
twice *adv.* 62
twig *n.* 374; *vb.* 419, 452
twilight *n.* 128, 799
twin *n.* 11, 28; *adj.* 13, 18, 61, 62; *vb.* 62
twine *n.* 207, 251; *vb.* 221, 251
twinge *n.* 828
twinkle *n.* 797, 818; *vb.* 326, 797, 818, 838
twinkling *n.* 115
twirl *n.* 323; *vb.* 251, 323
twist *n.* 245, 251; *vb.* 219, 221, 245, 247, 251, 323
twitch *vb.* 326
twitter *vb.* 789
two *n.* 61
two-edged *adj.* 454
two-faced *adj.* 477, 932
two-time *vb.* 932
tycoon *n.* 728
type *n.* 23, 97, 482, 522; *vb.* 521
typescript *n.* 521

321

unwise *adj.* 393, 416, 435, 578
unworthy *adj.* 918
unwrap *vb.* 324
unyielding *adj.* 112, 161, 334, 337, 534, 537
up *adv.* 208
update *vb.* 125, 587
upgrade *vb.* 587
upheaval *n.* 80, 148
uphill *adj.* 615, 633
uphold *vb.* 143, 145, 217, 929
upland *n.* 356
uplands *n.* 208
uplift *vb.* 318, 836
upper *adj.* 34
upper classes *n.* 870
uppermost *adj.* 212
upraised *adj.* 318
upright *adj.* 214, 248, 430, 915, 931, 935
uprising *n.* 358
uproar *n.* 80, 175, 780
uproot *vb.* 187, 312
upset *n.* 220, 414; *adj.* 837; *vb.* 82, 148, 830, 893
upshot *n.* 87, 156
upside-down *adj.* 220; *adv.* 80
upstanding *adj.* 214, 318
upstart *n.* 125, 880
upsurge *vb.* 36
uptight *adj.* 756, 894
up-to-date *adj.* 125
upward *adj.* 219, 316
urban *adj.* 183
urchin *n.* 970
urge *n.* 547, 861; *vb.* 468, 547, 613, 624, 674, 695
urgency *n.* 506, 562, 573, 613, 674, 695
urinate *vb.* 303, 310
urn *n.* 193, 372

usage *n.* 499, 501, 545, 606
use *n.* 606; *vb.* 575, 606, 707, 719
used *adj.* 126, 606
used to *adj.* 545
useful *adj.* 550, 575, 577
useless *adj.* 576, 662
usher in *vb.* 84
usual *adj.* 138, 545, 867
usurer *n.* 718
usurp *vb.* 918
utensil *n.* 565
utilitarian *adj.* 575
utilitarianism *n.* 903
utility *n.* 575, 606
utilize *vb.* 575, 606
utmost *n.* 235
utopia *n.* 449
utter *adj.* 56; *vb.* 512, 514, 788
utterance *n.* 492, 494, 498, 512, 514, 788

V

vacant *adj.* 189, 385, 435, 451
vacate *vb.* 187
vacation *n.* 144, 612, 614
vaccine *n.* 591
vacillate *vb.* 151, 325, 536
vacuity *n.* 2, 189
vacuum *n.* 2, 189, 333
vagabond *n.* 270, 697
vagrant *n.* 270
vague *adj.* 4, 243, 409, 454, 503, 799, 824
vain *adj.* 576, 662, 855, 875
valentine *n.* 523, 890
valiant *adj.* 857
valid *adj.* 413, 430, 915, 954

validate *vb.* 413, 954
validity *n.* 430, 954
valley *n.* 200, 209, 254
valour *n.* 857
valuable *adj.* 573, 575, 579
valuables *n.* 711
value *n.* 575, 579, 743; *vb.* 573, 743, 889, 922
valuer *n.* 415
valve *n.* 265
vampire *n.* 906, 969
van *n.* 276
vandal *n.* 167
vandalism *n.* 722
vanished *adj.* 2, 189, 706, **826**
vanity *n.* 576, 873, **875**, 934
vaporization *n.* 346
vaporous *adj.* 4, 344, 346
vapour *n.* 4, 343, 344, 346
variable *n.* 39; *adj.* 15, 17, 104, 142, **151**
variance *n.* 15, 425, 642
variant *n.* 15; *adj.* 15
variation *n.* 15, 19, 104, 142
variegation *n.* **817**
variety *n.* 19, 72, 104, 529
various *adj.* 104
varnish *vb.* 225, 257, 365
vary *vb.* 15, 142, 151
vase *n.* 193
vast *adj.* 32, 78, 182, 194
vastly *adv.* 32
vat *n.* 193
vault *n.* 252, 320, 329, 372, 732; *vb.* 320
vaulted *adj.* 247
vaunt *vb.* 879
veer *vb.* 142, 247, 285
vegetability *n.* 374

vegetable *n.* 306
vegetate *vb.* 169, 174, 612, 666
vegetation *n.* 374
vehement *adj.* 173, 175, 506, 759
vehicle *n.* 276, 563
veil *n.* 461, 463, 549, 801; *vb.* 225, 461, 801
veiled *adj.* 225, 459
velocity *n.* 266, 280
vendetta *n.* 425, 642
vendor *n.* 697, 727
veneer *n.* 211, 225; *vb.* 206, 225
venerable *adj.* 126, 130
venerate *vb.* 922, 982
vengeance *n.* 647, 912
venomous *adj.* 164, 580, 592
vent *n.* 262, 361, 600
ventilate *vb.* 348, 583
ventilation *n.* 348, 775
ventilator *n.* 361, 764
venture *n.* 269, 553, 604, 605; *vb.* 158, 553, 604, 918
veracity *n.* 476
verb *n.* 499
verbal *adj.* 450, 494, 514
verbalize *vb.* 498
verbose *adj.* 505, 516
verdict *n.* 415, 960
verge *n.* 233; *vb.* 233
verge on *vb.* 292
verify *vb.* 396, 401, 408, 413
veritable *adj.* 430
vermin *n.* 373
vernacular *n.* 492; *adj.* 190, 492
versatile *adj.* 151, 627
verse *n.* 528
versed *adj.* 602
version *n.* 456
vertebrate *n.* 373
vertical *adj.* 214, 248

verve *n.* 173, 368, 506, 611
very *adj.* 13; *adv.* 32
vespers *n.* 128, 988
vessel *n.* 193, 277
vestige *n.* 44
vestment *n.* 227, **989**
vet *n.* 377
veteran *n.* 132, 629, 655; *adj.* 627
veterinary science *n.* 377
veto *n.* 681, 691, 694; *vb.* 691
vexed *adj.* 828, 893
via *adv.* 284
viable *adj.* 404
vibration *n.* 325, 326, 778, 784
vicar *n.* 689, 986
vicarious *adj.* 149, 685, 943
vicarious authority *n.* **685**
vice *n.* **936**; *adj.* 689
vicinity *n.* 199, 229
vicious circle *n.* 412
vicissitude *n.* 142
victim *n.* 479, 716, 828, 853
victimize *vb.* 478, 900
victor *n.* 661
Victorian *adj.* 126, 951
victorious *adj.* 661
victory *n.* 661
video-recorder *n.* 484
videotape *n.* 483
view *n.* 415, 420, 624, 818; *vb.* 818
viewer *n.* 821
vie with *vb.* 649
viewpoint *n.* 818
vigilant *adj.* 390, 392, 818, 860
vigilante *n.* 593
vigour *n.* 159, 161, 173, 368, 506, 585, 611
vile *adj.* 580, 777, 892

vilify *vb.* 901, 928
villa *n.* 191
village *n.* 183
villain *n.* 906, 940
vindicate *vb.* 647, 912, 929, 961
vindication *n.* 929
vindictive *adj.* 908, 912
vinegar *n.* 773
vineyard *n.* 378
violate *vb.* 314, 608, 672, 703, 920, 952, 955, 981
violence *n.* 175, 674
violent *adj.* 175, 642
violet *n.* 814; *adj.* 814
VIP *n.* 868
viper *n.* 906
virgin *n.* 897; *adj.* 125, 427, 603, 897, 951
virgin territory *n.* 427
virile *adj.* 161, 380
virtual *adj.* 404
virtually *adv.* 199
virtue *n.* 876, 931, 935, 951
virtuoso *n.* 793
virtuous *adj.* 931, 935, 951
virus *n.* 167, 586, 592
visa *n.* 690
viscosity *n.* 362, 400
viscount *n.* 870
visibility *n.* **823**
visible *adj.* 3, 458, 823, 825
vision *n.* 449, 458, **818**, 854, 971, 976
visionary *n.* 449, 903; *adj.* 4, 449
visit *n.* 269, 884; *vb.* 188, 269, 300, 971
visitor *n.* 100, 270, 884
visual *adj.* 458, 818
visualize *vb.* 449
vital *adj.* 368, 562
vitality *n.* 161, 173, 368, 506, 585, 836

vitalize *vb.* 173, 368
vitreous *adj.* 802
vivacious *adj.* 368, 836
vivacity *n.* 514
vivid *adj.* 441, 506, 509, 525
vivisection *n.* 370
vocabulary *n.* 494, 501
vocal *adj.* 512, 792
vocalist *n.* 793
vocalize *vb.* 512, 514
vocation *n.* 557, 985
vociferous *adj.* 780, 788
vogue *n.* 125; *adj.* 495
voice *n.* 492, 512; *vb.* 512, 514
void *n.* 2, 74, 189; *adj.* 2, 333, 451; *vb.* 955
volatile *adj.* 151, 344, 346
volition *n.* 530
volte-face n. 147, 220, 289, 538
voluble *adj.* 509, 514, 516
volume *n.* 26, 194, 400, 524
voluntary *adj.* 530, 532
volunteer *vb.* 532, 693
voluptuous *adj.* 827, 945
vomit *vb.* 303
voodoo *n.* 984
voracity *n.* 750, 861, 948
vortex *n.* 323, 358
vote *n.* 540, 909; *vb.* 424, 540
voted *adj.* 424
voter *n.* 190, 540
vouch *vb.* 468
voucher *n.* 482, 741
vow *n.* 468, 698; *vb.* 468, 698
vowel *n.* 493, 512
voyage *n.* 271, 313; *vb.* 271
voyager *n.* 270

vulgar *adj.* 511, 849, 887, 952
vulnerable *adj.* 594, 753

W

wadding *n.* 226
wade *vb.* 271
wafer *n.* 306
waffle *vb.* 516
waft *n.* 359
wag *n.* 842; *vb.* 325
wager *n.* 553
wages *n.* 731, 738, 741
wagon *n.* 276
wail *n.* 788, 839; *vb.* 788, 839
wait *vb.* 443, 610
wait and see *vb.* 135, 610
waiter *n.* 676
wait on *vb.* 287, 676
waive *vb.* 556, 713
wake *n.* 237
walk *n.* 269, 559; *vb.* 269
walk away with *vb.* 661
walker *n.* 270
walkie-talkie *n.* 467
walk out *vb.* 144, 556, 687
walkout *n.* 144
walk-over *n.* 634, 661
wall *n.* 217, 230, 234
wallet *n.* 193, 732
wallop *vb.* 282, 963
wan *adj.* 807
wand *n.* 677
wander *vb.* 269, 285, 505
wanderer *n.* 270
wandering *n.* 391
wane *n.* 37; *vb.* 37, 799
want *n.* 57, 562, 706, 861; *vb.* 57, 189, 530, 532, 562, 571, **861**

wanted *adj.* 562, 600
wanton *adj.* 936, 952
war *n.* 649, **651**
warble *vb.* 789
ward *n.* 183, 540
warden *n.* 593, 683
warder *n.* 683
ward off *vb.* 646
wardrobe *n.* 227
wardship *n.* 129
warehouse *n.* 567
wares *n.* 729
warfare *n.* 649, 651
warlike *adj.* 651
warm *adj.* 419, 759, 805; *vb.* 306, 761, 836
warm-hearted *adj.* 882, 899
warmth *n.* 506, 752, 759, 805, 882
warm up *vb.* 306
warning *n.* 447, 460, 597, 902; *adj.* 597
warp *vb.* 219, 247, 416, 487
warrant *n.* 424, 671, 685; *vb.* 690, 698, 917
warranty *n.* 701
warren *n.* 234, 254
warrior *n.* 655
wart *n.* 252
wary *adj.* 390, 860
wash *n.* 358, 805; *vb* 583, 805
washed out *adj.* 612, 617, 806
wash-out *n.* 662
waste *n.* 44, 164, **569** 576; *vb.* 569, 608, 749
waste away *vb.* 53, 586 588
wasted *adj.* 205, 569
wasteful *adj.* 393, 569, 749
waste-pipe *n.* 600
waste time *vb.* 612
wastrel *n.* 612, 749, 940

watch *n.* 116, 646; *vb.*
  392, 818
watchdog *n.* 593
watcher *n.* 821
watchful *adj.* 392, 443,
  818, 860
watchman *n.* 683
watchword *n.* 432
water *n.* 309, 347; *vb.*
  378
water channel *n.* 360
water down *vb.* 45, 162
waterfall *n.* 358
water in motion *n.* 358
waterlogged *adj.* 349,
  355
waterproof *adj.* 350,
  593
watershed *n.* 230
water sports *n.* 271
watertight *adj.* 265, 350
water travel *n.* 271
waterway *n.* 358
watery *adj.* 343, 347
wave *n.* 325, 358, 482;
  vb. 325, 482, 886
wavering *n.* 142, 151,
  325, 409, 536; *adj.* 141,
  151, 326, 536
wavy *adj.* 251
wax *n.* 342, 800; *vb.* 36,
  225
way *n.* 198, 313, **559**
wayfarer *n.* 270
way out *n.* 301, 600
wayward *adj.* 151, 672
weak *adj.* 162, 507, 586,
  617, 628, 781, 858
weak-minded *adj.* 162,
  435
weakness *n.* 162, 178,
  315, 507, 586, 617, 858,
  936
weak spot *n.* 582, 594
wealth *n.* 168, 664, 711,
  731, **734**
wean from *vb.* 546, 548
weapons *n.* 657

wear *vb.* 227
wear and tear *n.* 569
wear away *vb.* 341
wear down *vb.* 160, 547
weariness *n.* 612, 617,
  841
wearisome *adj.* 633,
  841
wear out *vb.* 569, 617
weather *n.* 348
weave *n.* 339; *vb.* 221,
  313
web *n.* 221, 339
wed *adj.* 47; *vb.* 896
wedding *n.* 896
wedge *n.* 230, 246, 265
weed *n.* 374; *vb.* 378
weedy *adj.* 205
week *n.* 109
weep *vb.* 301, 833, 839,
  907
weigh *vb.* 330, 397, 415
weight *n.* 26, 177, 194,
  330, 400, 573; *vb.* 330
weighting *n.* 31
weightless *adj.* 331
weigh up *vb.* 384
weird *adj.* 971, 984
welcome *n.* 302; *adj.*
  827; *vb.* 302, 884, 886
welcoming *adj.* 716
weld *n.* 49; *vb.* 50
welfare *n.* 550, 664
well *n.* 254, 567; *adj.*
  585; *vb.* 301, 358
well-behaved *adj.* 673
well-being *n.* 550, 585,
  664
well-dressed *adj.* 227
well-formed *adj.* 499,
  844
well grounded *adj.* 426
well-meaning *adj.* 899
well-off *adj.* 664, 734
well-proportioned *adj.*
  244, 510, 844
well-read *adj.* 426, 472

well thought of *adj.*
  868, 922
well-turned *adj.* 510
well-versed *adj.* 426,
  627
weltschmerz *n.* 837
west *n.* 284
wet *n.* 347, 349; *adj.*
  347, 349; *vb.* 349
wet blanket *n.* 548, 841
whack *n.* 782; *vb.* 282,
  782, 963
whacked *adj.* 617
whale *n.* 194
what's-its-name *n.* 497
wheedle *vb.* 547, 927
wheel *n.* 250
wheeled *adj.* 276
wheeze *vb.* 359, 786
when *adv., prep.* 107
whereabouts *n.* 185
wherewithal *n.* 564, 566
whet *vb.* 255, 755
while *adv., prep.* 107
while away *vb.* 107, 612
whim *n.* 449, 539
whimper *vb.* 788, 839
whimsical *adj.* 449,
  539, 842, 851
whine *vb.* 784, 788, 789,
  839
whip *n.* 964; *vb.* 282,
  963
whip up *vb.* 175, 755
whirl *n.* 323; *vb.* 323,
  358, 359
whirlpool *n.* 323, 358
whirlwind *n.* 323, 359
whirr *n.* 783, 786; *vb.*
  783, 784, 786
whisk *n.* 359; *vb.* 359
whisper *n.* 460, 781; *vb.*
  781
whistle *n.* 482, 786,
  787; *vb.* 482, 786, 787,
  789
white *n.* 807, 951; *adj.*
  583, 806, 807

white flag   n. 652
whittle   vb. 203
whiz   vb. 280, 786
whizz-kid   n. 629
whole   n. 26, 54, 59; adj.
   39, 54, 56, 581, 585
wholehearted   adj. 534
wholesale   adj. 54, 56,
   98
wholesome   adj.   438,
   585
whoop   vb. 788, 840
whore   n. 953
wicked   adj.   551, 580,
   900, 916, 932, 936, 981
wickerwork   n. 221
wide   adj. 101, 182, 204
widen   vb. 36, 182, 204
widespread   adj. 32, 54,
   101, 182
widow   n. 898; vb. 898
widowhood   n. **898**
width   n. 26, **204**, 400
wife   n. 896
wiggle   vb. 251
wild   adj. 175, 433, 439,
   859, 889
wilful   adj. 530
will   n. **530**; vb. 530, 714
willies   n. 856
willingness   n. 532, 692
willpower   n. 530, 534
wilt   vb. 837
wily   adj. 478, 631
win   vb. 661, 705, 720
wince   vb. 283
wind   n. 359; vb. 251,
   322
windfall   n. 550, 715
window   n. 262
wind up   vb. 89, 116,
   739
windy   adj.   344, 348,
   359
wine   n. 309
wink   n. 482, 818; vb.
   482, 818
winner   n. 661

winnings   n. 724
winnow   vb. 46, 48, 378
win over   vb. 547
winsome   adj. 829, 889
winter   n. **128**; adj. 128
wintry   adj. 128, 760
wipe   vb. 341
wipe out   vb. 164, 485,
   911
wire   n. 207, 460, 467;
   adj. 611; vb. 460
wireless   n. 467
wiry   adj. 207
wisdom   n.   382, 392,
   426, **434**
wisecrack   n. 842
wish   n. 530, 854, 861;
   vb. 530, 854, 861
wishful thinking   n. 449,
   478, 854
wishy-washy   adj. 162,
   507, 666, 768
wisp   n. 4, 207
wit   n. 434, **842**
witchcraft   n. 984
withdraw   vb. 42, 289,
   293, 299, **312**, 538, 556,
   600, 687, 731, 826
withdrawn   adj.   681,
   885
wither   vb. 350, 588
withhold   vb. 461, 694,
   712
within hearing   adv. 199
within reach   adj. 404
without   adv., prep. 42;
   prep. 571
withstand   vb. 646, 648
with strings attached
   adj. 700
with the exception of
   adv., prep. 42
with young   adj. 163
witness   n. 401, 483; vb.
   401, 413
witty   adj. 840, 842

wizard   n. 447, 984
wizened   adj. 197, 205
wobble   n. 326; vb. 325,
   326
woe   n. 580
wold   n. 356
woman   n. 133, 381
woman-hater   n. 904
womanizer   n. 953
women's rights   n. 917
wonder   n. **866**; vb. 866
wonderful   adj. 32, 579,
   844
wont   n. 545
woo   vb. 882, 889, 890
wood   n. 374, 765
woodwind   n. 794
word   n. **494**, 698; vb.
   498
word for word   adj. 450,
   456
wording   n. 501
Word of God   n. 976
word order   n. 499
wordy   adj. 505
work   n. 163, 488, 521,
   524, **557**, 605, 615, 792;
   vb. 172, 557, 615, 676
workable   adj. 406
work against   vb. 181
worked up   adj. 893
worker   n. 609, 619, 676
work off   vb. 149
work oneself up   vb. 756
work one's way up   vb.
   316
work out   vb. 38, 452,
   552, 558, 659
workshop   n. **620**
work together   vb. 52,
   180
work up   vb. 755
world   n. 329, 379
worldliness   n. 327, 329,
   981
world-weariness   n. 837,
   841
worldwide   adj. 32, 101

worm in   *vb.* 300
worn   *adj.* 162, 588
worn out   *adj.* 612, 617, 841
worried   *adj.* 828
worry   *n.* 828, 856; *vb.* 830, 856
worse   *adj.* 35
worsen   *vb.* 588, 835
worship   *n.* 922, 980, **982**; *vb.* 922, 980, **982**, 983, 988
worth   *n.* 575, 579, 743; *adj.* 743
worthless   *adj.* 574, 576, 580, 924
worthwhile   *adj.* 965
worthy   *adj.* 917, 935
wound   *n.* 588, 828; *vb.* 580, 588, 830
wraith   *n.* 971
wrangle   *vb.* 642
wrap   *vb.* 225, 227, 234
wrapped up in   *adj.* 384, 934
wrap up   *vb.* 227, 659
wrath   *n.* 893
wreath   *n.* 250
wreathe   *vb.* 251
wreckage   *n.* 164
wrecker   *n.* 167
wrench   *vb.* 312
wretch   *n.* 828, 940
wretched   *adj.* 665, 828, 837
wriggle   *vb.* 251, 300

wrinkle   *n.* 260; *vb.* 197, 251, 260
wrinkled   *adj.* 130, 260
writ   *n.* 671, 960
write   *vb.* 58, 483, **521**, 528
write off   *vb.* 739
writer   *n.* 456, 521, 524, 528
write to   *vb.* 523
write up   *vb.* 526, 925
writhe   *vb.* 245, 251
writhing   *adj.* 828
writing   *n.* 501, **521**, 528
writing on the wall   *n.* 447, 597, 902
wrong   *n.* 431, 551, **916**, 955; *adj.* 137, 416, 431, 580, **916**, 938, 955; *vb.* 580, 608, 916
wrongdoer   *n.* 906, 940

X,Y,Z

yacht   *n.* 277
yap   *n.* 516; *vb.* 516, 789
yard   *n.* 184, 234, 620
yarn   *n.* 207, 525
yawn   *vb.* 262, 612
yawning   *adj.* 210, 262
year   *n.* 109, 122
yearning   *n.* 854, 861;

adj. 861, 889
yeast   *n.* 331
yell   *n.* 788; *vb.* 788
yellow   *n.* 813; *adj.* 813, 858
yelp   *n.* 782; *vb.* 787, 789
yes   *n.* 424
yes-man   *n.* 881
yesterday   *n.* 124; *adv.* 121, 124
yield   *n.* 163, 705; *vb.* 163, 335, 424, 654, 692
yoke   *vb.* 47
yokel   *n.* 871
young   *adj.* 129
youngster   *n.* 131
youth   *n.* 88, **129**, 131
zeal   *n.* 532, 759, 980
zealot   *n.* 611
zealous   *adj.* 532, 611, 980
zenith   *n.* 212
zephyr   *n.* 359
zero   *n.* 74; *adj.* 74
zest   *n.* 173, 611, 769, 827
zigzag   *n.* 246; *vb.* 246, 325
zip   *n.* 49, 173; *vb.* 280
zombie   *n.* 971
zone   *n.* 183, 184, 206
zoo   *n.* 377
zoology   *n.* 366, 373, 375
zoom   *vb.* 273, 613

List of categories

I Abstract Relations

A Existence

1 existence
2 non-existence
3 material existence
4 non-material existence
5 being according to internal form
6 being according to external form
7 absolute state
8 circumstance

B Relation

9 relation
10 absence of relation
11 kindred relations
12 correlation
13 identity
14 absolute difference
15 variance
16 uniformity
17 non-uniformity
18 similarity
19 dissimilarity
20 imitation
21 non-imitation
22 copy
23 prototype
24 agreement
25 disagreement

C Quantity

26 quantity
27 relative quantity
28 equality
29 inequality
30 mean
31 compensation
32 greatness
33 smallness

34 superiority
35 inferiority
36 increase
37 decrease
38 numeration
39 number
40 addition
41 thing added
42 subtraction
43 thing subtracted
44 remainder
45 mixture
46 freedom from mixture
47 junction
48 separation
49 bond
50 coherence
51 incoherence
52 combination
53 decomposition
54 whole
55 part
56 completeness
57 incompleteness
58 composition
59 unity
60 accompaniment
61 duality
62 duplication
63 bisection
64 triality
65 triplication
66 trisection
67 quaternity
68 quadruplication
69 quadrisection
70 five and over
71 multisection
72 plurality
73 fraction
74 zero
75 multitude

76 fewness
77 repetition
78 infinity

D Order

79 order
80 disorder
81 arrangement
82 disarrangement
83 list
85 precedence
85 sequence
86 precursor
87 sequel
88 beginning
89 end
90 middle
91 continuity
92 discontinuity
93 position in a series
94 assemblage
95 dispersion
96 focus
97 class
98 inclusion
99 exclusion
100 extraneousness
101 generality
102 speciality
103 rule
104 diversity
105 conformity
106 unconformity

E Time

107 time
108 absence of time
109 period
110 course of time
111 contingent duration
112 long duration
113 short duration
114 endless duration

321

485 obliteration
486 representation
487 misrepresentation
488 painting
489 sculpture
490 engraving
491 artist
492 language
493 letter
494 word
495 neologism
496 nomenclature
497 misnomer
498 phrase
499 grammar
500 solecism
501 style
502 lucidity
503 obscurity
504 conciseness
505 diffuseness
506 vigour
507 feebleness
508 plainness
509 ornament
510 elegance
511 inelegance
512 voice
513 muteness
514 speech
515 imperfect speech
516 talkativeness
517 taciturnity
518 address
519 conversation
520 monologue
521 writing
522 printing
523 correspondence
524 book
525 description
526 dissertation
527 compendium
528 poetry; prose
529 drama

V Volition

I Individual volition

A Volition in general
530 will
531 necessity
532 willingness
533 unwillingness
534 resolution
535 perseverance
536 irresolution
537 obstinacy
538 change of mind
539 caprice
540 choice
541 absence of choice
542 rejection
543 predetermination
544 spontaneity
545 habit
546 absence of habit
547 motive
548 dissuasion
549 pretext
550 good
551 evil

B Prospective volition
552 intention
553 chance
554 pursuit
555 avoidance
556 relinquishment
557 business
558 plan
559 way
560 mid-course
561 circuit
562 requirement
563 instrumentality
564 means
565 instrument
566 materials
567 store
568 provision
569 waste
570 sufficiency
571 insufficiency
572 excess
573 importance
574 unimportance
575 utility
576 inutility
577 expedience
578 inexpedience
579 goodness
580 badness
581 perfection
582 imperfection
583 cleanness
584 uncleanness
585 health
586 ill health
587 improvement
588 deterioration
589 restoration
590 relapse
591 remedy
592 bane
593 safety
594 danger
595 refuge
596 pitfall
597 warning
598 indication of danger
599 preservation
600 escape
601 deliverance
602 preparation
603 non-preparation
604 attempt
605 undertaking
606 use
607 disuse
608 misuse

C Voluntary action
609 action
610 inaction
611 activity
612 inactivity
613 haste
614 leisure
615 exertion

616	repose	661	success	703	non-observance
617	fatigue	662	failure	704	compromise
618	refreshment	663	trophy		
619	agent	664	prosperity	**D**	**Possessive**
620	workshop	665	adversity		**relations**
621	conduct	666	mediocrity	705	acquisition
622	management			706	loss
623	director	**2**	**Intersocial volition**	707	possession
624	advice			708	non-possession
625	council		**A General**	709	joint possession
626	precept	667	authority	710	possessor
627	skill	668	laxity	711	property
628	unskilfulness	669	severity	712	retention
629	expert	670	lenience	713	non-retention
630	bungler	671	command	714	transfer
631	cunning	672	disobedience	715	giving
632	artlessness	673	obedience	716	receiving
		674	compulsion	717	apportionment
D	**Antagonism**	675	master	718	lending
633	difficulty	676	servant	719	borrowing
634	ease	677	sign of authority	720	taking
635	hindrance	678	freedom	721	restitution
636	aid	679	subjection	722	stealing
637	opposition	680	liberation	723	thief
638	opponent	681	restraint	724	booty
639	cooperation	682	prison	725	business
640	auxiliary	683	keeper	726	purchase
641	party	684	prisoner	727	sale
642	discord	685	vicarious authority	728	trader
643	concord	686	annulment	729	merchandise
644	defiance	687	resignation	730	market
645	attack	688	consignee	731	money
646	defence	689	deputy	732	treasury
647	retaliation			733	treasurer
648	resistance		**B Special**	734	wealth
649	contest	690	permission	735	poverty
650	peace	691	prohibition	736	credit
651	war	692	consent	737	debt
652	pacification	693	offer	738	payment
653	mediation	694	refusal	739	non-payment
654	submission	695	request	740	expenditure
655	combatant	696	protest	741	income
656	non-combatant	697	petitioner	742	accounts
657	arms			743	price
658	arena		**C Conditional**	744	discount
		698	promise	745	dearness
E	**Results of action**	699	contract	746	cheapness
659	completion	700	conditions	747	liberality
660	non-completion	701	security		
		702	observance		

879 boasting	**E Moral**	954 legality
880 insolence	915 right	955 illegality
881 servility	916 wrong	956 jurisdiction
	917 dueness	957 tribunal
	918 undueness	958 judge
D Sympathetic	919 duty	959 lawyer
882 friendship	920 neglect of duty	960 lawsuit
883 enmity	921 exemption	961 acquittal
884 sociability	922 respect	962 condemnation
885 unsociability	923 disrespect	963 punishment
886 courtesy	924 contempt	964 means of punish-
887 discourtesy	925 approval	ment
888 congratulation	926 disapproval	965 reward
889 love	927 flattery	
890 endearment	928 disparagement	**F Religious**
891 darling; favourite	929 vindication	966 divinity
892 hate	930 accusation	967 God
893 resentment; anger	931 probity	968 good spirit
894 irritability	932 improbity	969 evil spirit
895 sullenness	933 disinterestedness	970 mythical being
896 marriage	934 selfishness	971 ghost
897 celibacy	935 virtue	972 heaven
898 divorce;	936 vice	973 hell
widowhood	937 innocence	974 religion
899 benevolence	938 guilt	975 irreligion
900 malevolence	939 good person	976 revelation
901 curse	940 bad person	977 orthodoxy
902 threat	941 penitence	978 heresy
903 philanthropy	942 impenitence	979 sectarianism
904 misanthropy	943 atonement	980 piety
905 benefactor	944 temperance	981 impiety
906 evildoer	945 intemperance	982 worship
907 pity	946 asceticism	983 idolatry
908 pitilessness	947 fasting	984 sorcery
909 gratitude	948 gluttony	985 churchdom
910 ingratitude	949 soberness	986 clergyman
911 forgiveness	950 drunkenness	987 laity
912 revenge	951 purity	988 religious service
913 jealousy	952 impurity	989 vestment
914 envy	953 libertine	990 church building

328